CQ's State Fact Finder

D1530000

CQ's State Fact Finder 2002
Rankings Across America

Kendra A. Hovey

Harold A. Hovey

Congressional Quarterly Inc.
Washington, D.C.

To the memory of Harold A. Hovey

CQ Press
1255 22nd Street, N.W., Washington, D.C. 20037
Copyright © 2002 Congressional Quarterly

(202) 729-1800; (800) 638-1710

www.cqpress.com

Copyright © 2002 by CQ Press, a Division of Congressional Quarterly Inc.

Printed and bound in the United States of America

06 05 04 03 02   5 4 3 2 1

♾ The paper used in this publication meets the minimum
requirements of the American National Standard for
Information Sciences—Permanence of Paper for Printed
Library Materials, ANSI Z39.48-1992.

ISBN 1-56802-732-X (cloth)
ISBN 1-56802-731-1 (paper)
ISSN 1079-7149

Contents

Detailed Contents of Subject Rankings

Geography

Government

Federal Impacts

Taxes

Revenues and Finances

Education

Health

Crime and Law Enforcement

Transportation

Welfare

Technology

Introduction

CQ's State Fact Finder is an important information source and analytical tool for any person interested in developments in America's fifty states and the District of Columbia. The series is a valuable reference source for anyone looking to uncover trends in the states, whether a policy expert seeking detailed data or an individual wishing to learn more about today's social, political, and economic currents.

The nation's economy, our population, and the government's actions are constantly changing. These changes affect states differently. So it is important that information be as up to date as possible. To meet this need, CQ Press publishes *State Fact Finder* annually; the 2002 book is the eighth edition.

State Fact Finder 2002 reflects our changing landscape by providing new data for more than 90 percent of the statistics covered in the 2001 edition. It is likely that about 90 percent of the statistics in this edition will be different by the time the next edition is issued early in 2003. Readers can make sure they will receive the next edition as soon as it is published by establishing a standing order with CQ Press. The data in this and previous editions of *State Fact Finder* are also available for purchase in electronic form directly from State Policy Research (614-262-9229).

Many readers will want to use the successive volumes of *State Fact Finder* as valuable tools for identifying trends over time. The tables and statistical concepts in this book are closely comparable with those found in the first edition (1993). They are so comparable in the 1996 through 2000 editions that readers will be able to use them for statistical analyses of changes at the state level.

About This Book

The book was prepared by experts who constantly work with data comparing states to analyze state policy options and to compare states in ways important to policy makers, such as the success of their efforts to promote economic development and the costs and apparent results of their decisions. As a result, this book differs considerably from ordinary compilations of statistics in several important ways.

First, *State Fact Finder* includes many statistics that are not contained in standard statistical reports of government agencies and thus don't appear in compilations of statistics that rely solely on such published reports. For example, many of the tables in the health and welfare sections comparing state programs for low-income people are based on unpublished statistics maintained by agencies that administer these programs. Also, there are tables such as B-28, the Index of State Economic Momentum, and G-21, a comparison of state spending "needs," that reflect original research by State Policy Research.

Second, information from other sources is converted to a basis that makes comparisons meaningful. For example, information on the headquarters of the largest companies in America in Table B-16 includes the number of companies in each state in relation to population as well as the total number of companies.

Third, each table provides a ranking of the states. This makes it easy for readers to see how the state or states that interest them relate to neighboring states and to other states throughout the nation.

Fourth, the volume begins with an essay ("Finding Information Users Want to Know") in which the authors guide readers through the use of the information. This section helps readers understand the scope of information available to them.

Fifth, each of the thirteen chapters in the subject rankings section begins with an outlook brief, two or three paragraphs in length, pointing to emerging trends in that subject area, including issues likely to be on the front-burner in the coming year. For instance, in this 2002 edition of *State Fact Finder*, the brief at the beginning of the welfare section identifies topics certain to be of importance when welfare laws, reformed in 1996, come up for reauthorization in 2002. The briefs also address the possible ramifications of two overreaching and dominant events as we enter 2002—(1) the terrorist attacks of September 11th, as well as the subsequent military actions; and (2) the faltering economy.

Finally, *State Fact Finder* offers carefully documented source notes that follow the tables in each section. These notes list the origins of the statistics in each table and guide readers to additional sources where more information on the same topic can be obtained.

New Technology Chapter

The 2002 edition includes, for the first time, a separate chapter on technology. Although a few tables on technology data have appeared previously, the editors believe the issue has become so important to states that a consolidated collection of tables is appropriate. Among the tables included are those showing the percentage of households with computers and with Internet access. Other tables show the percentage of zip codes with broadband telecommunications services and the number of high-tech jobs.

About the Publisher

State Fact Finder was first published by Congressional Quarterly Inc. in 1993 as part of CQ's fifty-six year tradition of providing comprehensive, reliable, and focused information about national public policy issues in America. This effort has broadened to include developments and trends in the states in recent years through the publication of such books as *State Fact Finder* and the creation of *Governing*, a magazine covering all aspects of state government.

About the Authors

State Policy Research is known to state government experts everywhere as one of the most reliable and knowledgeable organizations dealing with state-level information. For more than fifteen years State Policy Research published the periodicals *State Policy Reports* and *State Budget & Tax News*, and for a decade it published *States in Profile*, which has now merged into *State Fact Finder*. The organization also provides the tables that appear in *Governing* magazine's annual *State and Local Sourcebook*.

Information Development

Any data book is by definition a work in progress. What is useful one year may be less helpful the next, as new information needs arise. For these and many other reasons, the editors welcome reactions from readers, suggestions for additional information or changes in presentation, and, of course, any corrections or clarifications that come to the readers' attention. These should be sent to Kendra Hovey at State Policy Research, 73 Crestview Road, Columbus, Ohio 43202. She can be reached by phone at 614-262-9229, by fax at 614-268-2669, or by e-mail at SPR@columbus.rr.com.

Finding Information Users Want to Know

Readers differ in their preferences on many things—from what they value in a place to live to the amount of state government spending they consider appropriate. They will not agree on such subjects as where they should move or which state is governed best.

In this section, rather than imposing personal values as though they were facts by ranking some states as the "best places" to live or do business, the authors have provided guideposts on how to use the tables so that readers can obtain the information they need. Using a question-and-answer format, this section leads readers to groups of tables that can be consulted together to deal with the broad questions, such as which state might have the best schools or the best business opportunities.

The section is divided into three parts, each based on particular types of decisions people use state statistics to make. The first covers personal and family decisions, such as those concerning job opportunities. The second focuses on business decisions, such as where to locate a new plant. The third provides information about the government to assist people in voting and in influencing public policy.

Subject Rankings

This section forms the heart of the book. It is organized into thirteen subject areas that are challenging policy makers throughout the country: population, economies, geography, government, federal impacts, taxes, revenues and finances, education, health, crime and law enforcement, transportation, welfare, and technology. States are listed alphabetically in each table. The information also is presented in rankings that allow a reader to see how each state compares with the others.

Source Notes

The source notes that follow each section are designed to be used in tandem with the subject rankings to understand the specific usefulness of, and any caveats about, the data. The sources for all the statistics in the book are documented so that the calculations can be replicated or expanded upon by those who need more detail than space allows here. These source notes allow the reader to locate other information sources that may be useful.

State Rankings

The state rankings section provides the reader with a composite view of each state. In this section, the editors bring together the state rankings of most of the data included in the volume. This compilation gives readers a quick summary of their states' positions in each subject area.

Index

The index guides readers to topics presented in the various sections of the book.

Introduction to the Data

Rankings: There is nothing magical about rankings, though *State Fact Finder* generally follows the convention of most statisticians by ranking from highest to lowest. Most rankings can be interpreted similarly by reversing them. For example, a table showing tax burdens from highest to lowest can be reversed to show tax burdens from lowest to highest by ranking the fiftieth state first, the forty-ninth state second, and so on.

Data Accuracy: The statistics in this volume vary greatly in their accuracy. Some, such as the land area of states or the number of state legislators, can be measured precisely. Other data, such as birth rates or finances of local governments, are estimates. The source notes generally explain how the data were developed or direct readers to the statistical providers, who usually have available detailed technical papers on their methods.

Ranking Positions and Ties: In preparing this report, the editors worked with data as presented by the statistical source. In presenting the data in tables, figures were rounded to a manageable number of digits (such as by expressing financial data as $24.5 million rather than $24,515,078). As a result, the rankings that are based on detailed data will show one state ranked above another even though they are apparently tied in the data published in the table.

When available, the value shown for the United States reflects the value provided by the original statistical source. Some statistical agencies include U.S. territories such as Puerto Rico in their national total. In these cases, adding the fifty-state total to the District of Columbia total will not yield the exact U.S. total.

Junk Data: Many special interest groups have strong opinions about appropriate policies for governments. They translate these opinions into rankings of which states are "best" in their subject areas of interest, such as protecting the environment, providing mental health services, or keeping a favorable climate for business. Sometimes the resulting statistics themselves are unreliable. Sometimes they combine individually reliable statistics into measures that simply reflect the policy preferences of those who rank the composite results. Such reports are generally not included in *State Fact Finder*, but the editors are familiar with them and are willing to help readers deal with them.

Time Periods: The tables all deal with the specific time periods indicated in the headings. These are normally calendar years. In the case of fiscal data, the time periods are fiscal years that end in the years shown.

District of Columbia: The District of Columbia has a unique status in any statistical compilation. It is not a state in the sense that it has no voting representatives in Congress and is counted as a city, not a state, in all Census Bureau statistics on government finances. However, the Census Bureau does include District residents within the total population of the United States. Federal agencies and private data-gathering organizations differ on how they treat the District, Puerto Rico, the Virgin Islands, and other entities in their statistics.

State Fact Finder presents information for the District of Columbia in each table but does not include it in the state rankings. State Policy Research has consistently avoided including the District for two reasons. First, users of rankings find this inclusion cumbersome to explain, often having to resort to particular explanations of rankings (such as a state being ranked fifth, fourth among states and also behind the District of Columbia). Second, the District is economically and demographically a central city with fiscal and other attributes of most central cities (high taxes, high crime rates, large percentages of the population in poverty and receiving government benefits, and so forth). When ranked along with states, the District often ranks first or last in the tables, distorting other rankings.

Finding Information Users Want to Know

Most people look at state statistics to answer specific questions related to a decision they need to make but often discover that the statistics they seek do not appear in the reference books they consult. Alternatively, they find some comparisons that seem to be relevant but wonder if they are.

State Fact Finder contains a feature not found in other compilations of data about states. Besides finding tables, readers can consult this section to find a list of frequently asked questions. Under each question they will find information about which statistics in this book should be helpful in trying to find answers, as well as road maps to other statistics that might be useful. Readers sometimes will be informed that the statistics they seek are not available anywhere and why.

This section is divided into three parts, each based on particular types of decisions people use state statistics to make. The first covers personal and family decisions, such as finding the states with the best job opportunities, the best health care, and even the best chances for finding a spouse. The second covers business decisions, such as where to locate a new business or where to find the most productive workers. This section is also useful for investors. The third contains information about government to assist people in their roles as voters and in influencing public policy.

About Personal Decisions on Where to Live or Visit

1. Where is the best place to find a job?

As a general rule, people find it easier to get a job, higher pay, better opportunities for advancement, and better opportunities for building professional practices if they locate in rapidly expanding economies. If they go to places in economic decline they will find few job opportunities and stiff competition to get the positions that do exist.

To find states with rapidly expanding economies, look at measures of recent economic growth, particularly the Index of State Economic Momentum (B-28), population growth (A-3), job growth (B-29, B-30), and projections of future population growth (A-4). The Index (B-28) is especially useful because it summarizes the three elements of economic growth important to job-seekers: population growth, income growth, and increases in the number of jobs.

Growth rates are particularly important if you seek jobs that are inherently related to growth, such as jobs in the construction industry. Because the need for construction relates to *changes* in the need for homes and buildings, there are massive differences between fast- and slow-growing states. For example, in 2000 there were 16 new homes being built for every 1,000 residents of Nevada but only 2 for every 1,000 residents of New York (B-20).

When a state is classified as rapidly growing, this does not necessarily mean that all local areas in the state are growing. For example, the fast growth in Nevada is concentrated in the Las Vegas area. Growth in the Pacific Northwest is occurring along the Pacific Coast between Seattle and Portland, but there are few job opportunities in the eastern parts of Oregon and Washington. To find which areas are growing and in what types of industries and jobs, you can consult local sources, such as state economic development departments, local chambers of commerce, or even friends familiar with the area. For nationwide statistics on growth in metropolitan areas, you can get information on recent job growth from the

Bureau of Labor Statistics. Somewhat less current statistics on income and other economic factors are available from the Department of Commerce, including detailed books on major counties called *County Business Patterns*.

2. Where will tax burdens be least for me and my family?

The tables in the Taxes section (F) are good guides to average tax burdens. Table F-1 shows what share of personal income goes to state and local taxes in each state. Tables F-6, F-9, and F-13 do this for each of the major taxes: property, sales, and personal income. The range among states is very large. For example, New York governments take 14 percent of income in state and local taxes, while governments in Tennessee take only 8.8 percent.

The taxes you actually pay will depend on your circumstances, such as how much property you plan to own in relation to your income. You can see the major differences in Tables F-16 and F-23. For example, Florida and Texas have tax systems that wealthy retirees will like—no income, inheritance, or estate taxes. Young couples without much income will pay heavy sales taxes and find that renters do not share in special property tax breaks for homeowners. For them, states like Oregon, which have no sales tax but steep income taxes, might be a better deal.

The state and local taxes you pay will be a combination of state government taxes, which are uniform throughout entire states, and local taxes. These vary greatly from place to place within a state. There are about 50,000 local governments in the United States with the power to set tax rates and there are 50 states—an average of about 1,000 different local governments in each state.

Depending on where you decide to live, you may find you are paying property taxes that are the sum of individual taxes levied by a county; a municipality or township; a school district; perhaps a second school district, such as a community college or vocational district; and hosts of special districts, such as road districts, transit districts, mosquito control districts, and levee districts—to mention just a few of the possibilities. Local governments in many states also levy sales taxes and a few states have significant local income taxes, such as the steep income taxes of New York City and Philadelphia. All these taxes are reflected in the state averages.

Because of these differences, what you pay will depend on where you live even though state government taxes are uniform in each state. To find local areas with low taxes within a state, look for places that have large business sources of tax revenues combined with small numbers of

people to serve. In most metropolitan areas, there are suburbs with concentrations of office buildings, shopping centers, and businesses that have much lower property taxes than those of surrounding areas. Realtors in metropolitan regions will be able to identify them. For property taxes, check the county government where you want to locate. The county officials who collect property taxes will have rate information for each local area.

Most state tax departments, with offices in state capitals and major cities, publish free booklets describing all their state taxes and tax rates.

3. Which state has the best public schools?

To compare how well students do, consider the first five tables in the Education section. Use Tables H-1 and H-2 for overall comparisons, H-3 for students not going to college right away, and H-4 and H-5 for the college preparation programs. You can also use the tables to compare states on measures of what they spend per student (H-15), what they pay teachers (H-16), class sizes (H-9), and more.

Except in Hawaii, all schools are local. Expect to find immense variations within areas in every state; these are as important as the variations from state to state. All state education departments, located in state capitals, keep statistics for each school district on spending and number of teachers and pupils. Some states issue "report cards" comparing district performance measures, such as how students do on standardized tests. You can use these or research locally such indicators as percentage of graduates that go on to college, percentages winning National Merit Scholarships and other awards, and local reputations for good schools.

How well students do depends heavily on how much help and motivation they get at home, not just on what happens at school. Much of the difference among states is caused by differences in the students, not in the schools. This is true for districts within a state as well.

One key is getting a child into the right school, not just the right school district. Some of the best specialized programs, and some of the worst schools, are found in central cities.

If you want to send children to private schools, do not expect much help from government. Many states are considering "voucher" plans that would help with tuition, but such plans are available now only in Ohio and Wisconsin, where they mostly serve poor, inner-city children. Iowa and Minnesota provide limited income tax breaks if you pay private school tuition.

4. Which state is best for children?

Throughout *State Fact Finder* you will find many tables comparing states on aspects of life important to children, including health, education, crime, and economic opportunity. If you want even more comparisons, detailed ones are available from the Children's Defense Fund (25 E Street N.W., Washington, D.C. 20001, 202-628-8787) and from the Annie E. Casey Foundation (One Lafayette Place, Greenwich, CT 06830, 203-661-2773) in the annual *Kids Count Data Book*.

Children grow up in small worlds, such as school buildings and neighborhoods, so do not expect to rely totally on facts about states, metropolitan areas, or even individual cities and counties for information important to your child's life. Where your child is within one of these areas is often much more important than which geographical area the child is in. State differences are important in such fields as the quality of education and the possibilities for getting a job.

5. Which is the best state for retirement?

Most people retire within twenty miles of where they lived when they stopped working. For them, finding the right place is more a matter of finding the right house or apartment in the right community than of finding the right state. If you are thinking about retirement in another state, *State Fact Finder* can be helpful, but you will need to go beyond it to make an informed decision.

Do not start with statistics comparing places, unless your overriding concern is minimizing the taxes you will pay. Start with your own preferences. Decide first on how far you are willing to be from your family and old friends and on climate issues, such as whether you want to avoid ice and snow and whether you will like places that do not have changing seasons during the year. Most people will be able to narrow their choices considerably this way.

If you are willing to take the time to look systematically at what is important to you about a place, take a "preference inventory" such as the one found in *Retirement Places Rated*, by David Savageneau. It will force you to consider whether being able to get a part-time job, see and hear a symphony orchestra, follow a professional sports team, and other items are important to you.

In the tables in *State Fact Finder,* you will see systematic differences among the states in such characteristics as income and education levels of residents, living costs, crime, and taxes.

There are many books designed to help with retirement decisions. A library or good bookstore should be able to recommend some reference book choices. Some describe places to live and provide information on investments, Medicare, and estate planning. *The Only Retirement Guide You'll Ever Need* (1991), by Kathryn and Ross Petras, is an example. Some deal only with places to retire, often with different emphases, such as health (*The 50 Healthiest Places to Live and Retire in the United States* [1991] by Normal D. Ford) or specialized retirement areas (*Retirement Places Rated,* which covers Kauai, Hawaii, and Hilton Head, South Carolina, but not New York City or any place in Ohio or Illinois).

AARP is a good source for a variety of publications on retirement, including specialized guides on state taxes. One topic of particular interest to retirees is what percentage of income from Social Security is taxed by each state.

6. Which state universities are best?

State Fact Finder contains some important statistics that are relevant when selecting among state university systems. Look for them in Tables H-19 to H-24. State statistics alone cannot pick a university to attend because state systems include everything from community colleges to medical schools. California even has systems within systems. They vary from the University of California, with campuses at Berkeley and elsewhere, which contains some of the finest institutions in the country, to California State University, which enjoys less of a national reputation but has some outstanding specialized programs, to community colleges with diverse and varying strengths and weaknesses.

Students attend schools, not states. Consult guides and ratings on individual schools that contain information on the numbers of students, types of curriculum, costs, and attempted assessments of the quality of students and faculty.

7. Which state has the best cultural attractions and recreation?

Recreational opportunities cannot be adequately measured by statistics. Attempts to do so often are misleading. For example, you will find by far the best ratio of park land to people in Alaska, but much of the state is covered by glaciers that are not fit for hiking or camping. Some fine experiences—the "big sky" of Montana, the bustle of the streets of New York, and the beauty of fall foliage in New England—are not specific places and do not count attendance.

There are fairly good statistics about how many people participate in various sports in each state. Table C-6 is an example. See the notes to this table at the end of the chapter for how to obtain specific information on other sports. Most sports have specialized equipment stores, magazines, and guidebooks that are superior to state statistics for making personal recreational choices. For example, just because there are more golfers and courses per capita in one state than another does not mean you will have trouble finding more than enough courses and players to make foursomes in the lower-ranked states.

Cultural opportunities are listed in the many guidebooks and specialized magazines published in nearly every possible field of interest. Government spending on the arts, shown in Table C-8, is not a useful indicator of the extent or quality of arts in each state. States spend, on average, about $1 per year per capita funding the arts—amounts that are dwarfed by sales revenues, admissions, and donations.

8. Where is the best place to invest in property?

It is hard to pick a winner in a field of losers and hard to pick a loser in a field of winners. You want to pick the right state (and metropolitan area in that state) for your investment.

Nearly everyone interested in owning real estate has heard the old saw about the three keys to real estate investment: location, location, and location. This applies to states and metropolitan areas within states. For example, statistics in Table B-21 from the Office of Federal Housing Enterprise Oversight show that in the five years from 1996 to 2001, the average house in Massachusetts appreciated by 59.3 percent while the average house in Hawaii increased in value by only one percent. Of course, how much your investment will lose or appreciate depends on the property you buy, whether you pay the right price, and local market conditions.

Real estate prices depend on supply and demand. Supply does not go down much in poor markets—who would tear down a house or office building just because values were dropping? Supply responds to increased demand in good markets, but prices rise because new construction usually costs more than established buildings, prices of lots and construction labor tend to rise, and the most desirable locations generally already have buildings on them.

The best strategy for real estate investment is to pick an area with an expanding economy, where lots of new jobs are being created. Look at the answer to Question 1 (where to find a job) for tips on using *State Fact Finder* to identify those places.

9. Can picking the right states help pick winners in stocks and bonds?

Few economists or investment professionals would suggest picking which company's stocks to buy based on the states in which their headquarters or plants are found. The important questions are how good are the products and how well are they marketed. Some successful companies operate from unlikely places. For example, computer-maker Gateway is based in farm country in South Dakota and apparel seller L. L. Bean is based in rural Maine.

For making things, being in a fast-growing economy is bad news, not good news. In fast-growing economies, it is harder to get and keep good workers, their pay is often higher, and transportation facilities are often congested. Look for strong state and regional economies only when looking for regionally oriented companies that sell products, such as new homes and fast food, directly to consumers.

Most people who buy tax-exempt bonds do so through mutual funds or rely heavily on bond-rating agencies, such as Standard & Poor's and Moody's. Those professional investors rely heavily on the kinds of economic, population, and government statistics used in *State Fact Finder* and analyses of recent fiscal developments presented in publications like *State Budget & Tax News* and *State Policy Reports*. People who buy individual bonds or buy mutual funds of tax-exempt bonds issued from a single state, like those that invest solely in the bonds of New York or California, can use these same statistics.

10. Which state government will interfere least with my freedom?

People occasionally say they would like to live where government interferes less with their daily lives. Government intrusiveness cannot easily be compared because governments often restrict the freedom of some citizens to enhance that of others. The ultimate example is capital punishment, which is the most intrusive concept imaginable for the person being punished but is used in the name of increasing freedom from fear and crime for everyone else. State policies are not necessarily consistent on intrusiveness issues. For example, the states that are most likely to allow you to own weapons without restriction are least likely to let you grow marijuana on your own property for personal consumption.

Some elements of government intrusiveness can be measured. One is taxes, measured by the many comparisons in the Taxes section (F). *State Policy Reports* designed an experimental comparison of tax intrusiveness (Vol. 12, Issue 24, December 1994), giving extra weight to property taxes and counting only taxes paid by households, not businesses. With a national average set at 100, it showed variation from 142 in most-intrusive New York to 32 in least-intrusive Alaska.

Another way to look at intrusiveness is the ratio of state and local government employees to population (D-13). If you find local governments closer to citizens and less intrusive than state governments, look at measures of differences in state and local roles as indicated by public employees (D-15) and revenue raising (D-16).

11. Where are taxes likely to go up/down in the future?

Tax rates are set by state legislatures and local bodies (school boards, city councils, county commissions, etc.). Predicting where taxes will be raised or lowered would appear to be a matter of forecasting the views of those who now serve on or will subsequently be elected to these bodies. The economic and population statistics in *State Fact Finder* provide some excellent clues to future tax rates, as does common sense thinking about why some states have higher taxes than others.

Right now, the states with the lowest taxes on people who live there are the states that get lots of their money from other sources—tourists, oil and gas, and gaming casinos, for example. States amply endowed with these—such as Alaska, Nevada, Texas, and Wyoming—have been able to keep taxes low while still offering extensive government services. Some states have been able to keep taxes on their residents relatively low because they have been able to draw new residents who pay substantial taxes but do not have children in public schools, which is the biggest single cause of state and local spending. Fast-growing states of the Southwest and Florida have been the best examples.

These same states will be under the strongest pressures to raise tax levels in the future. As more people come to them, the amount that their unique resources contribute to revenues *per resident* drops. Furthermore, as time passes, their populations become more like the national averages. For example, the childless young people who flocked to Florida in large numbers to work at tourist attractions and to provide health care and other services to retirees are having children in large numbers. Florida has to pay for putting nearly 100,000 additional students in its classrooms every year. California and Texas face similar pressures.

12. Which states have the least/most pollution?

State Fact Finder presents summary statistics on air and water pollution and hazardous waste (C-10 to C-14). More important, the notes to the tables provide leads to where to get more details on local areas. State averages are misleading for people seeking to decide where to live or visit. For example, western cities, like Denver and Salt Lake City, have some of the worst air pollution problems in the nation, but away from urban areas the air in these states is about as pure as you will find. An average for California that lumps downtown Los Angeles with the forests of northern California and the state's deserts will not give an accurate picture of any of these places.

13. Where do I find the best health care?

Because much more money is spent in gathering them, state-by-state statistics on health and health care (section I) are quite comprehensive compared with statistics in other fields. The statistics cover (1) health of average people in a state's population, (2) apparent availability of care, (3) cost of care, and (4) government programs, which are generally oriented to poor people. These statistics suggest strong concentrations of health professionals in northeastern states.

People worried about whether they can find adequate health care for themselves and their family need not be guided by these statistics. Most people are limited to amounts their insurance will pay. Because insurers will not pay for long-distance travel and hotel bills except in rare cases, the doctors capable of performing all types of operations have been locating in the areas across the country where paying patients are found. One result is the development of top-flight facilities across the country, such as the University of Iowa hospital, which serves as a specialized facility for patients throughout that state, and the medical complex around Birmingham, Alabama. There is no reason for anyone to avoid an entire state because of concerns about health care, unless they have a very specialized medical problem. The main limits on health care are primarily those that people accept by their decisions on where to locate within a state. People who seek near-wilderness isolation by buying ranches in Colorado or locating on small islands off the Atlantic Ocean must accept the consequences of their isolation on the availability of health care.

14. Where will I be safest from crime?

State statistics, and even city statistics, on crime are not much help in looking for a safe place to live. In every state, crime is most prevalent in the low-income areas of central cities. Violent crimes are most prevalent in these areas after dark. Reported crime statistics overstate crime risks for people who do not spend evenings in low-income central city areas. A high crime rate for an entire state says more about the percentage of a state's population living in these areas than about safety in that state's suburban, small town, and rural areas as compared with similar areas in other states.

City and state crime rates are also misleading when used to consider which places are safe to visit on business or recreational trips. All statistics, like crime rates and per capita amounts, that relate a category to population use night-time population—the number of people whose regular beds are in a city or state. States such as Florida, Hawaii, and Nevada have many visitors for vacations and conventions. Cities have day-time commuters and business and vacation travelers. Crime rates in cities and these states are much lower for people at risk than when expressed in relation to the number of people who regularly sleep there.

15. Where is the best place to look for a mate?

People looking for an opposite sex partner can reasonably expect better opportunities in locations where they are outnumbered by persons of the opposite sex (A-13). However, aggregate statistics can be misleading for people under fifty-five looking for a partner about their own age. Because women live longer than men, the states with predominately older populations (A-6) also tend to have high ratios of women to men. Careful research by several women on the Federal Reserve Bank of Boston's research staff found the worst sex ratios (from the standpoint of women seeking men) in older northeastern cities and the states with a high percentage of jobs in health care, government, and financial services, which are disproportionately filled by women. The best ratios, again from the perspective of women seeking men, were in booming western states where economic growth draws large numbers of young men to occupations such as mining and construction.

16. Where can I find the lowest living costs?

State Fact Finder includes the best information in use on comparative living costs (B-8), but the data must be used with care. For reasons appearing in the table notes, these measures are not likely to be accurate for what they try to measure—average living costs—and more accurate data are not likely to be available. Also, there are substan-

tial variations within states. All costs, except state and local taxes, are about the same in midsize cities and rural areas throughout the nation. The major differences are taxes (see section F) and costs related to economic growth (see section B).

In booming communities and states, housing prices soar, wage rates tend to be higher, and ample and growing sales discourage everyone from doctors to corner store owners from engaging in price wars. In depressed communities and slow-growth states (for example, West Virginia and older industrial communities such as Syracuse and St. Louis), the reverse factors are reducing housing costs, wages, and prices.

Different people buy different things, so the costs they experience will differ from averages, often by wide margins. Business travelers experience enormous price differences in what they buy—downtown hotel rooms, rental cars, and meals at restaurants catering to expense-account travelers. Highly paid executives with downtown jobs will find large differentials, particularly if they hope to live within fifteen minutes commuting time of their work. The largest differentials are associated with the size of metropolitan areas, not with states. New York, Chicago, and Los Angeles are expensive places for these people, but Rochester, Joliet, and Fresno are not.

Most people will not see such large differences in living costs. Much of what they buy—cars, furniture, alcoholic beverages and soft drinks, packaged foods, motion pictures and videotapes, books, sports equipment, clothing, and more—is produced long distances away. The prices generally reflect only minor differences in shipping costs among states, except Alaska and Hawaii, where prices are higher. A large part of the housing costs will depend on mortgage rates, which are nearly uniform nationwide. Most will select homes far enough away from congested central cities so that older home prices cannot get too far out of line with what it costs to build new houses, which is about the same nationwide.

About Business Decisions on Where to Locate and Expand

1. Where is the best place to locate a business?

State Fact Finder provides useful statistics for some kinds of business but not all. Businesses that depend on local customers—from doctors' offices to fast-food franchises—will usually do better in rapidly growing areas. To use *State Fact Finder* to identify these areas, see Question 1 in the previous section. Some local businesses have specialized markets, appealing primarily to clearly defined groups, such as children or the retired. To identify where such populations are large and growing, study the tables in the sections on population and the economy.

Sophisticated investors in consumer-oriented businesses, like franchises, often do extensive market research before committing their money. The same is true for companies deciding how and where to market consumer products from cars to shampoo. The serious researchers are generally looking at geographic detail not found in sources like *State Fact Finder*—zip codes and even streets and census tracts, rather than states or metropolitan areas. They rely on their own publications, most notably *American Demographics.* Many private companies specialize in providing such information and the computer software to use it. These companies advertise in such publications.

Some businesses, such as manufacturing companies, can separate where they produce products from where their consumers are located. Their business often limits their location choices. Mining and oil production companies need to be on top of their raw materials. Manufacturing needs an ample supply of labor and may have special transportation requirements, such as access to a rail line or deep-water port.

Within these parameters, the additional factors that help determine the best location for a business relate to costs—labor costs, state and local taxes, electricity prices, and transportation costs. Every firm, indeed every plant, is different in where it gets supplies, where its customers are located, how much and what kind of energy it uses, and the relative use of labor and machinery. This means the best place to locate depends on the match between the needs of a particular firm and the attractions of a potential plant site.

State Fact Finder contains much useful information to compare business locations. The Population (A) and Economies (B) sections provide information about potential markets for selling products and hiring workers. The Government (D) section offers information about how states are governed. The Taxes (F) and Revenues and Finances (G) sections cover factors associated with each state's tax burdens. Elements of government-provided services that are important to business are discussed in the Education (H) and Transportation (K) sections.

In establishing a business oriented to local economic growth, the important question is what growth *will be,* not what growth was. Most statistics show what it *was.* As the warning about mutual funds goes, "past performance is no guarantee of future results." So, too, for state economic growth.

Future growth will depend on many factors, such as changes in oil prices, federal spending (particularly defense), and how well particular firms and industries (and thus the places where they are located) do in the marketplace. To make predictions on future growth, you can review trend statistics (A-2, B-29, and E-2) or look at the composite Index of State Economic Momentum (B-28). Forecasts can be purchased from firms specializing in forecasting or they can be obtained inexpensively from the Department of Commerce (14th Street and Constitution Avenue N.W., Washington, D.C. 20230).

2. Which state has the most productive workers?

In their industrial development ads in business magazines, some states try to convince firms to locate within their borders because their workers are more productive. Productivity in this context is an elusive concept. Many experts are not even sure that national figures about changes in worker productivity are right, much less state-by-state numbers on the same subject.

Employers' ideas of a productive worker may vary from situation to situation. For example, software design and advertising place a premium on creativity and originality, so employees that work irregular hours still may be considered highly productive. An assembly line, however, will not work unless all the workers show up at the same time. Having lots of formal schooling may make engineers productive, but experience may be better for those who repair plumbing or who fish for a living.

State Fact Finder has many statistics on factors employers may consider to be signs of productivity, particularly in the Education (H) and Health (I) sections. *State Fact Finder* also includes the statistics usually used to calculate productivity in states (B-7), but such data are misleading for the reasons explained in the notes to the table.

3. Which states have the lowest labor costs?

Most comparisons among states regarding labor costs are based on average annual pay (B-5), as well as annual averages in retailing (B-10) and manufacturing (B-9). However, they will not necessarily be correct for hiring new workers in a particular occupation in a particular location within a state. The wages that must be paid to get competent workers in such a situation will depend upon the supply of labor and the demand for it in that local labor market. Firms looking for low-wage workers should do just the opposite of workers looking for high-paying firms, as discussed in Question 1 of the Personal Decisions section.

The really important statistic is how much work an employer gets from a worker in relation to a dollar paid. That statistic is elusive because productivity per worker is hard to calculate accurately (see Question 2, above). For a sophisticated attempt to calculate this unit labor cost in relation to productivity, see the research presented by Regional Financial Associates (West Chester, Pa.), including *The High Costs of High Costs* (1995).

4. Where will my business pay the least taxes?

State taxes on business are a complex web of interlocking provisions made even more complex because many local governments have separate taxes on business. These combinations have different impacts on different types of business, depending on such factors as how profitable they are; how capital-intensive they are; whether they qualify for state and local economic development incentives; and whether they are organized as proprietorships, partnerships, S (small business) corporations, or C (regular) corporations.

There is no substitute for learning the tax rules for the states and localities where you might operate and applying them to the expected characteristics (payroll, profits, etc.) of the business you plan to start or move. These calculations are so complicated that a major consulting industry has been developed to make them.

State Fact Finder provides some good indicators of the possible results of these calculations. Start with the overall levels of taxes (F-1 to F-3). If these are high, you will pay them somewhere—if not in taxes on your firm, then in taxes on your salary, your house, and what your firm pays for utility services. Next, look at the burdens of the specific taxes important to your operations. If you will have high investments in property (plant and equipment), see Tables F-6 to F-8. If you are concerned about payroll taxes, see Tables F-13 to F-16. If you are concerned about taxes on your sales, see Tables F-9 to F-12.

If yours is a local service business, such as a bakery or retail store, you do not have to worry much about state taxes on your business. Unless you are near a border with another state, your competitors will be paying the same taxes as you. This may not be true with local taxes, so you have to check them specifically. If yours is a small business, you may not be as worried about some taxes, particularly corporate income and franchise taxes, as large firms. You may be more concerned with certain taxes on

individuals, such as income and estate taxes, as shown in Tables F-16 and F-23.

If yours is a nationally oriented business, such as manufacturing, you may be in for some pleasant and unpleasant surprises about taxes on your business. Some states with high overall tax levels, such as New York, are very competitive in taxes on manufacturing. Some states with low taxes on households, particularly those with no taxes on personal incomes, have relatively high taxes on firms. For multistate firms, opening a plant in one state affects corporate income taxes in all the states because of the way corporate income is apportioned among states for tax purposes. For samples of calculations of corporate taxes of different industries in many states, see studies that the accounting firm of KPMG Peat Marwick has prepared for states evaluating their "tax competitiveness." Recent studies have been made for Kentucky, New York, and North Carolina.

5. Which states provide the best incentives to locate in them?

The amounts and types of assistance available from state and local governments in tax breaks, grants, and loans for locating in their jurisdiction depend on the type of business. If your business inherently serves local customers—an auto dealership, restaurant, retail store, or repair business, for example—expect no significant help from these governments. Your new business is not going to increase the wealth or income of the area you serve but rather just move it from those already there and competing for the same business you want. You may get some technical assistance and even loans, but mostly from state and local agencies administering federal small business money. If you pick the right state and right local government within that state, you may get some tax breaks because local communities compete for tax base with other local communities.

If your business will draw money from out-of-state, your business (large or small) will likely be offered major incentives from just about any state. There are so many incentives and the number is growing so fast that directories of them, such as the one published by the Urban Institute in 1991, are obsolete the day they are released. Do not try to use national directories of these types. Even if you do, you will miss the deals that states might be willing to tailor to fit your business. Nearly every community of any size and all states employ "developers"—economic development professionals whose mission is to draw employers to their community or state by providing information and administering incentives. These people are eager to provide you with details about sites, taxes, worker availability, and state and local incentives. Look for state agencies with *development* in their titles, and find local agencies through county or city governments or chambers of commerce.

6. Which states have the lowest utility rates?

Statistics comparing state averages of electric rates for various consumers appear in Tables B-34. They are indicative of rate differentials for other fuels as well. In general, the farther you locate from the sources of inexpensive energy (the gas fields of the Southwest and hydroelectric sites), the more expensive energy will be. Taxes make a big difference in what you pay for energy. So do state policies that determine how the total bill is divided between household and industrial uses, as Table B-34 dramatically illustrates.

There are price variations within states among users of differing quantities and among types of industrial service (such as cheaper rates for those who will close their plants on high-use days). Many concessions are made to firms newly locating in an area or who demonstrate they can obtain service from a competitor utility. There is no substitute for checking the prices the local utilities charge.

7. Which states regulate business the least?

There is no statistical way to compare state and local regulation of business across the board because there are so many different ways government regulation touches business operations. There is also great variation in policies among states and local areas. Many of the regulatory differences are not systematic. For example, some southern states have less stringent regulation of workplace conditions while imposing more stringent regulation on how corporations are governed.

8. Where is the transportation system best?

The interstate transportation systems—road, rail, air, and even barge lines—form an interconnected network that reaches every state in some way. Once your products or raw materials reach this network, service is close to uniform until they leave it. For businesses with large shipping requirements, the key aspect is how easily you can connect with the national networks used by your particular business. This varies with geography, not state lines, and is critically dependent on exactly where your site is located relative to rail and other transportation access points. As every driver knows, the quality and capacity of roads depends on exactly which roads you use.

However, there are systematic differences among states. These appear most dramatically in measures of maintenance and construction, the condition of bridges (K-3), and highway pavement (K-2).

9. Which states have pro-business attitudes?

Like the rest of us, business owners and managers have differing needs and differing views of appropriate public policies. For example, a company engaged in a low-technology, labor-intensive activity such as poultry processing is not much concerned with the education of its workers but is highly concerned with pollution control costs, state labor regulations, and taxes. A company engaged in high-tech competition for improved designs of computer chips or software is not as affected by such state regulation or even taxes; it is highly sensitive to how well educated employees are and whether governments offer strong university systems and cultural and recreational opportunities. Thus, a state with relatively high taxes that is accustomed to paying for top-flight schools and state universities will appear anti-business to some business leaders and pro-business to others.

The phrase *business climate* was widely used in the 1980s in discussions of state policies for economic development, regulation, labor laws, and taxes. The statistics were developed by the Grant Thornton accounting firm, based on opinions of which characteristics were important to those manufacturing firms that participated in state manufacturing associations. The state rankings much favored southeastern states with low taxes, low wages, and little business regulation. The influence of these ratings on state policies encouraged the development of counter-statistics, particularly the annual *Development Report Card for the States,* published by the Corporation for Enterprise Development (777 North Capitol Street N.E., Suite 410, Washington D.C. 20002, 202-408-9788), whose sponsors include many unions. As the name implies, the *Report Card* gives letter grades, not aggregate rankings, to reflect the complexity and controversy associated with deciding which state policies are pro-business and which are successful in causing state economic development. The state grades are nearly a flip-flop from the business climate rankings. In CfED's evaluation, southeastern states tend to have the lowest grades.

The availability of these more sophisticated measures discouraged use of the old business climate rankings, which are no longer published. The term *business climate* has been appropriated by the publishers of the business-oriented quarterly *Site Selection*. Its ranking procedure, associated with the number of new jobs primarily in manufacturing, inherently favors large states over less populous ones. Using the test of which states are drawing the most new work, see Table B-30, which shows growth in manufacturing jobs. Using the test of where firms locate their headquarters, see Tables B-16 and B-17.

10. Which states are the best places to sell business-to-business?

Many companies do not sell to consumers; they sell goods and services to other businesses. Finding firms that might want to buy office supplies, parts, maintenance services, and other business-to-business offerings is different then finding individual consumers (which is discussed in Question 1). The statistics needed for finding business customers are too specialized for this book but exist in abundance from government sources. The Bureau of Labor Statistics in the Department of Labor keeps up-to-date statistics on the number of jobs in each state, with breakdowns by major industry. The Commerce Department keeps detailed data and publishes them on a county level in *County Business Patterns*. The Commerce Department also does major surveys of industries, such as the Census of Manufacturing and the Census of Retail Trade.

State governments have even more detailed information, though some do a better job than others in keeping it current and making it available in usable form. The state agencies that administer unemployment compensation (UC)—typically called the Department of Labor or Employment Services Administration—know details on all private firms because they collect UC payroll taxes from them every quarter. Corporations, from mom-and-pop stores to General Motors, are chartered by states and often need some kind of permit to operate in states where they are not chartered. Secretaries of state are the keepers of these records. Many state economic development departments have detailed statistics on businesses operating in the state, and some publish directories.

About Government and Public Policy

1. Which state is the best managed?

No one has ever found a way to use statistics to determine which states, or for that matter which private companies, are best managed. Bottom-line results—good

schools, low taxes, and high and growing business profits—count. But some companies and states face greater challenges than others in achieving them because of circumstances beyond the control of their managers. There are awards for well-managed companies and governments, but these are like civic awards. Who gets them depends on who is on the selection committees, the criteria those particular people think are important, and their personal knowledge of the award candidates.

Somewhat more objective measures of state financial management are available. Bond rating agencies, such as Moody's, assess credit risks (G-15) much like a bank would determine how much to loan a family seeking a mortgage. Like personal credit ratings, these concern only the likelihood that loans will be repaid, not whether the borrower is competent, efficient, or doing the right things.

States can also be compared in financial management practices, such as whether they conform to generally accepted accounting principles and whether they use performance-oriented budgeting. Most experts believe these practices improve the quality of state decisions. These comparisons can be found in Table G-20. For detailed comparisons of such state practices as balanced budget requirements, governors' item-veto powers, and use of stabilization or "rainy day" funds, see the National Association of State Budget Officers' publication, *Budget Processes in the States*.

2. Which state has the fairest tax system?

Fairness in taxes depends entirely on one's perspective about who should bear what share of tax burdens—a specific example of the old maxim, "Where you stand depends on where you sit." The data needed to form opinions are found in Tables F-6 through F-22 in the Taxes section. Included are tables on progressivity of taxes; relative reliance on sales, income, and other tax bases; and tax burdens on high- and low-income households.

A large group of experts and state officials—including governors, legislators, and tax commissioners—have jointly published a study about the elements of good tax systems. *Financing State Government in the 1990s* is available from the National Conference of State Legislatures in Denver or the National Governors' Association in Washington, D.C. The study advocates keeping rates of all taxes as low as possible, given the money to be raised, by avoiding lots of special exemptions and balancing reliance on property, income, and sales tax. Look for balance in percentage of three-tax revenue in Tables F-8, F-11, and F-15.

3. Which states keep the share of taxes paid by business low?

Economists argue that all taxes must reduce some person's income in order to make it available for government. They do not believe that legal abstractions, such as corporations and partnerships, bear the burden of any taxes. Instead, the tax burdens find their way into prices paid by customers, lower wages paid to workers, lower prices paid to suppliers, and lower profits credited to stockholders.

Many people do not agree with this. Public opinion polls usually show that voters would rather see taxes on corporations than taxes they *know* they pay, such as sales taxes and personal income taxes. While many business leaders do not agree with the economists' outlook, others believe it but want to protect everyone involved—stockholders, suppliers, workers, and customers—by avoiding taxes on their businesses. As a result there is a lot of interest in comparing how states distribute tax burdens between businesses and people.

Good data to make such comparisons will never exist because the people who might gather the information, the tax collectors, do not care about it. Most collect the same property tax on houses and stores whether they are owned by occupants, individual landlords, or a corporate landlord. When someone buys a pad of paper and pays sales tax no one asks if they are buying it for grocery lists or for a business project. The family farm is both a business and a home, but most states do not divide the value between the two or make the tax lower or higher if the family is organized as a sole proprietorship, partnership, or corporation.

Consequently, comparisons of states on the share of taxes paid by businesses inherently involve guesswork and arbitrary distinctions, such as calling all severance taxes business taxes and all farm taxes people taxes. The most recent comparison was published in *State Policy Reports* in September 1997. It found business paid the lowest share of state and local taxes in Maryland (25.6 percent) and the highest in Alaska (88.4 percent). These data deliberately are not included in *State Fact Finder*.

4. Which state has the highest taxes?

The three standard measures of tax burdens are found in the first three tables of the Taxes section (F-1, F-2, and F-3). None of them is as good as the other tables in this section for considering what taxes are likely to be on an individual household or business. For those answers, see the answers to Question 2 in the Personal Decisions section and Question 4 in the Business Decisions section.

5. Which state has the best education policies?

People disagree about the best policies in education and other public policy fields. To answer questions like these, there are sporadic publications of evaluations of aggregate policies that rank states, but these simply reflect the policy preferences of the interest group issuing them. The scores and rankings are useful to those who share their biases, misleading to those who do not. *State Fact Finder* provides statistics on education (section H) and lets you decide which ones are most important to you.

6. Which states help the poor the most?

There is much disagreement about what is truly helpful to the poor. For example, some people believe providing welfare cash helps, but others argue that this hurts in the long run because it discourages working and hinders the opportunity to rise out of poverty.

State Fact Finder has many tables on programs for the poor, including food stamps (L-3), welfare (L-2, L-9, L-15, and L-16), Medicaid (I-12, I-13, I-16, I-17, and I-18), and school aid for the disadvantaged (H-12), as well as on tax policies affecting low-income households (L-11).

If you want to look further into this question, consult the Center for Budget and Policy Priorities (820 1st Street N.E., Suite 510, Washington, D.C. 20002, 202-408-1080). This group has analyzed which states are most generous to the poor in their spending and how regressive state and local tax policies are—that is, whether they take away in taxes a larger percentage of the purchasing power of the poor than of the rich.

7. Which states have the best roads?

Comparing state policies on a topic such as education does not work well because different people have different ideas about what constitutes good or bad policy. However, for some services, such as providing well-maintained roads, people generally agree on what is good and bad. Even when people can agree on desirable results (for example, how children should perform on standard reading tests), it is difficult to judge states on these outcomes because so much of the result is determined by factors governments do not control. Because state and local governments maintain their own roads, few extraneous factors are involved.

Highways provide a good example of how services can be compared (see Tables K-2 and K-3). Truckers run their own surveys, which can be found in the special-interest magazine *Overdrive*.

8. Overall, which states use tax dollars in the most cost-effective manner?

For conceptual reasons, this question cannot be answered. Conceptual problems arise because people do not agree on what governments should do and how they should do it. For example, most people would agree that administrative costs for welfare should be kept at a minimum so that all available money can be devoted to real work. Most people would agree that it is bad for society if large numbers of people are allowed to cheat their governments, and most would also agree that welfare recipients should be encouraged to find jobs. These beliefs produce contradictory results when applied to available data, such as costs per case of administering welfare (L-17) and collecting child support (L-13). These costs are lowest if a state does little counseling and does not spend much money checking for fraud.

Another example of a conceptual problem is the size of elementary school classes (H-9); some people think really small classes are ideal for all schools, while others believe small classes result in unnecessary spending.

Conceptual problems are not unique to governments. How can a company effectively measure whether its public relations or shareholder relations departments are cost-effective?

Even if conceptual problems could be solved, there are enormous difficulties in collecting the relevant data. For many functions, we do not have good measures of effectiveness. Do you know an effective police officer when you meet one, or an effective state university professor, or an effective state legislator? If you do, can you think how you would apply your effectiveness tests to every police officer, state university professor, or legislator in the nation?

Often, good measures of costs are not available either—at least not ones that are related closely to particular services or outputs of government. This problem is not unique to government. What percentage of the cost of a steer goes with the beef and what percentage with the leather?

Most attempts to measure the cost-effectiveness of government are experimental, usually confined to activities that can be measured fairly easily, such as gathering refuse, maintaining highways, and collecting bills. For more information, see the many useful books by Harry Hatry,

published by the Urban Institute (2100 M Street N.W., Washington, D.C. 20037, 202-833-7200).

9. Which states have the best government institutions?

Beauty is clearly in the eye of the beholder when it comes to deciding how governments ought to be organized, their policies established, and their leaders selected. Some people have strong preferences on these matters, which are from time to time reflected in comparisons oriented to showing the states with the "best" practices.

For the past thirty years, experts have advocated and states have moved to organizing the executive branches of state government in ways that strengthen the power of governors. These moves include (1) strengthening the veto power, including "line-item" vetoes; (2) reducing the number of executive officials (comptrollers, education superintendents, and insurance commissioners, etc.) selected by elections rather than appointed; (3) increasing the governor's role in preparing and administering budgets; and (4) extending governors' terms by converting two-year terms to four-year terms and allowing governors to run for reelection. Information on these developments and classifications of which states have which practices appear in the Government section (D).

For decades state legislatures were criticized as citadels of corrupt power removed from popular control and unresponsive to the needs of citizens. One major change came with a Supreme Court decision on reapportionment, requiring "one man (or woman), one vote." Now the U.S. Senate is the only governing body in the nation where voting power is not proportional to population. The National Conference of State Legislatures and some business groups and foundations have sponsored research on "modern" legislatures emphasizing (1) longer annual sessions, (2) more staff, and (3) higher legislative pay and expenses. Three such measures of the results appear in Tables D-5, D-8, and D-9.

These ideas have come under considerable criticism recently. Some people saw more staffing and full-time legislators making the field a career as a move toward professionalizing the legislature; others saw this as a recipe for making bureaucrats out of legislators, creating "full-time politicians," and pulling legislators out of touch with the people they represent. One result has been a move to limit the number of terms legislators can serve (D-8), in effect encouraging turnover (D-7).

Surveys show that large numbers of Americans think corruption is common among elected officials at the state and federal levels. There is no statistical way to compare ethics, but laws on conflict of interest and disclosure of personal financial information can be compared. The National Conference of State Legislatures does this, with the organization Common Cause providing a kind of watchdog role.

There is no prevailing doctrine on whether "bigger is better" for business and government. Sometimes the fashion is consolidation—forming conglomerates for business and merging regional governments to reduce the roughly 85,000 different state and local governments. Sometimes the emphasis is decentralization and local control, with spin-offs for business and special districts (for example, downtown revitalization areas, police service districts) and decentralized control of neighborhood schools within large school systems.

One way to look at differing state policy is to compare the ratio of governments to people (D-4). Another approach is to examine the percentage of local government spending that local officials do not have to finance with their own taxes (D-16).

10. Overall, which states have the best policies?

For some people, picking the best policy is simple: the best state is the one with the lowest taxes, or the one that spends the most on schools or taking care of the poor, or that is active in some other area of interest to the person making the judgment. For most people, this question is too general to be answered meaningfully because opinions differ so markedly on what is "best." Even for a particular person, one state may combine "good" policies on one subject with "bad" policies on another.

One thing is clear: State officials have to play the hands they are dealt, balancing the needs of their population and the tax base available for revenue to meet those needs. Needs appear in the form of children to be educated (H-10), poor people potentially eligible for services (A-11), and more. Tax bases are apparent from economic differences, as shown in the Economies section (B). State differences are summarized in Table G-21 for spending needs and Table F-3 for tax bases.

By comparing these statistics, some conclusions are pretty obvious. For example, compared with most states, it is easy for Connecticut officials to look good, as the state has both low taxes and high spending in relation to what it does, such as spending per school pupil. The state has a rich tax base and a comparatively small percentage of people needing service. Mississippi faces the exact opposite situation.

11. All things considered, which state is run the best?

Readers are advised not to pay attention to magazine rankings purporting to show which state governments are best, or which states are governed the best by the combination of state and local officials responsible for their policies. You can get a pretty good idea that there is something slippery about these just by comparing results. For example, in the mid-1990s, two financial magazines, *Worth* and *Financial World*, published rankings. One said Wyoming was best and Alaska was second. The other ranked Wyoming forty-third and put Alaska next to last.

The rankings for cities and metropolitan areas are no better than those for states. For a good discussion of the pitfalls involved in such rankings, see "Why Nice Cities Finish Last" in *Governing* magazine (September 1995).

If you must rank states on something, pick some areas where they compete for the same prize, such as jobs (B-29); where residents are judged by the same test (H-3); or where the same objective criteria are being applied, such as tax levels (F-1).

There is widespread agreement on what constitutes a valuable football player or an outstanding actor. This is not true for governments. Many people think those that govern best govern least, but others are looking for good schools, good roads, and quick responses from police and fire departments.

Subject Rankings

Population

Since 1790, when U.S. Marshals set out on horseback to conduct the country's first headcount, the U.S. government has counted its population every ten years. The last such census was taken in the year 2000, the results of which appear in this chapter. The Census Bureau will continue to release more detailed results through 2003.

Not everyone gets counted in a census, but some groups are harder to count than others. In 1990, four million people, or 1.6 percent of the population, were missed. The undercount for the Hispanic and African American populations was much higher— 5.0 percent and 4.4 percent, respectively. The Census Bureau is reporting far better results for the 2000 census. In October of 2001, the Bureau announced a revised "preliminary estimated" net undercount of "virtually zero" (0.06%). This percentage increases to 0.78 percent for the African American population and 1.25 percent for Hispanics.

Census population numbers are used to reallocate seats in the U.S. House. They also help determine how large chunks of federal funds are divvied between the states. For these reasons, the numbers tend to generate controversy. Cities and states with a higher percentage of minorities claim that their populations aren't accurately represented by "unadjusted" numbers, translating into a loss of funds for programs such as Medicaid, foster care, and social service block grants, among others. These grievances often end up in the courts. In late 2001, a handful of cases were pending. The Census Bureau tends to win these court battles because though it admits to an undercount, it claims the count it made is still the most accurate available.

In addition to the lowest undercount in recent years, the 2000 census also marked the first year respondents were able to identify themselves as multi-racial, by checking one or more boxes classifying race (Hispanic is considered an ethnicity, not a race, by the Census Bureau). In 2000, 2.4 percent of the population, or 6.8 million people, reported being of one or more races.

A-1 Population and Percentage Distribution, 2000

State	Population 2000 (in thousands)	Percentage of national total 2000	Rank by percentage
Alabama	4,447	1.6	23
Alaska	627	0.2	48
Arizona	5,131	1.8	20
Arkansas	2,673	0.9	33
California	33,872	12.0	1
Colorado	4,301	1.5	24
Connecticut	3,406	1.2	29
Delaware	784	0.3	45
Florida	15,982	5.7	4
Georgia	8,186	2.9	10
Hawaii	1,212	0.4	42
Idaho	1,294	0.5	39
Illinois	12,419	4.4	5
Indiana	6,080	2.2	14
Iowa	2,926	1.0	30
Kansas	2,688	1.0	32
Kentucky	4,042	1.4	25
Louisiana	4,469	1.6	22
Maine	1,275	0.5	40
Maryland	5,296	1.9	19
Massachusetts	6,349	2.3	13
Michigan	9,938	3.5	8
Minnesota	4,919	1.7	21
Mississippi	2,845	1.0	31
Missouri	5,595	2.0	17
Montana	902	0.3	44
Nebraska	1,711	0.6	38
Nevada	1,998	0.7	35
New Hampshire	1,236	0.4	41
New Jersey	8,414	3.0	9
New Mexico	1,819	0.6	36
New York	18,976	6.7	3
North Carolina	8,049	2.9	11
North Dakota	642	0.2	47
Ohio	11,353	4.0	7
Oklahoma	3,451	1.2	27
Oregon	3,421	1.2	28
Pennsylvania	12,281	4.4	6
Rhode Island	1,048	0.4	43
South Carolina	4,012	1.4	26
South Dakota	755	0.3	46
Tennessee	5,689	2.0	16
Texas	20,852	7.4	2
Utah	2,233	0.8	34
Vermont	609	0.2	49
Virginia	7,079	2.5	12
Washington	5,894	2.1	15
West Virginia	1,808	0.6	37
Wisconsin	5,364	1.9	18
Wyoming	494	0.2	50
50 States	280,850	99.8	
DC	572	0.2	
United States	281,422	100.0	

Rank in order by percentage

1 California
2 Texas
3 New York
4 Florida
5 Illinois
6 Pennsylvania
7 Ohio
8 Michigan
9 New Jersey
10 Georgia
11 North Carolina
12 Virginia
13 Massachusetts
14 Indiana
15 Washington
16 Tennessee
17 Missouri
18 Wisconsin
19 Maryland
20 Arizona
21 Minnesota
22 Louisiana
23 Alabama
24 Colorado
25 Kentucky
26 South Carolina
27 Oklahoma
28 Oregon
29 Connecticut
30 Iowa
31 Mississippi
32 Kansas
33 Arkansas
34 Utah
35 Nevada
36 New Mexico
37 West Virginia
38 Nebraska
39 Idaho
40 Maine
41 New Hampshire
42 Hawaii
43 Rhode Island
44 Montana
45 Delaware
46 South Dakota
47 North Dakota
48 Alaska
49 Vermont
50 Wyoming

Note: Numbers that appear to be identical are rounded and vary slightly in actual value. The rankings reflect the actual values before rounding. See the introduction for more details.

A-2 Percentage Change in Population, 1999-2000

State	Adjusted Population 1999 (in thousands)	Percentage change in population 1999-2000	Rank by percentage change
Alabama	4,434	0.30	43
Alaska	626	0.22	44
Arizona	5,028	2.04	2
Arkansas	2,645	1.08	14
California	33,446	1.27	10
Colorado	4,223	1.86	3
Connecticut	3,381	0.72	21
Delaware	775	1.10	13
Florida	15,754	1.45	6
Georgia	8,041	1.81	4
Hawaii	1,217	-0.47	49
Idaho	1,276	1.39	8
Illinois	12,360	0.48	36
Indiana	6,048	0.54	32
Iowa	2,916	0.34	41
Kansas	2,679	0.36	39
Kentucky	4,019	0.57	31
Louisiana	4,462	0.16	45
Maine	1,269	0.50	34
Maryland	5,248	0.93	17
Massachusetts	6,312	0.58	30
Michigan	9,896	0.43	38
Minnesota	4,869	1.04	15
Mississippi	2,826	0.66	26
Missouri	5,562	0.60	29
Montana	898	0.48	35
Nebraska	1,706	0.33	42
Nevada	1,929	3.61	1
New Hampshire	1,222	1.17	12
New Jersey	8,346	0.82	20
New Mexico	1,811	0.43	37
New York	18,842	0.71	23
North Carolina	7,950	1.25	11
North Dakota	645	-0.50	50
Ohio	11,342	0.10	46
Oklahoma	3,428	0.66	25
Oregon	3,400	0.62	28
Pennsylvania	12,270	0.09	47
Rhode Island	1,038	0.95	16
South Carolina	3,976	0.91	18
South Dakota	750	0.63	27
Tennessee	5,640	0.87	19
Texas	20,534	1.55	5
Utah	2,202	1.44	7
Vermont	605	0.71	22
Virginia	6,989	1.29	9
Washington	5,853	0.70	24
West Virginia	1,812	-0.23	48
Wisconsin	5,335	0.53	33
Wyoming	492	0.35	40
50 States	278,324	0.91	
DC	566	1.00	
United States	278,890	0.91	

Rank in order by percentage change	
1	Nevada
2	Arizona
3	Colorado
4	Georgia
5	Texas
6	Florida
7	Utah
8	Idaho
9	Virginia
10	California
11	North Carolina
12	New Hampshire
13	Delaware
14	Arkansas
15	Minnesota
16	Rhode Island
17	Maryland
18	South Carolina
19	Tennessee
20	New Jersey
21	Connecticut
22	Vermont
23	New York
24	Washington
25	Oklahoma
26	Mississippi
27	South Dakota
28	Oregon
29	Missouri
30	Massachusetts
31	Kentucky
32	Indiana
33	Wisconsin
34	Maine
35	Montana
36	Illinois
37	New Mexico
38	Michigan
39	Kansas
40	Wyoming
41	Iowa
42	Nebraska
43	Alabama
44	Alaska
45	Louisiana
46	Ohio
47	Pennsylvania
48	West Virginia
49	Hawaii
50	North Dakota

Note: Numbers that appear to be identical are rounded and vary slightly in actual value. The rankings reflect the actual values before rounding. See the introduction for more details.

A-3 Percentage Change in Population, 1990-2000

State	Population 1990 (in thousands)	Percentage change in population 1990-2000	Rank by percentage change
Alabama	4,041	10.1	25
Alaska	550	14.0	17
Arizona	3,665	40.0	2
Arkansas	2,351	13.7	19
California	29,760	13.8	18
Colorado	3,294	30.6	3
Connecticut	3,287	3.6	47
Delaware	666	17.6	13
Florida	12,938	23.5	7
Georgia	6,478	26.4	6
Hawaii	1,108	9.3	31
Idaho	1,007	28.5	5
Illinois	11,431	8.6	34
Indiana	5,544	9.7	27
Iowa	2,777	5.4	43
Kansas	2,478	8.5	35
Kentucky	3,685	9.7	28
Louisiana	4,220	5.9	40
Maine	1,228	3.8	46
Maryland	4,781	10.8	23
Massachusetts	6,016	5.5	41
Michigan	9,295	6.9	39
Minnesota	4,375	12.4	21
Mississippi	2,573	10.5	24
Missouri	5,117	9.3	30
Montana	799	12.9	20
Nebraska	1,578	8.4	37
Nevada	1,202	66.3	1
New Hampshire	1,109	11.4	22
New Jersey	7,730	8.9	33
New Mexico	1,515	20.1	12
New York	17,990	5.5	42
North Carolina	6,629	21.4	9
North Dakota	639	0.5	50
Ohio	10,847	4.7	44
Oklahoma	3,146	9.7	26
Oregon	2,842	20.4	11
Pennsylvania	11,882	3.4	48
Rhode Island	1,003	4.5	45
South Carolina	3,487	15.1	15
South Dakota	696	8.5	36
Tennessee	4,877	16.7	14
Texas	16,987	22.8	8
Utah	1,723	29.6	4
Vermont	563	8.2	38
Virginia	6,187	14.4	16
Washington	4,867	21.1	10
West Virginia	1,793	0.8	49
Wisconsin	4,892	9.6	29
Wyoming	454	8.9	32
50 States	248,103	13.2	
DC	607	-5.7	
United States	248,710	13.2	

Rank in order by percentage change

1 Nevada
2 Arizona
3 Colorado
4 Utah
5 Idaho
6 Georgia
7 Florida
8 Texas
9 North Carolina
10 Washington
11 Oregon
12 New Mexico
13 Delaware
14 Tennessee
15 South Carolina
16 Virginia
17 Alaska
18 California
19 Arkansas
20 Montana
21 Minnesota
22 New Hampshire
23 Maryland
24 Mississippi
25 Alabama
26 Oklahoma
27 Indiana
28 Kentucky
29 Wisconsin
30 Missouri
31 Hawaii
32 Wyoming
33 New Jersey
34 Illinois
35 Kansas
36 South Dakota
37 Nebraska
38 Vermont
39 Michigan
40 Louisiana
41 Massachusetts
42 New York
43 Iowa
44 Ohio
45 Rhode Island
46 Maine
47 Connecticut
48 Pennsylvania
49 West Virginia
50 North Dakota

Note: Numbers that appear to be identical are rounded and vary slightly in actual value. The rankings reflect the actual values before rounding. See the introduction for more details.

A-4 Projected Population, 2005, and Population Change

State	Projected population 2005 (in thousands)	Percentage change in population 2000-2005	Rank by percentage change
Alabama	4,631	4.1	14
Alaska	700	11.7	3
Arizona	5,230	1.9	32
Arkansas	2,750	2.9	22
California	34,441	1.7	35
Colorado	4,468	3.9	15
Connecticut	3,317	-2.6	48
Delaware	800	2.1	31
Florida	16,279	1.9	33
Georgia	8,413	2.8	23
Hawaii	1,342	10.8	6
Idaho	1,480	14.4	2
Illinois	12,266	-1.2	46
Indiana	6,215	2.2	27
Iowa	2,941	0.5	42
Kansas	2,761	2.7	24
Kentucky	4,098	1.4	37
Louisiana	4,535	1.5	36
Maine	1,285	0.8	39
Maryland	5,467	3.2	19
Massachusetts	6,310	-0.6	45
Michigan	9,763	-1.8	47
Minnesota	5,005	1.7	34
Mississippi	2,908	2.2	26
Missouri	5,718	2.2	29
Montana	1,006	11.5	4
Nebraska	1,761	2.9	21
Nevada	2,070	3.6	17
New Hampshire	1,281	3.7	16
New Jersey	8,392	-0.3	44
New Mexico	2,016	10.8	5
New York	18,250	-3.8	50
North Carolina	8,227	2.2	28
North Dakota	677	5.4	11
Ohio	11,428	0.7	40
Oklahoma	3,491	1.2	38
Oregon	3,613	5.6	10
Pennsylvania	12,281	0.0	43
Rhode Island	1,012	-3.5	49
South Carolina	4,033	0.5	41
South Dakota	810	7.3	8
Tennessee	5,966	4.9	12
Texas	21,487	3.0	20
Utah	2,411	8.0	7
Vermont	638	4.8	13
Virginia	7,324	3.5	18
Washington	6,258	6.2	9
West Virginia	1,849	2.2	25
Wisconsin	5,479	2.2	30
Wyoming	568	15.0	1
50 States	285,451	1.6	
DC	529	-7.5	
United States*	285,981	1.6	

Rank in order by percentage change	
1	Wyoming
2	Idaho
3	Alaska
4	Montana
5	New Mexico
6	Hawaii
7	Utah
8	South Dakota
9	Washington
10	Oregon
11	North Dakota
12	Tennessee
13	Vermont
14	Alabama
15	Colorado
16	New Hampshire
17	Nevada
18	Virginia
19	Maryland
20	Texas
21	Nebraska
22	Arkansas
23	Georgia
24	Kansas
25	West Virginia
26	Mississippi
27	Indiana
28	North Carolina
29	Missouri
30	Wisconsin
31	Delaware
32	Arizona
33	Florida
34	Minnesota
35	California
36	Louisiana
37	Kentucky
38	Oklahoma
39	Maine
40	Ohio
41	South Carolina
42	Iowa
43	Pennsylvania
44	New Jersey
45	Massachusetts
46	Illinois
47	Michigan
48	Connecticut
49	Rhode Island
50	New York

Note: Numbers that appear to be identical are rounded and vary slightly in actual value. The rankings reflect the actual values before rounding. See the introduction for more details.

Due to rounding or data sources, the 50-state total plus D.C. may not equal the U.S. total. Please see introduction.

A-5 Projected Population for the Year 2015

State	Estimated 2015 population (in thousands)	Rank
Alabama	4,956	22
Alaska	791	47
Arizona	5,808	19
Arkansas	2,922	33
California	41,373	1
Colorado	4,833	24
Connecticut	3,506	29
Delaware	832	46
Florida	18,497	4
Georgia	9,200	9
Hawaii	1,553	40
Idaho	1,622	39
Illinois	12,808	5
Indiana	6,404	15
Iowa	2,994	31
Kansas	2,939	32
Kentucky	4,231	26
Louisiana	4,840	23
Maine	1,362	42
Maryland	5,862	18
Massachusetts	6,574	14
Michigan	9,917	8
Minnesota	5,283	21
Mississippi	3,035	30
Missouri	6,005	17
Montana	1069	44
Nebraska	1,850	38
Nevada	2,179	36
New Hampshire	1,372	41
New Jersey	8,924	10
New Mexico	2,300	35
New York	18,916	3
North Carolina	8,840	11
North Dakota	704	48
Ohio	11,588	7
Oklahoma	3,789	28
Oregon	3,992	27
Pennsylvania	12,449	6
Rhode Island	1070	43
South Carolina	4,369	25
South Dakota	840	45
Tennessee	6,365	16
Texas	24,280	2
Utah	2,670	34
Vermont	662	49
Virginia	7,921	12
Washington	7,058	13
West Virginia	1,851	37
Wisconsin	5,693	20
Wyoming	641	50
50 States	309,539	
DC	594	
United States*	310,134	

Rank in order by population	
1	California
2	Texas
3	New York
4	Florida
5	Illinois
6	Pennsylvania
7	Ohio
8	Michigan
9	Georgia
10	New Jersey
11	North Carolina
12	Virginia
13	Washington
14	Massachusetts
15	Indiana
16	Tennessee
17	Missouri
18	Maryland
19	Arizona
20	Wisconsin
21	Minnesota
22	Alabama
23	Louisiana
24	Colorado
25	South Carolina
26	Kentucky
27	Oregon
28	Oklahoma
29	Connecticut
30	Mississippi
31	Iowa
32	Kansas
33	Arkansas
34	Utah
35	New Mexico
36	Nevada
37	West Virginia
38	Nebraska
39	Idaho
40	Hawaii
41	New Hampshire
42	Maine
43	Rhode Island
44	Montana
45	South Dakota
46	Delaware
47	Alaska
48	North Dakota
49	Vermont
50	Wyoming

Due to rounding or data sources, the 50-state total plus D.C. may not equal the U.S. total. Please see introduction.

A-6 Population Age 65 and Over, 2000

State	Population 65 and over (in thousands)	Percentage of population 65 and over	Rank by percentage
Alabama	580	13.0	21
Alaska	36	5.7	50
Arizona	668	13.0	22
Arkansas	374	14.0	9
California	3,596	10.6	45
Colorado	416	9.7	47
Connecticut	470	13.8	10
Delaware	102	13.0	23
Florida	2,808	17.6	1
Georgia	785	9.6	48
Hawaii	161	13.3	16
Idaho	146	11.3	41
Illinois	1,500	12.1	33
Indiana	753	12.4	28
Iowa	436	14.9	4
Kansas	356	13.3	17
Kentucky	505	12.5	27
Louisiana	517	11.6	39
Maine	183	14.4	7
Maryland	599	11.3	40
Massachusetts	860	13.5	12
Michigan	1,219	12.3	30
Minnesota	594	12.1	32
Mississippi	344	12.1	34
Missouri	755	13.5	13
Montana	121	13.4	14
Nebraska	232	13.6	11
Nevada	219	11.0	44
New Hampshire	148	12.0	36
New Jersey	1,113	13.2	18
New Mexico	212	11.7	38
New York	2,448	12.9	24
North Carolina	969	12.0	35
North Dakota	94	14.7	5
Ohio	1,508	13.3	15
Oklahoma	456	13.2	19
Oregon	438	12.8	25
Pennsylvania	1,919	15.6	2
Rhode Island	152	14.5	6
South Carolina	485	12.1	31
South Dakota	108	14.3	8
Tennessee	703	12.4	29
Texas	2,073	9.9	46
Utah	190	8.5	49
Vermont	78	12.7	26
Virginia	792	11.2	43
Washington	662	11.2	42
West Virginia	277	15.3	3
Wisconsin	703	13.1	20
Wyoming	58	11.7	37
50 States	34,922	12.4	
DC	70	12.2	
United States	34,992	12.4	

Rank in order by percentage

1 Florida
2 Pennsylvania
3 West Virginia
4 Iowa
5 North Dakota
6 Rhode Island
7 Maine
8 South Dakota
9 Arkansas
10 Connecticut
11 Nebraska
12 Massachusetts
13 Missouri
14 Montana
15 Ohio
16 Hawaii
17 Kansas
18 New Jersey
19 Oklahoma
20 Wisconsin
21 Alabama
22 Arizona
23 Delaware
24 New York
25 Oregon
26 Vermont
27 Kentucky
28 Indiana
29 Tennessee
30 Michigan
31 South Carolina
32 Minnesota
33 Illinois
34 Mississippi
35 North Carolina
36 New Hampshire
37 Wyoming
38 New Mexico
39 Louisiana
40 Maryland
41 Idaho
42 Washington
43 Virginia
44 Nevada
45 California
46 Texas
47 Colorado
48 Georgia
49 Utah
50 Alaska

Note: Numbers that appear to be identical are rounded and vary slightly in actual value. The rankings reflect the actual values before rounding. See the introduction for more details.

A-7 Population Age 17 and Under, 2000

State	Population 17 and under (in thousands)	Percentage of population 17 and under	Rank by percentage
Alabama	1,123	25.3	29
Alaska	191	30.4	2
Arizona	1,367	26.6	10
Arkansas	680	25.4	27
California	9,250	27.3	6
Colorado	1,101	25.6	23
Connecticut	842	24.7	38
Delaware	195	24.8	34
Florida	3,646	22.8	49
Georgia	2,169	26.5	12
Hawaii	296	24.4	42
Idaho	369	28.5	3
Illinois	3,245	26.1	15
Indiana	1,574	25.9	18
Iowa	734	25.1	31
Kansas	713	26.5	11
Kentucky	995	24.6	39
Louisiana	1,220	27.3	7
Maine	301	23.6	47
Maryland	1,356	25.6	22
Massachusetts	1,500	23.6	48
Michigan	2,596	26.1	16
Minnesota	1,287	26.2	14
Mississippi	775	27.3	8
Missouri	1,428	25.5	25
Montana	230	25.5	26
Nebraska	450	26.3	13
Nevada	512	25.6	21
New Hampshire	310	25.0	32
New Jersey	2,088	24.8	35
New Mexico	509	28.0	5
New York	4,690	24.7	37
North Carolina	1,964	24.4	43
North Dakota	161	25.0	33
Ohio	2,888	25.4	28
Oklahoma	892	25.9	19
Oregon	847	24.7	36
Pennsylvania	2,922	23.8	45
Rhode Island	248	23.6	46
South Carolina	1,010	25.2	30
South Dakota	203	26.8	9
Tennessee	1,399	24.6	40
Texas	5,887	28.2	4
Utah	719	32.2	1
Vermont	148	24.2	44
Virginia	1,738	24.6	41
Washington	1,514	25.7	20
West Virginia	402	22.3	50
Wisconsin	1,369	25.5	24
Wyoming	129	26.1	17
50 States	72,179	25.7	
DC	115	20.1	
United States	72,294	25.7	

Rank in order by percentage

1 Utah
2 Alaska
3 Idaho
4 Texas
5 New Mexico
6 California
7 Louisiana
8 Mississippi
9 South Dakota
10 Arizona
11 Kansas
12 Georgia
13 Nebraska
14 Minnesota
15 Illinois
16 Michigan
17 Wyoming
18 Indiana
19 Oklahoma
20 Washington
21 Nevada
22 Maryland
23 Colorado
24 Wisconsin
25 Missouri
26 Montana
27 Arkansas
28 Ohio
29 Alabama
30 South Carolina
31 Iowa
32 New Hampshire
33 North Dakota
34 Delaware
35 New Jersey
36 Oregon
37 New York
38 Connecticut
39 Kentucky
40 Tennessee
41 Virginia
42 Hawaii
43 North Carolina
44 Vermont
45 Pennsylvania
46 Rhode Island
47 Maine
48 Massachusetts
49 Florida
50 West Virginia

Note: Numbers that appear to be identical are rounded and vary slightly in actual value. The rankings reflect the actual values before rounding. See the introduction for more details.

A-8 Median Age, 2000

State	Median age 2000	Rank
Alabama	35.8	26
Alaska	32.4	48
Arizona	34.2	42
Arkansas	36.0	19
California	33.3	46
Colorado	34.3	41
Connecticut	37.4	7
Delaware	36.0	19
Florida	38.7	2
Georgia	33.4	45
Hawaii	36.2	14
Idaho	33.2	47
Illinois	34.7	39
Indiana	35.2	36
Iowa	36.6	11
Kansas	35.2	36
Kentucky	35.9	23
Louisiana	34.0	43
Maine	38.6	3
Maryland	36.0	19
Massachusetts	36.5	12
Michigan	35.5	29
Minnesota	35.4	31
Mississippi	33.8	44
Missouri	36.1	18
Montana	37.5	6
Nebraska	35.3	33
Nevada	35.0	38
New Hampshire	37.1	8
New Jersey	36.7	9
New Mexico	34.6	40
New York	35.9	23
North Carolina	35.3	33
North Dakota	36.2	14
Ohio	36.2	14
Oklahoma	35.5	29
Oregon	36.3	13
Pennsylvania	38.0	4
Rhode Island	36.7	9
South Carolina	35.4	31
South Dakota	35.6	28
Tennessee	35.9	23
Texas	32.3	49
Utah	27.1	50
Vermont	37.7	5
Virginia	35.7	27
Washington	35.3	33
West Virginia	38.9	1
Wisconsin	36.0	19
Wyoming	36.2	14
50 States	n/a	
DC	34.6	
United States	35.3	

Rank in order by age	
1	West Virginia
2	Florida
3	Maine
4	Pennsylvania
5	Vermont
6	Montana
7	Connecticut
8	New Hampshire
9	New Jersey
9	Rhode Island
11	Iowa
12	Massachusetts
13	Oregon
14	Hawaii
14	North Dakota
14	Ohio
14	Wyoming
18	Missouri
19	Arkansas
19	Delaware
19	Maryland
19	Wisconsin
23	Kentucky
23	New York
23	Tennessee
26	Alabama
27	Virginia
28	South Dakota
29	Michigan
29	Oklahoma
31	Minnesota
31	South Carolina
33	Nebraska
33	North Carolina
33	Washington
36	Indiana
36	Kansas
38	Nevada
39	Illinois
40	New Mexico
41	Colorado
42	Arizona
43	Louisiana
44	Mississippi
45	Georgia
46	California
47	Idaho
48	Alaska
49	Texas
50	Utah

Note: Ties in ranking reflect ties in actual values.

A-9 African American Population, 2000

State	African American population of one race ("alone") (in thousands)	African American population alone and of more than one race ("in combination") (in thousands)	In combination population as a percentage of alone and in combination population	Alone and in combination population as a percentage of total population	Rank by percentage of total population
Alabama	1,156	1,169	1.1	26.3	6
Alaska	22	27	19.7	4.3	33
Arizona	159	186	14.4	3.6	36
Arkansas	419	427	1.9	16.0	12
California	2,264	2,513	9.9	7.4	26
Colorado	165	191	13.5	4.4	31
Connecticut	310	339	8.6	10.0	21
Delaware	151	157	4.1	20.1	9
Florida	2,336	2,472	5.5	15.5	14
Georgia	2,350	2,393	1.8	29.2	4
Hawaii	22	33	34.0	2.8	38
Idaho	5	8	32.9	0.6	49
Illinois	1,877	1,938	3.1	15.6	13
Indiana	510	538	5.2	8.8	22
Iowa	62	73	14.7	2.5	39
Kansas	154	171	9.6	6.3	27
Kentucky	296	312	5.1	7.7	24
Louisiana	1,452	1,468	1.1	32.9	2
Maine	7	10	29.2	0.7	47
Maryland	1,477	1,525	3.1	28.8	5
Massachusetts	343	398	13.8	6.3	28
Michigan	1,413	1,475	4.2	14.8	15
Minnesota	172	203	15.4	4.1	34
Mississippi	1,034	1,042	0.8	36.6	1
Missouri	629	655	4.0	11.7	19
Montana	3	4	39.4	0.5	50
Nebraska	69	76	9.6	4.4	32
Nevada	135	151	10.0	7.5	25
New Hampshire	9	12	26.1	1.0	43
New Jersey	1,142	1,212	5.8	14.4	16
New Mexico	34	42	19.0	2.3	40
New York	3,014	3,234	6.8	17.0	10
North Carolina	1,738	1,776	2.2	22.1	7
North Dakota	4	5	27.1	0.8	46
Ohio	1,301	1,373	5.2	12.1	17
Oklahoma	261	285	8.4	8.3	23
Oregon	56	73	23.4	2.1	41
Pennsylvania	1,225	1,289	5.0	10.5	20
Rhode Island	47	58	19.2	5.5	30
South Carolina	1,185	1,201	1.3	29.9	3
South Dakota	5	7	29.9	0.9	45
Tennessee	933	953	2.2	16.8	11
Texas	2,405	2,493	3.5	12.0	18
Utah	18	24	27.6	1.1	42
Vermont	3	4	31.8	0.7	48
Virginia	1,390	1,441	3.5	20.4	8
Washington	190	238	20.2	4.0	35
West Virginia	57	63	8.9	3.5	37
Wisconsin	304	327	6.8	6.1	29
Wyoming	4	5	23.5	1.0	44
50 States	34,315	36,069	n/a	12.8	
DC	343	350	2.0	61.3	
United States	34,658	36,419	4.8	12.9	

Rank in order by percentage of total population	
1	Mississippi
2	Louisiana
3	South Carolina
4	Georgia
5	Maryland
6	Alabama
7	North Carolina
8	Virginia
9	Delaware
10	New York
11	Tennessee
12	Arkansas
13	Illinois
14	Florida
15	Michigan
16	New Jersey
17	Ohio
18	Texas
19	Missouri
20	Pennsylvania
21	Connecticut
22	Indiana
23	Oklahoma
24	Kentucky
25	Nevada
26	California
27	Kansas
28	Massachusetts
29	Wisconsin
30	Rhode Island
31	Colorado
32	Nebraska
33	Alaska
34	Minnesota
35	Washington
36	Arizona
37	West Virginia
38	Hawaii
39	Iowa
40	New Mexico
41	Oregon
42	Utah
43	New Hampshire
44	Wyoming
45	South Dakota
46	North Dakota
47	Maine
48	Vermont
49	Idaho
50	Montana

Note: Numbers that appear to be identical are rounded and vary slightly in actual value. The rankings reflect the actual values before rounding. See the introduction for more details.

A-10 Hispanic Population, 2000

State	Hispanic population (in thousands)	Percentage of total population	Rank by percentage
Alabama	75.8	1.7	42
Alaska	25.9	4.1	28
Arizona	1,295.6	25.3	4
Arkansas	86.9	3.2	32
California	10,966.6	32.4	2
Colorado	735.6	17.1	6
Connecticut	320.3	9.4	11
Delaware	37.3	4.8	24
Florida	2,682.7	16.8	7
Georgia	435.2	5.3	22
Hawaii	87.7	7.2	17
Idaho	101.7	7.9	15
Illinois	1,530.3	12.3	10
Indiana	214.5	3.5	30
Iowa	82.5	2.8	35
Kansas	188.3	7.0	18
Kentucky	59.9	1.5	44
Louisiana	107.7	2.4	36
Maine	9.4	0.7	49
Maryland	227.9	4.3	27
Massachusetts	428.7	6.8	19
Michigan	323.9	3.3	31
Minnesota	143.4	2.9	34
Mississippi	39.6	1.4	46
Missouri	118.6	2.1	39
Montana	18.1	2.0	40
Nebraska	94.4	5.5	21
Nevada	394.0	19.7	5
New Hampshire	20.5	1.7	43
New Jersey	1,117.2	13.3	9
New Mexico	765.4	42.1	1
New York	2,867.6	15.1	8
North Carolina	379.0	4.7	25
North Dakota	7.8	1.2	47
Ohio	217.1	1.9	41
Oklahoma	179.3	5.2	23
Oregon	275.3	8.0	14
Pennsylvania	394.1	3.2	33
Rhode Island	90.8	8.7	13
South Carolina	95.1	2.4	37
South Dakota	10.9	1.4	45
Tennessee	123.8	2.2	38
Texas	6,669.7	32.0	3
Utah	201.6	9.0	12
Vermont	5.5	0.9	48
Virginia	329.5	4.7	26
Washington	441.5	7.5	16
West Virginia	12.3	0.7	50
Wisconsin	192.9	3.6	29
Wyoming	31.7	6.4	20
50 States	35,260.9	12.6	
DC	45.0	7.9	
United States*	35,305.8	12.5	

Rank in order by percentage	
1	New Mexico
2	California
3	Texas
4	Arizona
5	Nevada
6	Colorado
7	Florida
8	New York
9	New Jersey
10	Illinois
11	Connecticut
12	Utah
13	Rhode Island
14	Oregon
15	Idaho
16	Washington
17	Hawaii
18	Kansas
19	Massachusetts
20	Wyoming
21	Nebraska
22	Georgia
23	Oklahoma
24	Delaware
25	North Carolina
26	Virginia
27	Maryland
28	Alaska
29	Wisconsin
30	Indiana
31	Michigan
32	Arkansas
33	Pennsylvania
34	Minnesota
35	Iowa
36	Louisiana
37	South Carolina
38	Tennessee
39	Missouri
40	Montana
41	Ohio
42	Alabama
43	New Hampshire
44	Kentucky
45	South Dakota
46	Mississippi
47	North Dakota
48	Vermont
49	Maine
50	West Virginia

Note: Numbers that appear to be identical are rounded and vary slightly in actual value. The rankings reflect the actual values before rounding. See the introduction for more details.

Due to rounding or data sources, the 50-state total plus D.C. may not equal the U.S. total. Please see introduction.

A-11 Population in Poverty, 2000

State	Population in poverty (in thousands)	Percentage of population in poverty	Rank by percentage
Alabama	613	14.1	8
Alaska	49	8.0	42
Arizona	611	12.1	15
Arkansas	486	18.0	1
California	4,559	12.9	12
Colorado	307	7.9	43
Connecticut	189	6.3	48
Delaware	65	8.7	36
Florida	1,648	10.7	20
Georgia	901	11.3	18
Hawaii	106	9.7	28
Idaho	168	13.0	11
Illinois	1,458	11.6	17
Indiana	459	8.4	38
Iowa	192	7.1	47
Kansas	233	9.5	31
Kentucky	457	11.8	16
Louisiana	753	17.4	2
Maine	97	8.3	39
Maryland	362	7.6	45
Massachusetts	649	10.1	25
Michigan	1,028	10.1	25
Minnesota	266	5.9	49
Mississippi	369	12.9	12
Missouri	406	7.8	44
Montana	142	15.9	4
Nebraska	139	8.8	35
Nevada	151	8.2	40
New Hampshire	53	4.8	50
New Jersey	687	8.1	41
New Mexico	306	16.8	3
New York	2,528	13.4	10
North Carolina	935	12.2	14
North Dakota	58	10.0	27
Ohio	1,209	10.2	24
Oklahoma	504	15.4	5
Oregon	342	10.7	20
Pennsylvania	1,097	8.9	34
Rhode Island	74	8.6	37
South Carolina	377	10.4	23
South Dakota	64	9.5	31
Tennessee	814	14.6	7
Texas	3,085	14.7	6
Utah	211	9.6	30
Vermont	60	10.6	22
Virginia	520	7.6	45
Washington	526	9.7	28
West Virginia	243	13.9	9
Wisconsin	459	9.2	33
Wyoming	52	10.9	19
50 States	31,067	11.1	
DC	73	14.8	
United States*	31,139	11.3	

Rank in order by percentage	
1	Arkansas
2	Louisiana
3	New Mexico
4	Montana
5	Oklahoma
6	Texas
7	Tennessee
8	Alabama
9	West Virginia
10	New York
11	Idaho
12	California
12	Mississippi
14	North Carolina
15	Arizona
16	Kentucky
17	Illinois
18	Georgia
19	Wyoming
20	Florida
20	Oregon
22	Vermont
23	South Carolina
24	Ohio
25	Massachusetts
25	Michigan
27	North Dakota
28	Hawaii
28	Washington
30	Utah
31	Kansas
31	South Dakota
33	Wisconsin
34	Pennsylvania
35	Nebraska
36	Delaware
37	Rhode Island
38	Indiana
39	Maine
40	Nevada
41	New Jersey
42	Alaska
43	Colorado
44	Missouri
45	Maryland
45	Virginia
47	Iowa
48	Connecticut
49	Minnesota
50	New Hampshire

Note: Ties in ranking reflect ties in actual values.

*Due to rounding or data sources, the 50-state total plus D.C. may not equal the U.S. total. Please see introduction.

A-12 Number and Rate of Children in Poverty, 2000

State	Number of persons under 18 in poverty (in thousands)	Percentage in poverty	Rank by percentage
Alabama	209	20.1	7
Alaska	18	10.3	42
Arizona	285	19.3	9
Arkansas	212	27.1	1
California	1,962	18.9	10
Colorado	85	10.7	40
Connecticut	49	9.2	44
Delaware	29	16.4	17
Florida	599	15.9	20
Georgia	343	16.4	17
Hawaii	30	14.1	26
Idaho	71	18.5	12
Illinois	650	17.4	16
Indiana	106	10.0	43
Iowa	51	8.7	45
Kansas	68	13.1	32
Kentucky	130	15.1	23
Louisiana	259	23.3	4
Maine	16	8.6	47
Maryland	62	6.8	50
Massachusetts	238	13.7	28
Michigan	398	13.6	29
Minnesota	86	8.7	45
Mississippi	135	16.2	19
Missouri	119	10.5	41
Montana	56	24.8	2
Nebraska	44	11.8	35
Nevada	52	11.6	36
New Hampshire	14	7.5	49
New Jersey	261	10.9	39
New Mexico	127	23.2	5
New York	941	18.6	11
North Carolina	361	17.9	15
North Dakota	18	14.0	27
Ohio	543	15.1	23
Oklahoma	185	23.6	3
Oregon	119	18.4	13
Pennsylvania	362	11.0	38
Rhode Island	15	12.6	33
South Carolina	104	15.9	20
South Dakota	18	12.6	33
Tennessee	268	19.9	8
Texas	1,301	20.5	6
Utah	85	11.5	37
Vermont	17	15.4	22
Virginia	130	8.2	48
Washington	147	13.2	31
West Virginia	63	18.4	13
Wisconsin	151	13.5	30
Wyoming	17	14.4	25
50 States	11,609	16.2	
DC	21	23.4	
United States*	11,633	16.2	

Rank in order by percentage	
1	Arkansas
2	Montana
3	Oklahoma
4	Louisiana
5	New Mexico
6	Texas
7	Alabama
8	Tennessee
9	Arizona
10	California
11	New York
12	Idaho
13	Oregon
13	West Virginia
15	North Carolina
16	Illinois
17	Delaware
17	Georgia
19	Mississippi
20	Florida
20	South Carolina
22	Vermont
23	Kentucky
23	Ohio
25	Wyoming
26	Hawaii
27	North Dakota
28	Massachusetts
29	Michigan
30	Wisconsin
31	Washington
32	Kansas
33	Rhode Island
33	South Dakota
35	Nebraska
36	Nevada
37	Utah
38	Pennsylvania
39	New Jersey
40	Colorado
41	Missouri
42	Alaska
43	Indiana
44	Connecticut
45	Iowa
45	Minnesota
47	Maine
48	Virginia
49	New Hampshire
50	Maryland

Note: Ties in ranking reflect ties in actual values.

Due to rounding or data sources, the 50-state total plus D.C. may not equal the U.S. total. Please see introduction.

A-13 Female Population, 2000

State	Female population (in thousands)	Percentage of population	Rank by percentage
Alabama	2,301	51.7	4
Alaska	303	48.3	50
Arizona	2,570	50.1	43
Arkansas	1,369	51.2	19
California	16,997	50.2	40
Colorado	2,135	49.6	48
Connecticut	1,756	51.6	9
Delaware	403	51.4	12
Florida	8,185	51.2	18
Georgia	4,159	50.8	31
Hawaii	603	49.8	46
Idaho	645	49.9	45
Illinois	6,339	51.0	21
Indiana	3,098	51.0	26
Iowa	1,491	50.9	27
Kansas	1,360	50.6	34
Kentucky	2,066	51.1	20
Louisiana	2,306	51.6	8
Maine	655	51.3	16
Maryland	2,739	51.7	7
Massachusetts	3,290	51.8	2
Michigan	5,065	51.0	24
Minnesota	2,484	50.5	35
Mississippi	1,471	51.7	6
Missouri	2,875	51.4	14
Montana	453	50.2	41
Nebraska	868	50.7	32
Nevada	980	49.1	49
New Hampshire	628	50.8	30
New Jersey	4,332	51.5	10
New Mexico	925	50.8	29
New York	9,830	51.8	3
North Carolina	4,107	51.0	22
North Dakota	322	50.1	42
Ohio	5,841	51.4	11
Oklahoma	1,755	50.9	28
Oregon	1,725	50.4	36
Pennsylvania	6,351	51.7	5
Rhode Island	545	52.0	1
South Carolina	2,063	51.4	13
South Dakota	380	50.4	37
Tennessee	2,919	51.3	17
Texas	10,499	50.4	38
Utah	1,114	49.9	44
Vermont	310	51.0	23
Virginia	3,607	51.0	25
Washington	2,960	50.2	39
West Virginia	929	51.4	15
Wisconsin	2,715	50.6	33
Wyoming	245	49.7	47
50 States	143,065	50.9	
DC	303	52.9	
United States	143,368	50.9	

Rank in order by percentage

1 Rhode Island
2 Massachusetts
3 New York
4 Alabama
5 Pennsylvania
6 Mississippi
7 Maryland
8 Louisiana
9 Connecticut
10 New Jersey
11 Ohio
12 Delaware
13 South Carolina
14 Missouri
15 West Virginia
16 Maine
17 Tennessee
18 Florida
19 Arkansas
20 Kentucky
21 Illinois
22 North Carolina
23 Vermont
24 Michigan
25 Virginia
26 Indiana
27 Iowa
28 Oklahoma
29 New Mexico
30 New Hampshire
31 Georgia
32 Nebraska
33 Wisconsin
34 Kansas
35 Minnesota
36 Oregon
37 South Dakota
38 Texas
39 Washington
40 California
41 Montana
42 North Dakota
43 Arizona
44 Utah
45 Idaho
46 Hawaii
47 Wyoming
48 Colorado
49 Nevada
50 Alaska

Note: Numbers that appear to be identical are rounded and vary slightly in actual value. The rankings reflect the actual values before rounding. See the introduction for more details.

A-14 Birth Rates, 2000

State	Births per 1,000 population	Rank
Alabama	14.4	22
Alaska	16.1	6
Arizona	17.5	3
Arkansas	14.8	17
California	15.8	8
Colorado	15.8	8
Connecticut	13.1	39
Delaware	14.5	21
Florida	13.3	37
Georgia	16.7	4
Hawaii	14.9	15
Idaho	16.0	7
Illinois	15.2	14
Indiana	14.6	20
Iowa	13.4	36
Kansas	14.9	15
Kentucky	14.1	27
Louisiana	15.5	12
Maine	10.8	49
Maryland	14.2	25
Massachusetts	13.2	38
Michigan	13.7	34
Minnesota	14.0	29
Mississippi	15.8	8
Missouri	13.9	32
Montana	12.3	43
Nebraska	14.8	17
Nevada	16.4	5
New Hampshire	12.0	46
New Jersey	14.0	29
New Mexico	15.6	11
New York	14.1	27
North Carolina	15.5	12
North Dakota	12.2	44
Ohio	n/a	n/a
Oklahoma	14.8	17
Oregon	13.7	34
Pennsylvania	12.2	44
Rhode Island	12.5	42
South Carolina	14.3	24
South Dakota	14.0	29
Tennessee	14.4	22
Texas	18.0	2
Utah	21.9	1
Vermont	10.9	48
Virginia	14.2	25
Washington	13.9	32
West Virginia	11.6	47
Wisconsin	13.1	39
Wyoming	13.0	41
50 States	n/a	
DC	14.8	
United States	14.8	

Rank in order by rate	
1	Utah
2	Texas
3	Arizona
4	Georgia
5	Nevada
6	Alaska
7	Idaho
8	California
8	Colorado
8	Mississippi
11	New Mexico
12	Louisiana
12	North Carolina
14	Illinois
15	Hawaii
15	Kansas
17	Arkansas
17	Nebraska
17	Oklahoma
20	Indiana
21	Delaware
22	Alabama
22	Tennessee
24	South Carolina
25	Maryland
25	Virginia
27	Kentucky
27	New York
29	Minnesota
29	New Jersey
29	South Dakota
32	Missouri
32	Washington
34	Michigan
34	Oregon
36	Iowa
37	Florida
38	Massachusetts
39	Connecticut
39	Wisconsin
41	Wyoming
42	Rhode Island
43	Montana
44	North Dakota
44	Pennsylvania
46	New Hampshire
47	West Virginia
48	Vermont
49	Maine

Note: Ties in ranking reflect ties in actual values.

A-15 Death Rates (age-adjusted), 2000

State	Deaths per 1,000 population	Rank
Alabama	1,013.6	4
Alaska	863.0	24
Arizona	844.5	28
Arkansas	1,002.1	8
California	765.7	48
Colorado	789.7	44
Connecticut	799.6	42
Delaware	918.4	15
Florida	828.9	33
Georgia	1,004.2	7
Hawaii	666.9	49
Idaho	811.7	38
Illinois	877.5	22
Indiana	942.8	13
Iowa	802.9	41
Kansas	852.0	27
Kentucky	1,005.2	6
Louisiana	1,020.4	3
Maine	888.4	20
Maryland	912.1	16
Massachusetts	815.3	36
Michigan	892.8	19
Minnesota	767.2	46
Mississippi	1,074.8	1
Missouri	928.3	14
Montana	843.8	29
Nebraska	798.1	43
Nevada	951.5	12
New Hampshire	837.6	31
New Jersey	863.6	23
New Mexico	839.9	30
New York	808.3	39
North Carolina	964.5	11
North Dakota	766.9	47
Ohio	n/a	n/a
Oklahoma	991.7	10
Oregon	834.5	32
Pennsylvania	903.6	17
Rhode Island	827.2	35
South Carolina	993.4	9
South Dakota	813.5	37
Tennessee	1,021.2	2
Texas	887.8	21
Utah	786.7	45
Vermont	856.5	26
Virginia	897.9	18
Washington	807.2	40
West Virginia	1,010.7	5
Wisconsin	827.6	34
Wyoming	860.1	25
50 States	n/a	
DC	1,036.2	
United States	872.4	

Rank in order by rate

1	Mississippi
2	Tennessee
3	Louisiana
4	Alabama
5	West Virginia
6	Kentucky
7	Georgia
8	Arkansas
9	South Carolina
10	Oklahoma
11	North Carolina
12	Nevada
13	Indiana
14	Missouri
15	Delaware
16	Maryland
17	Pennsylvania
18	Virginia
19	Michigan
20	Maine
21	Texas
22	Illinois
23	New Jersey
24	Alaska
25	Wyoming
26	Vermont
27	Kansas
28	Arizona
29	Montana
30	New Mexico
31	New Hampshire
32	Oregon
33	Florida
34	Wisconsin
35	Rhode Island
36	Massachusetts
37	South Dakota
38	Idaho
39	New York
40	Washington
41	Iowa
42	Connecticut
43	Nebraska
44	Colorado
45	Utah
46	Minnesota
47	North Dakota
48	California
49	Hawaii

A-16 Population Density, 2000

State	Persons per square mile	Rank
Alabama	88	26
Alaska	1	50
Arizona	45	36
Arkansas	51	34
California	217	12
Colorado	42	37
Connecticut	703	4
Delaware	401	7
Florida	296	8
Georgia	141	18
Hawaii	189	13
Idaho	16	44
Illinois	223	11
Indiana	170	16
Iowa	52	33
Kansas	33	40
Kentucky	102	23
Louisiana	103	22
Maine	41	38
Maryland	542	5
Massachusetts	810	3
Michigan	175	15
Minnesota	62	31
Mississippi	61	32
Missouri	81	27
Montana	6	48
Nebraska	22	42
Nevada	18	43
New Hampshire	138	20
New Jersey	1,135	1
New Mexico	15	45
New York	402	6
North Carolina	165	17
North Dakota	9	47
Ohio	277	9
Oklahoma	50	35
Oregon	36	39
Pennsylvania	274	10
Rhode Island	1,003	2
South Carolina	133	21
South Dakota	10	46
Tennessee	138	19
Texas	80	28
Utah	27	41
Vermont	66	30
Virginia	179	14
Washington	89	25
West Virginia	75	29
Wisconsin	99	24
Wyoming	5	49
50 States	79	
DC	9,378	
United States	80	

Rank in order by density

1. New Jersey
2. Rhode Island
3. Massachusetts
4. Connecticut
5. Maryland
6. New York
7. Delaware
8. Florida
9. Ohio
10. Pennsylvania
11. Illinois
12. California
13. Hawaii
14. Virginia
15. Michigan
16. Indiana
17. North Carolina
18. Georgia
19. Tennessee
20. New Hampshire
21. South Carolina
22. Louisiana
23. Kentucky
24. Wisconsin
25. Washington
26. Alabama
27. Missouri
28. Texas
29. West Virginia
30. Vermont
31. Minnesota
32. Mississippi
33. Iowa
34. Arkansas
35. Oklahoma
36. Arizona
37. Colorado
38. Maine
39. Oregon
40. Kansas
41. Utah
42. Nebraska
43. Nevada
44. Idaho
45. New Mexico
46. South Dakota
47. North Dakota
48. Montana
49. Wyoming
50. Alaska

Note: Numbers that appear to be identical are rounded and vary slightly in actual value. The rankings reflect the actual values before rounding. See the introduction for more details.

A-17 Illegal Immigrant Population, 1996

State	Illegal immigrant population	Percentage of total illegal immigrant population	Percentage of total U.S. population	Rank by number of immigrants
Alabama	4,000	0.1	0.1	39
Alaska	3,700	0.1	0.6	40
Arizona	115,000	2.3	2.6	7
Arkansas	5,400	0.1	0.2	37
California	2,000,000	40.0	6.3	1
Colorado	45,000	0.9	1.2	11
Connecticut	29,000	0.6	0.9	18
Delaware	2,500	0.1	0.3	44
Florida	350,000	7.0	2.4	4
Georgia	32,000	0.6	0.4	17
Hawaii	9,000	0.2	0.8	31
Idaho	16,000	0.3	1.3	25
Illinois	290,000	5.8	2.4	5
Indiana	14,000	0.3	0.2	28
Iowa	6,400	0.1	0.2	35
Kansas	20,000	0.4	0.8	24
Kentucky	6,000	0.1	0.2	36
Louisiana	22,000	0.4	0.5	21
Maine	3,300	0.1	0.3	42
Maryland	44,000	0.9	0.9	12
Massachusetts	85,000	1.7	1.4	8
Michigan	37,000	0.7	0.4	13
Minnesota	7,200	0.1	0.2	34
Mississippi	3,700	0.1	0.1	41
Missouri	16,000	0.3	0.3	25
Montana	1,200	0.0	0.1	48
Nebraska	7,600	0.2	0.5	33
Nevada	24,000	0.5	1.5	19
New Hampshire	2,000	0.0	0.2	45
New Jersey	135,000	2.7	1.7	6
New Mexico	37,000	0.7	2.2	13
New York	540,000	10.8	3.0	3
North Carolina	22,000	0.4	0.3	21
North Dakota	800	0.0	0.1	49
Ohio	23,000	0.5	0.2	20
Oklahoma	21,000	0.4	0.6	23
Oregon	33,000	0.7	1.0	16
Pennsylvania	37,000	0.7	0.3	13
Rhode Island	12,000	0.2	1.2	30
South Carolina	4,800	0.1	0.1	38
South Dakota	800	0.0	0.1	49
Tennessee	13,000	0.3	0.2	29
Texas	700,000	14.0	3.7	2
Utah	15,000	0.3	0.7	27
Vermont	2,700	0.1	0.5	43
Virginia	55,000	1.1	0.8	9
Washington	52,000	1.0	0.9	10
West Virginia	2,000	0.0	0.1	45
Wisconsin	7,700	0.2	0.1	32
Wyoming	1,700	0.0	0.4	47
50 States	4,916,500	98.3	1.9	
DC	30,000	0.6	5.5	
United States*	5,000,000	100.0	1.9	

Rank in order by number	
1	California
2	Texas
3	New York
4	Florida
5	Illinois
6	New Jersey
7	Arizona
8	Massachusetts
9	Virginia
10	Washington
11	Colorado
12	Maryland
13	Michigan
13	New Mexico
13	Pennsylvania
16	Oregon
17	Georgia
18	Connecticut
19	Nevada
20	Ohio
21	Louisiana
21	North Carolina
23	Oklahoma
24	Kansas
25	Idaho
25	Missouri
27	Utah
28	Indiana
29	Tennessee
30	Rhode Island
31	Hawaii
32	Wisconsin
33	Nebraska
34	Minnesota
35	Iowa
36	Kentucky
37	Arkansas
38	South Carolina
39	Alabama
40	Alaska
41	Mississippi
42	Maine
43	Vermont
44	Delaware
45	New Hampshire
45	West Virginia
47	Wyoming
48	Montana
49	North Dakota
49	South Dakota

Note: Ties in ranking reflect ties in actual values.

Due to rounding or data sources, the 50-state total plus D.C. may not equal the U.S. total. Please see introduction.

Source Notes for Population (Section A)

A-1 Population and Percentage Distribution, 2000: The U.S. population is counted once every decade in years ending in zero. The population numbers shown here are from the most recent census. They were released in December, 2000 and are available on the Census Bureau website (www.census.gov). For all non-census years, the Census Bureau prepares estimates for July 1 of each year. Outside experts and the Census Bureau agree that the census undercounts the nation's population and that this undercount tends to be concentrated in low-income areas in major cities. The understatement of population is greatest for these communities and the states that contain them. Because population estimates are used to determine representation in Congress and how much state and local governments get from federal aid programs, some states and cities have gone to court seeking to force the federal government to use more correct estimates. In the past, the Census Bureau successfully resisted these challenges because, while it agrees the official count is inaccurate, it did not know what data might be substituted for that count.

A-2 Percentage Change in Population, 1999-2000: The Census Bureau counts the U.S. population every ten years. In the intervening years, the Bureau makes *estimates* of the U.S. population. When the next census is done, the Census Bureau changes the estimates for the previous nine years. Thus, population estimates for 1991-1999 will be revised, based on both the 1990 and 2000 census. Currently, the Census Bureau is not expected to release these revisions until the Spring of 2002. In the interim, to compute this table *State Fact Finder* has utilized adjusted 1999 population numbers from the Bureau of Economic Research. The adjusted 1999 numbers (available on the BEA website: www.bea.gov) are based on, and consistent with, the 1999 and 2000 census data. The adjustment allows for more meaningful year-to-year comparisons.

A-3 Percentage Change in Population, 1990-2000: The 1990 population data shown on this table are from the 1990 census, reflecting the count as of April 1, 1990.

A-4 Projected Population, 2005, and Population Change, 2000-2005: The population projections for 2005 were made by the Census Bureau and are available on their website (www.census.gov). See Table A-1 for the 2000 population numbers used to calculate the projected change over time. Many private market research and economic forecasting firms also make population projections. The projections reflect recent trends, so western states are predicted to gain population rapidly while the slowest growth appears in the Northeast and Midwest. Projections for short periods are quite reliable because they are based on events that are predictable for large groups, such as the percentage of persons who will die each year and the percentage of women of childbearing age who will have babies. Over longer periods, more guesswork is involved. Major economic shifts can be caused by changes in defense spending, fluctuations in oil and gas prices, and success or failure of particular firms or industries. Those shifts affect migration of workers and ultimately where they have children and die.

A-5 Projected Population for the Year 2015: See notes to Table A-4.

A-6 Population 65 and Over and as Percentage of Population, 2000: This Census Bureau count, issued in October, 2001, is available on the Bureau's website (see notes to Table A-1). In the ten years since the last census, the number of people 65 years and over has increased 12 percent, but their proportion of the total population has decreased since 1990 from 12.6 percent to 12.4. Two kinds of states have the largest percentage of elderly citizens. First, there are states, like Florida and Arkansas, that draw large numbers of retirees from other states. Second, there are states with slow population growth, such as Pennsylvania, that lose many of their working-age younger people through migration to other states.

A-7 Population Age 17 and Under and as Percentage of Population, 2000: This count, from the same source as Table A-6 and issued in September of 2001, shows the flip side of the high concentrations of elderly citizens shown in Table A-6. The highest-ranking states, typified by Utah, have a large percentage of adults of childbearing age and high birth rates.

A-8 Median Age, 2000: In each state, half the population was older than the age shown, while half was younger. This statistic, available on the Census Bureau's website (see notes to Table A-1) is a way to capture age differences among states in a single number for each state. The rankings are based on unrounded numbers.

A-9 African American Population and Percentage of Population, 2000: The Census Bureau identifies six race categories: White; Black or African-American; American Indian and Alaska Native; Asian; Native Hawaiian and Other Pacific Islander; and "some other race" (write-in answer). "Hispanic" is not considered a race by the Census Bureau, so Hispanics are asked to classify themselves using the above six race categories. The 2000 census marked the first year respondents were able to check one or more boxes identifying race. Thus, this *State Fact Finder* table presents two ways of counting the African-American population. The first column shows the number of people who classify themselves as African-American only (or, in Census Bureau terminology, "the alone population"). The second column also includes those who identify as African-American only, but added in are those who identified as African-American and some other race or races as well (the "alone" or "in combination" population). The numbers in the second column are used to determine African-Americans as a percentage of the total population, which is presented in the fourth column and the ranking table.

The values in the third column show what percentage of the alone and combined African-American population (second column) identify as being of two or more races. Nationally, 4.8 percent of African-Americans classify themselves as black plus some other race or races. This percentage varies significantly between states, however. The percentage jumps to 39.4 in Montana and dips to 0.8 in Mississippi.

These data come from a Census 2000 Brief, "The Black Population: 2000," released in August, 2001 and available on the Census Bureau's website (see notes to Table A-1). Counts for other federally recognized racial groups are available from the Census Bureau. The "undercount" (see notes to Table A-1) means that statistics probably undercount African Americans and Hispanics.

A-10 Hispanic Population and Percentage of Population, 2000: See notes to Table A-9. While the census theoretically accounts for every resident in the country, illegal immigrants (many of whom are Hispanic) have an understandable fear of being identified by any government agency. Therefore, the count of this group is probably not very accurate. The data come from the Census Bureau website (see notes to Table A-1).

A-11 Population in Poverty, 2000: The federal government has a uniform definition of the income families need to avoid poverty. The amount considered necessary varies with family size but not with rural or urban location or from state to state. The income used to calculate whether households are living in poverty does not include the value of non-cash benefits, such as free medical care, provided to the poor under government programs. The estimates shown are from the Census Bureau website (see notes to Table A-1). They are based in part on monthly household surveys of a small sample of the nation's population, not a full count. They reflect possible sampling errors, particularly for less populous states.

A-12 Number and Rate of Children in Poverty, 2000: These statistics are available on the Census Bureau's website (see notes to Table A-1). They were made available on September 12, 2000, and are subject to the same caveats as similar data for persons of all ages in Table A-11. The percentage of children in poverty exceeds the percentage of all persons in poverty because households with children are often headed by a parent or parents in their early earning years, and the income needed to avoid the poverty standard is higher for families with children than for adults without children. Children not related to heads of households, such as foster children, are not included in this count.

A-13 Female Population, 2000: More than half of newly born children are male, but women tend to outlive men. The result is about equal numbers of each in the population as a whole, but disproportionate numbers of women in states with more aged population (see Table A-8). These data come from the Census Bureau website (see notes to Table A-1).

A-14 Birth Rates, 2000: These data show that 14.8 children are born each year for every 1,000 people. The birth rate is nearly 67.6 per 1,000 when only women of childbearing age are considered. The data come from the National Center for Health Statistics publication, *National Vital Statistics Report* (Vol. 49, No. 5, July 24, 2001) available on the website for the Center for Disease Control (www.cdc.gov). See notes to Table A-15 below.

A-15 Death Rates (age-adjusted), 2000: Raw death rates, like raw birth rates (births related to population), are highly sensitive to the age distribution of a state's population. A state with large numbers of older persons will tend to have lower raw birth rates and higher death rates. The National Center for Health Statistics makes special calculations adjusting deaths for age and births for the numbers of women of childbearing age (called fertility rates).

State Fact Finder illustrates both approaches by using raw rates for births (Table A-14) and adjusted rates for deaths. Data showing raw rates for deaths are, like the age-adjusted death rates shown, available from the National Center for Health Statistics publication, *National Vital Statistics Reports, Vol. 49, No. 12, October 9, 2001*. This source also provides technical notes indicating exactly how adjustments are made. The notes also explain how a changed population standard in data year 1999 makes these rates not directly comparable to those of previous years. This table is indicating that, on average, people living in Mississippi die sooner than those in Hawaii.

A-16 Population Density, 2000: This table is calculated by taking the land area estimate from the 2000 census, available on the Census Bureau's website (see notes to A-1) and relating it to the 2000 population. The result is a rough measure of urban-rural characteristics of each state and is often cited as a proxy for possible crowding. However, in many states much of the land area is unusable for settlement because of lack of water, extraordinarily low or high elevation, and other factors. Consequently, much of the population of a low-density state may in fact be densely packed in a few small areas.

A-17 Illegal Immigrant Population, 1996: Counting illegal immigrants, many of whom fear being counted, is inherently difficult. These estimates come from an Immigration and Naturalization Service press release titled, *Estimates of the Unauthorized Immigrant Population Residing in the United States: October 1996*. While the estimates may not be accurate, they are useful in illustrating the large differences among states. These estimates, now six years old, are the most recent available.

Economies

In late November 2001, the recession became official. The arbiter of this decision, a private, non-profit group of university economists within the National Bureau of Economic Research (NBER), pinpointed March 2001 as the beginning of the recession, or, stated differently, the end of an unprecedented 10-years of economic expansion.

Though the economy began declining before September 11th, according to NBER, a full-blown recession may have been averted if not for the immediate impact of the terrorist attacks and the sustained drop in consumer and business confidence. Indicators included in this chapter such as employment and the Index of State Economic Momentum show that prior to September 11th, states of the industrial midwest and south and those with significant tech sectors, such as Oregon, were teetering towards recession. After September 11th, all states have felt the effects of layoffs and drops in sales. Previously strong regions, such as Florida and southern California have been hit particularly hard by the fall-off in travel. Problems in some states, particularly those of the south, may be somewhat mitigated by increases in defense spending. Unlike previous recessions, some analysts (see economy.com) are predicting that this one will not unfairly burden one region of the country.

Whatever final economic stimulus package Congress passes may or may not effect recovery, though it will have a bearing on how the economic downturn is shouldered by the states. The nation's recovery, in some eyes, will be driven by consumer and business confidence, as frequent admonishments to spend, spend, spend reveal. Others contend that perspectives on the role of government, post-September 11th, are shifting, and recovery will depend more on government spending—spending, not only on safety-net programs, but on public needs from transportation safety to public health to infrastructure and energy needs. The idea being: public investment could very well have a stimulating effect on the economy. Certainly unpredictable events like future terrorist attacks or prolonged conflict overseas will effect the length and depth of the current contraction.

If history serves as a guide, the country will be feeling better by March of 2002. The longest recession in recent decades lasted 16 months, the average duration has been one year.

B-1 Personal Income, 2000

State	Personal income $ (in millions)	Rank
Alabama	104,568	24
Alaska	18,612	47
Arizona	129,133	23
Arkansas	58,844	34
California	1,094,770	1
Colorado	140,353	21
Connecticut	139,305	22
Delaware	24,441	44
Florida	447,012	4
Georgia	228,692	11
Hawaii	33,776	40
Idaho	30,759	42
Illinois	396,239	5
Indiana	163,549	16
Iowa	77,283	30
Kansas	73,829	31
Kentucky	97,445	26
Louisiana	103,112	25
Maine	32,412	41
Maryland	178,506	15
Massachusetts	239,739	10
Michigan	289,390	9
Minnesota	157,430	17
Mississippi	59,467	33
Missouri	152,437	18
Montana	20,395	45
Nebraska	47,423	36
Nevada	59,640	32
New Hampshire	40,938	37
New Jersey	312,891	8
New Mexico	39,973	38
New York	655,583	2
North Carolina	217,011	13
North Dakota	15,916	49
Ohio	317,266	7
Oklahoma	81,554	29
Oregon	94,999	28
Pennsylvania	362,989	6
Rhode Island	30,599	43
South Carolina	96,411	27
South Dakota	19,659	46
Tennessee	147,752	20
Texas	580,736	3
Utah	52,474	35
Vermont	16,411	48
Virginia	220,583	12
Washington	184,280	14
West Virginia	39,370	39
Wisconsin	150,866	19
Wyoming	13,575	50
50 States	8,290,397	
DC	21,919	
United States*	8,312,312	

Rank in order by $	
1	California
2	New York
3	Texas
4	Florida
5	Illinois
6	Pennsylvania
7	Ohio
8	New Jersey
9	Michigan
10	Massachusetts
11	Georgia
12	Virginia
13	North Carolina
14	Washington
15	Maryland
16	Indiana
17	Minnesota
18	Missouri
19	Wisconsin
20	Tennessee
21	Colorado
22	Connecticut
23	Arizona
24	Alabama
25	Louisiana
26	Kentucky
27	South Carolina
28	Oregon
29	Oklahoma
30	Iowa
31	Kansas
32	Nevada
33	Mississippi
34	Arkansas
35	Utah
36	Nebraska
37	New Hampshire
38	New Mexico
39	West Virginia
40	Hawaii
41	Maine
42	Idaho
43	Rhode Island
44	Delaware
45	Montana
46	South Dakota
47	Alaska
48	Vermont
49	North Dakota
50	Wyoming

Due to rounding or data sources, the 50-state total plus D.C. may not equal the U.S. total. Please see introduction.

B-2 Gross State Product, Total and Per Capita, 1999

State	Gross state product $ (in millions)	Per capita $	Rank per capita
Alabama	115,071	26,333	45
Alaska	26,353	42,539	3
Arizona	143,683	30,070	32
Arkansas	64,773	25,388	47
California	1,229,098	37,082	9
Colorado	153,728	37,900	8
Connecticut	151,779	46,245	1
Delaware	34,669	46,008	2
Florida	442,895	29,309	38
Georgia	275,719	35,402	15
Hawaii	40,914	34,512	17
Idaho	34,025	27,183	43
Illinois	445,666	36,746	11
Indiana	182,202	30,659	30
Iowa	85,243	29,707	33
Kansas	80,843	30,460	31
Kentucky	113,539	28,665	40
Louisiana	128,959	29,496	35
Maine	34,064	27,185	42
Maryland	174,710	33,782	20
Massachusetts	262,564	42,519	4
Michigan	308,310	31,257	27
Minnesota	172,982	36,223	14
Mississippi	64,286	23,220	49
Missouri	170,470	31,174	28
Montana	20,636	23,376	48
Nebraska	53,744	32,259	23
Nevada	69,864	38,615	7
New Hampshire	44,229	36,823	10
New Jersey	331,544	40,713	6
New Mexico	51,026	29,328	37
New York	754,590	41,469	5
North Carolina	258,592	33,799	19
North Dakota	16,991	26,814	44
Ohio	361,981	32,157	24
Oklahoma	86,382	25,724	46
Oregon	109,694	33,079	21
Pennsylvania	382,980	31,931	25
Rhode Island	32,546	32,848	22
South Carolina	106,917	27,515	41
South Dakota	21,631	29,505	34
Tennessee	170,085	31,017	29
Texas	687,272	34,288	18
Utah	62,641	29,411	36
Vermont	17,164	28,908	39
Virginia	242,221	35,243	16
Washington	209,258	36,352	13
West Virginia	40,685	22,516	50
Wisconsin	166,481	31,708	26
Wyoming	17,448	36,380	12
50 States	**9,253,147**	**33,997**	
DC	55,832	107,576	
United States*	**9,308,983**	**34,138**	

Due to rounding or data sources, the 50-state total plus D.C. may not equal the U.S. total. Please see introduction.

Rank in order per capita	
1	Connecticut
2	Delaware
3	Alaska
4	Massachusetts
5	New York
6	New Jersey
7	Nevada
8	Colorado
9	California
10	New Hampshire
11	Illinois
12	Wyoming
13	Washington
14	Minnesota
15	Georgia
16	Virginia
17	Hawaii
18	Texas
19	North Carolina
20	Maryland
21	Oregon
22	Rhode Island
23	Nebraska
24	Ohio
25	Pennsylvania
26	Wisconsin
27	Michigan
28	Missouri
29	Tennessee
30	Indiana
31	Kansas
32	Arizona
33	Iowa
34	South Dakota
35	Louisiana
36	Utah
37	New Mexico
38	Florida
39	Vermont
40	Kentucky
41	South Carolina
42	Maine
43	Idaho
44	North Dakota
45	Alabama
46	Oklahoma
47	Arkansas
48	Montana
49	Mississippi
50	West Virginia

B-3 Per Capita Personal Income, 2000

State	Per capita personal income $	Rank
Alabama	23,460	43
Alaska	29,597	14
Arizona	24,991	37
Arkansas	21,945	47
California	32,225	8
Colorado	32,441	7
Connecticut	40,870	1
Delaware	31,074	12
Florida	27,836	21
Georgia	27,790	23
Hawaii	27,819	22
Idaho	23,640	41
Illinois	31,842	10
Indiana	26,838	32
Iowa	26,376	33
Kansas	27,408	28
Kentucky	24,057	39
Louisiana	23,041	45
Maine	25,399	36
Maryland	33,621	5
Massachusetts	37,710	2
Michigan	29,071	18
Minnesota	31,913	9
Mississippi	20,856	50
Missouri	27,186	29
Montana	22,541	46
Nebraska	27,658	25
Nevada	29,551	15
New Hampshire	33,042	6
New Jersey	37,112	3
New Mexico	21,883	48
New York	34,502	4
North Carolina	26,842	31
North Dakota	24,780	38
Ohio	27,914	20
Oklahoma	23,582	42
Oregon	27,649	26
Pennsylvania	29,533	16
Rhode Island	29,158	17
South Carolina	23,952	40
South Dakota	25,993	34
Tennessee	25,878	35
Texas	27,722	24
Utah	23,364	44
Vermont	26,904	30
Virginia	31,065	13
Washington	31,129	11
West Virginia	21,767	49
Wisconsin	28,066	19
Wyoming	27,436	27
50 States	n/a	
DC	38,374	
United States	29,451	

Rank in order per capita	
1	Connecticut
2	Massachusetts
3	New Jersey
4	New York
5	Maryland
6	New Hampshire
7	Colorado
8	California
9	Minnesota
10	Illinois
11	Washington
12	Delaware
13	Virginia
14	Alaska
15	Nevada
16	Pennsylvania
17	Rhode Island
18	Michigan
19	Wisconsin
20	Ohio
21	Florida
22	Hawaii
23	Georgia
24	Texas
25	Nebraska
26	Oregon
27	Wyoming
28	Kansas
29	Missouri
30	Vermont
31	North Carolina
32	Indiana
33	Iowa
34	South Dakota
35	Tennessee
36	Maine
37	Arizona
38	North Dakota
39	Kentucky
40	South Carolina
41	Idaho
42	Oklahoma
43	Alabama
44	Utah
45	Louisiana
46	Montana
47	Arkansas
48	New Mexico
49	West Virginia
50	Mississippi

Note: Numbers that appear to be identical are rounded and vary slightly in actual value. The rankings reflect the actual values before rounding. See the introduction for more details.

B-4 Personal Income from Wages and Salaries, 2000

State	Wages and salaries $ (in millions)	As percentage of personal income	Rank by percentage
Alabama	57,706	55.2	31
Alaska	10,752	57.8	22
Arizona	76,159	59.0	12
Arkansas	31,511	53.6	38
California	639,727	58.4	17
Colorado	86,011	61.3	6
Connecticut	79,064	56.8	26
Delaware	15,807	64.7	1
Florida	228,688	51.2	46
Georgia	141,096	61.7	4
Hawaii	19,254	57.0	24
Idaho	16,581	53.9	37
Illinois	236,583	59.7	10
Indiana	94,924	58.0	20
Iowa	42,324	54.8	32
Kansas	41,302	55.9	29
Kentucky	54,381	55.8	30
Louisiana	55,635	54.0	36
Maine	17,225	53.1	40
Maryland	93,992	52.7	42
Massachusetts	151,327	63.1	2
Michigan	175,747	60.7	8
Minnesota	96,658	61.4	5
Mississippi	30,795	51.8	44
Missouri	88,949	58.4	18
Montana	9,994	49.0	50
Nebraska	26,642	56.2	28
Nevada	35,172	59.0	13
New Hampshire	21,889	53.5	39
New Jersey	176,400	56.4	27
New Mexico	21,788	54.5	35
New York	399,246	60.9	7
North Carolina	127,585	58.8	16
North Dakota	8,432	53.0	41
Ohio	186,609	58.8	15
Oklahoma	41,949	51.4	45
Oregon	54,771	57.7	23
Pennsylvania	198,108	54.6	34
Rhode Island	16,079	52.5	43
South Carolina	54,776	56.8	25
South Dakota	9,691	49.3	49
Tennessee	85,376	57.8	21
Texas	342,171	58.9	14
Utah	32,683	62.3	3
Vermont	8,961	54.6	33
Virginia	131,858	59.8	9
Washington	109,665	59.5	11
West Virginia	19,409	49.3	48
Wisconsin	87,946	58.3	19
Wyoming	6,778	49.9	47
50 States	4,796,177	57.9	
DC	37,792	172.4	
United States	4,833,969	58.2	

Rank in order by percentage

1. Delaware
2. Massachusetts
3. Utah
4. Georgia
5. Minnesota
6. Colorado
7. New York
8. Michigan
9. Virginia
10. Illinois
11. Washington
12. Arizona
13. Nevada
14. Texas
15. Ohio
16. North Carolina
17. California
18. Missouri
19. Wisconsin
20. Indiana
21. Tennessee
22. Alaska
23. Oregon
24. Hawaii
25. South Carolina
26. Connecticut
27. New Jersey
28. Nebraska
29. Kansas
30. Kentucky
31. Alabama
32. Iowa
33. Vermont
34. Pennsylvania
35. New Mexico
36. Louisiana
37. Idaho
38. Arkansas
39. New Hampshire
40. Maine
41. North Dakota
42. Maryland
43. Rhode Island
44. Mississippi
45. Oklahoma
46. Florida
47. Wyoming
48. West Virginia
49. South Dakota
50. Montana

Note: Numbers that appear to be identical are rounded and vary slightly in actual value. The rankings reflect the actual values before rounding. See the introduction for more details.

B-5 Average Annual Pay, 2000

State	Average annual pay $	Rank
Alabama	29,037	33
Alaska	35,125	14
Arizona	32,606	21
Arkansas	26,307	46
California	41,194	5
Colorado	37,167	7
Connecticut	45,445	1
Delaware	36,677	10
Florida	30,549	30
Georgia	34,182	17
Hawaii	30,630	28
Idaho	27,709	39
Illinois	38,044	6
Indiana	31,015	26
Iowa	27,928	37
Kansas	29,357	31
Kentucky	28,829	35
Louisiana	27,877	38
Maine	27,664	40
Maryland	36,373	11
Massachusetts	44,326	3
Michigan	37,016	9
Minnesota	35,418	12
Mississippi	25,197	47
Missouri	31,386	24
Montana	24,264	50
Nebraska	27,662	41
Nevada	32,276	23
New Hampshire	34,731	16
New Jersey	43,691	4
New Mexico	27,498	42
New York	44,942	2
North Carolina	31,077	25
North Dakota	24,678	49
Ohio	32,510	22
Oklahoma	26,980	43
Oregon	32,765	19
Pennsylvania	33,999	18
Rhode Island	32,618	20
South Carolina	28,173	36
South Dakota	24,803	48
Tennessee	30,558	29
Texas	34,948	15
Utah	29,226	32
Vermont	28,920	34
Virginia	35,151	13
Washington	37,059	8
West Virginia	26,887	44
Wisconsin	30,697	27
Wyoming	26,837	45
50 States	n/a	
DC	53,018	
United States	35,296	

Rank in order by $

1	Connecticut
2	New York
3	Massachusetts
4	New Jersey
5	California
6	Illinois
7	Colorado
8	Washington
9	Michigan
10	Delaware
11	Maryland
12	Minnesota
13	Virginia
14	Alaska
15	Texas
16	New Hampshire
17	Georgia
18	Pennsylvania
19	Oregon
20	Rhode Island
21	Arizona
22	Ohio
23	Nevada
24	Missouri
25	North Carolina
26	Indiana
27	Wisconsin
28	Hawaii
29	Tennessee
30	Florida
31	Kansas
32	Utah
33	Alabama
34	Vermont
35	Kentucky
36	South Carolina
37	Iowa
38	Louisiana
39	Idaho
40	Maine
41	Nebraska
42	New Mexico
43	Oklahoma
44	West Virginia
45	Wyoming
46	Arkansas
47	Mississippi
48	South Dakota
49	North Dakota
50	Montana

B-6 Average Hourly Earnings, 2001

State	Average hourly earnings $	Rank
Alabama	13.37	38
Alaska	13.80	35
Arizona	13.07	41
Arkansas	12.42	45
California	14.64	27
Colorado	15.39	11
Connecticut	16.12	7
Delaware	16.77	4
Florida	12.70	43
Georgia	13.19	40
Hawaii	14.35	28
Idaho	14.86	21
Illinois	14.68	25
Indiana	16.16	6
Iowa	14.81	23
Kansas	15.16	17
Kentucky	15.30	12
Louisiana	15.88	8
Maine	15.16	17
Maryland	15.17	16
Massachusetts	15.24	14
Michigan	19.59	1
Minnesota	15.30	12
Mississippi	12.04	48
Missouri	14.87	20
Montana	14.66	26
Nebraska	13.38	37
Nevada	14.12	32
New Hampshire	13.94	33
New Jersey	15.77	9
New Mexico	14.33	29
New York	14.77	24
North Carolina	13.24	39
North Dakota	12.29	46
Ohio	17.26	3
Oklahoma	12.72	42
Oregon	15.53	10
Pennsylvania	14.85	22
Rhode Island	12.17	47
South Carolina	11.18	50
South Dakota	11.57	49
Tennessee	13.43	36
Texas	12.52	44
Utah	13.88	34
Vermont	14.25	30
Virginia	14.20	31
Washington	17.53	2
West Virginia	14.97	19
Wisconsin	15.19	15
Wyoming	16.52	5
50 States	n/a	
DC	15.76	
United States	14.79	

Rank in order by $	
1	Michigan
2	Washington
3	Ohio
4	Delaware
5	Wyoming
6	Indiana
7	Connecticut
8	Louisiana
9	New Jersey
10	Oregon
11	Colorado
12	Kentucky
12	Minnesota
14	Massachusetts
15	Wisconsin
16	Maryland
17	Kansas
17	Maine
19	West Virginia
20	Missouri
21	Idaho
22	Pennsylvania
23	Iowa
24	New York
25	Illinois
26	Montana
27	California
28	Hawaii
29	New Mexico
30	Vermont
31	Virginia
32	Nevada
33	New Hampshire
34	Utah
35	Alaska
36	Tennessee
37	Nebraska
38	Alabama
39	North Carolina
40	Georgia
41	Arizona
42	Oklahoma
43	Florida
44	Texas
45	Arkansas
46	North Dakota
47	Rhode Island
48	Mississippi
49	South Dakota
50	South Carolina

Note: Ties in ranking reflect ties in actual values.

B-7 Value Added in Manufacturing, 1999

State	Value added $ (in millions)	Per capita $	Rank per capita
Alabama	30,183	6,907	29
Alaska	1,111	1,793	49
Arizona	33,166	6,941	28
Arkansas	20,873	8,181	18
California	218,179	6,583	30
Colorado	19,407	4,785	41
Connecticut	27,075	8,249	17
Delaware	6,070	8,056	19
Florida	41,963	2,777	45
Georgia	62,640	8,043	20
Hawaii	1,311	1,106	50
Idaho	7,309	5,839	37
Illinois	96,829	7,984	21
Indiana	77,906	13,109	1
Iowa	28,434	9,909	7
Kansas	22,124	8,336	13
Kentucky	40,555	10,239	6
Louisiana	26,607	6,086	34
Maine	7,592	6,059	35
Maryland	19,144	3,702	43
Massachusetts	45,753	7,409	25
Michigan	101,570	10,297	5
Minnesota	40,302	8,439	12
Mississippi	23,790	8,593	11
Missouri	45,556	8,331	14
Montana	1,792	2,030	48
Nebraska	11,815	7,092	27
Nevada	3,827	2,115	47
New Hampshire	9,953	8,286	15
New Jersey	51,502	6,324	33
New Mexico	13,549	7,787	22
New York	80,440	4,421	42
North Carolina	90,442	11,821	2
North Dakota	2,264	3,572	44
Ohio	118,178	10,498	4
Oklahoma	17,995	5,359	39
Oregon	24,593	7,416	24
Pennsylvania	89,386	7,453	23
Rhode Island	5,811	5,864	36
South Carolina	35,287	9,081	9
South Dakota	6,988	9,532	8
Tennessee	47,602	8,681	10
Texas	131,146	6,543	31
Utah	11,845	5,562	38
Vermont	4,919	8,286	16
Virginia	49,194	7,158	26
Washington	36,924	6,414	32
West Virginia	9,190	5,086	40
Wisconsin	61,160	11,649	3
Wyoming	1,254	2,614	46
50 States	1,962,502	7,211	
DC	142	274	
United States	1,962,644	7,197	

Rank in order per capita	
1	Indiana
2	North Carolina
3	Wisconsin
4	Ohio
5	Michigan
6	Kentucky
7	Iowa
8	South Dakota
9	South Carolina
10	Tennessee
11	Mississippi
12	Minnesota
13	Kansas
14	Missouri
15	New Hampshire
16	Vermont
17	Connecticut
18	Arkansas
19	Delaware
20	Georgia
21	Illinois
22	New Mexico
23	Pennsylvania
24	Oregon
25	Massachusetts
26	Virginia
27	Nebraska
28	Arizona
29	Alabama
30	California
31	Texas
32	Washington
33	New Jersey
34	Louisiana
35	Maine
36	Rhode Island
37	Idaho
38	Utah
39	Oklahoma
40	West Virginia
41	Colorado
42	New York
43	Maryland
44	North Dakota
45	Florida
46	Wyoming
47	Nevada
48	Montana
49	Alaska
50	Hawaii

Note: Numbers that appear to be identical are rounded and vary slightly in actual value. The rankings reflect the actual values before rounding. See the introduction for more details.

B-8 Cost of Living, 1999

State	Cost of living index	Rank by index
Alabama	92.7	39
Alaska	111.4	6
Arizona	100.4	17
Arkansas	91.0	47
California	102.1	14
Colorado	101.1	15
Connecticut	112.2	5
Delaware	103.0	13
Florida	94.3	32
Georgia	91.7	45
Hawaii	121.7	1
Idaho	95.1	29
Illinois	100.3	18
Indiana	96.3	24
Iowa	93.4	34
Kansas	93.3	35
Kentucky	91.7	45
Louisiana	92.8	38
Maine	104.9	9
Maryland	97.4	23
Massachusetts	114.2	2
Michigan	95.0	30
Minnesota	95.0	30
Mississippi	90.4	50
Missouri	92.9	37
Montana	95.4	26
Nebraska	93.8	33
Nevada	100.8	16
New Hampshire	108.5	8
New Jersey	113.7	3
New Mexico	97.7	22
New York	113.2	4
North Carolina	92.0	43
North Dakota	93.1	36
Ohio	98.0	21
Oklahoma	92.2	42
Oregon	98.9	20
Pennsylvania	104.7	10
Rhode Island	110.7	7
South Carolina	92.3	41
South Dakota	92.0	43
Tennessee	92.7	39
Texas	90.9	48
Utah	100.3	18
Vermont	103.6	12
Virginia	95.4	26
Washington	104.1	11
West Virginia	90.8	49
Wisconsin	95.2	28
Wyoming	95.9	25
50 States	n/a	
DC	104.2	
United States	100.0	

Rank in order by index

1 Hawaii
2 Massachusetts
3 New Jersey
4 New York
5 Connecticut
6 Alaska
7 Rhode Island
8 New Hampshire
9 Maine
10 Pennsylvania
11 Washington
12 Vermont
13 Delaware
14 California
15 Colorado
16 Nevada
17 Arizona
18 Illinois
18 Utah
20 Oregon
21 Ohio
22 New Mexico
23 Maryland
24 Indiana
25 Wyoming
26 Montana
26 Virginia
28 Wisconsin
29 Idaho
30 Michigan
30 Minnesota
32 Florida
33 Nebraska
34 Iowa
35 Kansas
36 North Dakota
37 Missouri
38 Louisiana
39 Alabama
39 Tennessee
41 South Carolina
42 Oklahoma
43 North Carolina
43 South Dakota
45 Georgia
45 Kentucky
47 Arkansas
48 Texas
49 West Virginia
50 Mississippi

Note: Ties in ranking reflect ties in actual values.

B-9 Average Annual Pay in Manufacturing, 2000

State	Average annual pay in manufacturing $	Rank
Alabama	33,582	43
Alaska	32,107	45
Arizona	48,541	8
Arkansas	29,247	49
California	57,695	3
Colorado	47,450	9
Connecticut	59,987	1
Delaware	55,130	5
Florida	38,173	26
Georgia	37,448	31
Hawaii	34,404	41
Idaho	43,754	18
Illinois	45,818	14
Indiana	42,421	20
Iowa	36,416	35
Kansas	37,690	28
Kentucky	37,618	29
Louisiana	40,312	21
Maine	35,344	38
Maryland	45,853	12
Massachusetts	57,254	4
Michigan	54,706	6
Minnesota	44,952	16
Mississippi	28,505	50
Missouri	39,881	22
Montana	31,397	47
Nebraska	33,194	44
Nevada	37,937	27
New Hampshire	46,444	11
New Jersey	59,177	2
New Mexico	38,464	25
New York	51,462	7
North Carolina	37,004	34
North Dakota	30,515	48
Ohio	43,969	17
Oklahoma	35,006	40
Oregon	45,839	13
Pennsylvania	42,597	19
Rhode Island	37,436	32
South Carolina	35,158	39
South Dakota	31,939	46
Tennessee	36,054	36
Texas	45,089	15
Utah	35,464	37
Vermont	39,781	23
Virginia	37,334	33
Washington	47,072	10
West Virginia	37,500	30
Wisconsin	39,009	24
Wyoming	34,214	42
50 States	n/a	
DC	68,276	
United States	44,778	

Rank in order by $	
1	Connecticut
2	New Jersey
3	California
4	Massachusetts
5	Delaware
6	Michigan
7	New York
8	Arizona
9	Colorado
10	Washington
11	New Hampshire
12	Maryland
13	Oregon
14	Illinois
15	Texas
16	Minnesota
17	Ohio
18	Idaho
19	Pennsylvania
20	Indiana
21	Louisiana
22	Missouri
23	Vermont
24	Wisconsin
25	New Mexico
26	Florida
27	Nevada
28	Kansas
29	Kentucky
30	West Virginia
31	Georgia
32	Rhode Island
33	Virginia
34	North Carolina
35	Iowa
36	Tennessee
37	Utah
38	Maine
39	South Carolina
40	Oklahoma
41	Hawaii
42	Wyoming
43	Alabama
44	Nebraska
45	Alaska
46	South Dakota
47	Montana
48	North Dakota
49	Arkansas
50	Mississippi

B-10 Average Annual Pay in Retailing, 2000

State	Average annual pay in retailing $	Rank
Alabama	15,690	40
Alaska	19,729	8
Arizona	19,246	10
Arkansas	17,600	24
California	21,915	2
Colorado	19,074	12
Connecticut	23,584	1
Delaware	17,913	21
Florida	18,579	16
Georgia	18,194	20
Hawaii	18,231	19
Idaho	16,329	33
Illinois	18,885	13
Indiana	15,793	39
Iowa	14,755	43
Kansas	15,884	36
Kentucky	15,834	38
Louisiana	15,004	42
Maine	16,771	29
Maryland	19,109	11
Massachusetts	21,000	4
Michigan	17,312	26
Minnesota	18,552	17
Mississippi	14,737	44
Missouri	16,542	32
Montana	14,346	47
Nebraska	14,680	45
Nevada	20,951	5
New Hampshire	19,274	9
New Jersey	21,726	3
New Mexico	16,069	35
New York	20,537	7
North Carolina	17,466	25
North Dakota	13,870	50
Ohio	16,957	28
Oklahoma	15,011	41
Oregon	18,730	15
Pennsylvania	17,116	27
Rhode Island	18,791	14
South Carolina	16,329	33
South Dakota	14,270	49
Tennessee	17,824	22
Texas	18,472	18
Utah	16,632	30
Vermont	16,558	31
Virginia	17,814	23
Washington	20,877	6
West Virginia	14,274	48
Wisconsin	15,862	37
Wyoming	14,576	46
50 States	n/a	
DC	18,807	
United States	18,432	

Rank in order by $

1 Connecticut
2 California
3 New Jersey
4 Massachusetts
5 Nevada
6 Washington
7 New York
8 Alaska
9 New Hampshire
10 Arizona
11 Maryland
12 Colorado
13 Illinois
14 Rhode Island
15 Oregon
16 Florida
17 Minnesota
18 Texas
19 Hawaii
20 Georgia
21 Delaware
22 Tennessee
23 Virginia
24 Arkansas
25 North Carolina
26 Michigan
27 Pennsylvania
28 Ohio
29 Maine
30 Utah
31 Vermont
32 Missouri
33 Idaho
33 South Carolina
35 New Mexico
36 Kansas
37 Wisconsin
38 Kentucky
39 Indiana
40 Alabama
41 Oklahoma
42 Louisiana
43 Iowa
44 Mississippi
45 Nebraska
46 Wyoming
47 Montana
48 West Virginia
49 South Dakota
50 North Dakota

Note: Ties in ranking reflect ties in actual values.

B-11 Labor Force, 2001

State	Labor force (in thousands)	Labor force as percentage of population	Rank by percentage
Alabama	2,169	48.8	41
Alaska	329	52.5	21
Arizona	2,459	47.9	44
Arkansas	1270	47.5	45
California	17,478	51.6	25
Colorado	2,340	54.4	9
Connecticut	1,712	50.3	36
Delaware	419	53.4	13
Florida	7,796	48.8	40
Georgia	4,194	51.2	29
Hawaii	611	50.4	34
Idaho	689	53.2	14
Illinois	6,385	51.4	27
Indiana	3,125	51.4	28
Iowa	1,599	54.7	8
Kansas	1,440	53.6	12
Kentucky	1,992	49.3	39
Louisiana	2,055	46.0	48
Maine	691	54.2	10
Maryland	2,901	54.8	7
Massachusetts	3,370	53.1	17
Michigan	5,248	52.8	19
Minnesota	2,823	57.4	1
Mississippi	1,304	45.8	49
Missouri	2963	52.9	18
Montana	474	52.5	20
Nebraska	950	55.5	5
Nevada	1,047	52.4	23
New Hampshire	702	56.8	3
New Jersey	4,267	50.7	32
New Mexico	857	47.1	46
New York	8,912	47.0	47
North Carolina	4,029	50.1	37
North Dakota	337	52.4	22
Ohio	5,916	52.1	24
Oklahoma	1,674	48.5	42
Oregon	1,817	53.1	15
Pennsylvania	6,087	49.6	38
Rhode Island	506	48.3	43
South Carolina	2,018	50.3	35
South Dakota	408	54.1	11
Tennessee	2,877	50.6	33
Texas	10,656	51.1	30
Utah	1,140	51.0	31
Vermont	344	56.4	4
Virginia	3,759	53.1	16
Washington	3,032	51.4	26
West Virginia	806	44.6	50
Wisconsin	3,055	57.0	2
Wyoming	271	54.9	6
50 States	143,298	51.0	
DC	278	48.5	
United States	143,576	51.0	

Rank in order by percentage

1 Minnesota
2 Wisconsin
3 New Hampshire
4 Vermont
5 Nebraska
6 Wyoming
7 Maryland
8 Iowa
9 Colorado
10 Maine
11 South Dakota
12 Kansas
13 Delaware
14 Idaho
15 Oregon
16 Virginia
17 Massachusetts
18 Missouri
19 Michigan
20 Montana
21 Alaska
22 North Dakota
23 Nevada
24 Ohio
25 California
26 Washington
27 Illinois
28 Indiana
29 Georgia
30 Texas
31 Utah
32 New Jersey
33 Tennessee
34 Hawaii
35 South Carolina
36 Connecticut
37 North Carolina
38 Pennsylvania
39 Kentucky
40 Florida
41 Alabama
42 Oklahoma
43 Rhode Island
44 Arizona
45 Arkansas
46 New Mexico
47 New York
48 Louisiana
49 Mississippi
50 West Virginia

Note: Numbers that appear to be identical are rounded and vary slightly in actual value. The rankings reflect the actual values before rounding. See the introduction for more details.

B-12 Unemployed and Unemployment Rate, 2001

State	Unemployed (in thousands)	Unemployment rate (percentage of labor force unemployed)	Rank by rate
Alabama	114.0	5.3	14
Alaska	19.9	6.0	4
Arizona	128.3	5.2	15
Arkansas	54.5	4.3	31
California	995.8	5.7	6
Colorado	99.3	4.2	34
Connecticut	54.4	3.2	46
Delaware	12.5	3.0	48
Florida	384.9	4.9	20
Georgia	171.0	4.1	37
Hawaii	32.5	5.3	12
Idaho	33.4	4.8	21
Illinois	353.7	5.5	9
Indiana	148.8	4.8	23
Iowa	54.3	3.4	44
Kansas	57.9	4.0	38
Kentucky	101.1	5.1	17
Louisiana	115.0	5.6	7
Maine	29.6	4.3	32
Maryland	127.7	4.4	30
Massachusetts	140.1	4.2	35
Michigan	278.9	5.3	13
Minnesota	103.7	3.7	42
Mississippi	70.1	5.4	11
Missouri	132.2	4.5	27
Montana	21.4	4.5	24
Nebraska	28.3	3.0	49
Nevada	66.1	6.3	3
New Hampshire	26.4	3.8	40
New Jersey	203.3	4.8	22
New Mexico	49.5	5.8	5
New York	447.4	5.0	18
North Carolina	223.3	5.5	8
North Dakota	6.8	2.0	50
Ohio	262.3	4.4	28
Oklahoma	62.6	3.7	41
Oregon	118.9	6.5	2
Pennsylvania	301.3	5.0	19
Rhode Island	21.0	4.1	36
South Carolina	111.0	5.5	10
South Dakota	12.7	3.1	47
Tennessee	128.7	4.5	26
Texas	555.8	5.2	16
Utah	48.4	4.2	33
Vermont	11.0	3.2	45
Virginia	136.4	3.6	43
Washington	200.1	6.6	1
West Virginia	35.5	4.4	29
Wisconsin	137.2	4.5	25
Wyoming	10.4	3.8	39
50 States	7,039.4	4.9	
DC	17.4	6.3	
United States	7,056.8	4.9	

Rank in order by rate	
1	Washington
2	Oregon
3	Nevada
4	Alaska
5	New Mexico
6	California
7	Louisiana
8	North Carolina
9	Illinois
10	South Carolina
11	Mississippi
12	Hawaii
13	Michigan
14	Alabama
15	Arizona
16	Texas
17	Kentucky
18	New York
19	Pennsylvania
20	Florida
21	Idaho
22	New Jersey
23	Indiana
24	Montana
25	Wisconsin
26	Tennessee
27	Missouri
28	Ohio
29	West Virginia
30	Maryland
31	Arkansas
32	Maine
33	Utah
34	Colorado
35	Massachusetts
36	Rhode Island
37	Georgia
38	Kansas
39	Wyoming
40	New Hampshire
41	Oklahoma
42	Minnesota
43	Virginia
44	Iowa
45	Vermont
46	Connecticut
47	South Dakota
48	Delaware
49	Nebraska
50	North Dakota

Note: Numbers that appear to be identical are rounded and vary slightly in actual value. The rankings reflect the actual values before rounding. See the introduction for more details.

B-13 Employment and Employment Rate, 2001

State	Employed (in thousands)	Employment rate (percentage of labor force employed)	Rank by rate
Alabama	2,055	94.7	37
Alaska	309	94.0	47
Arizona	2,331	94.8	36
Arkansas	1,215	95.7	20
California	16,482	94.3	45
Colorado	2,241	95.8	17
Connecticut	1,657	96.8	5
Delaware	406	97.0	3
Florida	7,411	95.1	31
Georgia	4,023	95.9	14
Hawaii	578	94.7	39
Idaho	655	95.2	30
Illinois	6,031	94.5	42
Indiana	2,976	95.2	28
Iowa	1,545	96.6	7
Kansas	1,382	96.0	13
Kentucky	1,891	94.9	34
Louisiana	1,940	94.4	44
Maine	662	95.7	19
Maryland	2,773	95.6	21
Massachusetts	3,230	95.8	16
Michigan	4,969	94.7	38
Minnesota	2,719	96.3	9
Mississippi	1,234	94.6	40
Missouri	2,830	95.5	24
Montana	452	95.5	27
Nebraska	922	97.0	2
Nevada	981	93.7	48
New Hampshire	676	96.2	11
New Jersey	4,064	95.2	29
New Mexico	807	94.2	46
New York	8,465	95.0	33
North Carolina	3,806	94.5	43
North Dakota	330	98.0	1
Ohio	5,654	95.6	23
Oklahoma	1,611	96.3	10
Oregon	1,698	93.5	49
Pennsylvania	5,785	95.0	32
Rhode Island	485	95.9	15
South Carolina	1,907	94.5	41
South Dakota	396	96.9	4
Tennessee	2,748	95.5	25
Texas	10,100	94.8	35
Utah	1,091	95.8	18
Vermont	333	96.8	6
Virginia	3,622	96.4	8
Washington	2,832	93.4	50
West Virginia	771	95.6	22
Wisconsin	2,918	95.5	26
Wyoming	261	96.2	12
50 States	136,259	95.1	
DC	260	93.7	
United States	136,519	95.1	

Rank in order by rate	
1	North Dakota
2	Nebraska
3	Delaware
4	South Dakota
5	Connecticut
6	Vermont
7	Iowa
8	Virginia
9	Minnesota
10	Oklahoma
11	New Hampshire
12	Wyoming
13	Kansas
14	Georgia
15	Rhode Island
16	Massachusetts
17	Colorado
18	Utah
19	Maine
20	Arkansas
21	Maryland
22	West Virginia
23	Ohio
24	Missouri
25	Tennessee
26	Wisconsin
27	Montana
28	Indiana
29	New Jersey
30	Idaho
31	Florida
32	Pennsylvania
33	New York
34	Kentucky
35	Texas
36	Arizona
37	Alabama
38	Michigan
39	Hawaii
40	Mississippi
41	South Carolina
42	Illinois
43	North Carolina
44	Louisiana
45	California
46	New Mexico
47	Alaska
48	Nevada
49	Oregon
50	Washington

Note: Numbers that appear to be identical are rounded and vary slightly in actual value. The rankings reflect the actual values before rounding. See the introduction for more details.

B-14 Government Employment, 2001

State	Government employment (in thousands)	Percentage of total employment	Rank by percentage
Alabama	352	18.4	13
Alaska	76	26.0	1
Arizona	383	16.9	23
Arkansas	194	16.6	27
California	2,401	16.2	31
Colorado	347	15.5	33
Connecticut	246	14.6	38
Delaware	58	13.7	45
Florida	1,019	13.9	44
Georgia	606	15.3	34
Hawaii	117	21.1	5
Idaho	110	19.4	9
Illinois	832	13.9	43
Indiana	414	14.0	42
Iowa	243	16.3	30
Kansas	250	18.2	15
Kentucky	316	17.2	19
Louisiana	373	19.2	10
Maine	102	16.8	25
Maryland	452	18.3	14
Massachusetts	430	12.8	49
Michigan	700	15.0	35
Minnesota	396	14.9	37
Mississippi	238	21.0	6
Missouri	423	15.6	32
Montana	81	20.6	7
Nebraska	156	17.2	20
Nevada	126	11.9	50
New Hampshire	82	13.2	47
New Jersey	604	15.0	36
New Mexico	186	24.5	3
New York	1,473	17.1	21
North Carolina	650	16.4	29
North Dakota	73	22.3	4
Ohio	798	14.2	41
Oklahoma	293	19.4	8
Oregon	269	17.0	22
Pennsylvania	735	12.9	48
Rhode Island	65	13.6	46
South Carolina	318	16.9	24
South Dakota	71	18.7	12
Tennessee	399	14.5	40
Texas	1,599	16.6	28
Utah	191	17.5	18
Vermont	50	16.7	26
Virginia	629	17.7	17
Washington	492	18.0	16
West Virginia	140	19.1	11
Wisconsin	414	14.6	39
Wyoming	61	24.8	2
50 States	21,031	15.9	
DC	224	34.4	
United States	21,255	16.0	

Rank in order by percentage

1 Alaska
2 Wyoming
3 New Mexico
4 North Dakota
5 Hawaii
6 Mississippi
7 Montana
8 Oklahoma
9 Idaho
10 Louisiana
11 West Virginia
12 South Dakota
13 Alabama
14 Maryland
15 Kansas
16 Washington
17 Virginia
18 Utah
19 Kentucky
20 Nebraska
21 New York
22 Oregon
23 Arizona
24 South Carolina
25 Maine
26 Vermont
27 Arkansas
28 Texas
29 North Carolina
30 Iowa
31 California
32 Missouri
33 Colorado
34 Georgia
35 Michigan
36 New Jersey
37 Minnesota
38 Connecticut
39 Wisconsin
40 Tennessee
41 Ohio
42 Indiana
43 Illinois
44 Florida
45 Delaware
46 Rhode Island
47 New Hampshire
48 Pennsylvania
49 Massachusetts
50 Nevada

Note: Numbers that appear to be identical are rounded and vary slightly in actual value. The rankings reflect the actual values before rounding. See the introduction for more details.

B-15 Manufacturing Employment, 2001

State	Manufacturing employment (in thousands)	Percentage of total employment	Rank by percentage
Alabama	341	17.9	8
Alaska	13	4.6	47
Arizona	207	9.2	39
Arkansas	238	20.4	3
California	1,876	12.7	28
Colorado	198	8.8	41
Connecticut	253	15.0	19
Delaware	55	12.9	26
Florida	479	6.5	44
Georgia	561	14.1	22
Hawaii	17	3.1	50
Idaho	75	13.2	24
Illinois	904	15.1	18
Indiana	650	21.9	1
Iowa	257	17.2	11
Kansas	207	15.2	17
Kentucky	301	16.4	12
Louisiana	176	9.1	40
Maine	79	13.0	25
Maryland	173	7.0	43
Massachusetts	420	12.5	29
Michigan	926	19.9	4
Minnesota	424	16.0	15
Mississippi	215	19.0	5
Missouri	372	13.7	23
Montana	23	5.9	45
Nebraska	117	12.8	27
Nevada	46	4.3	49
New Hampshire	100	16.1	13
New Jersey	438	10.9	35
New Mexico	42	5.5	46
New York	827	9.6	38
North Carolina	726	18.3	7
North Dakota	25	7.6	42
Ohio	1,041	18.5	6
Oklahoma	175	11.7	33
Oregon	233	14.7	20
Pennsylvania	881	15.4	16
Rhode Island	69	14.4	21
South Carolina	327	17.4	10
South Dakota	45	11.7	32
Tennessee	483	17.6	9
Texas	1,066	11.0	34
Utah	128	11.8	31
Vermont	48	16.1	14
Virginia	371	10.4	37
Washington	333	12.2	30
West Virginia	77	10.4	36
Wisconsin	586	20.7	2
Wyoming	11	4.6	48
50 States	17,636	13.3	
DC	11	1.8	
United States	17,647	13.3	

Rank in order by percentage

1. Indiana
2. Wisconsin
3. Arkansas
4. Michigan
5. Mississippi
6. Ohio
7. North Carolina
8. Alabama
9. Tennessee
10. South Carolina
11. Iowa
12. Kentucky
13. New Hampshire
14. Vermont
15. Minnesota
16. Pennsylvania
17. Kansas
18. Illinois
19. Connecticut
20. Oregon
21. Rhode Island
22. Georgia
23. Missouri
24. Idaho
25. Maine
26. Delaware
27. Nebraska
28. California
29. Massachusetts
30. Washington
31. Utah
32. South Dakota
33. Oklahoma
34. Texas
35. New Jersey
36. West Virginia
37. Virginia
38. New York
39. Arizona
40. Louisiana
41. Colorado
42. North Dakota
43. Maryland
44. Florida
45. Montana
46. New Mexico
47. Alaska
48. Wyoming
49. Nevada
50. Hawaii

Note: Numbers that appear to be identical are rounded and vary slightly in actual value. The rankings reflect the actual values before rounding. See the introduction for more details.

B-16 *Fortune* 500 Companies, 2001

State	Number of *Fortune* 500 companies	*Fortune* 500 companies per million population	Rank per million
Alabama	7	1.6	24
Alaska	0	n/a	n/a
Arizona	5	1.0	30
Arkansas	5	1.9	18
California	55	1.6	22
Colorado	4	0.9	31
Connecticut	13	3.8	2
Delaware	3	3.8	1
Florida	12	0.8	33
Georgia	15	1.8	21
Hawaii	0	n/a	n/a
Idaho	3	2.3	12
Illinois	39	3.1	4
Indiana	5	0.8	32
Iowa	2	0.7	35
Kansas	2	0.7	34
Kentucky	4	1.0	29
Louisiana	1	0.2	40
Maine	0	n/a	n/a
Maryland	7	1.3	27
Massachusetts	13	2.0	15
Michigan	19	1.9	17
Minnesota	16	3.3	3
Mississippi	1	0.4	38
Missouri	13	2.3	11
Montana	0	n/a	n/a
Nebraska	5	2.9	5
Nevada	3	1.5	25
New Hampshire	0	n/a	n/a
New Jersey	22	2.6	9
New Mexico	0	n/a	n/a
New York	55	2.9	6
North Carolina	13	1.6	23
North Dakota	0	n/a	n/a
Ohio	29	2.6	10
Oklahoma	5	1.4	26
Oregon	2	0.6	36
Pennsylvania	25	2.0	16
Rhode Island	3	2.9	7
South Carolina	1	0.2	39
South Dakota	2	2.6	8
Tennessee	6	1.1	28
Texas	45	2.2	14
Utah	1	0.4	37
Vermont	0	n/a	n/a
Virginia	16	2.3	13
Washington	11	1.9	19
West Virginia	0	n/a	n/a
Wisconsin	10	1.9	20
Wyoming	0	n/a	n/a
50 States	498	1.8	
DC	2	3.5	
United States	500	1.8	

Rank in order per million

1 Delaware
2 Connecticut
3 Minnesota
4 Illinois
5 Nebraska
6 New York
7 Rhode Island
8 South Dakota
9 New Jersey
10 Ohio
11 Missouri
12 Idaho
13 Virginia
14 Texas
15 Massachusetts
16 Pennsylvania
17 Michigan
18 Arkansas
19 Washington
20 Wisconsin
21 Georgia
22 California
23 North Carolina
24 Alabama
25 Nevada
26 Oklahoma
27 Maryland
28 Tennessee
29 Kentucky
30 Arizona
31 Colorado
32 Indiana
33 Florida
34 Kansas
35 Iowa
36 Oregon
37 Utah
38 Mississippi
39 South Carolina
40 Louisiana

Note: Numbers that appear to be identical are rounded and vary slightly in actual value. The rankings reflect the actual values before rounding. See the introduction for more details.

B-17 *Forbes* 500 Companies, 2001

State	Number of *Forbes* 500 companies	*Forbes* 500 companies per million companies	Rank per million
Alabama	12	2.7	19
Alaska	0	n/a	n/a
Arizona	8	1.6	32
Arkansas	5	1.9	30
California	121	3.6	11
Colorado	9	2.1	29
Connecticut	22	6.5	1
Delaware	5	6.4	2
Florida	21	1.3	39
Georgia	23	2.8	16
Hawaii	3	2.5	23
Idaho	3	2.3	25
Illinois	50	4.0	5
Indiana	9	1.5	36
Iowa	4	1.4	37
Kansas	4	1.5	35
Kentucky	5	1.2	40
Louisiana	5	1.1	42
Maine	3	2.4	24
Maryland	14	2.6	21
Massachusetts	29	4.6	3
Michigan	29	2.9	15
Minnesota	19	3.9	8
Mississippi	3	1.1	44
Missouri	22	3.9	6
Montana	1	1.1	43
Nebraska	5	2.9	14
Nevada	5	2.5	22
New Hampshire	1	0.8	45
New Jersey	33	3.9	7
New Mexico	0	n/a	n/a
New York	80	4.2	4
North Carolina	18	2.2	28
North Dakota	1	1.6	33
Ohio	42	3.7	10
Oklahoma	8	2.3	26
Oregon	4	1.2	41
Pennsylvania	34	2.8	17
Rhode Island	4	3.8	9
South Carolina	6	1.5	34
South Dakota	2	2.6	20
Tennessee	10	1.8	31
Texas	71	3.4	12
Utah	3	1.3	38
Vermont	0	n/a	n/a
Virginia	22	3.1	13
Washington	16	2.7	18
West Virginia	1	0.6	46
Wisconsin	12	2.2	27
Wyoming	0	n/a	n/a
50 States	807	2.9	
DC	6	10.5	
United States*	817	2.9	

Rank in order per million	
1	Connecticut
2	Delaware
3	Massachusetts
4	New York
5	Illinois
6	Missouri
7	New Jersey
8	Minnesota
9	Rhode Island
10	Ohio
11	California
12	Texas
13	Virginia
14	Nebraska
15	Michigan
16	Georgia
17	Pennsylvania
18	Washington
19	Alabama
20	South Dakota
21	Maryland
22	Nevada
23	Hawaii
24	Maine
25	Idaho
26	Oklahoma
27	Wisconsin
28	North Carolina
29	Colorado
30	Arkansas
31	Tennessee
32	Arizona
33	North Dakota
34	South Carolina
35	Kansas
36	Indiana
37	Iowa
38	Utah
39	Florida
40	Kentucky
41	Oregon
42	Louisiana
43	Montana
44	Mississippi
45	New Hampshire
46	West Virginia

Note: Numbers that appear to be identical are rounded and vary slightly in actual value. The rankings reflect the actual values before rounding. See the introduction for more details.

Due to rounding or data sources, the 50-state total plus D.C. may not equal the U.S. total. Please see introduction.

B-18 Tourism Spending, 1999

State	Tourism spending $ (in millions)	Percentage of U.S. total	Per capita $	Rank per capita
Alabama	5,110	1.0	1,169	45
Alaska	1,507	0.3	2,433	5
Arizona	9,489	2.0	1,986	12
Arkansas	3,659	0.8	1,434	40
California	71,370	14.9	2,153	9
Colorado	9,355	2.0	2,306	7
Connecticut	5,243	1.1	1,597	30
Delaware	1,088	0.2	1,443	38
Florida	55,785	11.7	3,692	3
Georgia	14,538	3.0	1,867	16
Hawaii	14,224	3.0	11,998	1
Idaho	2,102	0.4	1,679	25
Illinois	22,147	4.6	1,826	20
Indiana	6,058	1.3	1,019	49
Iowa	4,172	0.9	1,454	36
Kansas	3,412	0.7	1,286	41
Kentucky	5,068	1.1	1,279	42
Louisiana	8,090	1.7	1,850	17
Maine	2,073	0.4	1,655	26
Maryland	8,043	1.7	1,555	33
Massachusetts	12,207	2.6	1,977	13
Michigan	11,512	2.4	1,167	46
Minnesota	6,919	1.4	1,449	37
Mississippi	4,348	0.9	1,570	31
Missouri	9,346	2.0	1,709	24
Montana	1,904	0.4	2,157	8
Nebraska	2,592	0.5	1,556	32
Nevada	21,034	4.4	11,626	2
New Hampshire	2,347	0.5	1,954	14
New Jersey	15,053	3.1	1,849	18
New Mexico	3,545	0.7	2,038	10
New York	36,315	7.6	1,996	11
North Carolina	11,868	2.5	1,551	34
North Dakota	1,148	0.2	1,812	22
Ohio	12,748	2.7	1,133	47
Oklahoma	3,735	0.8	1,112	48
Oregon	5,461	1.1	1,647	28
Pennsylvania	14,763	3.1	1,231	43
Rhode Island	1,425	0.3	1,438	39
South Carolina	7,046	1.5	1,813	21
South Dakota	1,189	0.2	1,622	29
Tennessee	9,752	2.0	1,778	23
Texas	33,131	6.9	1,653	27
Utah	3,924	0.8	1,842	19
Vermont	1,442	0.3	2,429	6
Virginia	12,863	2.7	1,872	15
Washington	8,499	1.8	1,476	35
West Virginia	1,642	0.3	909	50
Wisconsin	6,253	1.3	1,191	44
Wyoming	1,496	0.3	3,120	4
50 States	518,039	108.4	1,903	
DC	5,721	1.2	11,024	
United States	523,760	109.6	1,921	

Rank in order per capita	
1	Hawaii
2	Nevada
3	Florida
4	Wyoming
5	Alaska
6	Vermont
7	Colorado
8	Montana
9	California
10	New Mexico
11	New York
12	Arizona
13	Massachusetts
14	New Hampshire
15	Virginia
16	Georgia
17	Louisiana
18	New Jersey
19	Utah
20	Illinois
21	South Carolina
22	North Dakota
23	Tennessee
24	Missouri
25	Idaho
26	Maine
27	Texas
28	Oregon
29	South Dakota
30	Connecticut
31	Mississippi
32	Nebraska
33	Maryland
34	North Carolina
35	Washington
36	Iowa
37	Minnesota
38	Delaware
39	Rhode Island
40	Arkansas
41	Kansas
42	Kentucky
43	Pennsylvania
44	Wisconsin
45	Alabama
46	Michigan
47	Ohio
48	Oklahoma
49	Indiana
50	West Virginia

B-19 Exports, 2000

State	Exports $ (millions)	Exports per capita $	Rank per capita
Alabama	7,317	1,645	30
Alaska	2,464	3,930	4
Arizona	14,334	2,794	11
Arkansas	2,599	972	43
California	119,640	3,532	6
Colorado	6,593	1,533	31
Connecticut	8,047	2,363	16
Delaware	2,197	2,804	10
Florida	26,543	1,661	28
Georgia	14,925	1,823	27
Hawaii	387	319	50
Idaho	3,559	2,750	12
Illinois	31,438	2,531	13
Indiana	15,386	2,530	14
Iowa	4,466	1,526	33
Kansas	5,145	1,914	26
Kentucky	9,612	2,378	15
Louisiana	16,814	3,762	5
Maine	1,779	1,395	36
Maryland	4,593	867	47
Massachusetts	20,514	3,231	9
Michigan	33,845	3,405	7
Minnesota	10,303	2,094	22
Mississippi	2,726	958	44
Missouri	6,497	1,161	39
Montana	541	599	49
Nebraska	2,511	1,467	34
Nevada	1,482	742	48
New Hampshire	2,373	1,920	25
New Jersey	18,638	2,215	20
New Mexico	2,391	1,314	37
New York	42,846	2,258	18
North Carolina	17,946	2,229	19
North Dakota	626	975	42
Ohio	26,322	2,318	17
Oklahoma	3,072	890	46
Oregon	11,441	3,344	8
Pennsylvania	18,792	1,530	32
Rhode Island	1,186	1,131	40
South Carolina	8,565	2,135	21
South Dakota	679	900	45
Tennessee	11,592	2,037	23
Texas	103,866	4,981	3
Utah	3,221	1,442	35
Vermont	4,097	6,729	1
Virginia	11,698	1,653	29
Washington	32,215	5,466	2
West Virginia	2,219	1,227	38
Wisconsin	10,508	1,959	24
Wyoming	503	1,018	41
50 States	711,052	2,532	
DC	1,003	1,754	
United States*	782,429	2,780	

Rank in order per capita	
1	Vermont
2	Washington
3	Texas
4	Alaska
5	Louisiana
6	California
7	Michigan
8	Oregon
9	Massachusetts
10	Delaware
11	Arizona
12	Idaho
13	Illinois
14	Indiana
15	Kentucky
16	Connecticut
17	Ohio
18	New York
19	North Carolina
20	New Jersey
21	South Carolina
22	Minnesota
23	Tennessee
24	Wisconsin
25	New Hampshire
26	Kansas
27	Georgia
28	Florida
29	Virginia
30	Alabama
31	Colorado
32	Pennsylvania
33	Iowa
34	Nebraska
35	Utah
36	Maine
37	New Mexico
38	West Virginia
39	Missouri
40	Rhode Island
41	Wyoming
42	North Dakota
43	Arkansas
44	Mississippi
45	South Dakota
46	Oklahoma
47	Maryland
48	Nevada
49	Montana
50	Hawaii

Due to rounding or data sources, the 50-state total plus D.C. may not equal the U.S. total. Please see introduction.

B-20 Housing Permits, 2000

State	Housing permits	Permits per 10,000 population	Rank per 10,000
Alabama	17,406	39.1	37
Alaska	2,147	34.2	39
Arizona	61,485	119.8	3
Arkansas	9,203	34.4	38
California	145,575	43.0	30
Colorado	54,596	126.9	2
Connecticut	9,376	27.5	47
Delaware	4,611	58.8	16
Florida	155,269	97.2	6
Georgia	91,820	112.2	4
Hawaii	4,905	40.5	35
Idaho	10,915	84.4	7
Illinois	51,944	41.8	32
Indiana	37,903	62.3	15
Iowa	12,500	42.7	31
Kansas	12,542	46.7	26
Kentucky	18,460	45.7	27
Louisiana	14,720	32.9	42
Maine	6,177	48.4	25
Maryland	30,358	57.3	18
Massachusetts	18,000	28.4	46
Michigan	52,489	52.8	23
Minnesota	32,814	66.7	12
Mississippi	11,270	39.6	36
Missouri	24,321	43.5	29
Montana	2,572	28.5	45
Nebraska	9,105	53.2	22
Nevada	32,285	161.6	1
New Hampshire	6,680	54.1	21
New Jersey	34,585	41.1	34
New Mexico	8,869	48.8	24
New York	44,105	23.2	49
North Carolina	78,376	97.4	5
North Dakota	2,128	33.1	41
Ohio	49,745	43.8	28
Oklahoma	11,148	32.3	43
Oregon	19,877	58.1	17
Pennsylvania	41,076	33.4	40
Rhode Island	2,596	24.8	48
South Carolina	32,812	81.8	8
South Dakota	4,196	55.6	20
Tennessee	32,203	56.6	19
Texas	141,231	67.7	11
Utah	17,638	79.0	9
Vermont	2,506	41.2	33
Virginia	48,402	68.4	10
Washington	39,021	66.2	13
West Virginia	3,763	20.8	50
Wisconsin	34,154	63.7	14
Wyoming	1,582	32.0	44
50 States	1,591,461	56.7	
DC	806	14.1	
United States	1,592,267	56.6	

Rank in order per 10,000 population	
1	Nevada
2	Colorado
3	Arizona
4	Georgia
5	North Carolina
6	Florida
7	Idaho
8	South Carolina
9	Utah
10	Virginia
11	Texas
12	Minnesota
13	Washington
14	Wisconsin
15	Indiana
16	Delaware
17	Oregon
18	Maryland
19	Tennessee
20	South Dakota
21	New Hampshire
22	Nebraska
23	Michigan
24	New Mexico
25	Maine
26	Kansas
27	Kentucky
28	Ohio
29	Missouri
30	California
31	Iowa
32	Illinois
33	Vermont
34	New Jersey
35	Hawaii
36	Mississippi
37	Alabama
38	Arkansas
39	Alaska
40	Pennsylvania
41	North Dakota
42	Louisiana
43	Oklahoma
44	Wyoming
45	Montana
46	Massachusetts
47	Connecticut
48	Rhode Island
49	New York
50	West Virginia

B-21 Percentage Change in Home Prices, 1996-2001

State	Percentage change in price	Rank
Alabama	25.1	36
Alaska	18.3	47
Arizona	32.7	15
Arkansas	21.0	45
California	55.5	2
Colorado	51.7	4
Connecticut	32.8	14
Delaware	25.7	34
Florida	33.5	12
Georgia	37.9	7
Hawaii	1.0	50
Idaho	20.2	46
Illinois	25.6	35
Indiana	25.0	37
Iowa	27.2	27
Kansas	31.4	17
Kentucky	27.3	26
Louisiana	27.2	27
Maine	37.6	8
Maryland	23.2	40
Massachusetts	59.3	1
Michigan	42.1	6
Minnesota	49.6	5
Mississippi	26.5	30
Missouri	29.8	19
Montana	23.7	38
Nebraska	26.9	29
Nevada	18.2	48
New Hampshire	55.0	3
New Jersey	35.1	10
New Mexico	14.3	49
New York	37.0	9
North Carolina	28.8	22
North Dakota	21.4	43
Ohio	27.6	25
Oklahoma	26.4	31
Oregon	28.4	23
Pennsylvania	21.3	44
Rhode Island	32.5	16
South Carolina	33.3	13
South Dakota	27.7	24
Tennessee	25.9	32
Texas	30.4	18
Utah	23.5	39
Vermont	25.9	32
Virginia	29.1	20
Washington	34.4	11
West Virginia	21.5	42
Wisconsin	28.9	21
Wyoming	22.2	41
50 States	n/a	
DC	49.9	
United States	34.8	

Rank in order by percentage

1 Massachusetts
2 California
3 New Hampshire
4 Colorado
5 Minnesota
6 Michigan
7 Georgia
8 Maine
9 New York
10 New Jersey
11 Washington
12 Florida
13 South Carolina
14 Connecticut
15 Arizona
16 Rhode Island
17 Kansas
18 Texas
19 Missouri
20 Virginia
21 Wisconsin
22 North Carolina
23 Oregon
24 South Dakota
25 Ohio
26 Kentucky
27 Iowa
27 Louisiana
29 Nebraska
30 Mississippi
31 Oklahoma
32 Tennessee
32 Vermont
34 Delaware
35 Illinois
36 Alabama
37 Indiana
38 Montana
39 Utah
40 Maryland
41 Wyoming
42 West Virginia
43 North Dakota
44 Pennsylvania
45 Arkansas
46 Idaho
47 Alaska
48 Nevada
49 New Mexico
50 Hawaii

Note: Ties in ranking reflect ties in actual values.

B-22 Net Farm Income, 2000

State	Net farm income $ (in thousands)	Net farm income per capita $	Rank by total income
Alabama	1,196,212	269	13
Alaska	13,397	21	49
Arizona	616,638	120	25
Arkansas	1,578,125	590	8
California	5,348,996	158	1
Colorado	542,652	126	28
Connecticut	184,783	54	39
Delaware	135,909	173	41
Florida	2,712,956	170	4
Georgia	1,998,777	244	6
Hawaii	63,904	53	45
Idaho	832,094	643	19
Illinois	1,561,412	126	9
Indiana	821,529	135	20
Iowa	2,578,305	881	5
Kansas	956,147	356	17
Kentucky	1,662,695	411	7
Louisiana	488,360	109	30
Maine	96,510	76	43
Maryland	409,650	77	32
Massachusetts	59,778	9	46
Michigan	304,678	31	35
Minnesota	1,548,378	315	10
Mississippi	769,201	270	22
Missouri	971,899	174	16
Montana	291,794	323	36
Nebraska	1,419,762	830	11
Nevada	88,948	45	44
New Hampshire	15,837	13	48
New Jersey	221,698	26	37
New Mexico	494,239	272	29
New York	609,053	32	26
North Carolina	3,107,638	386	3
North Dakota	749,127	1,167	23
Ohio	1,177,321	104	14
Oklahoma	1,144,662	332	15
Oregon	342,656	100	34
Pennsylvania	949,161	77	18
Rhode Island	11,300	11	50
South Carolina	552,169	138	27
South Dakota	1,398,608	1,853	12
Tennessee	448,601	79	31
Texas	3,644,154	175	2
Utah	219,096	98	38
Vermont	163,143	268	40
Virginia	642,073	91	24
Washington	796,305	135	21
West Virginia	41,469	23	47
Wisconsin	347,614	65	33
Wyoming	114,239	231	42
50 States	46,443,651	165	
DC	n/a	n/a	
United States	46,443,651	165	

Rank in order by total income	
1	California
2	Texas
3	North Carolina
4	Florida
5	Iowa
6	Georgia
7	Kentucky
8	Arkansas
9	Illinois
10	Minnesota
11	Nebraska
12	South Dakota
13	Alabama
14	Ohio
15	Oklahoma
16	Missouri
17	Kansas
18	Pennsylvania
19	Idaho
20	Indiana
21	Washington
22	Mississippi
23	North Dakota
24	Virginia
25	Arizona
26	New York
27	South Carolina
28	Colorado
29	New Mexico
30	Louisiana
31	Tennessee
32	Maryland
33	Wisconsin
34	Oregon
35	Michigan
36	Montana
37	New Jersey
38	Utah
39	Connecticut
40	Vermont
41	Delaware
42	Wyoming
43	Maine
44	Nevada
45	Hawaii
46	Massachusetts
47	West Virginia
48	New Hampshire
49	Alaska
50	Rhode Island

B-23 Financial Institution Assets, 2000

State	Total assets $ (in millions)	Per capita assets $	Rank per capita		Rank in order per capita
Alabama	183,676	41,302	7	1	Delaware
Alaska	6,478	10,333	44	2	Rhode Island
Arizona	62,657	12,212	38	3	North Carolina
Arkansas	28,954	10,830	42	4	New York
California	673,563	19,886	18	5	South Dakota
Colorado	47,390	11,018	41	6	Utah
Connecticut	49,607	14,566	28	7	Alabama
Delaware	164,359	209,749	1	8	Minnesota
Florida	82,635	5,170	49	9	Ohio
Georgia	175,283	21,411	17	10	Illinois
Hawaii	30,862	25,473	15	11	North Dakota
Idaho	3,097	2,393	50	12	Massachusetts
Illinois	395,070	31,811	10	13	Nebraska
Indiana	101,485	16,690	25	14	New Hampshire
Iowa	48,997	16,744	24	15	Hawaii
Kansas	49,335	18,351	20	16	Pennsylvania
Kentucky	55,664	13,772	32	17	Georgia
Louisiana	56,137	12,561	35	18	California
Maine	15,050	11,805	39	19	Nevada
Maryland	55,406	10,461	43	20	Kansas
Massachusetts	173,693	27,357	12	21	Wisconsin
Michigan	170,016	17,107	22	22	Michigan
Minnesota	189,974	38,617	8	23	New Jersey
Mississippi	35,054	12,323	36	24	Iowa
Missouri	71,587	12,794	34	25	Indiana
Montana	12,489	13,843	31	26	Tennessee
Nebraska	45,177	26,400	13	27	Wyoming
Nevada	38,804	19,419	19	28	Connecticut
New Hampshire	31,646	25,608	14	29	Oklahoma
New Jersey	143,131	17,010	23	30	Vermont
New Mexico	18,569	10,208	45	31	Montana
New York	1,436,712	75,710	4	32	Kentucky
North Carolina	986,961	122,614	3	33	Virginia
North Dakota	18,516	28,832	11	34	Missouri
Ohio	434,246	38,249	9	35	Louisiana
Oklahoma	49,758	14,420	29	36	Mississippi
Oregon	19,475	5,692	48	37	Washington
Pennsylvania	265,335	21,605	16	38	Arizona
Rhode Island	184,034	175,552	2	39	Maine
South Carolina	31,658	7,891	47	40	Texas
South Dakota	38,308	50,750	5	41	Colorado
Tennessee	92,029	16,176	26	42	Arkansas
Texas	233,385	11,193	40	43	Maryland
Utah	104,465	46,779	6	44	Alaska
Vermont	8,621	14,160	30	45	New Mexico
Virginia	91,190	12,883	33	46	West Virginia
Washington	72,113	12,235	37	47	South Carolina
West Virginia	18,339	10,141	46	48	Oregon
Wisconsin	97,917	18,256	21	49	Florida
Wyoming	7,877	15,952	27	50	Idaho
50 States	7,406,784	26,373			
DC	1,011	1,767			
United States*	7,461,348	26,513			

Due to rounding or data sources, the 50-state total plus D.C. may not equal the U.S. total. Please see introduction.

B-24 Bankruptcy Filings by Individuals and Businesses, 2001

State	Bankruptcy petitions	Petitions per 1,000 residents	Rank per 1,000
Alabama	34,755	7.82	2
Alaska	1,436	2.29	50
Arizona	21,691	4.23	27
Arkansas	18,325	6.85	7
California	142,616	4.21	28
Colorado	16,333	3.80	33
Connecticut	10,922	3.21	41
Delaware	4,295	5.48	15
Florida	75,341	4.71	22
Georgia	62,563	7.64	3
Hawaii	4,647	3.84	32
Idaho	7,378	5.70	11
Illinois	64,038	5.16	18
Indiana	39,608	6.51	8
Iowa	8,917	3.05	45
Kansas	11,980	4.46	25
Kentucky	22,354	5.53	14
Louisiana	23,989	5.37	16
Maine	4,153	3.26	40
Maryland	31,709	5.99	9
Massachusetts	16,180	2.55	48
Michigan	39,176	3.94	30
Minnesota	16,109	3.27	38
Mississippi	19,669	6.91	6
Missouri	26,782	4.79	21
Montana	3,469	3.85	31
Nebraska	5,999	3.51	37
Nevada	14,745	7.38	4
New Hampshire	3,676	2.97	46
New Jersey	38,620	4.59	23
New Mexico	7,457	4.10	29
New York	61,872	3.26	39
North Carolina	28,922	3.59	35
North Dakota	2,026	3.15	42
Ohio	57,707	5.08	20
Oklahoma	20,501	5.94	10
Oregon	19,145	5.60	12
Pennsylvania	46,319	3.77	34
Rhode Island	4,606	4.39	26
South Carolina	12,450	3.10	44
South Dakota	2,188	2.90	47
Tennessee	52,252	9.18	1
Texas	65,191	3.13	43
Utah	16,090	7.21	5
Vermont	1,538	2.53	49
Virginia	37,597	5.31	17
Washington	32,757	5.56	13
West Virginia	9,217	5.10	19
Wisconsin	18,853	3.51	36
Wyoming	2,207	4.47	24
50 States	1,290,370	4.59	
DC	2,403	4.20	
United States*	1,307,857	4.65	

Due to rounding or data sources, the 50-state total plus D.C. may not equal the U.S. total. Please see introduction.

Rank in order per 1,000 residents	
1	Tennessee
2	Alabama
3	Georgia
4	Nevada
5	Utah
6	Mississippi
7	Arkansas
8	Indiana
9	Maryland
10	Oklahoma
11	Idaho
12	Oregon
13	Washington
14	Kentucky
15	Delaware
16	Louisiana
17	Virginia
18	Illinois
19	West Virginia
20	Ohio
21	Missouri
22	Florida
23	New Jersey
24	Wyoming
25	Kansas
26	Rhode Island
27	Arizona
28	California
29	New Mexico
30	Michigan
31	Montana
32	Hawaii
33	Colorado
34	Pennsylvania
35	North Carolina
36	Wisconsin
37	Nebraska
38	Minnesota
39	New York
40	Maine
41	Connecticut
42	North Dakota
43	Texas
44	South Carolina
45	Iowa
46	New Hampshire
47	South Dakota
48	Massachusetts
49	Vermont
50	Alaska

Note: Numbers that appear to be identical are rounded and vary slightly in actual value. The rankings reflect the actual values before rounding. See the introduction for more details.

B-25 Patents Issued, FY 2000

State	Patents issued	Patents per 100,000 population	Rank per 100,000
Alabama	432	9.7	46
Alaska	72	11.5	45
Arizona	1,707	33.3	22
Arkansas	245	9.2	47
California	20,401	60.2	6
Colorado	2,147	49.9	10
Connecticut	2,161	63.5	5
Delaware	459	58.6	7
Florida	3,217	20.1	28
Georgia	1,567	19.1	30
Hawaii	99	8.2	49
Idaho	1,608	124.3	1
Illinois	4,580	36.9	18
Indiana	1,781	29.3	24
Iowa	738	25.2	26
Kansas	511	19.0	31
Kentucky	540	13.4	42
Louisiana	557	12.5	44
Maine	161	12.6	43
Maryland	1,628	30.7	23
Massachusetts	4,065	64.0	3
Michigan	4,261	42.9	12
Minnesota	3,129	63.6	4
Mississippi	227	8.0	50
Missouri	1,036	18.5	32
Montana	146	16.2	38
Nebraska	309	18.1	35
Nevada	385	19.3	29
New Hampshire	711	57.5	8
New Jersey	4,526	53.8	9
New Mexico	377	20.7	27
New York	7,385	38.9	14
North Carolina	2,218	27.6	25
North Dakota	98	15.3	40
Ohio	4,193	36.9	17
Oklahoma	629	18.2	33
Oregon	1,526	44.6	11
Pennsylvania	4,227	34.4	20
Rhode Island	390	37.2	15
South Carolina	681	17.0	37
South Dakota	102	13.5	41
Tennessee	1,010	17.8	36
Texas	7,129	34.2	21
Utah	825	36.9	16
Vermont	426	70.0	2
Virginia	1,290	18.2	34
Washington	2,143	36.4	19
West Virginia	160	8.8	48
Wisconsin	2,157	40.2	13
Wyoming	77	15.6	39
50 States	100,449	35.8	
DC	56	9.8	
United States*	100,548	35.7	

Rank in order per 100,000 population

1	Idaho
2	Vermont
3	Massachusetts
4	Minnesota
5	Connecticut
6	California
7	Delaware
8	New Hampshire
9	New Jersey
10	Colorado
11	Oregon
12	Michigan
13	Wisconsin
14	New York
15	Rhode Island
16	Utah
17	Ohio
18	Illinois
19	Washington
20	Pennsylvania
21	Texas
22	Arizona
23	Maryland
24	Indiana
25	North Carolina
26	Iowa
27	New Mexico
28	Florida
29	Nevada
30	Georgia
31	Kansas
32	Missouri
33	Oklahoma
34	Virginia
35	Nebraska
36	Tennessee
37	South Carolina
38	Montana
39	Wyoming
40	North Dakota
41	South Dakota
42	Kentucky
43	Maine
44	Louisiana
45	Alaska
46	Alabama
47	Arkansas
48	West Virginia
49	Hawaii
50	Mississippi

Note: Numbers that appear to be identical are rounded and vary slightly in actual value. The rankings reflect the actual values before rounding. See the introduction for more details.

*Due to rounding or data sources, the 50-state total plus D.C. may not equal the U.S. total. Please see introduction.

B-26 Workers' Compensation Temporary Disability Payments, 2001

State	Maximum weekly benefit $	Rank
Alabama	510.00	30
Alaska	762.00	8
Arizona	373.94	49
Arkansas	410.00	44
California	490.00	37
Colorado	593.81	19
Connecticut	838.00	4
Delaware	449.60	40
Florida	571.00	23
Georgia	375.00	48
Hawaii	547.00	25
Idaho	445.50	42
Illinois	956.32	2
Indiana	508.00	31
Iowa	1031.00	1
Kansas	401.00	45
Kentucky	530.07	28
Louisiana	388.00	47
Maine	458.83	39
Maryland	668.00	10
Massachusetts	830.89	5
Michigan	644.00	12
Minnesota	750.00	9
Mississippi	316.46	50
Missouri	599.96	18
Montana	439.00	43
Nebraska	508.00	31
Nevada	580.72	22
New Hampshire	923.00	3
New Jersey	591.00	20
New Mexico	492.98	35
New York	400.00	46
North Carolina	620.00	15
North Dakota	497.00	34
Ohio	618.00	16
Oklahoma	473.00	38
Oregon	628.64	14
Pennsylvania	644.00	12
Rhode Island	653.00	11
South Carolina	532.77	27
South Dakota	448.00	41
Tennessee	562.00	24
Texas	533.00	26
Utah	529.00	29
Vermont	790.00	7
Virginia	606.00	17
Washington	821.77	6
West Virginia	490.55	36
Wisconsin	582.00	21
Wyoming	504.88	33
50 States	n/a	
DC	948.76	
United States	n/a	

Rank in order by $	
1	Iowa
2	Illinois
3	New Hampshire
4	Connecticut
5	Massachusetts
6	Washington
7	Vermont
8	Alaska
9	Minnesota
10	Maryland
11	Rhode Island
12	Michigan
12	Pennsylvania
14	Oregon
15	North Carolina
16	Ohio
17	Virginia
18	Missouri
19	Colorado
20	New Jersey
21	Wisconsin
22	Nevada
23	Florida
24	Tennessee
25	Hawaii
26	Texas
27	South Carolina
28	Kentucky
29	Utah
30	Alabama
31	Indiana
31	Nebraska
33	Wyoming
34	North Dakota
35	New Mexico
36	West Virginia
37	California
38	Oklahoma
39	Maine
40	Delaware
41	South Dakota
42	Idaho
43	Montana
44	Arkansas
45	Kansas
46	New York
47	Louisiana
48	Georgia
49	Arizona
50	Mississippi

Note: Ties in ranking reflect ties in actual values.

B-27 Average Unemployment Compensation Benefit, 2000

State	Average weekly UC benefit $	Rank
Alabama	159.41	49
Alaska	189.86	39
Arizona	162.51	47
Arkansas	210.08	31
California	160.00	48
Colorado	255.86	8
Connecticut	257.56	7
Delaware	214.85	26
Florida	220.21	23
Georgia	211.89	30
Hawaii	283.67	4
Idaho	209.46	33
Illinois	251.58	10
Indiana	222.19	22
Iowa	238.42	14
Kansas	247.09	12
Kentucky	224.78	20
Louisiana	182.06	44
Maine	202.29	36
Maryland	212.51	29
Massachusetts	293.45	1
Michigan	244.12	13
Minnesota	290.51	2
Mississippi	156.62	50
Missouri	186.22	43
Montana	187.92	42
Nebraska	188.00	41
Nevada	222.43	21
New Hampshire	217.21	24
New Jersey	289.61	3
New Mexico	180.43	46
New York	247.48	11
North Carolina	231.21	18
North Dakota	210.01	32
Ohio	236.40	15
Oklahoma	214.40	27
Oregon	232.62	17
Pennsylvania	264.76	6
Rhode Island	253.48	9
South Carolina	190.18	38
South Dakota	180.86	45
Tennessee	188.74	40
Texas	227.11	19
Utah	213.89	28
Vermont	215.55	25
Virginia	203.88	35
Washington	280.94	5
West Virginia	197.53	37
Wisconsin	233.11	16
Wyoming	207.10	34
50 States	n/a	
DC	241.03	
United States	221.00	

Rank in order by $

1 Massachusetts
2 Minnesota
3 New Jersey
4 Hawaii
5 Washington
6 Pennsylvania
7 Connecticut
8 Colorado
9 Rhode Island
10 Illinois
11 New York
12 Kansas
13 Michigan
14 Iowa
15 Ohio
16 Wisconsin
17 Oregon
18 North Carolina
19 Texas
20 Kentucky
21 Nevada
22 Indiana
23 Florida
24 New Hampshire
25 Vermont
26 Delaware
27 Oklahoma
28 Utah
29 Maryland
30 Georgia
31 Arkansas
32 North Dakota
33 Idaho
34 Wyoming
35 Virginia
36 Maine
37 West Virginia
38 South Carolina
39 Alaska
40 Tennessee
41 Nebraska
42 Montana
43 Missouri
44 Louisiana
45 South Dakota
46 New Mexico
47 Arizona
48 California
49 Alabama
50 Mississippi

B-28 Index of State Economic Momentum, September 2001

State	Index of state economic momentum September 2001	Rank
Alabama	-1.19	46
Alaska	-0.53	34
Arizona	0.08	18
Arkansas	-0.80	41
California	0.71	6
Colorado	2.00	2
Connecticut	-0.52	33
Delaware	0.45	11
Florida	1.28	3
Georgia	0.53	9
Hawaii	-0.43	29
Idaho	0.18	14
Illinois	-0.40	28
Indiana	-1.69	50
Iowa	-0.63	37
Kansas	-0.49	32
Kentucky	-0.17	23
Louisiana	-0.82	42
Maine	-0.16	22
Maryland	0.15	16
Massachusetts	0.13	17
Michigan	-1.61	49
Minnesota	0.63	8
Mississippi	-1.49	48
Missouri	-0.88	44
Montana	-0.04	19
Nebraska	-0.85	43
Nevada	2.22	1
New Hampshire	-0.11	21
New Jersey	0.22	13
New Mexico	0.48	10
New York	0.18	15
North Carolina	-0.22	24
North Dakota	-0.45	31
Ohio	-1.33	47
Oklahoma	-0.05	20
Oregon	-0.92	45
Pennsylvania	-0.59	36
Rhode Island	-0.28	25
South Carolina	-0.40	27
South Dakota	-0.57	35
Tennessee	-0.38	26
Texas	0.89	4
Utah	0.68	7
Vermont	-0.45	30
Virginia	0.75	5
Washington	-0.76	39
West Virginia	-0.76	40
Wisconsin	-0.71	38
Wyoming	0.40	12
50 States	0.00	
DC	-0.24	
United States	0.00	

Rank in order by index	
1	Nevada
2	Colorado
3	Florida
4	Texas
5	Virginia
6	California
7	Utah
8	Minnesota
9	Georgia
10	New Mexico
11	Delaware
12	Wyoming
13	New Jersey
14	Idaho
15	New York
16	Maryland
17	Massachusetts
18	Arizona
19	Montana
20	Oklahoma
21	New Hampshire
22	Maine
23	Kentucky
24	North Carolina
25	Rhode Island
26	Tennessee
27	South Carolina
28	Illinois
29	Hawaii
30	Vermont
31	North Dakota
32	Kansas
33	Connecticut
34	Alaska
35	South Dakota
36	Pennsylvania
37	Iowa
38	Wisconsin
39	Washington
40	West Virginia
41	Arkansas
42	Louisiana
43	Nebraska
44	Missouri
45	Oregon
46	Alabama
47	Ohio
48	Mississippi
49	Michigan
50	Indiana

Note: Numbers that appear to be identical are rounded and vary slightly in actual value. The rankings reflect the actual values before rounding. See the introduction for more details.

B-29 Employment Change, 2000-2001

State	Change in number of jobs June 2000-2001 (in thousands)	Percentage change in employment	Rank by percentage change
Alabama	-17.6	-0.91	48
Alaska	2.8	0.94	17
Arizona	19.2	0.86	19
Arkansas	-0.5	-0.04	40
California	261.8	1.79	6
Colorado	43.0	1.92	5
Connecticut	4.0	0.23	34
Delaware	3.7	0.87	18
Florida	218.6	3.08	2
Georgia	46.6	1.16	14
Hawaii	6.5	1.17	13
Idaho	7.5	1.32	10
Illinois	2.3	0.04	37
Indiana	-32.3	-1.07	49
Iowa	6.5	0.43	31
Kansas	11.7	0.86	20
Kentucky	15.4	0.84	21
Louisiana	12.7	0.66	24
Maine	6.7	1.08	15
Maryland	15.9	0.64	26
Massachusetts	40.0	1.19	12
Michigan	-7.6	-0.16	44
Minnesota	17.6	0.65	25
Mississippi	-18.5	-1.59	50
Missouri	-24.1	-0.86	47
Montana	6.9	1.75	8
Nebraska	-3.3	-0.36	45
Nevada	44.6	4.34	1
New Hampshire	3.7	0.59	29
New Jersey	24.2	0.60	28
New Mexico	13.3	1.78	7
New York	88.6	1.02	16
North Carolina	-4.4	-0.11	42
North Dakota	0.0	0.00	38
Ohio	3.7	0.06	36
Oklahoma	11.9	0.80	22
Oregon	-12.8	-0.79	46
Pennsylvania	19.8	0.34	32
Rhode Island	2.9	0.60	27
South Carolina	-0.8	-0.04	39
South Dakota	1.0	0.26	33
Tennessee	15.0	0.55	30
Texas	189.1	1.99	4
Utah	17.1	1.58	9
Vermont	-0.4	-0.13	43
Virginia	46.2	1.30	11
Washington	21.6	0.79	23
West Virginia	1.3	0.18	35
Wisconsin	-1.8	-0.06	41
Wyoming	6.9	2.78	3
50 States	1,136.2	0.86	
DC	3.2	0.49	
United States	1,139.4	0.86	

Rank in order by percentage change	
1	Nevada
2	Florida
3	Wyoming
4	Texas
5	Colorado
6	California
7	New Mexico
8	Montana
9	Utah
10	Idaho
11	Virginia
12	Massachusetts
13	Hawaii
14	Georgia
15	Maine
16	New York
17	Alaska
18	Delaware
19	Arizona
20	Kansas
21	Kentucky
22	Oklahoma
23	Washington
24	Louisiana
25	Minnesota
26	Maryland
27	Rhode Island
28	New Jersey
29	New Hampshire
30	Tennessee
31	Iowa
32	Pennsylvania
33	South Dakota
34	Connecticut
35	West Virginia
36	Ohio
37	Illinois
38	North Dakota
39	South Carolina
40	Arkansas
41	Wisconsin
42	North Carolina
43	Vermont
44	Michigan
45	Nebraska
46	Oregon
47	Missouri
48	Alabama
49	Indiana
50	Mississippi

Note: Numbers that appear to be identical are rounded and vary slightly in actual value. The rankings reflect the actual values before rounding. See the introduction for more details.

B-30 Manufacturing Employment Change, 2000-2001

State	Change in number of manufacturing jobs July 2000-2001 (in thousands)	Percentage change in manufacturing employment	Rank by percentage change
Alabama	-17.5	-4.84	42
Alaska	-1.5	-7.11	48
Arizona	-4.7	-2.17	13
Arkansas	-10.7	-4.25	35
California	-42.9	-2.19	15
Colorado	-4.9	-2.37	18
Connecticut	-5.7	-2.18	14
Delaware	-3.4	-5.81	45
Florida	-5.5	-1.13	8
Georgia	-20.0	-3.41	27
Hawaii	0.3	1.72	2
Idaho	-1.0	-1.28	9
Illinois	-36.4	-3.84	30
Indiana	-29.9	-4.33	36
Iowa	-2.9	-1.10	7
Kansas	-0.9	-0.43	3
Kentucky	-16.9	-5.25	44
Louisiana	-4.3	-2.34	17
Maine	-4.2	-4.90	43
Maryland	-5.4	-2.99	24
Massachusetts	-11.7	-2.70	21
Michigan	-45.5	-4.69	40
Minnesota	-10.2	-2.29	16
Mississippi	-17.5	-7.49	49
Missouri	-24.4	-6.01	46
Montana	-1.2	-4.78	41
Nebraska	-2.9	-2.39	19
Nevada	1.4	3.14	1
New Hampshire	-3.4	-3.25	25
New Jersey	-19.0	-4.13	34
New Mexico	-0.8	-1.85	12
New York	-28.8	-3.30	26
North Carolina	-47.7	-6.08	47
North Dakota	-0.4	-1.57	11
Ohio	-27.9	-2.59	20
Oklahoma	-5.4	-2.95	22
Oregon	-11.3	-4.52	37
Pennsylvania	-36.4	-3.91	31
Rhode Island	-2.7	-3.91	32
South Carolina	-11.9	-3.42	28
South Dakota	-3.9	-7.75	50
Tennessee	-23.5	-4.61	39
Texas	-10.5	-0.97	6
Utah	-1.8	-1.37	10
Vermont	-0.3	-0.61	4
Virginia	-11.5	-2.98	23
Washington	-13.0	-3.68	29
West Virginia	-3.3	-4.08	33
Wisconsin	-28.3	-4.52	38
Wyoming	-0.1	-0.87	5
50 States	**-622.3**	**-3.36**	
DC	0.0	0.00	
United States	**-622.3**	**-3.36**	

Rank in order by percentage change

1 Nevada
2 Hawaii
3 Kansas
4 Vermont
5 Wyoming
6 Texas
7 Iowa
8 Florida
9 Idaho
10 Utah
11 North Dakota
12 New Mexico
13 Arizona
14 Connecticut
15 California
16 Minnesota
17 Louisiana
18 Colorado
19 Nebraska
20 Ohio
21 Massachusetts
22 Oklahoma
23 Virginia
24 Maryland
25 New Hampshire
26 New York
27 Georgia
28 South Carolina
29 Washington
30 Illinois
31 Pennsylvania
32 Rhode Island
33 West Virginia
34 New Jersey
35 Arkansas
36 Indiana
37 Oregon
38 Wisconsin
39 Tennessee
40 Michigan
41 Montana
42 Alabama
43 Maine
44 Kentucky
45 Delaware
46 Missouri
47 North Carolina
48 Alaska
49 Mississippi
50 South Dakota

Note: Numbers that appear to be identical are rounded and vary slightly in actual value. The rankings reflect the actual values before rounding. See the introduction for more details.

B-31 Home Ownership, 1996-2000

State	Home ownership rate (as percentage)	Rank
Alabama	72.64	12
Alaska	65.84	39
Arizona	64.72	40
Arkansas	66.90	36
California	55.90	48
Colorado	66.04	38
Connecticut	69.10	27
Delaware	71.06	15
Florida	67.38	35
Georgia	70.50	19
Hawaii	53.08	49
Idaho	71.42	14
Illinois	67.86	33
Indiana	73.74	9
Iowa	73.34	10
Kansas	67.50	34
Kentucky	74.12	7
Louisiana	66.56	37
Maine	75.98	1
Maryland	69.12	26
Massachusetts	61.10	46
Michigan	74.94	4
Minnesota	75.68	2
Mississippi	74.38	6
Missouri	71.70	13
Montana	69.10	27
Nebraska	68.90	31
Nevada	62.28	45
New Hampshire	68.16	32
New Jersey	64.30	41
New Mexico	70.86	17
New York	52.86	50
North Carolina	70.94	16
North Dakota	69.02	29
Ohio	70.18	21
Oklahoma	70.16	22
Oregon	63.42	43
Pennsylvania	73.76	8
Rhode Island	59.44	47
South Carolina	75.44	3
South Dakota	68.92	30
Tennessee	70.62	18
Texas	62.50	44
Utah	73.26	11
Vermont	69.26	25
Virginia	70.28	20
Washington	63.86	42
West Virginia	74.88	5
Wisconsin	69.86	23
Wyoming	69.28	24
50 States	n/a	
DC	41.02	
United States	66.32	

Rank in order by rate

1	Maine
2	Minnesota
3	South Carolina
4	Michigan
5	West Virginia
6	Mississippi
7	Kentucky
8	Pennsylvania
9	Indiana
10	Iowa
11	Utah
12	Alabama
13	Missouri
14	Idaho
15	Delaware
16	North Carolina
17	New Mexico
18	Tennessee
19	Georgia
20	Virginia
21	Ohio
22	Oklahoma
23	Wisconsin
24	Wyoming
25	Vermont
26	Maryland
27	Connecticut
27	Montana
29	North Dakota
30	South Dakota
31	Nebraska
32	New Hampshire
33	Illinois
34	Kansas
35	Florida
36	Arkansas
37	Louisiana
38	Colorado
39	Alaska
40	Arizona
41	New Jersey
42	Washington
43	Oregon
44	Texas
45	Nevada
46	Massachusetts
47	Rhode Island
48	California
49	Hawaii
50	New York

Note: Ties in ranking reflect ties in actual values.

B-32 Gambling, 2000

State	Gambling gross revenue $ (in millions)	Per capita gambling revenue	Rank by total revenue
Alabama	58	13	41
Alaska	54	86	42
Arizona	196	38	33
Arkansas	52	19	43
California	2,629	78	6
Colorado	869	202	18
Connecticut	418	123	28
Delaware	576	735	22
Florida	1,618	101	10
Georgia	1,063	130	16
Hawaii	0	0	n/a
Idaho	45	34	44
Illinois	2,680	216	5
Indiana	2,049	337	8
Iowa	1,004	343	17
Kansas	127	47	36
Kentucky	507	125	25
Louisiana	2,194	491	7
Maine	104	81	38
Maryland	747	141	19
Massachusetts	1,347	212	12
Michigan	1,706	172	9
Minnesota	422	86	27
Mississippi	2,685	944	4
Missouri	1,262	226	13
Montana	302	335	29
Nebraska	120	70	37
Nevada	9,632	4,820	1
New Hampshire	158	128	35
New Jersey	5,451	648	2
New Mexico	161	89	34
New York	2,739	144	3
North Carolina	8	1	47
North Dakota	76	119	39
Ohio	1,199	106	14
Oklahoma	62	18	40
Oregon	607	178	21
Pennsylvania	1,134	92	15
Rhode Island	298	285	30
South Carolina	422	105	26
South Dakota	275	364	31
Tennessee	0	0	n/a
Texas	1,364	65	11
Utah	0	0	n/a
Vermont	34	57	45
Virginia	523	74	24
Washington	659	112	20
West Virginia	525	290	23
Wisconsin	241	45	32
Wyoming	8	16	46
50 States	50,411	179	
DC	117	205	
United States	50,528	180	

Rank in order by total revenue	
1	Nevada
2	New Jersey
3	New York
4	Mississippi
5	Illinois
6	California
7	Louisiana
8	Indiana
9	Michigan
10	Florida
11	Texas
12	Massachusetts
13	Missouri
14	Ohio
15	Pennsylvania
16	Georgia
17	Iowa
18	Colorado
19	Maryland
20	Washington
21	Oregon
22	Delaware
23	West Virginia
24	Virginia
25	Kentucky
26	South Carolina
27	Minnesota
28	Connecticut
29	Montana
30	Rhode Island
31	South Dakota
32	Wisconsin
33	Arizona
34	New Mexico
35	New Hampshire
36	Kansas
37	Nebraska
38	Maine
39	North Dakota
40	Oklahoma
41	Alabama
42	Alaska
43	Arkansas
44	Idaho
45	Vermont
46	Wyoming
47	North Carolina

Note: Numbers that appear to be identical are rounded and vary slightly in actual value. The rankings reflect the actual values before rounding. See the introduction for more details.

B-33 Annual Electricity Use Per Residential Customer, 2000

State	Average annual kwh use per residential customer	Rank
Alabama	14,919	3
Alaska	8,043	39
Arizona	12,668	15
Arkansas	12,601	17
California	7,047	45
Colorado	8,149	38
Connecticut	8,531	35
Delaware	10,746	26
Florida	13,790	7
Georgia	13,102	12
Hawaii	7,516	42
Idaho	13,146	11
Illinois	8,449	37
Indiana	11,151	24
Iowa	9,676	29
Kansas	9,051	33
Kentucky	13,260	10
Louisiana	15,185	2
Maine	6,524	48
Maryland	12,115	19
Massachusetts	6,437	49
Michigan	7,440	43
Minnesota	9,171	32
Mississippi	14,606	4
Missouri	12,519	18
Montana	10,161	27
Nebraska	11,409	23
Nevada	11,837	21
New Hampshire	6,706	47
New Jersey	7,698	40
New Mexico	6,996	46
New York	6,294	50
North Carolina	12,854	14
North Dakota	12,019	20
Ohio	9,851	28
Oklahoma	12,921	13
Oregon	12,659	16
Pennsylvania	9,452	30
Rhode Island	7,536	41
South Carolina	14,404	6
South Dakota	10,827	25
Tennessee	15,249	1
Texas	14,491	5
Utah	8,558	34
Vermont	7,229	44
Virginia	13,539	8
Washington	13,526	9
West Virginia	11,766	22
Wisconsin	8,491	36
Wyoming	9,427	31
50 States	n/a	
DC	8,109	
United States	10,623	

Rank in order by average use

1	Tennessee
2	Louisiana
3	Alabama
4	Mississippi
5	Texas
6	South Carolina
7	Florida
8	Virginia
9	Washington
10	Kentucky
11	Idaho
12	Georgia
13	Oklahoma
14	North Carolina
15	Arizona
16	Oregon
17	Arkansas
18	Missouri
19	Maryland
20	North Dakota
21	Nevada
22	West Virginia
23	Nebraska
24	Indiana
25	South Dakota
26	Delaware
27	Montana
28	Ohio
29	Iowa
30	Pennsylvania
31	Wyoming
32	Minnesota
33	Kansas
34	Utah
35	Connecticut
36	Wisconsin
37	Illinois
38	Colorado
39	Alaska
40	New Jersey
41	Rhode Island
42	Hawaii
43	Michigan
44	Vermont
45	California
46	New Mexico
47	New Hampshire
48	Maine
49	Massachusetts
50	New York

B-34 Average Cost Per Kilowatt Hour, 2000

State	Average cost for industrial customer (cents per kwh)	Average cost for residential customer (cents per kwh)	Residential cost as percentage of industrial cost	Rank by residential as percentage of industrial
Alabama	3.9	7.0	178.0	19
Alaska	7.9	11.4	143.7	45
Arizona	5.0	8.4	167.6	30
Arkansas	4.2	7.5	177.8	20
California	5.4	10.5	194.3	8
Colorado	4.4	7.4	166.2	33
Connecticut	7.3	10.9	148.3	42
Delaware	4.8	9.1	188.3	14
Florida	4.9	7.8	157.8	39
Georgia	4.0	7.8	191.6	12
Hawaii	11.7	16.4	139.8	47
Idaho	3.1	5.4	172.0	25
Illinois	4.2	8.8	209.1	4
Indiana	3.8	6.8	180.1	17
Iowa	3.9	8.1	207.6	5
Kansas	4.5	7.6	169.6	29
Kentucky	3.0	5.3	175.8	22
Louisiana	5.0	7.9	156.8	40
Maine	6.4	12.9	202.7	7
Maryland	4.1	8.0	192.5	11
Massachusetts	8.1	10.8	132.8	50
Michigan	5.1	8.5	166.7	31
Minnesota	4.6	7.4	162.2	36
Mississippi	4.2	7.0	166.5	32
Missouri	4.5	7.0	156.1	41
Montana	2.9	6.4	220.1	2
Nebraska	3.6	6.5	180.1	18
Nevada	4.9	7.3	148.0	43
New Hampshire	9.3	13.6	146.5	44
New Jersey	6.8	10.8	159.7	38
New Mexico	4.8	8.3	170.9	27
New York	4.9	14.1	287.0	1
North Carolina	4.6	8.0	174.3	24
North Dakota	4.0	6.5	162.6	35
Ohio	4.5	8.6	190.0	13
Oklahoma	4.2	7.1	171.0	26
Oregon	3.4	5.9	174.6	23
Pennsylvania	4.3	9.1	209.9	3
Rhode Island	8.5	11.5	136.1	49
South Carolina	3.6	7.4	204.0	6
South Dakota	4.6	7.4	161.3	37
Tennessee	4.6	6.3	138.9	48
Texas	4.5	7.9	177.1	21
Utah	3.3	6.3	188.2	16
Vermont	7.3	12.1	165.4	34
Virginia	3.9	7.5	193.6	10
Washington	3.6	5.2	143.6	46
West Virginia	3.8	6.4	170.4	28
Wisconsin	4.0	7.5	188.2	15
Wyoming	3.4	6.6	194.0	9
50 States	n/a	n/a	n/a	
DC	4.8	8.0	166.6	
United States	4.5	8.2	184.4	

Rank in order by percentage

1 New York
2 Montana
3 Pennsylvania
4 Illinois
5 Iowa
6 South Carolina
7 Maine
8 California
9 Wyoming
10 Virginia
11 Maryland
12 Georgia
13 Ohio
14 Delaware
15 Wisconsin
16 Utah
17 Indiana
18 Nebraska
19 Alabama
20 Arkansas
21 Texas
22 Kentucky
23 Oregon
24 North Carolina
25 Idaho
26 Oklahoma
27 New Mexico
28 West Virginia
29 Kansas
30 Arizona
31 Michigan
32 Mississippi
33 Colorado
34 Vermont
35 North Dakota
36 Minnesota
37 South Dakota
38 New Jersey
39 Florida
40 Louisiana
41 Missouri
42 Connecticut
43 Nevada
44 New Hampshire
45 Alaska
46 Washington
47 Hawaii
48 Tennessee
49 Rhode Island
50 Massachusetts

Note: Numbers that appear to be identical are rounded and vary slightly in actual value. The rankings reflect the actual values before rounding. See the introduction for more details.

B-35 New Companies, 2000

State	New companies	New companies per 1,000 employees	Rank per 1,000
Alabama	10,067	4.9	40
Alaska	2,333	7.8	14
Arizona	15,175	6.7	22
Arkansas	4,680	4.0	49
California	167,047	10.3	4
Colorado	25,462	11.5	3
Connecticut	9,910	5.8	30
Delaware	3,682	9.4	5
Florida	59,912	8.3	11
Georgia	28,925	7.2	20
Hawaii	3,745	6.6	23
Idaho	5,829	9.3	6
Illinois	28,875	4.7	44
Indiana	14,112	4.7	43
Iowa	5,668	3.7	50
Kansas	6,483	4.8	41
Kentucky	8,637	4.5	45
Louisiana	10,468	5.5	33
Maine	5,135	7.7	15
Maryland	20,539	7.6	16
Massachusetts	18,640	5.9	27
Michigan	23,760	4.7	42
Minnesota	13,906	5.2	36
Mississippi	6,439	5.1	37
Missouri	13,996	4.9	39
Montana	3,605	7.9	12
Nebraska	4,441	5.0	38
Nevada	8,587	9.1	8
New Hampshire	4,677	7.0	21
New Jersey	55,769	13.8	2
New Mexico	5,836	7.4	18
New York	61,507	7.2	19
North Carolina	23,310	6.1	26
North Dakota	1,493	4.5	46
Ohio	22,290	4.0	48
Oklahoma	8,979	5.6	31
Oregon	14,729	8.6	10
Pennsylvania	35,104	6.1	25
Rhode Island	3,675	7.6	17
South Carolina	11,114	5.8	29
South Dakota	2,138	5.5	34
Tennessee	15,793	5.9	28
Texas	54,330	5.5	32
Utah	9,875	9.2	7
Vermont	2,511	7.8	13
Virginia	22,219	6.3	24
Washington	40,357	14.0	1
West Virginia	4,177	5.4	35
Wisconsin	12,436	4.4	47
Wyoming	2,314	9.0	9
50 States	944,691	7.0	
DC	4,472	17.0	
United States*	954,510	7.1	

Rank in order per 1,000 employees	
1	Washington
2	New Jersey
3	Colorado
4	California
5	Delaware
6	Idaho
7	Utah
8	Nevada
9	Wyoming
10	Oregon
11	Florida
12	Montana
13	Vermont
14	Alaska
15	Maine
16	Maryland
17	Rhode Island
18	New Mexico
19	New York
20	Georgia
21	New Hampshire
22	Arizona
23	Hawaii
24	Virginia
25	Pennsylvania
26	North Carolina
27	Massachusetts
28	Tennessee
29	South Carolina
30	Connecticut
31	Oklahoma
32	Texas
33	Louisiana
34	South Dakota
35	West Virginia
36	Minnesota
37	Mississippi
38	Nebraska
39	Missouri
40	Alabama
41	Kansas
42	Michigan
43	Indiana
44	Illinois
45	Kentucky
46	North Dakota
47	Wisconsin
48	Ohio
49	Arkansas
50	Iowa

Note: Numbers that appear to be identical are rounded and vary slightly in actual value. The rankings reflect the actual values before rounding. See the introduction for more details.

Due to rounding or data sources, the 50-state total plus D.C. may not equal the U.S. total. Please see introduction.

Source Notes for Economies (Section B)

B-1 Personal Income, 2000: These data reflect income of residents of each state, including pensions, dividends, interest, and rent as well as amounts received from employers as wages and salaries. These estimates are made by the Department of Commerce each quarter. The calendar year 2000 estimates were released on September 24, 2001, and are available on the Department's website (www.bea.doc.gov).

B-2 Gross State Product, Total and Per Capita, 1999: The gross state product is the state counterpart of the gross national product (now called the gross domestic product). This is the single best measure of the size of a state's economy. It is the sum of all the value of production of goods and services. While estimates of national data are released on a current basis, state-by-state estimates are made by the Department of Commerce only with a substantial lag. These 1999 data were released in June 2001 and come from the same source as Table B-1.

B-3 Per Capita Personal Income, 2000: These data, from the same source as Table B-1, reflect personal income in relation to population. They are a common measure of the relative affluence of each state. The data are also used to determine what percentage the federal government pays of each state's Medicaid costs.

B-4 Personal Income from Wages and Salaries, 2000: These data show the portion of personal income that comes from wages and salaries. The data on origins of personal income were released by the Department of Commerce Bureau of Economic Analysis (BEA) on September 24, 2001. They are available on the BEA website (www.bea.doc.gov). The percentages, calculated for *State Fact Finder*, indicate relative reliance of states' economies on current work, as distinct from investments and government payments.

B-5 Average Annual Pay, 2000: These data reflect the average pay of workers in each state. They are prepared by the Department of Labor and available on-line at stats.bls.gov. They were released September 11, 2001.

B-6 Average Hourly Earnings, 2001: These data are often used to compare wage costs of the states. They are prepared by the Department of Labor monthly and released in the publication *Employment and Earnings*. These June 2001 data appeared in the September 2001 edition. These data only cover production workers, excluding service and retailing employees as well as government employees.

B-7 Value Added in Manufacturing, 1999: This table measures the value that is added by manufacturing operations in each state. Value added is calculated by subtracting the value of inputs to production from the value of the outputs. For example, the value of manufacturing a car is the value of

the car minus the value of components, such as engines, purchased to manufacture it. These data are from the Census Bureau's *1999 Annual Survey of Manufacturers (M99(AS)-3)*, issued April 2001. Value added per worker can be calculated from this report. This per worker statistic is sometimes used to compare the productivity of state work forces but is a misleading statistic because capital investments in machinery make massive contributions to adding values in highly automated operations such as chemical manufacturing.

B-8 Cost of Living, 1999: The federal government has not attempted to produce measures that compare living costs since the 1980s and, even then, provided the data only for selected large metropolitan areas, not states. Some researchers periodically try to produce such indices, but they are of doubtful statistical validity. The one shown was created by Herman B. Leonard and Jay H. Walder at the Kennedy School of Government at Harvard University and is published in *The Federal Budget and the States, Fiscal Year 1999*. For information on methodology consult Leonard and Monica Friar's paper, *Variations in Costs of Living Across States*.

B-9 Average Annual Pay in Manufacturing, 2000: This is the manufacturing component of the data described for Table B-5, from the same source. States with many jobs in high-wage industries, like chemical or vehicle manufacturing, rank highest.

B-10 Average Annual Pay in Retailing, 2000: This is the retailing component of the data described for Table B-5, from the same source. Because most retailing jobs are entry-level positions requiring little experience or formal training, these data are a good measure of the costs of obtaining new workers in the states.

B-11 Labor Force, 2001: About 143.6 million people, 51 percent of Americans, are either working or looking for work but not working (unemployed). These two groups make up the labor force. The rest of the population are not in the labor force because they are retired, too young to work, disabled, or have opted not to work. This group includes "discouraged workers" who indicate that they would like to work but have given up hope of finding a job.

The labor force data are available on the website of the Bureau of Labor Statistics (www.bls.gov). They are also available in their monthly publication *Regional and State Area Employment and Unemployment* released on November 20, 2001 with preliminary estimates for October. The data are seasonally adjusted to make month-to-month comparisons possible despite fluctuations associated with time of the year such as hiring by retail stores for the December holiday season and summertime hiring of students. The 2000 population estimates come from the Census Bureau (see

Table A-1). Labor force as a percentage of population varies among states because of differences in the percentage of population at working age and the percentage of people who want to work—the labor force participation rate.

B-12 Unemployed and Unemployment Rate, 2001: The estimates of persons unemployed and the unemployment rate (percentage of labor force unemployed) are from the same source as Table B-11. See notes to Table B-13 for an explanation of why the national unemployment rate shown in the table differs from the national value (5.4 percent) reported for October in the Bureau of Labor Statistics' November release, *The Employment Situation: 2001*.

B-13 Employment and Employment Rate, 2001: The Bureau of Labor Statistics faces a perpetual dilemma in presenting statistics on employment and unemployment. It must make national unemployment estimates based on a survey of households in which people are asked whether they are looking for work. This *household survey* also provides the national estimate of the people who are employed. But the sample is too small to provide reliable estimates of employment for less populous states. To provide estimates for those states, the Bureau obtains monthly reports from employers, called the *establishment survey*. The national totals from the two different surveys often diverge by hundreds of thousands of workers. Periodically, the Bureau "benchmarks" the totals and revises past estimates to make them consistent.

To make the matter even more complicated, the Bureau attempts in various complex ways to use the results of one survey to guide estimating procedures for the other. How this is done is explained in detail in various technical publications available from the Bureau. The net effect harmonizes the results of the two approaches better for large states than small ones. For example, the employment in Wyoming implicit in the Bureau's estimates is the labor force (Table B-11) minus the unemployed (Table B-12)—260,000—but the employment published in a different table in the report (see notes to Table B-11) is 246,000. For Table B-13, *State Fact Finder* uses the implicit estimate so that employment plus unemployment sum to the labor force for each state. The employment rate is the relationship between the employment shown and the labor force on Table B-11.

Because *State Fact Finder* contains many tables relying on employment data for individual states, it uses the best employment estimates available, those from the establishment survey, in Table B-14 and other tables showing state-by-state details of employment.

B-14 Government Employment, 2001: This table, from the same source as Table B-11, uses seasonally adjusted data from the establishment survey (see notes to Table B-13 on differences between the household and establishment surveys) which were made available by the Bureau of Labor

Statistics on November 20, 2001, with preliminary estimates for October. The employment reported on this table includes federal, state, and local employees.

These Bureau of Labor Statistics data on government employment covering 2001 are more current than data provided by the Census Bureau. The latest Census Bureau data, published in 2001, cover information on March 2000 payrolls. But the Census Bureau data are used often in *State Fact Finder* because the Bureau of Labor Statistics data do not include such details as how much employees are paid and the type of service (for example, education, transportation) they provide.

B-15 Manufacturing Employment, 2001: These data are comparable to those shown in Table B-14, but cover manufacturing.

B-16 *Fortune* 500 Companies, 2001: Two major business magazines—*Fortune* and *Forbes*—provide annual listings of the largest companies in America, using somewhat different criteria. This table reflects the list as published in *Fortune* (April 16, 2001). Because large states tend to have the most large companies, the rankings are based on a calculation of the representation of these companies' headquarters in each state in relation to population of that state.

B-17 *Forbes* 500 Companies, 2001: This table is the counterpart of Table B-16. This listing was published in *Forbes* magazine (April 16, 2001). Because *Forbes* uses four separate criteria for its listings, 817 American companies are included in the "500" list.

B-18 Tourism Spending, 1999: The travel industry is a major factor in the economies of all states and a dominant factor in a few. However, data on it are elusive. Many trips combine business and pleasure, so separating tourism from business is difficult. Other trips combine an activity, such as coming home for Christmas, with a tourist activity, such as visiting a museum. Restaurants and gift shops do not normally know whether their customers are tourists or local customers. Consequently, estimates of tourism spending have more guesswork than most of the statistics in *State Fact Finder*. The 1999 data shown in the table are the most up-to-date. They are prepared by the Travel Industry Association of America and are published in *Tourism Works for America, 10th Annual Edition 2001*.

B-19 Exports, 2000: National estimates of exports are made quarterly by the Department of Commerce to develop estimates of gross domestic product and balance of payments with other nations. Relatively current estimates by state are also made by the Commerce Department but are of doubtful reliability because of data-gathering limitations and conceptual problems. For example, does a shipment from a New York port of a product from an Ohio plant of items made from components from Ohio and Mississippi contained in boxes produced in South Carolina constitute an export from New York, Ohio, or somewhere else? The data shown came from the Census Bureau's website (www.census.gov) on August 2, 2001.

B-20 Housing Permits, 2000: No state-by-state system exists to report completion of single-family houses and apartment and condominium units, but there are good data on the issuance of permits for such construction. Although some builders obtain permits and then don't build, permits are expensive so most permits are followed by construction. The data shown were compiled by the National Association of Home Builders and are available on its website (www.nahb.com). The relationship to population shows which states have rapidly growing populations and which are more stagnant.

B-21 Percentage Change in Home Prices, 1996-2001: Most people are interested in changes in housing prices because of the implications for a specific existing home—usually the one they own. The data often cited in the media, which come from realtors' sales records, come from averages of homes sold. As a result, they include large percentages of new (and typically larger, better equipped, and more expensive) homes in fast-growing states. A preferable way to measure price changes is to examine prices for successive sales of the same homes. This has recently become possible with improvements in computing capacity and the increasing importance of secondary mortgage lenders, who buy massive numbers of mortgages from banks and other lenders. The data in the table reflect this approach.

The information comes from *House Price Index Second Quarter 2001* (August 31, 2001) published by the Office of Federal Housing Enterprise Oversight and available on its website (www.ofheo.gov).

B-22 Net Farm Income, 2000: These data reflect the net income derived from farming—the value of farm sales minus the cost of production. They are estimates made by the Department of Agriculture and are available on its website (www.ers.usda.gov). The *State Fact Finder* calculation of per capita amounts provides a basis for comparing the importance of agriculture to the economies of each state.

B-23 Financial Institution Assets, 2000: This table shows total assets of banks, trust companies, and savings institutions. These data, from the Federal Deposit Insurance Corporation's *Statistics on Banking: 2000*, provide a good measure of the importance of banking in each state. However, they provide no indication of the wealth of individuals in a state as deposits flow freely across state lines. States that have successfully tried to draw financial institutions, like Delaware and South Dakota, show large per capita

amounts, as do regional banking centers, such as the Boston banks that serve customers throughout New England.

B-24 Bankruptcy Filings by Individuals and Businesses, 2001: These data show how new bankruptcy cases (mostly individuals rather than businesses) were distributed among the states. These data cover the twelve-month period ending March 31, 2001, and come from the website of the Administrative Office of the U.S. Courts (www.uscourts.gov).

B-25 Patents Issued, FY 2000: The U.S. Patent Office issued 100,548 new patents in FY 2000 to residents (both corporations and individuals) in the states shown. When related to population, this statistic is often used to compare states in the degree to which they are on the forefront of new technology. The data come from the United States Patent and Trademark Office and are available on its website (www.uspto.gov) as *Performance and Accountability Report Fiscal Year 2000*. Because patent applications are often made by or for companies, headquarters of companies (for example, DuPont in Delaware and 3-M in Minnesota) affect the results.

B-26 Workers' Compensation Temporary Disability Payments, 2001: All states maintain a program that provides compensation for workers who are injured on the job. These programs differ massively from state to state in how much money is paid for certain injuries, how hard it is to prove disability and its relationship to the job, and how employers are forced to pay program costs. These differences, set by state policy, are not captured by aggregate statistics on workers' compensation costs because some industries (like construction and logging) are inherently more hazardous than others (like banking), so state-by-state costs will vary with the mix of industries. This table compares one major dimension of benefit generosity/parsimony, the maximum payment per month to a worker who is temporarily unable to work because of a job-related injury. The data come from the Department of Labor publication dated January 2001, *State Workers' Compensation Laws*.

B-27 Average Unemployment Compensation Benefit, 2000: All states maintain a federally supervised program of unemployment compensation. States have wide discretion in determining how large unemployment compensation payments will be, how long they will last, and how costs are distributed among employers. This table, from a September 14, 2001 e-mail from the Department of Labor Unemployment Insurance Service, shows the average weekly benefit paid in each state.

B-28 Index of State Economic Momentum, September 2001: Each quarter *State Policy Reports* publishes its Index of State Economic Momentum, a statistic created by State Policy Research to compare the recent economic performance of each state in relation to the national average. A state growing at the national average rate would show an index of 0.0 while one growing roughly 1.0 percent faster would show an index of 1.0. Negative numbers show states lagging behind national average growth. The index combines (with equal weights) the most recent known one-year changes in (1) employment, (2) personal income, and (3) population.

B-29 Employment Change, 2000-2001: This table uses Department of Labor data from June 2000 and 2001 (not seasonally adjusted) to show the change in the number of jobs in each state. The data, from the Bureau of Labor Statistics website (www.bls.gov), are one component of the state economic momentum index shown in Table B-28.

B-30 Manufacturing Employment Change, 2000-2001: This table uses Department of Labor (see source for Table B-29) data from July 2000 to July 2001 (not seasonally adjusted) to show the states experiencing job loss and those experiencing job growth in manufacturing. These data are released monthly and revised often, but differences in state economic performance tend to persist from month to month.

B-31 Home Ownership, 1996-2000: These data show the percentage of households living in homes they own. The data come from the *Housing Vacancy Survey*, available on the Census website (www.census.gov). These are estimates based on Census surveys averaged over five years. Because of the relatively small samples, the margin of error for less populous states is relatively large.

B-32 Gambling, 2000: Legal gambling establishments in the United States grossed over $50.5 billion in 2000—$180 per person, including people who do not gamble at all. The distribution of these revenues among the states is shown in the table, reflecting estimates made by Christiansen Capital Advisors.

These statistics dealing with the revenues of gaming establishments provide one indication of the amount of gambling activity. However, they should not be confused with amounts bet. While gamblers lose, on average, about 50 cents for every dollar spent on state lotteries and 20 cents for every dollar at horse tracks, they lose only about 2 cents of what they bet at casino table games and about 5 cents at slot machines. So, the same dollar is, in effect, bet many times before it is lost. Christiansen Capital Advisors has much more detailed estimates of gambling by state and type of gambling, as well as information on gambling taxes and revenues of gambling establishments.

B-33 Average Annual Electricity Use Per Residential Customer, 2000: These data from the Edison Electric Institute's *Statistical Yearbook of the Electric Utility Industry 2001* show differences in electricity use among the states. The results are heavily influenced by the relative importance of heating and air conditioning and the mix of fuels used for heating.

B-34 Average Cost Per Kilowatt Hour, 2000: These data also come from the Edison Electric Institute (see source for Table B-33), which maintains additional details on other years, types of consumers, and more. The data have many uses. The cost per kilowatt hour permits comparisons among states of electricity costs for households and businesses. The residential rate as a percentage of industrial rate is a useful indicator of the extent to which state regulatory policy (which controls rates charged by private companies) is tilted toward providing low industrial rates to stimulate economic development or low residential rates to keep prices low for voter/consumers at the potential expense of loss of industry. Based on costs of service, industrial users should pay less because they are cheaper per kilowatt to bill and often agree to have service curtailed when there is a shortage of power.

B-35 New Companies, 2000: These data show the number of companies that applied for new account numbers from state employment services. These data were made available to *State Fact Finder* by Tom Stengle of the Department of Labor Unemployment Insurance Service in an e-mail dated November 7, 2001. *State Fact Finder* then related these numbers to the total number of workers in each state. These employment numbers are annual averages and were released on the Bureau of Labor Statistics' website (www.bls.gov) on February 23, 2001.

Geography

When the Bush administration unveiled its energy plan in early 2001, rolling blackouts in California and energy price spikes had people talking about energy issues. Prices then began to stabilize and California's problems began to look more like a mishandling, rather than a shortage, of energy. But the events of September 11th and recent U.S. military actions again heightened long-term concerns about how we generate, acquire, and use energy.

While all parties agree on the goal of reducing dependence on foreign energy sources, exactly how this should be done has been the center of the energy debate during the 106th Congress. While the Bush plan promoted domestic oil and gas drilling, including drilling in the Arctic National Wildlife Refuge (ANWR), Democrats emphasized protecting ANWR and reducing dependency through energy efficiency and reduced demand.

During the energy policy debates, states paid particular attention to electric restructuring proposals that would increase federal authority. States are concerned that suggestions such as mandates and federal "eminent domain" over electricity transmission facilities and lines are draconian measures that unduly threaten state control.

On the deregulation front: heading into 2002, sixteen states plus the District of Columbia have opened their electricity market to competition, some through pilot programs. Seven states—Arkansas, Montana, Nevada, New Mexico, Oklahoma, Oregon, and West Virginia—have delayed deregulation. The California Public Utilities Commission suspended direct retail access in that state. The remaining twenty-six states remain inactive.

C-1 Total Land Area, 2000

State	Land area (in square miles)	Rank
Alabama	50,744	28
Alaska	571,951	1
Arizona	113,635	6
Arkansas	52,068	27
California	155,959	3
Colorado	103,718	8
Connecticut	4,845	48
Delaware	1,954	49
Florida	53,927	26
Georgia	57,906	21
Hawaii	6,423	47
Idaho	82,747	11
Illinois	55,584	24
Indiana	35,867	38
Iowa	55,869	23
Kansas	81,815	13
Kentucky	39,728	36
Louisiana	43,562	33
Maine	30,862	39
Maryland	9,774	42
Massachusetts	7,840	45
Michigan	56,804	22
Minnesota	79,610	14
Mississippi	46,907	31
Missouri	68,886	18
Montana	145,552	4
Nebraska	76,872	15
Nevada	109,826	7
New Hampshire	8,968	44
New Jersey	7,417	46
New Mexico	121,356	5
New York	47,214	30
North Carolina	48,711	29
North Dakota	68,976	17
Ohio	40,948	35
Oklahoma	68,667	19
Oregon	95,997	10
Pennsylvania	44,817	32
Rhode Island	1,045	50
South Carolina	30,110	40
South Dakota	75,885	16
Tennessee	41,217	34
Texas	261,797	2
Utah	82,144	12
Vermont	9,250	43
Virginia	39,594	37
Washington	66,544	20
West Virginia	24,078	41
Wisconsin	54,310	25
Wyoming	97,100	9
50 States	3,537,380	
DC	61	
United States	3,537,441	

Rank in order by square mile	
1	Alaska
2	Texas
3	California
4	Montana
5	New Mexico
6	Arizona
7	Nevada
8	Colorado
9	Wyoming
10	Oregon
11	Idaho
12	Utah
13	Kansas
14	Minnesota
15	Nebraska
16	South Dakota
17	North Dakota
18	Missouri
19	Oklahoma
20	Washington
21	Georgia
22	Michigan
23	Iowa
24	Illinois
25	Wisconsin
26	Florida
27	Arkansas
28	Alabama
29	North Carolina
30	New York
31	Mississippi
32	Pennsylvania
33	Louisiana
34	Tennessee
35	Ohio
36	Kentucky
37	Virginia
38	Indiana
39	Maine
40	South Carolina
41	West Virginia
42	Maryland
43	Vermont
44	New Hampshire
45	Massachusetts
46	New Jersey
47	Hawaii
48	Connecticut
49	Delaware
50	Rhode Island

C-2 Land Owned by Federal Government, 2000

State	Total acres of federally owned land (in thousands)	Percentage of land federally owned	Rank by total acres
Alabama	1,326	4.1	29
Alaska	220,852	60.4	1
Arizona	32,379	44.5	6
Arkansas	3,410	10.1	17
California	47,889	47.8	3
Colorado	24,108	36.3	11
Connecticut	14	0.5	49
Delaware	16	1.2	48
Florida	4,599	13.2	14
Georgia	2,027	5.4	23
Hawaii	639	15.6	37
Idaho	33,106	62.5	5
Illinois	590	1.6	38
Indiana	510	2.2	39
Iowa	230	0.6	42
Kansas	674	1.3	35
Kentucky	1,447	5.7	28
Louisiana	1,199	4.2	31
Maine	173	0.9	44
Maryland	166	2.6	45
Massachusetts	71	1.4	47
Michigan	4,076	11.2	16
Minnesota	4,217	8.2	15
Mississippi	1,672	5.5	26
Missouri	4,798	10.8	13
Montana	27,428	29.4	9
Nebraska	651	1.3	36
Nevada	58,319	83	2
New Hampshire	759	13.2	33
New Jersey	124	2.6	46
New Mexico	26,572	34.2	10
New York	222	0.7	43
North Carolina	1,989	6.3	24
North Dakota	2,316	5.2	19
Ohio	441	1.7	40
Oklahoma	1,666	3.8	27
Oregon	32,356	52.5	7
Pennsylvania	717	2.5	34
Rhode Island	4	0.5	50
South Carolina	1,110	5.7	32
South Dakota	3,120	6.4	18
Tennessee	2,115	7.9	22
Texas	2,307	1.4	20
Utah	34,001	64.5	4
Vermont	375	6.3	41
Virginia	2,280	8.9	21
Washington	12,176	28.5	12
West Virginia	1,222	7.9	30
Wisconsin	1,819	5.2	25
Wyoming	31,070	49.8	8
50 States	635,346	28.0	
DC	9	23.2	
United States	635,355	28.0	

Rank in order by total acres

1. Alaska
2. Nevada
3. California
4. Utah
5. Idaho
6. Arizona
7. Oregon
8. Wyoming
9. Montana
10. New Mexico
11. Colorado
12. Washington
13. Missouri
14. Florida
15. Minnesota
16. Michigan
17. Arkansas
18. South Dakota
19. North Dakota
20. Texas
21. Virginia
22. Tennessee
23. Georgia
24. North Carolina
25. Wisconsin
26. Mississippi
27. Oklahoma
28. Kentucky
29. Alabama
30. West Virginia
31. Louisiana
32. South Carolina
33. New Hampshire
34. Pennsylvania
35. Kansas
36. Nebraska
37. Hawaii
38. Illinois
39. Indiana
40. Ohio
41. Vermont
42. Iowa
43. New York
44. Maine
45. Maryland
46. New Jersey
47. Massachusetts
48. Delaware
49. Connecticut
50. Rhode Island

C-3 State Park Acreage, FY 2000

State	State park acreage	Acreage per 1,000 population	Rank by total acreage
Alabama	49,710	11.2	41
Alaska	3,291,209	5,249.7	1
Arizona	58,528	11.4	39
Arkansas	50,945	19.1	40
California	1,412,825	41.7	2
Colorado	347,176	80.7	7
Connecticut	182,993	53.7	17
Delaware	21,142	27.0	48
Florida	547,020	34.2	5
Georgia	75,712	9.2	33
Hawaii	26,689	22.0	46
Idaho	43456	33.6	43
Illinois	304,879	24.5	9
Indiana	178,315	29.3	18
Iowa	63,171	21.6	38
Kansas	32,300	12.0	45
Kentucky	43,508	10.8	42
Louisiana	36,099	8.1	44
Maine	94,970	74.5	28
Maryland	258,621	48.8	12
Massachusetts	288,801	45.5	10
Michigan	351,223	35.3	6
Minnesota	255,793	52.0	14
Mississippi	24,287	8.5	47
Missouri	137,120	24.5	21
Montana	64,916	72.0	37
Nebraska	133,044	77.7	22
Nevada	132,885	66.5	23
New Hampshire	74,471	60.3	34
New Jersey	345,425	41.1	8
New Mexico	90,693	49.9	30
New York	1,015,911	53.5	3
North Carolina	159,028	19.8	19
North Dakota	20,046	31.2	49
Ohio	205,047	18.1	15
Oklahoma	71,586	20.7	36
Oregon	94,869	27.7	29
Pennsylvania	288,486	23.5	11
Rhode Island	8,748	8.3	50
South Carolina	80,459	20.1	32
South Dakota	97,637	129.3	27
Tennessee	141,247	24.8	20
Texas	631,018	30.3	4
Utah	113,592	50.9	26
Vermont	84,007	138.0	31
Virginia	72,998	10.3	35
Washington	258,502	43.9	13
West Virginia	195,565	108.1	16
Wisconsin	129,353	24.1	24
Wyoming	121,170	245.4	25
50 States	12,807,195	45.6	
DC	n/a	n/a	
United States	12,807,195	45.5	

Rank in order by total acreage	
1	Alaska
2	California
3	New York
4	Texas
5	Florida
6	Michigan
7	Colorado
8	New Jersey
9	Illinois
10	Massachusetts
11	Pennsylvania
12	Maryland
13	Washington
14	Minnesota
15	Ohio
16	West Virginia
17	Connecticut
18	Indiana
19	North Carolina
20	Tennessee
21	Missouri
22	Nebraska
23	Nevada
24	Wisconsin
25	Wyoming
26	Utah
27	South Dakota
28	Maine
29	Oregon
30	New Mexico
31	Vermont
32	South Carolina
33	Georgia
34	New Hampshire
35	Virginia
36	Oklahoma
37	Montana
38	Iowa
39	Arizona
40	Arkansas
41	Alabama
42	Kentucky
43	Idaho
44	Louisiana
45	Kansas
46	Hawaii
47	Mississippi
48	Delaware
49	North Dakota
50	Rhode Island

C-4 State Park Visitors, FY 2000

State	State park total visitors (in thousands)	Visitors per capita	Rank per capita
Alabama	5,878	1.3	44
Alaska	3,888	6.2	5
Arizona	2,371	0.5	49
Arkansas	6,643	2.5	27
California	98,520	2.9	22
Colorado	10,284	2.4	28
Connecticut	7,567	2.2	30
Delaware	3,910	5.0	11
Florida	16,672	1.0	46
Georgia	16,124	2.0	33
Hawaii	18,171	15.0	1
Idaho	2,573	2.0	32
Illinois	44,484	3.6	16
Indiana	18,475	3.0	19
Iowa	15,152	5.2	9
Kansas	7,202	2.7	25
Kentucky	7,792	1.9	34
Louisiana	1,715	0.4	50
Maine	2,265	1.8	37
Maryland	10,004	1.9	35
Massachusetts	12,775	2.0	31
Michigan	27,534	2.8	24
Minnesota	8,496	1.7	40
Mississippi	4,198	1.5	43
Missouri	18,174	3.2	17
Montana	1,367	1.5	42
Nebraska	9,619	5.6	7
Nevada	3,451	1.7	39
New Hampshire	5,127	4.1	15
New Jersey	15,073	1.8	36
New Mexico	4,639	2.5	26
New York	59,126	3.1	18
North Carolina	12,400	1.5	41
North Dakota	1,111	1.7	38
Ohio	55,340	4.9	12
Oklahoma	16,148	4.7	13
Oregon	38,563	11.3	2
Pennsylvania	36,717	3.0	21
Rhode Island	6,231	5.9	6
South Carolina	9,247	2.3	29
South Dakota	7,038	9.3	3
Tennessee	30,182	5.3	8
Texas	18,751	0.9	47
Utah	6,737	3.0	20
Vermont	719	1.2	45
Virginia	5,717	0.8	48
Washington	46,444	7.9	4
West Virginia	7,990	4.4	14
Wisconsin	15,470	2.9	23
Wyoming	2,538	5.1	10
50 States	**786,610**	**2.8**	
DC	n/a	n/a	
United States	**786,610**	**2.8**	

Rank in order per capita	
1	Hawaii
2	Oregon
3	South Dakota
4	Washington
5	Alaska
6	Rhode Island
7	Nebraska
8	Tennessee
9	Iowa
10	Wyoming
11	Delaware
12	Ohio
13	Oklahoma
14	West Virginia
15	New Hampshire
16	Illinois
17	Missouri
18	New York
19	Indiana
20	Utah
21	Pennsylvania
22	California
23	Wisconsin
24	Michigan
25	Kansas
26	New Mexico
27	Arkansas
28	Colorado
29	South Carolina
30	Connecticut
31	Massachusetts
32	Idaho
33	Georgia
34	Kentucky
35	Maryland
36	New Jersey
37	Maine
38	North Dakota
39	Nevada
40	Minnesota
41	North Carolina
42	Montana
43	Mississippi
44	Alabama
45	Vermont
46	Florida
47	Texas
48	Virginia
49	Arizona
50	Louisiana

Note: Numbers that appear to be identical are rounded and vary slightly in actual value. The rankings reflect the actual values before rounding. See the introduction for more details.

C-5 Percentage of Population Not Physically Active, 2000

State	Percentage reporting not to be physically active	Rank
Alabama	31.6	8
Alaska	20.0	46
Arizona	34.2	4
Arkansas	28.1	20
California	26.5	28
Colorado	19.8	47
Connecticut	25.2	30
Delaware	28.0	22
Florida	28.8	16
Georgia	29.0	15
Hawaii	23.2	39
Idaho	19.8	47
Illinois	30.9	10
Indiana	25.4	29
Iowa	27.3	24
Kansas	30.4	11
Kentucky	41.1	1
Louisiana	36.2	2
Maine	27.2	25
Maryland	24.2	37
Massachusetts	24.6	34
Michigan	22.9	42
Minnesota	24.8	33
Mississippi	33.3	6
Missouri	28.8	16
Montana	23.3	38
Nebraska	29.6	13
Nevada	24.9	32
New Hampshire	26.7	26
New Jersey	28.6	18
New Mexico	24.4	35
New York	29.4	14
North Carolina	30.4	11
North Dakota	24.3	36
Ohio	31.3	9
Oklahoma	34.4	3
Oregon	20.1	45
Pennsylvania	23.0	41
Rhode Island	27.5	23
South Carolina	28.1	20
South Dakota	26.7	26
Tennessee	32.7	7
Texas	28.5	19
Utah	15.5	50
Vermont	23.2	39
Virginia	25.0	31
Washington	16.9	49
West Virginia	33.6	5
Wisconsin	22.1	44
Wyoming	22.6	43
50 States	n/a	
DC	20.8	
United States	26.9	

Rank in order by percentage	
1	Kentucky
2	Louisiana
3	Oklahoma
4	Arizona
5	West Virginia
6	Mississippi
7	Tennessee
8	Alabama
9	Ohio
10	Illinois
11	Kansas
11	North Carolina
13	Nebraska
14	New York
15	Georgia
16	Florida
16	Missouri
18	New Jersey
19	Texas
20	Arkansas
20	South Carolina
22	Delaware
23	Rhode Island
24	Iowa
25	Maine
26	New Hampshire
26	South Dakota
28	California
29	Indiana
30	Connecticut
31	Virginia
32	Nevada
33	Minnesota
34	Massachusetts
35	New Mexico
36	North Dakota
37	Maryland
38	Montana
39	Hawaii
39	Vermont
41	Pennsylvania
42	Michigan
43	Wyoming
44	Wisconsin
45	Oregon
46	Alaska
47	Colorado
47	Idaho
49	Washington
50	Utah

Note: Ties in ranking reflect ties in actual values.

C-6 Hunters with Firearms, 2000

State	Hunters with firearms (in thousands)	Percentage of population	Rank by percentage
Alabama	583	13.1	16
Alaska	n/a	n/a	n/a
Arizona	269	5.2	33
Arkansas	424	15.9	9
California	692	2.0	44
Colorado	405	9.4	22
Connecticut	129	3.8	40
Delaware	10	1.3	48
Florida	524	3.3	42
Georgia	404	4.9	36
Hawaii	n/a	n/a	n/a
Idaho	509	39.3	1
Illinois	414	3.3	41
Indiana	302	5.0	35
Iowa	291	9.9	18
Kansas	353	13.1	15
Kentucky	398	9.8	19
Louisiana	440	9.8	20
Maine	254	19.9	4
Maryland	296	5.6	32
Massachusetts	119	1.9	45
Michigan	778	7.8	25
Minnesota	685	13.9	13
Mississippi	493	17.3	7
Missouri	860	15.4	10
Montana	179	19.8	5
Nebraska	239	14.0	12
Nevada	97	4.9	37
New Hampshire	40	3.2	43
New Jersey	146	1.7	46
New Mexico	162	8.9	23
New York	809	4.3	39
North Carolina	510	6.3	29
North Dakota	121	18.8	6
Ohio	586	5.2	34
Oklahoma	454	13.2	14
Oregon	374	10.9	17
Pennsylvania	1,206	9.8	21
Rhode Island	18	1.7	47
South Carolina	172	4.3	38
South Dakota	158	20.9	3
Tennessee	354	6.2	30
Texas	1,184	5.7	31
Utah	317	14.2	11
Vermont	40	6.6	28
Virginia	552	7.8	26
Washington	443	7.5	27
West Virginia	441	24.4	2
Wisconsin	869	16.2	8
Wyoming	42	8.5	24
50 States	19,145	6.8	
DC	n/a	n/a	
United States*	19,144	6.8	

*Due to rounding or data sources, the 50-state total plus D.C. may not equal the U.S. total. Please see introduction.

Rank in order by percentage

1 Idaho
2 West Virginia
3 South Dakota
4 Maine
5 Montana
6 North Dakota
7 Mississippi
8 Wisconsin
9 Arkansas
10 Missouri
11 Utah
12 Nebraska
13 Minnesota
14 Oklahoma
15 Kansas
16 Alabama
17 Oregon
18 Iowa
19 Kentucky
20 Louisiana
21 Pennsylvania
22 Colorado
23 New Mexico
24 Wyoming
25 Michigan
26 Virginia
27 Washington
28 Vermont
29 North Carolina
30 Tennessee
31 Texas
32 Maryland
33 Arizona
34 Ohio
35 Indiana
36 Georgia
37 Nevada
38 South Carolina
39 New York
40 Connecticut
41 Illinois
42 Florida
43 New Hampshire
44 California
45 Massachusetts
46 New Jersey
47 Rhode Island
48 Delaware

Note: Numbers that appear to be identical are rounded and vary slightly in actual value. The rankings reflect the actual values before rounding. See the introduction for more details.

C-7 Registered Boats, 2000

State	Registered boats	Registered boats per 1,000 population	Rank by total number of boats
Alabama	265,458	60	18
Alaska	29,113	46	48
Arizona	148,748	29	29
Arkansas	177,912	67	27
California	904,863	27	2
Colorado	104,880	24	32
Connecticut	103,218	30	33
Delaware	46,719	60	45
Florida	840,684	53	3
Georgia	322,681	39	14
Hawaii	13,807	11	50
Idaho	85,438	66	36
Illinois	372,162	30	10
Indiana	219,189	36	24
Iowa	223,573	76	23
Kansas	103,190	38	34
Kentucky	169,670	42	28
Louisiana	314,321	70	15
Maine	119,243	94	31
Maryland	208,186	39	25
Massachusetts	138,861	22	30
Michigan	1,000,049	101	1
Minnesota	812,247	165	4
Mississippi	292,335	103	16
Missouri	334,460	60	13
Montana	51,325	57	42
Nebraska	73,638	43	38
Nevada	61,722	31	40
New Hampshire	97,925	79	35
New Jersey	243,281	29	20
New Mexico	70,464	39	39
New York	525,436	28	7
North Carolina	349,631	43	12
North Dakota	47,722	74	44
Ohio	416,798	37	8
Oklahoma	230,524	67	22
Oregon	195,691	57	26
Pennsylvania	359,360	29	11
Rhode Island	40,265	38	46
South Carolina	383,734	96	9
South Dakota	50,935	67	43
Tennessee	269,583	47	17
Texas	626,761	30	5
Utah	79,397	36	37
Vermont	33,686	55	47
Virginia	237,228	34	21
Washington	257,625	44	19
West Virginia	60,895	34	41
Wisconsin	573,920	107	6
Wyoming	26,926	55	49
50 States	12,715,479	45	
DC	2,791	5	
United States*	12,782,143	45	

Rank in order by total number	
1	Michigan
2	California
3	Florida
4	Minnesota
5	Texas
6	Wisconsin
7	New York
8	Ohio
9	South Carolina
10	Illinois
11	Pennsylvania
12	North Carolina
13	Missouri
14	Georgia
15	Louisiana
16	Mississippi
17	Tennessee
18	Alabama
19	Washington
20	New Jersey
21	Virginia
22	Oklahoma
23	Iowa
24	Indiana
25	Maryland
26	Oregon
27	Arkansas
28	Kentucky
29	Arizona
30	Massachusetts
31	Maine
32	Colorado
33	Connecticut
34	Kansas
35	New Hampshire
36	Idaho
37	Utah
38	Nebraska
39	New Mexico
40	Nevada
41	West Virginia
42	Montana
43	South Dakota
44	North Dakota
45	Delaware
46	Rhode Island
47	Vermont
48	Alaska
49	Wyoming
50	Hawaii

*Due to rounding or data sources, the 50-state total plus D.C. may not equal the U.S. total. Please see introduction.

C-8 State Spending on State Arts Agencies, FY 2001

State	State spending for the arts $ (in thousands)	Per capita $	Rank per capita		Rank in order per capita	
Alabama	6,121	1.38	16		1	Hawaii
Alaska	459	0.73	31		2	Connecticut
Arizona	3,898	0.76	29		3	New York
Arkansas	1,311	0.49	42		4	Massachusetts
California	68,063	2.01	12		5	Minnesota
Colorado	1,886	0.44	47		6	New Jersey
Connecticut	13,583	3.99	2		7	Michigan
Delaware	1,674	2.14	11		8	Maryland
Florida	36,935	2.31	9		9	Florida
Georgia	4,835	0.59	40		10	Missouri
Hawaii	6,006	4.96	1		11	Delaware
Idaho	951	0.74	30		12	California
Illinois	19,789	1.59	14		13	Rhode Island
Indiana	3,843	0.63	37		14	Illinois
Iowa	1,708	0.58	41		15	Ohio
Kansas	1,644	0.61	39		16	Alabama
Kentucky	4,073	1.01	24		17	South Carolina
Louisiana	4,898	1.10	22		18	West Virginia
Maine	797	0.63	38		19	Utah
Maryland	12,646	2.39	8		20	Oklahoma
Massachusetts	17,780	2.80	4		21	Pennsylvania
Michigan	25,836	2.60	7		22	Louisiana
Minnesota	13,094	2.66	5		23	New Mexico
Mississippi	2,430	0.85	27		24	Kentucky
Missouri	11,972	2.14	10		25	North Carolina
Montana	286	0.32	49		26	Vermont
Nebraska	1,455	0.85	28		27	Mississippi
Nevada	1,342	0.67	34		28	Nebraska
New Hampshire	589	0.48	45		29	Arizona
New Jersey	22,089	2.63	6		30	Idaho
New Mexico	1,921	1.06	23		31	Alaska
New York	56,739	2.99	3		32	Wyoming
North Carolina	7,856	0.98	25		33	South Dakota
North Dakota	422	0.66	36		34	Nevada
Ohio	16,280	1.43	15		35	Virginia
Oklahoma	4,235	1.23	20		36	North Dakota
Oregon	1,632	0.48	44		37	Indiana
Pennsylvania	14,000	1.14	21		38	Maine
Rhode Island	1,746	1.67	13		39	Kansas
South Carolina	5,422	1.35	17		40	Georgia
South Dakota	512	0.68	33		41	Iowa
Tennessee	2,307	0.41	48		42	Arkansas
Texas	4,739	0.23	50		43	Wisconsin
Utah	2,776	1.24	19		44	Oregon
Vermont	565	0.93	26		45	New Hampshire
Virginia	4,690	0.66	35		46	Washington
Washington	2,628	0.45	46		47	Colorado
West Virginia	2,343	1.30	18		48	Tennessee
Wisconsin	2,563	0.48	43		49	Montana
Wyoming	353	0.71	32		50	Texas
50 States	425,723	1.52				
DC	1,900	3.32				
United States*	446,506	1.59				

Note: Numbers that appear to be identical are rounded and vary slightly in actual value. The rankings reflect the actual values before rounding. See the introduction for more details.

Due to rounding or data sources, the 50-state total plus D.C. may not equal the U.S. total. Please see introduction.

C-9 Energy Consumption, Total and Per Capita, 1999

State	Energy consumption (in trillion BTUs)	BTUs per capita	Rank per capita
Alabama	2,004.8	458,779	10
Alaska	694.7	1,121,388	1
Arizona	1,219.8	255,277	45
Arkansas	1,203.7	471,785	6
California	8,375.4	252,689	48
Colorado	1,155.5	284,877	39
Connecticut	839.3	255,726	44
Delaware	278.8	369,988	22
Florida	3,852.9	254,969	46
Georgia	2,798.1	359,272	25
Hawaii	241.4	203,628	50
Idaho	518.3	414,077	13
Illinois	3,882.6	320,125	35
Indiana	2,735.8	460,348	9
Iowa	1,121.7	390,916	17
Kansas	1,050.0	395,621	16
Kentucky	1,830.2	462,075	8
Louisiana	3,615.4	826,938	3
Maine	528.6	421,854	12
Maryland	1,378.2	266,492	42
Massachusetts	1,569.1	254,098	47
Michigan	3,239.6	328,434	30
Minnesota	1,675.3	350,811	26
Mississippi	1,208.5	436,499	11
Missouri	1,768.0	323,316	34
Montana	412.4	467,161	7
Nebraska	602.0	361,338	24
Nevada	615.3	340,085	28
New Hampshire	335.4	279,236	40
New Jersey	2,588.7	317,889	37
New Mexico	635.0	364,975	23
New York	4,283.0	235,374	49
North Carolina	2,446.9	319,823	36
North Dakota	365.7	577,118	4
Ohio	4,323.4	384,075	20
Oklahoma	1,377.5	410,209	14
Oregon	1,109.2	334,484	29
Pennsylvania	3,715.5	309,779	38
Rhode Island	261.1	263,519	43
South Carolina	1,493.0	384,226	19
South Dakota	239.0	325,998	31
Tennessee	2,070.0	377,494	21
Texas	11,501.0	573,784	5
Utah	693.9	325,800	32
Vermont	165.0	277,899	41
Virginia	2,227.3	324,069	33
Washington	2,240.8	389,274	18
West Virginia	735.4	406,989	15
Wisconsin	1,810.5	344,828	27
Wyoming	421.8	879,479	2
50 States	95,454.5	350,714	
DC	169.8	327,168	
United States*	95,682.4	350,882	

Due to rounding or data sources, the 50-state total plus D.C. may not equal the U.S. total. Please see introduction.

Rank in order per capita	
1	Alaska
2	Wyoming
3	Louisiana
4	North Dakota
5	Texas
6	Arkansas
7	Montana
8	Kentucky
9	Indiana
10	Alabama
11	Mississippi
12	Maine
13	Idaho
14	Oklahoma
15	West Virginia
16	Kansas
17	Iowa
18	Washington
19	South Carolina
20	Ohio
21	Tennessee
22	Delaware
23	New Mexico
24	Nebraska
25	Georgia
26	Minnesota
27	Wisconsin
28	Nevada
29	Oregon
30	Michigan
31	South Dakota
32	Utah
33	Virginia
34	Missouri
35	Illinois
36	North Carolina
37	New Jersey
38	Pennsylvania
39	Colorado
40	New Hampshire
41	Vermont
42	Maryland
43	Rhode Island
44	Connecticut
45	Arizona
46	Florida
47	Massachusetts
48	California
49	New York
50	Hawaii

C-10 Toxic Chemical Release, 1999

State	Toxic chemical release in pounds (in thousands)	Per capita release in pounds	Rank per capita
Alabama	138,129	31.6	13
Alaska	433,018	699.0	1
Arizona	963,330	201.6	4
Arkansas	41,525	16.3	27
California	69,046	2.1	47
Colorado	26,085	6.4	39
Connecticut	7,835	2.4	45
Delaware	11,380	15.1	30
Florida	149,407	9.9	36
Georgia	126,924	16.3	26
Hawaii	2,575	2.2	46
Idaho	85,976	68.7	7
Illinois	165,055	13.6	32
Indiana	198,871	33.5	12
Iowa	48,792	17.0	23
Kansas	42,574	16.0	28
Kentucky	106,205	26.8	16
Louisiana	150,153	34.3	11
Maine	7,849	6.3	40
Maryland	43,981	8.5	37
Massachusetts	11,876	1.9	48
Michigan	142,287	14.4	31
Minnesota	31,223	6.5	38
Mississippi	75,796	27.4	14
Missouri	129,741	23.7	18
Montana	127,619	144.6	6
Nebraska	27,267	16.4	25
Nevada	1,168,408	645.8	2
New Hampshire	5,872	4.9	42
New Jersey	31,283	3.8	44
New Mexico	262,276	150.7	5
New York	71,814	3.9	43
North Carolina	158,351	20.7	20
North Dakota	23,656	37.3	10
Ohio	303,228	26.9	15
Oklahoma	37,069	11.0	35
Oregon	67,696	20.4	21
Pennsylvania	235,569	19.6	22
Rhode Island	1,391	1.4	49
South Carolina	84,061	21.6	19
South Dakota	12,129	16.5	24
Tennessee	144,311	26.3	17
Texas	313,866	15.7	29
Utah	1,161,787	545.5	3
Vermont	647	1.1	50
Virginia	80,570	11.7	33
Washington	28,475	4.9	41
West Virginia	100,492	55.6	8
Wisconsin	58,382	11.1	34
Wyoming	19,430	40.5	9
50 States	7,735,280	28.4	
DC	98	0.2	
United States*	7,754,830	28.4	

Rank in order per capita	
1	Alaska
2	Nevada
3	Utah
4	Arizona
5	New Mexico
6	Montana
7	Idaho
8	West Virginia
9	Wyoming
10	North Dakota
11	Louisiana
12	Indiana
13	Alabama
14	Mississippi
15	Ohio
16	Kentucky
17	Tennessee
18	Missouri
19	South Carolina
20	North Carolina
21	Oregon
22	Pennsylvania
23	Iowa
24	South Dakota
25	Nebraska
26	Georgia
27	Arkansas
28	Kansas
29	Texas
30	Delaware
31	Michigan
32	Illinois
33	Virginia
34	Wisconsin
35	Oklahoma
36	Florida
37	Maryland
38	Minnesota
39	Colorado
40	Maine
41	Washington
42	New Hampshire
43	New York
44	New Jersey
45	Connecticut
46	Hawaii
47	California
48	Massachusetts
49	Rhode Island
50	Vermont

Note: Numbers that appear to be identical are rounded and vary slightly in actual value. The rankings reflect the actual values before rounding. See the introduction for more details.

Due to rounding or data sources, the 50-state total plus D.C. may not equal the U.S. total. Please see introduction.

C-11 Hazardous Waste Sites, 2001

State	Hazardous waste sites #	Rank
Alabama	15	26
Alaska	7	44
Arizona	10	39
Arkansas	12	33
California	100	2
Colorado	17	22
Connecticut	16	24
Delaware	17	22
Florida	53	6
Georgia	15	26
Hawaii	3	46
Idaho	9	41
Illinois	44	8
Indiana	29	14
Iowa	15	26
Kansas	12	33
Kentucky	15	26
Louisiana	16	24
Maine	12	33
Maryland	18	21
Massachusetts	33	12
Michigan	69	5
Minnesota	24	18
Mississippi	4	45
Missouri	25	16
Montana	14	30
Nebraska	10	39
Nevada	1	49
New Hampshire	19	20
New Jersey	114	1
New Mexico	13	32
New York	90	4
North Carolina	26	15
North Dakota	0	50
Ohio	35	11
Oklahoma	12	33
Oregon	12	33
Pennsylvania	99	3
Rhode Island	12	33
South Carolina	25	16
South Dakota	2	47
Tennessee	14	30
Texas	40	10
Utah	21	19
Vermont	9	41
Virginia	31	13
Washington	48	7
West Virginia	9	41
Wisconsin	41	9
Wyoming	2	47
50 States	1,289	
DC	1	
United States*	1,303	

Rank in order by #	
1	New Jersey
2	California
3	Pennsylvania
4	New York
5	Michigan
6	Florida
7	Washington
8	Illinois
9	Wisconsin
10	Texas
11	Ohio
12	Massachusetts
13	Virginia
14	Indiana
15	North Carolina
16	Missouri
16	South Carolina
18	Minnesota
19	Utah
20	New Hampshire
21	Maryland
22	Colorado
22	Delaware
24	Connecticut
24	Louisiana
26	Alabama
26	Georgia
26	Iowa
26	Kentucky
30	Montana
30	Tennessee
32	New Mexico
33	Arkansas
33	Kansas
33	Maine
33	Oklahoma
33	Oregon
33	Rhode Island
39	Arizona
39	Nebraska
41	Idaho
41	Vermont
41	West Virginia
44	Alaska
45	Mississippi
46	Hawaii
47	South Dakota
47	Wyoming
49	Nevada
50	North Dakota

Note: Ties in ranking reflect ties in actual values.

*Due to rounding or data sources, the 50-state total plus D.C. may not equal the U.S. total. Please see introduction.

C-12 Polluted Rivers and Streams, 1998

State	Percentage of EPA-surveyed river and stream miles that are polluted	EPA-surveyed river and stream miles as a percentage of total river and stream miles	Rank by percentage polluted
Alabama	5.5	5	46
Alaska	99.4	0	2
Arizona	38.6	5	29
Arkansas	17.7	10	39
California	70.2	8	6
Colorado	4.4	27	47
Connecticut	28.2	16	35
Delaware	100.0	95	1
Florida	44.2	10	24
Georgia	60.6	12	16
Hawaii	69.2	100	7
Idaho	67.0	11	9
Illinois	44.1	33	25
Indiana	47.6	24	20
Iowa	23.2	14	38
Kansas	68.6	12	8
Kentucky	33.3	19	32
Louisiana	89.4	9	4
Maine	1.7	100	49
Maryland	5.7	39	45
Massachusetts	64.9	18	11
Michigan	8.3	40	44
Minnesota	62.3	13	15
Mississippi	96.4	47	3
Missouri	47.2	42	22
Montana	59.2	10	18
Nebraska	41.2	5	27
Nevada	47.3	1	21
New Hampshire	15.9	24	40
New Jersey	64.6	59	12
New Mexico	62.7	4	14
New York	2.0	100	48
North Carolina	13.6	89	42
North Dakota	39.9	22	28
Ohio	42.2	10	26
Oklahoma	65.9	14	10
Oregon	25.9	47	37
Pennsylvania	34.2	15	31
Rhode Island	36.6	54	30
South Carolina	74.6	65	5
South Dakota	63.8	32	13
Tennessee	28.1	88	36
Texas	31.0	7	34
Utah	32.1	10	33
Vermont	15.6	16	41
Virginia	13.6	39	43
Washington	59.4	98	17
West Virginia	58.2	24	19
Wisconsin	44.4	40	23
Wyoming	0.4	87	50
50 States	34.7	n/a	
DC	100.0	98	
United States	34.7	23	

Rank in order by percentage polluted

1 Delaware
2 Alaska
3 Mississippi
4 Louisiana
5 South Carolina
6 California
7 Hawaii
8 Kansas
9 Idaho
10 Oklahoma
11 Massachusetts
12 New Jersey
13 South Dakota
14 New Mexico
15 Minnesota
16 Georgia
17 Washington
18 Montana
19 West Virginia
20 Indiana
21 Nevada
22 Missouri
23 Wisconsin
24 Florida
25 Illinois
26 Ohio
27 Nebraska
28 North Dakota
29 Arizona
30 Rhode Island
31 Pennsylvania
32 Kentucky
33 Utah
34 Texas
35 Connecticut
36 Tennessee
37 Oregon
38 Iowa
39 Arkansas
40 New Hampshire
41 Vermont
42 North Carolina
43 Virginia
44 Michigan
45 Maryland
46 Alabama
47 Colorado
48 New York
49 Maine
50 Wyoming

Note: Numbers that appear to be identical are rounded and vary slightly in actual value. The rankings reflect the actual values before rounding. See the introduction for more details.

C-13 Expired Surface Water Pollution Discharge Permits, 2000

State	Percentage of major facilities with expired Clean Water Act permits	Rank
Alabama	13	39
Alaska	23	27
Arizona	24	23
Arkansas	12	40
California	36	15
Colorado	50	6
Connecticut	38	13
Delaware	29	18
Florida	17	35
Georgia	1	48
Hawaii	37	14
Idaho	36	15
Illinois	17	35
Indiana	46	9
Iowa	25	21
Kansas	19	33
Kentucky	2	47
Louisiana	47	8
Maine	24	23
Maryland	21	31
Massachusetts	50	6
Michigan	24	23
Minnesota	44	11
Mississippi	12	40
Missouri	24	23
Montana	20	32
Nebraska	67	3
Nevada	70	1
New Hampshire	44	11
New Jersey	29	18
New Mexico	59	5
New York	4	46
North Carolina	23	27
North Dakota	0	49
Ohio	35	17
Oklahoma	25	21
Oregon	67	3
Pennsylvania	11	43
Rhode Island	68	2
South Carolina	19	33
South Dakota	16	38
Tennessee	22	30
Texas	23	27
Utah	6	45
Vermont	12	40
Virginia	28	20
Washington	46	9
West Virginia	11	43
Wisconsin	17	35
Wyoming	0	50
50 States	n/a	
DC	100	
United States	25	

Rank in order by percentage	
1	Nevada
2	Rhode Island
3	Nebraska
3	Oregon
5	New Mexico
6	Colorado
6	Massachusetts
8	Louisiana
9	Indiana
9	Washington
11	Minnesota
11	New Hampshire
13	Connecticut
14	Hawaii
15	California
15	Idaho
17	Ohio
18	Delaware
18	New Jersey
20	Virginia
21	Iowa
21	Oklahoma
23	Arizona
23	Maine
23	Michigan
23	Missouri
27	Alaska
27	North Carolina
27	Texas
30	Tennessee
31	Maryland
32	Montana
33	Kansas
33	South Carolina
35	Florida
35	Illinois
35	Wisconsin
38	South Dakota
39	Alabama
40	Arkansas
40	Mississippi
40	Vermont
43	Pennsylvania
43	West Virginia
45	Utah
46	New York
47	Kentucky
48	Georgia
49	North Dakota
50	Wyoming

Note: Ties in ranking reflect ties in actual values.

C-14 Air Pollution Emissions, 1999

State	Emissions in short tons (in thousands)	Per capita	Rank by total emissions
Alabama	4,906	1.1	12
Alaska	3,166	5.1	24
Arizona	3,517	0.7	21
Arkansas	2,396	0.9	32
California	11,792	0.4	2
Colorado	2,714	0.7	29
Connecticut	1,356	0.4	41
Delaware	453	0.6	48
Florida	9,415	0.6	3
Georgia	7,144	0.9	5
Hawaii	567	0.5	47
Idaho	1,822	1.5	36
Illinois	7,003	0.6	6
Indiana	5,619	0.9	10
Iowa	2,482	0.9	30
Kansas	2,781	1.0	28
Kentucky	3,614	0.9	19
Louisiana	4,325	1.0	15
Maine	1,040	0.8	44
Maryland	2,180	0.4	35
Massachusetts	2,437	0.4	31
Michigan	6,272	0.6	9
Minnesota	3,724	0.8	17
Mississippi	2,924	1.1	27
Missouri	4,208	0.8	16
Montana	1,478	1.7	39
Nebraska	1,760	1.1	37
Nevada	1,169	0.6	43
New Hampshire	797	0.7	46
New Jersey	2,989	0.4	26
New Mexico	2,388	1.4	33
New York	6,299	0.3	8
North Carolina	5,467	0.7	11
North Dakota	1,405	2.2	40
Ohio	8,494	0.8	4
Oklahoma	3,273	1.0	23
Oregon	3,541	1.1	20
Pennsylvania	6,579	0.5	7
Rhode Island	378	0.4	50
South Carolina	3,163	0.8	25
South Dakota	895	1.2	45
Tennessee	4,597	0.8	13
Texas	13,615	0.7	1
Utah	1,635	0.8	38
Vermont	450	0.8	49
Virginia	4,330	0.6	14
Washington	3,702	0.6	18
West Virginia	2,371	1.3	34
Wisconsin	3,494	0.7	22
Wyoming	1,303	2.7	42
50 States	183,431	0.7	
DC	131	0.3	
United States*	183,561	0.7	

Rank in order by total emissions	
1	Texas
2	California
3	Florida
4	Ohio
5	Georgia
6	Illinois
7	Pennsylvania
8	New York
9	Michigan
10	Indiana
11	North Carolina
12	Alabama
13	Tennessee
14	Virginia
15	Louisiana
16	Missouri
17	Minnesota
18	Washington
19	Kentucky
20	Oregon
21	Arizona
22	Wisconsin
23	Oklahoma
24	Alaska
25	South Carolina
26	New Jersey
27	Mississippi
28	Kansas
29	Colorado
30	Iowa
31	Massachusetts
32	Arkansas
33	New Mexico
34	West Virginia
35	Maryland
36	Idaho
37	Nebraska
38	Utah
39	Montana
40	North Dakota
41	Connecticut
42	Wyoming
43	Nevada
44	Maine
45	South Dakota
46	New Hampshire
47	Hawaii
48	Delaware
49	Vermont
50	Rhode Island

Due to rounding or data sources, the 50-state total plus D.C. may not equal the U.S. total. Please see introduction.

Source Notes for Geography (Section C)

C-1 Total Land Area, 2000: This statistic comes from the 2000 census and is prepared by the geography division of the Census Bureau. It can be combined with population statistics to calculate the population "density" of each state (see Table A-16).

C-2 Land Owned by Federal Government, 2000: The federal government owns land for its buildings, military installations, and other facilities in every state, but these holdings are not major factors in the land use patterns of most states. The federal government also owns massive areas as part of the National Park Service and the Forest Service, and public lands managed by the U.S. Department of the Interior, primarily arid lands in Western states. These federal land holdings, measured in land area—not land usefulness—are more than half of the land in some states. The data are maintained by the individual federal agencies that own the land, and they are compiled in the U.S. General Services Administration's annual publication, *Inventory Report on Real Property Owned by the United States Throughout the World.*

C-3 State Park Acreage, FY 2000: These statistics show the acres of state parks and the number of acres of state parks per one thousand people. The data are for the year ending June 30, 2000. They come from the National Association of State Park Directors' statistical report titled, *The 2001 Annual Information Exchange.* The ratio was calculated by *State Fact Finder.*

C-4 State Park Visitors, FY 2000: State park agencies make estimates of the number of visitors to state parks maintained by the National Association of State Park Directors (see source for Table C-3). *State Fact Finder* related these visits to population using Census data. The data can be viewed as indicating that the average person visits a state park about 2.8 times a year.

C-5 Percentage of Population Not Physically Active, 2000: There are few reliable data on a state level on the participation of citizens in various forms of recreational activities, as no one maintains records of who hikes, plays tennis, or fishes except when they use facilities requiring admission. These data are from a survey of the Centers for Disease Control and Prevention (CDC). The data reflect the percentage of those surveyed who answered "no" to the question "During the past month, did you participate in any physical activities?" The numbers are available on the CDC website (www.cdc.gov) as "Online Prevalence Data" and were retrieved by *State Fact Finder* on August 11, 2000.

C-6 Hunters with Firearms, 2000: These data show the sharp differences among states in the use of firearms for hunting—statistics highly relevant to debates over use and control of firearms. Note that the participant for the state listed is a resident of that state even though they may not have hunted in that state. That is, a hunter with firearms in Texas is a resident of Texas even though he or she may have hunted in Louisiana. Estimates by state are made by the National Sporting Goods Association (Mt. Prospect, Illinois 60056) for all major recreation activities.

C-7 Registered Boats, 2000: All states require registration of motorboats and some require registration of other boats, such as canoes and sailboats. These data, collected from state authorities by the U.S. Coast Guard, show the number of registered boats and the relationship between the number of boats and population. The data come from the Consumer Affairs and Analysis Branch of the U.S. Coast Guard and were provided to *State Fact Finder* by e-mail on November 14, 2001.

C-8 State Spending on State Arts Agencies, FY 2001: The federal government subsidizes arts programs in the states and encourages states to do the same. Each state has an agency to act as the state government's primary means of funding the arts and encouraging cultural participation. State arts agencies receive state legislative dollars as well as federal funds. This table measures legislative support for state arts agencies in FY 2001. The National Assembly of State Arts Agencies collects and publishes this statistic and provided it to *State Fact Finder* by e-mail on November 15, 2001.

C-9 Energy Consumption, Total and Per Capita, 1999: At the time of the "energy crisis" of the 1970s, the federal government established a Department of Energy (DOE) and a vast data collection mechanism covering production and consumption of all forms of energy, including coal, oil, gas, and nuclear power. This table from the Energy Information Administration (EIA) of the DOE shows total energy consumption and relates it to the population of each state.

These data show consumption by all users, including businesses, by the state where energy is used, not necessarily where it was produced. States with relatively small populations and intensive energy use for mining and petrochemical manufacturing show the largest use. The EIA has detailed data by state on sources of energy and use in categories, such as residential and industrial. For those users interested in comparisons over time, the 1997 as well as the 1995 and 1994 data (which were published in the 1999 and the 1997 edition of *State Fact Finder,* respectively) are not comparable to previously released data for earlier years. As of the release of the 1994 data, the EIA has included renewable energy sources (wood and waste are examples) in energy consumption compilations. The EIA has revised 1990-1993 data to also include renewable energy. These numbers appear in the EIA's *State Energy Data Report 1994.* Data on 1999 energy consumption come from the *State Energy Data Report 1999.*

C-10 Toxic Chemical Release, 1999: The U.S. Environmental Protection Agency (EPA) requires detailed reporting of what it defines as "toxic" chemical releases into the atmosphere. These data, from the *1999 Toxics Release Inventory*, available on the EPA website (www.epa.gov), are frequently cited by the media as indicators of health risks and air pollution in particular states. They are of little value for this purpose. The effects of releases in a particular state often are not felt in that state because they are carried to an adjacent state or the oceans. High totals are generally associated with a few plants whose owners argue that their releases are not hazardous to health.

C-11 Hazardous Waste Sites, 2001: This table shows the number of sites the Environmental Protection Agency (EPA) has designated for cleanup under the Superfund program. The program and the designations are highly controversial, but the data are often cited as indicators of the relative prevalence of hazardous waste problems in particular states. The data are available on the EPA website (www.epa.gov/superfund).

C-12 Polluted Rivers and Streams, 1998: Under federal water pollution laws, each state reports to the Environmental Protection Agency (EPA) on the status of its rivers, specifically whether they are safe for fishing (and eating the catch) and swimming. The EPA compiles this data in its biannual publication *National Water Quality Inventory: Report to Congress.* These data are printed in the 1998 report that was released in June 2000. The percentages reflect not the total number of rivers and streams in a state but the total number that were surveyed. Nationwide, 23 percent of 3.6 million river and stream miles were surveyed in 2000. Impairment refers to reduced "aquatic life support."

This table and other available measures of the pollution of rivers are not particularly useful for many purposes. At this point, states are unable to survey all their bodies of water and thus tend to monitor areas with suspected problems. In addition, any compilation of river-miles includes many stretches in remote locations that are of little use for swimming or fishing because of inaccessibility, low flows, few fish, and insufficient depth for swimming. There is no statistic that allows comparing states on a basis more reflective of the extent to which pollution prevents safe fishing and swimming in relation to the fishing and swimming that would occur if there were no pollution at all.

C-13 Expired Surface Water Pollution Discharge Permits, 2000: Through the Clean Water Act a system of permits was created. These permits are issued to factories, utilities, sewage treatment plants and any other private or public entity that releases pollutants into the nation's waters. The purpose is to regulate and reduce pollution discharges. Permits come up for renewal at least every five years, at which time new requirements for pollution reduction or better treatment technologies are generally required. This table from the Environmental Working Group (ewg.org) based on data from the Environmental Protection Agency (EPA) provides a measure of the permit backlog in each state. EWG argues that while permits remain in limbo, a water pollution program cannot be operated effectively. The EPA has put forth the goal of reducing permit backlog to 10 percent by the end of 2001.

C-14 Air Pollution Emissions, 1999: Despite many years and millions of dollars put into efforts to measure air pollution on a state-by-state basis, no satisfactory method has been found to develop a summary measure. There are many problems. Air pollution affects people where they breathe, so for some purposes the relevant measure is what's in the ambient air, but there is little interest in measuring air quality in places with few or no people like mountains and deserts. So, such measures focus on metropolitan areas, not states. Within each state, there are dramatic differences in pollution levels associated with such factors as proximity to prevailing winds and pollution sources and elevation.

Air pollution can only be controlled where it originates, so measurement related to enforcement concentrates on place of origin, which is often not the same as the state where people are affected. Airborne pollutants don't recognize state lines, so the relevant concept is airsheds, not states.

State Fact Finder developed this table primarily to lead users to the vast quantities of data available. The table reflects added estimates of short tons of pollution emissions in each state for five pollutants — carbon monoxide, nitrogen oxide, volatile organic compounds, sulfur dioxide, and particulate matter. The per capita calculation is provided only as a subject of possible interest. The ranking based on total tons of emissions is not a proxy for the seriousness of air pollution to the residents of the states listed and not a recognized measure of how effectively states control pollution.

The data on each pollutant by state and major causes (for example, transportation, farming, utility operation) come from the Emission Factor and Inventory Group at the Environmental Protection Agency Office of Air Quality Planning and Standards. This office and its publication *National Air Pollutant Emission Trends* are good sources for other information useful to readers interested in comparing air pollution emissions of the various states.

Government

In the wake of September 11th, states and localities have been doubly concerned with public safety. Soon after the attacks, thirty-five states established new anti-terrorism task forces. Nineteen states created a security director position similar to the federal position now held by former Pennsylvania governor Tom Ridge. Border states, shoreline and coast line states, and those hosting major events such as the Olympics in Utah and the Super Bowl in Louisiana have additional security responsibilities, all of which come with additional costs. How states shoulder the financial burden, or share it with the federal government, will undoubtedly be raised in 2002.

The attacks on September 11th and the current focus on national security has engendered some discussion on the role of government at the local, state, and national level. In *Governing* Magazine (November, 2001) writer Jonathan Walters offers one perspective:

"Two images in particular stand out for me in the immediate confusion of the September 11th terrorism. One is the image of Rudolph Guiliani immersing himself in the danger and debris of ground zero as he rallied his troops for an emergency response. The other is of the President of the United States trying desperately to get out of harm's way as he flew from Florida, to Louisiana, to Nebraska, and finally that night back to the White House in Washington, D.C.

These observations are meant neither as praise for Guiliani nor as criticism of President Bush. They are offered simply to illustrate the different and clearly outlined roles of local, state, and federal government as they were thrown into stark relief by the disaster: When it comes to domestic issues and incidents, the buck really does stop with the states and localities."

Other issues still on the burner: redistricting and election reform. New census numbers mean new political boundaries. States are charged with the task of redrawing legislative district lines, a process often accompanied by dispute and litigation.

States remain mindful of election issues. Hoping to avoid repeating the situation in Florida, states continue to examine, revamp, and update their voting processes.

D-1 Members of the United States House, 2002

State	Number of House members	Change from 1990 census	Rank
Alabama	7	0	22
Alaska	1	0	44
Arizona	8	+2	18
Arkansas	4	0	31
California	53	+1	1
Colorado	7	+1	22
Connecticut	5	-1	27
Delaware	1	0	44
Florida	25	+2	4
Georgia	13	+2	9
Hawaii	2	0	39
Idaho	2	0	39
Illinois	19	-1	5
Indiana	9	-1	14
Iowa	5	0	27
Kansas	4	0	31
Kentucky	6	0	25
Louisiana	7	0	22
Maine	2	0	39
Maryland	8	0	18
Massachusetts	10	0	13
Michigan	15	-1	8
Minnesota	8	0	18
Mississippi	4	-1	31
Missouri	9	0	14
Montana	1	0	44
Nebraska	3	0	34
Nevada	3	+1	34
New Hampshire	2	0	39
New Jersey	13	0	9
New Mexico	3	0	34
New York	29	-2	3
North Carolina	13	+1	9
North Dakota	1	0	44
Ohio	18	-1	7
Oklahoma	5	-1	27
Oregon	5	0	27
Pennsylvania	19	-2	5
Rhode Island	2	0	39
South Carolina	6	0	25
South Dakota	1	0	44
Tennessee	9	0	14
Texas	32	+2	2
Utah	3	0	34
Vermont	1	0	44
Virginia	11	0	12
Washington	9	0	14
West Virginia	3	0	34
Wisconsin	8	-1	18
Wyoming	1	0	44
50 States	435		
DC	n/a		
United States	435		

Rank in order by #	
1	California
2	Texas
3	New York
4	Florida
5	Illinois
5	Pennsylvania
7	Ohio
8	Michigan
9	Georgia
9	New Jersey
9	North Carolina
12	Virginia
13	Massachusetts
14	Indiana
14	Missouri
14	Tennessee
14	Washington
18	Arizona
18	Maryland
18	Minnesota
18	Wisconsin
22	Alabama
22	Colorado
22	Louisiana
25	Kentucky
25	South Carolina
27	Connecticut
27	Iowa
27	Oklahoma
27	Oregon
31	Arkansas
31	Kansas
31	Mississippi
34	Nebraska
34	Nevada
34	New Mexico
34	Utah
34	West Virginia
39	Hawaii
39	Idaho
39	Maine
39	New Hampshire
39	Rhode Island
44	Alaska
44	Delaware
44	Montana
44	North Dakota
44	South Dakota
44	Vermont
44	Wyoming

Note: Ties in ranking reflect ties in actual values.

D-2 Members of State Legislatures, 2002

State	Senate members	House members	Total members	Rank by total members
Alabama	35	105	140	28
Alaska	20	40	60	49
Arizona	30	60	90	43
Arkansas	35	100	135	31
California	40	80	120	36
Colorado	35	65	100	42
Connecticut	36	151	187	9
Delaware	21	41	62	48
Florida	40	120	160	18
Georgia	56	180	236	3
Hawaii	25	51	76	46
Idaho	35	70	105	39
Illinois	59	118	177	13
Indiana	50	100	150	19
Iowa	50	100	150	19
Kansas	40	125	165	17
Kentucky	38	100	138	30
Louisiana	39	105	144	27
Maine	35	151	186	10
Maryland	47	141	188	8
Massachusetts	40	160	200	6
Michigan	38	110	148	24
Minnesota	67	134	201	5
Mississippi	52	122	174	14
Missouri	34	163	197	7
Montana	50	100	150	19
Nebraska	49	n/a	49	50
Nevada	21	42	63	47
New Hampshire	24	400	424	1
New Jersey	40	80	120	36
New Mexico	42	70	112	38
New York	61	150	211	4
North Carolina	50	120	170	15
North Dakota	49	98	147	25
Ohio	33	99	132	33
Oklahoma	48	101	149	23
Oregon	30	60	90	43
Pennsylvania	50	203	253	2
Rhode Island	50	100	150	19
South Carolina	46	124	170	15
South Dakota	35	70	105	40
Tennessee	33	99	132	33
Texas	31	150	181	11
Utah	29	75	104	41
Vermont	30	150	180	12
Virginia	40	100	140	28
Washington	49	98	147	25
West Virginia	34	100	134	32
Wisconsin	33	99	132	33
Wyoming	30	60	90	43
50 States	1,984	5,440	7,424	
DC	n/a	n/a	n/a	
United States	1,984	5,440	7,424	

Rank in order by total members

1	New Hampshire
2	Pennsylvania
3	Georgia
4	New York
5	Minnesota
6	Massachusetts
7	Missouri
8	Maryland
9	Connecticut
10	Maine
11	Texas
12	Vermont
13	Illinois
14	Mississippi
15	North Carolina
15	South Carolina
17	Kansas
18	Florida
19	Indiana
19	Iowa
19	Montana
19	Rhode Island
23	Oklahoma
24	Michigan
25	North Dakota
25	Washington
27	Louisiana
28	Alabama
28	Virginia
30	Kentucky
31	Arkansas
32	West Virginia
33	Ohio
33	Tennessee
33	Wisconsin
36	California
36	New Jersey
38	New Mexico
39	Idaho
40	South Dakota
41	Utah
42	Colorado
43	Arizona
43	Oregon
43	Wyoming
46	Hawaii
47	Nevada
48	Delaware
49	Alaska
50	Nebraska

Note: Ties in ranking reflect ties in actual values.

D-3 State Legislators Per Million Population, 2002

State	Legislators per million population	Rank
Alabama	31	30
Alaska	96	9
Arizona	18	42
Arkansas	50	19
California	4	50
Colorado	23	37
Connecticut	55	17
Delaware	79	11
Florida	10	48
Georgia	29	31
Hawaii	63	13
Idaho	81	10
Illinois	14	45
Indiana	25	35
Iowa	51	18
Kansas	61	15
Kentucky	34	26
Louisiana	32	27
Maine	146	6
Maryland	35	24
Massachusetts	32	29
Michigan	15	43
Minnesota	41	23
Mississippi	61	16
Missouri	35	25
Montana	166	5
Nebraska	29	32
Nevada	32	28
New Hampshire	343	1
New Jersey	14	44
New Mexico	62	14
New York	11	47
North Carolina	21	39
North Dakota	229	3
Ohio	12	46
Oklahoma	43	21
Oregon	26	33
Pennsylvania	21	40
Rhode Island	143	7
South Carolina	42	22
South Dakota	139	8
Tennessee	23	38
Texas	9	49
Utah	47	20
Vermont	296	2
Virginia	20	41
Washington	25	34
West Virginia	74	12
Wisconsin	25	36
Wyoming	182	4
50 States	26	
DC	n/a	
United States	26	

Rank in order per million population

1 New Hampshire
2 Vermont
3 North Dakota
4 Wyoming
5 Montana
6 Maine
7 Rhode Island
8 South Dakota
9 Alaska
10 Idaho
11 Delaware
12 West Virginia
13 Hawaii
14 New Mexico
15 Kansas
16 Mississippi
17 Connecticut
18 Iowa
19 Arkansas
20 Utah
21 Oklahoma
22 South Carolina
23 Minnesota
24 Maryland
25 Missouri
26 Kentucky
27 Louisiana
28 Nevada
29 Massachusetts
30 Alabama
31 Georgia
32 Nebraska
33 Oregon
34 Washington
35 Indiana
36 Wisconsin
37 Colorado
38 Tennessee
39 North Carolina
40 Pennsylvania
41 Virginia
42 Arizona
43 Michigan
44 New Jersey
45 Illinois
46 Ohio
47 New York
48 Florida
49 Texas
50 California

Note: Numbers that appear to be identical are rounded and vary slightly in actual value. The rankings reflect the actual values before rounding. See the introduction for more details.

D-4 Units of Government, 1997

State	Number of government units	Units per 10,000 population	Rank per 10,000 population
Alabama	1,132	2.6	32
Alaska	176	2.9	30
Arizona	638	1.4	42
Arkansas	1,517	6.0	13
California	4,608	1.4	40
Colorado	1,870	4.8	20
Connecticut	584	1.8	37
Delaware	337	4.6	22
Florida	1,082	0.7	48
Georgia	1,345	1.8	36
Hawaii	20	0.2	50
Idaho	1,148	9.5	8
Illinois	6,836	5.7	15
Indiana	3,199	5.5	16
Iowa	1,877	6.6	11
Kansas	3,951	15.2	4
Kentucky	1,367	3.5	25
Louisiana	468	1.1	46
Maine	833	6.7	10
Maryland	421	0.8	47
Massachusetts	862	1.4	41
Michigan	2,776	2.8	31
Minnesota	3,502	7.5	9
Mississippi	937	3.4	26
Missouri	3,417	6.3	12
Montana	1,145	13.0	6
Nebraska	2,895	17.5	3
Nevada	206	1.2	44
New Hampshire	576	4.9	19
New Jersey	1,422	1.8	38
New Mexico	882	5.1	18
New York	3,414	1.9	35
North Carolina	953	1.3	43
North Dakota	2,759	43.0	1
Ohio	3,598	3.2	29
Oklahoma	1,800	5.4	17
Oregon	1,494	4.6	21
Pennsylvania	5,071	4.2	23
Rhode Island	120	1.2	45
South Carolina	717	1.9	34
South Dakota	1,811	24.5	2
Tennessee	941	1.8	39
Texas	4,701	2.4	33
Utah	684	3.3	27
Vermont	692	11.8	7
Virginia	484	0.7	49
Washington	1,813	3.2	28
West Virginia	705	3.9	24
Wisconsin	3,060	5.9	14
Wyoming	655	13.6	5
50 States	87,501	3.3	
DC	2	0.0	
United States*	87,504	3.3	

*Due to rounding or data sources, the 50-state total plus D.C. may not equal the U.S. total. Please see introduction.

Rank in order per 10,000 population	
1	North Dakota
2	South Dakota
3	Nebraska
4	Kansas
5	Wyoming
6	Montana
7	Vermont
8	Idaho
9	Minnesota
10	Maine
11	Iowa
12	Missouri
13	Arkansas
14	Wisconsin
15	Illinois
16	Indiana
17	Oklahoma
18	New Mexico
19	New Hampshire
20	Colorado
21	Oregon
22	Delaware
23	Pennsylvania
24	West Virginia
25	Kentucky
26	Mississippi
27	Utah
28	Washington
29	Ohio
30	Alaska
31	Michigan
32	Alabama
33	Texas
34	South Carolina
35	New York
36	Georgia
37	Connecticut
38	New Jersey
39	Tennessee
40	California
41	Massachusetts
42	Arizona
43	North Carolina
44	Nevada
45	Rhode Island
46	Louisiana
47	Maryland
48	Florida
49	Virginia
50	Hawaii

Note: Numbers that appear to be identical are rounded and vary slightly in actual value. The rankings reflect the actual values before rounding. See the introduction for more details.

D-5 State Legislator Compensation, 2001

State	Salary $	Per diem during session $	Rank by salary
Alabama	1,040	2,280/month	48
Alaska	24,012	161/day	20
Arizona	24,000	35-60/day	21
Arkansas	12,769	95/day	32
California	99,000	121/day	1
Colorado	30,000	45-99/day	17
Connecticut	28,000	0	18
Delaware	33,400	0	11
Florida	27,900	99/day	19
Georgia	16,200	128/day	26
Hawaii	32,000	10-80/day	13
Idaho	15,646	38-99/day	27
Illinois	55,788	85/day	5
Indiana	11,600	112/day	37
Iowa	20,758	65-86/day	22
Kansas	9,173	85/day	42
Kentucky	12,654	93.50/day	33
Louisiana	16,800	103/day	24
Maine	10,815	70/day	39
Maryland	31,509	126/day	15
Massachusetts	50,123	10-100/day	7
Michigan	77,400	12,000/year	3
Minnesota	31,140	66-56/day	16
Mississippi	10,000	85/day	41
Missouri	31,561	68/day	14
Montana	7,830	87.25/day	43
Nebraska	12,000	30-85/day	35
Nevada	15,600	federal rate	28
New Hampshire	100	0	49
New Jersey	35,000	0	10
New Mexico	0	136/day	50
New York	79,500	varies	2
North Carolina	13,951	104/day	31
North Dakota	12,210	900/month	34
Ohio	51,674	0	6
Oklahoma	38,400	103/day	9
Oregon	15,396	85/day	29
Pennsylvania	61,890	124/day	4
Rhode Island	11,236	0	38
South Carolina	10,400	95/day	40
South Dakota	6,000	110/day	46
Tennessee	16,500	124/day	25
Texas	7,200	124/day	44
Utah	5,400	117/day	47
Vermont	11,639	87-32/day	36
Virginia	18,000	115/day	23
Washington	32,064	82/day	12
West Virginia	15,000	85/day	30
Wisconsin	44,333	88/day	8
Wyoming	6,500	80/day	45
50 States (average)	24,822	n/a	
DC	92,500	0	
United States (average)	26,149	n/a	

Rank in order by salary

1 California
2 New York
3 Michigan
4 Pennsylvania
5 Illinois
6 Ohio
7 Massachusetts
8 Wisconsin
9 Oklahoma
10 New Jersey
11 Delaware
12 Washington
13 Hawaii
14 Missouri
15 Maryland
16 Minnesota
17 Colorado
18 Connecticut
19 Florida
20 Alaska
21 Arizona
22 Iowa
23 Virginia
24 Louisiana
25 Tennessee
26 Georgia
27 Idaho
28 Nevada
29 Oregon
30 West Virginia
31 North Carolina
32 Arkansas
33 Kentucky
34 North Dakota
35 Nebraska
36 Vermont
37 Indiana
38 Rhode Island
39 Maine
40 South Carolina
41 Mississippi
42 Kansas
43 Montana
44 Texas
45 Wyoming
46 South Dakota
47 Utah
48 Alabama
49 New Hampshire
50 New Mexico

D-6 Percentage of Legislators Who Are Female, 2001

State	Percentage of female legislators	Rank
Alabama	7.9	50
Alaska	21.7	30
Arizona	35.6	2
Arkansas	13.3	45
California	28.3	13
Colorado	34.0	4
Connecticut	29.9	9
Delaware	25.8	16
Florida	23.8	21
Georgia	20.8	31
Hawaii	25.0	17
Idaho	24.8	18
Illinois	26.6	15
Indiana	17.3	36
Iowa	22.0	27
Kansas	32.7	6
Kentucky	10.9	47
Louisiana	16.0	39
Maine	30.1	8
Maryland	29.3	10
Massachusetts	24.5	19
Michigan	22.3	25
Minnesota	28.9	12
Mississippi	12.6	46
Missouri	23.4	22
Montana	22.7	23
Nebraska	18.4	35
Nevada	34.9	3
New Hampshire	29.2	11
New Jersey	15.0	43
New Mexico	31.3	7
New York	21.8	29
North Carolina	18.8	32
North Dakota	17.0	37
Ohio	22.0	27
Oklahoma	10.1	49
Oregon	33.3	5
Pennsylvania	13.4	44
Rhode Island	22.7	23
South Carolina	10.6	48
South Dakota	15.2	42
Tennessee	15.9	40
Texas	18.8	32
Utah	22.1	26
Vermont	27.8	14
Virginia	16.4	38
Washington	38.8	1
West Virginia	18.7	34
Wisconsin	24.2	20
Wyoming	15.6	41
50 States	22.4	
DC	n/a	
United States	22.4	

Rank in order by percentage	
1	Washington
2	Arizona
3	Nevada
4	Colorado
5	Oregon
6	Kansas
7	New Mexico
8	Maine
9	Connecticut
10	Maryland
11	New Hampshire
12	Minnesota
13	California
14	Vermont
15	Illinois
16	Delaware
17	Hawaii
18	Idaho
19	Massachusetts
20	Wisconsin
21	Florida
22	Missouri
23	Montana
23	Rhode Island
25	Michigan
26	Utah
27	Iowa
27	Ohio
29	New York
30	Alaska
31	Georgia
32	North Carolina
32	Texas
34	West Virginia
35	Nebraska
36	Indiana
37	North Dakota
38	Virginia
39	Louisiana
40	Tennessee
41	Wyoming
42	South Dakota
43	New Jersey
44	Pennsylvania
45	Arkansas
46	Mississippi
47	Kentucky
48	South Carolina
49	Oklahoma
50	Alabama

Note: Ties in ranking reflect ties in actual values.

D-7 Turnover in Legislatures, Pre-election 2001

State	Percentage of new legislators	Rank
Alabama	0.0	45
Alaska	26.7	14
Arizona	41.1	4
Arkansas	34.1	10
California	35.0	8
Colorado	36.0	6
Connecticut	12.3	29
Delaware	4.8	43
Florida	46.3	2
Georgia	11.9	32
Hawaii	19.7	18
Idaho	14.3	23
Illinois	6.8	40
Indiana	6.0	41
Iowa	17.3	20
Kansas	23.6	15
Kentucky	8.7	37
Louisiana	0.0	45
Maine	33.3	11
Maryland	0.0	45
Massachusetts	9.5	35
Michigan	14.2	25
Minnesota	15.4	22
Mississippi	0.0	45
Missouri	22.8	16
Montana	41.3	3
Nebraska	12.2	30
Nevada	3.2	44
New Hampshire	34.4	9
New Jersey	0.0	45
New Mexico	22.3	17
New York	8.5	38
North Carolina	12.9	28
North Dakota	16.3	21
Ohio	39.4	5
Oklahoma	10.7	33
Oregon	35.6	7
Pennsylvania	7.9	39
Rhode Island	12.0	31
South Carolina	14.1	26
South Dakota	48.6	1
Tennessee	9.1	36
Texas	5.5	42
Utah	27.9	13
Vermont	30.6	12
Virginia	0.0	45
Washington	14.3	23
West Virginia	19.4	19
Wisconsin	9.8	34
Wyoming	13.3	27
50 States	17.6	
DC	n/a	
United States	17.6	

Rank in order by percentage	
1	South Dakota
2	Florida
3	Montana
4	Arizona
5	Ohio
6	Colorado
7	Oregon
8	California
9	New Hampshire
10	Arkansas
11	Maine
12	Vermont
13	Utah
14	Alaska
15	Kansas
16	Missouri
17	New Mexico
18	Hawaii
19	West Virginia
20	Iowa
21	North Dakota
22	Minnesota
23	Idaho
23	Washington
25	Michigan
26	South Carolina
27	Wyoming
28	North Carolina
29	Connecticut
30	Nebraska
31	Rhode Island
32	Georgia
33	Oklahoma
34	Wisconsin
35	Massachusetts
36	Tennessee
37	Kentucky
38	New York
39	Pennsylvania
40	Illinois
41	Indiana
42	Texas
43	Delaware
44	Nevada
45	Alabama
45	Louisiana
45	Maryland
45	Mississippi
45	New Jersey
45	Virginia

Note: Ties in ranking reflect ties in actual values.

D-8 Term Limits (in years), 2001

State	Consecutive term limits Governor	Consecutive term limits House	Consecutive term limits Senate	Rank by House members
Alabama	8	n/a	n/a	n/a
Alaska	8	n/a	n/a	n/a
Arizona	8	8	8	6
Arkansas	8	6	8	15
California	8	6	8	15
Colorado	8	8	8	6
Connecticut	n/a	n/a	n/a	n/a
Delaware	8	n/a	n/a	n/a
Florida	8	8	8	6
Georgia	8	n/a	n/a	n/a
Hawaii	8	n/a	n/a	n/a
Idaho	8	8	8	6
Illinois	n/a	n/a	n/a	n/a
Indiana	8	n/a	n/a	n/a
Iowa	n/a	n/a	n/a	n/a
Kansas	8	n/a	n/a	n/a
Kentucky	8	n/a	n/a	n/a
Louisiana	8	12	12	1
Maine	8	8	8	6
Maryland	8	n/a	n/a	n/a
Massachusetts	n/a	n/a	n/a	n/a
Michigan	8	6	8	15
Minnesota	n/a	n/a	n/a	n/a
Mississippi	8	n/a	n/a	n/a
Missouri	8	8	8	6
Montana	8	8	8	6
Nebraska	8	n/a	8	n/a
Nevada	8	12	12	1
New Hampshire	n/a	n/a	n/a	n/a
New Jersey	8	n/a	n/a	n/a
New Mexico	8	n/a	n/a	n/a
New York	n/a	n/a	n/a	n/a
North Carolina	8	n/a	n/a	n/a
North Dakota	n/a	n/a	n/a	n/a
Ohio	8	8	8	6
Oklahoma	8	12	12	1
Oregon	8	6	8	15
Pennsylvania	8	n/a	n/a	n/a
Rhode Island	8	n/a	n/a	n/a
South Carolina	8	n/a	n/a	n/a
South Dakota	8	8	8	6
Tennessee	8	n/a	n/a	n/a
Texas	n/a	n/a	n/a	n/a
Utah	12	12	12	1
Vermont	n/a	n/a	n/a	n/a
Virginia	4	n/a	n/a	n/a
Washington	n/a	n/a	n/a	n/a
West Virginia	8	n/a	n/a	n/a
Wisconsin	n/a	n/a	n/a	n/a
Wyoming	8	12	12	1
50 States	n/a	n/a	n/a	
DC	n/a	n/a	n/a	
United States	n/a	n/a	n/a	

Rank in order by House members	
1	Louisiana
1	Nevada
1	Oklahoma
1	Utah
1	Wyoming
6	Arizona
6	Colorado
6	Florida
6	Idaho
6	Maine
6	Missouri
6	Montana
6	Ohio
6	South Dakota
15	Arkansas
15	California
15	Michigan
15	Oregon

Note: Ties in ranking reflect ties in actual values.

D-9 Legislative Session Length, 2002

State	Legislative length in calendar days #	Rank
Alabama	104	15
Alaska	120	7
Arizona	97	17
Arkansas	no regular session	n/a
California	236	1
Colorado	119	8
Connecticut	91	21
Delaware	173	3
Florida	59	28
Georgia	60	27
Hawaii	111	12
Idaho	73	25
Illinois	no limit	n/a
Indiana	59	28
Iowa	97	17
Kansas	113	11
Kentucky	97	17
Louisiana	44	33
Maine	105	14
Maryland	89	23
Massachusetts	no limit	n/a
Michigan	no limit	n/a
Minnesota	111	12
Mississippi	89	23
Missouri	141	6
Montana	no regular session	n/a
Nebraska	96	20
Nevada	no regular session	n/a
New Hampshire	180	2
New Jersey	no limit	n/a
New Mexico	29	34
New York	no limit	n/a
North Carolina	91	21
North Dakota	no regular session	n/a
Ohio	no limit	n/a
Oklahoma	115	10
Oregon	no regular session	n/a
Pennsylvania	no limit	n/a
Rhode Island	171	4
South Carolina	149	5
South Dakota	66	26
Tennessee	103	16
Texas	no regular session	n/a
Utah	28	35
Vermont	119	8
Virginia	59	28
Washington	59	28
West Virginia	59	28
Wisconsin	no limit	n/a
Wyoming	25	36
50 States	n/a	
DC	no limit	
United States	n/a	

Rank in order by #	
1	California
2	New Hampshire
3	Delaware
4	Rhode Island
5	South Carolina
6	Missouri
7	Alaska
8	Colorado
8	Vermont
10	Oklahoma
11	Kansas
12	Hawaii
12	Minnesota
14	Maine
15	Alabama
16	Tennessee
17	Arizona
17	Iowa
17	Kentucky
20	Nebraska
21	Connecticut
21	North Carolina
23	Maryland
23	Mississippi
25	Idaho
26	South Dakota
27	Georgia
28	Florida
28	Indiana
28	Virginia
28	Washington
28	West Virginia
33	Louisiana
34	New Mexico
35	Utah
36	Wyoming

Note: Ties in ranking reflect ties in actual values.

D-10 Party Control of State Legislatures, 2002

State	Democrats in combined house	Republicans in combined house	Legislative control	Percentage of members Democratic	Rank by percentage Democratic
Alabama	92	48	D	65.7	9
Alaska	19	41	R	31.7	45
Arizona	39	51	S	43.3	35
Arkansas	97	38	D	71.9	5
California	75	43	D	62.5	11
Colorado	45	55	S	45.0	33
Connecticut	121	66	D	64.7	10
Delaware	28	34	S	45.2	32
Florida	58	102	R	36.3	41
Georgia	137	98	D	58.1	15
Hawaii	54	22	D	71.1	6
Idaho	12	93	R	11.4	49
Illinois	89	88	S	50.3	26
Indiana	71	79	S	47.3	27
Iowa	64	86	R	42.7	37
Kansas	56	109	R	33.9	43
Kentucky	84	54	S	60.9	12
Louisiana	96	45	D	66.7	8
Maine	106	78	S	57.0	19
Maryland	140	48	D	74.5	4
Massachusetts	169	29	D	84.5	2
Michigan	67	80	R	45.3	31
Minnesota	104	96	S	51.7	23
Mississippi	119	51	D	68.4	7
Missouri	102	92	S	51.8	22
Montana	61	89	R	40.7	38
Nebraska	n/a	n/a	n/a	n/a	n/a
Nevada	36	27	S	57.1	17
New Hampshire	151	269	R	35.6	42
New Jersey	64	56	S	53.3	21
New Mexico	66	46	D	58.9	13
New York	124	87	S	58.8	14
North Carolina	97	73	D	57.1	18
North Dakota	46	101	R	31.3	46
Ohio	52	80	R	39.4	39
Oklahoma	82	67	D	55.0	20
Oregon	41	48	R	45.6	30
Pennsylvania	119	132	R	47.0	28
Rhode Island	128	21	D	85.3	1
South Carolina	76	94	R	44.7	34
South Dakota	31	74	R	29.5	47
Tennessee	76	56	D	57.6	16
Texas	93	88	S	51.4	24
Utah	33	71	R	31.7	44
Vermont	78	97	S	43.3	36
Virginia	52	85	R	37.1	40
Washington	75	72	D	51.0	25
West Virginia	103	31	D	76.9	3
Wisconsin	61	71	S	46.2	29
Wyoming	24	66	R	26.7	48
50 States	3,813	3,527	17 D, 17 R, 15 S	51.4	
DC	0	0		n/a	
United States	3,818	3,532		51.4	

Rank in order by percentage Democratic

1 Rhode Island
2 Massachusetts
3 West Virginia
4 Maryland
5 Arkansas
6 Hawaii
7 Mississippi
8 Louisiana
9 Alabama
10 Connecticut
11 California
12 Kentucky
13 New Mexico
14 New York
15 Georgia
16 Tennessee
17 Nevada
18 North Carolina
19 Maine
20 Oklahoma
21 New Jersey
22 Missouri
23 Minnesota
24 Texas
25 Washington
26 Illinois
27 Indiana
28 Pennsylvania
29 Wisconsin
30 Oregon
31 Michigan
32 Delaware
33 Colorado
34 South Carolina
35 Arizona
36 Vermont
37 Iowa
38 Montana
39 Ohio
40 Virginia
41 Florida
42 New Hampshire
43 Kansas
44 Utah
45 Alaska
46 North Dakota
47 South Dakota
48 Wyoming
49 Idaho

Note: Numbers that appear to be identical are rounded and vary slightly in actual value. The rankings reflect the actual values before rounding. See the introduction for more details.

D-11 Governor's Power Rating, 2001

State	Power rating	Rank
Alabama	3.2	36
Alaska	3.8	11
Arizona	3.6	21
Arkansas	3.1	39
California	3.5	28
Colorado	3.8	11
Connecticut	3.6	21
Delaware	3.5	28
Florida	3.6	21
Georgia	3.2	36
Hawaii	3.9	6
Idaho	3.5	28
Illinois	3.7	16
Indiana	2.9	44
Iowa	3.8	11
Kansas	3.7	16
Kentucky	3.7	16
Louisiana	3.1	39
Maine	3.1	39
Maryland	4.3	1
Massachusetts	3.6	21
Michigan	3.9	6
Minnesota	3.4	31
Mississippi	3.3	33
Missouri	3.4	31
Montana	3.7	16
Nebraska	3.8	11
Nevada	3.0	42
New Hampshire	2.8	46
New Jersey	3.9	6
New Mexico	3.3	33
New York	4.1	3
North Carolina	2.9	44
North Dakota	3.9	6
Ohio	3.9	6
Oklahoma	2.7	48
Oregon	3.2	36
Pennsylvania	4.0	4
Rhode Island	2.6	50
South Carolina	2.8	46
South Dakota	3.8	11
Tennessee	3.6	21
Texas	3.0	42
Utah	4.0	4
Vermont	2.7	48
Virginia	3.3	33
Washington	3.6	21
West Virginia	4.3	1
Wisconsin	3.7	16
Wyoming	3.6	21
50 States	3.5	
DC	n/a	
United States	3.5	

Rank in order by rating

1	Maryland
1	West Virginia
3	New York
4	Pennsylvania
4	Utah
6	Hawaii
6	Michigan
6	New Jersey
6	North Dakota
6	Ohio
11	Alaska
11	Colorado
11	Iowa
11	Nebraska
11	South Dakota
16	Illinois
16	Kansas
16	Kentucky
16	Montana
16	Wisconsin
21	Arizona
21	Connecticut
21	Florida
21	Massachusetts
21	Tennessee
21	Washington
21	Wyoming
28	California
28	Delaware
28	Idaho
31	Minnesota
31	Missouri
33	Mississippi
33	New Mexico
33	Virginia
36	Alabama
36	Georgia
36	Oregon
39	Arkansas
39	Louisiana
39	Maine
42	Nevada
42	Texas
44	Indiana
44	North Carolina
46	New Hampshire
46	South Carolina
48	Oklahoma
48	Vermont
50	Rhode Island

Note: Ties in ranking reflect ties in actual values.

D-12 Number of Statewide Elected Officials, 2000

State	Elected officials #	Rank
Alabama	9	4
Alaska	2	45
Arizona	6	21
Arkansas	6	21
California	8	9
Colorado	5	35
Connecticut	6	21
Delaware	6	21
Florida	10	2
Georgia	9	4
Hawaii	2	45
Idaho	7	16
Illinois	9	4
Indiana	8	9
Iowa	7	16
Kansas	7	16
Kentucky	8	9
Louisiana	8	9
Maine	1	48
Maryland	4	40
Massachusetts	6	21
Michigan	4	40
Minnesota	4	40
Mississippi	8	9
Missouri	6	21
Montana	7	16
Nebraska	6	21
Nevada	6	21
New Hampshire	1	48
New Jersey	1	48
New Mexico	7	16
New York	4	40
North Carolina	10	2
North Dakota	12	1
Ohio	5	35
Oklahoma	8	9
Oregon	6	21
Pennsylvania	5	35
Rhode Island	5	35
South Carolina	9	4
South Dakota	6	21
Tennessee	2	45
Texas	6	21
Utah	5	35
Vermont	6	21
Virginia	3	44
Washington	9	4
West Virginia	6	21
Wisconsin	6	21
Wyoming	8	9
50 States	n/a	
DC	n/a	
United States	n/a	

Rank in order by #	
1	North Dakota
2	Florida
2	North Carolina
4	Alabama
4	Georgia
4	Illinois
4	South Carolina
4	Washington
9	California
9	Indiana
9	Kentucky
9	Louisiana
9	Mississippi
9	Oklahoma
9	Wyoming
16	Idaho
16	Iowa
16	Kansas
16	Montana
16	New Mexico
21	Arizona
21	Arkansas
21	Connecticut
21	Delaware
21	Massachusetts
21	Missouri
21	Nebraska
21	Nevada
21	Oregon
21	South Dakota
21	Texas
21	Vermont
21	West Virginia
21	Wisconsin
35	Colorado
35	Ohio
35	Pennsylvania
35	Rhode Island
35	Utah
40	Maryland
40	Michigan
40	Minnesota
40	New York
44	Virginia
45	Alaska
45	Hawaii
45	Tennessee
48	Maine
48	New Hampshire
48	New Jersey

Note: Ties in ranking reflect ties in actual values.

D-13 State and Local Government Employees, 2000

State	Government employees #	Per 10,000 population	Rank per 10,000 population
Alabama	261,297	588	12
Alaska	48,240	769	2
Arizona	246,771	481	47
Arkansas	145,191	543	28
California	1,676,902	495	46
Colorado	230,059	535	30
Connecticut	176,373	518	39
Delaware	44,814	572	15
Florida	765,298	479	48
Georgia	453,736	554	23
Hawaii	69,078	570	17
Idaho	73,632	569	18
Illinois	620,353	500	44
Indiana	314,472	517	41
Iowa	175,887	601	9
Kansas	170,635	635	5
Kentucky	223,270	552	24
Louisiana	279,354	625	7
Maine	72,017	565	21
Maryland	273,939	517	40
Massachusetts	327,848	516	42
Michigan	492,461	496	45
Minnesota	279,334	568	19
Mississippi	188,259	662	3
Missouri	299,414	535	29
Montana	51,588	572	16
Nebraska	107,625	629	6
Nevada	83,896	420	50
New Hampshire	64,461	522	36
New Jersey	449,099	534	31
New Mexico	117,469	646	4
New York	1,174,570	619	8
North Carolina	451,010	560	22
North Dakota	38,305	596	11
Ohio	595,404	524	35
Oklahoma	198,843	576	14
Oregon	177,781	520	37
Pennsylvania	537,573	438	49
Rhode Island	55,714	531	32
South Carolina	233,796	583	13
South Dakota	41,473	549	25
Tennessee	299,002	526	34
Texas	1,178,291	565	20
Utah	122,159	547	27
Vermont	36,323	597	10
Virginia	387,644	548	26
Washington	305,466	518	38
West Virginia	92,954	514	43
Wisconsin	283,490	529	33
Wyoming	39,798	806	1
50 States	15,032,368	535	
DC	45,335	792	
United States	15,077,703	536	

Rank in order by 10,000 population

1	Wyoming
2	Alaska
3	Mississippi
4	New Mexico
5	Kansas
6	Nebraska
7	Louisiana
8	New York
9	Iowa
10	Vermont
11	North Dakota
12	Alabama
13	South Carolina
14	Oklahoma
15	Delaware
16	Montana
17	Hawaii
18	Idaho
19	Minnesota
20	Texas
21	Maine
22	North Carolina
23	Georgia
24	Kentucky
25	South Dakota
26	Virginia
27	Utah
28	Arkansas
29	Missouri
30	Colorado
31	New Jersey
32	Rhode Island
33	Wisconsin
34	Tennessee
35	Ohio
36	New Hampshire
37	Oregon
38	Washington
39	Connecticut
40	Maryland
41	Indiana
42	Massachusetts
43	West Virginia
44	Illinois
45	Michigan
46	California
47	Arizona
48	Florida
49	Pennsylvania
50	Nevada

Note: Numbers that appear to be identical are rounded and vary slightly in actual value. The rankings reflect the actual values before rounding. See the introduction for more details.

D-14 Average Salaries of State and Local Government Employees, 2000

State	Average salary $	Rank
Alabama	29,781	45
Alaska	44,014	5
Arizona	34,174	23
Arkansas	28,076	49
California	47,125	1
Colorado	37,481	16
Connecticut	44,529	4
Delaware	37,065	18
Florida	34,300	22
Georgia	32,051	30
Hawaii	35,747	20
Idaho	30,229	43
Illinois	37,775	14
Indiana	32,351	27
Iowa	33,699	24
Kansas	30,396	40
Kentucky	29,805	44
Louisiana	28,877	47
Maine	30,920	36
Maryland	40,234	10
Massachusetts	40,538	9
Michigan	40,060	11
Minnesota	37,738	15
Mississippi	26,838	50
Missouri	31,045	33
Montana	30,645	38
Nebraska	31,032	35
Nevada	42,243	6
New Hampshire	33,331	25
New Jersey	45,977	2
New Mexico	30,661	37
New York	45,391	3
North Carolina	32,677	26
North Dakota	31,819	32
Ohio	36,087	19
Oklahoma	28,992	46
Oregon	37,471	17
Pennsylvania	38,430	12
Rhode Island	41,780	7
South Carolina	30,255	42
South Dakota	28,449	48
Tennessee	31,039	34
Texas	32,128	29
Utah	32,021	31
Vermont	32,178	28
Virginia	34,687	21
Washington	41,580	8
West Virginia	30,468	39
Wisconsin	37,797	13
Wyoming	30,277	41
50 States	37,124	
DC	46,530	
United States	37,153	

Rank in order by $	
1	California
2	New Jersey
3	New York
4	Connecticut
5	Alaska
6	Nevada
7	Rhode Island
8	Washington
9	Massachusetts
10	Maryland
11	Michigan
12	Pennsylvania
13	Wisconsin
14	Illinois
15	Minnesota
16	Colorado
17	Oregon
18	Delaware
19	Ohio
20	Hawaii
21	Virginia
22	Florida
23	Arizona
24	Iowa
25	New Hampshire
26	North Carolina
27	Indiana
28	Vermont
29	Texas
30	Georgia
31	Utah
32	North Dakota
33	Missouri
34	Tennessee
35	Nebraska
36	Maine
37	New Mexico
38	Montana
39	West Virginia
40	Kansas
41	Wyoming
42	South Carolina
43	Idaho
44	Kentucky
45	Alabama
46	Oklahoma
47	Louisiana
48	South Dakota
49	Arkansas
50	Mississippi

D-15 Local Employment, 2000

State	Number of local employees	Local share of state and local employees %	Rank by percentage
Alabama	181,666	69.5	27
Alaska	25,355	52.6	48
Arizona	181,925	73.7	10
Arkansas	96,400	66.4	36
California	1,321,575	78.8	2
Colorado	164,333	71.4	20
Connecticut	110,553	62.7	43
Delaware	21,071	47.0	49
Florida	580,128	75.8	7
Georgia	333,708	73.5	12
Hawaii	14,246	20.6	50
Idaho	50,985	69.2	30
Illinois	492,692	79.4	1
Indiana	231,877	73.7	9
Iowa	120,687	68.6	31
Kansas	128,047	75.0	8
Kentucky	149,133	66.8	34
Louisiana	184,558	66.1	38
Maine	51,449	71.4	19
Maryland	182,452	66.6	35
Massachusetts	232,266	70.8	23
Michigan	350,570	71.2	21
Minnesota	205,913	73.7	11
Mississippi	132,718	70.5	24
Missouri	207,989	69.5	28
Montana	33,668	65.3	40
Nebraska	77,828	72.3	16
Nevada	61,452	73.2	13
New Hampshire	45,685	70.9	22
New Jersey	315,973	70.4	25
New Mexico	69,656	59.3	46
New York	923,596	78.6	3
North Carolina	327,708	72.7	15
North Dakota	22,533	58.8	47
Ohio	459,058	77.1	6
Oklahoma	134,424	67.6	33
Oregon	124,438	70.0	26
Pennsylvania	387,852	72.1	17
Rhode Island	36,145	64.9	41
South Carolina	155,099	66.3	37
South Dakota	28,097	67.7	32
Tennessee	217,927	72.9	14
Texas	909,367	77.2	5
Utah	72,828	59.6	45
Vermont	22,691	62.5	44
Virginia	269,056	69.4	29
Washington	192,990	63.2	42
West Virginia	60,920	65.5	39
Wisconsin	219,793	77.5	4
Wyoming	28,594	71.8	18
50 States	10,949,674	72.8	
DC	45,335	100.0	
United States	10,995,009	72.9	

Rank in order by percentage

1 Illinois
2 California
3 New York
4 Wisconsin
5 Texas
6 Ohio
7 Florida
8 Kansas
9 Indiana
10 Arizona
11 Minnesota
12 Georgia
13 Nevada
14 Tennessee
15 North Carolina
16 Nebraska
17 Pennsylvania
18 Wyoming
19 Maine
20 Colorado
21 Michigan
22 New Hampshire
23 Massachusetts
24 Mississippi
25 New Jersey
26 Oregon
27 Alabama
28 Missouri
29 Virginia
30 Idaho
31 Iowa
32 South Dakota
33 Oklahoma
34 Kentucky
35 Maryland
36 Arkansas
37 South Carolina
38 Louisiana
39 West Virginia
40 Montana
41 Rhode Island
42 Washington
43 Connecticut
44 Vermont
45 Utah
46 New Mexico
47 North Dakota
48 Alaska
49 Delaware
50 Hawaii

Note: Numbers that appear to be identical are rounded and vary slightly in actual value. The rankings reflect the actual values before rounding. See the introduction for more details.

D-16 Local Spending Accountability, FY 1999

State	Percentage of local spending raised by local government	Rank
Alabama	56.0	41
Alaska	58.5	34
Arizona	57.9	37
Arkansas	56.8	39
California	53.8	45
Colorado	75.9	3
Connecticut	68.6	13
Delaware	51.7	46
Florida	70.2	11
Georgia	70.9	8
Hawaii	82.2	2
Idaho	59.0	32
Illinois	66.2	18
Indiana	64.3	23
Iowa	62.1	28
Kansas	64.8	22
Kentucky	56.0	40
Louisiana	63.2	25
Maine	70.6	9
Maryland	71.6	6
Massachusetts	61.5	29
Michigan	47.7	48
Minnesota	55.3	42
Mississippi	53.9	44
Missouri	65.8	19
Montana	66.3	17
Nebraska	72.8	4
Nevada	58.2	36
New Hampshire	90.2	1
New Jersey	72.4	5
New Mexico	44.9	49
New York	70.4	10
North Carolina	58.7	33
North Dakota	58.2	35
Ohio	65.5	20
Oklahoma	63.5	24
Oregon	57.5	38
Pennsylvania	60.0	31
Rhode Island	71.5	7
South Carolina	67.5	15
South Dakota	68.5	14
Tennessee	62.3	26
Texas	68.9	12
Utah	62.3	27
Vermont	43.4	50
Virginia	65.1	21
Washington	60.1	30
West Virginia	54.9	43
Wisconsin	50.2	47
Wyoming	67.4	16
50 States	62.7	
DC	80.9	
United States	62.8	

Rank in order by percentage	
1	New Hampshire
2	Hawaii
3	Colorado
4	Nebraska
5	New Jersey
6	Maryland
7	Rhode Island
8	Georgia
9	Maine
10	New York
11	Florida
12	Texas
13	Connecticut
14	South Dakota
15	South Carolina
16	Wyoming
17	Montana
18	Illinois
19	Missouri
20	Ohio
21	Virginia
22	Kansas
23	Indiana
24	Oklahoma
25	Louisiana
26	Tennessee
27	Utah
28	Iowa
29	Massachusetts
30	Washington
31	Pennsylvania
32	Idaho
33	North Carolina
34	Alaska
35	North Dakota
36	Nevada
37	Arizona
38	Oregon
39	Arkansas
40	Kentucky
41	Alabama
42	Minnesota
43	West Virginia
44	Mississippi
45	California
46	Delaware
47	Wisconsin
48	Michigan
49	New Mexico
50	Vermont

Note: Numbers that appear to be identical are rounded and vary slightly in actual value. The rankings reflect the actual values before rounding. See the introduction for more details.

D-17 Percentage of Eligible Voters Registered, November 2000

State	Percentage of registered voters	Rank
Alabama	75.9	32
Alaska	110.0	1
Arizona	59.9	48
Arkansas	80.7	25
California	63.2	46
Colorado	74.1	38
Connecticut	75.0	36
Delaware	86.8	15
Florida	74.3	37
Georgia	65.5	44
Hawaii	70.1	41
Idaho	79.1	27
Illinois	79.4	26
Indiana	89.9	9
Iowa	85.1	18
Kansas	81.9	23
Kentucky	85.4	17
Louisiana	83.9	22
Maine	91.2	8
Maryland	69.2	42
Massachusetts	84.4	21
Michigan	93.3	5
Minnesota	92.1	7
Mississippi	84.9	20
Missouri	94.0	3
Montana	104.5	2
Nebraska	87.9	13
Nevada	64.6	45
New Hampshire	94.0	3
New Jersey	75.4	33
New Mexico	77.0	28
New York	81.6	24
North Carolina	88.4	11
North Dakota	n/a	n/a
Ohio	89.4	10
Oklahoma	88.2	12
Oregon	76.8	29
Pennsylvania	85.0	19
Rhode Island	87.0	14
South Carolina	72.5	39
South Dakota	86.8	15
Tennessee	75.4	33
Texas	69.1	43
Utah	76.7	30
Vermont	92.9	6
Virginia	71.6	40
Washington	76.4	31
West Virginia	75.4	33
Wisconsin	n/a	n/a
Wyoming	61.5	47
50 States	n/a	
DC	86.2	
United States	76.0	

Rank in order by percentage	
1	Alaska
2	Montana
3	Missouri
3	New Hampshire
5	Michigan
6	Vermont
7	Minnesota
8	Maine
9	Indiana
10	Ohio
11	North Carolina
12	Oklahoma
13	Nebraska
14	Rhode Island
15	Delaware
15	South Dakota
17	Kentucky
18	Iowa
19	Pennsylvania
20	Mississippi
21	Massachusetts
22	Louisiana
23	Kansas
24	New York
25	Arkansas
26	Illinois
27	Idaho
28	New Mexico
29	Oregon
30	Utah
31	Washington
32	Alabama
33	New Jersey
33	Tennessee
33	West Virginia
36	Connecticut
37	Florida
38	Colorado
39	South Carolina
40	Virginia
41	Hawaii
42	Maryland
43	Texas
44	Georgia
45	Nevada
46	California
47	Wyoming
48	Arizona

Note: Ties in ranking reflect ties in actual values.

D-18 Percentage of Population Voting, November 2000

State	Percentage voting	Rank
Alabama	50.0	36
Alaska	66.4	3
Arizona	42.3	49
Arkansas	47.8	41
California	44.1	45
Colorado	56.8	18
Connecticut	58.4	12
Delaware	56.3	20
Florida	50.6	33
Georgia	43.8	46
Hawaii	40.5	50
Idaho	54.5	22
Illinois	52.8	28
Indiana	49.0	38
Iowa	60.7	8
Kansas	54.1	25
Kentucky	51.6	30
Louisiana	54.2	24
Maine	67.3	2
Maryland	51.6	30
Massachusetts	57.6	14
Michigan	57.5	15
Minnesota	68.8	1
Mississippi	48.6	40
Missouri	57.5	15
Montana	61.5	7
Nebraska	56.5	19
Nevada	43.8	46
New Hampshire	62.5	6
New Jersey	51.0	32
New Mexico	47.4	42
New York	50.4	34
North Carolina	50.3	35
North Dakota	60.4	10
Ohio	55.8	21
Oklahoma	48.8	39
Oregon	60.6	9
Pennsylvania	53.7	26
Rhode Island	54.3	23
South Carolina	46.6	43
South Dakota	58.2	13
Tennessee	49.2	37
Texas	43.1	48
Utah	52.6	29
Vermont	64.0	5
Virginia	53.0	27
Washington	56.9	17
West Virginia	45.8	44
Wisconsin	66.1	4
Wyoming	59.7	11
50 States	n/a	
DC	49.1	
United States	51.3	

Rank in order by percentage

1	Minnesota
2	Maine
3	Alaska
4	Wisconsin
5	Vermont
6	New Hampshire
7	Montana
8	Iowa
9	Oregon
10	North Dakota
11	Wyoming
12	Connecticut
13	South Dakota
14	Massachusetts
15	Michigan
15	Missouri
17	Washington
18	Colorado
19	Nebraska
20	Delaware
21	Ohio
22	Idaho
23	Rhode Island
24	Louisiana
25	Kansas
26	Pennsylvania
27	Virginia
28	Illinois
29	Utah
30	Kentucky
30	Maryland
32	New Jersey
33	Florida
34	New York
35	North Carolina
36	Alabama
37	Tennessee
38	Indiana
39	Oklahoma
40	Mississippi
41	Arkansas
42	New Mexico
43	South Carolina
44	West Virginia
45	California
46	Georgia
46	Nevada
48	Texas
49	Arizona
50	Hawaii

Note: Ties in ranking reflect ties in actual values.

D-19 Statewide Initiatives, 2000 and 2001

State	Number of initiatives	Initiatives approved by voters	Rank by number of initiatives
Alabama	0	n/a	n/a
Alaska	3	1	7
Arizona	6	4	4
Arkansas	2	1	9
California	5	3	6
Colorado	7	3	3
Connecticut	0	n/a	n/a
Delaware	0	n/a	n/a
Florida	1	1	16
Georgia	0	n/a	n/a
Hawaii	0	n/a	n/a
Idaho	0	n/a	n/a
Illinois	0	n/a	n/a
Indiana	0	n/a	n/a
Iowa	0	n/a	n/a
Kansas	0	n/a	n/a
Kentucky	0	n/a	n/a
Louisiana	0	n/a	n/a
Maine	3	0	7
Maryland	0	n/a	n/a
Massachusetts	6	2	4
Michigan	2	0	9
Minnesota	0	n/a	n/a
Mississippi	0	n/a	n/a
Missouri	2	0	9
Montana	1	1	16
Nebraska	2	2	9
Nevada	2	2	9
New Hampshire	0	n/a	n/a
New Jersey	0	n/a	n/a
New Mexico	0	n/a	n/a
New York	0	n/a	n/a
North Carolina	0	n/a	n/a
North Dakota	0	n/a	n/a
Ohio	0	n/a	n/a
Oklahoma	0	n/a	n/a
Oregon	19	5	1
Pennsylvania	0	n/a	n/a
Rhode Island	0	n/a	n/a
South Carolina	0	n/a	n/a
South Dakota	2	1	9
Tennessee	0	n/a	n/a
Texas	0	n/a	n/a
Utah	2	2	9
Vermont	0	n/a	n/a
Virginia	0	n/a	n/a
Washington	9	7	2
West Virginia	0	n/a	n/a
Wisconsin	0	n/a	n/a
Wyoming	0	n/a	n/a
50 States	74	32	
DC	n/a	n/a	
United States	74	32	

Rank in order by #	
1	Oregon
2	Washington
3	Colorado
4	Arizona
4	Massachusetts
6	California
7	Alaska
7	Maine
9	Arkansas
9	Michigan
9	Missouri
9	Nebraska
9	Nevada
9	South Dakota
9	Utah
16	Florida
16	Montana

Note: Ties in ranking reflect ties in actual values.

D-20 Campaign Costs Per Vote in Most Recent Gubernatorial Election, 1997, 1998, 1999 or 2000

State	Number of candidates and election year	Winning party and margin of victory %	Partisan shift (yes or no) and type of race (incumbent or open seat)	Cost per vote $	Rank by cost per vote
Alabama	9 in 1998	D-16	Y-I[1]	18.35	4
Alaska	13 in 1998	D-34	N-I	12.04	9
Arizona	6 in 1998	R-25	N-I	3.67	43
Arkansas	4 in 1998	R-21	N-I	4.92	34
California	17 in 1998	D-20	Y-O	16.09	6
Colorado	6 in 1998	R-1	Y-O	2.95	46
Connecticut	5 in 1998	R-28	N-I	6.98	29
Delaware	4 in 2000	D-19	N-O	9.78	16
Florida	2 in 1998	R-10	Y-O	3.29	45
Georgia	11 in 1998	D-9	N-O	21.51	2
Hawaii	12 in 1998	D-1	N-I	19.27	3
Idaho	7 in 1998	R-39	N-O	4.75	36
Illinois	9 in 1998	R-4	N-O	7.82	26
Indiana	4 in 2000	D-14	N-I	8.45	21
Iowa	8 in 1998	D-5	Y-O	8.84	19
Kansas	6 in 1998	R-50	N-I	3.95	42
Kentucky	4 in 1999	D-39	N-I	2.49	50
Louisiana	13 in 1999	R-32	N-I	5.51	33
Maine	8 in 1998	In-40	N-I	2.59	49
Maryland	6 in 1998	D-12	N-I	7.24	28
Massachusetts	6 in 1998	R-4	N-I	10.42	13
Michigan	5 in 1998	R-24	N-I	4.69	38
Minnesota	11 in 1998	Rf-3	Y-O	4.55	39
Mississippi	11 in 1999	D-1	Y-O	11.47	10
Missouri	10 in 2000	D-1	N-O	8.37	22
Montana	6 in 2000	R-4	N-O	11.46	11
Nebraska	9 in 1998	R-8	Y-O	16.93	5
Nevada	16 in 1998	R-10	Y-O	24.89	1
New Hampshire	9 in 2000	D-5	N-I	8.29	23
New Jersey	7 in 1997	R-1	N-I	12.45	8
New Mexico	8 in 1998	R-10	N-I	12.77	7
New York	12 in 1998	R-23	N-I	8.8	20
North Carolina	14 in 2000	D-6	N-O	9.77	17
North Dakota	4 in 2000	R-10	N-O	8.12	24
Ohio	4 in 1998	R-5	N-O	7.55	27
Oklahoma	4 in 1998	R-17	N-I	3.66	44
Oregon	12 in 1998	D-33	N-I	4.9	35
Pennsylvania	6 in 1998	R-27	N-I	4.52	40
Rhode Island	5 in 1998	R-9	N-I	10.29	14
South Carolina	4 in 1998	D-8	Y-I[1]	9.28	18
South Dakota	4 in 1998	R-31	N-I	5.68	31
Tennessee	14 in 1998	R-40	N-I	5.63	32
Texas	5 in 1998	R-38	N-I	6.78	30
Utah	4 in 2000	R-14	N-I	2.92	47
Vermont	10 in 2000	D-12	N-I	7.85	25
Virginia	3 in 1997	R-13	N-O	11.2	12
Washington	6 in 2000	D-19	N-I	2.71	48
West Virginia	15 in 2000	D-3	Y-I[1]	10.28	15
Wisconsin	8 in 1998	R-21	N-I	4.27	41
Wyoming	5 in 1998	R-16	N-I	4.7	37
50 States (average)	7	16.9	n/a	8.51	
DC	n/a	n/a	n/a	n/a	
United States (average)	7	16.9	n/a	8.51	

[1] incumbent did not win

Source Notes for Government (Section D)

D-1 Members of the United States House, 2002: Each state is allocated two senators and representation in the House of Representatives based on population, as determined by the census, which is taken in every year ending in zero (for example, 2000 and 2010).

The data in the table list the number of representatives as of 2002, based on unadjusted population numbers (see notes to Table A-1) from the 2000 census. Reapportionment of the 435 house seats resulted in gains in some western and southern states and loses in some northeastern and midwestern states. This allocation will prevail until seats are reapportioned based on the results of the 2010 census.

D-2 Members of State Legislatures, 2002: Like the Congress, state legislatures—except Nebraska's one-house legislature—have an upper and lower house, generally called senates and assemblies. These data come from the organization of legislators nationwide, the National Conference of State Legislatures.

D-3 State Legislators Per Million Population, 2002: Some small population states, like New Hampshire, have large legislatures. Some large states, like California, have relatively small ones. This table highlights the differences by relating the number of legislators (see Table D-2) to the most recent population estimates (see Table A-1).

D-4 Units of Government, 1997: There are more than eighty thousand units of government in the United States, including counties, cities, towns, townships, school districts, and special districts that provide water, maintain sewage systems, build and maintain roads, control mosquitoes, and more. There are so many that they are only counted every five years in the Census Bureau's Census of Governments, the most recent of which was in 1997. The data are available on the Census Bureau website (www.census.gov) as *Volume 1, Government Organization 1997.*

D-5 State Legislator Compensation, 2001: These data show the major sources of cash compensation of legislators, annual salaries and per diem amounts. The data are drawn from the National Conference of State Legislatures' website (www.ncsl.org).

Comparisons of legislative pay from state to state are nearly impossible. Some states pay their legislators like most employers pay their employees—a regular salary plus reimbursement of employment-related travel expenses while on official business away from the normal place of work. In addition, because most legislators live in their districts, they are paid expenses when staying overnight in the state capitol. Some states compensate legislators at a per diem rate, often adding an expense allowance that can exceed expenses actually incurred. Additionally, some legislatures provide extra pay for committee chairpersons and legislative leaders. Pensions for legislative service are nonexistent or negligible in some states, while pension and other benefits, such as employer-paid health care, are an important part of legislative compensation in other states.

D-6 Percentage of Legislators Who Are Female, 2001: The percentage of legislators who are women passed 20 percent in 1993 from less than 10 percent in the 1970s and less than 5 percent in the 1960s. The percentages for each state were calculated by the Center for the American Woman and Politics, Eagleton Institute of Politics, at Rutgers University and are available on their website (www.rci.rutgers.edu).

D-7 Turnover in Legislatures, Pre-election 2001: This table, from a late November e-mail from the National Conference of State Legislatures, shows the percentage of new state legislators taking office after the 2000 elections. Presumably, turnover will increase as more states begin to feel the effects of new term limit laws.

D-8 Term Limits (in years), 2001: This table, from the website of U.S. Term Limits (www.termlimits.org), a national group favoring term limit laws, shows the maximum number of consecutive years governors and legislators can serve. The states shown with no limits allow elected officials to serve as long as voters approve. The states are ranked, with many ties, somewhat arbitrarily. Those with the longest allowable terms for members of their lower house are ranked highest.

In 2001, Oregon's law was successfully challenged in the courts. The state Supreme Court is expected to rule on the matter in early 2002.

D-9 Legislative Session Length, 2002: Many states have constitutional limits on the length of time the legislature meets in its regular sessions. Those shown in the table are calendar days (for example, a sixty-day limit would be about two months). Many of the states with short sessions exercise the option of having special sessions called by the legislative leadership or governor. These data are available on the website of the National Conference of State Legislatures (www.ncsl.org).

It is difficult to compare the varying practices of the states. For instance, states listed as having no regular session in 2002 meet biannually, convening in 2001 and 2003.

D-10 Party Control of State Legislatures, 2002: These data, developed by the National Conference of State Legislatures shortly after the November 2001 election, show the party affiliation of legislators taking office in 2002. The states are ranked by the percentage of Democrats (reading top to bottom) or Republicans (bottom to top) in the combined legislative houses. S represents a split in party control.

D-11 Governor's Power Rating, 2001: This table presents the results of an update of the on-going study by Dr. Thad Beyle of the University of North Carolina at Chapel Hill, included in *Politics in the American States: A Comparative Analysis* published by CQ Press. The ranking is based on six measures of institutional power — tenure, appointment power, the number of other statewide elected officials, budget power, veto power, and party control. Those interested in more detailed data on this and earlier studies of the governor's powers should visit Dr. Thad Beyle's website (www.unc.edu/~beyle).

D-12 Number of Statewide Elected Officials, 2000: The federal pattern of holding nationwide elections for only the chief executive and running mate (president and vice president) is not followed by the states. States often elect the attorneys general, secretaries of state, comptrollers, treasurers, and auditors. The count in the table, from the Council of State Government's *The Book of the States 2001-02*, excludes judges, who are also elected in many states. *The Book of the States* is a biannual publication.

D-13 State and Local Government Employees, 2000: These statistics, from the Census Bureau's count of public employees available on the Census Bureau's website (www.census.gov), express the full-time equivalent of part-time workers plus full-time workers in state and local governments and relate the totals to population.

D-14 Average Salaries of State and Local Government Employees, 2000: These statistics, from the same source as Table D-13, show annual average state and local government salaries, which were obtained by dividing compensation in March 2000 by the number of employees in 2000 and multiplying by twelve.

D-15 Local Employment, 2000: The count of local employees identified is substantially larger than the number of state employees. The table shows the percentage of local employees. See Table D-13 for the source of these data.

D-16 Local Spending Accountability, FY 1999: Since 1970 there has been a massive growth in both federal and state aid to local governments. As a result, local officials finance over one-third of what they spend with money they do not raise by their own local taxes and fees. Critics say this encourages government spending to be excessive because the elected officials who spend the money do not have to account to taxpayers for raising it. The Wisconsin Taxpayers Association has dubbed this difference "the accountability gap." The table shows a measure of this gap, as calculated by State Policy Research using data from the Census Bureau (see source note to Table F-1 for important details).

The numbers reflect the percentage of their spending local officials raised. New Hampshire ranks first by this measure because it has uniquely low state taxes (with no state sales or income tax) and only minor state aid programs by comparison with other states.

D-17 Percentage of Eligible Voters Registered, November 2000: These statistics, available on the website of the Federal Elections Commission (www.fec.gov), show the percentage of persons presumably eligible to vote in each state, based on the voting age population in relation to the number who have complied with that state's requirements to vote (that is, becoming and staying registered as voters).

Data are not available for North Dakota because the state has no voter registration and therefore reports no total registration figures. Wisconsin has election day registration at the polls. The unusual numbers for Alaska and Montana were not adequately explained by the FEC, but presumably have something to do with population numbers that are *estimates*, and do not include military or institutionalized persons.

D-18 Percentage of Population Voting, November 2000: Not all persons legally old enough to vote actually do so. The table shows the percentage who reported voting in the elections of November 2000. It comes from the same source as Table D-17.

D-19 Statewide Initiatives, 2000 and 2001: In most states, voters select candidates to make policy for them as legislators but never vote directly on policy except when changes in the state constitution are being made. Some states allow "direct democracy," including allowing voters to put up a measure for popular vote by collecting a minimum number of signatures (voter initiatives). This tabulation shows the number of such initiatives on state ballots in 2000 and 2001.

The numbers reflect (1) whether initiatives are permitted in the state; (2) the difficulty of putting measures on the ballot, as affected by the number for signatures required and other factors in the constitutions of each state; and (3) voter interest in making state policy by this direct democracy approach.

These statistics come from a compilation of ballot measure results available on the National Conference of State Legislatures' website (www.ncsl.org).

D-20 Campaign Costs Per Vote in Most Recent Gubernatorial Election, 1997, 1998, 1999 or 2000: This table was created by Thad Beyle (Department of Political Science, UNC at Chapel Hill, NC 27599-3265) and Jennifer M. Jensen (Department of Political Science, University of Albany-SUNY, Albany, NY 12222). The authors compiled data from the specific agency in each state that regulates elections and campaign finances. The result is a measure of the gubernatorial campaign costs (converted to 2001$) in each state per vote in each state. Variables that have potential effects on these costs are also presented in this table. These variables include (1) the number of candidates seeking office, (2) the election year, (3) the party that won the office and (4) by what margin of victory, (5) whether or not the election resulted in a partisan shift, (6) whether or not an incumbent was seeking reelection, and (7) whether or not the incumbent won. Anyone interested in more detailed data on these elections should visit the co-author's website (www.unc.edu/~beyle).

Federal Impacts

Federal spending in the states comes, largely, in four forms: 1) direct payments to individuals through programs such as Social Security and Medicare; 2) federal grants to state or local governments for a myriad of programs, including Medicaid, highway construction and social service programs, among others; 3) procurement contracts, primarily for military installations and defense spending; and 4) paychecks for employees from postal workers to FEMA staff to members of the military.

It is easy to see that states receiving a larger chunk of federal money tend to either have a greater percentage of elderly or poverty striken populations (though state eligibility standards also play a role), large areas of federal lands, or a large military or defense presence. Size, though, is also a factor. Some small states see a greater amount of federal funds per capita because various federal grants have set minimums, irrespective of population counts.

Though U.S. military actions and growing concern for public safety and public health will certainly effect where and how future federal monies are spent, recent trends showing increased spending to individuals through Social Security and Medicare, and to the Medicaid program, will no doubt continue. Spending for these programs is expected to increase faster than discretionary programs in which spending levels are set by annual federal appropriations. The result: less federal control over how the money is ultimately spent and fewer options for state officials and congressional delegates to attract federal money to their state.

While increasing costs have forced states to address the issue of Medicaid, so will changes to federal financing rules. While the federal government shares the cost of the program, states have been able to squeeze more out of it through creative, and heretofore legal, accounting. The federal government is now phasing out that loophole.

E-1 Federal Spending, Total and Per Capita, FY 2000

State	Total federal spending $ (in millions)	Per capita federal spending $	Rank per capita		Rank in order per capita
Alabama	29,217	6,570	8	1	Alaska
Alaska	5,953	9,495	1	2	Virginia
Arizona	29,244	5,700	26	3	Maryland
Arkansas	14,828	5,546	29	4	North Dakota
California	175,751	5,189	34	5	New Mexico
Colorado	22,918	5,328	32	6	Hawaii
Connecticut	19,517	5,731	25	7	South Dakota
Delaware	3,959	5,052	39	8	Alabama
Florida	92,776	5,805	23	9	Rhode Island
Georgia	42,460	5,187	35	10	Montana
Hawaii	9,015	7,441	6	11	Wyoming
Idaho	7,009	5,417	31	12	West Virginia
Illinois	60,008	4,832	43	13	Mississippi
Indiana	28,723	4,724	44	14	Massachusetts
Iowa	14,751	5,041	41	15	Missouri
Kansas	14,260	5,304	33	16	Maine
Kentucky	24,444	6,048	17	17	Kentucky
Louisiana	25,955	5,808	22	18	Pennsylvania
Maine	7,849	6,156	16	19	Oklahoma
Maryland	45,089	8,513	3	20	Tennessee
Massachusetts	40,824	6,430	14	21	New York
Michigan	46,823	4,711	45	22	Louisiana
Minnesota	22,992	4,674	47	23	Florida
Mississippi	18,358	6,453	13	24	Washington
Missouri	35,687	6,378	15	25	Connecticut
Montana	5,917	6,558	10	26	Arizona
Nebraska	9,611	5,616	27	27	Nebraska
Nevada	8,626	4,317	50	28	South Carolina
New Hampshire	5,802	4,695	46	29	Arkansas
New Jersey	43,469	5,166	36	30	Vermont
New Mexico	14,470	7,955	5	31	Idaho
New York	110,333	5,814	21	32	Colorado
North Carolina	41,367	5,139	37	33	Kansas
North Dakota	5,245	8,167	4	34	California
Ohio	57,355	5,052	40	35	Georgia
Oklahoma	20,613	5,974	19	36	New Jersey
Oregon	16,553	4,838	42	37	North Carolina
Pennsylvania	73,715	6,002	18	38	Texas
Rhode Island	6,876	6,559	9	39	Delaware
South Carolina	22,294	5,557	28	40	Ohio
South Dakota	5,138	6,807	7	41	Iowa
Tennessee	33,560	5,899	20	42	Oregon
Texas	106,493	5,107	38	43	Illinois
Utah	10,037	4,495	49	44	Indiana
Vermont	3,362	5,522	30	45	Michigan
Virginia	62,709	8,859	2	46	New Hampshire
Washington	33,897	5,751	24	47	Minnesota
West Virginia	11,739	6,492	12	48	Wisconsin
Wisconsin	24,300	4,530	48	49	Utah
Wyoming	3,220	6,521	11	50	Nevada
50 States	1,575,111	5,608			
DC	28,254	49,390			
United States*	1,637,170	5,817			

Note: Numbers that appear to be identical are rounded and vary slightly in actual value. The rankings reflect the actual values before rounding. See the introduction for more details.

*Due to rounding or data sources, the 50-state total plus D.C. may not equal the U.S. total. Please see introduction.

E-2 Increase in Total Federal Spending, FY 1995–FY 2000

State	Total federal spending FY 1995 $ (in millions)	Percentage increase in federal spending	Rank by percentage increase
Alabama	22,795	28.2	11
Alaska	4,230	40.7	1
Arizona	20,906	39.9	2
Arkansas	11,768	26.0	17
California	153,831	14.2	44
Colorado	19,062	20.2	30
Connecticut	17,505	11.5	50
Delaware	3,310	19.6	31
Florida	75,000	23.7	21
Georgia	33,414	27.1	13
Hawaii	7,450	21.0	28
Idaho	5,301	32.2	6
Illinois	50,889	17.9	37
Indiana	23,028	24.7	20
Iowa	13,008	13.4	48
Kansas	12,471	14.3	43
Kentucky	19,433	25.8	18
Louisiana	22,526	15.2	40
Maine	6,649	18.0	36
Maryland	37,089	21.6	26
Massachusetts	35,822	14.0	46
Michigan	39,567	18.3	34
Minnesota	19,015	20.9	29
Mississippi	14,251	28.8	9
Missouri	31,541	13.1	49
Montana	4,829	22.5	22
Nebraska	7,461	28.8	10
Nevada	6,665	29.4	7
New Hampshire	4,890	18.7	33
New Jersey	37,920	14.6	42
New Mexico	11,826	22.4	24
New York	94,664	16.6	39
North Carolina	30,692	34.8	4
North Dakota	3,779	38.8	3
Ohio	50,516	13.5	47
Oklahoma	16,132	27.8	12
Oregon	13,640	21.4	27
Pennsylvania	64,609	14.1	45
Rhode Island	5,789	18.8	32
South Carolina	17,839	25.0	19
South Dakota	3,865	32.9	5
Tennessee	26,611	26.1	16
Texas	83,863	27.0	14
Utah	8,486	18.3	35
Vermont	2,664	26.2	15
Virginia	51,487	21.8	25
Washington	28,831	17.6	38
West Virginia	10,208	15.0	41
Wisconsin	19,839	22.5	23
Wyoming	2,492	29.2	8
50 States	1,309,458	20.3	
DC	21,912	28.9	
United States*	1,368,202	19.7	

Rank in order by percentage increase	
1	Alaska
2	Arizona
3	North Dakota
4	North Carolina
5	South Dakota
6	Idaho
7	Nevada
8	Wyoming
9	Mississippi
10	Nebraska
11	Alabama
12	Oklahoma
13	Georgia
14	Texas
15	Vermont
16	Tennessee
17	Arkansas
18	Kentucky
19	South Carolina
20	Indiana
21	Florida
22	Montana
23	Wisconsin
24	New Mexico
25	Virginia
26	Maryland
27	Oregon
28	Hawaii
29	Minnesota
30	Colorado
31	Delaware
32	Rhode Island
33	New Hampshire
34	Michigan
35	Utah
36	Maine
37	Illinois
38	Washington
39	New York
40	Louisiana
41	West Virginia
42	New Jersey
43	Kansas
44	California
45	Pennsylvania
46	Massachusetts
47	Ohio
48	Iowa
49	Missouri
50	Connecticut

Note: Numbers that appear to be identical are rounded and vary slightly in actual value. The rankings reflect the actual values before rounding. See the introduction for more details.

Due to rounding or data sources, the 50-state total plus D.C. may not equal the U.S. total. Please see introduction.

E-3 Federal Spending on Grants, Total and Per Capita, FY 2000

State	Federal grants to state and local governments $ (in millions)	Per capita federal grants to state and local government $	Rank per capita
Alabama	4,833	1,087	21
Alaska	2,174	3,468	1
Arizona	4,704	917	42
Arkansas	2,778	1,039	28
California	36,080	1,065	25
Colorado	3,591	835	47
Connecticut	4,033	1,184	16
Delaware	838	1,069	24
Florida	12,149	760	48
Georgia	7,520	919	41
Hawaii	1,348	1,113	20
Idaho	1,270	981	34
Illinois	11,228	904	43
Indiana	5,108	840	46
Iowa	2,714	927	39
Kansas	2,323	864	45
Kentucky	4,687	1,160	17
Louisiana	5,300	1,186	15
Maine	1,770	1,388	12
Maryland	6,911	1,305	13
Massachusetts	9,070	1,429	11
Michigan	10,107	1,017	31
Minnesota	4,753	966	36
Mississippi	3,517	1,236	14
Missouri	5,939	1,061	26
Montana	1,474	1,634	6
Nebraska	1,720	1,005	32
Nevada	1,340	671	50
New Hampshire	1,238	1,002	33
New Jersey	7,876	936	38
New Mexico	3,032	1,667	4
New York	31,564	1,663	5
North Carolina	8,518	1,058	27
North Dakota	1,101	1,714	3
Ohio	10,665	939	37
Oklahoma	3,583	1,038	29
Oregon	3,684	1,077	22
Pennsylvania	13,940	1,135	18
Rhode Island	1,574	1,501	9
South Carolina	4,163	1,038	30
South Dakota	1,088	1,441	10
Tennessee	6,372	1,120	19
Texas	18,346	880	44
Utah	2,065	925	40
Vermont	929	1,526	7
Virginia	5,163	729	49
Washington	6,345	1,076	23
West Virginia	2,729	1,509	8
Wisconsin	5,254	980	35
Wyoming	1,022	2,070	2
50 States	299,530	1,067	
DC	4,675	8,172	
United States*	308,530	1,096	

Rank in order per capita	
1	Alaska
2	Wyoming
3	North Dakota
4	New Mexico
5	New York
6	Montana
7	Vermont
8	West Virginia
9	Rhode Island
10	South Dakota
11	Massachusetts
12	Maine
13	Maryland
14	Mississippi
15	Louisiana
16	Connecticut
17	Kentucky
18	Pennsylvania
19	Tennessee
20	Hawaii
21	Alabama
22	Oregon
23	Washington
24	Delaware
25	California
26	Missouri
27	North Carolina
28	Arkansas
29	Oklahoma
30	South Carolina
31	Michigan
32	Nebraska
33	New Hampshire
34	Idaho
35	Wisconsin
36	Minnesota
37	Ohio
38	New Jersey
39	Iowa
40	Utah
41	Georgia
42	Arizona
43	Illinois
44	Texas
45	Kansas
46	Indiana
47	Colorado
48	Florida
49	Virginia
50	Nevada

Due to rounding or data sources, the 50-state total plus D.C. may not equal the U.S. total. Please see introduction.

E-4 Federal Spending on Procurement, FY 2000

State	Total spending on procurement $ (in millions)	Per capita procurement spending $	Rank per capita
Alabama	4,691	1,055	7
Alaska	1,108	1,767	4
Arizona	5,286	1,030	9
Arkansas	587	220	49
California	26,955	796	14
Colorado	4,349	1,011	10
Connecticut	2,699	793	15
Delaware	149	190	50
Florida	8,594	538	27
Georgia	5,102	623	24
Hawaii	1,278	1,055	6
Idaho	1,347	1,041	8
Illinois	3,999	322	42
Indiana	2,192	360	40
Iowa	1,115	381	36
Kansas	1,297	482	31
Kentucky	2,747	680	22
Louisiana	3,096	693	19
Maine	881	691	21
Maryland	10,551	1,992	3
Massachusetts	6,006	946	11
Michigan	2,374	239	47
Minnesota	2,090	425	33
Mississippi	1,978	695	18
Missouri	6,053	1,082	5
Montana	288	319	43
Nebraska	486	284	45
Nevada	836	418	35
New Hampshire	523	423	34
New Jersey	4,106	488	30
New Mexico	4,134	2,273	2
New York	6,909	364	39
North Carolina	2,555	317	44
North Dakota	238	371	37
Ohio	4,867	429	32
Oklahoma	1,940	562	25
Oregon	790	231	48
Pennsylvania	6,284	512	29
Rhode Island	584	557	26
South Carolina	2,774	691	20
South Dakota	279	370	38
Tennessee	5,217	917	12
Texas	18,981	910	13
Utah	1,597	715	17
Vermont	320	526	28
Virginia	21,321	3,012	1
Washington	4,664	791	16
West Virginia	622	344	41
Wisconsin	1,460	272	46
Wyoming	323	654	23
50 States	198,622	707	
DC	7,491	13,095	
United States*	223,324	794	

Rank in order per capita	
1	Virginia
2	New Mexico
3	Maryland
4	Alaska
5	Missouri
6	Hawaii
7	Alabama
8	Idaho
9	Arizona
10	Colorado
11	Massachusetts
12	Tennessee
13	Texas
14	California
15	Connecticut
16	Washington
17	Utah
18	Mississippi
19	Louisiana
20	South Carolina
21	Maine
22	Kentucky
23	Wyoming
24	Georgia
25	Oklahoma
26	Rhode Island
27	Florida
28	Vermont
29	Pennsylvania
30	New Jersey
31	Kansas
32	Ohio
33	Minnesota
34	New Hampshire
35	Nevada
36	Iowa
37	North Dakota
38	South Dakota
39	New York
40	Indiana
41	West Virginia
42	Illinois
43	Montana
44	North Carolina
45	Nebraska
46	Wisconsin
47	Michigan
48	Oregon
49	Arkansas
50	Delaware

Note: Numbers that appear to be identical are rounded and vary slightly in actual value. The rankings reflect the actual values before rounding. See the introduction for more details.

Due to rounding or data sources, the 50-state total plus D.C. may not equal the U.S. total. Please see introduction.

E-5 Federal Spending on Payments to Individuals, FY 2000

State	Total federal payments to individuals $ (in millions)	Per capita federal payments to individuals $	Rank per capita
Alabama	16,820	3,782	10
Alaska	1,322	2,109	50
Arizona	16,390	3,195	30
Arkansas	10,284	3,847	7
California	94,881	2,801	45
Colorado	11,191	2,602	48
Connecticut	11,390	3,345	23
Delaware	2,550	3,254	28
Florida	63,899	3,998	4
Georgia	23,137	2,826	44
Hawaii	3,960	3,269	27
Idaho	3,664	2,832	43
Illinois	38,572	3,106	33
Indiana	19,220	3,161	31
Iowa	9,934	3,395	19
Kansas	8,797	3,272	26
Kentucky	14,286	3,535	14
Louisiana	15,296	3,423	18
Maine	4,419	3,466	17
Maryland	18,453	3,484	16
Massachusetts	22,661	3,569	13
Michigan	31,216	3,141	32
Minnesota	14,251	2,897	41
Mississippi	11,145	3,918	5
Missouri	20,260	3,621	12
Montana	3,466	3,842	8
Nebraska	6,370	3,722	11
Nevada	5,475	2,740	46
New Hampshire	3,570	2,889	42
New Jersey	27,748	3,298	24
New Mexico	5,612	3,085	34
New York	63,982	3,372	20
North Carolina	24,767	3,077	35
North Dakota	3,289	5,121	1
Ohio	37,196	3,276	25
Oklahoma	12,139	3,518	15
Oregon	10,491	3,066	36
Pennsylvania	47,877	3,898	6
Rhode Island	3,996	3,812	9
South Carolina	12,877	3,210	29
South Dakota	3,187	4,222	2
Tennessee	19,138	3,364	21
Texas	57,039	2,735	47
Utah	4,773	2,137	49
Vermont	1,793	2,945	40
Virginia	23,747	3,355	22
Washington	17,948	3,045	37
West Virginia	7,424	4,105	3
Wisconsin	15,986	2,980	38
Wyoming	1,457	2,951	39
50 States	909,345	3,238	
DC	3,881	6,784	
United States*	920,780	3,272	

Rank in order per capita	
1	North Dakota
2	South Dakota
3	West Virginia
4	Florida
5	Mississippi
6	Pennsylvania
7	Arkansas
8	Montana
9	Rhode Island
10	Alabama
11	Nebraska
12	Missouri
13	Massachusetts
14	Kentucky
15	Oklahoma
16	Maryland
17	Maine
18	Louisiana
19	Iowa
20	New York
21	Tennessee
22	Virginia
23	Connecticut
24	New Jersey
25	Ohio
26	Kansas
27	Hawaii
28	Delaware
29	South Carolina
30	Arizona
31	Indiana
32	Michigan
33	Illinois
34	New Mexico
35	North Carolina
36	Oregon
37	Washington
38	Wisconsin
39	Wyoming
40	Vermont
41	Minnesota
42	New Hampshire
43	Idaho
44	Georgia
45	California
46	Nevada
47	Texas
48	Colorado
49	Utah
50	Alaska

Due to rounding or data sources, the 50-state total plus D.C. may not equal the U.S. total. Please see introduction.

E-6 Federal Spending on Social Security and Medicare, FY 2000

State	Total Social Security and Medicare spending $ (in millions)	Per capita spending $	Rank per capita
Alabama	11,712	2,634	7
Alaska	669	1,067	50
Arizona	10,930	2,130	34
Arkansas	6,878	2,573	10
California	68,510	2,023	37
Colorado	7,201	1,674	48
Connecticut	9,157	2,689	6
Delaware	1,869	2,385	20
Florida	48,592	3,040	2
Georgia	15,420	1,884	45
Hawaii	2,411	1,990	41
Idaho	2,428	1,876	46
Illinois	28,831	2,321	24
Indiana	14,350	2,360	22
Iowa	7,185	2,455	17
Kansas	6,254	2,326	23
Kentucky	10,291	2,546	12
Louisiana	11,132	2,491	15
Maine	3,124	2,450	19
Maryland	11,109	2,097	36
Massachusetts	17,102	2,694	5
Michigan	25,347	2,550	11
Minnesota	9,816	1,995	40
Mississippi	7,044	2,476	16
Missouri	14,221	2,542	13
Montana	2,004	2,221	28
Nebraska	3,688	2,155	33
Nevada	3,772	1,888	44
New Hampshire	2,612	2,114	35
New Jersey	21,655	2,574	9
New Mexico	3,484	1,915	43
New York	49,731	2,621	8
North Carolina	17,589	2,185	32
North Dakota	1,445	2,251	26
Ohio	28,366	2,499	14
Oklahoma	8,223	2,383	21
Oregon	7,530	2,201	31
Pennsylvania	37,285	3,036	3
Rhode Island	2,833	2,703	4
South Carolina	8,986	2,240	27
South Dakota	1,671	2,214	29
Tennessee	13,968	2,455	18
Texas	37,944	1,820	47
Utah	3,089	1,383	49
Vermont	1,346	2,211	30
Virginia	13,769	1,945	42
Washington	11,780	1,999	39
West Virginia	5,695	3,149	1
Wisconsin	12,267	2,287	25
Wyoming	994	2,013	38
50 States	653,308	2,326	
DC	1,331	2,327	
United States*	660,012	2,345	

Rank in order per capita	
1	West Virginia
2	Florida
3	Pennsylvania
4	Rhode Island
5	Massachusetts
6	Connecticut
7	Alabama
8	New York
9	New Jersey
10	Arkansas
11	Michigan
12	Kentucky
13	Missouri
14	Ohio
15	Louisiana
16	Mississippi
17	Iowa
18	Tennessee
19	Maine
20	Delaware
21	Oklahoma
22	Indiana
23	Kansas
24	Illinois
25	Wisconsin
26	North Dakota
27	South Carolina
28	Montana
29	South Dakota
30	Vermont
31	Oregon
32	North Carolina
33	Nebraska
34	Arizona
35	New Hampshire
36	Maryland
37	California
38	Wyoming
39	Washington
40	Minnesota
41	Hawaii
42	Virginia
43	New Mexico
44	Nevada
45	Georgia
46	Idaho
47	Texas
48	Colorado
49	Utah
50	Alaska

Due to rounding or data sources, the 50-state total plus D.C. may not equal the U.S. total. Please see introduction.

E-7 Social Security Benefits Paid, 1999

State	Social security amounts paid $ (in thousands)	Number of recipients	Average monthly benefit $	Rank by average benefit
Alabama	545,204	810,196	673	44
Alaska	35,321	51,320	688	41
Arizona	577,385	772,631	747	15
Arkansas	343,274	517,826	663	48
California	3,049,247	4,105,728	743	20
Colorado	374,345	522,116	717	30
Connecticut	463,896	567,637	817	2
Delaware	99,678	128,935	773	6
Florida	2,327,961	3,139,437	742	21
Georgia	740,639	1,073,388	690	39
Hawaii	130,574	178,000	734	24
Idaho	136,187	190,674	714	31
Illinois	1,410,302	1,816,192	777	5
Indiana	758,107	986,207	769	7
Iowa	397,324	537,366	739	22
Kansas	328,469	435,613	754	14
Kentucky	487,490	729,134	669	47
Louisiana	462,691	702,105	659	49
Maine	166,313	246,214	675	43
Maryland	525,786	704,867	746	18
Massachusetts	780,607	1,046,655	746	19
Michigan	1,269,070	1,620,377	783	3
Minnesota	533,536	728,088	733	25
Mississippi	321,156	505,731	635	50
Missouri	714,848	993,174	720	28
Montana	109,770	155,072	708	33
Nebraska	205,252	282,661	726	27
Nevada	205109	271,205	756	11
New Hampshire	147382	195,065	756	12
New Jersey	1082787	1,322,550	819	1
New Mexico	181555	270,658	671	45
New York	2,313,824	2,966,658	780	4
North Carolina	928,246	1,322,399	702	35
North Dakota	78,380	114,171	687	42
Ohio	1,413,626	1,893,896	746	16
Oklahoma	410,870	586,802	700	36
Oregon	417,501	553,547	754	13
Pennsylvania	1,784,298	2,332,589	765	9
Rhode Island	142265	190,681	746	17
South Carolina	468205	672,353	696	38
South Dakota	90590	135,165	670	46
Tennessee	669,847	970,895	690	40
Texas	1,803,465	2,575,745	700	37
Utah	171,612	234,587	732	26
Vermont	73,890	102,729	719	29
Virginia	714,309	1,008,033	709	32
Washington	632,948	825,281	767	8
West Virginia	275,672	390,558	706	34
Wisconsin	678,353	890,588	762	10
Wyoming	54,983	74,688	736	23
50 States	32,034,149	43,448,187	737	
DC	45,932	73,176	628	
United States*	32,578,173	44,595,202	731	

Rank in order by average benefit

1 New Jersey
2 Connecticut
3 Michigan
4 New York
5 Illinois
6 Delaware
7 Indiana
8 Washington
9 Pennsylvania
10 Wisconsin
11 Nevada
12 New Hampshire
13 Oregon
14 Kansas
15 Arizona
16 Ohio
17 Rhode Island
18 Maryland
19 Massachusetts
20 California
21 Florida
22 Iowa
23 Wyoming
24 Hawaii
25 Minnesota
26 Utah
27 Nebraska
28 Missouri
29 Vermont
30 Colorado
31 Idaho
32 Virginia
33 Montana
34 West Virginia
35 North Carolina
36 Oklahoma
37 Texas
38 South Carolina
39 Georgia
40 Tennessee
41 Alaska
42 North Dakota
43 Maine
44 Alabama
45 New Mexico
46 South Dakota
47 Kentucky
48 Arkansas
49 Louisiana
50 Mississippi

Note: Numbers that appear to be identical are rounded and vary slightly in actual value. The rankings reflect the actual values before rounding. See the introduction for more details.

Due to rounding or data sources, the 50-state total plus D.C. may not equal the U.S. total. Please see introduction.

E-8 Federal Spending on Employee Wages and Salaries, FY 2000

State	Total federal spending on wages and salaries $ (in millions)	Per capita spending on wages and salaries $	Rank per capita
Alabama	2,873	646	19
Alaska	1,349	2,152	1
Arizona	2,865	558	27
Arkansas	1,178	441	41
California	17,835	527	30
Colorado	3,787	880	7
Connecticut	1,396	410	43
Delaware	422	539	28
Florida	8,135	509	32
Georgia	6,700	818	11
Hawaii	2,429	2,005	2
Idaho	728	563	26
Illinois	6,210	500	34
Indiana	2,204	362	47
Iowa	988	338	48
Kansas	1,844	686	17
Kentucky	2,724	674	18
Louisiana	2,264	507	33
Maine	779	611	22
Maryland	9,174	1,732	4
Massachusetts	3,087	486	37
Michigan	3,126	315	49
Minnesota	1,897	386	45
Mississippi	1,718	604	24
Missouri	3,437	614	21
Montana	689	764	13
Nebraska	1,035	605	23
Nevada	976	488	36
New Hampshire	471	381	46
New Jersey	3,739	444	40
New Mexico	1,692	930	6
New York	7,879	415	42
North Carolina	5,527	687	16
North Dakota	616	959	5
Ohio	4,627	408	44
Oklahoma	2,951	855	8
Oregon	1,589	464	38
Pennsylvania	5,615	457	39
Rhode Island	722	689	15
South Carolina	2,481	618	20
South Dakota	584	774	12
Tennessee	2,833	498	35
Texas	12,126	582	25
Utah	1,603	718	14
Vermont	320	526	31
Virginia	12,477	1,763	3
Washington	4,940	838	10
West Virginia	963	533	29
Wisconsin	1,600	298	50
Wyoming	417	845	9
50 States	167,621	597	
DC	12,208	21,340	
United States*	184,537	656	

Rank in order per capita

1 Alaska
2 Hawaii
3 Virginia
4 Maryland
5 North Dakota
6 New Mexico
7 Colorado
8 Oklahoma
9 Wyoming
10 Washington
11 Georgia
12 South Dakota
13 Montana
14 Utah
15 Rhode Island
16 North Carolina
17 Kansas
18 Kentucky
19 Alabama
20 South Carolina
21 Missouri
22 Maine
23 Nebraska
24 Mississippi
25 Texas
26 Idaho
27 Arizona
28 Delaware
29 West Virginia
30 California
31 Vermont
32 Florida
33 Louisiana
34 Illinois
35 Tennessee
36 Nevada
37 Massachusetts
38 Oregon
39 Pennsylvania
40 New Jersey
41 Arkansas
42 New York
43 Connecticut
44 Ohio
45 Minnesota
46 New Hampshire
47 Indiana
48 Iowa
49 Michigan
50 Wisconsin

Due to rounding or data sources, the 50-state total plus D.C. may not equal the U.S. total. Please see introduction.

E-9 Federal Grant Spending Per Dollar of State Tax Revenue, FY 1999

State	Federal aid per dollar of state tax revenue $	Rank
Alabama	0.70	8
Alaska	1.35	1
Arizona	0.45	31
Arkansas	0.53	21
California	0.43	35
Colorado	0.45	32
Connecticut	0.33	48
Delaware	0.36	44
Florida	0.37	43
Georgia	0.47	30
Hawaii	0.40	39
Idaho	0.44	34
Illinois	0.40	37
Indiana	0.44	33
Iowa	0.49	28
Kansas	0.40	36
Kentucky	0.52	23
Louisiana	0.70	9
Maine	0.56	19
Maryland	0.39	40
Massachusetts	0.35	46
Michigan	0.38	41
Minnesota	0.32	49
Mississippi	0.65	11
Missouri	0.55	20
Montana	0.84	5
Nebraska	0.53	22
Nevada	0.27	50
New Hampshire	0.88	4
New Jersey	0.40	38
New Mexico	0.58	16
New York	0.66	10
North Carolina	0.49	27
North Dakota	0.77	6
Ohio	0.50	25
Oklahoma	0.50	24
Oregon	0.65	12
Pennsylvania	0.47	29
Rhode Island	0.65	13
South Carolina	0.58	17
South Dakota	0.91	3
Tennessee	0.76	7
Texas	0.61	15
Utah	0.50	26
Vermont	0.58	18
Virginia	0.34	47
Washington	0.37	42
West Virginia	0.63	14
Wisconsin	0.36	45
Wyoming	1.08	2
50 States	0.48	
DC	n/a	
United States	0.48	

Rank in order by $	
1	Alaska
2	Wyoming
3	South Dakota
4	New Hampshire
5	Montana
6	North Dakota
7	Tennessee
8	Alabama
9	Louisiana
10	New York
11	Mississippi
12	Oregon
13	Rhode Island
14	West Virginia
15	Texas
16	New Mexico
17	South Carolina
18	Vermont
19	Maine
20	Missouri
21	Arkansas
22	Nebraska
23	Kentucky
24	Oklahoma
25	Ohio
26	Utah
27	North Carolina
28	Iowa
29	Pennsylvania
30	Georgia
31	Arizona
32	Colorado
33	Indiana
34	Idaho
35	California
36	Kansas
37	Illinois
38	New Jersey
39	Hawaii
40	Maryland
41	Michigan
42	Washington
43	Florida
44	Delaware
45	Wisconsin
46	Massachusetts
47	Virginia
48	Connecticut
49	Minnesota
50	Nevada

Note: Numbers that appear to be identical are rounded and vary slightly in actual value. The rankings reflect the actual values before rounding. See the introduction for more details.

E-10 State and Local General Revenue from Federal Government, FY 1999

State	Total general revenue from federal government $ (in millions)	Percentage of revenue from federal government	Rank by percentage
Alabama	4,651	24.1	10
Alaska	1,379	18.1	32
Arizona	3,952	18.9	28
Arkansas	2,593	22.8	12
California	35,955	19.4	26
Colorado	3,324	15.7	45
Connecticut	3,451	16.0	43
Delaware	784	16.1	42
Florida	10,692	14.7	48
Georgia	6,460	17.5	35
Hawaii	1,386	20.2	22
Idaho	1,030	18.0	33
Illinois	10,079	16.7	37
Indiana	4,624	16.6	38
Iowa	2,597	18.1	31
Kansas	1,969	15.9	44
Kentucky	4,179	22.7	13
Louisiana	4,856	22.4	15
Maine	1,533	22.0	16
Maryland	4,296	16.3	40
Massachusetts	5,965	16.6	39
Michigan	9,347	17.8	34
Minnesota	4,496	15.6	46
Mississippi	3,135	24.6	8
Missouri	5,117	20.7	19
Montana	1,253	28.1	2
Nebraska	1,549	18.6	29
Nevada	1,149	13.2	50
New Hampshire	1,033	18.9	27
New Jersey	7,377	15.1	47
New Mexico	2,271	24.3	9
New York	28,448	20.7	18
North Carolina	7,687	20.5	20
North Dakota	1,018	28.1	1
Ohio	10,183	18.5	30
Oklahoma	2,935	20.3	21
Oregon	4,207	22.7	14
Pennsylvania	11,857	19.5	25
Rhode Island	1,325	23.9	11
South Carolina	3,870	21.0	17
South Dakota	871	26.0	4
Tennessee	5,914	25.3	6
Texas	17,684	19.6	24
Utah	2,091	20.0	23
Vermont	829	25.3	7
Virginia	4,501	13.7	49
Washington	5,302	16.8	36
West Virginia	2,179	25.5	5
Wisconsin	4,618	16.2	41
Wyoming	919	26.7	3
50 States	268,921	18.8	
DC	1,707	31.3	
United States	270,628	18.9	

Rank in order by percentage	
1	North Dakota
2	Montana
3	Wyoming
4	South Dakota
5	West Virginia
6	Tennessee
7	Vermont
8	Mississippi
9	New Mexico
10	Alabama
11	Rhode Island
12	Arkansas
13	Kentucky
14	Oregon
15	Louisiana
16	Maine
17	South Carolina
18	New York
19	Missouri
20	North Carolina
21	Oklahoma
22	Hawaii
23	Utah
24	Texas
25	Pennsylvania
26	California
27	New Hampshire
28	Arizona
29	Nebraska
30	Ohio
31	Iowa
32	Alaska
33	Idaho
34	Michigan
35	Georgia
36	Washington
37	Illinois
38	Indiana
39	Massachusetts
40	Maryland
41	Wisconsin
42	Delaware
43	Connecticut
44	Kansas
45	Colorado
46	Minnesota
47	New Jersey
48	Florida
49	Virginia
50	Nevada

Note: Numbers that appear to be identical are rounded and vary slightly in actual value. The rankings reflect the actual values before rounding. See the introduction for more details.

E-11 Federal Tax Burden, Total and Per Capita, FY 2001

State	Federal tax burden total $ (in millions)	Federal tax burden per capita $	Rank per capita
Alabama	24,682	5,512	41
Alaska	4,564	6,915	23
Arizona	32,942	6,774	27
Arkansas	13,998	5,285	45
California	268,942	8,197	12
Colorado	35,616	8,454	9
Connecticut	41,409	12,590	1
Delaware	6,177	7,993	13
Florida	122,142	7,937	14
Georgia	56,631	7,118	22
Hawaii	7,351	5,790	38
Idaho	7,084	5,182	46
Illinois	106,007	8,773	5
Indiana	40,727	6,709	29
Iowa	18,444	6,346	34
Kansas	18,283	6,817	25
Kentucky	22,630	5,643	39
Louisiana	24,203	5,449	43
Maine	7,717	6,110	35
Maryland	44,498	8,390	10
Massachusetts	62,136	9,997	3
Michigan	75,504	7,791	16
Minnesota	40,015	8,240	11
Mississippi	13,418	4,742	49
Missouri	37,051	6,656	30
Montana	4,829	5,039	47
Nebraska	11,552	6,742	28
Nevada	16,589	8,727	7
New Hampshire	10,768	8,736	6
New Jersey	85,816	10,452	2
New Mexico	9,290	4,932	48
New York	167,144	9,203	4
North Carolina	51,469	6,561	32
North Dakota	3,656	5,503	42
Ohio	77,003	6,793	26
Oklahoma	18,266	5,387	44
Oregon	23,511	6,856	24
Pennsylvania	89,960	7,365	18
Rhode Island	7,568	7,567	17
South Carolina	22,927	5,902	36
South Dakota	4,577	5,854	37
Tennessee	36,472	6,395	33
Texas	146,409	7,204	20
Utah	12,414	5,548	40
Vermont	4,082	6,582	31
Virginia	55,346	7,855	15
Washington	51,235	8,657	8
West Virginia	8,661	4,701	50
Wisconsin	38,208	7,143	21
Wyoming	3,852	7,248	19
50 States	2,093,775	7,455	
DC	5,646	10,777	
United States*	2,099,418	7,597	

Rank in order per capita	
1	Connecticut
2	New Jersey
3	Massachusetts
4	New York
5	Illinois
6	New Hampshire
7	Nevada
8	Washington
9	Colorado
10	Maryland
11	Minnesota
12	California
13	Delaware
14	Florida
15	Virginia
16	Michigan
17	Rhode Island
18	Pennsylvania
19	Wyoming
20	Texas
21	Wisconsin
22	Georgia
23	Alaska
24	Oregon
25	Kansas
26	Ohio
27	Arizona
28	Nebraska
29	Indiana
30	Missouri
31	Vermont
32	North Carolina
33	Tennessee
34	Iowa
35	Maine
36	South Carolina
37	South Dakota
38	Hawaii
39	Kentucky
40	Utah
41	Alabama
42	North Dakota
43	Louisiana
44	Oklahoma
45	Arkansas
46	Idaho
47	Montana
48	New Mexico
49	Mississippi
50	West Virginia

*Due to rounding or data sources, the 50-state total plus D.C. may not equal the U.S. total. Please see introduction.

E-12 Federal Spending Per Dollar of Taxes Paid, FY 2000

State	Spending per dollar of taxes paid $	Rank
Alabama	1.54	8
Alaska	1.68	5
Arizona	1.18	21
Arkansas	1.38	14
California	0.86	38
Colorado	0.85	41
Connecticut	0.62	50
Delaware	0.84	42
Florida	1.00	31
Georgia	0.99	32
Hawaii	1.56	7
Idaho	1.30	17
Illinois	0.74	46
Indiana	0.92	36
Iowa	1.04	29
Kansas	1.02	30
Kentucky	1.41	12
Louisiana	1.39	13
Maine	1.32	15
Maryland	1.32	15
Massachusetts	0.86	38
Michigan	0.81	44
Minnesota	0.76	45
Mississippi	1.78	3
Missouri	1.26	19
Montana	1.59	6
Nebraska	1.09	23
Nevada	0.69	48
New Hampshire	0.71	47
New Jersey	0.66	49
New Mexico	2.03	1
New York	0.86	38
North Carolina	1.06	26
North Dakota	1.86	2
Ohio	0.97	33
Oklahoma	1.46	10
Oregon	0.93	35
Pennsylvania	1.06	26
Rhode Island	1.18	21
South Carolina	1.27	18
South Dakota	1.46	10
Tennessee	1.20	20
Texas	0.96	34
Utah	1.06	26
Vermont	1.08	25
Virginia	1.48	9
Washington	0.87	37
West Virginia	1.75	4
Wisconsin	0.83	43
Wyoming	1.09	23
50 States	n/a	
DC	6.49	
United States	1.00	

Rank in order by $	
1	New Mexico
2	North Dakota
3	Mississippi
4	West Virginia
5	Alaska
6	Montana
7	Hawaii
8	Alabama
9	Virginia
10	Oklahoma
10	South Dakota
12	Kentucky
13	Louisiana
14	Arkansas
15	Maine
15	Maryland
17	Idaho
18	South Carolina
19	Missouri
20	Tennessee
21	Arizona
21	Rhode Island
23	Nebraska
23	Wyoming
25	Vermont
26	North Carolina
26	Pennsylvania
26	Utah
29	Iowa
30	Kansas
31	Florida
32	Georgia
33	Ohio
34	Texas
35	Oregon
36	Indiana
37	Washington
38	California
38	Massachusetts
38	New York
41	Colorado
42	Delaware
43	Wisconsin
44	Michigan
45	Minnesota
46	Illinois
47	New Hampshire
48	Nevada
49	New Jersey
50	Connecticut

Note: Ties in ranking reflect ties in actual values.

E-13 Highway Charges Returned to States, FY 2000

State	Percentage of charges returned to states	Rank
Alabama	92	32
Alaska	574	1
Arizona	85	50
Arkansas	96	24
California	92	31
Colorado	87	46
Connecticut	141	12
Delaware	162	8
Florida	89	39
Georgia	86	47
Hawaii	223	2
Idaho	142	11
Illinois	94	28
Indiana	90	37
Iowa	98	22
Kansas	98	23
Kentucky	91	33
Louisiana	88	42
Maine	94	27
Maryland	88	43
Massachusetts	98	21
Michigan	90	38
Minnesota	109	17
Mississippi	85	49
Missouri	95	25
Montana	215	4
Nebraska	93	29
Nevada	106	19
New Hampshire	108	18
New Jersey	90	34
New Mexico	114	15
New York	119	13
North Carolina	90	36
North Dakota	192	6
Ohio	87	45
Oklahoma	89	41
Oregon	101	20
Pennsylvania	117	14
Rhode Island	220	3
South Carolina	87	44
South Dakota	209	5
Tennessee	90	35
Texas	85	48
Utah	114	16
Vermont	190	7
Virginia	89	40
Washington	93	30
West Virginia	149	10
Wisconsin	95	26
Wyoming	151	9
50 States	n/a	
DC	348	
United States	99	

Rank in order by percentage

1 Alaska
2 Hawaii
3 Rhode Island
4 Montana
5 South Dakota
6 North Dakota
7 Vermont
8 Delaware
9 Wyoming
10 West Virginia
11 Idaho
12 Connecticut
13 New York
14 Pennsylvania
15 New Mexico
16 Utah
17 Minnesota
18 New Hampshire
19 Nevada
20 Oregon
21 Massachusetts
22 Iowa
23 Kansas
24 Arkansas
25 Missouri
26 Wisconsin
27 Maine
28 Illinois
29 Nebraska
30 Washington
31 California
32 Alabama
33 Kentucky
34 New Jersey
35 Tennessee
36 North Carolina
37 Indiana
38 Michigan
39 Florida
40 Virginia
41 Oklahoma
42 Louisiana
43 Maryland
44 South Carolina
45 Ohio
46 Colorado
47 Georgia
48 Texas
49 Mississippi
50 Arizona

E-14 Terms of Trade with the Federal Government, FY 2000

State	Federal grants to state and local governments $ (in millions)	Terms of trade, ratio of federal grants to federal taxes paid	Rank by ratio
Alabama	4,833	1.35	16
Alaska	2,174	3.29	1
Arizona	4,704	0.99	31
Arkansas	2,778	1.37	14
California	36,080	0.93	35
Colorado	3,591	0.70	45
Connecticut	4,033	0.67	47
Delaware	838	0.94	34
Florida	12,149	0.69	46
Georgia	7,520	0.92	37
Hawaii	1,348	1.27	18
Idaho	1,270	1.24	20
Illinois	11,228	0.73	44
Indiana	5,108	0.87	39
Iowa	2,714	1.02	29
Kansas	2,323	0.88	38
Kentucky	4,687	1.43	13
Louisiana	5,300	1.51	11
Maine	1,770	1.58	9
Maryland	6,911	1.07	26
Massachusetts	9,070	1.01	30
Michigan	10,107	0.92	36
Minnesota	4,753	0.82	42
Mississippi	3,517	1.81	7
Missouri	5,939	1.11	24
Montana	1,474	2.11	4
Nebraska	1,720	1.03	28
Nevada	1,340	0.56	50
New Hampshire	1,238	0.79	43
New Jersey	7,876	0.63	49
New Mexico	3,032	2.25	2
New York	31,564	1.30	17
North Carolina	8,518	1.14	23
North Dakota	1,101	2.08	5
Ohio	10,665	0.96	32
Oklahoma	3,583	1.35	15
Oregon	3,684	1.08	25
Pennsylvania	13,940	1.07	27
Rhode Island	1,574	1.44	12
South Carolina	4,163	1.25	19
South Dakota	1,088	1.64	8
Tennessee	6,372	1.21	21
Texas	18,346	0.86	40
Utah	2,065	1.15	22
Vermont	929	1.57	10
Virginia	5,163	0.64	48
Washington	6,345	0.85	41
West Virginia	2,729	2.17	3
Wisconsin	5,254	0.95	33
Wyoming	1,022	1.83	6
50 States	299,530	0.99	
DC	4,675	5.71	
United States*	308,530	1.01	

Rank in order by ratio	
1	Alaska
2	New Mexico
3	West Virginia
4	Montana
5	North Dakota
6	Wyoming
7	Mississippi
8	South Dakota
9	Maine
10	Vermont
11	Louisiana
12	Rhode Island
13	Kentucky
14	Arkansas
15	Oklahoma
16	Alabama
17	New York
18	Hawaii
19	South Carolina
20	Idaho
21	Tennessee
22	Utah
23	North Carolina
24	Missouri
25	Oregon
26	Maryland
27	Pennsylvania
28	Nebraska
29	Iowa
30	Massachusetts
31	Arizona
32	Ohio
33	Wisconsin
34	Delaware
35	California
36	Michigan
37	Georgia
38	Kansas
39	Indiana
40	Texas
41	Washington
42	Minnesota
43	New Hampshire
44	Illinois
45	Colorado
46	Florida
47	Connecticut
48	Virginia
49	New Jersey
50	Nevada

Note: Numbers that appear to be identical are rounded and vary slightly in actual value. The rankings reflect the actual values before rounding. See the introduction for more details.

Due to rounding or data sources, the 50-state total plus D.C. may not equal the U.S. total. Please see introduction.

E-15 Federal Personal Income Taxes, 1999

State	Federal tax liability $ (in millions)	Federal tax liability per capita $	Rank per capita
Alabama	9.57	2,190	40
Alaska	2.01	3,241	17
Arizona	13.41	2,806	24
Arkansas	4.98	1,954	48
California	126.11	3,805	10
Colorado	16.28	4,014	8
Connecticut	20.69	6,303	1
Delaware	2.62	3,476	15
Florida	52.73	3,490	13
Georgia	23.55	3,024	22
Hawaii	2.99	2,522	35
Idaho	2.71	2,165	41
Illinois	47.35	3,904	9
Indiana	16.55	2,785	27
Iowa	7.09	2,470	36
Kansas	7.43	2,801	25
Kentucky	8.55	2,159	42
Louisiana	9.23	2,112	44
Maine	3.00	2,396	37
Maryland	19.39	3,750	11
Massachusetts	30.25	4,898	3
Michigan	31.57	3,200	18
Minnesota	16.60	3,476	16
Mississippi	4.80	1,734	49
Missouri	14.76	2,700	32
Montana	1.75	1,986	47
Nebraska	4.50	2,703	31
Nevada	7.27	4,020	7
New Hampshire	4.97	4,134	6
New Jersey	40.45	4,967	2
New Mexico	3.47	1,995	46
New York	76.91	4,226	5
North Carolina	20.55	2,685	33
North Dakota	1.35	2,131	43
Ohio	31.44	2,793	26
Oklahoma	6.87	2,044	45
Oregon	9.16	2,762	28
Pennsylvania	37.83	3,154	19
Rhode Island	3.02	3,049	21
South Carolina	8.84	2,274	38
South Dakota	1.88	2,568	34
Tennessee	14.88	2,713	30
Texas	62.37	3,112	20
Utah	4.81	2,257	39
Vermont	1.62	2,736	29
Virginia	25.04	3,644	12
Washington	25.43	4,418	4
West Virginia	3.10	1,715	50
Wisconsin	15.48	2,948	23
Wyoming	1.67	3,489	14
50 States	908.90	3,339	
DC	2.63	5,068	
United States*	918.60	3,369	

Due to rounding or data sources, the 50-state total plus D.C. may not equal the U.S. total. Please see introduction.

Rank in order per capita	
1	Connecticut
2	New Jersey
3	Massachusetts
4	Washington
5	New York
6	New Hampshire
7	Nevada
8	Colorado
9	Illinois
10	California
11	Maryland
12	Virginia
13	Florida
14	Wyoming
15	Delaware
16	Minnesota
17	Alaska
18	Michigan
19	Pennsylvania
20	Texas
21	Rhode Island
22	Georgia
23	Wisconsin
24	Arizona
25	Kansas
26	Ohio
27	Indiana
28	Oregon
29	Vermont
30	Tennessee
31	Nebraska
32	Missouri
33	North Carolina
34	South Dakota
35	Hawaii
36	Iowa
37	Maine
38	South Carolina
39	Utah
40	Alabama
41	Idaho
42	Kentucky
43	North Dakota
44	Louisiana
45	Oklahoma
46	New Mexico
47	Montana
48	Arkansas
49	Mississippi
50	West Virginia

Note: Numbers that appear to be identical are rounded and vary slightly in actual value. The rankings reflect the actual values before rounding. See the introduction for more details.

E-16 Federal Share of Welfare and Medicaid, 2001

State	Federal cost-sharing percentages for welfare and Medicaid	Rank
Alabama	69.99	12
Alaska	60.13	26
Arizona	65.77	16
Arkansas	73.02	5
California	51.25	38
Colorado	50.00	42
Connecticut	50.00	42
Delaware	50.00	42
Florida	56.62	32
Georgia	59.67	29
Hawaii	53.85	34
Idaho	70.76	8
Illinois	50.00	42
Indiana	62.04	22
Iowa	62.67	19
Kansas	59.85	28
Kentucky	70.39	11
Louisiana	70.53	9
Maine	66.12	15
Maryland	50.00	42
Massachusetts	50.00	42
Michigan	56.18	33
Minnesota	51.11	39
Mississippi	76.82	1
Missouri	61.03	23
Montana	73.04	4
Nebraska	60.38	25
Nevada	50.36	41
New Hampshire	50.00	42
New Jersey	50.00	42
New Mexico	73.80	3
New York	50.00	42
North Carolina	62.47	20
North Dakota	69.99	12
Ohio	59.03	31
Oklahoma	71.24	7
Oregon	60.00	27
Pennsylvania	53.62	36
Rhode Island	53.79	35
South Carolina	70.44	10
South Dakota	68.31	14
Tennessee	63.79	18
Texas	60.57	24
Utah	71.44	6
Vermont	62.40	21
Virginia	51.85	37
Washington	50.70	40
West Virginia	75.34	2
Wisconsin	59.29	30
Wyoming	64.60	17
50 States	n/a	
DC	70.00	
United States	n/a	

Rank in order by percentage	
1	Mississippi
2	West Virginia
3	New Mexico
4	Montana
5	Arkansas
6	Utah
7	Oklahoma
8	Idaho
9	Louisiana
10	South Carolina
11	Kentucky
12	Alabama
12	North Dakota
14	South Dakota
15	Maine
16	Arizona
17	Wyoming
18	Tennessee
19	Iowa
20	North Carolina
21	Vermont
22	Indiana
23	Missouri
24	Texas
25	Nebraska
26	Alaska
27	Oregon
28	Kansas
29	Georgia
30	Wisconsin
31	Ohio
32	Florida
33	Michigan
34	Hawaii
35	Rhode Island
36	Pennsylvania
37	Virginia
38	California
39	Minnesota
40	Washington
41	Nevada
42	Colorado
42	Connecticut
42	Delaware
42	Illinois
42	Maryland
42	Massachusetts
42	New Hampshire
42	New Jersey
42	New York

Note: Ties in ranking reflect ties in actual values.

Source Notes for Federal Impacts (Section E)

E-1 Federal Spending, Total and Per Capita, FY 2000: The federal government affects state economies and state finances through its massive spending, accounting for nearly one-quarter of all economic activity in the United States. The primary components of that spending are grants to state and local governments; payments to individuals, such as Social Security; wages and salaries of federal employees; and purchases of goods and services, such as weapons for the Defense Department.

Details of where these funds are spent are compiled by federal agencies and summarized by the Census Bureau in *Consolidated Federal Funds Report for Fiscal Year 2000*. Many tables in this section reflect the latest version of this report, covering federal spending in fiscal 2000, which for the federal government ended in September 2000.

This table reflects total federal spending of nearly $1.6 trillion, along with the results of dividing each state's total by its population to permit meaningful comparisons among states. The federal figures exclude certain forms of federal spending that cannot reasonably be associated with particular states, primarily interest on the federal debt and money spent in other countries.

E-2 Increase in Total Federal Spending, FY 1995-FY 2000: This table uses the Census Bureau reports for federal fiscal years 1995 and 2000 to show the percentage change in total federal spending in each state over a five-year period. The data come from the federal report described in the notes to Table E-1.

E-3 Federal Spending on Grants, Total and Per Capita, FY 2000: This table reflects the federal spending for grants that help state and local governments finance welfare, Medicaid, highway construction, and other activities. The data come from the federal report described in the notes to Table E-1.

E-4 Federal Spending on Procurement, Total and Per Capita, FY 2000: This table reflects the federal spending for purchases ranging from tanks and space shuttles to gasoline for federal vehicles. The data come from the federal report described in the notes to Table E-1.

E-5 Federal Spending on Payments to Individuals, FY 2000: This table reflects the federal spending for payments to individuals. The primary components are Social Security pensions, Medicare payments to health care providers, pensions for retired federal workers, and food stamps. The data come from the federal report described in the notes to Table E-1.

E-6 Federal Spending on Social Security and Medicare, FY 2000: This table reflects the federal spending for Social Security pensions and Medicare payments to health care providers. This spending is a part of the total covered by Table E-5. The per capita amounts suggest the massive impact that this flow of funds has among states. While revenues from payroll taxes are concentrated in states that are showing strong economic growth, states with slower growth (primarily those in the Northeast) receive large portions of personal income from these retirement-related federal payments and private pensions. The data come from the federal report described in the notes to Table E-1.

E-7 Social Security Benefits Paid, 1999: This table provides another perspective on Social Security payments, using tabulations for December 1999 payments prepared by the Social Security Administration and available on the SSA website (www.ssa.gov).

This agency can provide additional details on benefits paid in each state, such as the amounts paid to retired workers, to deceased workers' beneficiaries, and to workers and their families based on disability. Besides the amounts paid and number of recipient households, the table shows the average benefit per household. This amount is appreciably higher in states where salaries have been high (such as in the Northeast) than where they have been low (such as in the South).

E-8 Federal Spending on Employee Wages and Salaries, FY 2000: This table reflects the federal spending on payments for salaries of civilian and military federal employees. The largest amounts are found in states with major federal installations, such as military bases. Because the Postal Service is included and some agencies, such as the Department of Agriculture, which operate in every state, even states without major installations show substantial federal spending. The data come from the federal report described in the notes to Table E-1.

E-9 Federal Grant Spending Per Dollar of State Tax Revenue, FY 1999: Most federal grant spending is now concentrated on state-administered programs, such as welfare and Medicaid. The amounts are substantial when compared with the amount that states raise from state taxes, as shown by the table, which relates the amounts provided by federal grants to the amounts states raised from taxes. The data for fiscal 1999 are from "State Government Finances," available on the Census Bureau website (www.census.gov).

E-10 State and Local General Revenue from Federal Government, FY 1999: These data, covering both state and local government, show the amount of federal aid contributing to "general revenue" as defined by the Census Bureau in its annual survey of government finances. It excludes certain trust funds, such as unemployment insurance, but includes others, such as those used for highway construction. The data are calculated from the Census Bureau's "State and Local Government Finances: 1998-1999" available on the Census Bureau website (www.census.gov).

E-11 Federal Tax Burden, Total and Per Capita, FY 2001: This table shows where the burdens of federal taxes fell in federal fiscal year 2001. The data come from the Tax Foundation's *Special Report* (July 2001, No. 105), which uses formulas to spread the burden of certain taxes, such as the corporate income tax, among states and actual data from federal tax collectors to show the sources of major tax revenues, such as those from personal income and payroll taxes.

E-12 Federal Spending Per Dollar of Taxes Paid, FY 2000: These data relate how much taxpayers in each state pay in federal taxes to the amounts the federal government spends in each state. The information comes from calculations by the Tax Foundation using allocations of tax burdens (see Table E-11) and the Census Bureau report on federal spending (see Table E-1).

Many states get more than a dollar back in federal spending for every dollar sent to the federal government in taxes. This occurs primarily in states where federal installations and/or purchasing is concentrated. Because a substantial portion of federal spending is financed by borrowing (deficit spending), the nationwide total would show more money returned as spending than paid as taxes, so the Tax Foundation adjusted spending to eliminate the deficit-financed portion.

E-13 Highway Charges Returned to States, FY 2000: Federal spending for highways is financed by special user charges, such as federal taxes on gasoline and diesel fuel. Some states, such as Alaska and Hawaii, receive much more federal highway aid than federal user charges collected in their states. Others, which highway officials call "donor states," usually receive less than a dollar of aid from every dollar in federal highway taxes collected within their boundaries. Some states will appear as "donee states" because of large interstate projects underway in a particular period. Which states should "donate" how much is a subject of perpetual controversy in the Congress. The controversy spawns many different ways to measure the federal redistribution of highway revenues.

In FY 2000, federal collections of highway user charges were about $30.3 billion while allocations of spending authority to states were about $30 billion. Federal spending for highways is financed by special "user charges," such as federal taxes on gasoline and diesel fuel.

This table is parallel to Table E-12 but covers only highway spending. It was developed by the Federal Highway Administration and is published in *2000 Highway Statistics*. Data from this book and earlier editions of *Highway Statistics* are available on the FHWA website (www.fhwa.dot.gov).

E-14 Terms of Trade with the Federal Government, FY 2000: This table was developed by State Policy Research to show the relationship between amounts paid by taxpayers in each state to the federal grants to state and local government financed by their federal taxes. The table shows federal grants, identical to the amounts shown in Table E-3. Because all grants, even those paid currently out of money the federal government raises by borrowing, are ultimately paid for by taxpayers, the total federal tax revenue to pay for grants was stipulated as equal to the grants for the fifty states and the District of Columbia.

To determine how this tax burden to pay for grants was distributed among states, the total tax burden for grants was allocated based on the percentage of all federal taxes paid by citizens and corporations in each state, using the Tax Foundation's logic (also used to prepare Table E-11). The result is that the sum of grants and of taxes are identical for the fifty states plus the District of Columbia.

However, the amounts are by no means equal for individual states. States with relatively high personal incomes (and thus federal tax liabilities) but low grants will show ratios below one. Conceptually, for example, 0.95 can be considered as getting 95 cents back in grants for every dollar in federal taxes paid, or a 95 percent return. Conversely, states with lower incomes and high grants will show a ratio above one.

E-15 Federal Personal Income Taxes, 1999: This table shows how much households in each state were required to pay in federal income taxes on their income during 1999, as reported in tax returns filed in early 2000. The data are from the Internal Revenue Service as reported in the *SOI Bulletin* (Vol. 20, No. 4, Spring 2001).

E-16 Federal Share of Welfare and Medicaid, 2001: The federal grants to states for Medicaid are based on multiplying the total costs of these programs by the federal cost-sharing percentages shown in the table. The formula used to determine each state's share provides the largest federal shares for the states with the lowest per capita incomes. A special rule overrides the calculation for more affluent states, so no state has less than 50 percent of these costs paid by the federal government. The percentages were published in Federal Funds Information for States' *Issue Brief 01-56*, released October 19, 2001.

Federal welfare reform legislation, enacted in 1996, was partially implemented at the option of the states during late 1996 and early 1997. Effective in October of 1997, the block grants established under the legislation became fully effective. They are based on federal spending patterns from fiscal year 1994 which reflected federal cost sharing percentages similar to those shown on the table. However, under the block grants, the federal government no longer shares in additional welfare costs with matching money.

Taxes

Just months into fiscal year 2002, all but a handful of states were reporting lower than expected tax revenues. Particularly lagging were receipts from sales and personal and corporate income taxes. When the economic fallout from September 11th becomes clearer, tax collections are sure to show greater declines. Avoiding the subject of tax increases for now, state lawmakers are talking about cost-cutting, hiring freezes, and dipping into reserves.

With internet sales on the rise, state officials are showing a renewed interest in an old problem—the limited reach of the sales tax. Many of the "goods" of today's economy are beyond the grasp of the tax as it is currently structured. Without rate hikes sales tax collections would fall. Current discussions center around streamlining the tax—a complicated and politically controversial multi-state proposal that would simplify and unify the system of sales taxation, allowing states to collect revenue from mail orders and e-purchases. For more information consult the National Governors Association and the National Conference of State Legislatures. For dissenting opinions consult any of the six states that have not joined the cause.

In this chapter you will find the most complete picture of state and local government tax collections available. Although the data cover FY 1999 this statement remains true for two reasons. First, the fiscal information covers *combined* state and local governments. Because of mandates and shifted responsibilities the finances of the two levels of government are intertwined. Second, the source of the numbers, the U.S. Census Bureau, applies uniform definitions and accounting practices to each of the 50 states. Although states do release more updated fiscal information, they are free to use their own accounting measures. Only Census Bureau data provides reliable and consistent comparisons between states. Aware of the need for more current numbers, the Census Bureau plans to release only national government finance figures for FY 2000, the next state and local breakdown should be more timely, but will cover FY 2001.

F-1 State and Local Tax Revenue, FY 1999

State	State and local taxes $ (in millions)	State and local taxes as a percentage of personal income	Rank by percentage
Alabama	8,770	9.1	48
Alaska	1,762	10.3	39
Arizona	12,238	10.9	25
Arkansas	6,077	11.3	18
California	104,977	11.4	15
Colorado	12,117	10.2	40
Connecticut	14,889	12.1	8
Delaware	2,472	11.2	19
Florida	40,245	10.0	44
Georgia	21,503	10.8	29
Hawaii	3,914	12.3	5
Idaho	3,039	11.3	17
Illinois	37,970	10.5	34
Indiana	15,576	10.5	37
Iowa	7,673	10.8	28
Kansas	7,292	10.8	31
Kentucky	9,761	11.1	21
Louisiana	10,533	10.8	27
Maine	4,082	13.9	2
Maryland	16,559	10.5	38
Massachusetts	22,269	10.9	26
Michigan	29,905	11.4	14
Minnesota	17,188	12.3	4
Mississippi	6,087	11.1	22
Missouri	14,028	10.2	43
Montana	2,041	10.9	24
Nebraska	4,624	10.8	30
Nevada	5,291	10.2	41
New Hampshire	3,110	8.8	49
New Jersey	31,576	11.4	13
New Mexico	4,469	12.2	7
New York	82,154	14.0	1
North Carolina	20,266	10.6	33
North Dakota	1,668	11.5	12
Ohio	32,301	11.0	23
Oklahoma	7,768	10.5	35
Oregon	8,536	10.0	45
Pennsylvania	35,193	10.7	32
Rhode Island	3,197	11.6	11
South Carolina	9,067	10.5	36
South Dakota	1,653	9.5	47
Tennessee	11,748	8.8	50
Texas	49,232	9.7	46
Utah	5,469	11.7	9
Vermont	1,784	12.2	6
Virginia	19,558	10.2	42
Washington	18,118	11.1	20
West Virginia	4,279	11.7	10
Wisconsin	17,418	12.7	3
Wyoming	1,357	11.3	16
50 States	812,803	11.0	
DC	2,974	15.1	
United States	815,777	11.0	

Rank in order by percentage

1 New York
2 Maine
3 Wisconsin
4 Minnesota
5 Hawaii
6 Vermont
7 New Mexico
8 Connecticut
9 Utah
10 West Virginia
11 Rhode Island
12 North Dakota
13 New Jersey
14 Michigan
15 California
16 Wyoming
17 Idaho
18 Arkansas
19 Delaware
20 Washington
21 Kentucky
22 Mississippi
23 Ohio
24 Montana
25 Arizona
26 Massachusetts
27 Louisiana
28 Iowa
29 Georgia
30 Nebraska
31 Kansas
32 Pennsylvania
33 North Carolina
34 Illinois
35 Oklahoma
36 South Carolina
37 Indiana
38 Maryland
39 Alaska
40 Colorado
41 Nevada
42 Virginia
43 Missouri
44 Florida
45 Oregon
46 Texas
47 South Dakota
48 Alabama
49 New Hampshire
50 Tennessee

Note: Numbers that appear to be identical are rounded and vary slightly in actual value. The rankings reflect the actual values before rounding. See the introduction for more details.

F-2 Per Capita State and Local Tax Revenue, FY 1999

State	State and local taxes per capita $	State taxes per capita $	Local taxes per capita $	Rank by state and local taxes per capita
Alabama	2,007	1,380	627	50
Alaska	2,841	1,460	1,381	22
Arizona	2,561	1,579	983	37
Arkansas	2,382	1,807	575	42
California	3,167	2,184	983	12
Colorado	2,987	1,619	1,368	17
Connecticut	4,536	2,932	1,604	1
Delaware	3,278	2,693	585	8
Florida	2,663	1,575	1,088	28
Georgia	2,761	1,600	1,161	25
Hawaii	3,303	2,672	630	7
Idaho	2,428	1,734	693	40
Illinois	3,131	1,749	1,382	14
Indiana	2,621	1,638	983	31
Iowa	2,674	1,697	978	27
Kansas	2,748	1,729	1,018	26
Kentucky	2,464	1,857	607	38
Louisiana	2,409	1,485	925	41
Maine	3,258	2,028	1,230	9
Maryland	3,202	1,837	1,365	11
Massachusetts	3,606	2,386	1,221	4
Michigan	3,032	2,216	816	15
Minnesota	3,599	2,613	985	5
Mississippi	2,198	1,652	546	48
Missouri	2,565	1,566	999	36
Montana	2,312	1,524	788	46
Nebraska	2,775	1,598	1,178	24
Nevada	2,925	1,896	1,029	19
New Hampshire	2,590	892	1,698	32
New Jersey	3,878	2,079	1,799	3
New Mexico	2,568	1,985	583	34
New York	4,515	2,127	2,388	2
North Carolina	2,649	1,887	762	29
North Dakota	2,631	1,745	886	30
Ohio	2,869	1,615	1,255	20
Oklahoma	2,313	1,613	700	45
Oregon	2,574	1,611	963	33
Pennsylvania	2,934	1,800	1,134	18
Rhode Island	3,226	1,912	1,314	10
South Carolina	2,333	1,585	748	44
South Dakota	2,255	1,188	1,067	47
Tennessee	2,142	1,312	830	49
Texas	2,456	1,281	1,175	39
Utah	2,568	1,715	852	35
Vermont	3,004	2,337	667	16
Virginia	2,846	1,682	1,163	21
Washington	3,148	2,143	1,004	13
West Virginia	2,368	1,827	541	43
Wisconsin	3,318	2,215	1,103	6
Wyoming	2,827	1,691	1,136	23
50 States	2,986	1,837	1,149	
DC	5,729	0	5,729	
United States	2,992	1,833	1,158	

Rank in order by state and local taxes per capita

1 Connecticut
2 New York
3 New Jersey
4 Massachusetts
5 Minnesota
6 Wisconsin
7 Hawaii
8 Delaware
9 Maine
10 Rhode Island
11 Maryland
12 California
13 Washington
14 Illinois
15 Michigan
16 Vermont
17 Colorado
18 Pennsylvania
19 Nevada
20 Ohio
21 Virginia
22 Alaska
23 Wyoming
24 Nebraska
25 Georgia
26 Kansas
27 Iowa
28 Florida
29 North Carolina
30 North Dakota
31 Indiana
32 New Hampshire
33 Oregon
34 New Mexico
35 Utah
36 Missouri
37 Arizona
38 Kentucky
39 Texas
40 Idaho
41 Louisiana
42 Arkansas
43 West Virginia
44 South Carolina
45 Oklahoma
46 Montana
47 South Dakota
48 Mississippi
49 Tennessee
50 Alabama

Note: Numbers that appear to be identical are rounded and vary slightly in actual value. The rankings reflect the actual values before rounding. See the introduction for more details.

F-3 State and Local Tax Effort, 1996

State	Tax effort %	Rank
Alabama	83	43
Alaska	116	4
Arizona	93	28
Arkansas	92	29
California	101	15
Colorado	82	44
Connecticut	115	5
Delaware	90	32
Florida	90	32
Georgia	95	26
Hawaii	104	9
Idaho	92	29
Illinois	97	25
Indiana	88	39
Iowa	98	24
Kansas	99	20
Kentucky	99	20
Louisiana	86	41
Maine	113	7
Maryland	100	16
Massachusetts	104	9
Michigan	100	16
Minnesota	113	7
Mississippi	102	12
Missouri	87	40
Montana	79	45
Nebraska	99	20
Nevada	73	50
New Hampshire	74	48
New Jersey	114	6
New Mexico	102	12
New York	141	1
North Carolina	94	27
North Dakota	89	35
Ohio	100	16
Oklahoma	92	29
Oregon	85	42
Pennsylvania	102	12
Rhode Island	117	2
South Carolina	89	35
South Dakota	79	45
Tennessee	79	45
Texas	90	32
Utah	89	35
Vermont	100	16
Virginia	89	35
Washington	104	9
West Virginia	99	20
Wisconsin	117	3
Wyoming	74	48
50 States	n/a	
DC	141	
United States	100	

Rank in order by tax effort

1	New York
2	Rhode Island
3	Wisconsin
4	Alaska
5	Connecticut
6	New Jersey
7	Maine
7	Minnesota
9	Hawaii
9	Massachusetts
9	Washington
12	Mississippi
12	New Mexico
12	Pennsylvania
15	California
16	Maryland
16	Michigan
16	Ohio
16	Vermont
20	Kansas
20	Kentucky
20	Nebraska
20	West Virginia
24	Iowa
25	Illinois
26	Georgia
27	North Carolina
28	Arizona
29	Arkansas
29	Idaho
29	Oklahoma
32	Delaware
32	Florida
32	Texas
35	North Dakota
35	South Carolina
35	Utah
35	Virginia
39	Indiana
40	Missouri
41	Louisiana
42	Oregon
43	Alabama
44	Colorado
45	Montana
45	South Dakota
45	Tennessee
48	New Hampshire
48	Wyoming
50	Nevada

Note: Ties in ranking reflect ties in actual values.

F-4 State and Local Tax Capacity, 1996

State	Tax capacity %	Rank
Alabama	83	47
Alaska	127	3
Arizona	94	34
Arkansas	81	48
California	103	16
Colorado	114	10
Connecticut	129	2
Delaware	121	5
Florida	100	19
Georgia	96	29
Hawaii	120	6
Idaho	90	40
Illinois	110	11
Indiana	97	24
Iowa	97	24
Kansas	96	29
Kentucky	84	45
Louisiana	88	42
Maine	89	41
Maryland	108	13
Massachusetts	116	8
Michigan	98	23
Minnesota	107	14
Mississippi	72	50
Missouri	97	24
Montana	99	20
Nebraska	99	20
Nevada	141	1
New Hampshire	118	7
New Jersey	116	8
New Mexico	85	43
New York	109	12
North Carolina	92	35
North Dakota	97	24
Ohio	96	29
Oklahoma	84	45
Oregon	103	16
Pennsylvania	95	32
Rhode Island	91	38
South Carolina	85	43
South Dakota	95	32
Tennessee	92	35
Texas	91	38
Utah	92	35
Vermont	99	20
Virginia	101	18
Washington	104	15
West Virginia	78	49
Wisconsin	97	24
Wyoming	127	3
50 States	n/a	
DC	126	
United States	100	

Rank in order by tax capacity

1	Nevada
2	Connecticut
3	Alaska
3	Wyoming
5	Delaware
6	Hawaii
7	New Hampshire
8	Massachusetts
8	New Jersey
10	Colorado
11	Illinois
12	New York
13	Maryland
14	Minnesota
15	Washington
16	California
16	Oregon
18	Virginia
19	Florida
20	Montana
20	Nebraska
20	Vermont
23	Michigan
24	Indiana
24	Iowa
24	Missouri
24	North Dakota
24	Wisconsin
29	Georgia
29	Kansas
29	Ohio
32	Pennsylvania
32	South Dakota
34	Arizona
35	North Carolina
35	Tennessee
35	Utah
38	Rhode Island
38	Texas
40	Idaho
41	Maine
42	Louisiana
43	New Mexico
43	South Carolina
45	Kentucky
45	Oklahoma
47	Alabama
48	Arkansas
49	West Virginia
50	Mississippi

Note: Ties in ranking reflect ties in actual values.

F-5 Change in State and Local Taxes, FY 1994-FY 1999

State	Percentage change in state and local taxes	Percentage change per capita	Change as a percentage of personal income	Rank by percentage change in state and local taxes
Alabama	29.8	13.7	-3.4	26
Alaska	-9.9	20.6	-27.6	50
Arizona	37.9	0.2	-12.7	13
Arkansas	47.6	19.6	6.0	4
California	38.9	13.6	2.7	10
Colorado	47.6	10.9	-4.6	3
Connecticut	32.1	21.7	-1.2	20
Delaware	40.4	14.6	-2.9	8
Florida	32.0	7.9	-6.9	22
Georgia	44.1	10.3	-4.1	5
Hawaii	4.2	2.0	-10.3	49
Idaho	36.9	10.9	-2.2	16
Illinois	30.6	14.1	-4.9	24
Indiana	27.8	16.9	-6.0	32
Iowa	18.1	9.2	-14.3	46
Kansas	23.6	10.3	-8.3	42
Kentucky	32.2	16.4	-3.5	19
Louisiana	41.9	28.1	3.7	7
Maine	40.1	20.7	11.0	9
Maryland	24.5	8.0	-6.6	38
Massachusetts	30.0	14.9	-6.7	25
Michigan	23.4	5.7	-8.7	43
Minnesota	37.7	20.5	-6.2	14
Mississippi	37.9	17.1	-2.6	12
Missouri	42.5	24.4	5.6	6
Montana	22.2	12.0	-4.8	44
Nebraska	24.4	17.7	-8.0	39
Nevada	54.3	7.3	-6.2	1
New Hampshire	24.9	4.6	-11.4	36
New Jersey	24.2	4.6	-5.8	40
New Mexico	28.5	16.0	-7.6	30
New York	17.3	7.6	-9.7	47
North Carolina	35.8	9.9	-8.2	17
North Dakota	28.8	22.7	-3.6	29
Ohio	32.0	17.1	-2.3	21
Oklahoma	29.1	14.9	-4.1	27
Oregon	22.1	7.4	-15.5	45
Pennsylvania	24.7	13.5	-2.8	37
Rhode Island	28.4	17.8	-1.6	31
South Carolina	37.4	11.5	-2.8	15
South Dakota	26.1	9.8	-6.8	35
Tennessee	29.1	10.2	-9.2	28
Texas	32.2	7.2	-10.3	18
Utah	49.3	14.4	-4.3	2
Vermont	23.9	9.7	-5.3	41
Virginia	38.1	13.3	0.4	11
Washington	30.6	9.5	-8.2	23
West Virginia	27.7	15.9	2.3	33
Wisconsin	27.0	10.3	-7.5	34
Wyoming	13.4	2.8	-12.1	48
50 States	30.5	11.2	-5.4	
DC	17.8	14.8	3.4	
United States	30.4	11.2	-5.3	

Rank in order by percentage change	
1	Nevada
2	Utah
3	Colorado
4	Arkansas
5	Georgia
6	Missouri
7	Louisiana
8	Delaware
9	Maine
10	California
11	Virginia
12	Mississippi
13	Arizona
14	Minnesota
15	South Carolina
16	Idaho
17	North Carolina
18	Texas
19	Kentucky
20	Connecticut
21	Ohio
22	Florida
23	Washington
24	Illinois
25	Massachusetts
26	Alabama
27	Oklahoma
28	Tennessee
29	North Dakota
30	New Mexico
31	Rhode Island
32	Indiana
33	West Virginia
34	Wisconsin
35	South Dakota
36	New Hampshire
37	Pennsylvania
38	Maryland
39	Nebraska
40	New Jersey
41	Vermont
42	Kansas
43	Michigan
44	Montana
45	Oregon
46	Iowa
47	New York
48	Wyoming
49	Hawaii
50	Alaska

Note: Numbers that appear to be identical are rounded and vary slightly in actual value. The rankings reflect the actual values before rounding. See the introduction for more details.

F-6 Property Taxes, FY 1999

State	Property taxes $ (in millions)	Property taxes as a percentage of personal income	Rank by percentage
Alabama	1,192	1.24	50
Alaska	728	4.24	8
Arizona	3,584	3.18	24
Arkansas	1,402	2.60	36
California	25,425	2.75	33
Colorado	3,414	2.88	31
Connecticut	5,175	4.22	10
Delaware	349	1.58	49
Florida	13,901	3.46	20
Georgia	5,423	2.72	34
Hawaii	595	1.87	45
Idaho	816	3.02	27
Illinois	14,100	3.90	12
Indiana	5,177	3.48	19
Iowa	2,533	3.56	15
Kansas	2,115	3.12	26
Kentucky	1,666	1.89	44
Louisiana	1,620	1.66	47
Maine	1,547	5.27	2
Maryland	4,144	2.62	35
Massachusetts	7,301	3.56	16
Michigan	8,811	3.35	22
Minnesota	4,459	3.20	23
Mississippi	1,390	2.52	38
Missouri	3,305	2.39	40
Montana	891	4.75	5
Nebraska	1,567	3.65	14
Nevada	1,261	2.43	39
New Hampshire	2,014	5.72	1
New Jersey	14,336	5.16	4
New Mexico	588	1.60	48
New York	24,759	4.23	9
North Carolina	4,351	2.27	41
North Dakota	497	3.42	21
Ohio	9,334	3.17	25
Oklahoma	1,238	1.67	46
Oregon	2,558	3.00	28
Pennsylvania	9,659	2.94	30
Rhode Island	1,285	4.64	6
South Carolina	2,476	2.86	32
South Dakota	617	3.55	17
Tennessee	2,684	2.01	43
Texas	18,805	3.70	13
Utah	1,192	2.54	37
Vermont	766	5.23	3
Virginia	5,758	2.99	29
Washington	5,763	3.54	18
West Virginia	812	2.21	42
Wisconsin	5,525	4.03	11
Wyoming	523	4.37	7
50 States	239,427	3.25	
DC	680	3.46	
United States	240,107	3.25	

Rank in order by percentage	
1	New Hampshire
2	Maine
3	Vermont
4	New Jersey
5	Montana
6	Rhode Island
7	Wyoming
8	Alaska
9	New York
10	Connecticut
11	Wisconsin
12	Illinois
13	Texas
14	Nebraska
15	Iowa
16	Massachusetts
17	South Dakota
18	Washington
19	Indiana
20	Florida
21	North Dakota
22	Michigan
23	Minnesota
24	Arizona
25	Ohio
26	Kansas
27	Idaho
28	Oregon
29	Virginia
30	Pennsylvania
31	Colorado
32	South Carolina
33	California
34	Georgia
35	Maryland
36	Arkansas
37	Utah
38	Mississippi
39	Nevada
40	Missouri
41	North Carolina
42	West Virginia
43	Tennessee
44	Kentucky
45	Hawaii
46	Oklahoma
47	Louisiana
48	New Mexico
49	Delaware
50	Alabama

Note: Numbers that appear to be identical are rounded and vary slightly in actual value. The rankings reflect the actual values before rounding. See the introduction for more details.

F-7 Property Taxes Per Capita, FY 1999

State	Property tax per capita $	Rank
Alabama	273	50
Alaska	1,174	9
Arizona	750	32
Arkansas	550	40
California	767	31
Colorado	842	23
Connecticut	1,577	3
Delaware	462	44
Florida	920	18
Georgia	696	34
Hawaii	502	42
Idaho	651	35
Illinois	1,163	10
Indiana	871	21
Iowa	883	20
Kansas	797	28
Kentucky	421	46
Louisiana	371	47
Maine	1,235	7
Maryland	801	27
Massachusetts	1,182	8
Michigan	893	19
Minnesota	934	17
Mississippi	502	41
Missouri	604	37
Montana	1,009	13
Nebraska	941	15
Nevada	697	33
New Hampshire	1,677	2
New Jersey	1,761	1
New Mexico	338	49
New York	1,361	4
North Carolina	569	38
North Dakota	784	29
Ohio	829	25
Oklahoma	369	48
Oregon	771	30
Pennsylvania	805	26
Rhode Island	1,297	5
South Carolina	637	36
South Dakota	842	22
Tennessee	489	43
Texas	938	16
Utah	559	39
Vermont	1,289	6
Virginia	838	24
Washington	1,001	14
West Virginia	449	45
Wisconsin	1,052	12
Wyoming	1,089	11
50 States	880	
DC	1,309	
United States	881	

Rank in order per capita	
1	New Jersey
2	New Hampshire
3	Connecticut
4	New York
5	Rhode Island
6	Vermont
7	Maine
8	Massachusetts
9	Alaska
10	Illinois
11	Wyoming
12	Wisconsin
13	Montana
14	Washington
15	Nebraska
16	Texas
17	Minnesota
18	Florida
19	Michigan
20	Iowa
21	Indiana
22	South Dakota
23	Colorado
24	Virginia
25	Ohio
26	Pennsylvania
27	Maryland
28	Kansas
29	North Dakota
30	Oregon
31	California
32	Arizona
33	Nevada
34	Georgia
35	Idaho
36	South Carolina
37	Missouri
38	North Carolina
39	Utah
40	Arkansas
41	Mississippi
42	Hawaii
43	Tennessee
44	Delaware
45	West Virginia
46	Kentucky
47	Louisiana
48	Oklahoma
49	New Mexico
50	Alabama

Note: Numbers that appear to be identical are rounded and vary slightly in actual value. The rankings reflect the actual values before rounding. See the introduction for more details.

F-8 Property Tax Revenue as a Percentage of Three-Tax Revenue, FY 1999

State	Property tax as a percentage of three-tax revenue	Rank
Alabama	15.6	49
Alaska	71.9	2
Arizona	32.1	26
Arkansas	25.2	40
California	27.5	34
Colorado	30.6	30
Connecticut	38.0	14
Delaware	24.2	41
Florida	40.0	12
Georgia	27.3	36
Hawaii	16.2	48
Idaho	30.4	31
Illinois	41.8	10
Indiana	36.6	16
Iowa	37.0	15
Kansas	31.9	27
Kentucky	19.7	45
Louisiana	17.8	47
Maine	41.5	11
Maryland	27.7	33
Massachusetts	36.2	18
Michigan	34.4	22
Minnesota	29.4	32
Mississippi	25.5	39
Missouri	25.9	38
Montana	53.0	3
Nebraska	38.1	13
Nevada	27.4	35
New Hampshire	77.7	1
New Jersey	49.9	4
New Mexico	15.6	50
New York	34.3	23
North Carolina	24.2	42
North Dakota	36.2	17
Ohio	31.6	28
Oklahoma	19.3	46
Oregon	36.0	19
Pennsylvania	33.4	24
Rhode Island	43.2	8
South Carolina	30.7	29
South Dakota	44.0	7
Tennessee	26.9	37
Texas	42.9	9
Utah	23.9	43
Vermont	47.9	6
Virginia	32.9	25
Washington	35.0	20
West Virginia	23.0	44
Wisconsin	35.0	21
Wyoming	49.8	5
50 States	33.4	
DC	26.5	
United States	33.3	

Rank in order by percentage	
1	New Hampshire
2	Alaska
3	Montana
4	New Jersey
5	Wyoming
6	Vermont
7	South Dakota
8	Rhode Island
9	Texas
10	Illinois
11	Maine
12	Florida
13	Nebraska
14	Connecticut
15	Iowa
16	Indiana
17	North Dakota
18	Massachusetts
19	Oregon
20	Washington
21	Wisconsin
22	Michigan
23	New York
24	Pennsylvania
25	Virginia
26	Arizona
27	Kansas
28	Ohio
29	South Carolina
30	Colorado
31	Idaho
32	Minnesota
33	Maryland
34	California
35	Nevada
36	Georgia
37	Tennessee
38	Missouri
39	Mississippi
40	Arkansas
41	Delaware
42	North Carolina
43	Utah
44	West Virginia
45	Kentucky
46	Oklahoma
47	Louisiana
48	Hawaii
49	Alabama
50	New Mexico

Note: Numbers that appear to be identical are rounded and vary slightly in actual value. The rankings reflect the actual values before rounding. See the introduction for more details.

F-9 Sales Taxes, FY 1999

State	State and local sales taxes $ (in millions)	State and local taxes as a percentage of personal income	Rank by percentage
Alabama	4,386	4.56	15
Alaska	285	1.66	46
Arizona	5,471	4.86	13
Arkansas	2,729	5.06	9
California	36,268	3.92	25
Colorado	4,383	3.70	30
Connecticut	4,822	3.93	24
Delaware	277	1.26	49
Florida	20,855	5.19	8
Georgia	8,745	4.38	18
Hawaii	2,004	6.30	4
Idaho	1,021	3.78	28
Illinois	12,366	3.42	36
Indiana	4,745	3.19	39
Iowa	2,560	3.60	33
Kansas	2,824	4.17	20
Kentucky	3,568	4.06	21
Louisiana	5,965	6.12	5
Maine	1,163	3.96	23
Maryland	4,275	2.70	44
Massachusetts	4,841	2.36	45
Michigan	9,351	3.55	34
Minnesota	5,415	3.88	26
Mississippi	3,080	5.59	6
Missouri	5,602	4.06	22
Montana	308	1.64	47
Nebraska	1,478	3.44	35
Nevada	3,335	6.42	3
New Hampshire	517	1.47	48
New Jersey	8,014	2.89	43
New Mexico	2,376	6.47	2
New York	21,274	3.63	32
North Carolina	7,041	3.67	31
North Dakota	694	4.78	14
Ohio	9,936	3.38	37
Oklahoma	3,107	4.19	19
Oregon	839	0.98	50
Pennsylvania	10,423	3.17	40
Rhode Island	925	3.34	38
South Carolina	3,279	3.79	27
South Dakota	786	4.52	16
Tennessee	7,127	5.34	7
Texas	25,023	4.92	11
Utah	2,332	4.98	10
Vermont	448	3.06	41
Virginia	5,672	2.95	42
Washington	10,697	6.57	1
West Virginia	1,802	4.91	12
Wisconsin	5,098	3.72	29
Wyoming	526	4.40	17
50 States	290,059	3.94	
DC	934	4.75	
United States	290,993	3.94	

Rank in order by percentage

1. Washington
2. New Mexico
3. Nevada
4. Hawaii
5. Louisiana
6. Mississippi
7. Tennessee
8. Florida
9. Arkansas
10. Utah
11. Texas
12. West Virginia
13. Arizona
14. North Dakota
15. Alabama
16. South Dakota
17. Wyoming
18. Georgia
19. Oklahoma
20. Kansas
21. Kentucky
22. Missouri
23. Maine
24. Connecticut
25. California
26. Minnesota
27. South Carolina
28. Idaho
29. Wisconsin
30. Colorado
31. North Carolina
32. New York
33. Iowa
34. Michigan
35. Nebraska
36. Illinois
37. Ohio
38. Rhode Island
39. Indiana
40. Pennsylvania
41. Vermont
42. Virginia
43. New Jersey
44. Maryland
45. Massachusetts
46. Alaska
47. Montana
48. New Hampshire
49. Delaware
50. Oregon

Note: Numbers that appear to be identical are rounded and vary slightly in actual value. The rankings reflect the actual values before rounding. See the introduction for more details.

F-10 Sales Taxes Per Capita, FY 1999

State	Sales taxes per capita $	Rank per capita
Alabama	1,004	25
Alaska	459	46
Arizona	1,145	11
Arkansas	1,070	21
California	1,094	17
Colorado	1,081	19
Connecticut	1,469	4
Delaware	368	48
Florida	1,380	5
Georgia	1,123	13
Hawaii	1,691	3
Idaho	815	42
Illinois	1,020	24
Indiana	798	43
Iowa	892	35
Kansas	1,064	22
Kentucky	901	34
Louisiana	1,364	7
Maine	928	31
Maryland	827	40
Massachusetts	784	44
Michigan	948	29
Minnesota	1,134	12
Mississippi	1,112	14
Missouri	1,025	23
Montana	349	49
Nebraska	887	36
Nevada	1,844	2
New Hampshire	430	47
New Jersey	984	27
New Mexico	1,366	6
New York	1,169	10
North Carolina	920	33
North Dakota	1,094	18
Ohio	883	37
Oklahoma	925	32
Oregon	253	50
Pennsylvania	869	38
Rhode Island	934	30
South Carolina	844	39
South Dakota	1,073	20
Tennessee	1,300	8
Texas	1,248	9
Utah	1,095	16
Vermont	755	45
Virginia	825	41
Washington	1,858	1
West Virginia	997	26
Wisconsin	971	28
Wyoming	1,096	15
50 States	1,066	
DC	1,800	
United States	1,067	

Rank in order per capita	
1	Washington
2	Nevada
3	Hawaii
4	Connecticut
5	Florida
6	New Mexico
7	Louisiana
8	Tennessee
9	Texas
10	New York
11	Arizona
12	Minnesota
13	Georgia
14	Mississippi
15	Wyoming
16	Utah
17	California
18	North Dakota
19	Colorado
20	South Dakota
21	Arkansas
22	Kansas
23	Missouri
24	Illinois
25	Alabama
26	West Virginia
27	New Jersey
28	Wisconsin
29	Michigan
30	Rhode Island
31	Maine
32	Oklahoma
33	North Carolina
34	Kentucky
35	Iowa
36	Nebraska
37	Ohio
38	Pennsylvania
39	South Carolina
40	Maryland
41	Virginia
42	Idaho
43	Indiana
44	Massachusetts
45	Vermont
46	Alaska
47	New Hampshire
48	Delaware
49	Montana
50	Oregon

Note: Numbers that appear to be identical are rounded and vary slightly in actual value. The rankings reflect the actual values before rounding. See the introduction for more details.

F-11 Sales Tax Revenue as a Percentage of Three-Tax Revenue, FY 1999

State	Sales taxes as a percentage of three-tax revenue	Rank
Alabama	57.5	7
Alaska	28.1	43
Arizona	49.1	15
Arkansas	49.0	16
California	39.2	25
Colorado	39.3	24
Connecticut	35.4	34
Delaware	19.3	48
Florida	60.0	6
Georgia	44.0	19
Hawaii	54.6	11
Idaho	38.0	27
Illinois	36.7	29
Indiana	33.6	36
Iowa	37.4	28
Kansas	42.6	21
Kentucky	42.2	22
Louisiana	65.4	3
Maine	31.2	39
Maryland	28.5	42
Massachusetts	24.0	46
Michigan	36.5	30
Minnesota	35.7	33
Mississippi	56.5	9
Missouri	43.9	20
Montana	18.3	49
Nebraska	35.9	32
Nevada	72.6	1
New Hampshire	19.9	47
New Jersey	27.9	45
New Mexico	63.0	5
New York	29.5	41
North Carolina	39.2	26
North Dakota	50.5	13
Ohio	33.6	35
Oklahoma	48.4	17
Oregon	11.8	50
Pennsylvania	36.0	31
Rhode Island	31.1	40
South Carolina	40.7	23
South Dakota	56.0	10
Tennessee	71.5	2
Texas	57.1	8
Utah	46.8	18
Vermont	28.1	44
Virginia	32.4	37
Washington	65.0	4
West Virginia	51.0	12
Wisconsin	32.3	38
Wyoming	50.2	14
50 States	40.4	
DC	36.4	
United States	40.4	

Rank in order percentage	
1	Nevada
2	Tennessee
3	Louisiana
4	Washington
5	New Mexico
6	Florida
7	Alabama
8	Texas
9	Mississippi
10	South Dakota
11	Hawaii
12	West Virginia
13	North Dakota
14	Wyoming
15	Arizona
16	Arkansas
17	Oklahoma
18	Utah
19	Georgia
20	Missouri
21	Kansas
22	Kentucky
23	South Carolina
24	Colorado
25	California
26	North Carolina
27	Idaho
28	Iowa
29	Illinois
30	Michigan
31	Pennsylvania
32	Nebraska
33	Minnesota
34	Connecticut
35	Ohio
36	Indiana
37	Virginia
38	Wisconsin
39	Maine
40	Rhode Island
41	New York
42	Maryland
43	Alaska
44	Vermont
45	New Jersey
46	Massachusetts
47	New Hampshire
48	Delaware
49	Montana
50	Oregon

Note: Numbers that appear to be identical are rounded and vary slightly in actual value. The rankings reflect the actual values before rounding. See the introduction for more details.

F-12 Number of Services Reached by Sales Tax, 1996

State	Services subject to sales tax	Rank
Alabama	32	28
Alaska	1	49
Arizona	57	21
Arkansas	65	15
California	13	46
Colorado	14	45
Connecticut	87	8
Delaware	142	4
Florida	64	16
Georgia	34	27
Hawaii	157	1
Idaho	29	31
Illinois	17	44
Indiana	22	40
Iowa	94	7
Kansas	76	10
Kentucky	26	37
Louisiana	58	20
Maine	27	36
Maryland	39	26
Massachusetts	20	41
Michigan	29	31
Minnesota	61	18
Mississippi	70	13
Missouri	28	33
Montana	19	42
Nebraska	49	25
Nevada	11	47
New Hampshire	11	47
New Jersey	50	24
New Mexico	152	2
New York	74	11
North Carolina	28	33
North Dakota	25	38
Ohio	52	23
Oklahoma	32	28
Oregon	0	50
Pennsylvania	61	18
Rhode Island	28	33
South Carolina	32	28
South Dakota	141	5
Tennessee	71	12
Texas	78	9
Utah	54	22
Vermont	23	39
Virginia	18	43
Washington	152	2
West Virginia	110	6
Wisconsin	69	14
Wyoming	63	17
50 States	n/a	
DC	63	
United States	164	

Rank in order by number	
1	Hawaii
2	New Mexico
2	Washington
4	Delaware
5	South Dakota
6	West Virginia
7	Iowa
8	Connecticut
9	Texas
10	Kansas
11	New York
12	Tennessee
13	Mississippi
14	Wisconsin
15	Arkansas
16	Florida
17	Wyoming
18	Minnesota
18	Pennsylvania
20	Louisiana
21	Arizona
22	Utah
23	Ohio
24	New Jersey
25	Nebraska
26	Maryland
27	Georgia
28	Alabama
28	Oklahoma
28	South Carolina
31	Idaho
31	Michigan
33	Missouri
33	North Carolina
33	Rhode Island
36	Maine
37	Kentucky
38	North Dakota
39	Vermont
40	Indiana
41	Massachusetts
42	Montana
43	Virginia
44	Illinois
45	Colorado
46	California
47	Nevada
47	New Hampshire
49	Alaska
50	Oregon

Note: Ties in ranking reflect ties in actual values.

F-13 Individual Income Taxes, FY 1999

State	Individual income tax $ (in millions)	Income tax as a percentage of personal income	Rank by percentage
Alabama	2,045	2.12	36
Alaska	0	n/a	n/a
Arizona	2,098	1.86	38
Arkansas	1,434	2.66	26
California	30,732	3.33	13
Colorado	3,355	2.83	21
Connecticut	3,610	2.95	17
Delaware	814	3.70	7
Florida	0	n/a	n/a
Georgia	5,697	2.85	18
Hawaii	1,069	3.36	12
Idaho	847	3.14	15
Illinois	7,248	2.00	37
Indiana	4,215	2.83	20
Iowa	1,755	2.47	33
Kansas	1,696	2.50	31
Kentucky	3,221	3.66	8
Louisiana	1,536	1.57	40
Maine	1,020	3.47	10
Maryland	6,563	4.15	3
Massachusetts	8,037	3.92	4
Michigan	7,476	2.84	19
Minnesota	5,306	3.81	5
Mississippi	983	1.79	39
Missouri	3,856	2.79	23
Montana	483	2.58	29
Nebraska	1,072	2.50	32
Nevada	0	n/a	n/a
New Hampshire	63	0.18	42
New Jersey	6,354	2.29	34
New Mexico	810	2.21	35
New York	26,045	4.45	1
North Carolina	6,586	3.43	11
North Dakota	182	1.25	41
Ohio	10,288	3.50	9
Oklahoma	2,070	2.79	22
Oregon	3,710	4.35	2
Pennsylvania	8,846	2.69	25
Rhode Island	763	2.76	24
South Carolina	2,298	2.66	27
South Dakota	0	n/a	n/a
Tennessee	160	0.12	43
Texas	0	n/a	n/a
Utah	1,461	3.12	16
Vermont	383	2.62	28
Virginia	6,088	3.16	14
Washington	0	n/a	n/a
West Virginia	920	2.51	30
Wisconsin	5,162	3.77	6
Wyoming	0	n/a	n/a
50 States	188,357	2.56	
DC	952	4.84	
United States	189,309	2.56	

Rank in order by percentage

1 New York
2 Oregon
3 Maryland
4 Massachusetts
5 Minnesota
6 Wisconsin
7 Delaware
8 Kentucky
9 Ohio
10 Maine
11 North Carolina
12 Hawaii
13 California
14 Virginia
15 Idaho
16 Utah
17 Connecticut
18 Georgia
19 Michigan
20 Indiana
21 Colorado
22 Oklahoma
23 Missouri
24 Rhode Island
25 Pennsylvania
26 Arkansas
27 South Carolina
28 Vermont
29 Montana
30 West Virginia
31 Kansas
32 Nebraska
33 Iowa
34 New Jersey
35 New Mexico
36 Alabama
37 Illinois
38 Arizona
39 Mississippi
40 Louisiana
41 North Dakota
42 New Hampshire
43 Tennessee

Note: Numbers that appear to be identical are rounded and vary slightly in actual value. The rankings reflect the actual values before rounding. See the introduction for more details.

F-14 Individual Income Taxes Per Capita, FY 1999

State	Income taxes per capita $	Rank per capita
Alabama	468	36
Alaska	0	n/a
Arizona	439	38
Arkansas	562	33
California	927	9
Colorado	827	14
Connecticut	1,100	6
Delaware	1,079	7
Florida	0	n/a
Georgia	731	21
Hawaii	902	11
Idaho	677	25
Illinois	598	31
Indiana	709	22
Iowa	612	30
Kansas	639	28
Kentucky	813	16
Louisiana	351	40
Maine	814	15
Maryland	1,269	3
Massachusetts	1,301	2
Michigan	758	19
Minnesota	1,111	5
Mississippi	355	39
Missouri	705	23
Montana	547	34
Nebraska	643	27
Nevada	0	n/a
New Hampshire	53	42
New Jersey	780	17
New Mexico	465	37
New York	1,431	1
North Carolina	861	13
North Dakota	287	41
Ohio	914	10
Oklahoma	617	29
Oregon	1,119	4
Pennsylvania	738	20
Rhode Island	770	18
South Carolina	591	32
South Dakota	0	n/a
Tennessee	29	43
Texas	0	n/a
Utah	686	24
Vermont	646	26
Virginia	886	12
Washington	0	n/a
West Virginia	509	35
Wisconsin	983	8
Wyoming	0	n/a
50 States	692	
DC	1,835	
United States	694	

Rank in order per capita	
1	New York
2	Massachusetts
3	Maryland
4	Oregon
5	Minnesota
6	Connecticut
7	Delaware
8	Wisconsin
9	California
10	Ohio
11	Hawaii
12	Virginia
13	North Carolina
14	Colorado
15	Maine
16	Kentucky
17	New Jersey
18	Rhode Island
19	Michigan
20	Pennsylvania
21	Georgia
22	Indiana
23	Missouri
24	Utah
25	Idaho
26	Vermont
27	Nebraska
28	Kansas
29	Oklahoma
30	Iowa
31	Illinois
32	South Carolina
33	Arkansas
34	Montana
35	West Virginia
36	Alabama
37	New Mexico
38	Arizona
39	Mississippi
40	Louisiana
41	North Dakota
42	New Hampshire
43	Tennessee

F-15 Individual Income Tax Revenue as a Percentage of Three-Tax Revenue, FY 1999

State	Income tax as a percentage of three-tax revenue	Rank
Alabama	26.8	26
Alaska	n/a	n/a
Arizona	18.8	38
Arkansas	25.8	30
California	33.3	11
Colorado	30.1	17
Connecticut	26.5	27
Delaware	56.5	1
Florida	n/a	n/a
Georgia	28.7	23
Hawaii	29.1	21
Idaho	31.6	14
Illinois	21.5	36
Indiana	29.8	18
Iowa	25.6	32
Kansas	25.6	33
Kentucky	38.1	5
Louisiana	16.8	40
Maine	27.4	25
Maryland	43.8	3
Massachusetts	39.8	4
Michigan	29.2	20
Minnesota	35.0	8
Mississippi	18.0	39
Missouri	30.2	16
Montana	28.7	22
Nebraska	26.0	28
Nevada	n/a	n/a
New Hampshire	2.4	42
New Jersey	22.1	35
New Mexico	21.5	37
New York	36.1	7
North Carolina	36.6	6
North Dakota	13.3	41
Ohio	34.8	9
Oklahoma	32.3	13
Oregon	52.2	2
Pennsylvania	30.6	15
Rhode Island	25.7	31
South Carolina	28.5	24
South Dakota	0.0	n/a
Tennessee	1.6	43
Texas	0.0	n/a
Utah	29.3	19
Vermont	24.0	34
Virginia	34.8	10
Washington	n/a	n/a
West Virginia	26.0	29
Wisconsin	32.7	12
Wyoming	n/a	n/a
50 States	26.2	
DC	37.1	
United States	26.3	

Rank in order by percentage

1. Delaware
2. Oregon
3. Maryland
4. Massachusetts
5. Kentucky
6. North Carolina
7. New York
8. Minnesota
9. Ohio
10. Virginia
11. California
12. Wisconsin
13. Oklahoma
14. Idaho
15. Pennsylvania
16. Missouri
17. Colorado
18. Indiana
19. Utah
20. Michigan
21. Hawaii
22. Montana
23. Georgia
24. South Carolina
25. Maine
26. Alabama
27. Connecticut
28. Nebraska
29. West Virginia
30. Arkansas
31. Rhode Island
32. Iowa
33. Kansas
34. Vermont
35. New Jersey
36. Illinois
37. New Mexico
38. Arizona
39. Mississippi
40. Louisiana
41. North Dakota
42. New Hampshire
43. Tennessee

Note: Numbers that appear to be identical are rounded and vary slightly in actual value. The rankings reflect the actual values before rounding. See the introduction for more details.

F-16 Highest Personal Income Tax Rate, 2001

State	Highest rate %	Rank
Alabama	3.02	39
Alaska	no tax	n/a
Arizona	5.04	31
Arkansas	7.00	11
California	9.30	3
Colorado	4.63	34
Connecticut	4.50	35
Delaware	5.95	25
Florida	no tax	n/a
Georgia	6.00	22
Hawaii	8.75	5
Idaho	8.10	8
Illinois	3.00	40
Indiana	3.40	38
Iowa	5.42	30
Kansas	6.45	20
Kentucky	6.00	22
Louisiana	3.62	37
Maine	8.50	6
Maryland	4.85	33
Massachusetts	5.85	26
Michigan	4.20	36
Minnesota	7.85	9
Mississippi	5.00	32
Missouri	6.00	22
Montana	6.64	18
Nebraska	6.68	17
Nevada	no tax	n/a
New Hampshire	no tax	n/a
New Jersey	6.37	21
New Mexico	8.20	7
New York	6.85	14
North Carolina	7.75	10
North Dakota	5.54	29
Ohio	6.98	13
Oklahoma	6.75	15
Oregon	9.00	4
Pennsylvania	2.80	41
Rhode Island	10.10	1
South Carolina	7.00	11
South Dakota	no tax	n/a
Tennessee	no tax	n/a
Texas	no tax	n/a
Utah	5.61	28
Vermont	9.50	2
Virginia	5.75	27
Washington	no tax	n/a
West Virginia	6.50	19
Wisconsin	6.75	15
Wyoming	no tax	n/a
50 States	n/a	
DC	9.50	
United States	n/a	

Rank in order by percentage

1	Rhode Island
2	Vermont
3	California
4	Oregon
5	Hawaii
6	Maine
7	New Mexico
8	Idaho
9	Minnesota
10	North Carolina
11	Arkansas
11	South Carolina
13	Ohio
14	New York
15	Oklahoma
15	Wisconsin
17	Nebraska
18	Montana
19	West Virginia
20	Kansas
21	New Jersey
22	Georgia
22	Kentucky
22	Missouri
25	Delaware
26	Massachusetts
27	Virginia
28	Utah
29	North Dakota
30	Iowa
31	Arizona
32	Mississippi
33	Maryland
34	Colorado
35	Connecticut
36	Michigan
37	Louisiana
38	Indiana
39	Alabama
40	Illinois
41	Pennsylvania

Note: Ties in ranking reflect ties in actual values.

F-17 Corporate Income Taxes, Total and Per Capita, FY 1999

State	Corporate income taxes $ (in millions)	Corporate income taxes per capita $	Rank per capita
Alabama	233	53	44
Alaska	212	342	1
Arizona	545	114	19
Arkansas	212	83	29
California	5,459	165	9
Colorado	301	74	36
Connecticut	475	145	14
Delaware	233	308	3
Florida	1,267	84	27
Georgia	793	102	21
Hawaii	52	44	46
Idaho	96	77	35
Illinois	2,104	173	7
Indiana	990	167	8
Iowa	235	82	31
Kansas	254	96	24
Kentucky	312	79	33
Louisiana	286	65	41
Maine	147	118	18
Maryland	405	78	34
Massachusetts	1,250	202	6
Michigan	2,414	245	4
Minnesota	779	163	11
Mississippi	230	83	30
Missouri	277	51	45
Montana	90	101	22
Nebraska	135	81	32
Nevada	0	n/a	n/a
New Hampshire	256	213	5
New Jersey	1,334	164	10
New Mexico	164	94	25
New York	5,827	320	2
North Carolina	921	120	17
North Dakota	94	148	12
Ohio	752	67	39
Oklahoma	187	56	43
Oregon	324	98	23
Pennsylvania	1,538	128	15
Rhode Island	66	67	38
South Carolina	257	66	40
South Dakota	51	69	37
Tennessee	571	104	20
Texas	0	n/a	n/a
Utah	180	85	26
Vermont	50	84	28
Virginia	414	60	42
Washington	0	n/a	n/a
West Virginia	263	146	13
Wisconsin	671	128	16
Wyoming	0	n/a	n/a
50 States	33,704	124	
DC	218	419	
United States	33,922	124	

Rank in order per capita	
1	Alaska
2	New York
3	Delaware
4	Michigan
5	New Hampshire
6	Massachusetts
7	Illinois
8	Indiana
9	California
10	New Jersey
11	Minnesota
12	North Dakota
13	West Virginia
14	Connecticut
15	Pennsylvania
16	Wisconsin
17	North Carolina
18	Maine
19	Arizona
20	Tennessee
21	Georgia
22	Montana
23	Oregon
24	Kansas
25	New Mexico
26	Utah
27	Florida
28	Vermont
29	Arkansas
30	Mississippi
31	Iowa
32	Nebraska
33	Kentucky
34	Maryland
35	Idaho
36	Colorado
37	South Dakota
38	Rhode Island
39	Ohio
40	South Carolina
41	Louisiana
42	Virginia
43	Oklahoma
44	Alabama
45	Missouri
46	Hawaii

Note: Numbers that appear to be identical are rounded and vary slightly in actual value. The rankings reflect the actual values before rounding. See the introduction for more details.

F-18 Motor Fuel Taxes

State	Gasoline tax 2001 cents/gallons	Motor fuel taxes FY 1999 $ (in millions)	Fuel taxes as a percentage of personal income	Rank by gas tax
Alabama	18.00	538	0.56	34
Alaska	8.00	38	0.22	48
Arizona	18.00	585	0.52	34
Arkansas	20.60	380	0.70	23
California	18.00	3,034	0.33	34
Colorado	22.00	516	0.44	16
Connecticut	25.00	545	0.44	7
Delaware	23.00	103	0.47	14
Florida	13.30	2,094	0.52	46
Georgia	7.50	566	0.28	50
Hawaii	16.00	134	0.42	42
Idaho	26.00	212	0.79	4
Illinois	19.30	1,514	0.42	30
Indiana	15.00	664	0.45	44
Iowa	20.00	341	0.48	24
Kansas	20.00	326	0.48	24
Kentucky	16.40	445	0.51	41
Louisiana	20.00	537	0.55	24
Maine	22.00	173	0.59	16
Maryland	23.50	680	0.43	13
Massachusetts	21.00	637	0.31	21
Michigan	19.00	1,075	0.41	31
Minnesota	20.00	581	0.42	24
Mississippi	18.40	403	0.73	33
Missouri	17.05	666	0.48	39
Montana	27.00	160	0.86	2
Nebraska	24.80	265	0.62	8
Nevada	24.00	300	0.58	11
New Hampshire	19.00	120	0.34	31
New Jersey	10.54	483	0.17	47
New Mexico	18.00	247	0.67	34
New York	8.00	505	0.09	48
North Carolina	24.55	1,146	0.60	9
North Dakota	21.00	105	0.72	21
Ohio	22.00	1,378	0.47	16
Oklahoma	17.00	384	0.52	40
Oregon	24.00	406	0.48	11
Pennsylvania	25.90	747	0.23	5
Rhode Island	29.00	119	0.43	1
South Carolina	16.00	351	0.41	42
South Dakota	22.00	108	0.62	16
Tennessee	21.40	770	0.58	20
Texas	20.00	2,592	0.51	24
Utah	24.50	313	0.67	10
Vermont	20.00	57	0.39	24
Virginia	17.50	795	0.41	38
Washington	23.00	718	0.44	14
West Virginia	25.65	237	0.65	6
Wisconsin	26.40	909	0.66	3
Wyoming	14.00	63	0.52	45
50 States	n/a	30,063	0.41	
DC	20.00	31	0.16	
United States	n/a	30,094	0.41	

Rank in order by gas tax

1	Rhode Island
2	Montana
3	Wisconsin
4	Idaho
5	Pennsylvania
6	West Virginia
7	Connecticut
8	Nebraska
9	North Carolina
10	Utah
11	Nevada
11	Oregon
13	Maryland
14	Delaware
14	Washington
16	Colorado
16	Maine
16	Ohio
16	South Dakota
20	Tennessee
21	Massachusetts
21	North Dakota
23	Arkansas
24	Iowa
24	Kansas
24	Louisiana
24	Minnesota
24	Texas
24	Vermont
30	Illinois
31	Michigan
31	New Hampshire
33	Mississippi
34	Alabama
34	Arizona
34	California
34	New Mexico
38	Virginia
39	Missouri
40	Oklahoma
41	Kentucky
42	Hawaii
42	South Carolina
44	Indiana
45	Wyoming
46	Florida
47	New Jersey
48	Alaska
48	New York
50	Georgia

Note: Ties in ranking reflect ties in actual values.

F-19 Tobacco Taxes

State	Cigarette tax rate 2001 cents/pack	Tobacco taxes FY 1999 $ (in millions)	Tobacco taxes as a percentage of personal income	Rank by tax rate
Alabama	16.5	83.0	0.09	42
Alaska	100.0	51.8	0.30	2
Arizona	58.0	162.8	0.14	14
Arkansas	31.5	94.6	0.18	28
California	87.0	899.9	0.10	4
Colorado	20.0	69.8	0.06	37
Connecticut	50.0	130.5	0.11	18
Delaware	24.0	24.5	0.11	31
Florida	33.9	453.9	0.11	26
Georgia	12.0	92.5	0.05	45
Hawaii	100.0	42.3	0.13	2
Idaho	28.0	28.5	0.11	30
Illinois	58.0	573.3	0.16	14
Indiana	15.5	89.9	0.06	43
Iowa	36.0	98.3	0.14	23
Kansas	24.0	54.6	0.08	31
Kentucky	3.0	17.7	0.02	49
Louisiana	24.0	85.7	0.09	31
Maine	74.0	78.4	0.27	9
Maryland	66.0	128.8	0.08	12
Massachusetts	76.0	284.4	0.14	7
Michigan	75.0	615.4	0.23	8
Minnesota	48.0	184.9	0.13	19
Mississippi	18.0	57.0	0.10	38
Missouri	17.0	130.6	0.09	40
Montana	18.0	14.1	0.08	38
Nebraska	34.0	47.1	0.11	25
Nevada	35.0	64.0	0.12	24
New Hampshire	52.0	73.8	0.21	16
New Jersey	80.0	417.5	0.15	6
New Mexico	21.0	24.7	0.07	36
New York	111.0	696.2	0.12	1
North Carolina	5.0	44.7	0.02	48
North Dakota	44.0	23.0	0.16	20
Ohio	24.0	298.1	0.10	31
Oklahoma	23.0	77.8	0.10	35
Oregon	68.0	193.8	0.23	11
Pennsylvania	31.0	330.4	0.10	29
Rhode Island	71.0	61.5	0.22	10
South Carolina	7.0	30.2	0.03	47
South Dakota	33.0	20.4	0.12	27
Tennessee	13.0	84.9	0.06	44
Texas	41.0	624.1	0.12	22
Utah	51.5	50.5	0.11	17
Vermont	44.0	13.6	0.09	20
Virginia	2.5	50.3	0.03	50
Washington	82.5	278.5	0.17	5
West Virginia	17.0	33.1	0.09	40
Wisconsin	59.0	266.8	0.19	13
Wyoming	12.0	5.8	0.05	45
50 States	n/a	8357.8	0.11	
DC	65.0	17.1	0.09	
United States	34.0	8374.9	0.11	

Rank in order by tax rate	
1	New York
2	Alaska
2	Hawaii
4	California
5	Washington
6	New Jersey
7	Massachusetts
8	Michigan
9	Maine
10	Rhode Island
11	Oregon
12	Maryland
13	Wisconsin
14	Arizona
14	Illinois
16	New Hampshire
17	Utah
18	Connecticut
19	Minnesota
20	North Dakota
20	Vermont
22	Texas
23	Iowa
24	Nevada
25	Nebraska
26	Florida
27	South Dakota
28	Arkansas
29	Pennsylvania
30	Idaho
31	Delaware
31	Kansas
31	Louisiana
31	Ohio
35	Oklahoma
36	New Mexico
37	Colorado
38	Mississippi
38	Montana
40	Missouri
40	West Virginia
42	Alabama
43	Indiana
44	Tennessee
45	Georgia
45	Wyoming
47	South Carolina
48	North Carolina
49	Kentucky
50	Virginia

Note: Ties in ranking reflect ties in actual values.

F-20 Tax Burden on Wealthy Families, 1998

State	Tax burden $	Rank
Alabama	11,709	47
Alaska	18,248	28
Arizona	14,081	41
Arkansas	16,979	35
California	19,005	27
Colorado	13,477	44
Connecticut	25,413	14
Delaware	13,866	43
Florida	16,335	36
Georgia	20,377	22
Hawaii	13,972	42
Idaho	20,563	21
Illinois	27,493	9
Indiana	17,210	34
Iowa	26,415	13
Kansas	20,171	23
Kentucky	17,459	33
Louisiana	9,660	49
Maine	26,691	11
Maryland	19,304	26
Massachusetts	21,851	18
Michigan	21,354	20
Minnesota	26,642	12
Mississippi	18,198	29
Missouri	18,190	30
Montana	27,916	7
Nebraska	29,661	5
Nevada	11,264	48
New Hampshire	39,193	1
New Jersey	27,502	8
New Mexico	14,861	39
New York	30,728	4
North Carolina	19,957	25
North Dakota	28,512	6
Ohio	21,721	19
Oklahoma	17,861	32
Oregon	22,480	17
Pennsylvania	24,804	15
Rhode Island	35,610	2
South Carolina	17,918	31
South Dakota	20,046	24
Tennessee	11,867	46
Texas	23,134	16
Utah	14,210	40
Vermont	26,854	10
Virginia	16,132	37
Washington	13,429	45
West Virginia	15,231	38
Wisconsin	31,881	3
Wyoming	7,804	50
50 States	n/a	
DC	n/a	
United States	20,504	

Rank in order by $	
1	New Hampshire
2	Rhode Island
3	Wisconsin
4	New York
5	Nebraska
6	North Dakota
7	Montana
8	New Jersey
9	Illinois
10	Vermont
11	Maine
12	Minnesota
13	Iowa
14	Connecticut
15	Pennsylvania
16	Texas
17	Oregon
18	Massachusetts
19	Ohio
20	Michigan
21	Idaho
22	Georgia
23	Kansas
24	South Dakota
25	North Carolina
26	Maryland
27	California
28	Alaska
29	Mississippi
30	Missouri
31	South Carolina
32	Oklahoma
33	Kentucky
34	Indiana
35	Arkansas
36	Florida
37	Virginia
38	West Virginia
39	New Mexico
40	Utah
41	Arizona
42	Hawaii
43	Delaware
44	Colorado
45	Washington
46	Tennessee
47	Alabama
48	Nevada
49	Louisiana
50	Wyoming

F-21 State and Local Taxes in the Largest City in Each State, 2000

State	Taxes for family with $50,000/year income $	Percentage of income	Rank by $
Alabama	4,093	8.2	21
Alaska	1,665	3.3	49
Arizona	2,594	5.2	43
Arkansas	3,928	7.9	27
California	4,175	8.3	19
Colorado	2,632	5.3	42
Connecticut	10,054	20.1	1
Delaware	3,471	6.9	36
Florida	2,282	4.6	47
Georgia	3,847	7.7	29
Hawaii	4,340	8.7	15
Idaho	3,593	7.2	34
Illinois	4,016	8.0	22
Indiana	3,676	7.4	31
Iowa	4,452	8.9	12
Kansas	3,192	6.4	39
Kentucky	5,153	10.3	8
Louisiana	3,136	6.3	40
Maine	5,623	11.2	5
Maryland	5,352	10.7	6
Massachusetts	4,569	9.1	11
Michigan	4,587	9.2	10
Minnesota	4,216	8.4	18
Mississippi	3,661	7.3	32
Missouri	4,344	8.7	14
Montana	3,269	6.5	38
Nebraska	3,544	7.1	35
Nevada	2,200	4.4	48
New Hampshire	4,391	8.8	13
New Jersey	6,295	12.6	3
New Mexico	3,613	7.2	33
New York	5,244	10.5	7
North Carolina	4,125	8.2	20
North Dakota	3,442	6.9	37
Ohio	4,312	8.6	16
Oklahoma	3,941	7.9	26
Oregon	3,988	8.0	24
Pennsylvania	6,713	13.4	2
Rhode Island	5,921	11.8	4
South Carolina	3,954	7.9	25
South Dakota	2,424	4.8	46
Tennessee	2,516	5.0	45
Texas	2,584	5.2	44
Utah	4,281	8.6	17
Vermont	3,915	7.8	28
Virginia	3,988	8.0	23
Washington	3,133	6.3	41
West Virginia	3,750	7.5	30
Wisconsin	4,896	9.8	9
Wyoming	1,563	3.1	50
50 States	n/a	n/a	
DC	4,335	8.7	
United States	4,019	8.0	

Rank in order by $

1 Connecticut
2 Pennsylvania
3 New Jersey
4 Rhode Island
5 Maine
6 Maryland
7 New York
8 Kentucky
9 Wisconsin
10 Michigan
11 Massachusetts
12 Iowa
13 New Hampshire
14 Missouri
15 Hawaii
16 Ohio
17 Utah
18 Minnesota
19 California
20 North Carolina
21 Alabama
22 Illinois
23 Virginia
24 Oregon
25 South Carolina
26 Oklahoma
27 Arkansas
28 Vermont
29 Georgia
30 West Virginia
31 Indiana
32 Mississippi
33 New Mexico
34 Idaho
35 Nebraska
36 Delaware
37 North Dakota
38 Montana
39 Kansas
40 Louisiana
41 Washington
42 Colorado
43 Arizona
44 Texas
45 Tennessee
46 South Dakota
47 Florida
48 Nevada
49 Alaska
50 Wyoming

Note: Numbers that appear to be identical are rounded and vary slightly in actual value. The rankings reflect the actual values before rounding. See the introduction for more details.

F-22 Progressivity of Major State and Local Taxes, 2000

State	Progressivity index %	Rank by least progressive to most
Alabama	126.7	8
Alaska	127.1	7
Arizona	85.1	27
Arkansas	91.3	23
California	75.0	37
Colorado	79.5	34
Connecticut	96.0	19
Delaware	67.2	43
Florida	107.4	10
Georgia	70.4	42
Hawaii	88.6	24
Idaho	54.4	50
Illinois	102.3	14
Indiana	107.3	11
Iowa	81.1	31
Kansas	63.6	46
Kentucky	98.2	16
Louisiana	73.7	39
Maine	74.1	38
Maryland	64.1	44
Massachusetts	82.6	29
Michigan	95.1	20
Minnesota	57.0	48
Mississippi	82.1	30
Missouri	94.8	22
Montana	55.9	49
Nebraska	70.8	41
Nevada	153.1	3
New Hampshire	118.3	9
New Jersey	106.1	12
New Mexico	80.4	32
New York	58.6	47
North Carolina	79.7	33
North Dakota	104.1	13
Ohio	85.8	26
Oklahoma	98.9	15
Oregon	77.7	36
Pennsylvania	96.3	18
Rhode Island	85.0	28
South Carolina	63.9	45
South Dakota	156.4	2
Tennessee	157.8	1
Texas	140.2	6
Utah	96.5	17
Vermont	71.2	40
Virginia	94.9	21
Washington	145.5	5
West Virginia	88.4	25
Wisconsin	78.2	35
Wyoming	147.9	4
50 States	n/a	
DC	78.6	
United States	92.9	

Rank in order by percentage	
1	Tennessee
2	South Dakota
3	Nevada
4	Wyoming
5	Washington
6	Texas
7	Alaska
8	Alabama
9	New Hampshire
10	Florida
11	Indiana
12	New Jersey
13	North Dakota
14	Illinois
15	Oklahoma
16	Kentucky
17	Utah
18	Pennsylvania
19	Connecticut
20	Michigan
21	Virginia
22	Missouri
23	Arkansas
24	Hawaii
25	West Virginia
26	Ohio
27	Arizona
28	Rhode Island
29	Massachusetts
30	Mississippi
31	Iowa
32	New Mexico
33	North Carolina
34	Colorado
35	Wisconsin
36	Oregon
37	California
38	Maine
39	Louisiana
40	Vermont
41	Nebraska
42	Georgia
43	Delaware
44	Maryland
45	South Carolina
46	Kansas
47	New York
48	Minnesota
49	Montana
50	Idaho

F-23 State Death Taxes, 2001

State	Type of state death tax 2001	State death tax revenue FY 1999	Death taxes per capita FY 1999	Rank per capita
Alabama	Pick-up	62,784	14.37	37
Alaska	Pick-up	1,726	2.79	50
Arizona	Pick-up	89,088	18.64	30
Arkansas	Pick-up	32,572	12.77	40
California	Pick-up	877,901	26.49	13
Colorado	Pick-up	65,391	16.12	33
Connecticut	Inheritance	250,171	76.22	1
Delaware	Pick-up	27,058	35.91	10
Florida	Pick-up	649,521	42.98	6
Georgia	Pick-up	111,192	14.28	38
Hawaii	Pick-up	28,738	24.24	19
Idaho	Pick-up	11,128	8.89	48
Illinois	Pick-up	346,978	28.61	11
Indiana	Inheritance	148,712	25.02	17
Iowa	Inheritance	72,836	25.38	16
Kansas	Pick-up	70,239	26.46	14
Kentucky	Inheritance	81,483	20.57	28
Louisiana	Inheritance	95,973	21.95	25
Maine	Pick-up	29,768	23.76	21
Maryland	Inheritance	126,168	24.40	18
Massachusetts	Pick-up	173,867	28.16	12
Michigan	Pick-up	174,891	17.73	31
Minnesota	Pick-up	58,132	12.17	43
Mississippi	Pick-up	30,767	11.11	46
Missouri	Pick-up	118,670	21.70	26
Montana	Pick-up	18,302	20.73	27
Nebraska	Pick-up	17,449	10.47	47
Nevada	Pick-up	41,472	22.92	22
New Hampshire	Inheritance	49,368	41.10	7
New Jersey	Inheritance	423,015	51.95	4
New Mexico	Pick-up	21,912	12.59	41
New York	Pick-up	1,071,464	58.88	3
North Carolina	Pick-up	182,851	23.90	20
North Dakota	Pick-up	7,416	11.70	45
Ohio	Estate	141,456	12.57	42
Oklahoma	Estate	88,796	26.44	15
Oregon	Pick-up	47,979	14.47	36
Pennsylvania	Inheritance	760,698	63.42	2
Rhode Island	Pick-up	46,854	47.29	5
South Carolina	Pick-up	57,190	14.72	35
South Dakota	Pick-up	26,427	36.05	9
Tennessee	Inheritance	89,127	16.25	32
Texas	Pick-up	256,277	12.79	39
Utah	Pick-up	8,238	3.87	49
Vermont	Pick-up	23,358	39.34	8
Virginia	Pick-up	154,078	22.42	23
Washington	Pick-up	69,701	12.11	44
West Virginia	Pick-up	27,325	15.12	34
Wisconsin	Pick-up	116,898	22.26	24
Wyoming	Pick-up	9,731	20.29	29
50 States	n/a	7,493,136	27.53	
DC	Pick-up	26,200	50.48	
United States	n/a	7,519,336	27.57	

Rank in order per capita	
1	Connecticut
2	Pennsylvania
3	New York
4	New Jersey
5	Rhode Island
6	Florida
7	New Hampshire
8	Vermont
9	South Dakota
10	Delaware
11	Illinois
12	Massachusetts
13	California
14	Kansas
15	Oklahoma
16	Iowa
17	Indiana
18	Maryland
19	Hawaii
20	North Carolina
21	Maine
22	Nevada
23	Virginia
24	Wisconsin
25	Louisiana
26	Missouri
27	Montana
28	Kentucky
29	Wyoming
30	Arizona
31	Michigan
32	Tennessee
33	Colorado
34	West Virginia
35	South Carolina
36	Oregon
37	Alabama
38	Georgia
39	Texas
40	Arkansas
41	New Mexico
42	Ohio
43	Minnesota
44	Washington
45	North Dakota
46	Mississippi
47	Nebraska
48	Idaho
49	Utah
50	Alaska

Source Notes for Taxes (Section F)

F-1 State and Local Tax Revenue, Total and as a Percentage of Personal Income, FY 1999: This is the most common definition of the tax burdens of state and local governments. It is the tax component of "general revenue" used by the Census Bureau in its annual survey of government finances. It excludes taxes used to finance certain trust funds, such as unemployment insurance taxes, but includes other earmarked revenues, such as gasoline tax revenues for highway construction. Tax revenues are related to personal income as a common proxy for tax base or "ability to pay."

For decades, state officials, media, scholars, taxpayer groups, and others have been comparing tax burdens and spending patterns of states using data published by the Census Bureau in its annual volume *Governmental Finances*. These data were also republished in many secondary sources such as *Significant Features of Fiscal Federalism*, published by the Advisory Commission on Intergovernmental Relations; *Statistical Abstract of the United States*, published by the Census Bureau and U.S. Government Printing Office; and other secondary sources.

The Census Bureau and other federal statistical agencies have been responding to tight budgets by limiting the number of their printed publications and analyses, both statistical and narrative, of the data they produce. This has allowed them to concentrate their resources on what only they can do—collecting and refining the underlying data. Beginning with the data for 1993, the Census Bureau has stopped publishing state and local fiscal data in printed reports such as *Governmental Finances*, making them available only electronically. Also the Bureau has discontinued making popular analytical calculations such as those comparing taxes and spending with personal income and population. This change and budget restrictions have eliminated some secondary sources, such as *Significant Features*.

Anyone with access to the internet, computer capability, and the ability to "unzip" and download the Census data can make calculations such as taxes as a percentage of personal income and per capita spending on particular state and/or local functions. However, not everyone has these capabilities, and those that do can produce different data unless they are careful to follow particular complex conventions covering such matters as which concepts of taxing and spending to use, which revision of often-revised government data to use, and which years of population and personal income estimates to use.

No government agency, including the Census Bureau, will certify the resulting differing numbers as the appropriate ones or vouch for their accuracy in applying past concepts for calculating them. However, many users will demand that comparative numbers be consistent from user to user, from year to year, and from state to state. As a result, some publications are becoming more authoritative than others. Congressional Quarterly, Inc., in conjunction with State Policy Research, Inc., is committed to publishing these comparative data annually in such widely used publications as *State Fact Finder*, *State Policy Reports*, and *Governing* magazine. It is likely that these sources, which are using identical data, will become the standard sources for most users.

All of the tables in *State Fact Finder* which rely on Census Bureau data covering government finances in 1999 use the same conventions, based on past practices of the Census Bureau. The underlying data on tax revenues and spending come from the Census Bureau website (www.census.gov). These data reflect fiscal information for varying government fiscal years ending in 1999, which for most states is a fiscal year ending on June 30, 1999, and for many local governments is a fiscal year ending on December 31, 1999.

Following the historical practice of the Census Bureau not to use revised personal income and population numbers, the personal income numbers used for comparison with these fiscal data are calendar year data for 1998 representing the original 1998 estimates released by the Bureau of Economic Analysis. The population data used to calculate per capita amounts are estimates for July 1, 1999, as originally released by the Census Bureau in 2000.

The data on tax burdens and spending in relation to personal income and per capita are comparable with those of prior years, as published by the Census Bureau and secondary sources, to exactly the degree that Census data for earlier years have been comparable. Data for any year are not recalculated. While underlying data on government revenues and spending are not normally revised, the Census Bureau and Bureau of Economic Analysis do re-estimate historical estimates of population and personal income.

F-2 Per Capita State and Local Tax Revenue, FY 1999: This table relates total tax revenue to population, providing another measure of relative tax burdens (see Table F-1). It also shows the division of tax revenues between state and local governments in each state.

F-3 State and Local Tax Effort, FY 1996: The revenue-raising ability of states and their local governments varies markedly among the states. For example, Alaska and Texas get massive revenues by taxing oil and gas, and Nevada gets large revenues from taxing casino gambling, but most states get no revenue from these sources. What states will collect from particular tax rates applied to property, sales, and income is higher in states with more affluent citizens. Because of these differences, the revenue collected (see Tables F-1 and F-2) is not a good indicator of how high tax rates are in each state.

A more appropriate way to compare the relative burden of state and local taxes, or what is often called "tax effort," is to consider what each state would raise if it and its local governments applied national average tax rates to their own tax bases. Unfortunately, this methodology, known as the "representative tax system," is tedious and expensive to apply. The Advisory Commission on Intergovernmental Relations historically did this work but stopped with the 1991 calculations. The commission was phased out in 1996, and no one had stepped forward to do the work until recently, when a report, based on the FY 1994 Census data on state and local finances, was issued by the Federal Reserve Bank of Boston. Robert Tannenwald, the author of that report and assistant vice president and economist at the Federal Reserve Bank of Boston, has published a second report with statistics for FY 1996. "Fiscal Disparity Among the States Revisited" is the source for the FY 1996 tax effort statistics shown in this table.

The values reflect differences in tax effort. For example, New York state and local governments have taxes that raise 41 percent more than would be raised if tax rates in that state were equal to the national average.

While the best available data on tax effort and tax capacity are those appearing in Tables F-3 and F-4, they must be used with caution. For states which are quite close to the national average and to each other, the results are not what statisticians call "robust." The measurements of tax base and tax revenues are quite reliable, but not so reliable that they prevent a point or two difference in the index from potentially being explained by errors. Also the differences in tax rates associated with small differences in tax effort are likely to be too small to affect decisions of households and businesses. Finally, the data are for FY 1996, while decisions made today are in FY 2002. The relevant data, which are unavailable, would reflect changes already made and others already underway.

So, for example, the differences among Kansas (99), Iowa (98), and Michigan (100) and among Georgia (95), Arizona (93), and North Carolina (94) cannot appropriately be used as an argument for changing public policy in those states. This being said, large differences among the states and extreme differences from the national average permit substantial conclusions about differing state policies and their effects.

F-4 State and Local Tax Capacity, FY 1996: The representative tax system (see notes to Table F-3) also permits a comparison of the tax base, or fiscal capacity, of individual states. This is presented in what can be viewed either as percentages of the national average or as index numbers. Either way, the table indicates, for example, that if it applied national average tax rates, Alabama would raise only 83 percent of the amount that those same rates would in the average state. For reasons indicated in the notes to Table F-3, these data are not available for any year more recent than 1996.

F-5 Change in State and Local Taxes, FY 1994-FY 1999: In the five years covered by the table, the Census Bureau reports for each year indicate that state and local tax revenues have increased by just over 30 percent. However, growth has been much faster in some states than others. See Table F-1 for the source for 1999 figures; 1994 numbers come from *State Fact Finder 1998*.

The table shows increases in state and local taxes as would be expected because the nation's population has been growing and prices have increased due to inflation. Predictably, the increases tend to be largest in states where population and government workloads, such as children in public schools, have grown most rapidly, such as Nevada. However, on average, tax burdens (taxes in relation to personal income) have declined by 5.3 percent.

F-6 Property Taxes, Total and as a Percentage of Personal Income, FY 1999: This and subsequent tables deal with the total revenues raised by particular state and local taxes. They start with the revenues from those taxes as indicated by Census Bureau data (see notes to Table F-1). Those revenues are then related to both population and personal income to provide the two most common measures of the levels, or burdens, of those taxes in each state.

F-7 Property Taxes Per Capita, FY 1999: See notes to Table F-6.

F-8 Property Tax Revenue as a Percentage of Three-Tax Revenue, FY 1999: Some people feel that their total state and local taxes are too high, while others may not be sure about total tax burdens but feel that a particular revenue source, such as property taxes, is too heavily used in their state. This table, using Census data (see notes to Table F-1), relates the amount raised from taxing property with the amounts raised from the other two major tax bases—sales and income.

F-9 Sales Taxes, Total and as a Percentage of Personal Income, FY 1999: All states, including those which do not have state sales taxes, show some sales tax revenues. The Census Bureau counts as sales tax revenues both revenues from sales taxes levied on sales of most goods and special excise taxes on particular goods, such as tobacco and alcoholic beverages. See notes to Table F-6.

F-10 Sales Taxes Per Capita, FY 1999: See notes to Tables F-6 and F-9.

F-11 Sales Tax Revenue as a Percentage of Three-Tax Revenue, FY 1999: See notes to Tables F-8 and F-9.

F-12 Number of Services Reached by Sales Tax, 1996: Sales taxes of state and local governments typically apply to goods, such as cars and clothing, but not to services, such as barbering and landscaping. Many experts suggest that the sales tax would be fairer and a more productive revenue source if it applied equally to both goods and services. This table shows the number of services covered in 1996 by the sales tax in each state. It was compiled by the Federation of Tax Administrators (FTA) and is available on its website (www.taxadmin.org). The table includes states, such as Oregon, that have no general sales tax and ones, such as Alaska, that may have special excise taxes on a few services. Citing "little activity in that area," FTA has no plans to update the count of taxed services in the near future.

F-13 Individual Income Taxes, Total and as a Percentage of Personal Income, FY 1999: Some states which do not tax personal income from wages and salaries do have taxes based on income from other sources, such as dividends, interest, rent, and capital gains. Revenues from all these taxes appear in the table. For the source, see notes to Table F-6.

F-14 Individual Income Taxes Per Capita, FY 1999: See notes to Tables F-6 and F-13.

F-15 Individual Income Tax Revenue as a Percentage of Three-Tax Revenue, FY 1999: See notes to Tables F-8 and F-13.

F-16 Highest Personal Income Tax Rate, 2001: While some states have no income tax at all, the rates paid by high-income households in a few others states can go as high as 10 percent. This table, developed by State Policy Research from compilations of state tax laws published by CCH, Inc., shows the highest state personal income tax rates. A few states use low flat-rate income taxes with few deductions and exemptions, so the same rate is applicable to all taxable income. Most states use a graduated rate schedule. In most of the states showing the highest rates in the table, this "marginal" or "top bracket" rate is paid only on income exceeding a threshold of $100,000 or more.

The rates shown were those in effect in December 2001 on income earned in 2001, to be reported on tax returns filed in early 2002.

F-17 Corporate Income Taxes, Total and Per Capita, FY 1999: See notes to Table F-6. This table is now the best of many unsatisfactory ways of comparing corporate income taxes in the fifty states. However, since 1999 states have made more changes in corporate income taxes (tax base, tax rates, tax credits) than in any other single tax affecting business.

Because of the widespread use of special tax credits for investment, research and development, job expansion, and other purposes and because of differences among states in how much income of multistate corporations is attributed to the taxing state, comparisons of corporate income tax rates are not particularly meaningful.

The most appropriate way to compare corporate income taxes of states is to make calculations of tax liability for individual hypothetical corporations. Such calculations reflect the different state definitions of the tax base, different tax rates, and different tax credits as well as different characteristics of firms in particular industries which affect tax liability. These calculations are complex because taxes levied by one state depend in part on taxes levied by other states. Such calculations have been made in special studies prepared for individual states, but they are typically made only for those ten to twenty states that the requesting state considers to be its major competitors in economic development.

F-18 Motor Fuel Taxes: States tax motor fuels, such as gasoline and diesel fuel, mostly to provide funds for road construction and maintenance. The table shows the tax rate on gasoline from a special compilation prepared by the Federation of Tax Administrators (FTA), covering rates in effect January 1, 2001. This statistic is available on the FTA website (www.taxadmin.org). The table also includes total state and local revenues from motor fuel taxes in fiscal 1999, compiled by the Census Bureau and available on its website (see notes to Table F-1). *State Fact Finder* related those revenues to personal income.

F-19 Tobacco Taxes: These data come from the same sources as those of Table F-18 but cover cigarette and related tobacco taxes.

F-20 Tax Burden on Wealthy Families, 1998: The amounts shown are the liability to be faced by a hypothetical wealthy family with an adjusted yearly gross income of $100,000 and a home value of $1,000,000. The calculations were made by *Bloomberg Personal Finance* and were published in their April 1999 issue. The high home value accounts for New Hampshire's number one ranking, despite the state's lack of income tax. Other top ranking states are mostly those with graduated personal income taxes. This statistic is heavily influenced by assumed property tax rates, which in most states vary greatly between communities. The magazine used data from Runzheimer International, a firm that specializes in calculating living cost differences for corporate executives. Its data focus primarily on affluent suburbs.

F-21 State and Local Taxes in the Largest City in Each State, 2000: These data show the costs of state and local taxes in the largest city in each state to typical families with incomes of $50,000, as calculated by the District of Columbia Department of Finance and Revenue in *Tax Rates and Tax Burdens in the District of Columbia: A Nationwide Comparison*, dated August 2001. The calculations for each state's largest city are not necessarily representative of statewide averages.

F-22 Progressivity of Major State and Local Taxes, 2000: These data compare the tax burdens as a percentage of income on households of two income levels ($25,000 and $150,000), using data from the analysis described in the notes to Table F-21. Low numbers indicate that the percentage paid by higher-income households is significantly higher than the percentage paid by low-income households, making the state and local tax structure "progressive." States with no personal income tax and high reliance on sales and property taxes, such as Nevada, have tax systems that can be called regressive. Their progressivity percentages over one hundred indicate that poorer households pay a larger percentage of their income on state and local taxes than do higher-income households.

F-23 State Death Taxes, 2001: The federal government levies taxes on the estates of persons when they die. State governments also tax estates either directly by taxing the amount left to heirs (estate taxes) or by taxing the amounts received by particular heirs (inheritance taxes). Some of the state tax liability is allowed by the federal government as a 100 percent credit against federal taxes owed. This means that states can levy taxes up to the amount of the credit without making taxpayers pay more, so all states levy such "pick-up" taxes. Some states levy additional taxes, though the trend has been to eliminate the extra taxes out of fear that they encourage affluent older residents to move to other states. The table shows which states levy these extra taxes and the type of tax they use. The table also shows how $7.5 billion of state death tax revenues in FY 1999 were collected by the states. The data, plus discussion of how the potential repeal of the federal estate and gift tax will effect the states, are found in an FTA bulletin "Repeal of Federal Estate Tax Would Have Effect on States" released February 22, 2001 and available on the FTA website (www.taxadmin.org).

Revenues and Finances

While state revenues are already failing to meet FY 2002 projections, all but a handful of states are scrambling to make up the losses. Periodic surveys conducted by the National Conference of State Legislatures, provide a fiscal picture of the 50 states. NCSL's December 2001 survey, "State Fiscal Outlook for FY 2002" reports the following:

· Revenues continue to be anemic, although three states reported improvement. Forty-three states now report that revenues were below forecasted levels in the opening months of FY 2002.

· Twenty-one states and the District of Columbia report that spending is above budgeted levels. Medicaid continues to exceed budgeted levels, proving to be an ongoing problem.

· At least thirty-six states have implemented or are considering budget cuts or holdbacks to address fiscal problems.

· Twenty-four states may tap reserve funds to balance their FY 2002 budgets. Most states are eyeing their rainy day funds, and a handful may tap tobacco settlement money.

· Twenty-two states have implemented belt-tightening measures that include hiring freezes, capital project cancellations, and travel restrictions.

· Six states have convened in special sessions to address budget problems, and one will begin a special session on Dec. 4. Several others are considering special sessions.

A large portion of the finance data in this chapter comes from the U. S. Census Bureau. It is the only source for reliable, consistent, and comparable data on state and local government finances. See page 139 for the reasons why.

G-1 State and Local Total Revenue, FY 1999

State	Total revenue $ (in millions)	Per capita total revenue $	Total revenue as a percentage of personal income	Rank per capita
Alabama	23,621	5,405	24.5	45
Alaska	9,225	14,878	53.7	1
Arizona	25,714	5,382	22.8	46
Arkansas	13,867	5,436	25.7	43
California	242,469	7,315	26.2	8
Colorado	25,413	6,265	21.4	24
Connecticut	23,796	7,250	19.4	11
Delaware	5,526	7,328	25.1	7
Florida	88,422	5,851	22.0	33
Georgia	46,265	5,940	23.2	30
Hawaii	8,094	6,830	25.4	13
Idaho	6,868	5,485	25.4	41
Illinois	73,603	6,069	20.3	27
Indiana	30,890	5,198	20.8	49
Iowa	17,270	6,019	24.3	29
Kansas	14,141	5,328	20.9	48
Kentucky	22,769	5,748	25.9	37
Louisiana	25,698	5,878	26.4	31
Maine	8,096	6,461	27.6	19
Maryland	31,268	6,046	19.8	28
Massachusetts	41,425	6,709	20.2	14
Michigan	66,078	6,699	25.1	15
Minnesota	36,637	7,671	26.3	4
Mississippi	14,973	5,407	27.2	44
Missouri	29,960	5,479	21.7	42
Montana	5,134	5,814	27.4	34
Nebraska	10,947	6,571	25.5	17
Nevada	11,721	6,479	22.6	18
New Hampshire	6,454	5,374	18.3	47
New Jersey	59,121	7,260	21.3	10
New Mexico	11,238	6,459	30.6	20
New York	172,301	9,469	29.4	2
North Carolina	49,073	6,414	25.5	22
North Dakota	4,091	6,453	28.2	21
Ohio	75,103	6,672	25.5	16
Oklahoma	17,440	5,194	23.5	50
Oregon	23,040	6,948	27.0	12
Pennsylvania	74,569	6,217	22.7	26
Rhode Island	7,203	7,268	26.0	9
South Carolina	21,640	5,569	25.0	40
South Dakota	4,224	5,763	24.3	36
Tennessee	31,368	5,720	23.5	38
Texas	117,493	5,862	23.1	32
Utah	13,292	6,240	28.4	25
Vermont	3,759	6,329	25.7	23
Virginia	39,931	5,810	20.8	35
Washington	43,831	7,615	26.9	5
West Virginia	10,154	5,619	27.7	39
Wisconsin	38,789	7,388	28.3	6
Wyoming	4,422	9,212	37.0	3
50 States	1,788,426	6,571	24.3	
DC	6,131	11,813	31.2	
United States	1,794,557	6,581	24.3	

Rank in order per capita

1. Alaska
2. New York
3. Wyoming
4. Minnesota
5. Washington
6. Wisconsin
7. Delaware
8. California
9. Rhode Island
10. New Jersey
11. Connecticut
12. Oregon
13. Hawaii
14. Massachusetts
15. Michigan
16. Ohio
17. Nebraska
18. Nevada
19. Maine
20. New Mexico
21. North Dakota
22. North Carolina
23. Vermont
24. Colorado
25. Utah
26. Pennsylvania
27. Illinois
28. Maryland
29. Iowa
30. Georgia
31. Louisiana
32. Texas
33. Florida
34. Montana
35. Virginia
36. South Dakota
37. Kentucky
38. Tennessee
39. West Virginia
40. South Carolina
41. Idaho
42. Missouri
43. Arkansas
44. Mississippi
45. Alabama
46. Arizona
47. New Hampshire
48. Kansas
49. Indiana
50. Oklahoma

G-2 State and Local General Revenue, FY 1999

State	General revenue $ (in millions)	Per capita general revenue $	General revenue as percentage of personal income	Rank per capita
Alabama	19,322	4,422	20.1	47
Alaska	7,612	12,277	44.3	1
Arizona	20,958	4,386	18.6	48
Arkansas	11,376	4,459	21.1	46
California	185,731	5,604	20.1	11
Colorado	21,137	5,211	17.8	20
Connecticut	21,505	6,552	17.5	4
Delaware	4,872	6,462	22.1	5
Florida	72,658	4,808	18.1	32
Georgia	36,878	4,735	18.5	34
Hawaii	6,879	5,805	21.6	9
Idaho	5,715	4,564	21.2	42
Illinois	60,334	4,975	16.7	26
Indiana	27,802	4,678	18.7	37
Iowa	14,314	4,989	20.1	24
Kansas	12,343	4,651	18.2	38
Kentucky	18,377	4,639	20.9	39
Louisiana	21,639	4,950	22.2	27
Maine	6,968	5,561	23.7	14
Maryland	26,329	5,091	16.6	21
Massachusetts	35,965	5,824	17.5	8
Michigan	52,377	5,310	19.9	19
Minnesota	28,846	6,040	20.7	6
Mississippi	12,720	4,594	23.1	40
Missouri	24,687	4,515	17.9	44
Montana	4,458	5,049	23.8	23
Nebraska	8,304	4,985	19.3	25
Nevada	8,728	4,825	16.8	31
New Hampshire	5,472	4,556	15.5	43
New Jersey	48,996	6,017	17.6	7
New Mexico	9,334	5,364	25.4	18
New York	137,114	7,535	23.4	2
North Carolina	37,545	4,907	19.5	28
North Dakota	3,619	5,708	24.9	10
Ohio	54,974	4,884	18.7	30
Oklahoma	14,450	4,303	19.5	49
Oregon	18,511	5,582	21.7	13
Pennsylvania	60,656	5,057	18.5	22
Rhode Island	5,550	5,601	20.1	12
South Carolina	18,400	4,735	21.3	35
South Dakota	3,348	4,567	19.2	41
Tennessee	23,364	4,260	17.5	50
Texas	90,327	4,506	17.8	45
Utah	10,443	4,903	22.3	29
Vermont	3,279	5,521	22.4	15
Virginia	32,804	4,773	17.0	33
Washington	31,563	5,483	19.4	16
West Virginia	8,541	4,727	23.3	36
Wisconsin	28,445	5,418	20.8	17
Wyoming	3,445	7,176	28.8	3
50 States	1,429,012	5,250	19.4	
DC	5,452	10,504	27.7	
United States	1,434,464	5,260	19.4	

Rank in order per capita

1 Alaska
2 New York
3 Wyoming
4 Connecticut
5 Delaware
6 Minnesota
7 New Jersey
8 Massachusetts
9 Hawaii
10 North Dakota
11 California
12 Rhode Island
13 Oregon
14 Maine
15 Vermont
16 Washington
17 Wisconsin
18 New Mexico
19 Michigan
20 Colorado
21 Maryland
22 Pennsylvania
23 Montana
24 Iowa
25 Nebraska
26 Illinois
27 Louisiana
28 North Carolina
29 Utah
30 Ohio
31 Nevada
32 Florida
33 Virginia
34 Georgia
35 South Carolina
36 West Virginia
37 Indiana
38 Kansas
39 Kentucky
40 Mississippi
41 South Dakota
42 Idaho
43 New Hampshire
44 Missouri
45 Texas
46 Arkansas
47 Alabama
48 Arizona
49 Oklahoma
50 Tennessee

Note: Numbers that appear to be identical are rounded and vary slightly in actual value. The rankings reflect the actual values before rounding. See the introduction for more details.

G-3 State and Local "Own-source" General Revenue, FY 1999

State	"Own-source" general revenue $ (in millions)	Per capita "own-source" general revenue $	"Own-source" general revenue as a percentage of personal income	Rank per capita
Alabama	14,671	3,357	15.2	49
Alaska	6,232	10,052	36.3	1
Arizona	17,005	3,559	15.1	43
Arkansas	8,783	3,443	16.3	46
California	149,776	4,519	16.2	12
Colorado	17,813	4,392	15.0	13
Connecticut	18,054	5,501	14.7	3
Delaware	4,088	5,422	18.6	4
Florida	61,966	4,101	15.4	24
Georgia	30,418	3,906	15.2	32
Hawaii	5,493	4,635	17.3	9
Idaho	4,684	3,741	17.4	36
Illinois	50,254	4,144	13.9	20
Indiana	23,178	3,900	15.6	34
Iowa	11,716	4,084	16.5	25
Kansas	10,374	3,909	15.3	31
Kentucky	14,198	3,585	16.1	41
Louisiana	16,784	3,839	17.2	35
Maine	5,435	4,338	18.5	15
Maryland	22,033	4,260	13.9	18
Massachusetts	30,000	4,858	14.6	8
Michigan	43,031	4,362	16.3	14
Minnesota	24,350	5,098	17.5	7
Mississippi	9,585	3,462	17.4	45
Missouri	19,569	3,579	14.2	42
Montana	3,205	3,629	17.1	39
Nebraska	6,756	4,055	15.7	28
Nevada	7,579	4,190	14.6	19
New Hampshire	4,438	3,695	12.6	38
New Jersey	41,619	5,111	15.0	6
New Mexico	7,063	4,059	19.2	27
New York	108,665	5,972	18.6	2
North Carolina	29,858	3,902	15.5	33
North Dakota	2,601	4,103	17.9	23
Ohio	44,790	3,979	15.2	29
Oklahoma	11,515	3,429	15.5	47
Oregon	14,304	4,314	16.8	16
Pennsylvania	48,799	4,069	14.9	26
Rhode Island	4,225	4,263	15.3	17
South Carolina	14,530	3,739	16.8	37
South Dakota	2,476	3,378	14.2	48
Tennessee	17,450	3,182	13.1	50
Texas	72,643	3,624	14.3	40
Utah	8,353	3,921	17.8	30
Vermont	2,450	4,125	16.7	21
Virginia	28,303	4,118	14.7	22
Washington	26,260	4,562	16.1	10
West Virginia	6,362	3,521	17.3	44
Wisconsin	23,827	4,538	17.4	11
Wyoming	2,526	5,262	21.1	5
50 States	1,160,091	4,262	15.8	
DC	3,745	7,215	19.0	
United States	1,163,836	4,268	15.8	

Rank in order per capita	
1	Alaska
2	New York
3	Connecticut
4	Delaware
5	Wyoming
6	New Jersey
7	Minnesota
8	Massachusetts
9	Hawaii
10	Washington
11	Wisconsin
12	California
13	Colorado
14	Michigan
15	Maine
16	Oregon
17	Rhode Island
18	Maryland
19	Nevada
20	Illinois
21	Vermont
22	Virginia
23	North Dakota
24	Florida
25	Iowa
26	Pennsylvania
27	New Mexico
28	Nebraska
29	Ohio
30	Utah
31	Kansas
32	Georgia
33	North Carolina
34	Indiana
35	Louisiana
36	Idaho
37	South Carolina
38	New Hampshire
39	Montana
40	Texas
41	Kentucky
42	Missouri
43	Arizona
44	West Virginia
45	Mississippi
46	Arkansas
47	Oklahoma
48	South Dakota
49	Alabama
50	Tennessee

G-4 State and Local Non-tax "Own-source" Revenue, FY 1999

State	Non-tax "own-source" revenue $ (in millions)	Per capita non-tax "own-source" revenue $	Non-tax "own-source" revenue as a percentage of personal income	Rank per capita
Alabama	5,900	1,350	6.1	17
Alaska	4,471	7,211	26.0	1
Arizona	4,767	998	4.2	49
Arkansas	2,706	1,061	5.0	43
California	44,799	1,352	4.8	16
Colorado	5,696	1,404	4.8	14
Connecticut	3,165	964	2.6	50
Delaware	1,617	2,144	7.3	3
Florida	21,721	1,437	5.4	9
Georgia	8,915	1,145	4.5	34
Hawaii	1,579	1,333	5.0	18
Idaho	1,645	1,314	6.1	21
Illinois	12,284	1,013	3.4	48
Indiana	7,602	1,279	5.1	23
Iowa	4,043	1,409	5.7	12
Kansas	3,082	1,161	4.5	32
Kentucky	4,438	1,120	5.0	38
Louisiana	6,250	1,430	6.4	10
Maine	1,353	1,080	4.6	42
Maryland	5,475	1,059	3.5	44
Massachusetts	7,731	1,252	3.8	28
Michigan	13,126	1,331	5.0	19
Minnesota	7,162	1,500	5.1	5
Mississippi	3,498	1,263	6.4	26
Missouri	5,542	1,013	4.0	47
Montana	1,163	1,317	6.2	20
Nebraska	2,132	1,280	5.0	22
Nevada	2,288	1,265	4.4	25
New Hampshire	1,328	1,106	3.8	41
New Jersey	10,043	1,233	3.6	29
New Mexico	2,594	1,491	7.1	6
New York	26,511	1,457	4.5	8
North Carolina	9,592	1,254	5.0	27
North Dakota	933	1,471	6.4	7
Ohio	12,489	1,109	4.2	40
Oklahoma	3,747	1,116	5.1	39
Oregon	5,768	1,739	6.8	4
Pennsylvania	13,606	1,134	4.1	35
Rhode Island	1,028	1,037	3.7	46
South Carolina	5,463	1,406	6.3	13
South Dakota	823	1,123	4.7	36
Tennessee	5,702	1,040	4.3	45
Texas	23,411	1,168	4.6	31
Utah	2,884	1,354	6.2	15
Vermont	666	1,121	4.5	37
Virginia	8,746	1,272	4.5	24
Washington	8,142	1,415	5.0	11
West Virginia	2,083	1,153	5.7	33
Wisconsin	6,409	1,221	4.7	30
Wyoming	1,169	2,435	9.8	2
50 States	347,289	1,276	4.7	
DC	771	1,486	3.9	
United States	348,060	1,276	4.7	

Rank in order per capita	
1	Alaska
2	Wyoming
3	Delaware
4	Oregon
5	Minnesota
6	New Mexico
7	North Dakota
8	New York
9	Florida
10	Louisiana
11	Washington
12	Iowa
13	South Carolina
14	Colorado
15	Utah
16	California
17	Alabama
18	Hawaii
19	Michigan
20	Montana
21	Idaho
22	Nebraska
23	Indiana
24	Virginia
25	Nevada
26	Mississippi
27	North Carolina
28	Massachusetts
29	New Jersey
30	Wisconsin
31	Texas
32	Kansas
33	West Virginia
34	Georgia
35	Pennsylvania
36	South Dakota
37	Vermont
38	Kentucky
39	Oklahoma
40	Ohio
41	New Hampshire
42	Maine
43	Arkansas
44	Maryland
45	Tennessee
46	Rhode Island
47	Missouri
48	Illinois
49	Arizona
50	Connecticut

G-5 State and Local Total Expenditures, FY 1999

State	Total expenditures $ (in millions)	Per capita total expenditures $	Total expenditure as a percentage of personal income	Rank per capita
Alabama	23,378	5,350	24.3	34
Alaska	8,085	13,041	47.1	1
Arizona	24,062	5,036	21.4	41
Arkansas	11,752	4,607	21.8	50
California	217,970	6,576	23.6	9
Colorado	23,503	5,795	19.8	21
Connecticut	22,262	6,783	18.2	5
Delaware	4,889	6,484	22.2	11
Florida	80,663	5,338	20.1	35
Georgia	41,057	5,272	20.6	36
Hawaii	7,789	6,573	24.5	10
Idaho	6,195	4,948	23.0	45
Illinois	69,283	5,713	19.2	23
Indiana	29,540	4,971	19.9	44
Iowa	16,138	5,625	22.7	26
Kansas	13,366	5,036	19.7	42
Kentucky	20,421	5,155	23.2	40
Louisiana	23,810	5,446	24.4	30
Maine	6,963	5,557	23.7	28
Maryland	27,941	5,402	17.7	32
Massachusetts	40,986	6,637	20.0	7
Michigan	57,058	5,784	21.7	22
Minnesota	31,874	6,674	22.9	6
Mississippi	14,299	5,164	26.0	39
Missouri	26,585	4,862	19.2	47
Montana	4,739	5,367	25.3	33
Nebraska	9,983	5,992	23.2	17
Nevada	10,848	5,997	20.9	16
New Hampshire	5,890	4,904	16.7	46
New Jersey	51,265	6,296	18.5	12
New Mexico	10,578	6,079	28.8	14
New York	160,937	8,844	27.5	2
North Carolina	42,198	5,515	22.0	29
North Dakota	3,783	5,967	26.1	18
Ohio	63,475	5,639	21.6	25
Oklahoma	15,682	4,670	21.2	49
Oregon	21,911	6,608	25.7	8
Pennsylvania	70,689	5,894	21.5	19
Rhode Island	6,137	6,192	22.2	13
South Carolina	21,159	5,445	24.4	31
South Dakota	3,552	4,846	20.4	48
Tennessee	30,641	5,587	22.9	27
Texas	100,327	5,005	19.7	43
Utah	12,370	5,807	26.4	20
Vermont	3,352	5,643	22.9	24
Virginia	35,499	5,165	18.4	38
Washington	40,177	6,980	24.7	4
West Virginia	9,389	5,196	25.6	37
Wisconsin	31,673	6,033	23.1	15
Wyoming	3,542	7,379	29.6	3
50 States	1,619,666	5,951	22.0	
DC	6,273	12,087	31.9	
United States	1,625,939	5,963	22.0	

Rank in order per capita	
1	Alaska
2	New York
3	Wyoming
4	Washington
5	Connecticut
6	Minnesota
7	Massachusetts
8	Oregon
9	California
10	Hawaii
11	Delaware
12	New Jersey
13	Rhode Island
14	New Mexico
15	Wisconsin
16	Nevada
17	Nebraska
18	North Dakota
19	Pennsylvania
20	Utah
21	Colorado
22	Michigan
23	Illinois
24	Vermont
25	Ohio
26	Iowa
27	Tennessee
28	Maine
29	North Carolina
30	Louisiana
31	South Carolina
32	Maryland
33	Montana
34	Alabama
35	Florida
36	Georgia
37	West Virginia
38	Virginia
39	Mississippi
40	Kentucky
41	Arizona
42	Kansas
43	Texas
44	Indiana
45	Idaho
46	New Hampshire
47	Missouri
48	South Dakota
49	Oklahoma
50	Arkansas

Note: Numbers that appear to be identical are rounded and vary slightly in actual value. The rankings reflect the actual values before rounding. See the introduction for more details.

G-6 State and Local General Expenditures, FY 1999

State	General expenditures $ (in millions)	General expenditures as a percentage of personal income	Rank by percentage
Alabama	20,119	20.9	15
Alaska	7,131	41.5	1
Arizona	20,302	18.0	34
Arkansas	10,662	19.8	24
California	180,875	19.6	25
Colorado	20,068	16.9	44
Connecticut	19,688	16.1	47
Delaware	4,483	20.4	21
Florida	71,631	17.8	39
Georgia	35,831	18.0	36
Hawaii	6,889	21.7	12
Idaho	5,612	20.8	16
Illinois	59,727	16.5	46
Indiana	26,642	17.9	37
Iowa	14,687	20.7	18
Kansas	12,066	17.8	40
Kentucky	18,062	20.5	19
Louisiana	21,118	21.7	11
Maine	6,388	21.8	10
Maryland	24,876	15.7	49
Massachusetts	35,000	17.1	43
Michigan	50,558	19.2	26
Minnesota	28,160	20.2	22
Mississippi	12,940	23.5	5
Missouri	23,881	17.3	41
Montana	4,293	22.9	6
Nebraska	7,716	18.0	35
Nevada	9,296	17.9	38
New Hampshire	5,329	15.1	50
New Jersey	44,326	16.0	48
New Mexico	9,466	25.8	3
New York	133,769	22.9	7
North Carolina	36,769	19.1	27
North Dakota	3,487	24.0	4
Ohio	53,150	18.1	33
Oklahoma	13,555	18.3	31
Oregon	18,301	21.5	13
Pennsylvania	61,226	18.6	30
Rhode Island	5,281	19.1	28
South Carolina	18,232	21.1	14
South Dakota	3,245	18.7	29
Tennessee	24,172	18.1	32
Texas	87,375	17.2	42
Utah	10,440	22.3	9
Vermont	3,030	20.7	17
Virginia	32,299	16.8	45
Washington	32,334	19.9	23
West Virginia	8,227	22.4	8
Wisconsin	28,043	20.5	20
Wyoming	3,152	26.3	2
50 States	1,393,903	18.9	
DC	4,630	23.5	
United States	1,398,533	18.9	

Rank in order by percentage	
1	Alaska
2	Wyoming
3	New Mexico
4	North Dakota
5	Mississippi
6	Montana
7	New York
8	West Virginia
9	Utah
10	Maine
11	Louisiana
12	Hawaii
13	Oregon
14	South Carolina
15	Alabama
16	Idaho
17	Vermont
18	Iowa
19	Kentucky
20	Wisconsin
21	Delaware
22	Minnesota
23	Washington
24	Arkansas
25	California
26	Michigan
27	North Carolina
28	Rhode Island
29	South Dakota
30	Pennsylvania
31	Oklahoma
32	Tennessee
33	Ohio
34	Arizona
35	Nebraska
36	Georgia
37	Indiana
38	Nevada
39	Florida
40	Kansas
41	Missouri
42	Texas
43	Massachusetts
44	Colorado
45	Virginia
46	Illinois
47	Connecticut
48	New Jersey
49	Maryland
50	New Hampshire

Note: Numbers that appear to be identical are rounded and vary slightly in actual value. The rankings reflect the actual values before rounding. See the introduction for more details.

G-7 State and Local General Expenditures Per Capita, FY 1999

State	State and local general expenditure per capita $	State general expenditure per capita $	Local general expenditure per capita $	Rank by state and local expenditure per capita
Alabama	4,604	2,210	2,394	36
Alaska	11,502	7,327	4,175	1
Arizona	4,249	1,503	2,746	48
Arkansas	4,179	2,243	1,936	49
California	5,457	1,865	3,592	12
Colorado	4,948	2,017	2,931	23
Connecticut	5,999	3,208	2,791	4
Delaware	5,946	3,913	2,033	5
Florida	4,740	1,740	3,000	30
Georgia	4,601	1,913	2,687	37
Hawaii	5,813	4,639	1,174	7
Idaho	4,482	2,048	2,435	42
Illinois	4,925	1,942	2,982	24
Indiana	4,483	1,883	2,600	41
Iowa	5,119	2,325	2,794	19
Kansas	4,546	1,836	2,711	40
Kentucky	4,560	2,544	2,016	38
Louisiana	4,830	2,380	2,450	27
Maine	5,098	2,816	2,282	22
Maryland	4,810	2,219	2,591	28
Massachusetts	5,668	3,088	2,580	8
Michigan	5,125	1,936	3,190	18
Minnesota	5,896	2,388	3,508	6
Mississippi	4,673	2,186	2,487	34
Missouri	4,367	1,994	2,373	46
Montana	4,861	2,749	2,112	26
Nebraska	4,631	2,085	2,546	35
Nevada	5,139	1,764	3,375	17
New Hampshire	4,437	2,184	2,253	43
New Jersey	5,443	2,214	3,229	13
New Mexico	5,440	2,913	2,527	14
New York	7,351	2,656	4,695	2
North Carolina	4,806	2,100	2,706	29
North Dakota	5,500	3,000	2,500	11
Ohio	4,722	1,889	2,832	31
Oklahoma	4,037	1,866	2,170	50
Oregon	5,519	2,401	3,118	10
Pennsylvania	5,105	2,299	2,806	20
Rhode Island	5,329	3,163	2,165	16
South Carolina	4,692	2,390	2,302	33
South Dakota	4,428	2,229	2,198	44
Tennessee	4,408	1,956	2,452	45
Texas	4,359	1,725	2,635	47
Utah	4,901	2,536	2,365	25
Vermont	5,100	2,958	2,142	21
Virginia	4,699	2,132	2,567	32
Washington	5,617	2,519	3,098	9
West Virginia	4,553	2,637	1,916	39
Wisconsin	5,342	1,986	3,355	15
Wyoming	6,567	2,802	3,765	3
50 States	5,121	2,148	2,974	
DC	8,920	n/a	8,920	
United States	5,129	2,144	2,985	

Rank in order by state and local per capita	
1	Alaska
2	New York
3	Wyoming
4	Connecticut
5	Delaware
6	Minnesota
7	Hawaii
8	Massachusetts
9	Washington
10	Oregon
11	North Dakota
12	California
13	New Jersey
14	New Mexico
15	Wisconsin
16	Rhode Island
17	Nevada
18	Michigan
19	Iowa
20	Pennsylvania
21	Vermont
22	Maine
23	Colorado
24	Illinois
25	Utah
26	Montana
27	Louisiana
28	Maryland
29	North Carolina
30	Florida
31	Ohio
32	Virginia
33	South Carolina
34	Mississippi
35	Nebraska
36	Alabama
37	Georgia
38	Kentucky
39	West Virginia
40	Kansas
41	Indiana
42	Idaho
43	New Hampshire
44	South Dakota
45	Tennessee
46	Missouri
47	Texas
48	Arizona
49	Arkansas
50	Oklahoma

G-8 Percentage Change in State and Local Expenditures, FY 1994-FY 1999

State	Percentage change	Rank
Alabama	36.1	17
Alaska	15.8	49
Arizona	35.0	18
Arkansas	43.1	7
California	30.6	26
Colorado	33.7	21
Connecticut	18.2	45
Delaware	41.7	10
Florida	37.2	15
Georgia	37.4	13
Hawaii	3.6	50
Idaho	48.9	3
Illinois	34.7	20
Indiana	25.1	36
Iowa	31.4	24
Kansas	24.2	39
Kentucky	42.1	8
Louisiana	25.3	35
Maine	29.7	28
Maryland	26.9	33
Massachusetts	24.4	38
Michigan	28.4	29
Minnesota	27.5	32
Mississippi	50.1	2
Missouri	48.0	5
Montana	30.1	27
Nebraska	23.7	41
Nevada	48.0	4
New Hampshire	20.0	44
New Jersey	16.2	48
New Mexico	37.3	14
New York	18.0	46
North Carolina	47.6	6
North Dakota	34.9	19
Ohio	26.4	34
Oklahoma	28.2	30
Oregon	41.9	9
Pennsylvania	30.7	25
Rhode Island	16.5	47
South Carolina	31.9	23
South Dakota	21.9	42
Tennessee	40.4	11
Texas	36.7	16
Utah	51.4	1
Vermont	24.9	37
Virginia	37.5	12
Washington	33.6	22
West Virginia	20.0	43
Wisconsin	27.9	31
Wyoming	24.0	40
50 States	30.3	
DC	1.2	
United States	30.2	

Rank in order by percentage	
1	Utah
2	Mississippi
3	Idaho
4	Nevada
5	Missouri
6	North Carolina
7	Arkansas
8	Kentucky
9	Oregon
10	Delaware
11	Tennessee
12	Virginia
13	Georgia
14	New Mexico
15	Florida
16	Texas
17	Alabama
18	Arizona
19	North Dakota
20	Illinois
21	Colorado
22	Washington
23	South Carolina
24	Iowa
25	Pennsylvania
26	California
27	Montana
28	Maine
29	Michigan
30	Oklahoma
31	Wisconsin
32	Minnesota
33	Maryland
34	Ohio
35	Louisiana
36	Indiana
37	Vermont
38	Massachusetts
39	Kansas
40	Wyoming
41	Nebraska
42	South Dakota
43	West Virginia
44	New Hampshire
45	Connecticut
46	New York
47	Rhode Island
48	New Jersey
49	Alaska
50	Hawaii

Note: Numbers that appear to be identical are rounded and vary slightly in actual value. The rankings reflect the actual values before rounding. See the introduction for more details.

G-9 State Government General Revenue, FY 1999

State	State government general revenue $ (in millions)	State government general revenue per capita $	Rank per capita
Alabama	13,093	2,996	35
Alaska	5,941	9,582	1
Arizona	13,077	2,737	46
Arkansas	8,449	3,312	24
California	119,408	3,603	18
Colorado	11,747	2,896	40
Connecticut	14,920	4,546	6
Delaware	4,060	5,385	2
Florida	39,222	2,596	49
Georgia	21,445	2,754	45
Hawaii	5,615	4,738	3
Idaho	3,847	3,073	32
Illinois	35,686	2,942	39
Indiana	17,729	2,983	36
Iowa	9,208	3,209	29
Kansas	7,597	2,863	43
Kentucky	13,584	3,429	22
Louisiana	14,603	3,340	23
Maine	4,857	3,876	13
Maryland	16,240	3,140	31
Massachusetts	25,664	4,156	8
Michigan	36,791	3,730	14
Minnesota	19,131	4,006	12
Mississippi	8,972	3,240	27
Missouri	15,770	2,884	41
Montana	3,121	3,534	20
Nebraska	5,089	3,055	33
Nevada	5,013	2,771	44
New Hampshire	3,108	2,588	50
New Jersey	29,708	3,648	16
New Mexico	7,161	4,115	9
New York	80,042	4,399	7
North Carolina	25,312	3,308	25
North Dakota	2,552	4,025	11
Ohio	33,207	2,950	38
Oklahoma	9,684	2,884	42
Oregon	11,889	3,585	19
Pennsylvania	38,859	3,240	28
Rhode Island	3,994	4,030	10
South Carolina	12,378	3,185	30
South Dakota	2,179	2,972	37
Tennessee	14,635	2,669	47
Texas	52,545	2,621	48
Utah	7,043	3,307	26
Vermont	2,730	4,596	5
Virginia	20,867	3,036	34
Washington	20,242	3,517	21
West Virginia	6,584	3,644	17
Wisconsin	19,262	3,669	15
Wyoming	2,215	4,614	4
50 States	906,076	3,329	
DC	n/a	n/a	
United States	906,076	3,323	

Rank in order per capita	
1	Alaska
2	Delaware
3	Hawaii
4	Wyoming
5	Vermont
6	Connecticut
7	New York
8	Massachusetts
9	New Mexico
10	Rhode Island
11	North Dakota
12	Minnesota
13	Maine
14	Michigan
15	Wisconsin
16	New Jersey
17	West Virginia
18	California
19	Oregon
20	Montana
21	Washington
22	Kentucky
23	Louisiana
24	Arkansas
25	North Carolina
26	Utah
27	Mississippi
28	Pennsylvania
29	Iowa
30	South Carolina
31	Maryland
32	Idaho
33	Nebraska
34	Virginia
35	Alabama
36	Indiana
37	South Dakota
38	Ohio
39	Illinois
40	Colorado
41	Missouri
42	Oklahoma
43	Kansas
44	Nevada
45	Georgia
46	Arizona
47	Tennessee
48	Texas
49	Florida
50	New Hampshire

Note: Numbers that appear to be identical are rounded and vary slightly in actual value. The rankings reflect the actual values before rounding. See the introduction for more details.

G-10 State Government General Spending, FY 1999

State	State government general spending $ (in millions)	State government general spending per capita $	Rank per capita
Alabama	13,289	3,041	32
Alaska	5,572	8,987	1
Arizona	13,127	2,747	46
Arkansas	8,372	3,282	24
California	120,178	3,626	13
Colorado	11,699	2,884	40
Connecticut	13,340	4,064	9
Delaware	3,671	4,869	2
Florida	39,735	2,630	48
Georgia	21,579	2,771	44
Hawaii	5,651	4,769	3
Idaho	3,777	3,017	33
Illinois	34,358	2,833	42
Indiana	17,437	2,934	37
Iowa	9,543	3,326	23
Kansas	7,678	2,893	39
Kentucky	13,327	3,365	22
Louisiana	14,051	3,214	28
Maine	4,386	3,501	19
Maryland	15,540	3,005	34
Massachusetts	25,820	4,181	7
Michigan	35,123	3,561	15
Minnesota	18,410	3,855	11
Mississippi	9,073	3,276	25
Missouri	15,346	2,806	43
Montana	3,136	3,551	16
Nebraska	4,962	2,978	35
Nevada	5,280	2,919	38
New Hampshire	3,101	2,582	49
New Jersey	25,831	3,172	30
New Mexico	7,434	4,273	6
New York	78,720	4,326	5
North Carolina	24,611	3,217	27
North Dakota	2,459	3,879	10
Ohio	33,285	2,957	36
Oklahoma	9,249	2,754	45
Oregon	11,635	3,509	18
Pennsylvania	38,517	3,211	29
Rhode Island	3,730	3,764	12
South Carolina	12,641	3,253	26
South Dakota	2,106	2,873	41
Tennessee	14,900	2,717	47
Texas	49,591	2,474	50
Utah	7,214	3,387	21
Vermont	2,456	4,135	8
Virginia	21,155	3,078	31
Washington	20,616	3,582	14
West Virginia	6,343	3,510	17
Wisconsin	18,315	3,489	20
Wyoming	2,107	4,389	4
50 States	889,475	3,268	
DC	n/a	n/a	
United States	889,475	3,262	

Rank in order per capita

1	Alaska
2	Delaware
3	Hawaii
4	Wyoming
5	New York
6	New Mexico
7	Massachusetts
8	Vermont
9	Connecticut
10	North Dakota
11	Minnesota
12	Rhode Island
13	California
14	Washington
15	Michigan
16	Montana
17	West Virginia
18	Oregon
19	Maine
20	Wisconsin
21	Utah
22	Kentucky
23	Iowa
24	Arkansas
25	Mississippi
26	South Carolina
27	North Carolina
28	Louisiana
29	Pennsylvania
30	New Jersey
31	Virginia
32	Alabama
33	Idaho
34	Maryland
35	Nebraska
36	Ohio
37	Indiana
38	Nevada
39	Kansas
40	Colorado
41	South Dakota
42	Illinois
43	Missouri
44	Georgia
45	Oklahoma
46	Arizona
47	Tennessee
48	Florida
49	New Hampshire
50	Texas

G-11 State Government General Fund Spending, FY 2000

State	State government general fund spending $ (in millions)	As a percentage of personal income	Rank by percentage
Alabama	14,730	14.1	14
Alaska	5,245	28.2	1
Arizona	14,924	11.6	29
Arkansas	10,093	17.2	7
California	122,167	11.2	34
Colorado	12,267	8.7	46
Connecticut	18,096	13.0	19
Delaware	5,015	20.5	3
Florida	48,808	10.9	36
Georgia	25,865	11.3	31
Hawaii	6,784	20.1	4
Idaho	3,636	11.8	26
Illinois	35,084	8.9	45
Indiana	16,881	10.3	41
Iowa	11,652	15.1	11
Kansas	8,416	11.4	30
Kentucky	12,653	13.0	20
Louisiana	15,636	15.2	10
Maine	4,846	15.0	12
Maryland	18,316	10.3	42
Massachusetts	26,532	11.1	35
Michigan	34,947	12.1	24
Minnesota	18,447	11.7	27
Mississippi	9,655	16.2	9
Missouri	16,015	10.5	40
Montana	2,783	13.6	16
Nebraska	5,801	12.2	23
Nevada	4,594	7.7	49
New Hampshire	3,395	8.3	48
New Jersey	29,672	9.5	44
New Mexico	8,269	20.7	2
New York	73,573	11.2	32
North Carolina	25,837	11.9	25
North Dakota	2,256	14.2	13
Ohio	38,816	12.2	22
Oklahoma	10,595	13.0	18
Oregon	10,655	11.2	33
Pennsylvania	38,465	10.6	39
Rhode Island	4,271	14.0	15
South Carolina	16,892	17.5	5
South Dakota	2,109	10.7	37
Tennessee	15,809	10.7	38
Texas	49,465	8.5	47
Utah	6,561	12.5	21
Vermont	2,231	13.6	17
Virginia	22,364	10.1	43
Washington	21,481	11.7	28
West Virginia	6,482	16.5	8
Wisconsin	26,185	17.4	6
Wyoming	n/a	n/a	n/a
50 States	945,271	11.4	
DC	n/a	n/a	
United States	945,271	11.4	

Rank in order by percentage

1 Alaska
2 New Mexico
3 Delaware
4 Hawaii
5 South Carolina
6 Wisconsin
7 Arkansas
8 West Virginia
9 Mississippi
10 Louisiana
11 Iowa
12 Maine
13 North Dakota
14 Alabama
15 Rhode Island
16 Montana
17 Vermont
18 Oklahoma
19 Connecticut
20 Kentucky
21 Utah
22 Ohio
23 Nebraska
24 Michigan
25 North Carolina
26 Idaho
27 Minnesota
28 Washington
29 Arizona
30 Kansas
31 Georgia
32 New York
33 Oregon
34 California
35 Massachusetts
36 Florida
37 South Dakota
38 Tennessee
39 Pennsylvania
40 Missouri
41 Indiana
42 Maryland
43 Virginia
44 New Jersey
45 Illinois
46 Colorado
47 Texas
48 New Hampshire
49 Nevada

Note: Numbers that appear to be identical are rounded and vary slightly in actual value. The rankings reflect the actual values before rounding. See the introduction for more details.

G-12 State and Local Debt, FY 1999

State	State and local debt $ (in millions)	State and local debt per capita $	State and local debt as a percentage of personal income	Rank per capita
Alabama	14,250	3,261	14.8	42
Alaska	7,434	11,991	43.3	1
Arizona	22,913	4,795	20.3	21
Arkansas	6,937	2,719	12.9	48
California	168,344	5,079	18.2	18
Colorado	22,059	5,439	18.6	16
Connecticut	22,238	6,776	18.1	5
Delaware	4,916	6,519	22.3	7
Florida	75,706	5,010	18.9	19
Georgia	26,273	3,373	13.2	40
Hawaii	7,651	6,457	24.0	9
Idaho	3,144	2,511	11.7	49
Illinois	62,897	5,186	17.4	17
Indiana	18,464	3,107	12.4	46
Iowa	7,156	2,494	10.1	50
Kansas	9,737	3,669	14.4	38
Kentucky	22,516	5,685	25.6	13
Louisiana	17,316	3,961	17.8	34
Maine	5,585	4,457	19.0	27
Maryland	23,852	4,612	15.1	24
Massachusetts	50,319	8,149	24.5	3
Michigan	44,095	4,470	16.7	26
Minnesota	26,864	5,625	19.3	15
Mississippi	8,577	3,098	15.6	47
Missouri	17,605	3,220	12.7	44
Montana	3,561	4,033	19.0	32
Nebraska	6,290	3,776	14.6	37
Nevada	12,300	6,800	23.7	4
New Hampshire	6,776	5,642	19.3	14
New Jersey	47,930	5,886	17.3	11
New Mexico	7,198	4,137	19.6	30
New York	171,419	9,420	29.3	2
North Carolina	27,401	3,581	14.3	39
North Dakota	2,464	3,887	17.0	36
Ohio	36,510	3,243	12.4	43
Oklahoma	11,173	3,327	15.1	41
Oregon	14,346	4,326	16.8	29
Pennsylvania	69,465	5,792	21.2	12
Rhode Island	6,620	6,680	23.9	6
South Carolina	15,584	4,010	18.0	33
South Dakota	3,004	4,099	17.3	31
Tennessee	17,437	3,180	13.1	45
Texas	90,558	4,518	17.8	25
Utah	12,941	6,076	27.6	10
Vermont	2,786	4,690	19.0	23
Virginia	30,410	4,425	15.8	28
Washington	37,198	6,463	22.8	8
West Virginia	7,098	3,928	19.4	35
Wisconsin	24,643	4,694	18.0	22
Wyoming	2,350	4,896	19.6	20
50 States	1,364,314	5,013	18.5	
DC	4,939	9,517	25.1	
United States	1,369,253	5,021	18.5	

Rank in order per capita

1 Alaska
2 New York
3 Massachusetts
4 Nevada
5 Connecticut
6 Rhode Island
7 Delaware
8 Washington
9 Hawaii
10 Utah
11 New Jersey
12 Pennsylvania
13 Kentucky
14 New Hampshire
15 Minnesota
16 Colorado
17 Illinois
18 California
19 Florida
20 Wyoming
21 Arizona
22 Wisconsin
23 Vermont
24 Maryland
25 Texas
26 Michigan
27 Maine
28 Virginia
29 Oregon
30 New Mexico
31 South Dakota
32 Montana
33 South Carolina
34 Louisiana
35 West Virginia
36 North Dakota
37 Nebraska
38 Kansas
39 North Carolina
40 Georgia
41 Oklahoma
42 Alabama
43 Ohio
44 Missouri
45 Tennessee
46 Indiana
47 Mississippi
48 Arkansas
49 Idaho
50 Iowa

G-13 State and Local Debt Related to Revenue, FY 1999

State	State and local debt as a percentage of general revenue	Rank
Alabama	60.3	37
Alaska	80.6	18
Arizona	89.1	11
Arkansas	50.0	47
California	69.4	27
Colorado	86.8	13
Connecticut	93.5	8
Delaware	89.0	12
Florida	85.6	14
Georgia	56.8	43
Hawaii	94.5	7
Idaho	45.8	49
Illinois	85.5	15
Indiana	59.8	39
Iowa	41.4	50
Kansas	68.9	30
Kentucky	98.9	5
Louisiana	67.4	31
Maine	69.0	29
Maryland	76.3	20
Massachusetts	121.5	1
Michigan	66.7	32
Minnesota	73.3	23
Mississippi	57.3	42
Missouri	58.8	40
Montana	69.4	28
Nebraska	57.5	41
Nevada	104.9	3
New Hampshire	105.0	2
New Jersey	81.1	17
New Mexico	64.0	34
New York	99.5	4
North Carolina	55.8	44
North Dakota	60.2	38
Ohio	48.6	48
Oklahoma	64.1	33
Oregon	62.3	36
Pennsylvania	93.2	9
Rhode Island	91.9	10
South Carolina	72.0	24
South Dakota	71.1	25
Tennessee	55.6	45
Texas	77.1	19
Utah	97.4	6
Vermont	74.1	22
Virginia	76.2	21
Washington	84.9	16
West Virginia	69.9	26
Wisconsin	63.5	35
Wyoming	53.1	46
50 States	76.3	
DC	80.6	
United States	76.3	

Rank in order by percentage

1 Massachusetts
2 New Hampshire
3 Nevada
4 New York
5 Kentucky
6 Utah
7 Hawaii
8 Connecticut
9 Pennsylvania
10 Rhode Island
11 Arizona
12 Delaware
13 Colorado
14 Florida
15 Illinois
16 Washington
17 New Jersey
18 Alaska
19 Texas
20 Maryland
21 Virginia
22 Vermont
23 Minnesota
24 South Carolina
25 South Dakota
26 West Virginia
27 California
28 Montana
29 Maine
30 Kansas
31 Louisiana
32 Michigan
33 Oklahoma
34 New Mexico
35 Wisconsin
36 Oregon
37 Alabama
38 North Dakota
39 Indiana
40 Missouri
41 Nebraska
42 Mississippi
43 Georgia
44 North Carolina
45 Tennessee
46 Wyoming
47 Arkansas
48 Ohio
49 Idaho
50 Iowa

Note: Numbers that appear to be identical are rounded and vary slightly in actual value. The rankings reflect the actual values before rounding. See the introduction for more details.

G-14 State and Local Full Faith and Credit Debt, FY 1999

State	Full faith and credit debt $ (in millions)	Per capita $	As a percentage of personal income	Rank per capita
Alabama	5,481	1,254	5.7	30
Alaska	2,409	3,886	14.0	4
Arizona	8,811	1,844	7.8	18
Arkansas	1,709	670	3.2	43
California	38,776	1,170	4.2	35
Colorado	8,268	2,038	7.0	15
Connecticut	14,411	4,391	11.8	1
Delaware	1,331	1,766	6.1	20
Florida	13,093	866	3.3	39
Georgia	9,638	1,238	4.8	31
Hawaii	5,070	4,279	15.9	2
Idaho	759	606	2.8	46
Illinois	31,613	2,607	8.7	9
Indiana	2,893	487	1.9	49
Iowa	2,738	954	3.9	37
Kansas	3,637	1,370	5.4	28
Kentucky	1,932	488	2.2	48
Louisiana	5,897	1,349	6.0	29
Maine	1,731	1,382	5.9	27
Maryland	11,497	2,223	7.3	12
Massachusetts	21,277	3,446	10.4	5
Michigan	17,889	1,814	6.8	19
Minnesota	12,973	2,716	9.3	8
Mississippi	4,508	1,628	8.2	21
Missouri	4,935	903	3.6	38
Montana	549	622	2.9	45
Nebraska	1,431	859	3.3	40
Nevada	7,059	3,902	13.6	3
New Hampshire	1,871	1,558	5.3	23
New Jersey	15,844	1,946	5.7	16
New Mexico	1,758	1,010	4.8	36
New York	62,241	3,420	10.6	6
North Carolina	9,003	1,177	4.7	33
North Dakota	425	671	2.9	42
Ohio	13,244	1,177	4.5	34
Oklahoma	1,858	553	2.5	47
Oregon	6,992	2,109	8.2	14
Pennsylvania	27,124	2,261	8.3	11
Rhode Island	1,839	1,855	6.6	17
South Carolina	4,629	1,191	5.3	32
South Dakota	548	747	3.1	41
Tennessee	8,370	1,526	6.3	24
Texas	42,269	2,109	8.3	13
Utah	3,039	1,427	6.5	25
Vermont	955	1,607	6.5	22
Virginia	9,598	1,396	5.0	26
Washington	17,612	3,060	10.8	7
West Virginia	634	351	1.7	50
Wisconsin	12,621	2,404	9.2	10
Wyoming	320	666	2.7	44
50 States	485,110	1,782	6.6	
DC	3,758	7,242	19.1	
United States	488,868	1,793	6.6	

Rank in order per capita	
1	Connecticut
2	Hawaii
3	Nevada
4	Alaska
5	Massachusetts
6	New York
7	Washington
8	Minnesota
9	Illinois
10	Wisconsin
11	Pennsylvania
12	Maryland
13	Texas
14	Oregon
15	Colorado
16	New Jersey
17	Rhode Island
18	Arizona
19	Michigan
20	Delaware
21	Mississippi
22	Vermont
23	New Hampshire
24	Tennessee
25	Utah
26	Virginia
27	Maine
28	Kansas
29	Louisiana
30	Alabama
31	Georgia
32	South Carolina
33	North Carolina
34	Ohio
35	California
36	New Mexico
37	Iowa
38	Missouri
39	Florida
40	Nebraska
41	South Dakota
42	North Dakota
43	Arkansas
44	Wyoming
45	Montana
46	Idaho
47	Oklahoma
48	Kentucky
49	Indiana
50	West Virginia

Note: Numbers that appear to be identical are rounded and vary slightly in actual value. The rankings reflect the actual values before rounding. See the introduction for more details.

G-15 State Government Bond Ratings, 2001

State	State bond ratings	Rank
Alabama	Aa3	4
Alaska	Aa2	3
Arizona	no general obligation debt	n/a
Arkansas	Aa2	3
California	Aa3	4
Colorado	no general obligation debt	n/a
Connecticut	Aa2	3
Delaware	Aaa	1
Florida	Aa2	3
Georgia	Aaa	1
Hawaii	Aa3	4
Idaho	no general obligation debt	n/a
Illinois	Aa2	3
Indiana	no general obligation debt	n/a
Iowa	no general obligation debt	n/a
Kansas	no general obligation debt	n/a
Kentucky	Aa2	3
Louisiana	A2	5
Maine	Aa2	3
Maryland	Aaa	1
Massachusetts	Aa2	3
Michigan	Aaa	1
Minnesota	Aaa	1
Mississippi	Aa3	4
Missouri	Aaa	1
Montana	Aa3	4
Nebraska	no general obligation debt	n/a
Nevada	Aa2	3
New Hampshire	Aa2	3
New Jersey	Aa1	2
New Mexico	Aa1	2
New York	A2	5
North Carolina	Aaa	1
North Dakota	Aa3	4
Ohio	Aa1	2
Oklahoma	Aa3	4
Oregon	Aa2	3
Pennsylvania	Aa2	3
Rhode Island	Aa3	4
South Carolina	Aaa	1
South Dakota	no general obligation debt	n/a
Tennessee	Aa2	3
Texas	Aa1	2
Utah	Aaa	1
Vermont	Aa1	2
Virginia	Aaa	1
Washington	Aa1	2
West Virginia	Aa3	4
Wisconsin	Aa3	4
Wyoming	no general obligation debt	n/a
50 States	n/a	
DC	n/a	
United States	n/a	

Rank in order by rating

1	Delaware
1	Georgia
1	Maryland
1	Michigan
1	Minnesota
1	Missouri
1	North Carolina
1	South Carolina
1	Utah
1	Virginia
2	New Jersey
2	New Mexico
2	Ohio
2	Texas
2	Vermont
2	Washington
3	Alaska
3	Arkansas
3	Connecticut
3	Florida
3	Illinois
3	Kentucky
3	Maine
3	Massachusetts
3	Nevada
3	New Hampshire
3	Oregon
3	Pennsylvania
3	Tennessee
4	Alabama
4	California
4	Hawaii
4	Mississippi
4	Montana
4	North Dakota
4	Oklahoma
4	Rhode Island
4	West Virginia
4	Wisconsin
5	Louisiana
5	New York

Note: Ties in ranking reflect ties in actual values.

G-16 State Solvency Index, 1993

State	State solvency index	Rank by index
Alabama	46	23
Alaska	21,344	1
Arizona	97	22
Arkansas	483	12
California	-512	34
Colorado	784	6
Connecticut	-2,895	49
Delaware	200	17
Florida	-424	32
Georgia	139	20
Hawaii	-1,119	44
Idaho	137	21
Illinois	-854	38
Indiana	-233	27
Iowa	723	7
Kansas	582	8
Kentucky	-339	31
Louisiana	-2,206	48
Maine	-1,802	47
Maryland	-951	41
Massachusetts	-2,943	50
Michigan	-1,097	43
Minnesota	179	18
Mississippi	-256	28
Missouri	-19	24
Montana	259	15
Nebraska	498	11
Nevada	-319	30
New Hampshire	-624	35
New Jersey	-886	40
New Mexico	2,812	3
New York	-134	25
North Carolina	545	9
North Dakota	1,018	5
Ohio	-178	26
Oklahoma	-782	37
Oregon	1,138	4
Pennsylvania	-474	33
Rhode Island	-1,649	45
South Carolina	-877	39
South Dakota	527	10
Tennessee	142	19
Texas	352	14
Utah	359	13
Vermont	-1,061	42
Virginia	-292	29
Washington	-767	36
West Virginia	-1,657	46
Wisconsin	251	16
Wyoming	5,572	2
50 States	-304	
DC	n/a	
United States	-304	

Rank in order by index

1	Alaska
2	Wyoming
3	New Mexico
4	Oregon
5	North Dakota
6	Colorado
7	Iowa
8	Kansas
9	North Carolina
10	South Dakota
11	Nebraska
12	Arkansas
13	Utah
14	Texas
15	Montana
16	Wisconsin
17	Delaware
18	Minnesota
19	Tennessee
20	Georgia
21	Idaho
22	Arizona
23	Alabama
24	Missouri
25	New York
26	Ohio
27	Indiana
28	Mississippi
29	Virginia
30	Nevada
31	Kentucky
32	Florida
33	Pennsylvania
34	California
35	New Hampshire
36	Washington
37	Oklahoma
38	Illinois
39	South Carolina
40	New Jersey
41	Maryland
42	Vermont
43	Michigan
44	Hawaii
45	Rhode Island
46	West Virginia
47	Maine
48	Louisiana
49	Connecticut
50	Massachusetts

G-17 Assets of State-administered Pension Plans, 2000

State	Total assets $ (in millions)	Total membership #	Average assets per member	Rank by average
Alabama	22,733	247,766	91,753	38
Alaska	11,337	61,099	185,559	5
Arizona	31,097	314,261	98,954	33
Arkansas	13,523	121,109	111,661	23
California	376,114	1,824,276	206,171	1
Colorado	25,720	280,184	91,797	37
Connecticut	20,884	147,176	141,899	14
Delaware	6,115	40,134	152,363	11
Florida	83,411	686,011	121,589	20
Georgia	43,182	564,254	76,530	42
Hawaii	8,420	232,297	36,248	49
Idaho	7,360	60,490	121,671	19
Illinois	88,101	851,240	103,497	31
Indiana	18,241	365,723	49,877	48
Iowa	20,237	251,931	80,328	41
Kansas	10,621	177,963	59,681	45
Kentucky	23,627	242,165	97,567	36
Louisiana	27,698	282,946	97,891	35
Maine	7,570	53,022	142,765	13
Maryland	44,409	266,507	166,635	8
Massachusetts	43,122	327,548	131,652	17
Michigan	75,772	448,224	169,050	7
Minnesota	45,366	450,674	100,662	32
Mississippi	17,158	259,919	66,012	44
Missouri	39,907	275,188	145,018	12
Montana	5,635	75,988	74,159	43
Nebraska	7,258	82,513	87,964	39
Nevada	14,348	86,510	165,854	9
New Hampshire	4,615	44,007	104,872	29
New Jersey	56,733	459,111	123,571	18
New Mexico	14,519	133,669	108,621	27
New York	242,911	1,196,615	202,999	2
North Carolina	57,551	494,158	116,463	21
North Dakota	2,787	104,333	26,712	50
Ohio	112,517	1,086,938	103,518	30
Oklahoma	15,988	161,983	98,700	34
Oregon	21,997	203,494	108,097	28
Pennsylvania	98,361	510,576	192,647	3
Rhode Island	7,251	38,914	186,326	4
South Carolina	19,395	354,271	54,745	46
South Dakota	5,948	44,739	132,938	16
Tennessee	30,210	226,467	133,396	15
Texas	140,924	1,279,606	110,130	26
Utah	13,058	113,955	114,585	22
Vermont	2,496	29,051	85,926	40
Virginia	48,749	440,579	110,648	24
Washington	51,522	323,665	159,183	10
West Virginia	4,172	80,548	51,790	47
Wisconsin	69,669	383,828	181,512	6
Wyoming	3,922	35,481	110,534	25
50 States	2,164,263	16,823,106	128,648	
DC	4,380	11,069	395,736	
United States*	2,168,643	16,833,698	128,827	

Rank in order by average	
1	California
2	New York
3	Pennsylvania
4	Rhode Island
5	Alaska
6	Wisconsin
7	Michigan
8	Maryland
9	Nevada
10	Washington
11	Delaware
12	Missouri
13	Maine
14	Connecticut
15	Tennessee
16	South Dakota
17	Massachusetts
18	New Jersey
19	Idaho
20	Florida
21	North Carolina
22	Utah
23	Arkansas
24	Virginia
25	Wyoming
26	Texas
27	New Mexico
28	Oregon
29	New Hampshire
30	Ohio
31	Illinois
32	Minnesota
33	Arizona
34	Oklahoma
35	Louisiana
36	Kentucky
37	Colorado
38	Alabama
39	Nebraska
40	Vermont
41	Iowa
42	Georgia
43	Montana
44	Mississippi
45	Kansas
46	South Carolina
47	West Virginia
48	Indiana
49	Hawaii
50	North Dakota

Due to rounding or data sources, the 50-state total plus D.C. may not equal the U.S. total. Please see introduction.

G-18 State Reserves at the End of FY 2001

State	Balances as a percentage of expenditures	Rank
Alabama	0.5	48
Alaska	124.9	1
Arizona	5.2	32
Arkansas	0.0	49
California	8.2	18
Colorado	8.0	20
Connecticut	5.0	33
Delaware	4.1	36
Florida	5.6	30
Georgia	7.6	24
Hawaii	10.4	9
Idaho	12.6	7
Illinois	5.7	29
Indiana	9.9	10
Iowa	9.8	11
Kansas	9.7	12
Kentucky	3.6	37
Louisiana	1.3	46
Maine	6.1	26
Maryland	12.7	6
Massachusetts	8.5	16
Michigan	12.9	4
Minnesota	8.4	17
Mississippi	7.5	25
Missouri	3.3	38
Montana	8.2	18
Nebraska	15.2	3
Nevada	12.9	4
New Hampshire	2.2	45
New Jersey	6.1	26
New Mexico	8.7	15
New York	2.8	40
North Carolina	1.1	47
North Dakota	4.6	35
Ohio	6.1	26
Oklahoma	12.1	8
Oregon	9.5	13
Pennsylvania	7.7	23
Rhode Island	7.8	22
South Carolina	2.7	41
South Dakota	5.5	31
Tennessee	2.5	43
Texas	n/a	n/a
Utah	2.9	39
Vermont	4.8	34
Virginia	8.0	20
Washington	9.5	13
West Virginia	2.4	44
Wisconsin	2.7	41
Wyoming	23.3	2
50 States	n/a	
DC	n/a	
United States	7.2	

Rank in order by percentage	
1	Alaska
2	Wyoming
3	Nebraska
4	Michigan
4	Nevada
6	Maryland
7	Idaho
8	Oklahoma
9	Hawaii
10	Indiana
11	Iowa
12	Kansas
13	Oregon
13	Washington
15	New Mexico
16	Massachusetts
17	Minnesota
18	California
18	Montana
20	Colorado
20	Virginia
22	Rhode Island
23	Pennsylvania
24	Georgia
25	Mississippi
26	Maine
26	New Jersey
26	Ohio
29	Illinois
30	Florida
31	South Dakota
32	Arizona
33	Connecticut
34	Vermont
35	North Dakota
36	Delaware
37	Kentucky
38	Missouri
39	Utah
40	New York
41	South Carolina
41	Wisconsin
43	Tennessee
44	West Virginia
45	New Hampshire
46	Louisiana
47	North Carolina
48	Alabama
49	Arkansas

Note: Ties in ranking reflect ties in actual values.

G-19 State and Local Capital Outlays and Interest, FY 1999

State	Outlays and interest per capita $	Capital outlays per capita $	Interest per capita $	Rank by outlays and interest per capita
Alabama	746	580	166	44
Alaska	2,694	1,970	724	1
Arizona	1,179	920	259	11
Arkansas	668	519	149	49
California	959	683	276	22
Colorado	1,165	852	312	12
Connecticut	976	572	404	20
Delaware	1,249	841	408	9
Florida	1,084	778	306	15
Georgia	1,042	836	207	17
Hawaii	1,312	806	507	6
Idaho	745	601	144	45
Illinois	1,009	705	305	18
Indiana	751	586	165	43
Iowa	924	805	119	29
Kansas	867	688	179	36
Kentucky	1,112	746	366	13
Louisiana	893	669	224	32
Maine	612	392	220	50
Maryland	866	639	227	37
Massachusetts	1,310	885	425	7
Michigan	888	648	240	34
Minnesota	1,197	868	329	10
Mississippi	846	675	172	39
Missouri	789	607	182	41
Montana	954	689	265	24
Nebraska	1,094	875	219	14
Nevada	1,524	1,127	397	2
New Hampshire	828	486	342	40
New Jersey	881	592	289	35
New Mexico	954	713	241	23
New York	1,490	940	550	4
North Carolina	925	722	203	28
North Dakota	898	689	209	31
Ohio	850	665	185	38
Oklahoma	703	523	180	48
Oregon	1,050	845	205	16
Pennsylvania	939	579	360	26
Rhode Island	761	433	328	42
South Carolina	891	647	243	33
South Dakota	944	721	223	25
Tennessee	973	794	178	21
Texas	933	679	255	27
Utah	1,253	939	314	8
Vermont	710	438	273	47
Virginia	921	651	270	30
Washington	1,456	1,116	341	5
West Virginia	723	487	237	46
Wisconsin	990	736	254	19
Wyoming	1,518	1,242	277	3
50 States	1,010	727	284	
DC	1,817	1,300	517	
United States	1,012	728	284	

Rank in order per capita	
1	Alaska
2	Nevada
3	Wyoming
4	New York
5	Washington
6	Hawaii
7	Massachusetts
8	Utah
9	Delaware
10	Minnesota
11	Arizona
12	Colorado
13	Kentucky
14	Nebraska
15	Florida
16	Oregon
17	Georgia
18	Illinois
19	Wisconsin
20	Connecticut
21	Tennessee
22	California
23	New Mexico
24	Montana
25	South Dakota
26	Pennsylvania
27	Texas
28	North Carolina
29	Iowa
30	Virginia
31	North Dakota
32	Louisiana
33	South Carolina
34	Michigan
35	New Jersey
36	Kansas
37	Maryland
38	Ohio
39	Mississippi
40	New Hampshire
41	Missouri
42	Rhode Island
43	Indiana
44	Alabama
45	Idaho
46	West Virginia
47	Vermont
48	Oklahoma
49	Arkansas
50	Maine

Note: Numbers that appear to be identical are rounded and vary slightly in actual value. The rankings reflect the actual values before rounding. See the Introduction for more details.

G-20 Index of State Budget Process Quality, 1999

State	Index of state budget process quality	Rank
Alabama	58.9	40
Alaska	64.0	32
Arizona	63.0	35
Arkansas	52.0	45
California	54.5	42
Colorado	83.0	6
Connecticut	76.0	11
Delaware	72.0	14
Florida	71.0	15
Georgia	91.2	1
Hawaii	68.0	22
Idaho	47.2	47
Illinois	56.5	41
Indiana	41.0	48
Iowa	83.0	6
Kansas	59.0	39
Kentucky	69.7	19
Louisiana	70.4	18
Maine	83.0	6
Maryland	68.0	22
Massachusetts	87.0	3
Michigan	88.0	2
Minnesota	85.0	4
Mississippi	64.0	32
Missouri	75.7	12
Montana	65.7	29
Nebraska	64.0	32
Nevada	71.0	15
New Hampshire	33.3	50
New Jersey	84.0	5
New Mexico	68.0	22
New York	73.0	13
North Carolina	50.3	46
North Dakota	65.3	30
Ohio	68.0	22
Oklahoma	67.0	27
Oregon	80.0	9
Pennsylvania	64.9	31
Rhode Island	77.3	10
South Carolina	60.4	38
South Dakota	69.7	19
Tennessee	54.1	43
Texas	66.0	28
Utah	70.7	17
Vermont	37.4	49
Virginia	54.0	44
Washington	68.0	22
West Virginia	60.5	37
Wisconsin	63.0	35
Wyoming	68.1	21
50 States	**68.9**	
DC	n/a	
United States	**68.9**	

Rank in order by index	
1	Georgia
2	Michigan
3	Massachusetts
4	Minnesota
5	New Jersey
6	Colorado
6	Iowa
6	Maine
9	Oregon
10	Rhode Island
11	Connecticut
12	Missouri
13	New York
14	Delaware
15	Florida
15	Nevada
17	Utah
18	Louisiana
19	Kentucky
19	South Dakota
21	Wyoming
22	Hawaii
22	Maryland
22	New Mexico
22	Ohio
22	Washington
27	Oklahoma
28	Texas
29	Montana
30	North Dakota
31	Pennsylvania
32	Alaska
32	Mississippi
32	Nebraska
35	Arizona
35	Wisconsin
37	West Virginia
38	South Carolina
39	Kansas
40	Alabama
41	Illinois
42	California
43	Tennessee
44	Virginia
45	Arkansas
46	North Carolina
47	Idaho
48	Indiana
49	Vermont
50	New Hampshire

Note: Ties in ranking reflect ties in actual values.

Revenues and Finances   187

G-21 Relative State Spending "Needs," FY 1996

State	Additional spending needed to meet national average %	Rank
Alabama	4	41
Alaska	2	38
Arizona	5	45
Arkansas	0	30
California	10	48
Colorado	-10	8
Connecticut	2	38
Delaware	-11	4
Florida	-4	24
Georgia	4	41
Hawaii	-10	8
Idaho	0	30
Illinois	1	33
Indiana	-8	12
Iowa	-11	4
Kansas	-5	18
Kentucky	1	33
Louisiana	9	47
Maine	-12	2
Maryland	-5	18
Massachusetts	-7	14
Michigan	1	33
Minnesota	-6	16
Mississippi	10	48
Missouri	-8	12
Montana	-2	29
Nebraska	-12	2
Nevada	-6	16
New Hampshire	-16	1
New Jersey	-5	18
New Mexico	15	50
New York	4	41
North Carolina	-5	18
North Dakota	-4	24
Ohio	-3	28
Oklahoma	4	41
Oregon	-9	11
Pennsylvania	-7	14
Rhode Island	-11	4
South Carolina	1	33
South Dakota	-4	24
Tennessee	2	38
Texas	8	46
Utah	-5	18
Vermont	-10	8
Virginia	-4	24
Washington	-5	18
West Virginia	0	30
Wisconsin	-11	4
Wyoming	1	33
50 States	n/a	
DC	26	
United States	0	

Rank in order by percentage	
1	New Hampshire
2	Maine
2	Nebraska
4	Delaware
4	Iowa
4	Rhode Island
4	Wisconsin
8	Colorado
8	Hawaii
8	Vermont
11	Oregon
12	Indiana
12	Missouri
14	Massachusetts
14	Pennsylvania
16	Minnesota
16	Nevada
18	Kansas
18	Maryland
18	New Jersey
18	North Carolina
18	Utah
18	Washington
24	Florida
24	North Dakota
24	South Dakota
24	Virginia
28	Ohio
29	Montana
30	Arkansas
30	Idaho
30	West Virginia
33	Illinois
33	Kentucky
33	Michigan
33	South Carolina
33	Wyoming
38	Alaska
38	Connecticut
38	Tennessee
41	Alabama
41	Georgia
41	New York
41	Oklahoma
45	Arizona
46	Texas
47	Louisiana
48	California
48	Mississippi
50	New Mexico

Note: Ties in ranking reflect ties in actual values.

G-22 Structural Deficits

State	Projected state surplus or shortfall as a percentage of baseline revenues	Rank
Alabama	-4.8	31
Alaska	-16.4	49
Arizona	-10.5	44
Arkansas	-2.3	21
California	-2.8	23
Colorado	-7	38
Connecticut	0.4	6
Delaware	-3	25
Florida	-8.8	42
Georgia	-6.5	35
Hawaii	-15.1	48
Idaho	-13.2	47
Illinois	-0.4	13
Indiana	-5.7	33
Iowa	2.7	1
Kansas	-1.9	18
Kentucky	0.5	5
Louisiana	-2.5	22
Maine	0.1	9
Maryland	-7.1	39
Massachusetts	0	11
Michigan	0.4	6
Minnesota	0.1	9
Mississippi	-2	19
Missouri	-1.8	17
Montana	-5.7	33
Nebraska	1.5	2
Nevada	-18.3	50
New Hampshire	-8.2	41
New Jersey	-3.3	26
New Mexico	-12	46
New York	0.3	8
North Carolina	-3.7	27
North Dakota	0.9	3
Ohio	0.9	3
Oklahoma	-2.1	20
Oregon	-0.1	12
Pennsylvania	-1.3	14
Rhode Island	-2.9	24
South Carolina	-4.6	29
South Dakota	-5	32
Tennessee	-9.1	43
Texas	-7.8	40
Utah	-4.3	28
Vermont	-4.6	29
Virginia	-6.8	37
Washington	-6.7	36
West Virginia	-1.4	15
Wisconsin	-1.5	16
Wyoming	-10.6	45
50 States	n/a	
DC	n/a	
United States	-3.8	

Rank in order by percentage	
1	Iowa
2	Nebraska
3	North Dakota
3	Ohio
5	Kentucky
6	Connecticut
6	Michigan
8	New York
9	Maine
9	Minnesota
11	Massachusetts
12	Oregon
13	Illinois
14	Pennsylvania
15	West Virginia
16	Wisconsin
17	Missouri
18	Kansas
19	Mississippi
20	Oklahoma
21	Arkansas
22	Louisiana
23	California
24	Rhode Island
25	Delaware
26	New Jersey
27	North Carolina
28	Utah
29	South Carolina
29	Vermont
31	Alabama
32	South Dakota
33	Indiana
33	Montana
35	Georgia
36	Washington
37	Virginia
38	Colorado
39	Maryland
40	Texas
41	New Hampshire
42	Florida
43	Tennessee
44	Arizona
45	Wyoming
46	New Mexico
47	Idaho
48	Hawaii
49	Alaska
50	Nevada

Note: Ties in ranking reflect ties in actual values.

Source Notes for Revenues and Finances (Section G)

G-1 State and Local Total Revenue, FY 1999: This table and many others in this section of *State Fact Finder* rely on analysis of data collected by the Census Bureau for FY 1999. For sources of the fiscal data and the population and personal income estimates used to build the tables, see the extensive note associated with Table F-1.

Total revenue, shown in this table, is the most inclusive definition of the financial size of state and local governments used by the Census Bureau in its annual survey of government finances. It includes utilities run by state and local governments and many categories of trust funds. Such funds typically collect revenues, such as unemployment insurance taxes, for a particular purpose, such as paying unemployment compensation benefits, and are not commingled with other public funds. The revenues included come from state and local taxes, fees such as hospital charges and university tuition, and from the federal government.

G-2 State and Local General Revenue, FY 1999: From the same source as Table F-1, this table relates general revenue to population and personal income in each state. Because general revenue eliminates difficult to compare proprietary functions, such as utility and trust fund revenues, it allows for more appropriate state-by-state comparisons.

G-3 State and Local "Own-source" General Revenue, FY 1999: These data reflect the concept often used to measure the fiscal burdens associated with state and local activity. Revenues from federal aid are excluded, along with the revenues of trust funds and utilities. For source see the notes to Table F-1.

G-4 State and Local Non-tax "Own-source" Revenue, FY 1999: The principal sources of non-tax revenues are (1) fees related to use of state facilities and services, such as those charged by public hospitals and universities, and (2) interest earned on money held by governments in anticipation of spending. For source see the notes to Table F-1.

G-5 State and Local Total Expenditures, FY 1999: This is the spending counterpart of the revenues shown on Table G-1. For source see the notes to Table F-1.

G-6 State and Local General Expenditures, FY 1999: This concept of "general" spending (see notes to Table G-2) is the most appropriate for comparing spending among states. For source see the notes to Table F-1.

G-7 State and Local General Expenditures Per Capita, FY 1999: This table relates general expenditures to population with separate totals for state governments and local governments. State aid to local governments is included only when local officials spend the resources, to avoid double counting. For source see the notes to Table F-1.

G-8 Percentage Change in State and Local General Expenditures, FY 1994-FY 1999: This statistic shows the differences among states in the five-year growth of state and local spending. The changes shown are not adjusted for factors that might account for some of the differences in growth rates, such as growth in population and other factors affecting needs for government services. FY 1994 data come from the Census Bureau and are published in *State Fact Finder 1998*. See source for Table F-1 for FY 1999 data.

G-9 State Government General Revenue, FY 1999: Unlike Tables G-1 through G-8, these data deal with state governments alone, not state and local governments combined. They are from the 1999 version of "State Government Finances," available on the Census Bureau website (www.census.gov).

For most purposes, comparisons of finances among states need to include state and local revenues and spending because of major differences in the division of state and local responsibilities between states. For example, New York local governments pay nearly half of all state and local welfare costs, but local governments in most other states have almost no responsibility for paying these costs. Comparisons of states alone would make New York spending look artificially small. In Hawaii, the state alone pays for schools, while in other states local governments pay half these costs. Comparisons of states alone would make Hawaii's spending look artificially large.

However, comparisons of state governments alone are useful for those attempting to evaluate state officeholders and aspirants and for discussions of state government spending priorities and tax burdens.

This table and Table G-10 show "general" revenues and expenditures, a less inclusive measure than "total" expenditures. The difference is primarily associated with enterprises run by some state governments and not others, particularly liquor sales monopolies run by about a third of the states and the electric power marketing operations run by a few states. State impacts on utility services and liquor prices and sales are similar from state to state but some states achieve them by directly managing these functions. Because huge amounts of money are involved, inclusion of these operations in state comparisons would artificially distort the spending comparisons, so the concepts of general expenditures and general revenues exclude them.

G-10 State Government General Spending, FY 1999: See notes to Table G-9.

G-11 State Government General Fund Spending, FY 2000: These data reflect other estimates of state government spending. They come from a survey of state executive branch budget offices reported in the *2000 State Expenditure Report* by the National Association of State Budget Officers (NASBO). They reflect state fiscal 2000 definitions.

The year ended on June 30, 2000, for forty-six states, while one state ended the fiscal year in the spring and three ended in the fall.

The NASBO report differs from Census Bureau reports in many ways. The Census Bureau reports include all funds, while the NASBO report covers primarily funds subject to appropriation by legislatures and therefore for most states excludes funds of quasi-independent entities such as toll highway authorities. The Census Bureau does not distinguish among funds within state government, while the NASBO report presents data separately for state general funds, federal funds, and other state funds. The data shown in the table reflect the total of all reported funds. The NASBO data use different definitions of spending categories than do the Census Bureau data. See the notes for Table G-9 on the hazards of considering state spending without also considering local spending.

G-12 State and Local Debt, FY 1999: These data, from the Census Bureau (see notes to Table F-1), reflect the total debt of all state and local governments at the end of fiscal 1999, including debt of special authorities.

G-13 State and Local Debt Related to Revenue, FY 1999: This table relates total debt (see Table G-12) to total revenue (see Table G-1). Consequently, it offers a measure of how state and local budgets are strained by the costs of paying principal and interest on past obligations.

G-14 State and Local Full Faith and Credit Debt, FY 1999: These data reflect the component of total debt (see Table G-12) that is backed by the "full faith and credit" of the governments that issued the debt. This debt, commonly known as "general obligation" debt, is backed by all revenue sources of the issuing government. The debt not included in these totals, often known as revenue bonds, is backed only by specified revenues, not general taxes.

G-15 State Government Bond Ratings, 2001: Because thousands of individual state and local governments issue bonds, purchasers such as individuals and mutual funds find it difficult to analyze the risks associated with each individual issue. As a result, three rating agencies (Fitch, Moody's, and Standard & Poor's) evaluate the quality of individual bond issues. The ratings of revenue bonds are unique to the bonds and the revenue sources that back them. The ratings of general obligation bonds shown in this table are reflections of the fiscal soundness of state governments overall. As a result, they affect perceptions of fiscal soundness of states by voters as well as by potential bond purchasers.

The ratings shown come from Moody's and are dated September 1, 2001. Ratings from the other two agencies would show about the same ranking of states. Moody's system considers Aaa highest, followed by Aa1, Aa2, Aa3, A1, A2, and so on, down to lower ratings, which are awarded to some local governments but no states, which are generally considered good credit risks. Some states have so little general obligation debt that they have no recent ratings and therefore are not ranked in this table. While there is no clearly appropriate way to insert them in the rankings, many of these states have strong credit and would rank above many of the states shown in the rankings.

G-16 State Solvency Index, 1993: While state financial reports and Census Bureau data provide substantial detail about state finances, they do not provide answers to some common sense questions about state financial status. One of these questions is equivalent to "net worth," a fundamental concept in viewing the finances of individuals and companies. This table reflects a special study by State Policy Research, Inc. reported in its *State Policy Reports* (September 1993), using data from a variety of dates as close to late 1993 as possible.

Conceptually, the number shown is an answer to the question: If each state were to cease operations tomorrow and pay off all debts (including pension promises to employees), how much money would be left over? For most states, the answer is that nothing would be left. Instead, they would have to levy a special assessment on each citizen (the amounts shown as negative numbers) in order to cease operations. Some states, particularly Alaska with its large reserves built from oil revenues, would have money left over that could be distributed to taxpayers. The calculations exclude the value of physical assets, such as state park lands, trucks, and computers.

When estimates of unfunded pension liabilities are updated, the resulting revised solvency index should show significant differences from the 1993 index published here. In the late 1990s state solvency was substantially improved from the situation shown in this table because state balances and rainy day funds have grown substantially, and rising stock and bond markets had increased the value of investments by state-administered employee pension funds.

G-17 Assets of State-administered Pension Plans, 2000: States run pension plans for their own employees and, in most states, for teachers, city workers, and other local employees as well. To be considered actuarially sound, these plans must have built up enough assets from contributions of employees and their government employers to be able to cover the amounts needed to pay retired workers plus current workers when they retire. How much this amounts to depends on many factors, such as the exact benefits promised and the life expectancy of workers. There is no substitute for actuarial studies of each plan for determining the right amount each plan should have to cover future obligations.

This table shows the assets of state-administered plans and the persons who are considered members of these plans—retirees and active workers accruing retirement benefits. Dividing these two numbers produces average assets per member, which is a rough measure of the relative solvency of the public pension plans in each state. The data come from the Census Bureau website (www.census.gov).

G-18 State Reserves at the End of FY 2001: These data reflect the projected cash reserves of state governments as they finished fiscal year 2001, generally in the summer of 2001. These reserves come in two primary forms—balances (equivalent to the balances people show in their checkbooks) and "rainy day" or stabilization funds (formal reserves, somewhat akin to the savings accounts maintained by individuals). The data come from a survey of state budget officers by the National Association of State Budget Officers (NASBO) published in June 2001, titled *The Fiscal Survey of States*, and available on the NASBO website (www.nasbo.org).

Relating balances to spending provides a basis for comparisons among states of different sizes and financial responsibilities. Nationwide, this table indicates that states have enough in reserve to pay their normal bills for about 7.2 percent of their fiscal years, or roughly twenty-six days, with no additional revenue coming in.

With forty-three states reporting revenues coming in under expectations half way through FY 2002, these numbers are bound to be reduced in most states at the end of FY 2002. But, the percentages shown in the table show the extent of state reserves as states headed into the the fiscally troubled new fiscal year.

G-19 State and Local Capital Outlays and Interest, FY 1999: This table, from the same source as Table F-1, shows per capita amounts of spending in fiscal 1999 for interest and capital outlays. The outlays reflect the pace of activity in financing new facilities, such as roads and schools. The interest reflects the extent to which taxpayers of each state are seeing their tax funds used to pay interest on past spending, normally borrowing to finance capital outlays.

G-20 Index of State Budget Process Quality, 1999: Experts in public administration and budgeting generally agree on criteria of best budgeting practices, such as considering the impacts of spending and tax decisions over a longer period than one year. The numbers shown in the table are scores, with a perfect score being 100, developed by State Policy Research by comparing these criteria with actual state budget practices, as reported by the National Association of State Budget Officers in its special report *Budget Processes in the States* (October 1999).

G-21 Relative State Spending "Needs," FY 1996: Individual states have quite different population characteristics, as shown by many of the tables in *State Fact Finder*. For example, school-age children are an extraordinarily large proportion of the population of Utah, but a smaller-than-average proportion of Pennsylvania's population. As a result, some states would have higher per capita spending than others, even if all states spent identical amounts per pupil, had identical welfare payments, and identical levels of other services. These differences are important to consider in viewing differences in per capita spending among states.

The table was created by Robert Tannenwald of the Federal Reserve Bank of Boston and published in "Fiscal Disparity Among the States Revisited." Tannenwald calculated what state and local governments in each state would have to spend if they applied national average spending (for example, spending per pupil) to their own particular mix of population using government services. For example, to match national average spending patterns, Louisiana would have to spend nine percent more than the national average. Why? Because the state has extra burdens associated with large percentages of welfare recipients and school children.

These data are conceptually similar to concepts of tax capacity shown in Table F-4. Together, these data reflect a consistent pattern of strains that circumstances put on taxpayers and decision makers of individual states. More affluent states, such as Connecticut, often combine above-average tax bases with below-average spending needs while less affluent states, like Mississippi, show the reverse.

G-22 Structural Deficits: Even with their current prosperity, many state officials worry about *structural* deficits—long-term shortfalls because revenues from current taxes will be insufficient to cover the spending needed to maintain current programs. If such deficits exist, they would be obscured by extraordinary performance of the economy and tax collections, but would be magnified by *cyclical deficits* during any economic downturn.

This table shows the result of subtracting projected spending from projected revenues eight years from now. A budget gap or structural deficit is indicated by all the negative results. A value of zero indicates that state and local governments could cover the future costs of their current policies, including adjustments for inflation and workload changes, with revenues from their current tax system, with no change in tax rates or the definition of bases. A positive value means covering costs with money left.

The data were prepared by State Policy Research, Inc., and are published in *The Outlook for State and Local Finances* (National Education Association, 1998).

Education

At the top of the list of education issues is accountability. Specifically, accountability measured by testing of public school students. Testing is by no means new (see the first two tables in this chapter for results from the most recent national tests), but making tests mandatory and then tying the results to federal rewards or sanctions is.

Support for the concept has been bi-partisan, though critics have also been vocal. Those less enamored with testing contend that tests are not an accurate measure of student performance. They argue that, at the very least, tests tell only part of the education story, and that schools and their funding should be evaluated using a mix of accountability measures. Some parents and teachers in school systems that currently emphasize testing are concerned that students are spending more time on test-taking skills than on higher-level learning.

The practicalities of standardized testing will mean additional costs for the states, according to the National Association of State Boards of Education (NASBE). The organization estimates that states will spend as much as $7 billion to implement annual assessments in grades 3-8 in reading and math. A more conservative estimate, assuming simpler, cheaper tests, puts the cost at $2.7 billion.

In higher education, the troubling issue in 2002 will be the budget pinch. As state revenues slip, public colleges and universities are often the first to feel the strain, as recent cuts in Alabama and Ohio illustrate. The reasons higher education spending is the favorite victim of budget cutters are outlined in a 1999 report by *State Fact Finder* co-author Hal Hovey. The report, for the National Center for Public Policy and Higher Education, is entitled *State Spending for Higher Education in the Next Decade.*

H-1 Average Proficiency in Math, Eighth Grade, 2000

State	Average math score	Rank
Alabama	262	34
Alaska	n/a	n/a
Arizona	271	27
Arkansas	261	36
California	262	34
Colorado	n/a	n/a
Connecticut	282	10
Delaware	n/a	n/a
Florida	n/a	n/a
Georgia	266	30
Hawaii	263	32
Idaho	278	14
Illinois	277	16
Indiana	283	5
Iowa	n/a	n/a
Kansas	284	3
Kentucky	272	25
Louisiana	259	38
Maine	284	3
Maryland	276	19
Massachusetts	283	5
Michigan	278	14
Minnesota	288	1
Mississippi	254	39
Missouri	274	23
Montana	287	2
Nebraska	281	11
Nevada	268	29
New Hampshire	n/a	n/a
New Jersey	n/a	n/a
New Mexico	260	37
New York	276	19
North Carolina	280	13
North Dakota	283	5
Ohio	283	5
Oklahoma	272	25
Oregon	281	11
Pennsylvania	n/a	n/a
Rhode Island	273	24
South Carolina	266	30
South Dakota	n/a	n/a
Tennessee	263	32
Texas	275	21
Utah	275	21
Vermont	283	5
Virginia	277	16
Washington	n/a	n/a
West Virginia	271	27
Wisconsin	n/a	n/a
Wyoming	277	16
50 States	n/a	
DC	234	
United States	274	

	Rank in order by score
1	Minnesota
2	Montana
3	Kansas
3	Maine
5	Indiana
5	Massachusetts
5	North Dakota
5	Ohio
5	Vermont
10	Connecticut
11	Nebraska
11	Oregon
13	North Carolina
14	Idaho
14	Michigan
16	Illinois
16	Virginia
16	Wyoming
19	Maryland
19	New York
21	Texas
21	Utah
23	Missouri
24	Rhode Island
25	Kentucky
25	Oklahoma
27	Arizona
27	West Virginia
29	Nevada
30	Georgia
30	South Carolina
32	Hawaii
32	Tennessee
34	Alabama
34	California
36	Arkansas
37	New Mexico
38	Louisiana
39	Mississippi

Note: Ties in ranking reflect ties in actual values.

H-2 Average Proficiency in Science, Eighth Grade, 2000

State	Reading score	Rank
Alabama	141	33
Alaska	n/a	n/a
Arizona	146	26
Arkansas	143	30
California	132	37
Colorado	n/a	n/a
Connecticut	154	15
Delaware	n/a	n/a
Florida	n/a	n/a
Georgia	144	28
Hawaii	132	37
Idaho	159	8
Illinois	150	19
Indiana	156	11
Iowa	n/a	n/a
Kansas	n/a	n/a
Kentucky	152	17
Louisiana	136	35
Maine	160	6
Maryland	149	22
Massachusetts	161	2
Michigan	156	11
Minnesota	160	6
Mississippi	134	36
Missouri	156	11
Montana	165	1
Nebraska	157	10
Nevada	143	30
New Hampshire	n/a	n/a
New Jersey	n/a	n/a
New Mexico	140	34
New York	149	22
North Carolina	147	25
North Dakota	161	2
Ohio	161	2
Oklahoma	149	22
Oregon	154	15
Pennsylvania	n/a	n/a
Rhode Island	150	19
South Carolina	142	32
South Dakota	n/a	n/a
Tennessee	146	26
Texas	144	28
Utah	155	14
Vermont	161	2
Virginia	152	17
Washington	n/a	n/a
West Virginia	150	19
Wisconsin	n/a	n/a
Wyoming	158	9
50 States	n/a	
DC	n/a	
United States	149	

Rank in order by score

1	Montana
2	Massachusetts
2	North Dakota
2	Ohio
2	Vermont
6	Maine
6	Minnesota
8	Idaho
9	Wyoming
10	Nebraska
11	Indiana
11	Michigan
11	Missouri
14	Utah
15	Connecticut
15	Oregon
17	Kentucky
17	Virginia
19	Illinois
19	Rhode Island
19	West Virginia
22	Maryland
22	New York
22	Oklahoma
25	North Carolina
26	Arizona
26	Tennessee
28	Georgia
28	Texas
30	Arkansas
30	Nevada
32	South Carolina
33	Alabama
34	New Mexico
35	Louisiana
36	Mississippi
37	California
37	Hawaii

Note: Ties in ranking reflect ties in actual values.

H-3 Armed Forces Qualification Test Ranks, FY 1999

State	AFQT rank	Rank
Alabama	55.8	46
Alaska	61.5	17
Arizona	60.0	21
Arkansas	56.4	44
California	57.6	39
Colorado	61.9	15
Connecticut	59.1	27
Delaware	58.3	33
Florida	56.2	45
Georgia	55.3	48
Hawaii	63.5	4
Idaho	58.6	31
Illinois	62.0	14
Indiana	63.1	8
Iowa	61.0	18
Kansas	57.7	38
Kentucky	54.3	49
Louisiana	58.1	36
Maine	59.4	25
Maryland	62.6	12
Massachusetts	53.4	50
Michigan	59.1	27
Minnesota	62.6	12
Mississippi	62.7	10
Missouri	60.4	20
Montana	57.3	42
Nebraska	58.0	37
Nevada	58.3	33
New Hampshire	57.4	41
New Jersey	64.6	1
New Mexico	59.8	23
New York	58.4	32
North Carolina	63.2	6
North Dakota	59.9	22
Ohio	55.4	47
Oklahoma	62.9	9
Oregon	59.3	26
Pennsylvania	58.8	30
Rhode Island	62.7	10
South Carolina	58.2	35
South Dakota	63.3	5
Tennessee	57.1	43
Texas	63.2	6
Utah	61.9	15
Vermont	59.0	29
Virginia	61.0	18
Washington	59.8	23
West Virginia	64.0	3
Wisconsin	57.6	39
Wyoming	64.4	2
50 States	n/a	
DC	52.0	
United States	58.8	

Rank in order by rank

Rank	State
1	New Jersey
2	Wyoming
3	West Virginia
4	Hawaii
5	South Dakota
6	North Carolina
6	Texas
8	Indiana
9	Oklahoma
10	Mississippi
10	Rhode Island
12	Maryland
12	Minnesota
14	Illinois
15	Colorado
15	Utah
17	Alaska
18	Iowa
18	Virginia
20	Missouri
21	Arizona
22	North Dakota
23	New Mexico
23	Washington
25	Maine
26	Oregon
27	Connecticut
27	Michigan
29	Vermont
30	Pennsylvania
31	Idaho
32	New York
33	Delaware
33	Nevada
35	South Carolina
36	Louisiana
37	Nebraska
38	Kansas
39	California
39	Wisconsin
41	New Hampshire
42	Montana
43	Tennessee
44	Arkansas
45	Florida
46	Alabama
47	Ohio
48	Georgia
49	Kentucky
50	Massachusetts

Note: Ties in ranking reflect ties in actual values.

H-4 SAT Scores, 2001

State	Average SAT score	Percentage of graduates tested	Rank by score
Alabama	n/a	n/a	n/a
Alaska	1,024	51	6
Arizona	1,048	34	3
Arkansas	n/a	n/a	n/a
California	1,015	51	10
Colorado	n/a	n/a	n/a
Connecticut	1,019	82	7
Delaware	1,000	67	15
Florida	997	54	20
Georgia	980	63	23
Hawaii	1,001	52	14
Idaho	n/a	n/a	n/a
Illinois	n/a	n/a	n/a
Indiana	1,000	60	15
Iowa	n/a	n/a	n/a
Kansas	n/a	n/a	n/a
Kentucky	n/a	n/a	n/a
Louisiana	n/a	n/a	n/a
Maine	1,006	69	13
Maryland	1,018	65	8
Massachusetts	1,026	79	5
Michigan	n/a	n/a	n/a
Minnesota	n/a	n/a	n/a
Mississippi	n/a	n/a	n/a
Missouri	n/a	n/a	n/a
Montana	n/a	n/a	n/a
Nebraska	n/a	n/a	n/a
Nevada	n/a	n/a	n/a
New Hampshire	1,036	72	4
New Jersey	1,012	81	11
New Mexico	n/a	n/a	n/a
New York	1,000	77	15
North Carolina	992	65	21
North Dakota	n/a	n/a	n/a
Ohio	n/a	n/a	n/a
Oklahoma	n/a	n/a	n/a
Oregon	1,052	55	2
Pennsylvania	999	71	19
Rhode Island	1,000	71	15
South Carolina	974	57	24
South Dakota	n/a	n/a	n/a
Tennessee	n/a	n/a	n/a
Texas	992	53	21
Utah	n/a	n/a	n/a
Vermont	1,017	69	9
Virginia	1,011	68	12
Washington	1,054	53	1
West Virginia	n/a	n/a	n/a
Wisconsin	n/a	n/a	n/a
Wyoming	n/a	n/a	n/a
50 States	n/a	n/a	
DC	956	56	
United States	1,020	45	

Rank in order by score

1	Washington
2	Oregon
3	Arizona
4	New Hampshire
5	Massachusetts
6	Alaska
7	Connecticut
8	Maryland
9	Vermont
10	California
11	New Jersey
12	Virginia
13	Maine
14	Hawaii
15	Delaware
15	Indiana
15	New York
15	Rhode Island
19	Pennsylvania
20	Florida
21	North Carolina
21	Texas
23	Georgia
24	South Carolina

Note: Ties in ranking reflect ties in actual values.

H-5 ACT Scores, 2001

State	ACT composite scores	Percentage of graduates tested	Rank by score
Alabama	20.1	69	20
Alaska	n/a	n/a	n/a
Arizona	n/a	n/a	n/a
Arkansas	20.1	75	20
California	n/a	n/a	n/a
Colorado	21.5	62	8
Connecticut	n/a	n/a	n/a
Delaware	n/a	n/a	n/a
Florida	n/a	n/a	n/a
Georgia	n/a	n/a	n/a
Hawaii	n/a	n/a	n/a
Idaho	21.5	59	8
Illinois	21.6	71	5
Indiana	n/a	n/a	n/a
Iowa	22.0	67	3
Kansas	21.6	78	5
Kentucky	20.1	72	20
Louisiana	19.6	80	25
Maine	n/a	n/a	n/a
Maryland	n/a	n/a	n/a
Massachusetts	n/a	n/a	n/a
Michigan	21.3	69	16
Minnesota	22.1	66	2
Mississippi	18.5	89	26
Missouri	21.4	70	11
Montana	21.7	55	4
Nebraska	21.6	74	5
Nevada	21.3	39	16
New Hampshire	n/a	n/a	n/a
New Jersey	n/a	n/a	n/a
New Mexico	19.9	64	24
New York	n/a	n/a	n/a
North Carolina	n/a	n/a	n/a
North Dakota	21.4	80	11
Ohio	21.4	63	11
Oklahoma	20.5	71	18
Oregon	n/a	n/a	n/a
Pennsylvania	n/a	n/a	n/a
Rhode Island	n/a	n/a	n/a
South Carolina	n/a	n/a	n/a
South Dakota	21.4	70	11
Tennessee	20.0	79	23
Texas	n/a	n/a	n/a
Utah	21.4	69	11
Vermont	n/a	n/a	n/a
Virginia	n/a	n/a	n/a
Washington	n/a	n/a	n/a
West Virginia	20.2	61	19
Wisconsin	22.2	68	1
Wyoming	21.5	64	8
50 States	n/a	n/a	
DC	n/a	n/a	
United States	21.0	38	

Rank in order by score	
1	Wisconsin
2	Minnesota
3	Iowa
4	Montana
5	Illinois
5	Kansas
5	Nebraska
8	Colorado
8	Idaho
8	Wyoming
11	Missouri
11	North Dakota
11	Ohio
11	South Dakota
11	Utah
16	Michigan
16	Nevada
18	Oklahoma
19	West Virginia
20	Alabama
20	Arkansas
20	Kentucky
23	Tennessee
24	New Mexico
25	Louisiana
26	Mississippi

Note: Ties in ranking reflect ties in actual values.

H-6 Percentage of Population Over 25 with a High School Diploma, 2000

State	High school graduates %	Rank by percentage
Alabama	77.5	49
Alaska	90.4	5
Arizona	85.1	31
Arkansas	81.7	40
California	81.2	42
Colorado	89.7	9
Connecticut	88.2	13
Delaware	86.1	25
Florida	84.0	34
Georgia	82.6	37
Hawaii	87.4	17
Idaho	86.2	23
Illinois	85.5	29
Indiana	84.6	33
Iowa	89.7	9
Kansas	88.1	14
Kentucky	78.7	48
Louisiana	80.8	43
Maine	89.3	12
Maryland	85.7	27
Massachusetts	85.1	31
Michigan	86.2	23
Minnesota	90.8	3
Mississippi	80.3	44
Missouri	86.6	21
Montana	89.6	11
Nebraska	90.4	5
Nevada	82.8	36
New Hampshire	88.1	14
New Jersey	87.3	18
New Mexico	82.2	39
New York	82.5	38
North Carolina	79.2	46
North Dakota	85.5	29
Ohio	87.0	19
Oklahoma	86.1	25
Oregon	88.1	14
Pennsylvania	85.7	27
Rhode Island	81.3	41
South Carolina	83.0	35
South Dakota	91.8	1
Tennessee	79.9	45
Texas	79.2	46
Utah	90.7	4
Vermont	90.0	7
Virginia	86.6	21
Washington	91.8	1
West Virginia	77.1	50
Wisconsin	86.7	20
Wyoming	90.0	7
50 States	n/a	
DC	83.2	
United States	84.1	

Rank in order by percentage	
1	South Dakota
1	Washington
3	Minnesota
4	Utah
5	Alaska
5	Nebraska
7	Vermont
7	Wyoming
9	Colorado
9	Iowa
11	Montana
12	Maine
13	Connecticut
14	Kansas
14	New Hampshire
14	Oregon
17	Hawaii
18	New Jersey
19	Ohio
20	Wisconsin
21	Missouri
21	Virginia
23	Idaho
23	Michigan
25	Delaware
25	Oklahoma
27	Maryland
27	Pennsylvania
29	Illinois
29	North Dakota
31	Arizona
31	Massachusetts
33	Indiana
34	Florida
35	South Carolina
36	Nevada
37	Georgia
38	New York
39	New Mexico
40	Arkansas
41	Rhode Island
42	California
43	Louisiana
44	Mississippi
45	Tennessee
46	North Carolina
46	Texas
48	Kentucky
49	Alabama
50	West Virginia

Note: Ties in ranking reflect ties in actual values.

H-7 Students in Private Schools, 1999-2000

State	Private school enrollment	As a percentage of total enrollment	Rank by percentage
Alabama	73,352	9.1	26
Alaska	6,172	4.3	46
Arizona	44,060	4.9	44
Arkansas	26,424	5.6	40
California	619,067	9.4	23
Colorado	52,142	6.9	36
Connecticut	70,058	11.2	15
Delaware	22,779	16.7	1
Florida	290,872	10.9	16
Georgia	116,407	7.6	33
Hawaii	32,193	14.8	4
Idaho	10,209	4.0	48
Illinois	299,871	12.9	10
Indiana	105,533	9.7	21
Iowa	49,565	9.1	27
Kansas	43,113	8.4	28
Kentucky	75,084	10.6	17
Louisiana	138,135	15.5	3
Maine	18,287	8.0	30
Maryland	144,131	14.5	5
Massachusetts	132,154	12.0	14
Michigan	179,579	9.5	22
Minnesota	92,795	9.7	20
Mississippi	51,369	9.3	25
Missouri	122,387	12.0	13
Montana	8,711	5.2	42
Nebraska	42,141	12.8	11
Nevada	13,926	4.1	47
New Hampshire	23,383	10.2	19
New Jersey	198,631	13.7	8
New Mexico	23,055	6.6	38
New York	475,942	14.3	6
North Carolina	96,262	7.2	34
North Dakota	7,148	5.8	39
Ohio	254,494	12.3	12
Oklahoma	31,276	4.8	45
Oregon	45,352	7.7	32
Pennsylvania	339,484	15.7	2
Rhode Island	24,738	13.7	7
South Carolina	55,612	7.8	31
South Dakota	9,364	6.8	37
Tennessee	93,680	9.4	24
Texas	227,645	5.4	41
Utah	12,614	2.6	49
Vermont	12,170	10.4	18
Virginia	100,171	8.1	29
Washington	76,885	7.1	35
West Virginia	15,895	5.2	43
Wisconsin	139,455	13.7	9
Wyoming	2,221	2.4	50
50 States	5,145,994	10.0	
DC	16,690	17.8	
United States	5,162,684	10.0	

Rank in order by percentage

1 Delaware
2 Pennsylvania
3 Louisiana
4 Hawaii
5 Maryland
6 New York
7 Rhode Island
8 New Jersey
9 Wisconsin
10 Illinois
11 Nebraska
12 Ohio
13 Missouri
14 Massachusetts
15 Connecticut
16 Florida
17 Kentucky
18 Vermont
19 New Hampshire
20 Minnesota
21 Indiana
22 Michigan
23 California
24 Tennessee
25 Mississippi
26 Alabama
27 Iowa
28 Kansas
29 Virginia
30 Maine
31 South Carolina
32 Oregon
33 Georgia
34 North Carolina
35 Washington
36 Colorado
37 South Dakota
38 New Mexico
39 North Dakota
40 Arkansas
41 Texas
42 Montana
43 West Virginia
44 Arizona
45 Oklahoma
46 Alaska
47 Nevada
48 Idaho
49 Utah
50 Wyoming

Note: Numbers that appear to be identical are rounded and vary slightly in actual value. The rankings reflect the actual values before rounding. See the introduction for more details.

H-8 High School Completion Rates, 1998-2000

State	Percentage of 18 to 24 year-olds completing high school	Rank
Alabama	81.6	46
Alaska	93.3	3
Arizona	73.5	50
Arkansas	84.1	39
California	82.5	42
Colorado	81.6	46
Connecticut	91.7	8
Delaware	91.0	11
Florida	84.6	38
Georgia	83.5	40
Hawaii	91.8	7
Idaho	86.4	31
Illinois	87.1	29
Indiana	89.4	20
Iowa	90.8	13
Kansas	90.4	15
Kentucky	86.2	33
Louisiana	82.1	45
Maine	94.5	1
Maryland	87.4	26
Massachusetts	90.9	12
Michigan	89.2	21
Minnesota	91.9	6
Mississippi	82.3	43
Missouri	92.6	4
Montana	91.1	10
Nebraska	91.3	9
Nevada	77.9	49
New Hampshire	85.1	36
New Jersey	90.1	16
New Mexico	83.0	41
New York	86.3	32
North Carolina	86.1	34
North Dakota	94.4	2
Ohio	87.7	25
Oklahoma	85.7	35
Oregon	82.3	43
Pennsylvania	89.0	22
Rhode Island	87.9	24
South Carolina	85.1	36
South Dakota	92.0	5
Tennessee	89.0	22
Texas	79.4	48
Utah	90.0	17
Vermont	90.8	13
Virginia	87.3	28
Washington	87.4	26
West Virginia	89.6	19
Wisconsin	90.0	17
Wyoming	86.5	30
50 States	n/a	
DC	88.0	
United States	85.7	

Rank in order by percentage	
1	Maine
2	North Dakota
3	Alaska
4	Missouri
5	South Dakota
6	Minnesota
7	Hawaii
8	Connecticut
9	Nebraska
10	Montana
11	Delaware
12	Massachusetts
13	Iowa
13	Vermont
15	Kansas
16	New Jersey
17	Utah
17	Wisconsin
19	West Virginia
20	Indiana
21	Michigan
22	Pennsylvania
22	Tennessee
24	Rhode Island
25	Ohio
26	Maryland
26	Washington
28	Virginia
29	Illinois
30	Wyoming
31	Idaho
32	New York
33	Kentucky
34	North Carolina
35	Oklahoma
36	New Hampshire
36	South Carolina
38	Florida
39	Arkansas
40	Georgia
41	New Mexico
42	California
43	Mississippi
43	Oregon
45	Louisiana
46	Alabama
46	Colorado
48	Texas
49	Nevada
50	Arizona

Note: Ties in ranking reflect ties in actual values.

H-9 Pupil-Teacher Ratio, 2000-2001

State	Pupils per teacher in public K-12 schools	Rank by ratio
Alabama	15.3	25
Alaska	16.6	12
Arizona	19.0	4
Arkansas	15.4	24
California	20.7	2
Colorado	18.0	7
Connecticut	13.5	44
Delaware	15.3	25
Florida	18.0	7
Georgia	15.9	17
Hawaii	16.6	12
Idaho	17.8	9
Illinois	15.8	19
Indiana	16.9	11
Iowa	14.4	35
Kansas	14.3	36
Kentucky	16.6	12
Louisiana	15.0	29
Maine	13.2	46
Maryland	16.3	15
Massachusetts	13.9	39
Michigan	17.6	10
Minnesota	15.2	27
Mississippi	16.0	16
Missouri	13.8	40
Montana	15.0	29
Nebraska	13.8	40
Nevada	18.7	6
New Hampshire	14.5	34
New Jersey	13.2	46
New Mexico	15.8	19
New York	14.0	38
North Carolina	15.6	22
North Dakota	14.1	37
Ohio	15.7	21
Oklahoma	15.1	28
Oregon	18.9	5
Pennsylvania	15.5	23
Rhode Island	12.5	49
South Carolina	15.0	29
South Dakota	13.8	40
Tennessee	15.9	17
Texas	14.8	33
Utah	22.0	1
Vermont	11.8	50
Virginia	12.8	48
Washington	19.7	3
West Virginia	13.8	40
Wisconsin	15.0	29
Wyoming	13.3	45
50 States	n/a	
DC	15.6	
United States	16.0	

Rank in order by ratio	
1	Utah
2	California
3	Washington
4	Arizona
5	Oregon
6	Nevada
7	Colorado
7	Florida
9	Idaho
10	Michigan
11	Indiana
12	Alaska
12	Hawaii
12	Kentucky
15	Maryland
16	Mississippi
17	Georgia
17	Tennessee
19	Illinois
19	New Mexico
21	Ohio
22	North Carolina
23	Pennsylvania
24	Arkansas
25	Alabama
25	Delaware
27	Minnesota
28	Oklahoma
29	Louisiana
29	Montana
29	South Carolina
29	Wisconsin
33	Texas
34	New Hampshire
35	Iowa
36	Kansas
37	North Dakota
38	New York
39	Massachusetts
40	Missouri
40	Nebraska
40	South Dakota
40	West Virginia
44	Connecticut
45	Wyoming
46	Maine
46	New Jersey
48	Virginia
49	Rhode Island
50	Vermont

Note: Ties in ranking reflect ties in actual values.

H-10 Public School Enrollment, 2000-2001

State	Enrollment (in thousands)	As a percentage of total population	Rank by percentage
Alabama	733	16.5	28
Alaska	133	21.3	2
Arizona	868	16.9	18
Arkansas	449	16.8	23
California	6,046	17.9	7
Colorado	725	16.8	21
Connecticut	559	16.4	30
Delaware	115	14.6	50
Florida	2,428	15.2	44
Georgia	1,445	17.7	10
Hawaii	182	15.0	47
Idaho	246	19.0	4
Illinois	2,049	16.5	26
Indiana	993	16.3	32
Iowa	495	16.9	19
Kansas	468	17.4	13
Kentucky	630	15.6	42
Louisiana	737	16.5	27
Maine	207	16.2	34
Maryland	853	16.1	35
Massachusetts	977	15.4	43
Michigan	1,716	17.3	15
Minnesota	869	17.7	8
Mississippi	497	17.5	12
Missouri	894	16.0	36
Montana	156	17.3	14
Nebraska	285	16.6	25
Nevada	341	17.1	16
New Hampshire	208	16.9	20
New Jersey	1,268	15.1	46
New Mexico	320	17.6	11
New York	2,873	15.1	45
North Carolina	1,278	15.9	40
North Dakota	113	17.7	9
Ohio	1,810	15.9	38
Oklahoma	623	18.1	6
Oregon	546	16.0	37
Pennsylvania	1,814	14.8	49
Rhode Island	157	14.9	48
South Carolina	661	16.5	29
South Dakota	127	16.8	22
Tennessee	905	15.9	39
Texas	4,060	19.5	3
Utah	475	21.3	1
Vermont	102	16.8	24
Virginia	1,150	16.2	33
Washington	1,005	17.0	17
West Virginia	286	15.8	41
Wisconsin	879	16.4	31
Wyoming	90	18.1	5
50 States	46,848	16.7	
DC	69	12.0	
United States	46,917	16.7	

Rank in order by percentage

1 Utah
2 Alaska
3 Texas
4 Idaho
5 Wyoming
6 Oklahoma
7 California
8 Minnesota
9 North Dakota
10 Georgia
11 New Mexico
12 Mississippi
13 Kansas
14 Montana
15 Michigan
16 Nevada
17 Washington
18 Arizona
19 Iowa
20 New Hampshire
21 Colorado
22 South Dakota
23 Arkansas
24 Vermont
25 Nebraska
26 Illinois
27 Louisiana
28 Alabama
29 South Carolina
30 Connecticut
31 Wisconsin
32 Indiana
33 Virginia
34 Maine
35 Maryland
36 Missouri
37 Oregon
38 Ohio
39 Tennessee
40 North Carolina
41 West Virginia
42 Kentucky
43 Massachusetts
44 Florida
45 New York
46 New Jersey
47 Hawaii
48 Rhode Island
49 Pennsylvania
50 Delaware

Note: Numbers that appear to be identical are rounded and vary slightly in actual value. The rankings reflect the actual values before rounding. See the introduction for more details.

H-11 Public Library Holdings Per Capita, FY 1998

State	Holdings per capita	Rank per capita
Alabama	2.1	38
Alaska	3.3	20
Arizona	1.8	48
Arkansas	2.1	38
California	1.9	45
Colorado	2.7	28
Connecticut	4.4	10
Delaware	2.0	41
Florida	1.8	48
Georgia	1.9	45
Hawaii	2.5	32
Idaho	3.2	21
Illinois	3.8	15
Indiana	4.4	10
Iowa	4.0	13
Kansas	4.7	5
Kentucky	2.1	38
Louisiana	2.4	34
Maine	5.4	1
Maryland	2.9	24
Massachusetts	4.9	4
Michigan	2.8	26
Minnesota	3.2	21
Mississippi	2.0	41
Missouri	4.7	5
Montana	3.0	23
Nebraska	3.8	15
Nevada	2.3	35
New Hampshire	4.5	9
New Jersey	3.7	18
New Mexico	2.9	24
New York	4.6	8
North Carolina	2.0	41
North Dakota	3.8	15
Ohio	4.0	13
Oklahoma	2.2	36
Oregon	2.5	32
Pennsylvania	2.2	36
Rhode Island	4.1	12
South Carolina	1.9	45
South Dakota	5.0	2
Tennessee	1.6	50
Texas	2.0	41
Utah	2.7	28
Vermont	5.0	2
Virginia	2.6	31
Washington	2.7	28
West Virginia	2.8	26
Wisconsin	3.4	19
Wyoming	4.7	5
50 States	n/a	
DC	5.7	
United States	2.9	

Rank in order per capita

1	Maine
2	South Dakota
2	Vermont
4	Massachusetts
5	Kansas
5	Missouri
5	Wyoming
8	New York
9	New Hampshire
10	Connecticut
10	Indiana
12	Rhode Island
13	Iowa
13	Ohio
15	Illinois
15	Nebraska
15	North Dakota
18	New Jersey
19	Wisconsin
20	Alaska
21	Idaho
21	Minnesota
23	Montana
24	Maryland
24	New Mexico
26	Michigan
26	West Virginia
28	Colorado
28	Utah
28	Washington
31	Virginia
32	Hawaii
32	Oregon
34	Louisiana
35	Nevada
36	Oklahoma
36	Pennsylvania
38	Alabama
38	Arkansas
38	Kentucky
41	Delaware
41	Mississippi
41	North Carolina
41	Texas
45	California
45	Georgia
45	South Carolina
48	Arizona
48	Florida
50	Tennessee

Note: Ties in ranking reflect ties in actual values.

H-12 Children with Disabilities, 1998-1999

State	Children with disabilities #	Percentage of public school enrollment	Rank by percentage
Alabama	99,813	13.2	25
Alaska	17,712	13.2	24
Arizona	88,598	10.7	50
Arkansas	59,110	13.0	27
California	623,651	10.7	49
Colorado	75,134	10.7	47
Connecticut	76,740	14.1	18
Delaware	16,233	14.3	12
Florida	345,171	14.8	11
Georgia	155,754	11.1	44
Hawaii	20,551	11.0	46
Idaho	27,553	11.2	43
Illinois	283,698	14.0	19
Indiana	146,559	14.8	10
Iowa	70,958	14.1	16
Kansas	58,425	12.4	34
Kentucky	87,973	13.6	21
Louisiana	95,245	12.6	30
Maine	34,294	15.6	6
Maryland	111,688	13.3	22
Massachusetts	168,964	17.5	2
Michigan	208,403	12.3	36
Minnesota	106,194	12.4	35
Mississippi	61,778	12.3	37
Missouri	131,565	14.3	13
Montana	18,797	11.7	39
Nebraska	43,400	14.9	9
Nevada	33,319	10.7	48
New Hampshire	27,502	14.1	14
New Jersey	210,114	16.2	4
New Mexico	52,113	15.9	5
New York	432,119	15.2	8
North Carolina	165,333	13.3	23
North Dakota	13,181	11.6	41
Ohio	230,155	12.4	33
Oklahoma	80,289	12.8	29
Oregon	69,919	12.9	28
Pennsylvania	226,378	12.5	32
Rhode Island	27,911	18.1	1
South Carolina	99,033	15.4	7
South Dakota	15,702	11.1	45
Tennessee	128,273	14.1	17
Texas	486,749	12.5	31
Utah	55,252	11.6	40
Vermont	12,709	12.1	38
Virginia	153,716	13.7	20
Washington	114,144	11.4	42
West Virginia	49,934	16.9	3
Wisconsin	116,328	13.1	26
Wyoming	13,333	14.1	15
50 States	6,047,467	13.1	
DC	8,162	11.4	
United States*	6,114,803	13.0	

Due to rounding or data sources, the 50-state total plus D.C. may not equal the U.S. total. Please see introduction.

Rank in order by percentage	
1	Rhode Island
2	Massachusetts
3	West Virginia
4	New Jersey
5	New Mexico
6	Maine
7	South Carolina
8	New York
9	Nebraska
10	Indiana
11	Florida
12	Delaware
13	Missouri
14	New Hampshire
15	Wyoming
16	Iowa
17	Tennessee
18	Connecticut
19	Illinois
20	Virginia
21	Kentucky
22	Maryland
23	North Carolina
24	Alaska
25	Alabama
26	Wisconsin
27	Arkansas
28	Oregon
29	Oklahoma
30	Louisiana
31	Texas
32	Pennsylvania
33	Ohio
34	Kansas
35	Minnesota
36	Michigan
37	Mississippi
38	Vermont
39	Montana
40	Utah
41	North Dakota
42	Washington
43	Idaho
44	Georgia
45	South Dakota
46	Hawaii
47	Colorado
48	Nevada
49	California
50	Arizona

Note: Numbers that appear to be identical are rounded and vary slightly in actual value. The rankings reflect the actual values before rounding. See the introduction for more details.

H-13 State and Local Education Spending, FY 1999

State	Education spending $ (in millions)	Education spending per capita	Education spending as a percentage of personal income	Rank per capita
Alabama	7,174	1,642	7.5	36
Alaska	1,743	2,811	10.2	1
Arizona	7,402	1,549	6.6	45
Arkansas	3,985	1,562	7.4	43
California	56,688	1,710	6.1	29
Colorado	7,242	1,786	6.1	23
Connecticut	6,201	1,889	5.1	14
Delaware	1,611	2,137	7.3	4
Florida	21,321	1,411	5.3	50
Georgia	13,833	1,776	6.9	24
Hawaii	1,778	1,501	5.6	48
Idaho	2,024	1,616	7.5	39
Illinois	21,190	1,747	5.9	27
Indiana	10,689	1,799	7.2	20
Iowa	5,692	1,984	8.0	10
Kansas	4,770	1,797	7.0	21
Kentucky	5,980	1,510	6.8	47
Louisiana	6,870	1,571	7.0	41
Maine	2,068	1,650	7.0	35
Maryland	9,169	1,773	5.8	25
Massachusetts	10,456	1,693	5.1	31
Michigan	21,213	2,151	8.1	3
Minnesota	9,755	2,043	7.0	9
Mississippi	4,420	1,596	8.0	40
Missouri	8,559	1,565	6.2	42
Montana	1,603	1,815	8.5	19
Nebraska	3,124	1,875	7.3	16
Nevada	2,939	1,625	5.7	38
New Hampshire	1,848	1,538	5.2	46
New Jersey	16,874	2,072	6.1	8
New Mexico	3,331	1,914	9.1	12
New York	37,769	2,076	6.5	6
North Carolina	12,953	1,693	6.7	32
North Dakota	1,194	1,883	8.2	15
Ohio	19,161	1,702	6.5	30
Oklahoma	5,493	1,636	7.4	37
Oregon	6,211	1,873	7.3	17
Pennsylvania	22,234	1,854	6.8	18
Rhode Island	1,774	1,790	6.4	22
South Carolina	6,551	1,686	7.6	33
South Dakota	1,139	1,554	6.5	44
Tennessee	8,016	1,462	6.0	49
Texas	35,323	1,762	6.9	26
Utah	4,063	1,908	8.7	13
Vermont	1,233	2,076	8.4	5
Virginia	11,790	1,715	6.1	28
Washington	11,045	1,919	6.8	11
West Virginia	3,024	1,673	8.2	34
Wisconsin	10,892	2,075	7.9	7
Wyoming	1,068	2,226	8.9	2
50 States	482,482	1,773	6.6	
DC	777	1,497	4.0	
United States	483,259	1,772	6.5	

Rank in order per capita	
1	Alaska
2	Wyoming
3	Michigan
4	Delaware
5	Vermont
6	New York
7	Wisconsin
8	New Jersey
9	Minnesota
10	Iowa
11	Washington
12	New Mexico
13	Utah
14	Connecticut
15	North Dakota
16	Nebraska
17	Oregon
18	Pennsylvania
19	Montana
20	Indiana
21	Kansas
22	Rhode Island
23	Colorado
24	Georgia
25	Maryland
26	Texas
27	Illinois
28	Virginia
29	California
30	Ohio
31	Massachusetts
32	North Carolina
33	South Carolina
34	West Virginia
35	Maine
36	Alabama
37	Oklahoma
38	Nevada
39	Idaho
40	Mississippi
41	Louisiana
42	Missouri
43	Arkansas
44	South Dakota
45	Arizona
46	New Hampshire
47	Kentucky
48	Hawaii
49	Tennessee
50	Florida

Note: Numbers that appear to be identical are rounded and vary slightly in actual value. The rankings reflect the actual values before rounding. See the introduction for more details.

H-14 State and Local Education Spending as a Percentage of General Spending, FY 1999

State	Education spending as a percentage of general spending	Rank by percentage
Alabama	35.7	26
Alaska	24.4	50
Arizona	36.5	18
Arkansas	37.4	13
California	31.3	45
Colorado	36.1	20
Connecticut	31.5	44
Delaware	35.9	23
Florida	29.8	47
Georgia	38.6	11
Hawaii	25.8	49
Idaho	36.1	21
Illinois	35.5	27
Indiana	40.1	6
Iowa	38.8	10
Kansas	39.5	7
Kentucky	33.1	40
Louisiana	32.5	41
Maine	32.4	42
Maryland	36.9	15
Massachusetts	29.9	46
Michigan	42.0	1
Minnesota	34.6	32
Mississippi	34.2	35
Missouri	35.8	25
Montana	37.3	14
Nebraska	40.5	4
Nevada	31.6	43
New Hampshire	34.7	31
New Jersey	38.1	12
New Mexico	35.2	29
New York	28.2	48
North Carolina	35.2	28
North Dakota	34.2	33
Ohio	36.1	22
Oklahoma	40.5	3
Oregon	33.9	36
Pennsylvania	36.3	19
Rhode Island	33.6	38
South Carolina	35.9	24
South Dakota	35.1	30
Tennessee	33.2	39
Texas	40.4	5
Utah	38.9	8
Vermont	40.7	2
Virginia	36.5	17
Washington	34.2	34
West Virginia	36.8	16
Wisconsin	38.8	9
Wyoming	33.9	37
50 States	34.6	
DC	16.8	
United States	34.6	

Rank in order by percentage

1 Michigan
2 Vermont
3 Oklahoma
4 Nebraska
5 Texas
6 Indiana
7 Kansas
8 Utah
9 Wisconsin
10 Iowa
11 Georgia
12 New Jersey
13 Arkansas
14 Montana
15 Maryland
16 West Virginia
17 Virginia
18 Arizona
19 Pennsylvania
20 Colorado
21 Idaho
22 Ohio
23 Delaware
24 South Carolina
25 Missouri
26 Alabama
27 Illinois
28 North Carolina
29 New Mexico
30 South Dakota
31 New Hampshire
32 Minnesota
33 North Dakota
34 Washington
35 Mississippi
36 Oregon
37 Wyoming
38 Rhode Island
39 Tennessee
40 Kentucky
41 Louisiana
42 Maine
43 Nevada
44 Connecticut
45 California
46 Massachusetts
47 Florida
48 New York
49 Hawaii
50 Alaska

Note: Numbers that appear to be identical are rounded and vary slightly in actual value. The rankings reflect the actual values before rounding. See the introduction for more details.

H-15 Spending Per Pupil, 2000-2001

State	Spending per pupil $	Rank
Alabama	5,267	47
Alaska	9,410	4
Arizona	4,676	48
Arkansas	5,604	43
California	7,036	20
Colorado	5,333	45
Connecticut	10,163	1
Delaware	8,952	6
Florida	6,049	36
Georgia	6,869	24
Hawaii	6,570	27
Idaho	5,667	41
Illinois	7,946	10
Indiana	7,118	19
Iowa	6,362	30
Kansas	6,568	28
Kentucky	6,846	25
Louisiana	5,902	38
Maine	7,907	11
Maryland	7,469	16
Massachusetts	9,222	5
Michigan	7,458	17
Minnesota	7,830	13
Mississippi	5,301	46
Missouri	6,198	35
Montana	6,352	31
Nebraska	6,393	29
Nevada	5,600	44
New Hampshire	7,033	21
New Jersey	9,897	3
New Mexico	6,278	34
New York	10,049	2
North Carolina	6,021	37
North Dakota	4,431	49
Ohio	6,962	22
Oklahoma	5,752	39
Oregon	7,558	15
Pennsylvania	7,440	18
Rhode Island	8,392	8
South Carolina	6,346	32
South Dakota	5,680	40
Tennessee	5,616	42
Texas	6,600	26
Utah	4,425	50
Vermont	8,529	7
Virginia	6,323	33
Washington	6,913	23
West Virginia	7,859	12
Wisconsin	8,148	9
Wyoming	7,644	14
50 States	n/a	
DC	11,717	
United States	7,095	

Rank in order by $	
1	Connecticut
2	New York
3	New Jersey
4	Alaska
5	Massachusetts
6	Delaware
7	Vermont
8	Rhode Island
9	Wisconsin
10	Illinois
11	Maine
12	West Virginia
13	Minnesota
14	Wyoming
15	Oregon
16	Maryland
17	Michigan
18	Pennsylvania
19	Indiana
20	California
21	New Hampshire
22	Ohio
23	Washington
24	Georgia
25	Kentucky
26	Texas
27	Hawaii
28	Kansas
29	Nebraska
30	Iowa
31	Montana
32	South Carolina
33	Virginia
34	New Mexico
35	Missouri
36	Florida
37	North Carolina
38	Louisiana
39	Oklahoma
40	South Dakota
41	Idaho
42	Tennessee
43	Arkansas
44	Nevada
45	Colorado
46	Mississippi
47	Alabama
48	Arizona
49	North Dakota
50	Utah

H-16 Average Teacher Salary, 2000-2001

State	Average teacher salary $	Rank
Alabama	37,956	28
Alaska	46,986	11
Arizona	36,302	38
Arkansas	34,476	43
California	49,283	6
Colorado	40,887	20
Connecticut	52,100	2
Delaware	47,047	10
Florida	37,824	29
Georgia	42,216	15
Hawaii	40,052	24
Idaho	36,375	36
Illinois	48,053	8
Indiana	43,055	13
Iowa	36,479	34
Kansas	35,784	40
Kentucky	36,589	33
Louisiana	34,253	45
Maine	36,373	37
Maryland	45,963	12
Massachusetts	47,870	9
Michigan	50,694	4
Minnesota	40,577	21
Mississippi	31,954	48
Missouri	36,722	32
Montana	33,249	47
Nebraska	34,258	44
Nevada	40,443	22
New Hampshire	38,301	26
New Jersey	53,281	1
New Mexico	33,785	46
New York	50,920	3
North Carolina	41,151	19
North Dakota	30,891	49
Ohio	42,764	14
Oklahoma	34,499	42
Oregon	41,726	18
Pennsylvania	49,528	5
Rhode Island	48,474	7
South Carolina	37,328	30
South Dakota	30,265	50
Tennessee	37,074	31
Texas	38,361	25
Utah	36,441	35
Vermont	38,254	27
Virginia	40,197	23
Washington	42,108	17
West Virginia	35,888	39
Wisconsin	42,122	16
Wyoming	34,679	41
50 States	n/a	
DC	48,704	
United States	42,929	

Rank in order by $	
1	New Jersey
2	Connecticut
3	New York
4	Michigan
5	Pennsylvania
6	California
7	Rhode Island
8	Illinois
9	Massachusetts
10	Delaware
11	Alaska
12	Maryland
13	Indiana
14	Ohio
15	Georgia
16	Wisconsin
17	Washington
18	Oregon
19	North Carolina
20	Colorado
21	Minnesota
22	Nevada
23	Virginia
24	Hawaii
25	Texas
26	New Hampshire
27	Vermont
28	Alabama
29	Florida
30	South Carolina
31	Tennessee
32	Missouri
33	Kentucky
34	Iowa
35	Utah
36	Idaho
37	Maine
38	Arizona
39	West Virginia
40	Kansas
41	Wyoming
42	Oklahoma
43	Arkansas
44	Nebraska
45	Louisiana
46	New Mexico
47	Montana
48	Mississippi
49	North Dakota
50	South Dakota

H-17 Sources of School Funds, 1999-2000

State	Percentage from federal	Percentage from state	Percentage from local	Rank by percentage local
Alabama	10.4	64.5	25.0	44
Alaska	12.5	63.6	23.9	45
Arizona	7.3	49.2	43.5	22
Arkansas	8.2	62.9	28.9	39
California	7.7	62.9	29.4	37
Colorado	5.5	44.6	49.9	15
Connecticut	4.7	42.7	52.6	11
Delaware	7.4	66.0	26.6	42
Florida	8.1	50.8	41.1	27
Georgia	6.6	51.5	41.9	26
Hawaii	9.8	87.8	2.3	50
Idaho	7.0	60.9	32.0	33
Illinois	6.5	27.3	66.2	2
Indiana	4.5	50.7	44.8	20
Iowa	4.3	52.8	42.9	23
Kansas	6.2	64.4	29.4	37
Kentucky	8.0	63.2	28.8	40
Louisiana	11.7	50.8	37.5	30
Maine	6.2	46.3	47.6	17
Maryland	5.4	39.9	54.8	8
Massachusetts	5.0	43.0	52.0	12
Michigan	6.7	72.2	21.1	47
Minnesota	4.7	60.0	35.3	32
Mississippi	14.0	54.7	31.3	34
Missouri	6.8	37.7	55.5	7
Montana	11.1	44.8	44.1	21
Nebraska	5.3	43.3	51.5	13
Nevada	5.0	30.5	64.5	3
New Hampshire	3.7	8.5	87.8	1
New Jersey	3.2	38.1	58.7	4
New Mexico	12.6	74.7	12.7	49
New York	6.6	45.7	47.6	17
North Carolina	7.6	68.6	23.9	45
North Dakota	11.5	40.3	48.2	16
Ohio	5.8	43.3	50.9	14
Oklahoma	8.7	61.5	29.9	36
Oregon	6.3	57.0	36.7	31
Pennsylvania	5.5	41.0	53.5	9
Rhode Island	4.4	38.1	57.6	5
South Carolina	7.9	51.3	40.8	28
South Dakota	10.4	36.6	53.1	10
Tennessee	9.0	48.1	42.9	23
Texas	8.4	44.0	47.6	19
Utah	6.9	62.4	30.7	35
Vermont	4.5	76.6	19.0	48
Virginia	5.4	37.8	56.7	6
Washington	7.7	65.8	26.5	43
West Virginia	9.0	62.8	28.2	41
Wisconsin	4.6	53.4	42.0	25
Wyoming	7.6	52.1	40.3	29
50 States	n/a	n/a	n/a	
DC	16.6	n/a	83.4	
United States	6.9	50.7	42.4	

Rank in order by percentage local	
1	New Hampshire
2	Illinois
3	Nevada
4	New Jersey
5	Rhode Island
6	Virginia
7	Missouri
8	Maryland
9	Pennsylvania
10	South Dakota
11	Connecticut
12	Massachusetts
13	Nebraska
14	Ohio
15	Colorado
16	North Dakota
17	Maine
17	New York
19	Texas
20	Indiana
21	Montana
22	Arizona
23	Iowa
23	Tennessee
25	Wisconsin
26	Georgia
27	Florida
28	South Carolina
29	Wyoming
30	Louisiana
31	Oregon
32	Minnesota
33	Idaho
34	Mississippi
35	Utah
36	Oklahoma
37	California
37	Kansas
39	Arkansas
40	Kentucky
41	West Virginia
42	Delaware
43	Washington
44	Alabama
45	Alaska
45	North Carolina
47	Michigan
48	Vermont
49	New Mexico
50	Hawaii

Note: Ties in ranking reflect ties in actual values.

H-18 State Aid Per Pupil in Average Daily Attendance, 2000-2001

State	State aid per pupil $ (in thousands)	Rank
Alabama	3,902	30
Alaska	6,903	4
Arizona	2,867	46
Arkansas	3,837	32
California	5,507	11
Colorado	2,964	44
Connecticut	5,094	17
Delaware	7,086	3
Florida	4,560	22
Georgia	3,949	28
Hawaii	7,094	2
Idaho	4,166	26
Illinois	2,944	45
Indiana	4,835	18
Iowa	4,206	25
Kansas	5,213	15
Kentucky	5,382	13
Louisiana	3,414	38
Maine	4,240	23
Maryland	3,288	39
Massachusetts	4,709	20
Michigan	6,301	5
Minnesota	5,567	7
Mississippi	3,429	37
Missouri	3,040	43
Montana	3,493	36
Nebraska	3,161	41
Nevada	2,235	50
New Hampshire	4,691	21
New Jersey	4,155	27
New Mexico	5,698	6
New York	5,548	8
North Carolina	5,117	16
North Dakota	2,533	48
Ohio	4,207	24
Oklahoma	3,787	33
Oregon	5,542	9
Pennsylvania	3,877	31
Rhode Island	3,247	40
South Carolina	3,932	29
South Dakota	2,802	47
Tennessee	3,049	42
Texas	3,658	34
Utah	3,586	35
Vermont	7,289	1
Virginia	2,431	49
Washington	5,327	14
West Virginia	5,513	10
Wisconsin	5,501	12
Wyoming	4,800	19
50 States	4,427	
DC	n/a	
United States	4,420	

Rank in order by $	
1	Vermont
2	Hawaii
3	Delaware
4	Alaska
5	Michigan
6	New Mexico
7	Minnesota
8	New York
9	Oregon
10	West Virginia
11	California
12	Wisconsin
13	Kentucky
14	Washington
15	Kansas
16	North Carolina
17	Connecticut
18	Indiana
19	Wyoming
20	Massachusetts
21	New Hampshire
22	Florida
23	Maine
24	Ohio
25	Iowa
26	Idaho
27	New Jersey
28	Georgia
29	South Carolina
30	Alabama
31	Pennsylvania
32	Arkansas
33	Oklahoma
34	Texas
35	Utah
36	Montana
37	Mississippi
38	Louisiana
39	Maryland
40	Rhode Island
41	Nebraska
42	Tennessee
43	Missouri
44	Colorado
45	Illinois
46	Arizona
47	South Dakota
48	North Dakota
49	Virginia
50	Nevada

H-19 State and Local Spending for Higher Education, FY 1999

State	Higher education spending $ (in millions)	Per capita $	As a percentage of personal income	Rank per capita
Alabama	2,198	503	2.3	22
Alaska	341	550	2.0	16
Arizona	2,265	474	2.0	25
Arkansas	1,124	441	2.1	32
California	15,527	468	1.7	26
Colorado	2,281	562	1.9	13
Connecticut	1,113	339	0.9	47
Delaware	539	715	2.4	2
Florida	4,768	316	1.2	48
Georgia	3,137	403	1.6	36
Hawaii	686	579	2.2	11
Idaho	583	465	2.2	28
Illinois	4,623	381	1.3	41
Indiana	3,281	552	2.2	15
Iowa	1,940	676	2.7	4
Kansas	1,637	617	2.4	8
Kentucky	1,846	466	2.1	27
Louisiana	1,805	413	1.9	35
Maine	446	356	1.5	45
Maryland	2,510	485	1.6	23
Massachusetts	1,947	315	0.9	49
Michigan	6,232	632	2.4	6
Minnesota	2,445	512	1.8	20
Mississippi	1,403	507	2.5	21
Missouri	2,151	393	1.6	39
Montana	475	538	2.5	19
Nebraska	1,052	632	2.4	7
Nevada	683	378	1.3	43
New Hampshire	418	348	1.2	46
New Jersey	3,089	379	1.1	42
New Mexico	1,144	658	3.1	5
New York	5,736	315	1.0	50
North Carolina	4,122	539	2.1	18
North Dakota	436	688	3.0	3
Ohio	4,672	415	1.6	34
Oklahoma	1,610	479	2.2	24
Oregon	1,937	584	2.3	10
Pennsylvania	4,667	389	1.4	40
Rhode Island	369	372	1.3	44
South Carolina	1,737	447	2.0	31
South Dakota	289	395	1.7	38
Tennessee	2,205	402	1.7	37
Texas	8,978	448	1.8	30
Utah	1,528	717	3.3	1
Vermont	340	573	2.3	12
Virginia	3,140	457	1.6	29
Washington	3,166	550	1.9	17
West Virginia	769	426	2.1	33
Wisconsin	2,949	562	2.2	14
Wyoming	294	613	2.5	9
50 States	122,634	451	1.7	
DC	82	159	0.4	
United States	122,716	450	1.7	

Rank in order per capita

1 Utah
2 Delaware
3 North Dakota
4 Iowa
5 New Mexico
6 Michigan
7 Nebraska
8 Kansas
9 Wyoming
10 Oregon
11 Hawaii
12 Vermont
13 Colorado
14 Wisconsin
15 Indiana
16 Alaska
17 Washington
18 North Carolina
19 Montana
20 Minnesota
21 Mississippi
22 Alabama
23 Maryland
24 Oklahoma
25 Arizona
26 California
27 Kentucky
28 Idaho
29 Virginia
30 Texas
31 South Carolina
32 Arkansas
33 West Virginia
34 Ohio
35 Louisiana
36 Georgia
37 Tennessee
38 South Dakota
39 Missouri
40 Pennsylvania
41 Illinois
42 New Jersey
43 Nevada
44 Rhode Island
45 Maine
46 New Hampshire
47 Connecticut
48 Florida
49 Massachusetts
50 New York

Note: Numbers that appear to be identical are rounded and vary slightly in actual value. The rankings reflect the actual values before rounding. See the introduction for more details.

H-20 State and Local Spending for Higher Education as a Percentage of General Spending, FY 1999

State	Higher education spending as a percentage of general spending	Rank
Alabama	10.9	16
Alaska	4.8	49
Arizona	11.2	14
Arkansas	10.5	19
California	8.6	37
Colorado	11.4	11
Connecticut	5.7	47
Delaware	12.0	9
Florida	6.7	46
Georgia	8.8	35
Hawaii	10.0	25
Idaho	10.4	21
Illinois	7.7	40
Indiana	12.3	7
Iowa	13.2	4
Kansas	13.6	3
Kentucky	10.2	23
Louisiana	8.5	38
Maine	7.0	43
Maryland	10.1	24
Massachusetts	5.6	48
Michigan	12.3	6
Minnesota	8.7	36
Mississippi	10.8	17
Missouri	9.0	32
Montana	11.1	15
Nebraska	13.6	2
Nevada	7.3	42
New Hampshire	7.8	39
New Jersey	7.0	45
New Mexico	12.1	8
New York	4.3	50
North Carolina	11.2	13
North Dakota	12.5	5
Ohio	8.8	34
Oklahoma	11.9	10
Oregon	10.6	18
Pennsylvania	7.6	41
Rhode Island	7.0	44
South Carolina	9.5	28
South Dakota	8.9	33
Tennessee	9.1	31
Texas	10.3	22
Utah	14.6	1
Vermont	11.2	12
Virginia	9.7	27
Washington	9.8	26
West Virginia	9.4	29
Wisconsin	10.5	20
Wyoming	9.3	30
50 States	8.8	
DC	1.8	
United States	8.8	

Rank in order by percentage

1 Utah
2 Nebraska
3 Kansas
4 Iowa
5 North Dakota
6 Michigan
7 Indiana
8 New Mexico
9 Delaware
10 Oklahoma
11 Colorado
12 Vermont
13 North Carolina
14 Arizona
15 Montana
16 Alabama
17 Mississippi
18 Oregon
19 Arkansas
20 Wisconsin
21 Idaho
22 Texas
23 Kentucky
24 Maryland
25 Hawaii
26 Washington
27 Virginia
28 South Carolina
29 West Virginia
30 Wyoming
31 Tennessee
32 Missouri
33 South Dakota
34 Ohio
35 Georgia
36 Minnesota
37 California
38 Louisiana
39 New Hampshire
40 Illinois
41 Pennsylvania
42 Nevada
43 Maine
44 Rhode Island
45 New Jersey
46 Florida
47 Connecticut
48 Massachusetts
49 Alaska
50 New York

Note: Numbers that appear to be identical are rounded and vary slightly in actual value. The rankings reflect the actual values before rounding. See the introduction for more details.

H-21 Public Higher Education Enrollment, 1999

State	Higher education enrollment #	As a percentage of total population	Rank
Alabama	197,173	4.5	19
Alaska	25,687	4.1	31
Arizona	276,268	5.8	4
Arkansas	103,326	4.0	32
California	1,692,607	5.1	9
Colorado	219,436	5.4	7
Connecticut	96,834	3.0	47
Delaware	36,895	4.9	10
Florida	540,967	3.6	40
Georgia	237,411	3.0	46
Hawaii	46,479	3.9	34
Idaho	52,615	4.2	29
Illinois	533,522	4.4	21
Indiana	230,810	3.9	36
Iowa	133,753	4.7	15
Kansas	157,088	5.9	2
Kentucky	146,558	3.7	37
Louisiana	188,573	4.3	25
Maine	40,349	3.2	44
Maryland	220,809	4.3	27
Massachusetts	181,514	2.9	48
Michigan	461,825	4.7	13
Minnesota	207,474	4.3	23
Mississippi	121,369	4.4	22
Missouri	199,324	3.6	39
Montana	38,336	4.3	24
Nebraska	88,386	5.3	8
Nevada	85,270	4.7	12
New Hampshire	34,927	2.9	49
New Jersey	263,752	3.2	43
New Mexico	103,125	5.9	1
New York	566,306	3.1	45
North Carolina	321,311	4.2	30
North Dakota	35,940	5.7	5
Ohio	411,541	3.7	38
Oklahoma	155,361	4.6	16
Oregon	148,177	4.5	20
Pennsylvania	336,930	2.8	50
Rhode Island	38,650	3.9	35
South Carolina	153,496	4.0	33
South Dakota	34,197	4.7	14
Tennessee	193,646	3.5	41
Texas	862,271	4.3	26
Utah	120,558	5.7	6
Vermont	20,580	3.5	42
Virginia	311,536	4.5	18
Washington	263,415	4.6	17
West Virginia	76,777	4.2	28
Wisconsin	249,608	4.8	11
Wyoming	27,944	5.8	3
50 States	11,290,706	4.1	
DC	5,349	1.0	
United States*	11,309,399	4.1	

Rank in order by percentage	
1	New Mexico
2	Kansas
3	Wyoming
4	Arizona
5	North Dakota
6	Utah
7	Colorado
8	Nebraska
9	California
10	Delaware
11	Wisconsin
12	Nevada
13	Michigan
14	South Dakota
15	Iowa
16	Oklahoma
17	Washington
18	Virginia
19	Alabama
20	Oregon
21	Illinois
22	Mississippi
23	Minnesota
24	Montana
25	Louisiana
26	Texas
27	Maryland
28	West Virginia
29	Idaho
30	North Carolina
31	Alaska
32	Arkansas
33	South Carolina
34	Hawaii
35	Rhode Island
36	Indiana
37	Kentucky
38	Ohio
39	Missouri
40	Florida
41	Tennessee
42	Vermont
43	New Jersey
44	Maine
45	New York
46	Georgia
47	Connecticut
48	Massachusetts
49	New Hampshire
50	Pennsylvania

Note: Numbers that appear to be identical are rounded and vary slightly in actual value. The rankings reflect the actual values before rounding. See the introduction for more details.

Due to rounding or data sources, the 50-state total plus D.C. may not equal the U.S. total. Please see introduction.

H-22 Per Pupil State Support of Higher Education, 2000-2001

State	Per pupil support $	Rank
Alabama	5,879	16
Alaska	7,419	2
Arizona	3,231	49
Arkansas	5,982	13
California	5,328	25
Colorado	3,388	47
Connecticut	7,336	3
Delaware	5,037	34
Florida	5,230	28
Georgia	6,741	7
Hawaii	7,294	4
Idaho	5,668	19
Illinois	5,059	32
Indiana	5,560	20
Iowa	6,363	9
Kansas	4,331	42
Kentucky	6,834	6
Louisiana	4,667	39
Maine	5,673	18
Maryland	5,320	26
Massachusetts	6,308	11
Michigan	4,832	36
Minnesota	6,503	8
Mississippi	7,266	5
Missouri	5,155	29
Montana	3,696	46
Nebraska	5,952	15
Nevada	3,713	45
New Hampshire	2,826	50
New Jersey	6,335	10
New Mexico	5,511	21
New York	6,097	12
North Carolina	7,465	1
North Dakota	5,137	30
Ohio	5,361	24
Oklahoma	5,018	35
Oregon	4,503	41
Pennsylvania	5,952	14
Rhode Island	4,213	43
South Carolina	5,734	17
South Dakota	3,942	44
Tennessee	5,367	23
Texas	4,673	38
Utah	4,510	40
Vermont	3,292	48
Virginia	5,231	27
Washington	5,064	31
West Virginia	5,046	33
Wisconsin	4,688	37
Wyoming	5,496	22
50 States	5,364	
DC	n/a	
United States	5,356	

Rank in order by $	
1	North Carolina
2	Alaska
3	Connecticut
4	Hawaii
5	Mississippi
6	Kentucky
7	Georgia
8	Minnesota
9	Iowa
10	New Jersey
11	Massachusetts
12	New York
13	Arkansas
14	Pennsylvania
15	Nebraska
16	Alabama
17	South Carolina
18	Maine
19	Idaho
20	Indiana
21	New Mexico
22	Wyoming
23	Tennessee
24	Ohio
25	California
26	Maryland
27	Virginia
28	Florida
29	Missouri
30	North Dakota
31	Washington
32	Illinois
33	West Virginia
34	Delaware
35	Oklahoma
36	Michigan
37	Wisconsin
38	Texas
39	Louisiana
40	Utah
41	Oregon
42	Kansas
43	Rhode Island
44	South Dakota
45	Nevada
46	Montana
47	Colorado
48	Vermont
49	Arizona
50	New Hampshire

H-23 Average Tuition and Fees at Public Universities, 1999-2000

State	Average tuition and fees $	Rank
Alabama	2,833	31
Alaska	2,855	30
Arizona	2,252	45
Arkansas	2,785	32
California	2,559	37
Colorado	2,775	33
Connecticut	4,435	9
Delaware	4,642	5
Florida	2,244	46
Georgia	2,524	39
Hawaii	2,965	27
Idaho	2,458	40
Illinois	4,038	13
Indiana	3,646	18
Iowa	2,998	25
Kansas	2,439	41
Kentucky	2,723	34
Louisiana	2,430	42
Maine	4,122	11
Maryland	4,552	6
Massachusetts	4,105	12
Michigan	4,538	7
Minnesota	3,800	15
Mississippi	2,872	29
Missouri	3,701	17
Montana	3,011	24
Nebraska	2,930	28
Nevada	2,034	50
New Hampshire	6,083	2
New Jersey	5,255	4
New Mexico	2,340	44
New York	3,983	14
North Carolina	2,054	49
North Dakota	2,990	26
Ohio	4,495	8
Oklahoma	2,183	47
Oregon	3,582	20
Pennsylvania	5,610	3
Rhode Island	4,318	10
South Carolina	3,638	19
South Dakota	3,210	23
Tennessee	2,698	35
Texas	2,644	36
Utah	2,147	48
Vermont	6,913	1
Virginia	3,733	16
Washington	3,357	21
West Virginia	2,549	38
Wisconsin	3,313	22
Wyoming	2,416	43
50 States	n/a	
DC	2,070	
United States	3,351	

Rank in order by $

1 Vermont
2 New Hampshire
3 Pennsylvania
4 New Jersey
5 Delaware
6 Maryland
7 Michigan
8 Ohio
9 Connecticut
10 Rhode Island
11 Maine
12 Massachusetts
13 Illinois
14 New York
15 Minnesota
16 Virginia
17 Missouri
18 Indiana
19 South Carolina
20 Oregon
21 Washington
22 Wisconsin
23 South Dakota
24 Montana
25 Iowa
26 North Dakota
27 Hawaii
28 Nebraska
29 Mississippi
30 Alaska
31 Alabama
32 Arkansas
33 Colorado
34 Kentucky
35 Tennessee
36 Texas
37 California
38 West Virginia
39 Georgia
40 Idaho
41 Kansas
42 Louisiana
43 Wyoming
44 New Mexico
45 Arizona
46 Florida
47 Oklahoma
48 Utah
49 North Carolina
50 Nevada

H-24 Average Salary of Associate Professors at "Flagship" State Universities, 2000-2001

State	Associate professor average salary $ (in thousands)	Rank
Alabama	55.2	40
Alaska	54.8	42
Arizona	60.9	23
Arkansas	57.1	33
California	72.4	3
Colorado	62.4	19
Connecticut	71.8	4
Delaware	67.1	10
Florida	61.4	21
Georgia	60.5	26
Hawaii	57.9	32
Idaho	52.5	45
Illinois	66.3	11
Indiana	61.1	22
Iowa	62.5	18
Kansas	56.1	34
Kentucky	58.5	30
Louisiana	53.6	44
Maine	55.3	37
Maryland	69.2	7
Massachusetts	68.7	8
Michigan	73.3	1
Minnesota	66.1	12
Mississippi	52.3	46
Missouri	61.8	20
Montana	49.1	48
Nebraska	58.4	31
Nevada	62.6	16
New Hampshire	60.4	27
New Jersey	72.8	2
New Mexico	54.3	43
New York	63.4	14
North Carolina	71.4	5
North Dakota	48.6	49
Ohio	63.8	13
Oklahoma	55.7	35
Oregon	55.4	36
Pennsylvania	63.4	14
Rhode Island	59.5	29
South Carolina	60.6	25
South Dakota	45.1	50
Tennessee	60.1	28
Texas	60.8	24
Utah	55.2	40
Vermont	55.3	37
Virginia	71.4	5
Washington	62.6	16
West Virginia	55.3	37
Wisconsin	68.0	9
Wyoming	51.6	47
50 States	60.5	
DC	68.0	
United States	60.6	

Rank in order by $	
1	Michigan
2	New Jersey
3	California
4	Connecticut
5	North Carolina
5	Virginia
7	Maryland
8	Massachusetts
9	Wisconsin
10	Delaware
11	Illinois
12	Minnesota
13	Ohio
14	New York
14	Pennsylvania
16	Nevada
16	Washington
18	Iowa
19	Colorado
20	Missouri
21	Florida
22	Indiana
23	Arizona
24	Texas
25	South Carolina
26	Georgia
27	New Hampshire
28	Tennessee
29	Rhode Island
30	Kentucky
31	Nebraska
32	Hawaii
33	Arkansas
34	Kansas
35	Oklahoma
36	Oregon
37	Maine
37	Vermont
37	West Virginia
40	Alabama
40	Utah
42	Alaska
43	New Mexico
44	Louisiana
45	Idaho
46	Mississippi
47	Wyoming
48	Montana
49	North Dakota
50	South Dakota

Note: Ties in ranking reflect ties in actual values.

H-25 State and Local Education Employees, 2000

State	Education employees #	Per 10,000 population	Rank per 10,000 population
Alabama	96,618	217	33
Alaska	18,712	298	2
Arizona	97,610	190	44
Arkansas	64,211	240	16
California	632,942	187	46
Colorado	85,228	198	43
Connecticut	78,756	231	25
Delaware	15,613	199	42
Florida	287,133	180	48
Georgia	201,031	246	10
Hawaii	24,918	206	39
Idaho	30,195	233	24
Illinois	258,541	208	37
Indiana	132,087	217	34
Iowa	69,544	238	18
Kansas	72,810	271	5
Kentucky	102,542	254	8
Louisiana	107,224	240	17
Maine	35,536	279	4
Maryland	106,841	202	41
Massachusetts	143,613	226	28
Michigan	207,567	209	36
Minnesota	123,507	251	9
Mississippi	72,918	256	7
Missouri	122,647	219	31
Montana	22,085	245	11
Nebraska	41,163	241	15
Nevada	27,827	139	50
New Hampshire	29,287	237	19
New Jersey	198,638	236	22
New Mexico	41,976	231	26
New York	444,199	234	23
North Carolina	175,844	218	32
North Dakota	14,424	225	30
Ohio	237,702	209	35
Oklahoma	83,877	243	13
Oregon	64,876	190	45
Pennsylvania	222,289	181	47
Rhode Island	25,307	241	14
South Carolina	90,122	225	29
South Dakota	18,467	245	12
Tennessee	115,772	203	40
Texas	558,310	268	6
Utah	46,118	207	38
Vermont	18,031	296	3
Virginia	167,541	237	21
Washington	93,678	159	49
West Virginia	42,803	237	20
Wisconsin	121,793	227	27
Wyoming	15,104	306	1
50 States	6,105,577	217	
DC	10,534	184	
United States	6,116,111	217	

Rank in order per 10,000 population	
1	Wyoming
2	Alaska
3	Vermont
4	Maine
5	Kansas
6	Texas
7	Mississippi
8	Kentucky
9	Minnesota
10	Georgia
11	Montana
12	South Dakota
13	Oklahoma
14	Rhode Island
15	Nebraska
16	Arkansas
17	Louisiana
18	Iowa
19	New Hampshire
20	West Virginia
21	Virginia
22	New Jersey
23	New York
24	Idaho
25	Connecticut
26	New Mexico
27	Wisconsin
28	Massachusetts
29	South Carolina
30	North Dakota
31	Missouri
32	North Carolina
33	Alabama
34	Indiana
35	Ohio
36	Michigan
37	Illinois
38	Utah
39	Hawaii
40	Tennessee
41	Maryland
42	Delaware
43	Colorado
44	Arizona
45	Oregon
46	California
47	Pennsylvania
48	Florida
49	Washington
50	Nevada

Note: Numbers that appear to be identical are rounded and vary slightly in actual value. The rankings reflect the actual values before rounding. See the introduction for more details.

H-26 Federal Research and Development Spending, FY 1999

State	Federal R&D spending $ (in thousands)	Federal R&D spending per capita $	Rank per capita
Alabama	1,806,956	414	6
Alaska	115,015	186	17
Arizona	1,116,946	234	13
Arkansas	106,422	42	49
California	15,600,123	471	5
Colorado	1,438,682	355	8
Connecticut	655,191	200	15
Delaware	52,255	69	43
Florida	2,284,405	151	24
Georgia	2,023,240	260	11
Hawaii	198,808	168	20
Idaho	200,672	160	21
Illinois	1,316,085	109	33
Indiana	413,864	70	42
Iowa	264,060	92	37
Kansas	191,603	72	40
Kentucky	146,845	37	50
Louisiana	219,218	50	47
Maine	150,569	120	32
Maryland	8,094,369	1,565	1
Massachusetts	3,129,401	507	4
Michigan	839,757	85	38
Minnesota	885,141	185	18
Mississippi	351,571	127	28
Missouri	928,681	170	19
Montana	95,446	108	34
Nebraska	94,089	56	44
Nevada	279,129	154	23
New Hampshire	291,723	243	12
New Jersey	2,661,153	327	10
New Mexico	2,068,291	1,189	2
New York	2,689,016	148	25
North Carolina	1,007,518	132	27
North Dakota	59,947	95	36
Ohio	3,687,855	328	9
Oklahoma	165,818	49	48
Oregon	408,099	123	31
Pennsylvania	1,907,139	159	22
Rhode Island	391,717	395	7
South Carolina	215,941	56	45
South Dakota	38,951	53	46
Tennessee	684,712	125	30
Texas	3,853,339	192	16
Utah	305,019	143	26
Vermont	61,707	104	35
Virginia	5,750,372	837	3
Washington	1,306,757	227	14
West Virginia	227,023	126	29
Wisconsin	377,801	72	41
Wyoming	35,219	73	39
50 States	71,193,660	262	
DC	2,451,606	4,724	
United States*	73,798,199	271	

Rank in order per capita	
1	Maryland
2	New Mexico
3	Virginia
4	Massachusetts
5	California
6	Alabama
7	Rhode Island
8	Colorado
9	Ohio
10	New Jersey
11	Georgia
12	New Hampshire
13	Arizona
14	Washington
15	Connecticut
16	Texas
17	Alaska
18	Minnesota
19	Missouri
20	Hawaii
21	Idaho
22	Pennsylvania
23	Nevada
24	Florida
25	New York
26	Utah
27	North Carolina
28	Mississippi
29	West Virginia
30	Tennessee
31	Oregon
32	Maine
33	Illinois
34	Montana
35	Vermont
36	North Dakota
37	Iowa
38	Michigan
39	Wyoming
40	Kansas
41	Wisconsin
42	Indiana
43	Delaware
44	Nebraska
45	South Carolina
46	South Dakota
47	Louisiana
48	Oklahoma
49	Arkansas
50	Kentucky

Note: Numbers that appear to be identical are rounded and vary slightly in actual value. The rankings reflect the actual values before rounding. See the introduction for more details.

Due to rounding or data sources, the 50-state total plus D.C. may not equal the U.S. total. Please see introduction.

H-27 Total Library Operating Expenditures, FY 1998

State	Library spending $ (in thousands)	Library spending per capita	Rank per capita
Alabama	54,362	12.5	44
Alaska	21,273	34.6	4
Arizona	89,636	19.2	26
Arkansas	28,420	11.2	49
California	650,574	19.9	24
Colorado	114,365	28.8	10
Connecticut	116,205	35.5	3
Delaware	11,188	15.0	39
Florida	278,010	18.6	28
Georgia	127,288	16.7	34
Hawaii	20,381	17.1	33
Idaho	19,420	15.8	35
Illinois	367,400	30.4	8
Indiana	193,006	32.7	6
Iowa	59,461	20.8	23
Kansas	56,669	21.5	22
Kentucky	56,694	14.4	40
Louisiana	82,921	19.0	27
Maine	22,085	17.7	30
Maryland	148,661	29.0	9
Massachusetts	174,582	28.4	11
Michigan	218,418	22.2	21
Minnesota	129,692	27.4	13
Mississippi	28,318	10.3	50
Missouri	108,111	19.9	25
Montana	11,543	13.1	43
Nebraska	30,018	18.1	29
Nevada	40,685	23.3	18
New Hampshire	27,787	23.4	17
New Jersey	267,159	33.0	5
New Mexico	24,407	14.1	41
New York	694,650	38.3	2
North Carolina	118,317	15.7	37
North Dakota	7,347	11.5	47
Ohio	474,325	42.2	1
Oklahoma	43,841	13.1	42
Oregon	78,225	23.8	16
Pennsylvania	207,990	17.3	32
Rhode Island	27,512	27.9	12
South Carolina	60,414	15.7	36
South Dakota	11,047	15.1	38
Tennessee	63,575	11.7	46
Texas	243,892	12.4	45
Utah	48,292	23.0	19
Vermont	10,435	17.7	31
Virginia	153,692	22.6	20
Washington	180,519	31.7	7
West Virginia	20,641	11.4	48
Wisconsin	136,819	26.2	14
Wyoming	11,934	24.9	15
50 States	6,172,205	22.9	
DC	21,435	41.1	
United States	6,193,640	22.9	

Rank in order per capita	
1	Ohio
2	New York
3	Connecticut
4	Alaska
5	New Jersey
6	Indiana
7	Washington
8	Illinois
9	Maryland
10	Colorado
11	Massachusetts
12	Rhode Island
13	Minnesota
14	Wisconsin
15	Wyoming
16	Oregon
17	New Hampshire
18	Nevada
19	Utah
20	Virginia
21	Michigan
22	Kansas
23	Iowa
24	California
25	Missouri
26	Arizona
27	Louisiana
28	Florida
29	Nebraska
30	Maine
31	Vermont
32	Pennsylvania
33	Hawaii
34	Georgia
35	Idaho
36	South Carolina
37	North Carolina
38	South Dakota
39	Delaware
40	Kentucky
41	New Mexico
42	Oklahoma
43	Montana
44	Alabama
45	Texas
46	Tennessee
47	North Dakota
48	West Virginia
49	Arkansas
50	Mississippi

Note: Numbers that appear to be identical are rounded and vary slightly in actual value. The rankings reflect the actual values before rounding. See the introduction for more details.

Source Notes for Education (Section H)

H-1 Average Proficiency in Math, Eighth Grade, 2000: These statistics reflect scores on national tests administered to eighth graders to determine their ability to deal with basic concepts of mathematics. Because some states choose different assessment methods, only thirty-nine states participated in this study. The statistics are representative of those being developed through the National Assessment of Educational Progress, as administered by the U.S. Department of Education and cooperating states. They were printed in the *NAEP 2000 Mathematics Report Card.*

Statistics comparing the educational achievements of students in individual states, school districts, and schools are a response to the widespread criticism that taxpayers and parents have few ways to assess how well schools are educating children. Many states have established their own tests and print comparisons, often called "report cards," among school districts and schools within the state. Supporters of these statistics and tests argue that it is much more appropriate to compare results in education programs than the common statistics that just compare costs, such as how much is spent per pupil. Statistics on test results measure achievement of pupils, not that of teachers or school systems. Experts disagree on the relative influence of factors affecting student achievement, but all agree that it is heavily influenced by such out-of-school factors as early childhood training in the home, children's physical and mental health, and participation of parents in the educational process.

H-2 Average Proficiency in Science, Eighth Grade, 2000: These data are comparable to those shown in Table H-1, except they cover science. Through the National Assessment of Educational Progress, the Department of Education conducts mathematics, reading, and science assessments every other year on different timelines. *State Fact Finder* will publish the most recent assessment statistics available. These statistics, while not available for all states (see notes to Table H-1), come from the *NAEP 2000 Science Report Card.*

H-3 Armed Forces Qualification Test Ranks, FY 1999: Many employers test potential employees to determine their suitability for work, as indicated by such factors as ability to read and understand instructions and perform simple calculations. One of the most widely used tests is offered nationwide to persons seeking to enlist in the armed forces. These data reflect average scores of test-takers in the period from October 1998 to the end of September 1999. These data are prepared by the Department of Defense and published annually, along with other information about persons in uniform, in *Population Representation in the Military Services.*

The Defense Department, which does not want to become an arbitrator of which states prepare students best for jobs, tries to discourage the use of these results to rank states. Regardless, the results provide the best single measure of performance of high school graduates being tested by an employer using criteria approximating aptitude for work.

H-4 SAT Scores, 2001: College-bound students are generally required to take an achievement test to gain admission to the college or university of their choice. There are two major tests used for this purpose, the Scholastic Aptitude Test (SAT), which is administered by the College Board (www.collegeboard.org), and the ACT test, which is administered by the American College Testing Program (www.act.org). Both organizations seek to discourage the use of their test scores as a way to compare education systems of states, but they are commonly used because of the lack of other comparisons indicating how well states and individual school districts and schools compare in meeting these standards for college admissions. The test scores are presented here and in Table H-5, with neither table including all states. Each state's results are given only for the test that is most often taken in that state. Failure to sort in this way would produce highly misleading results. For example, many southern states rely primarily on the ACT, but their students who seek admission to exclusive private universities in the Northeast and California must take the SAT. As a result, the SAT is taken by a small fraction of high school graduates, but those who take it score extraordinarily high.

H-5 ACT Scores, 2001: See notes to Table H-4.

H-6 Percentage of Population Over 25 with a High School Diploma, 2000: These data reflect the percentage of the total population over age twenty-five that has a high school degree. Because each generation of Americans has, on average, attended school longer than its predecessors, the states with the highest ranks tend to be those with the fastest growth and thus youngest population. The data are available on the Census Bureau website (www.census.gov).

H-7 Students in Private Schools, 1999-2000: Just over five million students in kindergarten through the twelfth grade attend private schools. The private enrollment statistics were released in August 2001 by the Department of Education, National Center for Education Statistics (NCES). The data are posted on the NCES website (nces.ed.gov). Public enrollment statistics are gathered every two years as part of the National Education Association's Private School Survey (PSS).

H-8 High School Completion Rates, 1998-2000: An average over a three year period shows that, nationwide, 85.7 percent of eighteen- to twenty-four-year-olds have graduated from high school. Subtracting this figure from a 100 percent graduation rate suggests a "dropout" rate of 14.3 percent. This approach is one of several ways of comparing dropout rates among the states. The Department of Education has produced a dropout rate statistic that relies on a count of dropouts. Currently only thirty-seven states have reliable data that use this concept. The data printed here are from the Census Bureau and are available in a Department of Education, National Center for Education Statistics report titled *Dropout Rates in the United States: 2000*, released on the NCES website (nces.ed.gov) on November 15, 2001.

H-9 Pupil-Teacher Ratio, 2000-2001: Small classes are generally believed to be more beneficial to students than large ones, so pupil-teacher ratios are commonly used as a proxy measure of educational quality. The statistic shows a ratio lower than typical class sizes because some specialized teachers, such as those teaching art or special education, are included. These data come from the National Education Association's *Rankings and Estimates Update* released in September of 2001.

For these and other commonly used educational statistics comparing states, there are three primary sources: the Department of Education, the National Education Association (NEA), and the American Federation of Teachers (which, like the NEA, represents teachers). These organizations produce somewhat different data, using different concepts and different schedules. However, the rankings of states on any particular indicator are about the same regardless of the source used.

H-10 Public School Enrollment, 2000-2001: These statistics show how the nation's 46.9 million public school pupils are distributed among the states. The comparison with each state's population is a rough indicator of the differences among states in the financial burdens of providing free public education. The data come from the National Education Association's September 2001 report *Rankings and Estimates Update*.

H-11 Public Library Holdings Per Capita, FY 1998: These data, from *Public Libraries in the United States: FY 1998*, published by the National Center of Educational Statistics, relate the holdings of books (and related materials) to the population of each state. Nationally, public libraries hold about three books for every person. The reports exclude significant sources of reading materials not in public libraries, such as collections of private and university libraries and certain public school systems.

H-12 Children with Disabilities, 1998-1999: A substantial percentage of the nation's public school students are given special financing by state and federal programs because of something unique about them. The table reflects a Department of Education count of students in the 1998-1999 school year classified as disabled or receiving extra school money because of poverty. These data come from the De-

partment of Education's *Twenty-second Annual Report to Congress on the Implementation of the Individuals with Disabilities Education Act*, available on the education department's website (www.ed.gov).

H-13 State and Local Education Spending, FY 1999: This table relates spending data to population and personal income in each state. The data come from the Census Bureau's electronic publication "State and Local Government Finance Estimates, by State," available on the Census website (www.census.gov). Population numbers, also from the census, are as of July 1, 1999, and personal income numbers are from the Department of Commerce. Based on census historical practices, *State Fact Finder* used calendar year 1998 numbers. See notes to Table F-1 for more extensive information on the source of the data.

H-14 State and Local Education Spending as a Percentage of General Spending, FY 1999: This table, from the same source as Table H-13, shows the relative importance of education spending in state and local budgets. It is derived by comparing this spending with total "general" spending. General spending includes essentially all other spending, except municipal electric and other utilities and trust funds, such as those for workers' compensation.

H-15 Spending Per Pupil, 2000-2001: This table, from the same source as Table H-9, shows spending in public schools for operations (excluding capital outlays) in relation to the number of pupils enrolled.

H-16 Average Teacher Salary, 2000-2001: These average salary calculations, from the same source as Table H-9, show the average gross wage of teachers, not including special pay for leading student activities or teaching in summer sessions.

H-17 Sources of School Funds, 1999-2000: Except in a few states, federal aid covers less than 10 percent of public school costs. State and local governments divide the remainder in proportions that vary considerably from state to state, as shown in the table. The data come from the National Education Association's *Rankings and Estimates* released May 17, 2001.

H-18 State Aid Per Pupil in Average Daily Attendance, 2000-2001: These data, calculated from statistics in the National Education Association's May 2001 release *Rankings and Estimates* and the September 2001 update, show the amount each state government spends on supporting local public schools, expressed in relation to the number of pupils attending school.

H-19 State and Local Spending for Higher Education, FY 1999: This table relates spending data to population and personal income in each state. For source, see notes to Table H-13.

H-20 State and Local Spending for Higher Education as a Percentage of General Spending, FY 1999: This table, from the same source as Table H-13, shows the relative importance of higher education in state and local budgets. It is derived by comparing this spending with total "general" spending. General spending includes essentially all other spending excepting municipal electric and other utilities and trust funds, such as those for workers' compensation.

H-21 Public Higher Education Enrollment, 1999: This table shows the total number of students enrolled in public universities and colleges in fall 1999 and relates this number to the total population of each state. This percentage is an indicator of the relative costs of supporting public higher education in each state. The enrollment data are from the Department of Education and were provided to *State Fact Finder* on November 11, 2001.

H-22 Per Pupil State Support of Higher Education, 2000-2001: There are a variety of different statistics seeking to measure state outlays for higher education on a per pupil basis. None are totally satisfactory for complex reasons, such as difficulty in classifying pupils as private or public in institutions that receive public support for some of their programs but are truly private in financing other programs. This table relates state government spending for fiscal year 2000-2001 to fall 1999 enrollment. The enrollment data are from the Department of Education (see Table H-21). The amount of state support comes from a survey of Fiscal Year 2001 state appropriations for higher education conducted by the Center for Higher Education at Illinois State University.

H-23 Average Tuition and Fees at Public Universities, 1999-2000: These data, from the same source as Table H-21, reflect a composite of average tuition and general fees charged by public four-year institutions of higher education in the 1999-2000 academic year.

H-24 Average Salary of Associate Professors at "Flagship" State Universities, 2000-2001: These statistics were developed for *State Fact Finder* based on detailed salary surveys by the American Association of University Professors as printed in its magazine *Academe* (March/April 2001).

To make the comparisons, the "flagship" university salary for an associate professor was used. Usually the "flagship" is the largest, oldest state university, but in some states several institutions can be considered flagships, such as the University of Michigan and Michigan State. In those cases, *State Fact Finder* generally selected the university originally constituted as the general land-grant institution (for example, the University of Michigan) rather than the one initially designated as an agricultural and mechanical school (for example, Michigan State).

H-25 State and Local Education Employees, 2000: This statistic comes from a Census Bureau survey of state and local government employment, available on the internet (www.census.gov, "Public Employment"). It covers employees of public schools, from janitors to principals, but it does not include higher education employees.

H-26 Federal Research and Development Spending, FY 1999: The federal government is a major supplier of funds for research and development of new products and processes. This federally supported research provides an important source of income for state and private universities and a base from which state economies can develop in high technology industries. The table shows how federal R&D spending in fiscal 1999 was distributed among the states and relates that spending to the population of each state. The data were developed by the National Science Foundation in its *Survey of Federal Funds for Research and Development*.

H-27 Total Library Operating Expenditures, FY 1998: These data are from the same source as Table H-11.

Health

"Bracing for a new wave of medical inflation." This title of one session at the National Conference of State Legislatures' 5th Health Policy Conference aptly identifies the country's continuing hot-button healthcare issue. Costs are rising. Services are more expensive, as are insurance premiums, and state budgets are feeling the burden of mushrooming Medicaid costs. The Congressional Budget Office projects a rise in Medicaid expenditures of 9.2 percent in 2002. This is well above the expected increase in gross domestic product which, in CBO's August 2001 report, was projected to grow at a rate of 4.5 percent.

Soaring prescription drug costs are partially to blame for the increased costs. Higher wages due to a shortage of medical workers, especially nurses, is also a contributing factor. But the full picture is more complicated. Whatever the set of reasons driving healthcare costs (and some have yet to be figured out), states are feeling the pressure to act.

The economic situation will only exacerbate the issue. Feeling the pinch, many employers, Ford Motor Co. is one example, will pass on increased costs of insurance premiums to their employees. In recent years, a competitive market encouraged employers to cover these costs as a benefit to attract workers. Higher unemployment rates are likely to change this. Some workers will be unable or unwilling to pay the premiums, adding to the rolls of the uninsured. Of course, many of those who lost jobs in the softening economy also lost employer-sponsored health plans.

According to one of NCSL's session speakers, Scott Leitz, Director of Minnesota's Health Economics Program, the impossible problem for states is balancing "consumers' needs and desires for few limits on consumption of health services, with business and consumer desire for lower health costs."

While healthcare debates continue, and some new programs are emerging—such as Maine Rx, an attempt to control drug prices for elderly and near-poor residents—long-term solutions in 2002 remain extremely unlikely.

I-1 Immunization Rates, 2000

State	Vaccination coverage %	Rank
Alabama	81.1	16
Alaska	77.6	28
Arizona	74.4	45
Arkansas	73.6	46
California	77.3	30
Colorado	76.3	35
Connecticut	85.3	4
Delaware	76.2	37
Florida	74.7	42
Georgia	82.3	11
Hawaii	76.2	37
Idaho	74.6	44
Illinois	76.8	31
Indiana	77.7	27
Iowa	84.0	7
Kansas	76.5	34
Kentucky	81.4	13
Louisiana	75.7	41
Maine	84.1	6
Maryland	80.3	19
Massachusetts	85.7	3
Michigan	76.3	35
Minnesota	86.9	2
Mississippi	83.1	8
Missouri	78.9	23
Montana	78.4	25
Nebraska	80.4	18
Nevada	74.7	42
New Hampshire	84.8	5
New Jersey	76.8	31
New Mexico	71.7	49
New York	76.6	33
North Carolina	87.6	1
North Dakota	81.4	13
Ohio	72.5	47
Oklahoma	72.2	48
Oregon	80.3	19
Pennsylvania	81.2	15
Rhode Island	83.0	9
South Carolina	80.6	17
South Dakota	78.4	25
Tennessee	82.0	12
Texas	69.5	50
Utah	77.4	29
Vermont	82.7	10
Virginia	76.2	37
Washington	78.7	24
West Virginia	75.8	40
Wisconsin	80.1	21
Wyoming	79.7	22
50 States	n/a	
DC	72.8	
United States	77.6	

Rank in order by percentage

1	North Carolina
2	Minnesota
3	Massachusetts
4	Connecticut
5	New Hampshire
6	Maine
7	Iowa
8	Mississippi
9	Rhode Island
10	Vermont
11	Georgia
12	Tennessee
13	Kentucky
13	North Dakota
15	Pennsylvania
16	Alabama
17	South Carolina
18	Nebraska
19	Maryland
19	Oregon
21	Wisconsin
22	Wyoming
23	Missouri
24	Washington
25	Montana
25	South Dakota
27	Indiana
28	Alaska
29	Utah
30	California
31	Illinois
31	New Jersey
33	New York
34	Kansas
35	Colorado
35	Michigan
37	Delaware
37	Hawaii
37	Virginia
40	West Virginia
41	Louisiana
42	Florida
42	Nevada
44	Idaho
45	Arizona
46	Arkansas
47	Ohio
48	Oklahoma
49	New Mexico
50	Texas

Note: Ties in ranking reflect ties in actual values.

I-2 Infant Mortality Rates, 1999

State	Infant deaths per 1,000 live births	Rank
Alabama	9.8	3
Alaska	5.7	43
Arizona	6.8	27
Arkansas	8.0	13
California	5.4	46
Colorado	6.7	30
Connecticut	6.1	39
Delaware	7.4	18
Florida	7.4	18
Georgia	8.2	10
Hawaii	7.0	24
Idaho	6.7	30
Illinois	8.5	7
Indiana	8.0	13
Iowa	5.7	43
Kansas	7.3	21
Kentucky	7.6	17
Louisiana	9.2	4
Maine	4.8	49
Maryland	8.4	9
Massachusetts	5.2	47
Michigan	8.1	12
Minnesota	6.2	37
Mississippi	10.1	2
Missouri	7.8	15
Montana	6.7	30
Nebraska	6.8	27
Nevada	6.6	35
New Hampshire	5.8	40
New Jersey	6.7	30
New Mexico	6.9	25
New York	6.4	36
North Carolina	9.1	5
North Dakota	6.8	27
Ohio	8.2	10
Oklahoma	8.5	7
Oregon	5.8	40
Pennsylvania	7.3	21
Rhode Island	5.7	43
South Carolina	10.2	1
South Dakota	8.9	6
Tennessee	7.7	16
Texas	6.2	37
Utah	4.8	49
Vermont	5.8	40
Virginia	7.3	21
Washington	5.0	48
West Virginia	7.4	18
Wisconsin	6.7	30
Wyoming	6.9	25
50 States	n/a	
DC	15.0	
United States	7.1	

Rank in order by rate	
1	South Carolina
2	Mississippi
3	Alabama
4	Louisiana
5	North Carolina
6	South Dakota
7	Illinois
7	Oklahoma
9	Maryland
10	Georgia
10	Ohio
12	Michigan
13	Arkansas
13	Indiana
15	Missouri
16	Tennessee
17	Kentucky
18	Delaware
18	Florida
18	West Virginia
21	Kansas
21	Pennsylvania
21	Virginia
24	Hawaii
25	New Mexico
25	Wyoming
27	Arizona
27	Nebraska
27	North Dakota
30	Colorado
30	Idaho
30	Montana
30	New Jersey
30	Wisconsin
35	Nevada
36	New York
37	Minnesota
37	Texas
39	Connecticut
40	New Hampshire
40	Oregon
40	Vermont
43	Alaska
43	Iowa
43	Rhode Island
46	California
47	Massachusetts
48	Washington
49	Maine
49	Utah

Note: Ties in ranking reflect ties in actual values.

I-3 State Health Rankings, 2001

State	State health rankings	Rank
Alabama	-11.0	45
Alaska	2.4	25
Arizona	-4.4	35
Arkansas	-9.3	42
California	5.2	22
Colorado	13.6	10
Connecticut	16.5	4
Delaware	-5.9	38
Florida	-12.5	46
Georgia	-4.8	36
Hawaii	14.4	7
Idaho	6.8	19
Illinois	-1.6	30
Indiana	4.5	23
Iowa	13.7	8
Kansas	6.9	18
Kentucky	-6.1	39
Louisiana	-21.4	50
Maine	13.7	8
Maryland	1.6	28
Massachusetts	15.4	5
Michigan	0.1	29
Minnesota	23.1	1
Mississippi	-19.1	49
Missouri	-2.1	32
Montana	1.9	27
Nebraska	9.4	16
Nevada	-9.3	42
New Hampshire	20.2	2
New Jersey	6.5	20
New Mexico	-7.6	40
New York	-3.1	33
North Carolina	-3.8	34
North Dakota	11.4	13
Ohio	3.4	24
Oklahoma	-7.7	41
Oregon	7.8	17
Pennsylvania	2.2	26
Rhode Island	9.7	14
South Carolina	-14.6	48
South Dakota	5.7	21
Tennessee	-10.1	44
Texas	-4.8	36
Utah	19.0	3
Vermont	15.3	6
Virginia	9.6	15
Washington	12.3	12
West Virginia	-12.6	47
Wisconsin	12.4	11
Wyoming	-1.8	31
50 States	n/a	
DC	n/a	
United States	n/a	

Rank in order by ranking

1	Minnesota
2	New Hampshire
3	Utah
4	Connecticut
5	Massachusetts
6	Vermont
7	Hawaii
8	Iowa
8	Maine
10	Colorado
11	Wisconsin
12	Washington
13	North Dakota
14	Rhode Island
15	Virginia
16	Nebraska
17	Oregon
18	Kansas
19	Idaho
20	New Jersey
21	South Dakota
22	California
23	Indiana
24	Ohio
25	Alaska
26	Pennsylvania
27	Montana
28	Maryland
29	Michigan
30	Illinois
31	Wyoming
32	Missouri
33	New York
34	North Carolina
35	Arizona
36	Georgia
36	Texas
38	Delaware
39	Kentucky
40	New Mexico
41	Oklahoma
42	Arkansas
42	Nevada
44	Tennessee
45	Alabama
46	Florida
47	West Virginia
48	South Carolina
49	Mississippi
50	Louisiana

Note: Ties in ranking reflect ties in actual values.

I-4 Percentage of Non-Elderly Population Without Health Insurance, 2000

State	Percentage of non-elderly without health insurance	Rank
Alabama	15.3	19
Alaska	20.4	7
Arizona	17.8	10
Arkansas	15.9	15
California	19.7	8
Colorado	15.0	20
Connecticut	10.2	44
Delaware	12.1	36
Florida	20.5	6
Georgia	15.8	17
Hawaii	11.9	38
Idaho	17.4	11
Illinois	14.8	21
Indiana	13.9	29
Iowa	10.2	44
Kansas	13.7	31
Kentucky	14.6	23
Louisiana	21.6	4
Maine	13.6	32
Maryland	11.6	39
Massachusetts	10.7	43
Michigan	10.8	42
Minnesota	10.0	46
Mississippi	14.8	21
Missouri	12.2	35
Montana	21.3	5
Nebraska	11.5	41
Nevada	17.9	9
New Hampshire	7.9	49
New Jersey	14.2	26
New Mexico	26.7	1
New York	17.0	12
North Carolina	14.6	23
North Dakota	13.3	33
Ohio	12.1	36
Oklahoma	22.4	3
Oregon	15.9	15
Pennsylvania	8.5	47
Rhode Island	7.3	50
South Carolina	13.8	30
South Dakota	14.0	28
Tennessee	11.6	39
Texas	23.6	2
Utah	14.5	25
Vermont	12.6	34
Virginia	14.2	26
Washington	15.4	18
West Virginia	16.9	13
Wisconsin	8.2	48
Wyoming	16.5	14
50 States	n/a	
DC	16.6	
United States	15.8	

Rank in order by percentage

1	New Mexico
2	Texas
3	Oklahoma
4	Louisiana
5	Montana
6	Florida
7	Alaska
8	California
9	Nevada
10	Arizona
11	Idaho
12	New York
13	West Virginia
14	Wyoming
15	Arkansas
15	Oregon
17	Georgia
18	Washington
19	Alabama
20	Colorado
21	Illinois
21	Mississippi
23	Kentucky
23	North Carolina
25	Utah
26	New Jersey
26	Virginia
28	South Dakota
29	Indiana
30	South Carolina
31	Kansas
32	Maine
33	North Dakota
34	Vermont
35	Missouri
36	Delaware
36	Ohio
38	Hawaii
39	Maryland
39	Tennessee
41	Nebraska
42	Michigan
43	Massachusetts
44	Connecticut
44	Iowa
46	Minnesota
47	Pennsylvania
48	Wisconsin
49	New Hampshire
50	Rhode Island

Note: Ties in ranking reflect ties in actual values.

I-5 Abortions, 1997

State	Abortions #	Per 1,000 births	Rank per 1,000 births
Alabama	13,063	214	28
Alaska	1,632	164	34
Arizona	11,266	149	38
Arkansas	5,782	159	36
California	275,739	525	2
Colorado	9,183	162	35
Connecticut	13,802	320	9
Delaware	5,138	501	3
Florida	81692	425	5
Georgia	35,702	302	10
Hawaii	4520	260	18
Idaho	878	47	49
Illinois	50,147	277	15
Indiana	13,208	158	37
Iowa	10,022	273	16
Kansas	11,249	302	10
Kentucky	7,033	132	45
Louisiana	11,739	178	32
Maine	2,545	186	31
Maryland	9,869	141	41
Massachusetts	28,477	354	6
Michigan	29,528	221	25
Minnesota	14,229	221	25
Mississippi	4,325	104	46
Missouri	10,202	138	42
Montana	2,809	259	19
Nebraska	5,129	220	27
Nevada	6,887	256	21
New Hampshire	2,069	145	40
New Jersey	30,654	271	17
New Mexico	5,382	200	29
New York	140,834	547	1
North Carolina	31,495	294	13
North Dakota	1,226	147	39
Ohio	38,242	252	23
Oklahoma	6,428	133	44
Oregon	14,834	339	8
Pennsylvania	37,135	257	20
Rhode Island	5,478	440	4
South Carolina	9,212	176	33
South Dakota	919	90	47
Tennessee	18,283	245	24
Texas	84,680	254	22
Utah	3,408	79	48
Vermont	1,955	296	12
Virginia	26,089	284	14
Washington	26,932	344	7
West Virginia	2,808	135	43
Wisconsin	13,218	199	30
Wyoming	192	30	50
50 States	1,177,268	n/a	
DC	8,771	n/a	
United States	1,186,039	306	

Rank in order per 1,000 births

1	New York
2	California
3	Delaware
4	Rhode Island
5	Florida
6	Massachusetts
7	Washington
8	Oregon
9	Connecticut
10	Georgia
10	Kansas
12	Vermont
13	North Carolina
14	Virginia
15	Illinois
16	Iowa
17	New Jersey
18	Hawaii
19	Montana
20	Pennsylvania
21	Nevada
22	Texas
23	Ohio
24	Tennessee
25	Michigan
25	Minnesota
27	Nebraska
28	Alabama
29	New Mexico
30	Wisconsin
31	Maine
32	Louisiana
33	South Carolina
34	Alaska
35	Colorado
36	Arkansas
37	Indiana
38	Arizona
39	North Dakota
40	New Hampshire
41	Maryland
42	Missouri
43	West Virginia
44	Oklahoma
45	Kentucky
46	Mississippi
47	South Dakota
48	Utah
49	Idaho
50	Wyoming

Note: Ties in ranking reflect ties in actual values.

I-6 Alcohol Consumption Per Capita, 1998

State	Per capita consumption in gallons	Rank
Alabama	1.83	44
Alaska	2.77	4
Arizona	2.59	7
Arkansas	1.79	46
California	2.18	30
Colorado	2.64	6
Connecticut	2.24	25
Delaware	2.87	3
Florida	2.58	8
Georgia	2.21	26
Hawaii	2.28	22
Idaho	2.28	22
Illinois	2.29	21
Indiana	1.94	39
Iowa	1.92	40
Kansas	1.80	45
Kentucky	1.74	47
Louisiana	2.47	9
Maine	2.16	32
Maryland	2.10	35
Massachusetts	2.44	11
Michigan	2.11	34
Minnesota	2.41	14
Mississippi	2.12	33
Missouri	2.21	26
Montana	2.46	10
Nebraska	2.21	26
Nevada	3.90	2
New Hampshire	4.03	1
New Jersey	2.17	31
New Mexico	2.37	16
New York	1.92	40
North Carolina	1.95	38
North Dakota	2.42	13
Ohio	1.98	36
Oklahoma	1.71	48
Oregon	2.30	19
Pennsylvania	1.89	42
Rhode Island	2.35	18
South Carolina	2.38	15
South Dakota	2.28	22
Tennessee	1.88	43
Texas	2.30	19
Utah	1.25	50
Vermont	2.36	17
Virginia	1.96	37
Washington	2.21	26
West Virginia	1.63	49
Wisconsin	2.69	5
Wyoming	2.44	11
50 States	n/a	
DC	3.81	
United States	2.19	

Rank in order per capita

1	New Hampshire
2	Nevada
3	Delaware
4	Alaska
5	Wisconsin
6	Colorado
7	Arizona
8	Florida
9	Louisiana
10	Montana
11	Massachusetts
11	Wyoming
13	North Dakota
14	Minnesota
15	South Carolina
16	New Mexico
17	Vermont
18	Rhode Island
19	Oregon
19	Texas
21	Illinois
22	Hawaii
22	Idaho
22	South Dakota
25	Connecticut
26	Georgia
26	Missouri
26	Nebraska
26	Washington
30	California
31	New Jersey
32	Maine
33	Mississippi
34	Michigan
35	Maryland
36	Ohio
37	Virginia
38	North Carolina
39	Indiana
40	Iowa
40	New York
42	Pennsylvania
43	Tennessee
44	Alabama
45	Kansas
46	Arkansas
47	Kentucky
48	Oklahoma
49	West Virginia
50	Utah

Note: Ties in ranking reflect ties in actual values.

I-7 Percentage of Adult Smokers, 2000

State	Percentage of adult smokers	Rank
Alabama	25.2	10
Alaska	25.0	12
Arizona	18.6	48
Arkansas	25.1	11
California	17.2	49
Colorado	20.0	42
Connecticut	19.9	43
Delaware	22.9	28
Florida	23.2	25
Georgia	23.5	21
Hawaii	19.7	46
Idaho	22.3	29
Illinois	22.3	29
Indiana	26.9	4
Iowa	23.2	25
Kansas	21.0	37
Kentucky	30.5	1
Louisiana	24.1	15
Maine	23.8	18
Maryland	20.5	41
Massachusetts	19.9	43
Michigan	24.1	15
Minnesota	19.8	45
Mississippi	23.5	21
Missouri	27.2	3
Montana	18.8	47
Nebraska	21.2	36
Nevada	29.0	2
New Hampshire	25.3	9
New Jersey	21.0	37
New Mexico	23.6	20
New York	21.6	33
North Carolina	26.1	6
North Dakota	23.2	25
Ohio	26.2	5
Oklahoma	23.3	24
Oregon	20.7	39
Pennsylvania	24.3	14
Rhode Island	23.4	23
South Carolina	24.9	13
South Dakota	21.9	31
Tennessee	25.7	8
Texas	21.9	31
Utah	12.9	50
Vermont	21.5	34
Virginia	21.4	35
Washington	20.7	39
West Virginia	26.1	6
Wisconsin	24.1	15
Wyoming	23.8	18
50 States	20.9	
DC	23.2	
United States	22.6	

Rank in order by percentage

1	Kentucky
2	Nevada
3	Missouri
4	Indiana
5	Ohio
6	North Carolina
6	West Virginia
8	Tennessee
9	New Hampshire
10	Alabama
11	Arkansas
12	Alaska
13	South Carolina
14	Pennsylvania
15	Louisiana
15	Michigan
15	Wisconsin
18	Maine
18	Wyoming
20	New Mexico
21	Georgia
21	Mississippi
23	Rhode Island
24	Oklahoma
25	Florida
25	Iowa
25	North Dakota
28	Delaware
29	Idaho
29	Illinois
31	South Dakota
31	Texas
33	New York
34	Vermont
35	Virginia
36	Nebraska
37	Kansas
37	New Jersey
39	Oregon
39	Washington
41	Maryland
42	Colorado
43	Connecticut
43	Massachusetts
45	Minnesota
46	Hawaii
47	Montana
48	Arizona
49	California
50	Utah

Note: Ties in ranking reflect ties in actual values.

I-8 Percentage of Population Obese, 2000

State	Percentage of population obese	Rank
Alabama	23.5	2
Alaska	20.5	21
Arizona	18.8	30
Arkansas	22.6	7
California	19.2	27
Colorado	13.8	50
Connecticut	16.9	43
Delaware	16.2	47
Florida	18.1	35
Georgia	20.9	16
Hawaii	15.1	49
Idaho	18.4	34
Illinois	20.9	16
Indiana	21.3	12
Iowa	20.8	18
Kansas	20.1	22
Kentucky	22.3	8
Louisiana	22.8	3
Maine	19.7	24
Maryland	19.5	25
Massachusetts	16.4	46
Michigan	21.8	9
Minnesota	16.8	44
Mississippi	24.3	1
Missouri	21.6	10
Montana	15.2	48
Nebraska	20.6	20
Nevada	17.2	40
New Hampshire	17.1	42
New Jersey	17.6	37
New Mexico	18.8	30
New York	17.2	40
North Carolina	21.3	12
North Dakota	19.8	23
Ohio	21.0	14
Oklahoma	19.0	29
Oregon	21.0	14
Pennsylvania	20.7	19
Rhode Island	16.8	44
South Carolina	21.5	11
South Dakota	19.2	27
Tennessee	22.7	5
Texas	22.7	5
Utah	18.5	32
Vermont	17.7	36
Virginia	17.5	39
Washington	18.5	32
West Virginia	22.8	3
Wisconsin	19.4	26
Wyoming	17.6	37
50 States	n/a	
DC	21.2	
United States	19.8	

Rank in order by percentage

1	Mississippi
2	Alabama
3	Louisiana
3	West Virginia
5	Tennessee
5	Texas
7	Arkansas
8	Kentucky
9	Michigan
10	Missouri
11	South Carolina
12	Indiana
12	North Carolina
14	Ohio
14	Oregon
16	Georgia
16	Illinois
18	Iowa
19	Pennsylvania
20	Nebraska
21	Alaska
22	Kansas
23	North Dakota
24	Maine
25	Maryland
26	Wisconsin
27	California
27	South Dakota
29	Oklahoma
30	Arizona
30	New Mexico
32	Utah
32	Washington
34	Idaho
35	Florida
36	Vermont
37	New Jersey
37	Wyoming
39	Virginia
40	Nevada
40	New York
42	New Hampshire
43	Connecticut
44	Minnesota
44	Rhode Island
46	Massachusetts
47	Delaware
48	Montana
49	Hawaii
50	Colorado

Note: Ties in ranking reflect ties in actual values.

I-9 AIDS Cases, 2000

State	AIDS cases #	Rate per 100,000 residents	Rank by rate
Alabama	483	10.9	19
Alaska	22	3.5	41
Arizona	460	9.0	23
Arkansas	194	7.3	29
California	4,737	14.0	15
Colorado	313	7.3	29
Connecticut	620	18.2	8
Delaware	221	28.2	3
Florida	4,976	31.3	2
Georgia	1,237	15.1	12
Hawaii	115	9.5	22
Idaho	22	1.7	48
Illinois	1,761	14.2	14
Indiana	389	6.4	32
Iowa	94	3.2	43
Kansas	128	4.8	37
Kentucky	212	5.2	36
Louisiana	679	15.2	9
Maine	40	3.1	44
Maryland	1,465	27.7	4
Massachusetts	1,197	18.9	7
Michigan	767	7.7	28
Minnesota	185	3.8	40
Mississippi	431	15.2	9
Missouri	459	8.2	26
Montana	16	1.8	47
Nebraska	79	4.6	38
Nevada	286	14.3	13
New Hampshire	31	2.5	45
New Jersey	1,929	22.9	5
New Mexico	144	7.9	27
New York	6,204	32.7	1
North Carolina	696	8.6	25
North Dakota	3	0.5	50
Ohio	599	5.3	35
Oklahoma	352	10.2	20
Oregon	210	6.1	34
Pennsylvania	1,692	13.8	16
Rhode Island	102	9.7	21
South Carolina	810	20.2	6
South Dakota	8	1.1	49
Tennessee	863	15.2	9
Texas	2,667	12.8	17
Utah	151	6.8	31
Vermont	38	6.2	33
Virginia	891	12.6	18
Washington	515	8.7	24
West Virginia	63	3.5	41
Wisconsin	218	4.1	39
Wyoming	11	2.2	46
50 States	39,785	14.4	
DC	875	153.0	
United States*	42,156	14.7	

Rank in order by rate	
1	New York
2	Florida
3	Delaware
4	Maryland
5	New Jersey
6	South Carolina
7	Massachusetts
8	Connecticut
9	Louisiana
9	Mississippi
9	Tennessee
12	Georgia
13	Nevada
14	Illinois
15	California
16	Pennsylvania
17	Texas
18	Virginia
19	Alabama
20	Oklahoma
21	Rhode Island
22	Hawaii
23	Arizona
24	Washington
25	North Carolina
26	Missouri
27	New Mexico
28	Michigan
29	Arkansas
29	Colorado
31	Utah
32	Indiana
33	Vermont
34	Oregon
35	Ohio
36	Kentucky
37	Kansas
38	Nebraska
39	Wisconsin
40	Minnesota
41	Alaska
41	West Virginia
43	Iowa
44	Maine
45	New Hampshire
46	Wyoming
47	Montana
48	Idaho
49	South Dakota
50	North Dakota

Note: Ties in ranking reflect ties in actual values.

Due to rounding or data sources, the 50-state total plus D.C. may not equal the U.S. total. Please see introduction.

I-10 Physicians Per 100,000 Population, 2001

State	Physicians per 100,000 population	Rank
Alabama	206	40
Alaska	204	42
Arizona	216	34
Arkansas	196	46
California	250	20
Colorado	244	23
Connecticut	347	4
Delaware	259	14
Florida	251	19
Georgia	215	36
Hawaii	281	9
Idaho	162	50
Illinois	267	11
Indiana	205	41
Iowa	203	43
Kansas	228	31
Kentucky	216	35
Louisiana	255	16
Maine	264	12
Maryland	397	2
Massachusetts	403	1
Michigan	267	10
Minnesota	252	18
Mississippi	175	49
Missouri	254	17
Montana	207	39
Nebraska	229	30
Nevada	188	47
New Hampshire	243	24
New Jersey	320	8
New Mexico	219	33
New York	377	3
North Carolina	232	27
North Dakota	230	28
Ohio	263	13
Oklahoma	198	45
Oregon	229	29
Pennsylvania	322	7
Rhode Island	335	5
South Carolina	219	32
South Dakota	208	38
Tennessee	247	22
Texas	213	37
Utah	201	44
Vermont	325	6
Virginia	259	15
Washington	239	25
West Virginia	248	21
Wisconsin	236	26
Wyoming	178	48
50 States	261	
DC	685	
United States	265	

Rank in order per 100,000 population	
1	Massachusetts
2	Maryland
3	New York
4	Connecticut
5	Rhode Island
6	Vermont
7	Pennsylvania
8	New Jersey
9	Hawaii
10	Michigan
11	Illinois
12	Maine
13	Ohio
14	Delaware
15	Virginia
16	Louisiana
17	Missouri
18	Minnesota
19	Florida
20	California
21	West Virginia
22	Tennessee
23	Colorado
24	New Hampshire
25	Washington
26	Wisconsin
27	North Carolina
28	North Dakota
29	Oregon
30	Nebraska
31	Kansas
32	South Carolina
33	New Mexico
34	Arizona
35	Kentucky
36	Georgia
37	Texas
38	South Dakota
39	Montana
40	Alabama
41	Indiana
42	Alaska
43	Iowa
44	Utah
45	Oklahoma
46	Arkansas
47	Nevada
48	Wyoming
49	Mississippi
50	Idaho

Note: Numbers that appear to be identical are rounded and vary slightly in actual value. The rankings reflect the actual values before rounding. See the introduction for more details.

I-11 Hospital Beds Per 1,000 Population, 2000

State	Hospital beds per 1,000 population	Rank
Alabama	3.7	11
Alaska	2.3	41
Arizona	2.1	44
Arkansas	3.7	13
California	2.1	43
Colorado	2.2	42
Connecticut	2.3	40
Delaware	2.3	37
Florida	3.2	20
Georgia	2.9	25
Hawaii	2.5	35
Idaho	2.7	31
Illinois	3.0	23
Indiana	3.2	21
Iowa	4.0	7
Kansas	4.0	8
Kentucky	3.7	12
Louisiana	3.9	9
Maine	2.9	26
Maryland	2.1	45
Massachusetts	2.6	34
Michigan	2.6	33
Minnesota	3.4	18
Mississippi	4.8	3
Missouri	3.6	15
Montana	4.7	5
Nebraska	4.8	4
Nevada	1.9	49
New Hampshire	2.3	38
New Jersey	3.0	22
New Mexico	1.9	48
New York	3.5	16
North Carolina	2.9	28
North Dakota	6.0	1
Ohio	3.0	24
Oklahoma	3.2	19
Oregon	1.9	47
Pennsylvania	3.4	17
Rhode Island	2.3	39
South Carolina	2.9	27
South Dakota	5.7	2
Tennessee	3.6	14
Texas	2.7	32
Utah	1.9	46
Vermont	2.7	30
Virginia	2.4	36
Washington	1.9	50
West Virginia	4.4	6
Wisconsin	2.9	29
Wyoming	3.9	10
50 States	2.9	
DC	5.8	
United States	2.9	

Rank in order per 1,000 population	
1	North Dakota
2	South Dakota
3	Mississippi
4	Nebraska
5	Montana
6	West Virginia
7	Iowa
8	Kansas
9	Louisiana
10	Wyoming
11	Alabama
12	Kentucky
13	Arkansas
14	Tennessee
15	Missouri
16	New York
17	Pennsylvania
18	Minnesota
19	Oklahoma
20	Florida
21	Indiana
22	New Jersey
23	Illinois
24	Ohio
25	Georgia
26	Maine
27	South Carolina
28	North Carolina
29	Wisconsin
30	Vermont
31	Idaho
32	Texas
33	Michigan
34	Massachusetts
35	Hawaii
36	Virginia
37	Delaware
38	New Hampshire
39	Rhode Island
40	Connecticut
41	Alaska
42	Colorado
43	California
44	Arizona
45	Maryland
46	Utah
47	Oregon
48	New Mexico
49	Nevada
50	Washington

Note: Numbers that appear to be identical are rounded and vary slightly in actual value. The rankings reflect the actual values before rounding. See the introduction for more details.

I-12 Medicaid Recipients, FY 1999

State	Medicaid recipients # (in thousands)	As a percentage of population	Rank by percentage
Alabama	650	14.9	24
Alaska	99	16.0	16
Arizona	644	13.5	29
Arkansas	483	18.9	6
California	6,217	18.8	7
Colorado	352	8.7	48
Connecticut	410	12.5	33
Delaware	113	15.0	23
Florida	2,116	14.0	26
Georgia	1,237	15.9	18
Hawaii	203	17.1	11
Idaho	94	7.5	50
Illinois	1,699	14.0	27
Indiana	668	11.2	37
Iowa	313	10.9	38
Kansas	260	9.8	44
Kentucky	664	16.8	13
Louisiana	775	17.7	10
Maine	200	16.0	17
Maryland	628	12.2	36
Massachusetts	1,049	17.0	12
Michigan	1,335	13.5	28
Minnesota	585	12.3	35
Mississippi	545	19.7	5
Missouri	877	16.0	15
Montana	96	10.9	39
Nebraska	223	13.4	30
Nevada	143	7.9	49
New Hampshire	105	8.8	47
New Jersey	844	10.4	42
New Mexico	370	21.3	3
New York	3,327	18.3	9
North Carolina	1,205	15.8	19
North Dakota	62	9.8	45
Ohio	1,390	12.3	34
Oklahoma	525	15.6	20
Oregon	544	16.4	14
Pennsylvania	1,773	14.8	25
Rhode Island	155	15.6	21
South Carolina	725	18.6	8
South Dakota	92	12.5	32
Tennessee	1,533	27.9	1
Texas	2,676	13.4	31
Utah	202	9.5	46
Vermont	140	23.6	2
Virginia	699	10.2	43
Washington	895	15.6	22
West Virginia	377	20.9	4
Wisconsin	563	10.7	41
Wyoming	52	10.8	40
50 States	40,933	15.0	
DC	145	27.9	
United States*	42,062	15.4	

Rank in order by percentage	
1	Tennessee
2	Vermont
3	New Mexico
4	West Virginia
5	Mississippi
6	Arkansas
7	California
8	South Carolina
9	New York
10	Louisiana
11	Hawaii
12	Massachusetts
13	Kentucky
14	Oregon
15	Missouri
16	Alaska
17	Maine
18	Georgia
19	North Carolina
20	Oklahoma
21	Rhode Island
22	Washington
23	Delaware
24	Alabama
25	Pennsylvania
26	Florida
27	Illinois
28	Michigan
29	Arizona
30	Nebraska
31	Texas
32	South Dakota
33	Connecticut
34	Ohio
35	Minnesota
36	Maryland
37	Indiana
38	Iowa
39	Montana
40	Wyoming
41	Wisconsin
42	New Jersey
43	Virginia
44	Kansas
45	North Dakota
46	Utah
47	New Hampshire
48	Colorado
49	Nevada
50	Idaho

Note: Numbers that appear to be identical are rounded and vary slightly in actual value. The rankings reflect the actual values before rounding. See the introduction for more details.

Due to rounding or data sources, the 50-state total plus D.C. may not equal the U.S. total. Please see introduction.

I-13 Medicaid Recipients as a Percentage of Poverty Population, FY 1999

State	Recipients as a percentage of poverty population	Rank
Alabama	96.8	42
Alaska	211.0	3
Arizona	111.3	37
Arkansas	128.9	27
California	132.9	25
Colorado	100.4	40
Connecticut	174.3	4
Delaware	143.4	18
Florida	113.4	36
Georgia	123.1	32
Hawaii	153.9	14
Idaho	53.7	50
Illinois	140.8	20
Indiana	169.2	7
Iowa	148.5	15
Kansas	81.9	46
Kentucky	141.2	19
Louisiana	94.1	43
Maine	148.2	16
Maryland	170.8	5
Massachusetts	145.3	17
Michigan	136.6	23
Minnesota	169.2	8
Mississippi	122.6	33
Missouri	138.6	21
Montana	68.5	48
Nebraska	123.7	31
Nevada	66.2	49
New Hampshire	109.9	38
New Jersey	133.7	24
New Mexico	99.7	41
New York	127.8	28
North Carolina	118.5	35
North Dakota	77.4	47
Ohio	103.2	39
Oklahoma	126.8	30
Oregon	127.5	29
Pennsylvania	161.0	12
Rhode Island	159.3	13
South Carolina	162.8	11
South Dakota	170.3	6
Tennessee	232.6	2
Texas	89.0	45
Utah	165.6	10
Vermont	241.9	1
Virginia	129.0	26
Washington	166.1	9
West Virginia	136.8	22
Wisconsin	122.1	34
Wyoming	92.6	44
50 States	127.4	
DC	188.0	
United States	130.4	

Rank in order by percentage

1 Vermont
2 Tennessee
3 Alaska
4 Connecticut
5 Maryland
6 South Dakota
7 Indiana
8 Minnesota
9 Washington
10 Utah
11 South Carolina
12 Pennsylvania
13 Rhode Island
14 Hawaii
15 Iowa
16 Maine
17 Massachusetts
18 Delaware
19 Kentucky
20 Illinois
21 Missouri
22 West Virginia
23 Michigan
24 New Jersey
25 California
26 Virginia
27 Arkansas
28 New York
29 Oregon
30 Oklahoma
31 Nebraska
32 Georgia
33 Mississippi
34 Wisconsin
35 North Carolina
36 Florida
37 Arizona
38 New Hampshire
39 Ohio
40 Colorado
41 New Mexico
42 Alabama
43 Louisiana
44 Wyoming
45 Texas
46 Kansas
47 North Dakota
48 Montana
49 Nevada
50 Idaho

Note: Numbers that appear to be identical are rounded and vary slightly in actual value. The rankings reflect the actual values before rounding. See the introduction for more details.

I-14 State and Local Spending for Health and Hospitals, FY 1999

State	Total spending $ (in millions)	Per capita $	As a percentage of personal income	Rank per capita
Alabama	3,234	740	3.4	2
Alaska	250	404	1.5	23
Arizona	987	207	0.9	47
Arkansas	1,080	423	2.0	20
California	16,764	506	1.8	11
Colorado	998	246	0.8	43
Connecticut	1,547	471	1.3	13
Delaware	260	345	1.2	32
Florida	6,600	437	1.6	17
Georgia	3,669	471	1.8	14
Hawaii	548	462	1.7	15
Idaho	545	436	2.0	18
Illinois	4,176	344	1.2	33
Indiana	2,482	418	1.7	21
Iowa	1,619	564	2.3	8
Kansas	1,005	379	1.5	26
Kentucky	1,096	277	1.2	41
Louisiana	3,078	704	3.2	4
Maine	393	314	1.3	37
Maryland	1,206	233	0.8	45
Massachusetts	2,186	354	1.1	30
Michigan	4,235	429	1.6	19
Minnesota	1,725	361	1.2	29
Mississippi	1,929	696	3.5	5
Missouri	2,102	384	1.5	25
Montana	299	338	1.6	35
Nebraska	543	326	1.3	36
Nevada	675	373	1.3	28
New Hampshire	156	130	0.4	48
New Jersey	2,072	254	0.7	42
New Mexico	846	486	2.3	12
New York	11,018	605	1.9	7
North Carolina	5,298	693	2.8	6
North Dakota	52	82	0.4	50
Ohio	4,472	397	1.5	24
Oklahoma	1,261	375	1.7	27
Oregon	1,453	438	1.7	16
Pennsylvania	3,611	301	1.1	39
Rhode Island	242	244	0.9	44
South Carolina	2,826	727	3.3	3
South Dakota	152	207	0.9	46
Tennessee	2,953	539	2.2	10
Texas	8,198	409	1.6	22
Utah	722	339	1.5	34
Vermont	61	103	0.4	49
Virginia	2,432	354	1.3	31
Washington	3,221	560	2.0	9
West Virginia	517	286	1.4	40
Wisconsin	1,609	306	1.2	38
Wyoming	448	934	3.7	1
50 States	118,851	437	1.6	
DC	510	982	2.6	
United States	119,361	438	1.6	

Rank in order per capita	
1	Wyoming
2	Alabama
3	South Carolina
4	Louisiana
5	Mississippi
6	North Carolina
7	New York
8	Iowa
9	Washington
10	Tennessee
11	California
12	New Mexico
13	Connecticut
14	Georgia
15	Hawaii
16	Oregon
17	Florida
18	Idaho
19	Michigan
20	Arkansas
21	Indiana
22	Texas
23	Alaska
24	Ohio
25	Missouri
26	Kansas
27	Oklahoma
28	Nevada
29	Minnesota
30	Massachusetts
31	Virginia
32	Delaware
33	Illinois
34	Utah
35	Montana
36	Nebraska
37	Maine
38	Wisconsin
39	Pennsylvania
40	West Virginia
41	Kentucky
42	New Jersey
43	Colorado
44	Rhode Island
45	Maryland
46	South Dakota
47	Arizona
48	New Hampshire
49	Vermont
50	North Dakota

Note: Numbers that appear to be identical are rounded and vary slightly in actual value. The rankings reflect the actual values before rounding. See the introduction for more details.

I-15 State and Local Health and Hospital Spending as a Percentage of General Spending, FY 1999

State	Health and hospital spending as a percentage of general spending	Rank
Alabama	16.1	1
Alaska	3.5	47
Arizona	4.9	42
Arkansas	10.1	10
California	9.3	16
Colorado	5.0	41
Connecticut	7.9	26
Delaware	5.8	39
Florida	9.2	17
Georgia	10.2	9
Hawaii	8.0	24
Idaho	9.7	12
Illinois	7.0	30
Indiana	9.3	14
Iowa	11.0	8
Kansas	8.3	22
Kentucky	6.1	37
Louisiana	14.6	4
Maine	6.2	35
Maryland	4.8	43
Massachusetts	6.2	34
Michigan	8.4	21
Minnesota	6.1	36
Mississippi	14.9	3
Missouri	8.8	19
Montana	7.0	31
Nebraska	7.0	29
Nevada	7.3	28
New Hampshire	2.9	48
New Jersey	4.7	44
New Mexico	8.9	18
New York	8.2	23
North Carolina	14.4	5
North Dakota	1.5	50
Ohio	8.4	20
Oklahoma	9.3	15
Oregon	7.9	25
Pennsylvania	5.9	38
Rhode Island	4.6	46
South Carolina	15.5	2
South Dakota	4.7	45
Tennessee	12.2	7
Texas	9.4	13
Utah	6.9	32
Vermont	2.0	49
Virginia	7.5	27
Washington	10.0	11
West Virginia	6.3	33
Wisconsin	5.7	40
Wyoming	14.2	6
50 States	8.5	
DC	11.0	
United States	8.5	

Rank in order by percentage	
1	Alabama
2	South Carolina
3	Mississippi
4	Louisiana
5	North Carolina
6	Wyoming
7	Tennessee
8	Iowa
9	Georgia
10	Arkansas
11	Washington
12	Idaho
13	Texas
14	Indiana
15	Oklahoma
16	California
17	Florida
18	New Mexico
19	Missouri
20	Ohio
21	Michigan
22	Kansas
23	New York
24	Hawaii
25	Oregon
26	Connecticut
27	Virginia
28	Nevada
29	Nebraska
30	Illinois
31	Montana
32	Utah
33	West Virginia
34	Massachusetts
35	Maine
36	Minnesota
37	Kentucky
38	Pennsylvania
39	Delaware
40	Wisconsin
41	Colorado
42	Arizona
43	Maryland
44	New Jersey
45	South Dakota
46	Rhode Island
47	Alaska
48	New Hampshire
49	Vermont
50	North Dakota

Note: Numbers that appear to be identical are rounded and vary slightly in actual value. The rankings reflect the actual values before rounding. See the introduction for more details.

I-16 Per Capita Medicaid Spending, FY 1999

State	Per capita Medicaid spending $	Rank
Alabama	558	30
Alaska	663	14
Arizona	420	45
Arkansas	573	28
California	612	24
Colorado	452	41
Connecticut	907	5
Delaware	606	25
Florida	447	42
Georgia	472	39
Hawaii	494	37
Idaho	411	47
Illinois	532	32
Indiana	508	36
Iowa	487	38
Kansas	461	40
Kentucky	681	12
Louisiana	751	9
Maine	919	4
Maryland	567	29
Massachusetts	942	3
Michigan	634	21
Minnesota	645	17
Mississippi	652	15
Missouri	665	13
Montana	437	44
Nebraska	592	26
Nevada	300	50
New Hampshire	648	16
New Jersey	709	11
New Mexico	635	20
New York	1,579	1
North Carolina	639	18
North Dakota	535	31
Ohio	614	22
Oklahoma	440	43
Oregon	588	27
Pennsylvania	803	6
Rhode Island	1,059	2
South Carolina	637	19
South Dakota	513	35
Tennessee	762	8
Texas	519	34
Utah	348	49
Vermont	790	7
Virginia	360	48
Washington	613	23
West Virginia	749	10
Wisconsin	525	33
Wyoming	418	46
50 States	660	
DC	1,769	
United States	664	

Rank in order per capita	
1	New York
2	Rhode Island
3	Massachusetts
4	Maine
5	Connecticut
6	Pennsylvania
7	Vermont
8	Tennessee
9	Louisiana
10	West Virginia
11	New Jersey
12	Kentucky
13	Missouri
14	Alaska
15	Mississippi
16	New Hampshire
17	Minnesota
18	North Carolina
19	South Carolina
20	New Mexico
21	Michigan
22	Ohio
23	Washington
24	California
25	Delaware
26	Nebraska
27	Oregon
28	Arkansas
29	Maryland
30	Alabama
31	North Dakota
32	Illinois
33	Wisconsin
34	Texas
35	South Dakota
36	Indiana
37	Hawaii
38	Iowa
39	Georgia
40	Kansas
41	Colorado
42	Florida
43	Oklahoma
44	Montana
45	Arizona
46	Wyoming
47	Idaho
48	Virginia
49	Utah
50	Nevada

I-17 Average Medicaid Spending Per Aged Recipient, FY 1998

State	Average spending per aged recipient $	Rank
Alabama	8,513	34
Alaska	10,765	21
Arizona	11,801	17
Arkansas	8,474	35
California	4,900	48
Colorado	10,117	28
Connecticut	20,258	1
Delaware	14,325	6
Florida	8,336	36
Georgia	5,531	47
Hawaii	9,238	31
Idaho	10,195	27
Illinois	10,217	26
Indiana	11,853	16
Iowa	11,641	18
Kansas	9,239	30
Kentucky	8,870	33
Louisiana	7,165	43
Maine	10,556	22
Maryland	13,571	8
Massachusetts	12,954	11
Michigan	10,258	25
Minnesota	16,923	5
Mississippi	6,857	45
Missouri	10,445	24
Montana	12,593	14
Nebraska	10,511	23
Nevada	7,439	41
New Hampshire	18,451	3
New Jersey	14,063	7
New Mexico	7,440	40
New York	20,000	2
North Carolina	7,520	39
North Dakota	12,660	13
Ohio	13,345	9
Oklahoma	n/a	n/a
Oregon	2,867	49
Pennsylvania	11,283	20
Rhode Island	16,996	4
South Carolina	6,631	46
South Dakota	11,315	19
Tennessee	7,588	38
Texas	7,771	37
Utah	9,276	29
Vermont	6,893	44
Virginia	7,377	42
Washington	9,236	32
West Virginia	12,322	15
Wisconsin	12,880	12
Wyoming	13,037	10
50 States	10,228	
DC	18,901	
United States	10,242	

Rank in order by $	
1	Connecticut
2	New York
3	New Hampshire
4	Rhode Island
5	Minnesota
6	Delaware
7	New Jersey
8	Maryland
9	Ohio
10	Wyoming
11	Massachusetts
12	Wisconsin
13	North Dakota
14	Montana
15	West Virginia
16	Indiana
17	Arizona
18	Iowa
19	South Dakota
20	Pennsylvania
21	Alaska
22	Maine
23	Nebraska
24	Missouri
25	Michigan
26	Illinois
27	Idaho
28	Colorado
29	Utah
30	Kansas
31	Hawaii
32	Washington
33	Kentucky
34	Alabama
35	Arkansas
36	Florida
37	Texas
38	Tennessee
39	North Carolina
40	New Mexico
41	Nevada
42	Virginia
43	Louisiana
44	Vermont
45	Mississippi
46	South Carolina
47	Georgia
48	California
49	Oregon

I-18 Average Medicaid Spending Per Child, FY 1998

State	Average spending per child $	Rank
Alabama	711	48
Alaska	2,297	2
Arizona	1,436	10
Arkansas	1,462	8
California	797	46
Colorado	970	41
Connecticut	1,529	7
Delaware	1,372	13
Florida	896	43
Georgia	874	44
Hawaii	1,554	5
Idaho	906	42
Illinois	1,268	19
Indiana	1,273	18
Iowa	1,293	16
Kansas	1,096	32
Kentucky	1,417	11
Louisiana	1,075	33
Maine	1,300	15
Maryland	1,459	9
Massachusetts	1,369	14
Michigan	836	45
Minnesota	1,550	6
Mississippi	1,034	36
Missouri	1,067	34
Montana	1,239	21
Nebraska	1,015	38
Nevada	1,209	24
New Hampshire	1,928	3
New Jersey	1,164	28
New Mexico	1,290	17
New York	1,766	4
North Carolina	1,176	26
North Dakota	1,212	23
Ohio	1,202	25
Oklahoma	n/a	n/a
Oregon	2,832	1
Pennsylvania	1,374	12
Rhode Island	1,254	20
South Carolina	1,132	30
South Dakota	1,169	27
Tennessee	741	47
Texas	1,053	35
Utah	1,134	29
Vermont	1,020	37
Virginia	1,009	39
Washington	697	49
West Virginia	1,004	40
Wisconsin	1,106	31
Wyoming	1,236	22
50 States	1,117	
DC	1,340	
United States	1,117	

Rank in order by $	
1	Oregon
2	Alaska
3	New Hampshire
4	New York
5	Hawaii
6	Minnesota
7	Connecticut
8	Arkansas
9	Maryland
10	Arizona
11	Kentucky
12	Pennsylvania
13	Delaware
14	Massachusetts
15	Maine
16	Iowa
17	New Mexico
18	Indiana
19	Illinois
20	Rhode Island
21	Montana
22	Wyoming
23	North Dakota
24	Nevada
25	Ohio
26	North Carolina
27	South Dakota
28	New Jersey
29	Utah
30	South Carolina
31	Wisconsin
32	Kansas
33	Louisiana
34	Missouri
35	Texas
36	Mississippi
37	Vermont
38	Nebraska
39	Virginia
40	West Virginia
41	Colorado
42	Idaho
43	Florida
44	Georgia
45	Michigan
46	California
47	Tennessee
48	Alabama
49	Washington

I-19 Medicare Payment Per Hospital Day, FY 1999

State	Average payment per hospital day $	Rank
Alabama	2,615	13
Alaska	2,645	10
Arizona	3,465	3
Arkansas	1,932	42
California	4,139	1
Colorado	2,991	6
Connecticut	2,455	17
Delaware	1,915	43
Florida	3,087	4
Georgia	2,259	25
Hawaii	2,641	11
Idaho	2,272	24
Illinois	2,740	8
Indiana	2,069	37
Iowa	1,915	44
Kansas	2,318	22
Kentucky	2,041	38
Louisiana	2,400	19
Maine	2,096	36
Maryland	1,541	50
Massachusetts	2,199	30
Michigan	2,252	26
Minnesota	2,574	14
Mississippi	1,810	48
Missouri	2,501	16
Montana	2,013	39
Nebraska	2,521	15
Nevada	3,826	2
New Hampshire	2,199	29
New Jersey	3,078	5
New Mexico	2,359	21
New York	1,884	45
North Carolina	1,949	41
North Dakota	1,983	40
Ohio	2,186	32
Oklahoma	2,106	35
Oregon	2,427	18
Pennsylvania	2,756	7
Rhode Island	2,138	34
South Carolina	2,295	23
South Dakota	1,883	46
Tennessee	2,209	27
Texas	2,692	9
Utah	2,640	12
Vermont	1,858	47
Virginia	2,191	31
Washington	2,393	20
West Virginia	1,637	49
Wisconsin	2,158	33
Wyoming	2,204	28
50 States	2,490	
DC	3,125	
United States	2,472	

Rank in order by $	
1	California
2	Nevada
3	Arizona
4	Florida
5	New Jersey
6	Colorado
7	Pennsylvania
8	Illinois
9	Texas
10	Alaska
11	Hawaii
12	Utah
13	Alabama
14	Minnesota
15	Nebraska
16	Missouri
17	Connecticut
18	Oregon
19	Louisiana
20	Washington
21	New Mexico
22	Kansas
23	South Carolina
24	Idaho
25	Georgia
26	Michigan
27	Tennessee
28	Wyoming
29	New Hampshire
30	Massachusetts
31	Virginia
32	Ohio
33	Wisconsin
34	Rhode Island
35	Oklahoma
36	Maine
37	Indiana
38	Kentucky
39	Montana
40	North Dakota
41	North Carolina
42	Arkansas
43	Delaware
44	Iowa
45	New York
46	South Dakota
47	Vermont
48	Mississippi
49	West Virginia
50	Maryland

Note: Numbers that appear to be identical are rounded and vary slightly in actual value. The rankings reflect the actual values before rounding. See the introduction for more details.

I-20 Hospital Expense Per Inpatient Day, 2000

State	Expense per inpatient day $	Rank
Alabama	1,666	49
Alaska	3,198	1
Arizona	2,069	29
Arkansas	1,702	47
California	2,247	23
Colorado	2,504	9
Connecticut	2,415	14
Delaware	2,478	10
Florida	1,793	45
Georgia	2,176	25
Hawaii	1,984	34
Idaho	2,317	18
Illinois	2,378	15
Indiana	2,331	17
Iowa	2,217	24
Kansas	2,022	33
Kentucky	1,808	43
Louisiana	1,770	46
Maine	2,296	20
Maryland	2,140	26
Massachusetts	2,779	3
Michigan	2,425	13
Minnesota	2,301	19
Mississippi	1,396	50
Missouri	2,253	22
Montana	2,573	6
Nebraska	2,032	31
Nevada	1,872	40
New Hampshire	2,662	5
New Jersey	1,827	41
New Mexico	2,365	16
New York	1,944	36
North Carolina	2,027	32
North Dakota	1,794	44
Ohio	2,277	21
Oklahoma	1,684	48
Oregon	2,767	4
Pennsylvania	1,938	37
Rhode Island	2,449	11
South Carolina	1,930	38
South Dakota	2,126	28
Tennessee	1,967	35
Texas	2,033	30
Utah	2,446	12
Vermont	2,138	27
Virginia	1,875	39
Washington	2,872	2
West Virginia	1,821	42
Wisconsin	2,539	8
Wyoming	2,544	7
50 States	2,099	
DC	2,271	
United States	2,100	

Rank in order by $

1	Alaska
2	Washington
3	Massachusetts
4	Oregon
5	New Hampshire
6	Montana
7	Wyoming
8	Wisconsin
9	Colorado
10	Delaware
11	Rhode Island
12	Utah
13	Michigan
14	Connecticut
15	Illinois
16	New Mexico
17	Indiana
18	Idaho
19	Minnesota
20	Maine
21	Ohio
22	Missouri
23	California
24	Iowa
25	Georgia
26	Maryland
27	Vermont
28	South Dakota
29	Arizona
30	Texas
31	Nebraska
32	North Carolina
33	Kansas
34	Hawaii
35	Tennessee
36	New York
37	Pennsylvania
38	South Carolina
39	Virginia
40	Nevada
41	New Jersey
42	West Virginia
43	Kentucky
44	North Dakota
45	Florida
46	Louisiana
47	Arkansas
48	Oklahoma
49	Alabama
50	Mississippi

I-21 Percentage of Population in Health Maintenance Organizations, 2001

State	Percentage of population in HMOs	Rank
Alabama	6.5	43
Alaska	0.0	50
Arizona	32.4	13
Arkansas	10.5	38
California	53.4	1
Colorado	36.1	6
Connecticut	39.7	3
Delaware	22.8	25
Florida	29.8	18
Georgia	15.9	32
Hawaii	31.8	14
Idaho	4.3	45
Illinois	19.2	27
Indiana	11.7	36
Iowa	6.5	43
Kansas	16.1	31
Kentucky	30.4	17
Louisiana	15.6	33
Maine	27.9	21
Maryland	38.4	5
Massachusetts	44.3	2
Michigan	26.7	23
Minnesota	28.2	20
Mississippi	0.9	49
Missouri	31.0	16
Montana	7.7	42
Nebraska	9.9	39
Nevada	20.4	26
New Hampshire	39.3	4
New Jersey	31.7	15
New Mexico	27.9	21
New York	35.0	9
North Carolina	16.3	29
North Dakota	1.3	48
Ohio	23.4	24
Oklahoma	13.9	35
Oregon	35.5	7
Pennsylvania	33.4	11
Rhode Island	35.0	9
South Carolina	9.5	41
South Dakota	9.7	40
Tennessee	33.0	12
Texas	17.5	28
Utah	35.5	7
Vermont	4.2	46
Virginia	16.2	30
Washington	15.3	34
West Virginia	10.9	37
Wisconsin	29.6	19
Wyoming	1.7	47
50 States	n/a	
DC	31.0	
United States	27.9	

Rank in order by percentage	
1	California
2	Massachusetts
3	Connecticut
4	New Hampshire
5	Maryland
6	Colorado
7	Oregon
7	Utah
9	New York
9	Rhode Island
11	Pennsylvania
12	Tennessee
13	Arizona
14	Hawaii
15	New Jersey
16	Missouri
17	Kentucky
18	Florida
19	Wisconsin
20	Minnesota
21	Maine
21	New Mexico
23	Michigan
24	Ohio
25	Delaware
26	Nevada
27	Illinois
28	Texas
29	North Carolina
30	Virginia
31	Kansas
32	Georgia
33	Louisiana
34	Washington
35	Oklahoma
36	Indiana
37	West Virginia
38	Arkansas
39	Nebraska
40	South Dakota
41	South Carolina
42	Montana
43	Alabama
43	Iowa
45	Idaho
46	Vermont
47	Wyoming
48	North Dakota
49	Mississippi
50	Alaska

Note: Ties in ranking reflect ties in actual values.

Source Notes for Health (Section I)

I-1 Immunization Rates, 2000: Information on immunization is collected by the Centers for Disease Control and Prevention (CDC) as part of their National Immunization Survey and are available on the CDC website (www.cdc.gov).

I-2 Infant Mortality Rates, 1999: These data are collected by the Centers for Disease Control and Prevention and are available on the CDC website (www.cdc.gov). They cover deaths of all children under one year of age, expressed in relation to each one thousand live births. This statistic is considered one of the best indicators with which to compare health among states and local areas. Higher death rates are associated with poor health of the mother, absence of medical care during pregnancy, and lack of medical treatment for infants.

I-3 State Health Rankings, 2001: These scores and rankings are developed annually for UnitedHealth Group (Minneapolis, Minn.) by Arundel Street Consulting, Inc. (175 Arundel Street, St. Paul, MN 55102). The results are from *America's Health: UnitedHealth Foundation State Health Rankings 2001 Edition*. They reflect a composite of indicators, including unemployment, health practices (such as smoking), the availability of health services, and outcomes (such as death rates). Probably no two researchers would use identical lists to produce such rankings, but the state rankings would likely be similar. While decisions by states have some impact on health rankings, decisions on health practices by individual citizens have more of an impact.

I-4 Percentage of Non-Elderly Population Without Health Insurance, 2000: Most Americans get health insurance coverage through their employers. All Americans over age sixty-four are covered by Medicare. About 12 percent of the non-elderly, including all welfare recipients, get coverage paid for by state and federal governments through Medicaid. Non-elderly citizens who have no health insurance comprise 15.8 percent of the population. These data are part of a compilation titled "Table HI-6" from the Housing and Household Economic Statistics Division of the Census Bureau.

I-5 Abortions, 1997: There are about 1.2 million legal abortions performed each year. The count comes from the Centers for Disease Control and Prevention (www.cdc.gov). The abortion rate compares the number of abortions with the number of live births.

I-6 Alcohol Consumption Per Capita, 1998: Some public health authorities consider high levels of alcoholic beverage consumption an indicator of poor health of a state's population. The data show the number of gallons of pure ethanol (typical liquor is about 43 percent ethanol or ethanol alcohol, wine 14 percent, and beer about 6 percent) consumed per resident age fourteen and over. The data are derived by dividing sales of alcoholic beverages by population. Those shown were developed by the Department of Health and Human Services (National Institute on Alcohol Abuse and Alcoholism) and published in *Surveillance Report #55*, December 2000. They are called "apparent" alcohol consumption because some alcoholic beverages are bought in one state for consumption by residents of another. This raises the apparent consumption of tourist-destination states, like Nevada, and states with low prices, like New Hampshire, which draw purchasers from other states.

I-7 Percentage of Adult Smokers, 2000: These estimates, results of sample surveys, are developed by the Centers for Disease Control and Prevention (CDC) and are available on the CDC website (www.cdc.gov). The estimates shown here are derived from answers to the question "Do you smoke cigarettes now?"

I-8 Percentage of Population Obese, 2000: These data are part of the Centers for Disease Control and Prevention's (CDC) behavioral risk factor surveillance system. Different definitions of how high a person's body mass index (BMI) can be without being considered a health risk would produce different percentages for every state, but not appreciably affect the rankings. These statistics were retrieved from the CDC website (www.cdc.gov). A person with a BMI of 30 or more is considered *obese*, while a BMI of 25 to 29.9 is considered *overweight*. The CDC also produces overweight statistics, but at press time the most recent available were the data published in *State Fact Finder 2001* covering calendar year 1999.

I-9 AIDS Cases, 2000: These data are developed by the Centers for Disease Control and Prevention (CDC) and reported in the *HIV/AIDS Surveillance Report (Vol. 12, No. 2)*. They cover cases newly reported in calendar year 2000. The rate shown is cases per one hundred thousand residents. Because persons at most risk of contracting AIDS are predominantly found in larger metropolitan areas, states containing those areas typically show the highest rates.

I-10 Physicians Per 100,000 Population, 2001: This table shows the number of physicians in relation to population. Rural states will show below-average numbers in part because intensive medical care, such as that received from major hospitals, is often sought in nearby states with large metropolitan areas. The statistics are based on data from Medical Marketing Service, Inc. (www.mmslists.com).

I-11 Hospital Beds Per 1,000 Population, 2000: This table shows the number of community hospital beds in relation to population. The data come from *Hospital Statistics, 2002 Edition*, a publication of the American Hospital Association. As of 1998, the AHA state data no longer cover all hospitals. Thus, the data shown here reflect only community (nonfederal, short-term, general and other special) hospitals.

I-12 Medicaid Recipients, FY 1999: Over 42 million people receive health care through the Medicaid program each year. The federal government sets minimum standards for this program and pays about 60 percent of the costs nationwide through a formula that provides 50 percent of the costs in the most affluent states and up to 76 percent in the poorest states. Within federal guidelines, states set the rules for eligibility, the health services covered, and the amount of reimbursements to the providers of care.

The primary recipients are families that receive cash assistance from states through Temporary Assistance for Needy Families or from the federal government through Supplemental Security Income. These data come from tabulations of the Department of Health and Human Services' Centers for Medicare and Medicaid Services (CMS) and are available on the internet (cms.hhs.gov).

I-13 Medicaid Recipients as a Percentage of Poverty Population, FY 1999: These data, from the same source as Table I-12, relate the number of Medicaid recipients to the number of persons in households with income below federally defined poverty levels (see Table A-11). The differences among states are a good indication of how inclusive are the eligibility criteria set by the individual states.

I-14 State and Local Spending for Health and Hospitals, FY 1999: This table relates spending data to population and personal income in each state. The data come from the Census Bureau's electronic publication "State and Local Government Finance Estimates, by State," available on the Census website (www.census.gov). See notes to Table F-1 for more extensive information on the source of the data.

The spending includes public health activities plus the gross outlays of hospitals and nursing homes run by state and local governments, including costs defrayed by the charges such as hospitals make to patients and their health insurance providers. The largest outlays appear in states that rely heavily on government-owned hospitals.

I-15 State and Local Health and Hospital Spending as a Percentage of General Spending, FY 1999: This table shows the relative importance of health and hospital outlays in state and local budgets. It is derived by comparing this spending (see Table I-14) with total "general" spending. General spending includes essentially all other spending except municipal electric and other utilities and trust funds, such as those for workers' compensation.

I-16 Per Capita Medicaid Spending, FY 1999: These data, from the same source as the number of recipients in Table I-12, reflect the major impact that Medicaid costs are having on government budgets. The amounts shown reflect primarily federal grants spent by states, about 60 percent of the total with differences among the states, and state government matching funds. In a few states, particularly New York, some

of the federally required state match is provided by local governments.

I-17 Average Medicaid Spending Per Aged Recipient, FY 1998: These data, from the same source as Table I-12, illustrate differences among the states in this component of Medicaid costs. They relate total spending on all Medicaid recipients age sixty-five and over to the number of recipients. Over half of the nursing home residents in the United States are having their bills paid by Medicaid. States differ in the extent and success of programs designed to encourage people to live at home and with relatives rather than enter nursing homes. Those programs typically provide visiting nurses and homemakers who assist frail elderly persons in their homes, thereby reducing the need for institutionalization.

I-18 Average Medicaid Spending Per Child, FY 1998: These data reflect the same concepts and come from the same source as those shown in Table I-17. Differences among states primarily reflect differences in how much doctors and other providers of health care are compensated for providing services.

I-19 Medicare Payment Per Hospital Day, FY 1999: These data are one way to measure healthcare cost differences among states. They reflect the cost of a day in short-stay hospitals as reimbursed by the federal Medicare program. The data come from the Centers for Medicare and Medicaid Services (CMS) and are available on the internet (cms.hhs.gov). These data include both the basic rate for staying in the hospital (see Table I-20) and charges for specific services.

I-20 Hospital Expense Per Inpatient Day, 2000: These data result from a comparison of inpatient days and hospital unit total expenses at community hospitals as reported by the American Hospital Association. See source for Table I-11.

I-21 Percentage of Population in Health Maintenance Organizations, 2001: Most Americans receive their health care by purchasing it from individual doctors, hospitals, pharmacies, and others. However, a growing percentage are served by health maintenance organizations that provide complete packages of care for one monthly fee. Many people believe that this approach to buying care will reduce healthcare costs because the service providers cannot increase their incomes by providing additional services. Many companies providing health insurance to their employees and government programs have been shifting to this approach. The statistics, reflecting enrollment in January 2001 as a percentage of population, come from InterStudy (Saint Paul, Minn.) and are published in *InterStudy Competitive Edge 11.2 Part II: HMO Industry Report*.

Crime and Law Enforcement

The crime story of the mid-to-late 1990s was told by two seemingly conflicting statistics: the FBI's crime rates, which reported declines, and prisoner counts, which reported increases. States have been responding to crime with longer sentences and tougher consequences for repeat offenders (the so-called "three-strikes law"). The result: more people in jail and more spending on corrections at a time when the national crime rate was dropping. Critics called for relaxed sentencing and treatment programs for non-violent criminals. Proponents credited the drop in crime to the stiffer penalties.

The story of the aughts remains to be told. New data from the FBI (see the first six tables in this chapter) show crime rates in 2000 still decreasing but at only a marginal rate—three percent rather than the nearly eight percent decline between 1998 and 1999. Prison populations (see tables J7-J9) which grew at an average annual rate of 6 percent in the 1990s increased by only 1.3 percent in 2000, the lowest rate reported since 1972.

In the last decade, the growing number of prisoners put pressure on state corrections spending. In an effort to keep up with exploding inmate populations about half the states turned to private incarceration facilities. Some of these privatization projects have been plagued by criticisms of inadequate care and security. In 2000, 5.8 percent of inmates were held in private facilities. This percentage jumps to 40 in New Mexico and 33 in Alaska. The reduction in prisoner growth, as well as the recent trend of making more crimes "federal offenses," should help ease the burden of costs for the states. According to the Bureau of Justice Statistics, the state sentenced prison population grew 0.5 percent in 2000, while the sentenced federal prison population grew 9.4 percent.

The question in the air remains: will the sag in the economy be prolonged, and will it be accompanied by mounting crime rates? If the answers are affirmative, pressures on corrections spending will add to the states budgetary woes.

J-1 Total Crime Rate, 2000

State	Crime rate (per 100,000 population)	Rank
Alabama	4,546	15
Alaska	4,249	22
Arizona	5,830	1
Arkansas	4,116	23
California	3,740	30
Colorado	3,983	28
Connecticut	3,233	36
Delaware	4,478	17
Florida	5,695	2
Georgia	4,751	13
Hawaii	5,199	6
Idaho	3,186	38
Illinois	4,286	20
Indiana	3,752	29
Iowa	3,234	35
Kansas	4,409	19
Kentucky	2,960	45
Louisiana	5,423	4
Maine	2,620	46
Maryland	4,816	12
Massachusetts	3,026	42
Michigan	4,110	24
Minnesota	3,488	32
Mississippi	4,004	27
Missouri	4,528	16
Montana	3,533	31
Nebraska	4,096	25
Nevada	4,269	21
New Hampshire	2,433	48
New Jersey	3,161	39
New Mexico	5,519	3
New York	3,100	40
North Carolina	4,919	9
North Dakota	2,288	50
Ohio	4,042	26
Oklahoma	4,559	14
Oregon	4,845	11
Pennsylvania	2,995	43
Rhode Island	3,476	33
South Carolina	5,221	5
South Dakota	2,320	49
Tennessee	4,890	10
Texas	4,956	8
Utah	4,476	18
Vermont	2,987	44
Virginia	3,028	41
Washington	5,106	7
West Virginia	2,603	47
Wisconsin	3,209	37
Wyoming	3,298	34
50 States	n/a	
DC	7,277	
United States	4,124	

Rank in order by rate	
1	Arizona
2	Florida
3	New Mexico
4	Louisiana
5	South Carolina
6	Hawaii
7	Washington
8	Texas
9	North Carolina
10	Tennessee
11	Oregon
12	Maryland
13	Georgia
14	Oklahoma
15	Alabama
16	Missouri
17	Delaware
18	Utah
19	Kansas
20	Illinois
21	Nevada
22	Alaska
23	Arkansas
24	Michigan
25	Nebraska
26	Ohio
27	Mississippi
28	Colorado
29	Indiana
30	California
31	Montana
32	Minnesota
33	Rhode Island
34	Wyoming
35	Iowa
36	Connecticut
37	Wisconsin
38	Idaho
39	New Jersey
40	New York
41	Virginia
42	Massachusetts
43	Pennsylvania
44	Vermont
45	Kentucky
46	Maine
47	West Virginia
48	New Hampshire
49	South Dakota
50	North Dakota

J-2 Violent Crime Rate, 2000

State	Violent crime rate (per 100,000 population)	Rank
Alabama	486	20
Alaska	567	10
Arizona	532	14
Arkansas	445	22
California	622	9
Colorado	334	31
Connecticut	325	33
Delaware	684	6
Florida	812	1
Georgia	505	16
Hawaii	244	43
Idaho	253	42
Illinois	657	8
Indiana	349	29
Iowa	266	40
Kansas	389	24
Kentucky	295	36
Louisiana	681	7
Maine	110	49
Maryland	787	3
Massachusetts	476	21
Michigan	555	11
Minnesota	281	38
Mississippi	361	27
Missouri	490	19
Montana	241	44
Nebraska	328	32
Nevada	524	15
New Hampshire	175	46
New Jersey	384	25
New Mexico	758	4
New York	554	12
North Carolina	498	18
North Dakota	81	50
Ohio	334	30
Oklahoma	498	17
Oregon	351	28
Pennsylvania	420	23
Rhode Island	298	35
South Carolina	805	2
South Dakota	167	47
Tennessee	707	5
Texas	545	13
Utah	256	41
Vermont	114	48
Virginia	282	37
Washington	370	26
West Virginia	317	34
Wisconsin	237	45
Wyoming	267	39
50 States	n/a	
DC	1,508	
United States	506	

Rank in order by rate	
1	Florida
2	South Carolina
3	Maryland
4	New Mexico
5	Tennessee
6	Delaware
7	Louisiana
8	Illinois
9	California
10	Alaska
11	Michigan
12	New York
13	Texas
14	Arizona
15	Nevada
16	Georgia
17	Oklahoma
18	North Carolina
19	Missouri
20	Alabama
21	Massachusetts
22	Arkansas
23	Pennsylvania
24	Kansas
25	New Jersey
26	Washington
27	Mississippi
28	Oregon
29	Indiana
30	Ohio
31	Colorado
32	Nebraska
33	Connecticut
34	West Virginia
35	Rhode Island
36	Kentucky
37	Virginia
38	Minnesota
39	Wyoming
40	Iowa
41	Utah
42	Idaho
43	Hawaii
44	Montana
45	Wisconsin
46	New Hampshire
47	South Dakota
48	Vermont
49	Maine
50	North Dakota

Note: Numbers that appear to be identical are rounded and vary slightly in actual value. The rankings reflect the actual values before rounding. See the introduction for more details.

J-3 Murder and Rape Rates, 2000

State	Murder rate (per 100,000 population)	Rape rate (per 100,000 population)	Rank by murder rate
Alabama	7.4	33.3	5
Alaska	4.3	79.3	26
Arizona	7.0	30.7	9
Arkansas	6.3	31.7	13
California	6.1	28.9	16
Colorado	3.1	41.2	34
Connecticut	2.9	19.9	36
Delaware	3.2	54.1	32
Florida	5.6	44.2	21
Georgia	8.0	24.0	4
Hawaii	2.9	28.6	36
Idaho	1.2	29.7	47
Illinois	7.2	32.9	7
Indiana	5.8	28.9	18
Iowa	1.6	23.1	45
Kansas	6.3	38.0	13
Kentucky	4.8	27.0	25
Louisiana	12.5	33.5	1
Maine	1.2	25.1	47
Maryland	8.1	29.1	3
Massachusetts	2.0	26.7	40
Michigan	6.7	50.6	11
Minnesota	3.1	45.5	34
Mississippi	9.0	35.8	2
Missouri	6.2	24.1	15
Montana	1.8	33.4	43
Nebraska	3.7	25.5	28
Nevada	6.5	43.0	12
New Hampshire	1.8	42.2	43
New Jersey	3.4	16.1	30
New Mexico	7.4	50.7	5
New York	5.0	18.6	23
North Carolina	7.0	27.1	9
North Dakota	0.6	26.3	50
Ohio	3.7	37.6	28
Oklahoma	5.3	41.2	22
Oregon	2.0	37.6	40
Pennsylvania	4.9	26.4	24
Rhode Island	4.3	39.3	26
South Carolina	5.8	37.7	18
South Dakota	0.9	40.4	49
Tennessee	7.2	38.4	7
Texas	5.9	37.7	17
Utah	1.9	38.6	42
Vermont	1.5	23.0	46
Virginia	5.7	22.8	20
Washington	3.3	46.4	31
West Virginia	2.5	18.3	38
Wisconsin	3.2	21.7	32
Wyoming	2.4	32.4	39
50 States	n/a	n/a	
DC	41.8	43.9	
United States	5.5	32.0	

Rank in order by murder rate	
1	Louisiana
2	Mississippi
3	Maryland
4	Georgia
5	Alabama
5	New Mexico
7	Illinois
7	Tennessee
9	Arizona
9	North Carolina
11	Michigan
12	Nevada
13	Arkansas
13	Kansas
15	Missouri
16	California
17	Texas
18	Indiana
18	South Carolina
20	Virginia
21	Florida
22	Oklahoma
23	New York
24	Pennsylvania
25	Kentucky
26	Alaska
26	Rhode Island
28	Nebraska
28	Ohio
30	New Jersey
31	Washington
32	Delaware
32	Wisconsin
34	Colorado
34	Minnesota
36	Connecticut
36	Hawaii
38	West Virginia
39	Wyoming
40	Massachusetts
40	Oregon
42	Utah
43	Montana
43	New Hampshire
45	Iowa
46	Vermont
47	Idaho
47	Maine
49	South Dakota
50	North Dakota

Note: Ties in ranking reflect ties in actual values.

J-4 Property Crime Rate, 2000

State	Property crime rate (per 100,000 population)	Rank
Alabama	4,060	15
Alaska	3,683	23
Arizona	5,298	1
Arkansas	3,670	24
California	3,118	33
Colorado	3,649	25
Connecticut	2,908	38
Delaware	3,794	19
Florida	4,883	3
Georgia	4,246	11
Hawaii	4,955	2
Idaho	2,934	37
Illinois	3,629	27
Indiana	3,403	29
Iowa	2,967	36
Kansas	4,019	18
Kentucky	2,665	42
Louisiana	4,742	5
Maine	2,510	46
Maryland	4,030	17
Massachusetts	2,550	44
Michigan	3,555	28
Minnesota	3,208	31
Mississippi	3,644	26
Missouri	4,038	16
Montana	3,293	30
Nebraska	3,768	20
Nevada	3,744	21
New Hampshire	2,258	48
New Jersey	2,777	40
New Mexico	4,761	4
New York	2,546	45
North Carolina	4,422	8
North Dakota	2,207	49
Ohio	3,708	22
Oklahoma	4,061	14
Oregon	4,495	7
Pennsylvania	2,575	43
Rhode Island	3,179	32
South Carolina	4,417	9
South Dakota	2,153	50
Tennessee	4,183	13
Texas	4,410	10
Utah	4,220	12
Vermont	2,873	39
Virginia	2,746	41
Washington	4,736	6
West Virginia	2,286	47
Wisconsin	2,972	35
Wyoming	3,032	34
50 States	n/a	
DC	5,769	
United States	3,618	

Rank in order by rate	
1	Arizona
2	Hawaii
3	Florida
4	New Mexico
5	Louisiana
6	Washington
7	Oregon
8	North Carolina
9	South Carolina
10	Texas
11	Georgia
12	Utah
13	Tennessee
14	Oklahoma
15	Alabama
16	Missouri
17	Maryland
18	Kansas
19	Delaware
20	Nebraska
21	Nevada
22	Ohio
23	Alaska
24	Arkansas
25	Colorado
26	Mississippi
27	Illinois
28	Michigan
29	Indiana
30	Montana
31	Minnesota
32	Rhode Island
33	California
34	Wyoming
35	Wisconsin
36	Iowa
37	Idaho
38	Connecticut
39	Vermont
40	New Jersey
41	Virginia
42	Kentucky
43	Pennsylvania
44	Massachusetts
45	New York
46	Maine
47	West Virginia
48	New Hampshire
49	North Dakota
50	South Dakota

J-5 Motor Vehicle Theft Rate, 2000

State	Motor vehicle theft rate (per 100,000 population)	Rank
Alabama	288	32
Alaska	375	24
Arizona	842	1
Arkansas	259	36
California	537	7
Colorado	394	21
Connecticut	385	22
Delaware	402	20
Florida	558	5
Georgia	473	11
Hawaii	505	8
Idaho	161	45
Illinois	452	12
Indiana	347	26
Iowa	184	42
Kansas	242	39
Kentucky	230	40
Louisiana	476	10
Maine	104	50
Maryland	540	6
Massachusetts	408	16
Michigan	561	4
Minnesota	273	34
Mississippi	245	38
Missouri	441	15
Montana	217	41
Nebraska	306	29
Nevada	659	2
New Hampshire	174	44
New Jersey	406	18
New Mexico	404	19
New York	286	33
North Carolina	314	28
North Dakota	154	46
Ohio	344	27
Oklahoma	358	25
Oregon	407	17
Pennsylvania	296	30
Rhode Island	445	14
South Carolina	379	23
South Dakota	106	49
Tennessee	484	9
Texas	447	13
Utah	289	31
Vermont	133	47
Virginia	252	37
Washington	594	3
West Virginia	183	43
Wisconsin	273	35
Wyoming	116	48
50 States	n/a	
DC	1,154	
United States	414	

Rank in order by rate

1 Arizona
2 Nevada
3 Washington
4 Michigan
5 Florida
6 Maryland
7 California
8 Hawaii
9 Tennessee
10 Louisiana
11 Georgia
12 Illinois
13 Texas
14 Rhode Island
15 Missouri
16 Massachusetts
17 Oregon
18 New Jersey
19 New Mexico
20 Delaware
21 Colorado
22 Connecticut
23 South Carolina
24 Alaska
25 Oklahoma
26 Indiana
27 Ohio
28 North Carolina
29 Nebraska
30 Pennsylvania
31 Utah
32 Alabama
33 New York
34 Minnesota
35 Wisconsin
36 Arkansas
37 Virginia
38 Mississippi
39 Kansas
40 Kentucky
41 Montana
42 Iowa
43 West Virginia
44 New Hampshire
45 Idaho
46 North Dakota
47 Vermont
48 Wyoming
49 South Dakota
50 Maine

Note: Ties in ranking reflect ties in actual values.

J-6 Violent Crime Rate Change, 1995-2000

State	1995 violent crime rate (per 100,000 population)	Percentage increase in violent crime 1995-2000	Rank by percentage increase
Alabama	632	-23.1	29
Alaska	771	-26.5	38
Arizona	713	-25.5	36
Arkansas	553	-19.5	20
California	966	-35.7	47
Colorado	440	-24.1	32
Connecticut	406	-20.0	22
Delaware	725	-5.6	6
Florida	1,071	-24.2	33
Georgia	657	-23.2	30
Hawaii	296	-17.5	14
Idaho	322	-21.6	25
Illinois	996	-34.1	45
Indiana	525	-33.5	44
Iowa	354	-24.8	34
Kansas	421	-7.4	8
Kentucky	365	-19.3	18
Louisiana	1,007	-32.4	42
Maine	131	-16.6	13
Maryland	987	-20.3	23
Massachusetts	687	-30.7	40
Michigan	688	-19.3	19
Minnesota	356	-21.1	24
Mississippi	503	-28.2	39
Missouri	664	-26.2	37
Montana	171	41.1	2
Nebraska	382	-14.2	11
Nevada	945	-44.5	49
New Hampshire	114	n/a	n/a
New Jersey	600	-36.0	48
New Mexico	819	-7.5	9
New York	842	-34.2	46
North Carolina	646	-23.0	28
North Dakota	87	-6.2	7
Ohio	482	-30.8	41
Oklahoma	664	-25.0	35
Oregon	522	-32.9	43
Pennsylvania	427	-1.7	4
Rhode Island	368	-19.1	17
South Carolina	982	-18.0	16
South Dakota	208	-19.6	21
Tennessee	772	-8.3	10
Texas	664	-17.9	15
Utah	329	-22.2	27
Vermont	118	-4.0	5
Virginia	361	-22.1	26
Washington	484	-23.7	31
West Virginia	210	50.6	1
Wisconsin	281	-15.7	12
Wyoming	254	4.9	3
50 States	n/a	n/a	
DC	2,661	-43.3	
United States	685	-26.1	

Rank in order by percentage increase	
1	West Virginia
2	Montana
3	Wyoming
4	Pennsylvania
5	Vermont
6	Delaware
7	North Dakota
8	Kansas
9	New Mexico
10	Tennessee
11	Nebraska
12	Wisconsin
13	Maine
14	Hawaii
15	Texas
16	South Carolina
17	Rhode Island
18	Kentucky
19	Michigan
20	Arkansas
21	South Dakota
22	Connecticut
23	Maryland
24	Minnesota
25	Idaho
26	Virginia
27	Utah
28	North Carolina
29	Alabama
30	Georgia
31	Washington
32	Colorado
33	Florida
34	Iowa
35	Oklahoma
36	Arizona
37	Missouri
38	Alaska
39	Mississippi
40	Massachusetts
41	Ohio
42	Louisiana
43	Oregon
44	Indiana
45	Illinois
46	New York
47	California
48	New Jersey
49	Nevada

Note: Numbers that appear to be identical are rounded and vary slightly in actual value. The rankings reflect the actual values before rounding. See the introduction for more details.

Crime and Law Enforcement 255

J-7 Prisoners, 2000

State	Prisoners #	Rank
Alabama	26,225	16
Alaska	4,173	40
Arizona	26,510	15
Arkansas	11,915	28
California	163,001	1
Colorado	16,833	25
Connecticut	18,355	24
Delaware	6,921	34
Florida	71,319	3
Georgia	44,232	8
Hawaii	5,053	39
Idaho	5,526	37
Illinois	45,281	7
Indiana	20,125	23
Iowa	7,955	33
Kansas	8,344	32
Kentucky	14,919	26
Louisiana	35,047	10
Maine	1,679	49
Maryland	23,538	17
Massachusetts	10,722	29
Michigan	47,718	5
Minnesota	6,238	35
Mississippi	20,241	22
Missouri	27,323	14
Montana	3,105	44
Nebraska	3,895	41
Nevada	10,012	31
New Hampshire	2,257	46
New Jersey	29,784	13
New Mexico	5,342	38
New York	70,198	4
North Carolina	31,266	11
North Dakota	1,076	50
Ohio	45,833	6
Oklahoma	23,181	18
Oregon	10,630	30
Pennsylvania	36,847	9
Rhode Island	3,286	43
South Carolina	21,778	20
South Dakota	2,616	45
Tennessee	22,166	19
Texas	157,997	2
Utah	5,630	36
Vermont	1,697	47
Virginia	30,168	12
Washington	14,915	27
West Virginia	3,856	42
Wisconsin	20,612	21
Wyoming	1,680	48
50 States	1,229,020	
DC	7,456	
United States	1,236,476	

Rank in order by #	
1	California
2	Texas
3	Florida
4	New York
5	Michigan
6	Ohio
7	Illinois
8	Georgia
9	Pennsylvania
10	Louisiana
11	North Carolina
12	Virginia
13	New Jersey
14	Missouri
15	Arizona
16	Alabama
17	Maryland
18	Oklahoma
19	Tennessee
20	South Carolina
21	Wisconsin
22	Mississippi
23	Indiana
24	Connecticut
25	Colorado
26	Kentucky
27	Washington
28	Arkansas
29	Massachusetts
30	Oregon
31	Nevada
32	Kansas
33	Iowa
34	Delaware
35	Minnesota
36	Utah
37	Idaho
38	New Mexico
39	Hawaii
40	Alaska
41	Nebraska
42	West Virginia
43	Rhode Island
44	Montana
45	South Dakota
46	New Hampshire
47	Vermont
48	Wyoming
49	Maine
50	North Dakota

J-8 Change in Prisoners, 1990-2000

State	Percentage change in prisoners	Rank
Alabama	57.0	36
Alaska	15.0	48
Arizona	84.4	18
Arkansas	62.9	32
California	70.4	22
Colorado	119.4	7
Connecticut	69.3	25
Delaware	75.7	21
Florida	60.7	33
Georgia	103.7	11
Hawaii	108.0	10
Idaho	181.8	1
Illinois	64.6	30
Indiana	59.2	35
Iowa	100.5	12
Kansas	44.5	39
Kentucky	65.3	29
Louisiana	88.4	17
Maine	10.5	49
Maryland	34.4	43
Massachusetts	20.0	47
Michigan	39.3	42
Minnesota	96.4	13
Mississippi	138.0	4
Missouri	82.7	20
Montana	117.9	8
Nebraska	66.9	27
Nevada	70.4	22
New Hampshire	68.2	26
New Jersey	41.0	41
New Mexico	59.3	34
New York	27.9	45
North Carolina	52.2	37
North Dakota	128.5	5
Ohio	44.0	40
Oklahoma	88.7	16
Oregon	63.3	31
Pennsylvania	65.4	28
Rhode Island	24.0	46
South Carolina	29.7	44
South Dakota	94.9	14
Tennessee	113.4	9
Texas	164.3	2
Utah	123.4	6
Vermont	92.8	15
Virginia	70.2	24
Washington	83.4	19
West Virginia	142.5	3
Wisconsin	n/a	n/a
Wyoming	51.4	38
50 States	n/a	
DC	-26.3	
United States	71.7	

Rank in order by percentage

1	Idaho
2	Texas
3	West Virginia
4	Mississippi
5	North Dakota
6	Utah
7	Colorado
8	Montana
9	Tennessee
10	Hawaii
11	Georgia
12	Iowa
13	Minnesota
14	South Dakota
15	Vermont
16	Oklahoma
17	Louisiana
18	Arizona
19	Washington
20	Missouri
21	Delaware
22	California
22	Nevada
24	Virginia
25	Connecticut
26	New Hampshire
27	Nebraska
28	Pennsylvania
29	Kentucky
30	Illinois
31	Oregon
32	Arkansas
33	Florida
34	New Mexico
35	Indiana
36	Alabama
37	North Carolina
38	Wyoming
39	Kansas
40	Ohio
41	New Jersey
42	Michigan
43	Maryland
44	South Carolina
45	New York
46	Rhode Island
47	Massachusetts
48	Alaska
49	Maine

Note: Ties in ranking reflect ties in actual values.

J-9 Incarceration Rate, 2000

State	Incarceration rate (per 100,000 population)	Rank
Alabama	549	6
Alaska	341	32
Arizona	515	9
Arkansas	458	15
California	474	13
Colorado	403	20
Connecticut	398	22
Delaware	513	10
Florida	462	14
Georgia	550	5
Hawaii	302	37
Idaho	430	16
Illinois	371	26
Indiana	335	33
Iowa	276	39
Kansas	312	35
Kentucky	373	25
Louisiana	801	1
Maine	129	49
Maryland	429	17
Massachusetts	252	41
Michigan	480	12
Minnesota	128	50
Mississippi	688	3
Missouri	494	11
Montana	348	30
Nebraska	228	43
Nevada	518	8
New Hampshire	185	47
New Jersey	362	27
New Mexico	279	38
New York	383	23
North Carolina	347	31
North Dakota	158	48
Ohio	406	19
Oklahoma	685	4
Oregon	316	34
Pennsylvania	307	36
Rhode Island	197	46
South Carolina	532	7
South Dakota	353	28
Tennessee	399	21
Texas	730	2
Utah	254	40
Vermont	218	44
Virginia	422	18
Washington	251	42
West Virginia	211	45
Wisconsin	376	24
Wyoming	349	29
50 States	n/a	
DC	971	
United States	432	

Rank in order by rate

1. Louisiana
2. Texas
3. Mississippi
4. Oklahoma
5. Georgia
6. Alabama
7. South Carolina
8. Nevada
9. Arizona
10. Delaware
11. Missouri
12. Michigan
13. California
14. Florida
15. Arkansas
16. Idaho
17. Maryland
18. Virginia
19. Ohio
20. Colorado
21. Tennessee
22. Connecticut
23. New York
24. Wisconsin
25. Kentucky
26. Illinois
27. New Jersey
28. South Dakota
29. Wyoming
30. Montana
31. North Carolina
32. Alaska
33. Indiana
34. Oregon
35. Kansas
36. Pennsylvania
37. Hawaii
38. New Mexico
39. Iowa
40. Utah
41. Massachusetts
42. Washington
43. Nebraska
44. Vermont
45. West Virginia
46. Rhode Island
47. New Hampshire
48. North Dakota
49. Maine
50. Minnesota

J-10 Juvenile Violent Crime Index, 1999

State	Juvenile crime rate (per 100,000 youths)	Rank
Alabama	148	40
Alaska	279	23
Arizona	316	17
Arkansas	228	31
California	498	5
Colorado	300	21
Connecticut	339	13
Delaware	766	2
Florida	672	3
Georgia	188	38
Hawaii	220	32
Idaho	196	34
Illinois	1,058	1
Indiana	393	11
Iowa	267	25
Kansas	n/a	n/a
Kentucky	516	4
Louisiana	461	6
Maine	n/a	n/a
Maryland	304	20
Massachusetts	454	7
Michigan	195	35
Minnesota	275	24
Mississippi	189	37
Missouri	312	19
Montana	315	18
Nebraska	119	43
Nevada	288	22
New Hampshire	124	42
New Jersey	409	9
New Mexico	357	12
New York	336	14
North Carolina	334	16
North Dakota	92	45
Ohio	248	28
Oklahoma	n/a	n/a
Oregon	203	33
Pennsylvania	422	8
Rhode Island	246	29
South Carolina	400	10
South Dakota	167	39
Tennessee	250	27
Texas	235	30
Utah	253	26
Vermont	60	46
Virginia	191	36
Washington	335	15
West Virginia	95	44
Wisconsin	n/a	n/a
Wyoming	146	41
50 States	n/a	
DC	n/a	
United States	366	

Rank in order by rate	
1	Illinois
2	Delaware
3	Florida
4	Kentucky
5	California
6	Louisiana
7	Massachusetts
8	Pennsylvania
9	New Jersey
10	South Carolina
11	Indiana
12	New Mexico
13	Connecticut
14	New York
15	Washington
16	North Carolina
17	Arizona
18	Montana
19	Missouri
20	Maryland
21	Colorado
22	Nevada
23	Alaska
24	Minnesota
25	Iowa
26	Utah
27	Tennessee
28	Ohio
29	Rhode Island
30	Texas
31	Arkansas
32	Hawaii
33	Oregon
34	Idaho
35	Michigan
36	Virginia
37	Mississippi
38	Georgia
39	South Dakota
40	Alabama
41	Wyoming
42	New Hampshire
43	Nebraska
44	West Virginia
45	North Dakota
46	Vermont

J-11 Proportion of Sentence Served, 1997

State	Percentage of sentence served	Rank
Alabama	n/a	n/a
Alaska	67	7
Arizona	74	3
Arkansas	25	45
California	58	15
Colorado	51	22
Connecticut	68	6
Delaware	n/a	n/a
Florida	59	13
Georgia	62	11
Hawaii	46	30
Idaho	49	25
Illinois	44	35
Indiana	48	27
Iowa	38	43
Kansas	n/a	n/a
Kentucky	49	25
Louisiana	51	22
Maine	n/a	n/a
Maryland	56	18
Massachusetts	58	15
Michigan	n/a	n/a
Minnesota	69	5
Mississippi	46	30
Missouri	86	2
Montana	47	28
Nebraska	45	32
Nevada	45	32
New Hampshire	44	35
New Jersey	45	32
New Mexico	57	17
New York	60	12
North Carolina	40	42
North Dakota	64	9
Ohio	33	44
Oklahoma	43	39
Oregon	63	10
Pennsylvania	59	13
Rhode Island	66	8
South Carolina	51	22
South Dakota	47	28
Tennessee	44	35
Texas	52	20
Utah	43	39
Vermont	87	1
Virginia	52	20
Washington	74	3
West Virginia	41	41
Wisconsin	55	19
Wyoming	44	35
50 States	54	
DC	n/a	
United States	54	

Rank in order by percentage

1	Vermont
2	Missouri
3	Arizona
3	Washington
5	Minnesota
6	Connecticut
7	Alaska
8	Rhode Island
9	North Dakota
10	Oregon
11	Georgia
12	New York
13	Florida
13	Pennsylvania
15	California
15	Massachusetts
17	New Mexico
18	Maryland
19	Wisconsin
20	Texas
20	Virginia
22	Colorado
22	Louisiana
22	South Carolina
25	Idaho
25	Kentucky
27	Indiana
28	Montana
28	South Dakota
30	Hawaii
30	Mississippi
32	Nebraska
32	Nevada
32	New Jersey
35	Illinois
35	New Hampshire
35	Tennessee
35	Wyoming
39	Oklahoma
39	Utah
41	West Virginia
42	North Carolina
43	Iowa
44	Ohio
45	Arkansas

Note: Ties in ranking reflect ties in actual values.

J-12 State and Local Law Enforcement Employees, 2000

State	Law enforcement employees #	Per 10,000 population #	Rank per 10,000 population
Alabama	13,123	29.5	24
Alaska	1,628	26.0	35
Arizona	16,141	31.5	15
Arkansas	7,871	29.4	26
California	96,858	28.6	29
Colorado	12,042	28.0	31
Connecticut	10,502	30.8	17
Delaware	2,378	30.3	19
Florida	55,163	34.5	6
Georgia	24,261	29.6	23
Hawaii	3,612	29.8	21
Idaho	3,346	25.9	37
Illinois	44,092	35.5	5
Indiana	15,779	26.0	36
Iowa	7,251	24.8	40
Kansas	8,984	33.4	11
Kentucky	9,784	24.2	43
Louisiana	16,058	35.9	4
Maine	3,110	24.4	42
Maryland	16,628	31.4	16
Massachusetts	23,868	37.6	3
Michigan	25,814	26.0	34
Minnesota	10,636	21.6	48
Mississippi	8,627	30.3	20
Missouri	17,083	30.5	18
Montana	2,216	24.6	41
Nebraska	4,495	26.3	33
Nevada	6,751	33.8	10
New Hampshire	4,227	34.2	8
New Jersey	33,441	39.7	2
New Mexico	5,417	29.8	22
New York	86,256	45.5	1
North Carolina	23,053	28.6	28
North Dakota	1,440	22.4	47
Ohio	33,476	29.5	25
Oklahoma	11,048	32.0	13
Oregon	8,627	25.2	39
Pennsylvania	31,447	25.6	38
Rhode Island	3,358	32.0	12
South Carolina	13,598	33.9	9
South Dakota	1,700	22.5	46
Tennessee	18,057	31.7	14
Texas	58,854	28.2	30
Utah	5,400	24.2	44
Vermont	1,303	21.4	49
Virginia	18,750	26.5	32
Washington	14,137	24.0	45
West Virginia	3,767	20.8	50
Wisconsin	15,615	29.1	27
Wyoming	1,695	34.3	7
50 States	862,767	30.7	
DC	4,458	77.9	
United States	867,225	30.8	

Rank in order per 10,000 population

1	New York
2	New Jersey
3	Massachusetts
4	Louisiana
5	Illinois
6	Florida
7	Wyoming
8	New Hampshire
9	South Carolina
10	Nevada
11	Kansas
12	Rhode Island
13	Oklahoma
14	Tennessee
15	Arizona
16	Maryland
17	Connecticut
18	Missouri
19	Delaware
20	Mississippi
21	Hawaii
22	New Mexico
23	Georgia
24	Alabama
25	Ohio
26	Arkansas
27	Wisconsin
28	North Carolina
29	California
30	Texas
31	Colorado
32	Virginia
33	Nebraska
34	Michigan
35	Alaska
36	Indiana
37	Idaho
38	Pennsylvania
39	Oregon
40	Iowa
41	Montana
42	Maine
43	Kentucky
44	Utah
45	Washington
46	South Dakota
47	North Dakota
48	Minnesota
49	Vermont
50	West Virginia

Note: Numbers that appear to be identical are rounded and vary slightly in actual value. The rankings reflect the actual values before rounding. See the introduction for more details.

J-13 State and Local Corrections Employees, 2000

State	Correction employees #	Per 10,000 population #	Rank per 10,000 population
Alabama	7,103	16.0	45
Alaska	1,713	27.3	10
Arizona	13,556	26.4	14
Arkansas	5,345	20.0	31
California	77,838	23.0	20
Colorado	9,410	21.9	25
Connecticut	9,003	26.4	13
Delaware	2,423	30.9	5
Florida	42,666	26.7	12
Georgia	26,595	32.5	2
Hawaii	2,396	19.8	32
Idaho	2,627	20.3	29
Illinois	25,178	20.3	30
Indiana	11,278	18.5	36
Iowa	4,418	15.1	46
Kansas	6,137	22.8	21
Kentucky	6,682	16.5	41
Louisiana	13,412	30.0	7
Maine	1,767	13.9	48
Maryland	14,365	27.1	11
Massachusetts	10,364	16.3	42
Michigan	23,749	23.9	17
Minnesota	7,867	16.0	44
Mississippi	6,254	22.0	24
Missouri	13,811	24.7	15
Montana	1,619	17.9	37
Nebraska	2,998	17.5	39
Nevada	4,536	22.7	22
New Hampshire	1,740	14.1	47
New Jersey	15,899	18.9	34
New Mexico	5,498	30.2	6
New York	61,377	32.3	3
North Carolina	22,892	28.4	8
North Dakota	804	12.5	49
Ohio	26,386	23.2	19
Oklahoma	7,131	20.7	28
Oregon	8,159	23.8	18
Pennsylvania	26,321	21.4	26
Rhode Island	1,822	17.4	40
South Carolina	11,366	28.3	9
South Dakota	1,354	17.9	38
Tennessee	10,733	18.9	35
Texas	69,116	33.1	1
Utah	4,292	19.2	33
Vermont	988	16.2	43
Virginia	22,180	31.3	4
Washington	12,379	21.0	27
West Virginia	1,597	8.8	50
Wisconsin	12,857	24.0	16
Wyoming	1,109	22.5	23
50 States	681,110	24.3	
DC	2,365	41.3	
United States	683,475	24.3	

Rank in order per 10,000 population

1 Texas
2 Georgia
3 New York
4 Virginia
5 Delaware
6 New Mexico
7 Louisiana
8 North Carolina
9 South Carolina
10 Alaska
11 Maryland
12 Florida
13 Connecticut
14 Arizona
15 Missouri
16 Wisconsin
17 Michigan
18 Oregon
19 Ohio
20 California
21 Kansas
22 Nevada
23 Wyoming
24 Mississippi
25 Colorado
26 Pennsylvania
27 Washington
28 Oklahoma
29 Idaho
30 Illinois
31 Arkansas
32 Hawaii
33 Utah
34 New Jersey
35 Tennessee
36 Indiana
37 Montana
38 South Dakota
39 Nebraska
40 Rhode Island
41 Kentucky
42 Massachusetts
43 Vermont
44 Minnesota
45 Alabama
46 Iowa
47 New Hampshire
48 Maine
49 North Dakota
50 West Virginia

Note: Numbers that appear to be identical are rounded and vary slightly in actual value. The rankings reflect the actual values before rounding. See the introduction for more details.

J-14 State Corrections Spending, FY 2000

State	Corrections spending $ (in millions)	Corrections spending per prisoner $	Rank per prisoner
Alabama	258	9,838	49
Alaska	165	39,540	7
Arizona	622	23,463	33
Arkansas	161	13,512	47
California	4,748	29,129	21
Colorado	382	22,694	34
Connecticut	471	25,661	28
Delaware	169	24,418	32
Florida	1,554	21,789	36
Georgia	1,091	24,665	30
Hawaii	132	26,123	25
Idaho	110	19,906	38
Illinois	1,113	24,580	31
Indiana	522	25,938	27
Iowa	238	29,918	18
Kansas	263	31,520	17
Kentucky	338	22,656	35
Louisiana	517	14,752	45
Maine	84	50,030	3
Maryland	696	29,569	20
Massachusetts	723	67,431	1
Michigan	1,596	33,446	15
Minnesota	342	54,825	2
Mississippi	245	12,104	48
Missouri	423	15,481	44
Montana	90	28,986	22
Nebraska	144	36,970	9
Nevada	147	14,682	46
New Hampshire	57	25,255	29
New Jersey	1,010	33,911	13
New Mexico	154	28,828	23
New York	2,367	33,719	14
North Carolina	900	28,785	24
North Dakota	28	26,022	26
Ohio	1,512	32,989	16
Oklahoma	365	15,746	43
Oregon	484	45,532	4
Pennsylvania	1,323	35,905	11
Rhode Island	138	41,996	5
South Carolina	431	19,791	39
South Dakota	44	16,820	41
Tennessee	395	17,820	40
Texas	2,629	16,640	42
Utah	230	40,853	6
Vermont	67	39,481	8
Virginia	899	29,800	19
Washington	548	36,742	10
West Virginia	79	20,488	37
Wisconsin	710	34,446	12
Wyoming	n/a	n/a	n/a
50 States	31,714	25,804	
DC	n/a	n/a	
United States	31,714	25,649	

Rank in order per prisoner	
1	Massachusetts
2	Minnesota
3	Maine
4	Oregon
5	Rhode Island
6	Utah
7	Alaska
8	Vermont
9	Nebraska
10	Washington
11	Pennsylvania
12	Wisconsin
13	New Jersey
14	New York
15	Michigan
16	Ohio
17	Kansas
18	Iowa
19	Virginia
20	Maryland
21	California
22	Montana
23	New Mexico
24	North Carolina
25	Hawaii
26	North Dakota
27	Indiana
28	Connecticut
29	New Hampshire
30	Georgia
31	Illinois
32	Delaware
33	Arizona
34	Colorado
35	Kentucky
36	Florida
37	West Virginia
38	Idaho
39	South Carolina
40	Tennessee
41	South Dakota
42	Texas
43	Oklahoma
44	Missouri
45	Louisiana
46	Nevada
47	Arkansas
48	Mississippi
49	Alabama

J-15 Percentage Increase in State Corrections Spending, FY 1998-FY2000

State	Percentage increase in state corrections spending	Rank
Alabama	58.3	3
Alaska	6.5	46
Arizona	7.8	42
Arkansas	10.3	37
California	26.3	12
Colorado	172.9	1
Connecticut	20.2	17
Delaware	40.8	5
Florida	6.8	45
Georgia	56.1	4
Hawaii	17.9	25
Idaho	8.9	40
Illinois	20.3	15
Indiana	22.0	14
Iowa	20.2	16
Kansas	18.5	24
Kentucky	13.0	30
Louisiana	20.0	19
Maine	15.1	29
Maryland	7.6	43
Massachusetts	12.6	32
Michigan	22.2	13
Minnesota	7.9	41
Mississippi	27.6	9
Missouri	-18.7	49
Montana	20.0	18
Nebraska	67.4	2
Nevada	-5.8	48
New Hampshire	18.8	22
New Jersey	10.7	35
New Mexico	9.2	38
New York	0.8	47
North Carolina	9.1	39
North Dakota	33.3	7
Ohio	16.9	26
Oklahoma	29.9	8
Oregon	16.3	27
Pennsylvania	15.1	28
Rhode Island	10.4	36
South Carolina	12.8	31
South Dakota	7.3	44
Tennessee	11.0	34
Texas	19.4	21
Utah	19.8	20
Vermont	34.0	6
Virginia	18.6	23
Washington	12.1	33
West Virginia	27.4	11
Wisconsin	27.5	10
Wyoming	n/a	n/a
50 States	17.4	
DC	n/a	
United States	17.4	

Rank in order by percentage

1 Colorado
2 Nebraska
3 Alabama
4 Georgia
5 Delaware
6 Vermont
7 North Dakota
8 Oklahoma
9 Mississippi
10 Wisconsin
11 West Virginia
12 California
13 Michigan
14 Indiana
15 Illinois
16 Iowa
17 Connecticut
18 Montana
19 Louisiana
20 Utah
21 Texas
22 New Hampshire
23 Virginia
24 Kansas
25 Hawaii
26 Ohio
27 Oregon
28 Pennsylvania
29 Maine
30 Kentucky
31 South Carolina
32 Massachusetts
33 Washington
34 Tennessee
35 New Jersey
36 Rhode Island
37 Arkansas
38 New Mexico
39 North Carolina
40 Idaho
41 Minnesota
42 Arizona
43 Maryland
44 South Dakota
45 Florida
46 Alaska
47 New York
48 Nevada
49 Missouri

Note: Numbers that appear to be identical are rounded and vary slightly in actual value. The rankings reflect the actual values before rounding. See the introduction for more details.

J-16 State and Local Spending for Law Enforcement, FY 1999

State	Law enforcement spending $ (in millions)	Law enforcement spending per capita $	Rank per capita
Alabama	1,054	241	40
Alaska	332	536	2
Arizona	1,885	395	9
Arkansas	618	242	39
California	14,661	442	6
Colorado	1,565	386	11
Connecticut	1,183	360	15
Delaware	354	469	4
Florida	6,699	443	5
Georgia	2,470	317	28
Hawaii	355	300	30
Idaho	399	319	27
Illinois	4,318	356	17
Indiana	1,418	239	41
Iowa	679	237	43
Kansas	743	280	33
Kentucky	944	238	42
Louisiana	1,495	342	21
Maine	263	210	47
Maryland	1,924	372	13
Massachusetts	2,197	356	18
Michigan	3,538	359	16
Minnesota	1,370	287	32
Mississippi	679	245	38
Missouri	1,501	275	34
Montana	242	274	35
Nebraska	393	236	45
Nevada	869	480	3
New Hampshire	283	236	44
New Jersey	3,398	417	7
New Mexico	646	372	14
New York	9,803	539	1
North Carolina	2,357	308	29
North Dakota	114	179	48
Ohio	3,731	331	25
Oklahoma	859	256	37
Oregon	1,331	401	8
Pennsylvania	4,235	353	19
Rhode Island	328	331	24
South Carolina	1,152	296	31
South Dakota	165	225	46
Tennessee	1,440	263	36
Texas	6,831	341	22
Utah	714	335	23
Vermont	101	171	50
Virginia	2,268	330	26
Washington	1,971	342	20
West Virginia	312	172	49
Wisconsin	1,981	377	12
Wyoming	189	393	10
50 States	98,359	361	
DC	606	1,168	
United States	98,965	363	

Rank in order per capita	
1	New York
2	Alaska
3	Nevada
4	Delaware
5	Florida
6	California
7	New Jersey
8	Oregon
9	Arizona
10	Wyoming
11	Colorado
12	Wisconsin
13	Maryland
14	New Mexico
15	Connecticut
16	Michigan
17	Illinois
18	Massachusetts
19	Pennsylvania
20	Washington
21	Louisiana
22	Texas
23	Utah
24	Rhode Island
25	Ohio
26	Virginia
27	Idaho
28	Georgia
29	North Carolina
30	Hawaii
31	South Carolina
32	Minnesota
33	Kansas
34	Missouri
35	Montana
36	Tennessee
37	Oklahoma
38	Mississippi
39	Arkansas
40	Alabama
41	Indiana
42	Kentucky
43	Iowa
44	New Hampshire
45	Nebraska
46	South Dakota
47	Maine
48	North Dakota
49	West Virginia
50	Vermont

Note: Numbers that appear to be identical are rounded and vary slightly in actual value. The rankings reflect the actual values before rounding. See the introduction for more details.

J-17 State and Local Law Enforcement Spending as a Percentage of General Spending, FY 1999

State	Law enforcement spending as a percentage of general spending	Rank
Alabama	5.24	39
Alaska	4.66	45
Arizona	9.29	3
Arkansas	5.80	34
California	8.11	4
Colorado	7.80	7
Connecticut	6.01	31
Delaware	7.89	5
Florida	9.35	1
Georgia	6.89	20
Hawaii	5.16	41
Idaho	7.11	13
Illinois	7.23	12
Indiana	5.32	36
Iowa	4.62	46
Kansas	6.16	29
Kentucky	5.23	40
Louisiana	7.08	14
Maine	4.12	47
Maryland	7.73	8
Massachusetts	6.28	27
Michigan	7.00	18
Minnesota	4.86	44
Mississippi	5.24	38
Missouri	6.29	26
Montana	5.64	35
Nebraska	5.09	42
Nevada	9.35	2
New Hampshire	5.32	37
New Jersey	7.66	9
New Mexico	6.83	22
New York	7.33	10
North Carolina	6.41	23
North Dakota	3.26	50
Ohio	7.02	17
Oklahoma	6.34	24
Oregon	7.27	11
Pennsylvania	6.92	19
Rhode Island	6.22	28
South Carolina	6.32	25
South Dakota	5.09	43
Tennessee	5.96	33
Texas	7.82	6
Utah	6.84	21
Vermont	3.35	49
Virginia	7.02	16
Washington	6.10	30
West Virginia	3.79	48
Wisconsin	7.06	15
Wyoming	5.98	32
50 States	7.06	
DC	13.09	
United States	7.08	

Rank in order by percentage	
1	Florida
2	Nevada
3	Arizona
4	California
5	Delaware
6	Texas
7	Colorado
8	Maryland
9	New Jersey
10	New York
11	Oregon
12	Illinois
13	Idaho
14	Louisiana
15	Wisconsin
16	Virginia
17	Ohio
18	Michigan
19	Pennsylvania
20	Georgia
21	Utah
22	New Mexico
23	North Carolina
24	Oklahoma
25	South Carolina
26	Missouri
27	Massachusetts
28	Rhode Island
29	Kansas
30	Washington
31	Connecticut
32	Wyoming
33	Tennessee
34	Arkansas
35	Montana
36	Indiana
37	New Hampshire
38	Mississippi
39	Alabama
40	Kentucky
41	Hawaii
42	Nebraska
43	South Dakota
44	Minnesota
45	Alaska
46	Iowa
47	Maine
48	West Virginia
49	Vermont
50	North Dakota

Note: Numbers that appear to be identical are rounded and vary slightly in actual value. The rankings reflect the actual values before rounding. See the introduction for more details.

266   Crime and Law Enforcement

Source Notes for Crime and Law Enforcement (Section J)

J-1 Total Crime Rate, 2000: This table reflects the total crime rate as defined by the uniform crime reporting system of the U.S. Department of Justice (Federal Bureau of Investigation). The reports are compiled by individual law enforcement agencies throughout the nation and summarized in the Justice Department publication *Crime in the United States, 2000.*

These statistics inherently cover only crime known to law enforcement agencies, so they are often cited as "crime reported to the police." Certain crimes, such as murder and thefts for which victims seek insurance reimbursement, are almost always reported to police. Victims often fail to report other categories of crime, ranging from rape to thefts of small items. To capture information on crimes actually committed, the Justice Department does a survey (known as the "victimization survey") of U.S. households. Because that survey is based on nationwide samples, data from it are not available on a state-by-state basis.

The FBI has worked for years to make the statistics reported from different states and cities more comparable. However, some significant differences remain. Some reflect differences among states in their criminal laws and crime reporting systems. Some reflect inherent differences among citizens in reporting crime that are in turn related to differences in perceptions of whether law enforcement authorities will be able to solve the crimes. Small thefts, for example, are often not reported in large cities but are commonly reported in some smaller communities.

J-2 Violent Crime Rate, 2000: Crimes fall into two major classes. Some, such as murder and assault, involve violence or the threat of violence. Others, such as auto theft and burglary, do not. This table, from the same source as Table J-1, shows the rates for all violent crimes combined. West Virginia's large jump is likely explained, in part, by reporting changes.

J-3 Murder and Rape Rates, 2000: This table, from the same source as Table J-1, shows the rates for two specific crimes.

J-4 Property Crime Rate, 2000: This table, from the same source as Table J-1, shows the rates for crimes against property, such as burglary and auto theft.

J-5 Motor Vehicle Theft Rate, 2000: This table combines auto theft with theft of other vehicles, such as pickup trucks, using the same source as Table J-1.

J-6 Violent Crime Rate Change, 1995-2000: In the five-year period from 1995 to 2000 there was a nationwide decrease in the crime rate (crimes per one hundred thousand people) of 26.1 percent. The data come from the 1995 and 2000 editions of the Justice Department's *Crime in the United States.*

Because of a change in reporting procedures, rates before 1997 in New Hampshire are not comparable to current rates.

J-7 Prisoners, 2000: This table shows the total number of prisoners held in state penal institutions at the end of 2000. These data are developed by the Department of Justice from statistical reports of state and federal corrections agencies. The data shown come from the Department's website (www.ojp.usdoj.gov). They reflect state prisoners only. Federal prisoners constitute about 10 percent of all prisoners. The count of total state prisoners covers only those sentenced for more than a year and thus excludes persons who are being held for short periods in local jails.

J-8 Change in Prisoners, 1990-2000: This table, from the same source as Table J-7, shows the percentage change in the number of prisoners, reflecting an increase of 71.7 percent over this ten-year period. Wisconsin, shown as not having data available, did know how many prisoners they had, but the Department of Justice concluded that changes in methods of counting between 1990 and 1999 made comparisons inappropriate.

J-9 Incarceration Rate, 2000: This table measures the relationship between state prison populations (see Table J-7) and total population. While the national rate is equivalent to having 0.4 percent of the population in prison, the percentages are much higher for certain age and ethnic groups and for males.

J-10 Juvenile Violent Crime Index, 1999: This table is from *Juvenile Arrests 1999*, a publication of the Office of Juvenile Justice and Delinquency Prevention of the U.S. Department of Justice available on the internet (www.ncjrs.org). It reflects the number of violent crime arrests during 1999 of youths between the ages of ten and seventeen per one hundred thousand youths in the population of each state.

J-11 Proportion of Sentence Served, 1997: Because of parole and time off for good behavior, violent offenders typically serve only about half of the time they are sentenced to serve. These statistics, not available for all states, show the proportion of time served based on data reported in the January 1999 Department of Justice publication *Truth in Sentencing in State Prisons*. The United States total reflects only the states participating in the survey. The states with high percentages are not necessarily the toughest on criminals. They may have shorter sentences but force prisoners to serve a longer percentage of their sentences.

J-12 State and Local Law Enforcement Employees, 2000: These statistics come from a Census Bureau survey of state and local government employment, *Public Employment in 2000.*

The survey is available only on the Census Bureau website (www.census.gov).

J-13 State and Local Corrections Employees, 2000: This statistic comes from the same source as Table J-12.

J-14 State Corrections Spending, FY 2000: These data provide one way to look at the costs of maintaining prison systems in each state. The total spending shown is the general fund spending reported by state budget offices in the National Association of State Budget Officers' *2000 State Expenditure Report*. These general fund data showing about $31.7 billion for the fifty states exclude about $4.4 billion financed outside state general funds, primarily by bond funds used to finance prison construction. The per-inmate spending is the result of dividing the spending in fiscal 2000 by the number of inmates in prison at the end of 2000.

The resulting calculation is somewhat arbitrary as it does not separately account for the supervision of inmates on parole, which is another major function of corrections agencies not associated directly with inmates in prison.

J-15 Percentage Increase in State Corrections Spending, FY 1998-FY 2000: These data, from the same source as Table J-14, reflect the major impact that growing prison populations are having on state government budgets. Large deviations from one year to the next are often associated with large one-time expenditures for capital outlays in one of the years being compared. *State Fact Finder* has accounted for this by comparing spending over a two-year interval. Presumably, the large increase in Colorado is the result of new reporting measures.

J-16 State and Local Spending for Law Enforcement, FY 1999: This table relates spending on police and corrections to population in each state. The data come from the Census Bureau's electronic publication "State and Local Government Finance Estimates, by State," available on the Census website (www.census.gov). Population numbers, also from the census, are as of July 1, 1999, and personal income numbers are from the Department of Commerce. Based on census historical practices, *State Fact Finder* used calendar year 1998 numbers. See notes to Table F-1 for more extensive information on the source of the data.

J-17 State and Local Law Enforcement Spending as a Percentage of General Spending, FY 1999: This table shows the relative importance of law enforcement outlays in state and local budgets. It is derived by comparing this spending (see Table J-16) with total "general" spending. General spending includes essentially all other spending except municipal electric and other utilities and trust funds, such as those for workers' compensation.

Transportation

Though suburban growth continues to put pressure on new highway development, America's highways, for the most part, have been built. The era of construction has been replaced by an era of maintenance and operations. Today's question is how to get the best out of current roadways. Congestion relief is a top concern, as is increasing mobility through technology.

"Context-sensitive design"—making urban freeways more friendly to urban life—has seen activity in some states. Cincinnati's Fort Washington Way freeway, once a canyon separating downtown and the riverfront, is an example. Reconstruction of the highway narrowed its so-called "footprint" and reconnected the city grid, so that streets that once dead-ended into the freeway are now connected by bridges. Similar projects are under review in Milwaukee, San Francisco, and Philadelphia.

While safety is always a top concern of transportation officials, September 11th has shifted that concern to include terrorism. Federal actions have mostly impacted air transportation, but also include tighter restrictions on the movement of hazardous materials on the nation's roads. State transportation departments have been reassessing risks and reexamining preparedness.

In other safety news: while many states are reviewing the potential hazards of cell phone use while driving, New York is still the only state to issue a ban. In late 2001, New Jersey, not without controversy, instituted the most restrictive child passenger safety law. Children under the age of 8 and weighing less than 80 pounds must be in a car seat or booster seat.

On the funding front, more than halfway through the Transportation Equity Act of the 21st Century (TEA-21), debates over the next TEA-21 are starting to shape up. For at least a short term, TEA-21, and the general prosperity of the late 1990s, loosened the squeeze on federal money that had spawned a broad array of innovative financing mechanisms such as GARVEE (Grant Anticipation Revenue Vehicles) bonds and state infrastructure banks. The nation's economic outlook—and attendant fuel tax receipts—will play a large role in shaping the next federal authorization bill.

K-1 Travel on Interstate Highways, 2000

State	Annual interstate vehicle-miles (in millions)	Percentage of travel on interstates	Rank by percentage
Alabama	11,989	21.2	39
Alaska	1,394	30.2	5
Arizona	12,682	25.5	21
Arkansas	7,347	25.2	23
California	78,900	25.7	20
Colorado	9,706	23.2	27
Connecticut	9,985	32.5	3
Delaware	1,393	16.9	50
Florida	30,253	19.9	44
Georgia	27,544	26.2	16
Hawaii	1,766	20.7	41
Idaho	3,141	23.2	28
Illinois	29,088	28.3	10
Indiana	15,612	22.0	36
Iowa	6,626	22.5	33
Kansas	6,509	23.1	29
Kentucky	12,045	25.7	19
Louisiana	10,375	25.4	22
Maine	2,885	20.3	43
Maryland	15,208	30.3	4
Massachusetts	15,557	29.5	6
Michigan	21,682	22.2	35
Minnesota	11,906	22.6	32
Mississippi	6,370	17.9	48
Missouri	18,693	27.9	13
Montana	2,442	24.7	24
Nebraska	3,721	20.6	42
Nevada	4,147	23.5	26
New Hampshire	2,726	22.7	31
New Jersey	12,594	18.7	47
New Mexico	6,439	28.3	9
New York	24,672	19.1	46
North Carolina	17,647	19.7	45
North Dakota	1,536	21.3	38
Ohio	30,019	28.3	8
Oklahoma	8,969	20.7	40
Oregon	8,423	24.1	25
Pennsylvania	22,509	22.0	37
Rhode Island	2,174	26.0	18
South Carolina	11,938	26.2	17
South Dakota	2,292	27.2	14
Tennessee	18,445	28.1	11
Texas	49,012	22.3	34
Utah	7,627	33.8	1
Vermont	1,559	22.9	30
Virginia	21,524	28.8	7
Washington	14,889	27.9	12
West Virginia	5,165	26.8	15
Wisconsin	10,256	17.9	49
Wyoming	2,696	33.3	2
50 States	662,077	24.1	
DC	463	13.2	
United States	662,540	24.1	

Rank in order by percentage	
1	Utah
2	Wyoming
3	Connecticut
4	Maryland
5	Alaska
6	Massachusetts
7	Virginia
8	Ohio
9	New Mexico
10	Illinois
11	Tennessee
12	Washington
13	Missouri
14	South Dakota
15	West Virginia
16	Georgia
17	South Carolina
18	Rhode Island
19	Kentucky
20	California
21	Arizona
22	Louisiana
23	Arkansas
24	Montana
25	Oregon
26	Nevada
27	Colorado
28	Idaho
29	Kansas
30	Vermont
31	New Hampshire
32	Minnesota
33	Iowa
34	Texas
35	Michigan
36	Indiana
37	Pennsylvania
38	North Dakota
39	Alabama
40	Oklahoma
41	Hawaii
42	Nebraska
43	Maine
44	Florida
45	North Carolina
46	New York
47	New Jersey
48	Mississippi
49	Wisconsin
50	Delaware

Note: Numbers that appear to be identical are rounded and vary slightly in actual value. The rankings reflect the actual values before rounding. See the introduction for more details.

K-2 Percentage of Interstate Mileage in "Unacceptable" Condition, 2000

State	Percentage of interstate mileage in "unacceptable" condition	Rank
Alabama	1.1	28
Alaska	0.1	39
Arizona	0.1	39
Arkansas	26.3	2
California	13.6	3
Colorado	0.0	43
Connecticut	5.8	10
Delaware	28.2	1
Florida	0.8	32
Georgia	0.0	43
Hawaii	n/a	n/a
Idaho	2.3	18
Illinois	2.3	18
Indiana	0.5	36
Iowa	2.0	22
Kansas	0.2	38
Kentucky	1.6	24
Louisiana	9.3	5
Maine	0.3	37
Maryland	3.9	15
Massachusetts	1.1	28
Michigan	7.8	6
Minnesota	0.0	43
Mississippi	4.7	13
Missouri	4.1	14
Montana	1.1	28
Nebraska	7.7	7
Nevada	1.6	24
New Hampshire	0.0	43
New Jersey	6.6	9
New Mexico	3.7	16
New York	12.0	4
North Carolina	5.5	11
North Dakota	0.0	43
Ohio	0.6	34
Oklahoma	7.1	8
Oregon	0.0	43
Pennsylvania	2.3	18
Rhode Island	1.5	26
South Carolina	0.1	39
South Dakota	3.2	17
Tennessee	0.6	34
Texas	0.8	32
Utah	2.0	22
Vermont	2.2	21
Virginia	0.9	31
Washington	1.4	27
West Virginia	5.3	12
Wisconsin	0.0	43
Wyoming	0.1	39
50 States	3.4	
DC	53.8	
United States	3.4	

Rank in order by percentage

1 Delaware
2 Arkansas
3 California
4 New York
5 Louisiana
6 Michigan
7 Nebraska
8 Oklahoma
9 New Jersey
10 Connecticut
11 North Carolina
12 West Virginia
13 Mississippi
14 Missouri
15 Maryland
16 New Mexico
17 South Dakota
18 Idaho
18 Illinois
18 Pennsylvania
21 Vermont
22 Iowa
22 Utah
24 Nevada
24 Kentucky
26 Rhode Island
27 Washington
28 Alabama
28 Montana
28 Massachusetts
31 Virginia
32 Florida
32 Texas
34 Ohio
34 Tennessee
36 Indiana
37 Maine
38 Kansas
39 South Carolina
39 Wyoming
39 Alaska
39 Arizona
43 Colorado
43 Georgia
43 Minnesota
43 New Hampshire
43 North Dakota
43 Oregon
43 Wisconsin

Note: Ties in ranking reflect ties in actual values.

K-3 Deficient Bridges, 2001

State	Total deficient bridges #	Percentage of bridges deficient	Rank by percentage
Alabama	4,922	31.5	15
Alaska	412	28.8	23
Arizona	735	10.6	50
Arkansas	3,475	27.9	26
California	6,840	28.8	22
Colorado	1,443	17.9	46
Connecticut	1,305	31.3	16
Delaware	129	15.6	47
Florida	2,114	18.7	43
Georgia	3,502	24.3	33
Hawaii	537	50.1	2
Idaho	756	18.6	44
Illinois	4,824	18.9	42
Indiana	4,418	24.5	32
Iowa	7,096	28.3	24
Kansas	6,424	25.1	31
Kentucky	4,053	30.2	18
Louisiana	4,591	34.2	12
Maine	866	36.6	10
Maryland	1,446	29.2	20
Massachusetts	2,488	49.9	3
Michigan	3,366	31.7	14
Minnesota	1,784	13.9	49
Mississippi	5,002	29.7	19
Missouri	8,830	37.4	8
Montana	1,130	22.6	38
Nebraska	4,337	28.0	25
Nevada	221	14.6	48
New Hampshire	802	34.1	13
New Jersey	2,350	36.9	9
New Mexico	703	18.5	45
New York	6,588	37.9	7
North Carolina	5,307	31.2	17
North Dakota	1,137	25.2	30
Ohio	7,166	25.6	29
Oklahoma	9,123	40.2	5
Oregon	1,653	22.6	37
Pennsylvania	9,440	42.7	4
Rhode Island	379	50.6	1
South Carolina	2,056	22.7	36
South Dakota	1,744	29.1	21
Tennessee	4,701	24.3	34
Texas	10,555	22.0	39
Utah	634	23.1	35
Vermont	955	35.2	11
Virginia	3,465	27.1	27
Washington	2,142	27.0	28
West Virginia	2,667	39.4	6
Wisconsin	2,657	19.7	41
Wyoming	642	20.9	40
50 States	163,912	27.9	
DC	161	66.3	
United States*	165,099	28.0	

Rank in order by percentage

1 Rhode Island
2 Hawaii
3 Massachusetts
4 Pennsylvania
5 Oklahoma
6 West Virginia
7 New York
8 Missouri
9 New Jersey
10 Maine
11 Vermont
12 Louisiana
13 New Hampshire
14 Michigan
15 Alabama
16 Connecticut
17 North Carolina
18 Kentucky
19 Mississippi
20 Maryland
21 South Dakota
22 California
23 Alaska
24 Iowa
25 Nebraska
26 Arkansas
27 Virginia
28 Washington
29 Ohio
30 North Dakota
31 Kansas
32 Indiana
33 Georgia
34 Tennessee
35 Utah
36 South Carolina
37 Oregon
38 Montana
39 Texas
40 Wyoming
41 Wisconsin
42 Illinois
43 Florida
44 Idaho
45 New Mexico
46 Colorado
47 Delaware
48 Nevada
49 Minnesota
50 Arizona

Note: Numbers that appear to be identical are rounded and vary slightly in actual value. The rankings reflect the actual values before rounding. See the introduction for more details.

Due to rounding or data sources, the 50-state total plus D.C. may not equal the U.S. total. Please see introduction.

K-4 Traffic Deaths Per 100 Million Vehicle-miles, 2000

State	Traffic deaths per 100 million vehicle-miles	Rank
Alabama	1.76	16
Alaska	2.23	6
Arizona	2.08	8
Arkansas	2.24	5
California	1.22	38
Colorado	1.63	23
Connecticut	1.11	46
Delaware	1.49	28
Florida	1.97	12
Georgia	1.47	30
Hawaii	1.53	24
Idaho	2.04	10
Illinois	1.38	33
Indiana	1.23	37
Iowa	1.51	26
Kansas	1.64	22
Kentucky	1.75	17
Louisiana	2.29	4
Maine	1.19	40
Maryland	1.17	43
Massachusetts	0.82	50
Michigan	1.41	31
Minnesota	1.19	41
Mississippi	2.67	1
Missouri	1.72	18
Montana	2.40	2
Nebraska	1.53	25
Nevada	1.83	15
New Hampshire	1.05	48
New Jersey	1.08	47
New Mexico	1.89	13
New York	1.13	45
North Carolina	1.64	21
North Dakota	1.19	39
Ohio	1.28	35
Oklahoma	1.50	27
Oregon	1.29	34
Pennsylvania	1.49	29
Rhode Island	0.96	49
South Carolina	2.34	3
South Dakota	2.05	9
Tennessee	1.99	11
Texas	1.71	19
Utah	1.65	20
Vermont	1.16	44
Virginia	1.24	36
Washington	1.19	42
West Virginia	2.13	7
Wisconsin	1.40	32
Wyoming	1.88	14
50 States	1.52	
DC	1.40	
United States	1.52	

Rank in order by rate

1	Mississippi
2	Montana
3	South Carolina
4	Louisiana
5	Arkansas
6	Alaska
7	West Virginia
8	Arizona
9	South Dakota
10	Idaho
11	Tennessee
12	Florida
13	New Mexico
14	Wyoming
15	Nevada
16	Alabama
17	Kentucky
18	Missouri
19	Texas
20	Utah
21	North Carolina
22	Kansas
23	Colorado
24	Hawaii
25	Nebraska
26	Iowa
27	Oklahoma
28	Delaware
29	Pennsylvania
30	Georgia
31	Michigan
32	Wisconsin
33	Illinois
34	Oregon
35	Ohio
36	Virginia
37	Indiana
38	California
39	North Dakota
40	Maine
41	Minnesota
42	Washington
43	Maryland
44	Vermont
45	New York
46	Connecticut
47	New Jersey
48	New Hampshire
49	Rhode Island
50	Massachusetts

Note: Numbers that appear to be identical are rounded and vary slightly in actual value. The rankings reflect the actual values before rounding. See the introduction for more details.

K-5 Percentage of Drivers Using Seat Belts, 2000

State	Percentage of drivers using seat belts	Rank
Alabama	70.6	22
Alaska	61.0	39
Arizona	75.2	16
Arkansas	52.4	44
California	88.9	1
Colorado	65.1	33
Connecticut	76.3	13
Delaware	66.1	30
Florida	64.8	34
Georgia	73.6	19
Hawaii	80.4	8
Idaho	58.6	42
Illinois	70.2	24
Indiana	62.1	36
Iowa	78.0	10
Kansas	61.6	37
Kentucky	60.0	40
Louisiana	68.2	26
Maine	n/a	n/a
Maryland	85.0	3
Massachusetts	50.0	46
Michigan	83.5	5
Minnesota	73.4	20
Mississippi	50.4	45
Missouri	67.7	27
Montana	75.6	15
Nebraska	70.5	23
Nevada	78.5	9
New Hampshire	n/a	n/a
New Jersey	74.2	17
New Mexico	86.6	2
New York	77.3	11
North Carolina	80.5	7
North Dakota	47.7	48
Ohio	65.3	32
Oklahoma	67.5	28
Oregon	83.6	4
Pennsylvania	70.7	21
Rhode Island	64.4	35
South Carolina	73.9	18
South Dakota	53.4	43
Tennessee	59.0	41
Texas	76.6	12
Utah	75.7	14
Vermont	61.6	37
Virginia	69.9	25
Washington	81.6	6
West Virginia	49.5	47
Wisconsin	65.4	31
Wyoming	66.8	29
50 States	n/a	
DC	82.6	
United States	73.0	

Rank in order by percentage	
1	California
2	New Mexico
3	Maryland
4	Oregon
5	Michigan
6	Washington
7	North Carolina
8	Hawaii
9	Nevada
10	Iowa
11	New York
12	Texas
13	Connecticut
14	Utah
15	Montana
16	Arizona
17	New Jersey
18	South Carolina
19	Georgia
20	Minnesota
21	Pennsylvania
22	Alabama
23	Nebraska
24	Illinois
25	Virginia
26	Louisiana
27	Missouri
28	Oklahoma
29	Wyoming
30	Delaware
31	Wisconsin
32	Ohio
33	Colorado
34	Florida
35	Rhode Island
36	Indiana
37	Kansas
37	Vermont
39	Alaska
40	Kentucky
41	Tennessee
42	Idaho
43	South Dakota
44	Arkansas
45	Mississippi
46	Massachusetts
47	West Virginia
48	North Dakota

Note: Ties in ranking reflect ties in actual values.

K-6 Vehicle-miles Traveled Per Capita, 2000

State	Vehicle-miles traveled (in millions)	Vehicle-miles traveled per capita	Rank per capita
Alabama	56,534	12,713	3
Alaska	4,613	7,358	48
Arizona	49,768	9,700	34
Arkansas	29,167	10,910	18
California	306,649	9,053	39
Colorado	41,771	9,711	33
Connecticut	30,756	9,031	41
Delaware	8,240	10,516	25
Florida	152,136	9,519	35
Georgia	105,010	12,827	2
Hawaii	8,543	7,051	49
Idaho	13,534	10,459	27
Illinois	102,866	8,283	45
Indiana	70,862	11,654	8
Iowa	29,433	10,058	30
Kansas	28,130	10,463	26
Kentucky	46,803	11,580	9
Louisiana	40,849	9,141	38
Maine	14,190	11,130	15
Maryland	50,174	9,473	36
Massachusetts	52,796	8,316	44
Michigan	97,792	9,840	31
Minnesota	52601	10,692	19
Mississippi	35,536	12,492	6
Missouri	67,083	11,989	7
Montana	9,882	10,953	17
Nebraska	18,081	10,566	23
Nevada	17,639	8,827	42
New Hampshire	12,021	9,727	32
New Jersey	67,446	8,016	46
New Mexico	22,760	12,512	5
New York	129,057	6,801	50
North Carolina	89,504	11,119	16
North Dakota	7,217	11,238	12
Ohio	105,898	9,328	37
Oklahoma	43,355	12,564	4
Oregon	35,010	10,233	28
Pennsylvania	102,337	8,333	43
Rhode Island	8,359	7,974	47
South Carolina	45,538	11,350	11
South Dakota	8,432	11,171	14
Tennessee	65,732	11,554	10
Texas	220,064	10,554	24
Utah	22,597	10,119	29
Vermont	6,811	11,187	13
Virginia	74,801	10,567	22
Washington	53,330	9,048	40
West Virginia	19,242	10,641	21
Wisconsin	57,266	10,677	20
Wyoming	8,090	16,384	1
50 States	2,746,305	9,779	
DC	3,498	6,115	
United States	2,749,803	9,771	

Rank in order per capita

1 Wyoming
2 Georgia
3 Alabama
4 Oklahoma
5 New Mexico
6 Mississippi
7 Missouri
8 Indiana
9 Kentucky
10 Tennessee
11 South Carolina
12 North Dakota
13 Vermont
14 South Dakota
15 Maine
16 North Carolina
17 Montana
18 Arkansas
19 Minnesota
20 Wisconsin
21 West Virginia
22 Virginia
23 Nebraska
24 Texas
25 Delaware
26 Kansas
27 Idaho
28 Oregon
29 Utah
30 Iowa
31 Michigan
32 New Hampshire
33 Colorado
34 Arizona
35 Florida
36 Maryland
37 Ohio
38 Louisiana
39 California
40 Washington
41 Connecticut
42 Nevada
43 Pennsylvania
44 Massachusetts
45 Illinois
46 New Jersey
47 Rhode Island
48 Alaska
49 Hawaii
50 New York

K-7 Percentage of Workers Using Public Transportation, 2000

State	Percentage of workers using public transportation	Rank
Alabama	0.4	48
Alaska	2.8	17
Arizona	2.2	22
Arkansas	0.4	49
California	5.4	8
Colorado	3.4	14
Connecticut	4.4	10
Delaware	3.0	16
Florida	2.1	23
Georgia	2.7	18
Hawaii	6.5	6
Idaho	1.2	29
Illinois	9.3	4
Indiana	1.1	33
Iowa	0.8	40
Kansas	0.4	50
Kentucky	1.4	27
Louisiana	2.6	19
Maine	0.8	39
Maryland	8.4	5
Massachusetts	10.0	3
Michigan	1.1	32
Minnesota	3.2	15
Mississippi	0.6	42
Missouri	1.2	28
Montana	0.4	47
Nebraska	1.0	35
Nevada	3.8	13
New Hampshire	0.6	43
New Jersey	11.4	2
New Mexico	1.2	30
New York	26.9	1
North Carolina	0.7	41
North Dakota	0.5	45
Ohio	2.4	21
Oklahoma	0.5	44
Oregon	3.8	12
Pennsylvania	5.8	7
Rhode Island	2.1	24
South Carolina	1.0	34
South Dakota	0.4	46
Tennessee	0.9	36
Texas	1.9	25
Utah	2.4	20
Vermont	0.8	38
Virginia	4.2	11
Washington	5.0	9
West Virginia	0.9	37
Wisconsin	1.7	26
Wyoming	1.1	31
50 States	5.1	
DC	34.7	
United States	5.2	

Rank in order by percentage	
1	New York
2	New Jersey
3	Massachusetts
4	Illinois
5	Maryland
6	Hawaii
7	Pennsylvania
8	California
9	Washington
10	Connecticut
11	Virginia
12	Oregon
13	Nevada
14	Colorado
15	Minnesota
16	Delaware
17	Alaska
18	Georgia
19	Louisiana
20	Utah
21	Ohio
22	Arizona
23	Florida
24	Rhode Island
25	Texas
26	Wisconsin
27	Kentucky
28	Missouri
29	Idaho
30	New Mexico
31	Wyoming
32	Michigan
33	Indiana
34	South Carolina
35	Nebraska
36	Tennessee
37	West Virginia
38	Vermont
39	Maine
40	Iowa
41	North Carolina
42	Mississippi
43	New Hampshire
44	Oklahoma
45	North Dakota
46	South Dakota
47	Montana
48	Alabama
49	Arkansas
50	Kansas

Note: Numbers that appear to be identical are rounded and vary slightly in actual value. The rankings reflect the actual values before rounding. See the introduction for more details.

K-8 Road and Street Miles, 2000

State	Total road and street miles #	Total miles under state control #	Percentage under state control	Rank by percentage
Alabama	94,311	10,892	11.5	32
Alaska	12,823	5,509	43.0	6
Arizona	55,193	6,611	12.0	30
Arkansas	97,600	16,373	16.8	21
California	168,077	15,180	9.0	43
Colorado	85,411	9,086	10.6	37
Connecticut	20,845	3,718	17.8	19
Delaware	5,781	5,096	88.2	2
Florida	116,651	11,961	10.3	39
Georgia	114,726	17,837	15.5	24
Hawaii	4,279	944	22.1	15
Idaho	46,458	4,955	10.7	36
Illinois	138,371	16,298	11.8	31
Indiana	93,607	11,215	12.0	29
Iowa	113,376	10,243	9.0	42
Kansas	134,583	10,384	7.7	49
Kentucky	79,266	27,474	34.7	8
Louisiana	60,900	16,696	27.4	10
Maine	22,669	8,406	37.1	7
Maryland	30,497	5,130	16.8	20
Massachusetts	35,312	2,848	8.1	47
Michigan	121,980	9,713	8.0	48
Minnesota	132,251	11,928	9.0	44
Mississippi	73,500	10,653	14.5	25
Missouri	123,037	32,407	26.3	11
Montana	69,567	6,710	9.6	40
Nebraska	92,792	9,970	10.7	35
Nevada	37,855	5,457	14.4	26
New Hampshire	15,210	3,984	26.2	13
New Jersey	36,023	2,308	6.4	50
New Mexico	59,926	11,416	19.1	17
New York	112,783	15,026	13.3	28
North Carolina	99,814	78,267	78.4	4
North Dakota	86,611	7,378	8.5	46
Ohio	116,965	19,290	16.5	22
Oklahoma	112,634	12,270	10.9	34
Oregon	66,904	7,590	11.3	33
Pennsylvania	119,642	40,051	33.5	9
Rhode Island	6,053	1,169	19.3	16
South Carolina	64,920	41,529	64.0	5
South Dakota	83,471	7,793	9.3	41
Tennessee	87,418	13,790	15.8	23
Texas	301,034	79,261	26.3	12
Utah	41,855	5,835	13.9	27
Vermont	14,275	2,631	18.4	18
Virginia	70,391	57,853	82.2	3
Washington	80,209	7,046	8.8	45
West Virginia	37,276	33,930	91.0	1
Wisconsin	112,360	11,753	10.5	38
Wyoming	27,325	6,759	24.7	14
50 States	3,934,817	770,623	19.6	
DC	1,424	1,370	96.2	
United States	3,936,241	771,993	19.6	

Rank in order by percentage

1 West Virginia
2 Delaware
3 Virginia
4 North Carolina
5 South Carolina
6 Alaska
7 Maine
8 Kentucky
9 Pennsylvania
10 Louisiana
11 Missouri
12 Texas
13 New Hampshire
14 Wyoming
15 Hawaii
16 Rhode Island
17 New Mexico
18 Vermont
19 Connecticut
20 Maryland
21 Arkansas
22 Ohio
23 Tennessee
24 Georgia
25 Mississippi
26 Nevada
27 Utah
28 New York
29 Indiana
30 Arizona
31 Illinois
32 Alabama
33 Oregon
34 Oklahoma
35 Nebraska
36 Idaho
37 Colorado
38 Wisconsin
39 Florida
40 Montana
41 South Dakota
42 Iowa
43 California
44 Minnesota
45 Washington
46 North Dakota
47 Massachusetts
48 Michigan
49 Kansas
50 New Jersey

Note: Numbers that appear to be identical are rounded and vary slightly in actual value. The rankings reflect the actual values before rounding. See the introduction for more details.

K-9 State and Local Highway Employees, 2000

State	Highway employees #	Per 10,000 population	Rank per 10,000 population
Alabama	10,890	24.5	19
Alaska	3,494	55.7	1
Arizona	7,293	14.2	47
Arkansas	7,042	26.3	17
California	43,393	12.8	50
Colorado	8,258	19.2	35
Connecticut	7,793	22.9	23
Delaware	2,172	27.7	14
Florida	24,510	15.3	46
Georgia	13,794	16.8	41
Hawaii	1,721	14.2	48
Idaho	3,438	26.6	16
Illinois	21,040	16.9	40
Indiana	11,186	18.4	38
Iowa	8,518	29.1	13
Kansas	8,710	32.4	8
Kentucky	9,125	22.6	24
Louisiana	10,794	24.2	20
Maine	4,791	37.6	3
Maryland	9,805	18.5	37
Massachusetts	10,981	17.3	39
Michigan	13,215	13.3	49
Minnesota	12,519	25.4	18
Mississippi	8,617	30.3	11
Missouri	13,127	23.5	21
Montana	3,286	36.4	4
Nebraska	5,127	30.0	12
Nevada	3,227	16.1	43
New Hampshire	3,807	30.8	9
New Jersey	17,479	20.8	29
New Mexico	4,203	23.1	22
New York	38,909	20.5	31
North Carolina	16,109	20.0	32
North Dakota	1,976	30.8	10
Ohio	21,808	19.2	34
Oklahoma	9,348	27.1	15
Oregon	7,683	22.5	25
Pennsylvania	25,197	20.5	30
Rhode Island	1,671	15.9	44
South Carolina	7,575	18.9	36
South Dakota	2,559	33.9	6
Tennessee	11,153	19.6	33
Texas	35,034	16.8	42
Utah	3,430	15.4	45
Vermont	2,203	36.2	5
Virginia	15,042	21.3	27
Washington	12,986	22.0	26
West Virginia	5,970	33.0	7
Wisconsin	11,376	21.2	28
Wyoming	2,413	48.9	2
50 States	545,797	19.4	
DC	418	7.3	
United States	546,215	19.4	

Rank in order per 10,000 population

1 Alaska
2 Wyoming
3 Maine
4 Montana
5 Vermont
6 South Dakota
7 West Virginia
8 Kansas
9 New Hampshire
10 North Dakota
11 Mississippi
12 Nebraska
13 Iowa
14 Delaware
15 Oklahoma
16 Idaho
17 Arkansas
18 Minnesota
19 Alabama
20 Louisiana
21 Missouri
22 New Mexico
23 Connecticut
24 Kentucky
25 Oregon
26 Washington
27 Virginia
28 Wisconsin
29 New Jersey
30 Pennsylvania
31 New York
32 North Carolina
33 Tennessee
34 Ohio
35 Colorado
36 South Carolina
37 Maryland
38 Indiana
39 Massachusetts
40 Illinois
41 Georgia
42 Texas
43 Nevada
44 Rhode Island
45 Utah
46 Florida
47 Arizona
48 Hawaii
49 Michigan
50 California

Note: Numbers that appear to be identical are rounded and vary slightly in actual value. The rankings reflect the actual values before rounding. See the introduction for more details.

K-10 State and Local Public Transit Employees, 2000

State	Transit employees #	Per 10,000 population	Rank per 10,000 population
Alabama	209	0.5	46
Alaska	229	3.7	23
Arizona	128	0.2	49
Arkansas	242	0.9	38
California	29,237	8.6	8
Colorado	2,850	6.6	11
Connecticut	450	1.3	34
Delaware	554	7.1	9
Florida	6,452	4.0	21
Georgia	5,226	6.4	12
Hawaii	43	0.4	47
Idaho	33	0.3	48
Illinois	15,860	12.8	2
Indiana	1,526	2.5	26
Iowa	804	2.7	25
Kansas	234	0.9	39
Kentucky	959	2.4	28
Louisiana	1,389	3.1	24
Maine	101	0.8	40
Maryland	2,706	5.1	17
Massachusetts	6,053	9.5	6
Michigan	4,690	4.7	19
Minnesota	2,578	5.2	16
Mississippi	139	0.5	45
Missouri	2,943	5.3	15
Montana	167	1.9	31
Nebraska	407	2.4	27
Nevada	246	1.2	35
New Hampshire	90	0.7	41
New Jersey	10,420	12.4	3
New Mexico	681	3.7	22
New York	56,003	29.5	1
North Carolina	586	0.7	42
North Dakota	38	0.6	44
Ohio	6,453	5.7	14
Oklahoma	239	0.7	43
Oregon	3,035	8.9	7
Pennsylvania	13,115	10.7	5
Rhode Island	634	6.0	13
South Carolina	406	1.0	36
South Dakota	16	0.2	50
Tennessee	891	1.6	33
Texas	10,254	4.9	18
Utah	1,553	7.0	10
Vermont	126	2.1	30
Virginia	1,299	1.8	32
Washington	6,513	11.0	4
West Virginia	393	2.2	29
Wisconsin	2,331	4.3	20
Wyoming	49	1.0	37
50 States	201,580	7.2	
DC	8,864	154.9	
United States	210,444	7.5	

Rank in order per 10,000 population	
1	New York
2	Illinois
3	New Jersey
4	Washington
5	Pennsylvania
6	Massachusetts
7	Oregon
8	California
9	Delaware
10	Utah
11	Colorado
12	Georgia
13	Rhode Island
14	Ohio
15	Missouri
16	Minnesota
17	Maryland
18	Texas
19	Michigan
20	Wisconsin
21	Florida
22	New Mexico
23	Alaska
24	Louisiana
25	Iowa
26	Indiana
27	Nebraska
28	Kentucky
29	West Virginia
30	Vermont
31	Montana
32	Virginia
33	Tennessee
34	Connecticut
35	Nevada
36	South Carolina
37	Wyoming
38	Arkansas
39	Kansas
40	Maine
41	New Hampshire
42	North Carolina
43	Oklahoma
44	North Dakota
45	Mississippi
46	Alabama
47	Hawaii
48	Idaho
49	Arizona
50	South Dakota

Note: Numbers that appear to be identical are rounded and vary slightly in actual value. The rankings reflect the actual values before rounding. See the introduction for more details.

K-11 State and Local Spending for Highways, FY 1999

State	Highway spending $ (in millions)	Highway spending per capita $	Highway spending as a percentage of personal income	Rank by percentage
Alabama	1,248	286	1.30	47
Alaska	748	1,207	4.36	1
Arizona	1,738	364	1.54	27
Arkansas	860	337	1.59	33
California	7,383	223	0.80	50
Colorado	1,765	435	1.49	17
Connecticut	1,107	337	0.90	32
Delaware	388	515	1.76	10
Florida	5,055	335	1.26	34
Georgia	2,477	318	1.24	37
Hawaii	403	340	1.27	31
Idaho	525	419	1.94	18
Illinois	3,814	314	1.05	40
Indiana	1,827	307	1.23	43
Iowa	1,607	560	2.26	6
Kansas	1,339	505	1.98	11
Kentucky	1,581	399	1.80	22
Louisiana	1,548	354	1.59	29
Maine	512	409	1.75	21
Maryland	1,471	284	0.93	48
Massachusetts	2,720	440	1.33	16
Michigan	3,043	308	1.16	41
Minnesota	2,223	465	1.59	13
Mississippi	1,142	412	2.07	19
Missouri	1,923	352	1.39	30
Montana	481	545	2.57	7
Nebraska	802	481	1.87	12
Nevada	959	530	1.85	9
New Hampshire	458	381	1.30	25
New Jersey	2,391	294	0.86	45
New Mexico	1,132	651	3.08	4
New York	6,556	360	1.12	28
North Carolina	2,512	328	1.31	36
North Dakota	413	651	2.84	3
Ohio	3,555	316	1.21	38
Oklahoma	1,123	334	1.51	35
Oregon	1,240	374	1.46	26
Pennsylvania	3,782	315	1.15	39
Rhode Island	298	301	1.08	44
South Carolina	1,034	266	1.19	49
South Dakota	473	645	2.72	5
Tennessee	1,689	308	1.27	42
Texas	5,855	292	1.15	46
Utah	875	411	1.87	20
Vermont	316	532	2.16	8
Virginia	2,710	394	1.41	23
Washington	2,197	382	1.35	24
West Virginia	837	463	2.28	14
Wisconsin	2,387	455	1.74	15
Wyoming	397	827	3.32	2
50 States	92,917	341	1.26	
DC	101	195	0.51	
United States	93,018	341	1.26	

Rank in order by percentage

1 Alaska
2 Wyoming
3 North Dakota
4 New Mexico
5 South Dakota
6 Iowa
7 Montana
8 Vermont
9 Nevada
10 Delaware
11 Kansas
12 Nebraska
13 Minnesota
14 West Virginia
15 Wisconsin
16 Massachusetts
17 Colorado
18 Idaho
19 Mississippi
20 Utah
21 Maine
22 Kentucky
23 Virginia
24 Washington
25 New Hampshire
26 Oregon
27 Arizona
28 New York
29 Louisiana
30 Missouri
31 Hawaii
32 Connecticut
33 Arkansas
34 Florida
35 Oklahoma
36 North Carolina
37 Georgia
38 Ohio
39 Pennsylvania
40 Illinois
41 Michigan
42 Tennessee
43 Indiana
44 Rhode Island
45 New Jersey
46 Texas
47 Alabama
48 Maryland
49 South Carolina
50 California

Note: Numbers that appear to be identical are rounded and vary slightly in actual value. The rankings reflect the actual values before rounding. See the introduction for more details.

K-12 State and Local Highway Spending as a Percentage of General Spending, FY 1999

State	Highway spending as a percentage of general spending	Rank
Alabama	6.21	40
Alaska	10.49	8
Arizona	8.56	19
Arkansas	8.06	24
California	4.08	50
Colorado	8.79	15
Connecticut	5.62	47
Delaware	8.65	17
Florida	7.06	30
Georgia	6.91	32
Hawaii	5.85	44
Idaho	9.35	13
Illinois	6.39	39
Indiana	6.86	33
Iowa	10.94	7
Kansas	11.10	6
Kentucky	8.75	16
Louisiana	7.33	29
Maine	8.02	26
Maryland	5.91	43
Massachusetts	7.77	28
Michigan	6.02	42
Minnesota	7.89	27
Mississippi	8.83	14
Missouri	8.05	25
Montana	11.21	5
Nebraska	10.39	10
Nevada	10.32	11
New Hampshire	8.59	18
New Jersey	5.39	48
New Mexico	11.96	3
New York	4.90	49
North Carolina	6.83	34
North Dakota	11.84	4
Ohio	6.69	38
Oklahoma	8.28	23
Oregon	6.77	36
Pennsylvania	6.18	41
Rhode Island	5.65	46
South Carolina	5.67	45
South Dakota	14.56	1
Tennessee	6.99	31
Texas	6.70	37
Utah	8.38	22
Vermont	10.44	9
Virginia	8.39	21
Washington	6.79	35
West Virginia	10.18	12
Wisconsin	8.51	20
Wyoming	12.60	2
50 States	6.67	
DC	2.18	
United States	6.65	

Rank in order by percentage	
1	South Dakota
2	Wyoming
3	New Mexico
4	North Dakota
5	Montana
6	Kansas
7	Iowa
8	Alaska
9	Vermont
10	Nebraska
11	Nevada
12	West Virginia
13	Idaho
14	Mississippi
15	Colorado
16	Kentucky
17	Delaware
18	New Hampshire
19	Arizona
20	Wisconsin
21	Virginia
22	Utah
23	Oklahoma
24	Arkansas
25	Missouri
26	Maine
27	Minnesota
28	Massachusetts
29	Louisiana
30	Florida
31	Tennessee
32	Georgia
33	Indiana
34	North Carolina
35	Washington
36	Oregon
37	Texas
38	Ohio
39	Illinois
40	Alabama
41	Pennsylvania
42	Michigan
43	Maryland
44	Hawaii
45	South Carolina
46	Rhode Island
47	Connecticut
48	New Jersey
49	New York
50	California

Source Notes for Transportation (Section K)

K-1 Travel on Interstate Highways, 2000: Use of highways is measured by vehicle-miles (travel by one vehicle for one mile). By this measure, interstate highways account for nearly one-fourth of the nation's highway travel, according to calculations based on the U.S. Department of Transportation's *2000 Highway Statistics*. The federal government provides 90 percent of the money used to build interstates, but lower percentages for other highways. Having a large percentage of travel on interstates is good fiscal news as well as an indication of highway quality.

K-2 Percentage of Interstate Mileage in "Unacceptable" Condition, 2000: This table provides one measurement of pavement conditions. It is based on the International Roughness Index (IRI) which is an objective, equipment-based (as opposed to human observation) rating of the smoothness/bumpiness of interstate pavement. The IRI does not measure deterioration of other types. This table shows the percentage of interstate mileage given an IRI rating of 170 or above, the level identified as "unacceptable" in the Federal Highway Administration's *Conditions and Performance Report 1999*. The IRI data come from FHA's *2000 Highway Statistics*.

K-3 Deficient Bridges, 2001: This table shows the total number of deficient bridges on major highways in each state. Details appear in the complete inventory, *The Status of the Nation's Highway Bridges* to be published by the Department of Transportation (DOT) and updated biannually. The statistics are also posted on the DOT website (wwwcf.fhwa.dot.gov). Bridges can be classified as deficient as a result of deterioration, poor maintenance, or by original design (for example, too narrow for modern traffic).

K-4 Traffic Deaths Per 100 Million Vehicle-miles, 2000: Relating deaths to total miles traveled is a common way of measuring the safety of highways. Many factors could affect the totals, including weather conditions, highway designs, congestion, and traffic law enforcement by the states. The figures come from the Department of Transportation (see notes to Table K-1).

K-5 Percentage of Drivers Using Seat Belts, 2000: These data come from periodic checks of safety belt usage, as reported by the Department of Transportation. *State Fact Finder* received the information from the National Highway Traffic Safety Administration on November 2, 2001.

K-6 Vehicle-miles Traveled Per Capita, 2000: Vehicle-miles of travel, as reported by the Department of Transportation in *2000 Highway Statistics*, show the intensity of use of state highway systems. Vehicle-miles per capita show that the average American travels 9,771 miles a year. Short distances between homes, stores, and offices plus mass transit make usage lowest in northern urban areas.

K-7 Percentage of Workers Using Public Transportation, 2000: This table shows the percentage of workers who used public transportation systems for their journeys to work in 2000. The estimates come from questions about transportation usage from the Census 2000 Supplementary Survey.

K-8 Road and Street Miles, 2000: These data, from the same source as Table K-1, reflect total road and street (as distinct from highway) miles. They show the percentage of these miles that are controlled and maintained by state governments. Some states, such as Delaware and Virginia, maintain many local service roads that are controlled and maintained by counties and municipalities in other states.

K-9 State and Local Highway Employees, 2000: This statistic comes from a Census Bureau survey of state and local government employment, *Public Employment in 2000*. It is available on the internet at the Census Bureau website (www.census.gov). The data show the higher levels of employees, and thus costs, associated with maintaining highways in rural states.

K-10 State and Local Public Transit Employees, 2000: This statistic, from the same source as Table K-9, shows the higher levels of employees, and thus costs, associated with transit in urbanized states.

K-11 State and Local Spending for Highways, FY 1999: This table relates spending data to population and personal income in each state. The spending data, which cover local streets as well as state highways, come from the Census Bureau's electronic publication "State and Local Government Finance Estimates, by State," available on the Census Bureau's website (www.census.gov). Population numbers, also from the census, are as of July 1, 1999, and personal income numbers are from the Department of Commerce. Based on census historical practices, *State Fact Finder* used calendar year 1998 numbers. See notes to Table F-1 for more extensive information on the source of the data.

K-12 State and Local Highway Spending as a Percentage of General Spending, FY 1999: This table shows the relative importance of highway outlays in state and local budgets. It is derived by comparing highway spending with total "general" spending (see notes to Table K-11). General spending includes essentially all other spending excepting municipal electric and other utilities and trust funds, such as those for workers' compensation.

Welfare

When welfare was reformed in 1996, Congress "struck a deal with the states," according to *State Policy Reports* editor Marcia Howard: "Welfare reform provided states with a guaranteed level of funding along with flexibility in exchange for accepting the financial risks of the new welfare program. Under the old system, federal funding automatically increased when welfare caseloads increased. The new law provided states with a fixed funding level, regardless of welfare caseloads."

In one sense, states got lucky (if some former welfare recipients didn't): caseloads dropped. But, because spending needs were reduced, states were able to squirrel away TANF (Temporary Assistance for Needy Families) monies for future use, prompting suggestions from Congress to reduce funding levels. So far, states have avoided this.

When welfare is up for reauthorization in 2002, the issue of unspent funds is certain to be reevaluated, as will the troubling statistics that show that poverty rolls, especially for single-mother families, are not declining alongside welfare rolls. Again, from Howard:

"Focus has shifted from the number of people receiving public assistance to the number living in poverty. For most states, strict time limits and improving state economies resulted in a dramatic reduction in welfare caseloads. However, the caseload reductions were not necessarily accompanied by a sharp decline in poverty rates.

Under the current welfare law, many states have found it difficult to spend their federal welfare block grants on allowable activities. This results mainly from the law's focus on putting people to work rather than lifting them out of poverty. As the debate around reauthorization gets underway, states can be expected to argue that the second round of welfare reform needs to provide states the flexibility to spend federal welfare funds on anti-poverty initiatives."

Also, in 2002, the five-year limit on benefits may see some tweaking in response to the difficult economic conditions.

L-1 Percentage of Births to Unwed Mothers, 2000

State	Percentage of births to unwed mothers	Rank
Alabama	34.3	17
Alaska	33.0	23
Arizona	39.3	5
Arkansas	35.7	11
California	32.6	25
Colorado	25.0	46
Connecticut	29.1	35
Delaware	38.0	7
Florida	38.3	6
Georgia	37.0	8
Hawaii	32.2	26
Idaho	21.6	48
Illinois	34.5	15
Indiana	34.8	12
Iowa	28.0	42
Kansas	29.0	36
Kentucky	30.9	29
Louisiana	45.7	2
Maine	31.1	28
Maryland	34.6	13
Massachusetts	26.5	44
Michigan	33.4	21
Minnesota	25.8	45
Mississippi	46.0	1
Missouri	34.6	13
Montana	30.8	30
Nebraska	27.2	43
Nevada	36.0	10
New Hampshire	24.7	47
New Jersey	28.9	37
New Mexico	45.5	3
New York	36.3	9
North Carolina	33.3	22
North Dakota	28.3	39
Ohio	n/a	n/a
Oklahoma	33.8	19
Oregon	30.1	32
Pennsylvania	32.7	24
Rhode Island	34.3	17
South Carolina	39.8	4
South Dakota	33.5	20
Tennessee	34.5	15
Texas	30.2	31
Utah	17.2	49
Vermont	28.2	40
Virginia	29.9	33
Washington	28.2	40
West Virginia	31.8	27
Wisconsin	29.3	34
Wyoming	28.8	38
50 States	n/a	
DC	60.3	
United States	33.1	

Rank in order by percentage	
1	Mississippi
2	Louisiana
3	New Mexico
4	South Carolina
5	Arizona
6	Florida
7	Delaware
8	Georgia
9	New York
10	Nevada
11	Arkansas
12	Indiana
13	Maryland
13	Missouri
15	Illinois
15	Tennessee
17	Alabama
17	Rhode Island
19	Oklahoma
20	South Dakota
21	Michigan
22	North Carolina
23	Alaska
24	Pennsylvania
25	California
26	Hawaii
27	West Virginia
28	Maine
29	Kentucky
30	Montana
31	Texas
32	Oregon
33	Virginia
34	Wisconsin
35	Connecticut
36	Kansas
37	New Jersey
38	Wyoming
39	North Dakota
40	Vermont
40	Washington
42	Iowa
43	Nebraska
44	Massachusetts
45	Minnesota
46	Colorado
47	New Hampshire
48	Idaho
49	Utah

Note: Ties in ranking reflect ties in actual values.

L-2 Temporary Assistance for Needy Families (TANF) Recipients, 2000

State	Average monthly number of recipients	Recipients as a percentage of population	Rank by percentage
Alabama	55,098	1.2	34
Alaska	21,690	3.5	5
Arizona	89,915	1.8	22
Arkansas	28,259	1.1	40
California	1,275,366	3.8	2
Colorado	26,962	0.6	48
Connecticut	62,470	1.8	19
Delaware	17,124	2.2	12
Florida	135,559	0.8	46
Georgia	135,788	1.7	26
Hawaii	41,465	3.4	6
Idaho	2,262	0.2	50
Illinois	226322	1.8	21
Indiana	105,128	1.7	23
Iowa	48,647	1.7	25
Kansas	37,306	1.4	31
Kentucky	84,629	2.1	13
Louisiana	81,624	1.8	20
Maine	25,814	2.0	14
Maryland	71,146	1.3	33
Massachusetts	98,534	1.6	28
Michigan	191,630	1.9	16
Minnesota	115,271	2.3	10
Mississippi	35,186	1.2	35
Missouri	125,675	2.2	11
Montana	13,877	1.5	29
Nebraska	27,240	1.6	27
Nevada	17,100	0.9	45
New Hampshire	13,748	1.1	38
New Jersey	119,377	1.4	30
New Mexico	67,279	3.7	3
New York	673,033	3.5	4
North Carolina	96328	1.2	36
North Dakota	8,732	1.4	32
Ohio	224,594	2.0	15
Oklahoma	33,432	1.0	41
Oregon	38,667	1.1	37
Pennsylvania	229,326	1.9	17
Rhode Island	43,669	4.2	1
South Carolina	37,246	0.9	43
South Dakota	6,598	0.9	44
Tennessee	150,157	2.6	7
Texas	358,529	1.7	24
Utah	24,839	1.1	39
Vermont	15,350	2.5	8
Virginia	67,121	0.9	42
Washington	142,542	2.4	9
West Virginia	33,688	1.9	18
Wisconsin	38,784	0.7	47
Wyoming	999	0.2	49
50 States	5,621,125	2.0	
DC	44,574	7.8	
United States*	5,760,476	2.0	

Rank in order by percentage	
1	Rhode Island
2	California
3	New Mexico
4	New York
5	Alaska
6	Hawaii
7	Tennessee
8	Vermont
9	Washington
10	Minnesota
11	Missouri
12	Delaware
13	Kentucky
14	Maine
15	Ohio
16	Michigan
17	Pennsylvania
18	West Virginia
19	Connecticut
20	Louisiana
21	Illinois
22	Arizona
23	Indiana
24	Texas
25	Iowa
26	Georgia
27	Nebraska
28	Massachusetts
29	Montana
30	New Jersey
31	Kansas
32	North Dakota
33	Maryland
34	Alabama
35	Mississippi
36	North Carolina
37	Oregon
38	New Hampshire
39	Utah
40	Arkansas
41	Oklahoma
42	Virginia
43	South Carolina
44	South Dakota
45	Nevada
46	Florida
47	Wisconsin
48	Colorado
49	Wyoming
50	Idaho

Note: Numbers that appear to be identical are rounded and vary slightly in actual value. The rankings reflect the actual values before rounding. See the introduction for more details.

Due to rounding or data sources, the 50-state total plus D.C. may not equal the U.S. total. Please see introduction.

L-3 Food Stamp Recipients, FY 2000

State	Food stamp recipients # (in thousands)	Recipients as a percentage of population	Rank by percentage
Alabama	396	8.9	8
Alaska	38	6.0	25
Arizona	259	5.0	30
Arkansas	247	9.2	7
California	1,832	5.4	28
Colorado	156	3.6	47
Connecticut	165	4.8	34
Delaware	32	4.1	42
Florida	882	5.5	27
Georgia	559	6.8	17
Hawaii	118	9.7	4
Idaho	58	4.5	38
Illinois	779	6.3	22
Indiana	300	4.9	33
Iowa	123	4.2	40
Kansas	117	4.3	39
Kentucky	403	10.0	3
Louisiana	500	11.2	2
Maine	102	8.0	10
Maryland	219	4.1	41
Massachusetts	232	3.7	46
Michigan	603	6.1	23
Minnesota	196	4.0	44
Mississippi	276	9.7	5
Missouri	423	7.6	12
Montana	59	6.6	19
Nebraska	82	4.8	35
Nevada	61	3.0	49
New Hampshire	36	2.9	50
New Jersey	345	4.1	43
New Mexico	169	9.3	6
New York	1,439	7.6	11
North Carolina	488	6.1	24
North Dakota	32	5.0	32
Ohio	610	5.4	29
Oklahoma	253	7.3	14
Oregon	234	6.9	16
Pennsylvania	777	6.3	21
Rhode Island	74	7.1	15
South Carolina	295	7.4	13
South Dakota	43	5.7	26
Tennessee	496	8.7	9
Texas	1,333	6.4	20
Utah	82	3.7	45
Vermont	41	6.7	18
Virginia	336	4.7	36
Washington	295	5.0	31
West Virginia	227	12.5	1
Wisconsin	193	3.6	48
Wyoming	22	4.5	37
50 States	17,039	6.1	
DC	81	14.1	
United States*	17,158	6.1	

Rank in order by percentage	
1	West Virginia
2	Louisiana
3	Kentucky
4	Hawaii
5	Mississippi
6	New Mexico
7	Arkansas
8	Alabama
9	Tennessee
10	Maine
11	New York
12	Missouri
13	South Carolina
14	Oklahoma
15	Rhode Island
16	Oregon
17	Georgia
18	Vermont
19	Montana
20	Texas
21	Pennsylvania
22	Illinois
23	Michigan
24	North Carolina
25	Alaska
26	South Dakota
27	Florida
28	California
29	Ohio
30	Arizona
31	Washington
32	North Dakota
33	Indiana
34	Connecticut
35	Nebraska
36	Virginia
37	Wyoming
38	Idaho
39	Kansas
40	Iowa
41	Maryland
42	Delaware
43	New Jersey
44	Minnesota
45	Utah
46	Massachusetts
47	Colorado
48	Wisconsin
49	Nevada
50	New Hampshire

Note: Numbers that appear to be identical are rounded and vary slightly in actual value. The rankings reflect the actual values before rounding. See the introduction for more details.

Due to rounding or data sources, the 50-state total plus D.C. may not equal the U.S. total. Please see introduction.

L-4 Supplemental Security Income (SSI) Recipients, 2000

State	SSI recipients #	Recipients as a percentage of population	Rank by percentage
Alabama	159,486	3.6	5
Alaska	8,672	1.4	40
Arizona	81,493	1.6	32
Arkansas	85,410	3.2	8
California	1,086,333	3.2	7
Colorado	53,776	1.3	46
Connecticut	48,767	1.4	38
Delaware	11,984	1.5	35
Florida	377,218	2.4	16
Georgia	196,907	2.4	14
Hawaii	21,019	1.7	28
Idaho	18,381	1.4	39
Illinois	248,777	2.0	24
Indiana	88,041	1.4	37
Iowa	40,282	1.4	41
Kansas	36,282	1.3	42
Kentucky	174,349	4.3	2
Louisiana	165,577	3.7	4
Maine	29,727	2.3	17
Maryland	88,138	1.7	31
Massachusetts	167,559	2.6	12
Michigan	209,539	2.1	20
Minnesota	64,059	1.3	43
Mississippi	128,910	4.5	1
Missouri	112,213	2.0	23
Montana	13,877	1.5	34
Nebraska	21,249	1.2	47
Nevada	25,540	1.3	44
New Hampshire	11,592	0.9	49
New Jersey	146,112	1.7	27
New Mexico	46,660	2.6	13
New York	616,502	3.2	6
North Carolina	191,137	2.4	15
North Dakota	8,166	1.3	45
Ohio	240,002	2.1	19
Oklahoma	72,204	2.1	21
Oregon	52,046	1.5	36
Pennsylvania	283,785	2.3	18
Rhode Island	27,729	2.6	11
South Carolina	107,558	2.7	10
South Dakota	12,648	1.7	30
Tennessee	164,288	2.9	9
Texas	409,502	2.0	25
Utah	20,174	0.9	50
Vermont	12,492	2.1	22
Virginia	132,064	1.9	26
Washington	100,572	1.7	29
West Virginia	71,414	3.9	3
Wisconsin	84,892	1.6	33
Wyoming	5,827	1.2	48
50 States	6,580,931	2.3	
DC	20,073	3.5	
United States*	6,601,686	2.3	

Rank in order by percentage	
1	Mississippi
2	Kentucky
3	West Virginia
4	Louisiana
5	Alabama
6	New York
7	California
8	Arkansas
9	Tennessee
10	South Carolina
11	Rhode Island
12	Massachusetts
13	New Mexico
14	Georgia
15	North Carolina
16	Florida
17	Maine
18	Pennsylvania
19	Ohio
20	Michigan
21	Oklahoma
22	Vermont
23	Missouri
24	Illinois
25	Texas
26	Virginia
27	New Jersey
28	Hawaii
29	Washington
30	South Dakota
31	Maryland
32	Arizona
33	Wisconsin
34	Montana
35	Delaware
36	Oregon
37	Indiana
38	Connecticut
39	Idaho
40	Alaska
41	Iowa
42	Kansas
43	Minnesota
44	Nevada
45	North Dakota
46	Colorado
47	Nebraska
48	Wyoming
49	New Hampshire
50	Utah

Note: Numbers that appear to be identical are rounded and vary slightly in actual value. The rankings reflect the actual values before rounding. See the introduction for more details.

*Due to rounding or data sources, the 50-state total plus D.C. may not equal the U.S. total. Please see introduction.

L-5 Change in TANF/AFDC Recipients, FY 1995-FY 2000

State	Average monthly AFDC recipients FY 1995	Percentage decrease FY 1995-FY 2000	Rank by percentage decrease
Alabama	121,837	-54.7	32
Alaska	37,264	-34.6	47
Arizona	195,082	-57.5	27
Arkansas	65,325	-57.0	28
California	2,692,202	-52.7	33
Colorado	110,742	-75.0	8
Connecticut	170,719	-62.8	19
Delaware	26,314	-34.4	48
Florida	657,313	-79.3	5
Georgia	388,913	-65.2	16
Hawaii	65,207	-34.3	49
Idaho	24,050	-94.3	1
Illinois	710,032	-63.5	18
Indiana	197,225	-50.9	36
Iowa	103,108	-49.3	38
Kansas	81,504	-55.1	30
Kentucky	193,722	-55.8	29
Louisiana	258,180	-69.1	12
Maine	60973	-75.7	7
Maryland	227887	-68.9	13
Massachusetts	286175	-67.2	15
Michigan	612,224	-68.1	14
Minnesota	180,490	-35.4	45
Mississippi	146,319	-76.9	6
Missouri	259,595	-52.6	34
Montana	34,313	-59.2	26
Nebraska	42,038	-36.2	44
Nevada	41,846	-60.6	25
New Hampshire	28,671	-51.7	35
New Jersey	321,151	-61.0	23
New Mexico	105,114	-35.4	46
New York	1,266,350	-45.3	42
North Carolina	317,836	-69.4	11
North Dakota	14,920	-48.2	41
Ohio	629,719	-62.1	20
Oklahoma	127,336	-89.3	3
Oregon	107,610	-60.6	24
Pennsylvania	611,215	-61.9	22
Rhode Island	62,407	-28.2	50
South Carolina	133,567	-73.3	9
South Dakota	17,652	-62.0	21
Tennessee	281,982	-49.0	40
Texas	765,460	-55.1	31
Utah	47,472	-49.2	39
Vermont	27,716	-44.0	43
Virginia	189,493	-64.4	17
Washington	290,940	-49.7	37
West Virginia	107,668	-70.7	10
Wisconsin	214,404	-82.6	4
Wyoming	15,434	-92.9	2
50 States	13,674,716	-58.8	
DC	72,330	-38.5	
United States*	13,930,953	-58.5	

Rank in order by percentage decrease	
1	Idaho
2	Wyoming
3	Oklahoma
4	Wisconsin
5	Florida
6	Mississippi
7	Maine
8	Colorado
9	South Carolina
10	West Virginia
11	North Carolina
12	Louisiana
13	Maryland
14	Michigan
15	Massachusetts
16	Georgia
17	Virginia
18	Illinois
19	Connecticut
20	Ohio
21	South Dakota
22	Pennsylvania
23	New Jersey
24	Oregon
25	Nevada
26	Montana
27	Arizona
28	Arkansas
29	Kentucky
30	Kansas
31	Texas
32	Alabama
33	California
34	Missouri
35	New Hampshire
36	Indiana
37	Washington
38	Iowa
39	Utah
40	Tennessee
41	North Dakota
42	New York
43	Vermont
44	Nebraska
45	Minnesota
46	New Mexico
47	Alaska
48	Delaware
49	Hawaii
50	Rhode Island

Note: Numbers that appear to be identical are rounded and vary slightly in actual value. The rankings reflect the actual values before rounding. See the introduction for more details.

Due to rounding or data sources, the 50-state total plus D.C. may not equal the U.S. total. Please see introduction.

L-6 Condition of Children Index, 2001

State	Condition of Children Index "child well-being" ranked from 1 (highest) to 50 (lowest)
Alabama	46
Alaska	26
Arizona	45
Arkansas	47
California	27
Colorado	22
Connecticut	12
Delaware	34
Florida	35
Georgia	44
Hawaii	16
Idaho	23
Illinois	32
Indiana	15
Iowa	6
Kansas	17
Kentucky	36
Louisiana	49
Maine	10
Maryland	19
Massachusetts	4
Michigan	28
Minnesota	2
Mississippi	50
Missouri	31
Montana	29
Nebraska	8
Nevada	40
New Hampshire	1
New Jersey	7
New Mexico	48
New York	33
North Carolina	41
North Dakota	11
Ohio	25
Oklahoma	37
Oregon	20
Pennsylvania	14
Rhode Island	21
South Carolina	42
South Dakota	24
Tennessee	43
Texas	38
Utah	3
Vermont	13
Virginia	18
Washington	9
West Virginia	39
Wisconsin	5
Wyoming	30
50 States	n/a
DC	n/a
United States	n/a

Rank in order by Index ranked highest (1) to lowest (50)	
1	New Hampshire
2	Minnesota
3	Utah
4	Massachusetts
5	Wisconsin
6	Iowa
7	New Jersey
8	Nebraska
9	Washington
10	Maine
11	North Dakota
12	Connecticut
13	Vermont
14	Pennsylvania
15	Indiana
16	Hawaii
17	Kansas
18	Virginia
19	Maryland
20	Oregon
21	Rhode Island
22	Colorado
23	Idaho
24	South Dakota
25	Ohio
26	Alaska
27	California
28	Michigan
29	Montana
30	Wyoming
31	Missouri
32	Illinois
33	New York
34	Delaware
35	Florida
36	Kentucky
37	Oklahoma
38	Texas
39	West Virginia
40	Nevada
41	North Carolina
42	South Carolina
43	Tennessee
44	Georgia
45	Arizona
46	Alabama
47	Arkansas
48	New Mexico
49	Louisiana
50	Mississippi

L-7 Percentage of Families with Children Headed by a Single Parent, 1997-1999 (three-year average)

State	Percentage of families headed by single parent	Rank
Alabama	29	10
Alaska	27	18
Arizona	28	12
Arkansas	28	12
California	26	30
Colorado	24	42
Connecticut	27	18
Delaware	33	3
Florida	30	8
Georgia	31	4
Hawaii	26	30
Idaho	20	49
Illinois	28	12
Indiana	22	46
Iowa	24	42
Kansas	27	18
Kentucky	26	30
Louisiana	37	1
Maine	27	18
Maryland	27	18
Massachusetts	27	18
Michigan	28	12
Minnesota	21	48
Mississippi	34	2
Missouri	26	30
Montana	26	30
Nebraska	24	42
Nevada	27	18
New Hampshire	25	37
New Jersey	23	45
New Mexico	31	4
New York	31	4
North Carolina	28	12
North Dakota	22	46
Ohio	27	18
Oklahoma	27	18
Oregon	27	18
Pennsylvania	25	37
Rhode Island	30	8
South Carolina	29	10
South Dakota	25	37
Tennessee	31	4
Texas	27	18
Utah	17	50
Vermont	26	30
Virginia	28	12
Washington	26	30
West Virginia	27	18
Wisconsin	25	37
Wyoming	25	37
50 States	n/a	
DC	61	
United States	27	

Rank in order by percentage

1	Louisiana
2	Mississippi
3	Delaware
4	Georgia
4	New Mexico
4	New York
4	Tennessee
8	Florida
8	Rhode Island
10	Alabama
10	South Carolina
12	Arizona
12	Arkansas
12	Illinois
12	Michigan
12	North Carolina
12	Virginia
18	Alaska
18	Connecticut
18	Kansas
18	Maine
18	Maryland
18	Massachusetts
18	Nevada
18	Ohio
18	Oklahoma
18	Oregon
18	Texas
18	West Virginia
30	California
30	Hawaii
30	Kentucky
30	Missouri
30	Montana
30	Vermont
30	Washington
37	New Hampshire
37	Pennsylvania
37	South Dakota
37	Wisconsin
37	Wyoming
42	Colorado
42	Iowa
42	Nebraska
45	New Jersey
46	Indiana
46	North Dakota
48	Minnesota
49	Idaho
50	Utah

Note: Ties in ranking reflect ties in actual values.

L-8 Average Monthly TANF Cash Assistance Per Family, FY 2000

State	Average monthly TANF payment $	Rank
Alabama	166	48
Alaska	746	1
Arizona	282	32
Arkansas	216	42
California	623	3
Colorado	372	21
Connecticut	513	9
Delaware	277	35
Florida	317	28
Georgia	224	41
Hawaii	584	4
Idaho	213	43
Illinois	336	25
Indiana	172	46
Iowa	324	27
Kansas	276	37
Kentucky	239	38
Louisiana	234	40
Maine	521	7
Maryland	416	16
Massachusetts	468	14
Michigan	385	20
Minnesota	420	15
Mississippi	113	50
Missouri	237	39
Montana	350	24
Nebraska	292	30
Nevada	202	44
New Hampshire	478	11
New Jersey	391	19
New Mexico	498	10
New York	671	2
North Carolina	277	34
North Dakota	328	26
Ohio	364	23
Oklahoma	392	18
Oregon	372	22
Pennsylvania	519	8
Rhode Island	474	12
South Carolina	135	49
South Dakota	311	29
Tennessee	189	45
Texas	170	47
Utah	397	17
Vermont	537	5
Virginia	279	33
Washington	471	13
West Virginia	276	36
Wisconsin	292	31
Wyoming	532	6
50 States	433	
DC	368	
United States	426	

Rank in order by $

1	Alaska
2	New York
3	California
4	Hawaii
5	Vermont
6	Wyoming
7	Maine
8	Pennsylvania
9	Connecticut
10	New Mexico
11	New Hampshire
12	Rhode Island
13	Washington
14	Massachusetts
15	Minnesota
16	Maryland
17	Utah
18	Oklahoma
19	New Jersey
20	Michigan
21	Colorado
22	Oregon
23	Ohio
24	Montana
25	Illinois
26	North Dakota
27	Iowa
28	Florida
29	South Dakota
30	Nebraska
31	Wisconsin
32	Arizona
33	Virginia
34	North Carolina
35	Delaware
36	West Virginia
37	Kansas
38	Kentucky
39	Missouri
40	Louisiana
41	Georgia
42	Arkansas
43	Idaho
44	Nevada
45	Tennessee
46	Indiana
47	Texas
48	Alabama
49	South Carolina
50	Mississippi

Note: Numbers that appear to be identical are rounded and vary slightly in actual value. The rankings reflect the actual values before rounding. See the introduction for more details.

L-9 Welfare Assistance and Earnings of Three-person TANF Family as a Percentage of Poverty-level Income, 2000

State	Welfare and estimated part-time minimum wage earnings as a percentage of poverty-level income	Rank
Alabama	76.8	41
Alaska	140.5	1
Arizona	82.8	36
Arkansas	91.9	22
California	112.4	4
Colorado	80.1	40
Connecticut	136.4	2
Delaware	95.5	14
Florida	88.0	29
Georgia	80.9	39
Hawaii	123.5	3
Idaho	83.8	35
Illinois	91.0	24
Indiana	76.8	41
Iowa	92.2	21
Kansas	90.2	25
Kentucky	76.8	41
Louisiana	76.8	41
Maine	103.5	8
Maryland	84.7	34
Massachusetts	92.3	20
Michigan	93.1	19
Minnesota	105.7	5
Mississippi	76.8	41
Missouri	76.8	41
Montana	94.5	16
Nebraska	76.8	41
Nevada	76.8	41
New Hampshire	98.7	13
New Jersey	89.3	26
New Mexico	95.3	15
New York	100.8	9
North Carolina	76.8	41
North Dakota	84.9	32
Ohio	93.9	18
Oklahoma	84.8	33
Oregon	99.2	11
Pennsylvania	89.1	27
Rhode Island	105.6	6
South Carolina	81.8	38
South Dakota	85.8	31
Tennessee	88.3	28
Texas	76.8	41
Utah	94.1	17
Vermont	100.5	10
Virginia	98.9	12
Washington	104.6	7
West Virginia	86.1	30
Wisconsin	91.2	23
Wyoming	82.5	37
50 States	n/a	
DC	95.3	
United States	n/a	

Rank in order by percentage	
1	Alaska
2	Connecticut
3	Hawaii
4	California
5	Minnesota
6	Rhode Island
7	Washington
8	Maine
9	New York
10	Vermont
11	Oregon
12	Virginia
13	New Hampshire
14	Delaware
15	New Mexico
16	Montana
17	Utah
18	Ohio
19	Michigan
20	Massachusetts
21	Iowa
22	Arkansas
23	Wisconsin
24	Illinois
25	Kansas
26	New Jersey
27	Pennsylvania
28	Tennessee
29	Florida
30	West Virginia
31	South Dakota
32	North Dakota
33	Oklahoma
34	Maryland
35	Idaho
36	Arizona
37	Wyoming
38	South Carolina
39	Georgia
40	Colorado
41	Alabama
41	Indiana
41	Kentucky
41	Louisiana
41	Mississippi
41	Missouri
41	Nebraska
41	Nevada
41	North Carolina
41	Texas

Note: Ties in ranking reflect ties in actual values.

L-10 Supplemental Security Income (SSI) State Supplements, 2000

State	SSI state supplements per recipient $	Rank
Alabama	55	34
Alaska	312	3
Arizona	50	35
Arkansas	100	18
California	185	13
Colorado	197	11
Connecticut	307	4
Delaware	128	16
Florida	147	15
Georgia	67	28
Hawaii	56	32
Idaho	73	25
Illinois	66	29
Indiana	261	7
Iowa	260	8
Kansas	0	46
Kentucky	287	6
Louisiana	8	44
Maine	22	42
Maryland	192	12
Massachusetts	86	22
Michigan	47	36
Minnesota	181	14
Mississippi	0	46
Missouri	234	9
Montana	79	23
Nebraska	93	21
Nevada	56	32
New Hampshire	59	31
New Jersey	47	36
New Mexico	101	17
New York	78	24
North Carolina	510	1
North Dakota	451	2
Ohio	31	40
Oklahoma	44	38
Oregon	99	19
Pennsylvania	40	39
Rhode Island	73	25
South Carolina	307	4
South Dakota	73	25
Tennessee	0	46
Texas	0	46
Utah	3	45
Vermont	63	30
Virginia	232	10
Washington	27	41
West Virginia	0	46
Wisconsin	97	20
Wyoming	20	43
50 States	116	
DC	169	
United States	116	

Rank in order by $	
1	North Carolina
2	North Dakota
3	Alaska
4	Connecticut
4	South Carolina
6	Kentucky
7	Indiana
8	Iowa
9	Missouri
10	Virginia
11	Colorado
12	Maryland
13	California
14	Minnesota
15	Florida
16	Delaware
17	New Mexico
18	Arkansas
19	Oregon
20	Wisconsin
21	Nebraska
22	Massachusetts
23	Montana
24	New York
25	Rhode Island
25	South Dakota
25	Idaho
28	Georgia
29	Illinois
30	Vermont
31	New Hampshire
32	Nevada
32	Hawaii
34	Alabama
35	Arizona
36	Michigan
36	New Jersey
38	Oklahoma
39	Pennsylvania
40	Ohio
41	Washington
42	Maine
43	Wyoming
44	Louisiana
45	Utah
46	Kansas
46	Mississippi
46	Tennessee
46	Texas
46	West Virginia

Note: Ties in ranking reflect ties in actual values.

L-11 State Income Tax Liability of Typical Family in Poverty, 2000

State	Income tax liability $	Rank
Alabama	368	1
Alaska	n/a	n/a
Arizona	0	17
Arkansas	14	16
California	0	17
Colorado	-367	35
Connecticut	0	17
Delaware	0	17
Florida	n/a	n/a
Georgia	36	13
Hawaii	292	3
Idaho	0	17
Illinois	49	12
Indiana	263	4
Iowa	0	17
Kansas	-359	34
Kentucky	347	2
Louisiana	105	9
Maine	0	17
Maryland	-355	32
Massachusetts	-367	35
Michigan	161	7
Minnesota	-972	39
Mississippi	0	17
Missouri	22	15
Montana	175	6
Nebraska	0	17
Nevada	n/a	n/a
New Hampshire	n/a	n/a
New Jersey	-367	35
New Mexico	-85	31
New York	-776	38
North Carolina	0	17
North Dakota	n/a	n/a
Ohio	55	11
Oklahoma	127	8
Oregon	75	10
Pennsylvania	0	17
Rhode Island	0	17
South Carolina	0	17
South Dakota	n/a	n/a
Tennessee	n/a	n/a
Texas	n/a	n/a
Utah	23	14
Vermont	-1,174	40
Virginia	0	17
Washington	n/a	n/a
West Virginia	233	5
Wisconsin	-355	32
Wyoming	n/a	n/a
50 States	n/a	
DC	-53	
United States	n/a	

Rank in order by $	
1	Alabama
2	Kentucky
3	Hawaii
4	Indiana
5	West Virginia
6	Montana
7	Michigan
8	Oklahoma
9	Louisiana
10	Oregon
11	Ohio
12	Illinois
13	Georgia
14	Utah
15	Missouri
16	Arkansas
17	Arizona
17	California
17	Connecticut
17	Delaware
17	Idaho
17	Iowa
17	Maine
17	Mississippi
17	Nebraska
17	North Carolina
17	Pennsylvania
17	Rhode Island
17	South Carolina
17	Virginia
31	New Mexico
32	Maryland
32	Wisconsin
34	Kansas
35	Colorado
35	Massachusetts
35	New Jersey
38	New York
39	Minnesota
40	Vermont

Note: Ties in ranking reflect ties in actual values.

L-12 Child Support Collections, FY 2000

State	Total collections $ (in thousands)	Per capita collections $	Rank per capita
Alabama	192,137	43.20	43
Alaska	71,102	113.41	3
Arizona	196,762	38.35	47
Arkansas	120,493	45.07	40
California	2,059,473	60.80	19
Colorado	176,120	40.95	44
Connecticut	190,849	56.04	26
Delaware	49,010	62.55	18
Florida	648,007	40.55	45
Georgia	361,895	44.21	41
Hawaii	66,548	54.93	28
Idaho	75,069	58.02	23
Illinois	361,276	29.09	49
Indiana	366,155	60.22	21
Iowa	218,722	74.74	11
Kansas	139,182	51.77	30
Kentucky	226,433	56.02	27
Louisiana	213,901	47.86	35
Maine	89,399	70.12	13
Maryland	367,930	69.47	14
Massachusetts	318,570	50.18	32
Michigan	1,347,411	135.58	1
Minnesota	477,368	97.04	5
Mississippi	144,398	50.76	31
Missouri	338,989	60.59	20
Montana	40,752	45.17	39
Nebraska	142,452	83.24	9
Nevada	79,309	39.69	46
New Hampshire	71,390	57.77	24
New Jersey	679,194	80.72	10
New Mexico	39,543	21.74	50
New York	1,101,982	58.07	22
North Carolina	395,598	49.15	33
North Dakota	41,828	65.13	16
Ohio	1,411,209	124.30	2
Oklahoma	107,182	31.06	48
Oregon	248,206	72.55	12
Pennsylvania	1,167,422	95.06	6
Rhode Island	48,446	46.21	38
South Carolina	188,234	46.92	36
South Dakota	43,519	57.65	25
Tennessee	248,195	43.63	42
Texas	964,935	46.28	37
Utah	118,100	52.88	29
Vermont	38,738	63.63	17
Virginia	347,764	49.13	34
Washington	548,675	93.09	7
West Virginia	120,349	66.55	15
Wisconsin	569,046	106.09	4
Wyoming	41,896	84.85	8
50 States	17,621,166	62.74	
DC	35,030	61.23	
United States*	17,854,272	63.44	

Rank in order per capita	
1	Michigan
2	Ohio
3	Alaska
4	Wisconsin
5	Minnesota
6	Pennsylvania
7	Washington
8	Wyoming
9	Nebraska
10	New Jersey
11	Iowa
12	Oregon
13	Maine
14	Maryland
15	West Virginia
16	North Dakota
17	Vermont
18	Delaware
19	California
20	Missouri
21	Indiana
22	New York
23	Idaho
24	New Hampshire
25	South Dakota
26	Connecticut
27	Kentucky
28	Hawaii
29	Utah
30	Kansas
31	Mississippi
32	Massachusetts
33	North Carolina
34	Virginia
35	Louisiana
36	South Carolina
37	Texas
38	Rhode Island
39	Montana
40	Arkansas
41	Georgia
42	Tennessee
43	Alabama
44	Colorado
45	Florida
46	Nevada
47	Arizona
48	Oklahoma
49	Illinois
50	New Mexico

Due to rounding or data sources, the 50-state total plus D.C. may not equal the U.S. total. Please see introduction.

L-13 Child Support Collections Per Dollar of Administrative Costs, FY 2000

State	Collections per dollar of costs $	Rank
Alabama	3.66	35
Alaska	3.89	29
Arizona	3.72	33
Arkansas	3.28	42
California	3.23	43
Colorado	3.23	43
Connecticut	3.75	32
Delaware	3.19	45
Florida	3.45	40
Georgia	3.72	33
Hawaii	4.54	19
Idaho	4.32	23
Illinois	2.42	49
Indiana	7.69	1
Iowa	4.24	24
Kansas	2.91	46
Kentucky	4.02	27
Louisiana	4.92	10
Maine	4.90	12
Maryland	3.60	36
Massachusetts	3.50	38
Michigan	5.52	6
Minnesota	4.11	26
Mississippi	4.92	10
Missouri	3.37	41
Montana	3.58	37
Nebraska	3.78	31
Nevada	2.52	48
New Hampshire	4.82	15
New Jersey	4.60	18
New Mexico	1.31	50
New York	4.90	12
North Carolina	3.86	30
North Dakota	4.61	17
Ohio	4.82	15
Oklahoma	2.83	47
Oregon	5.54	5
Pennsylvania	6.05	4
Rhode Island	4.44	21
South Carolina	5.08	7
South Dakota	6.95	2
Tennessee	4.85	14
Texas	4.96	9
Utah	3.47	39
Vermont	4.02	27
Virginia	5.00	8
Washington	4.53	20
West Virginia	4.15	25
Wisconsin	6.51	3
Wyoming	4.33	22
50 States	n/a	
DC	2.64	
United States	4.21	

Rank in order by $	
1	Indiana
2	South Dakota
3	Wisconsin
4	Pennsylvania
5	Oregon
6	Michigan
7	South Carolina
8	Virginia
9	Texas
10	Louisiana
10	Mississippi
12	Maine
12	New York
14	Tennessee
15	New Hampshire
15	Ohio
17	North Dakota
18	New Jersey
19	Hawaii
20	Washington
21	Rhode Island
22	Wyoming
23	Idaho
24	Iowa
25	West Virginia
26	Minnesota
27	Kentucky
27	Vermont
29	Alaska
30	North Carolina
31	Nebraska
32	Connecticut
33	Arizona
33	Georgia
35	Alabama
36	Maryland
37	Montana
38	Massachusetts
39	Utah
40	Florida
41	Missouri
42	Arkansas
43	California
43	Colorado
45	Delaware
46	Kansas
47	Oklahoma
48	Nevada
49	Illinois
50	New Mexico

Note: Ties in ranking reflect ties in actual values.

L-14 Children in Foster Care, FY 1999

State	Children in foster care #	Children in foster care per 10,000 children #	Rank per 10,000 children
Alabama	5,180	47.8	35
Alaska	1,361	70.8	25
Arizona	6,999	55.4	32
Arkansas	2,675	40.9	42
California	119,246	133.8	2
Colorado	7,902	75.9	21
Connecticut	6,020	76.1	20
Delaware	1,395	77.9	19
Florida	24,930	70.4	26
Georgia	7,509	37.1	43
Hawaii	2,213	74.2	22
Idaho	1,099	31.3	45
Illinois	45,820	143.8	1
Indiana	3,911	25.8	47
Iowa	208	2.9	50
Kansas	6,334	90.8	9
Kentucky	6,386	64.6	30
Louisiana	5,637	47.3	37
Maine	3,167	108.6	5
Maryland	13,411	104.2	7
Massachusetts	12,836	88.1	12
Michigan	26,135	102.4	8
Minnesota	8,699	69.1	27
Mississippi	3,209	42.4	39
Missouri	12,312	87.5	13
Montana	2,031	90.5	10
Nebraska	4,789	107.5	6
Nevada	2,215	47.4	36
New Hampshire	1,262	42.3	40
New Jersey	9,229	46.4	38
New Mexico	796	15.8	49
New York	53,180	118.1	4
North Carolina	11,196	58.3	31
North Dakota	1,157	71.2	24
Ohio	14,779	52.0	33
Oklahoma	7,537	85.7	14
Oregon	6,797	82.4	16
Pennsylvania	22,466	78.6	18
Rhode Island	3,153	132.5	3
South Carolina	4,931	51.4	34
South Dakota	1,680	83.6	15
Tennessee	10,948	82.2	17
Texas	17,340	30.8	46
Utah	2,226	31.7	44
Vermont	1,278	90.4	11
Virginia	6,930	42.1	41
Washington	3,440	23.4	48
West Virginia	2,939	72.7	23
Wisconsin	9,198	68.1	28
Wyoming	876	67.7	29
50 States	536,967	77.0	
DC	3,188	309.6	
United States	540,155	77.3	

Rank in order per 10,000 children	
1	Illinois
2	California
3	Rhode Island
4	New York
5	Maine
6	Nebraska
7	Maryland
8	Michigan
9	Kansas
10	Montana
11	Vermont
12	Massachusetts
13	Missouri
14	Oklahoma
15	South Dakota
16	Oregon
17	Tennessee
18	Pennsylvania
19	Delaware
20	Connecticut
21	Colorado
22	Hawaii
23	West Virginia
24	North Dakota
25	Alaska
26	Florida
27	Minnesota
28	Wisconsin
29	Wyoming
30	Kentucky
31	North Carolina
32	Arizona
33	Ohio
34	South Carolina
35	Alabama
36	Nevada
37	Louisiana
38	New Jersey
39	Mississippi
40	New Hampshire
41	Virginia
42	Arkansas
43	Georgia
44	Utah
45	Idaho
46	Texas
47	Indiana
48	Washington
49	New Mexico
50	Iowa

Note: Numbers that appear to be identical are rounded and vary slightly in actual value. The rankings reflect the actual values before rounding. See the introduction for more details.

L-15 State and Local Welfare Spending, FY 1999

State	Welfare spending $ (in millions)	Per capita $	As a percentage of personal income	Rank per capita
Alabama	3,231	739	3.4	25
Alaska	689	1,112	4.0	4
Arizona	1,885	394	1.7	50
Arkansas	1,904	746	3.5	23
California	27,133	819	2.9	15
Colorado	2,576	635	2.2	37
Connecticut	2,930	893	2.4	12
Delaware	503	667	2.3	34
Florida	8,848	586	2.2	42
Georgia	4,921	632	2.5	39
Hawaii	956	807	3.0	16
Idaho	721	576	2.7	44
Illinois	8,657	714	2.4	28
Indiana	3,894	655	2.6	35
Iowa	2,078	724	2.9	27
Kansas	1,296	488	1.9	48
Kentucky	3,595	907	4.1	11
Louisiana	2,982	682	3.1	32
Maine	1,422	1,135	4.8	3
Maryland	3,675	710	2.3	29
Massachusetts	5,843	946	2.8	7
Michigan	6,452	654	2.5	36
Minnesota	5,501	1,152	3.9	2
Mississippi	2,041	737	3.7	26
Missouri	3,809	697	2.8	31
Montana	511	579	2.7	43
Nebraska	1,130	678	2.6	33
Nevada	852	471	1.6	49
New Hampshire	986	821	2.8	14
New Jersey	5,701	700	2.1	30
New Mexico	1,382	794	3.8	19
New York	28,053	1,542	4.8	1
North Carolina	5,691	744	3.0	24
North Dakota	622	981	4.3	6
Ohio	8,848	786	3.0	22
Oklahoma	1,739	518	2.3	47
Oregon	2,771	836	3.3	13
Pennsylvania	11,311	943	3.4	8
Rhode Island	1,042	1,052	3.8	5
South Carolina	3,131	806	3.6	17
South Dakota	446	609	2.6	40
Tennessee	4,324	789	3.2	20
Texas	11,260	562	2.2	45
Utah	1,349	633	2.9	38
Vermont	550	926	3.8	9
Virginia	4,046	589	2.1	41
Washington	4,609	801	2.8	18
West Virginia	1,669	924	4.5	10
Wisconsin	4,128	786	3.0	21
Wyoming	251	522	2.1	46
50 States	213,943	786	2.9	
DC	1,247	2,402	6.3	
United States	215,190	789	2.9	

Rank in order per capita	
1	New York
2	Minnesota
3	Maine
4	Alaska
5	Rhode Island
6	North Dakota
7	Massachusetts
8	Pennsylvania
9	Vermont
10	West Virginia
11	Kentucky
12	Connecticut
13	Oregon
14	New Hampshire
15	California
16	Hawaii
17	South Carolina
18	Washington
19	New Mexico
20	Tennessee
21	Wisconsin
22	Ohio
23	Arkansas
24	North Carolina
25	Alabama
26	Mississippi
27	Iowa
28	Illinois
29	Maryland
30	New Jersey
31	Missouri
32	Louisiana
33	Nebraska
34	Delaware
35	Indiana
36	Michigan
37	Colorado
38	Utah
39	Georgia
40	South Dakota
41	Virginia
42	Florida
43	Montana
44	Idaho
45	Texas
46	Wyoming
47	Oklahoma
48	Kansas
49	Nevada
50	Arizona

Note: Numbers that appear to be identical are rounded and vary slightly in actual value. The rankings reflect the actual values before rounding. See the introduction for more details.

L-16 State and Local Welfare Spending as a Percentage of General Spending, FY 1999

State	Welfare spending as a percentage of general spending	Rank by percentage
Alabama	16.1	16
Alaska	9.7	47
Arizona	9.3	48
Arkansas	17.9	11
California	15.0	21
Colorado	12.8	39
Connecticut	14.9	22
Delaware	11.2	45
Florida	12.4	43
Georgia	13.7	34
Hawaii	13.9	32
Idaho	12.9	38
Illinois	14.5	28
Indiana	14.6	26
Iowa	14.1	30
Kansas	10.7	46
Kentucky	19.9	4
Louisiana	14.1	31
Maine	22.3	1
Maryland	14.8	23
Massachusetts	16.7	14
Michigan	12.8	41
Minnesota	19.5	6
Mississippi	15.8	18
Missouri	16.0	17
Montana	11.9	44
Nebraska	14.6	25
Nevada	9.2	49
New Hampshire	18.5	7
New Jersey	12.9	37
New Mexico	14.6	27
New York	21.0	2
North Carolina	15.5	19
North Dakota	17.8	12
Ohio	16.6	15
Oklahoma	12.8	40
Oregon	15.1	20
Pennsylvania	18.5	8
Rhode Island	19.7	5
South Carolina	17.2	13
South Dakota	13.7	33
Tennessee	17.9	10
Texas	12.9	36
Utah	12.9	35
Vermont	18.1	9
Virginia	12.5	42
Washington	14.3	29
West Virginia	20.3	3
Wisconsin	14.7	24
Wyoming	8.0	50
50 States	15.3	
DC	26.9	
United States	15.4	

Rank in order per capita

1. Maine
2. New York
3. West Virginia
4. Kentucky
5. Rhode Island
6. Minnesota
7. New Hampshire
8. Pennsylvania
9. Vermont
10. Tennessee
11. Arkansas
12. North Dakota
13. South Carolina
14. Massachusetts
15. Ohio
16. Alabama
17. Missouri
18. Mississippi
19. North Carolina
20. Oregon
21. California
22. Connecticut
23. Maryland
24. Wisconsin
25. Nebraska
26. Indiana
27. New Mexico
28. Illinois
29. Washington
30. Iowa
31. Louisiana
32. Hawaii
33. South Dakota
34. Georgia
35. Utah
36. Texas
37. New Jersey
38. Idaho
39. Colorado
40. Oklahoma
41. Michigan
42. Virginia
43. Florida
44. Montana
45. Delaware
46. Kansas
47. Alaska
48. Arizona
49. Nevada
50. Wyoming

Note: Numbers that appear to be identical are rounded and vary slightly in actual value. The rankings reflect the actual values before rounding. See the introduction for more details.

L-17 Average Monthly Administrative Costs Per TANF Case, FY 2000

State	Costs per case $	Rank
Alabama	62.34	42
Alaska	131.20	17
Arizona	119.21	21
Arkansas	118.61	22
California	75.66	36
Colorado	139.42	12
Connecticut	127.85	18
Delaware	123.67	19
Florida	140.56	11
Georgia	1.67	50
Hawaii	74.34	37
Idaho	195.28	3
Illinois	132.62	15
Indiana	81.41	34
Iowa	98.15	28
Kansas	297.95	1
Kentucky	56.67	45
Louisiana	60.29	43
Maine	48.25	46
Maryland	82.62	32
Massachusetts	92.47	30
Michigan	119.60	20
Minnesota	93.64	29
Mississippi	41.42	49
Missouri	41.88	47
Montana	147.60	10
Nebraska	109.68	23
Nevada	182.08	4
New Hampshire	230.39	2
New Jersey	70.90	38
New Mexico	41.52	48
New York	136.10	13
North Carolina	77.75	35
North Dakota	158.82	7
Ohio	156.50	8
Oklahoma	151.48	9
Oregon	99.75	27
Pennsylvania	102.38	26
Rhode Island	65.94	40
South Carolina	131.23	16
South Dakota	82.43	33
Tennessee	56.86	44
Texas	64.64	41
Utah	181.77	5
Vermont	104.94	25
Virginia	88.35	31
Washington	70.54	39
West Virginia	105.88	24
Wisconsin	163.84	6
Wyoming	134.60	14
50 States	95.10	
DC	94.25	
United States	93.77	

Rank in order by $

1 Kansas
2 New Hampshire
3 Idaho
4 Nevada
5 Utah
6 Wisconsin
7 North Dakota
8 Ohio
9 Oklahoma
10 Montana
11 Florida
12 Colorado
13 New York
14 Wyoming
15 Illinois
16 South Carolina
17 Alaska
18 Connecticut
19 Delaware
20 Michigan
21 Arizona
22 Arkansas
23 Nebraska
24 West Virginia
25 Vermont
26 Pennsylvania
27 Oregon
28 Iowa
29 Minnesota
30 Massachusetts
31 Virginia
32 Maryland
33 South Dakota
34 Indiana
35 North Carolina
36 California
37 Hawaii
38 New Jersey
39 Washington
40 Rhode Island
41 Texas
42 Alabama
43 Louisiana
44 Tennessee
45 Kentucky
46 Maine
47 Missouri
48 New Mexico
49 Mississippi
50 Georgia

Source Notes for Welfare (Section L)

L-1 Percentage of Births to Unwed Mothers, 2000: These data come from state reports summarized by the National Center for Health Statistics in its *National Vital Statistics Report* (vol. 49, no. 5, July 24, 2001). The birth data, which come from hospitals, are highly reliable, but some states report the marital status of mothers somewhat differently.

L-2 TANF Recipients, Total and as a Percentage of Population, 2000: The primary federal welfare program has been Aid to Families with Dependent Children (AFDC) for households with children and income below stipulated levels. During 1997 and 1998 states made the transition to new programs under federal welfare reform legislation passed in 1996.

The table, from the U.S. Department of Health and Human Services website (www.acf.dhhs.gov), expresses the total number of people in households receiving Temporary Assistance to Needy Families (TANF) as of September 2000 as a percentage of population. Because states set their own eligibility standards, states with high percentages of persons in poverty do not necessarily have a larger-than-average percentage.

L-3 Food Stamp Recipients, Total and as a Percentage of Population, FY 2000: Unlike those for Temporary Assistance for Needy Families, food stamp standards of eligibility are uniform nationwide, so participation in this program tends to resemble closely the percentage of state population in poverty. The data are compiled by the U.S. Department of Agriculture, Food and Nutrition Service and are available on their website (www.fns.usda.gov).

L-4 SSI Recipients, Total and as a Percentage of Population, 2000: The Supplemental Security Income (SSI) program provides federal cash payments to persons eligible by reason of a combination of low incomes and disability, blindness, or age over sixty-five. The eligibility standards are uniform nationwide, as are the cash payments, except in about half the states that supplement the federal payments with state money (see Table L-10).

The data, reflecting recipients at year-end 2000, were calculated from information posted on the Social Security Administration's website (www.ssa.gov).

L-5 Change in TANF/AFDC Recipients, FY 1995-FY 2000: This table compares the 1995 average monthly number of recipients in each state with the 2000 average to show changes in welfare participation over the past five years. The data come from the same source as Table L-2. Since 1996 there has been a dramatic reduction in welfare caseloads as the result of a strong national economy and implementation of welfare reform.

L-6 Condition of Children Index, 2001: This is a ranking of states and the District of Columbia (1 highest, 50 lowest)

prepared by the Annie E. Casey Foundation based on ten indicators of health, income, education, and other factors. The details behind the rankings are found in *Kids Count Data Book* for 2001, the foundation's annual comprehensive publication.

L-7 Percentage of Families with Children Headed by a Single Parent, 1997-1999 (three-year average): A large and growing number of American children do not live in households with two parents. These statistics (from *Kids Count*; see notes to Table L-6) are averaged over three years and include only children in households with a single parent present.

L-8 Average Monthly TANF Cash Assistance Per Family, FY 2000: These data (reflecting the situation over the year ending in September 2000) show what a welfare family would receive to cover basic needs in a month. Assistance comes largely in the form of cash payments but can also include vouchers. Each state sets its own level of benefits. In addition to these cash payments, a typical welfare household would receive food stamps, assistance in paying heating and cooling bills, and free medical care under the Medicaid program. Some households would also receive additional cash as "emergency assistance" and reduced rents under various federal housing subsidy programs. For the source see Table L-2.

L-9 Welfare Assistance and Earnings of Three-person TANF Family as a Percentage of Poverty-level Income, 2000: These data are from a special compilation of the Congressional Research Service (CRS) and are included in the 2000 "Green Book" of the Ways and Means Committee of the U.S. House of Representatives available on the internet (www.access.gpo.gov). Because of TANF's work trigger (after 2 years of benefits) this table differs from previous years. Assumed earnings from part-time minimum wage employment (approximately $5,000 annually in most states) and an assumed earned income credit are combined with TANF cash payments and food stamps. The total is compared with poverty level income, which, in 2000, was $13,738 for a family of three.

The TANF cash payments are set by the states (see notes to Table L-8). Federally determined food stamp values differ from state to state, as greater amounts are provided in states with low cash welfare payments. The poverty level is uniform nationwide. CRS provides two numbers for the states of Michigan, New York, and California. *State Fact Finder* included the data for Wayne County, Michigan, rather than Washtenaw County (95%), New York City rather than Suffolk County (108.6%) and those for Region 1 in California rather than Region 2 (110.5%).

L-10 SSI State Supplements, 2000: These data compare the extent to which states supplement benefits under the federal Supplemental Security Income (SSI) program. For a description of the program see the notes to Table L-4. The complex rules for determining who receives supplements and how large they are mean that the averages shown are not necessarily indicative of the average supplement received. Some states provide relatively large supplements to some beneficiaries and none to the rest. However, the extreme differences among states show marked differences in their willingness to add to federally funded benefits using their own funds. The data were calculated from information from the Social Security Administration available on their website (www.ssa.gov).

L-11 State Income Tax Liability of Typical Family in Poverty, 2000: States have quite different approaches toward taxes on poor working families. The table illustrates these by showing how much state income tax a family of three making the poverty-level income ($13,737) would have to pay in tax on their 2000 income. A few states, like the federal government, supplement the income of poverty-level families with a refundable credit indicated by the minus amounts shown in the table. Some states do not have income taxes (n/a on the table) or have a tax but do not make such families pay it (shown as zeros on the table). The others charge the taxes shown. The calculations were performed by the Center on Budget and Policy Priorities and are available on their website (www.cbpp.org).

L-12 Child Support Collections, FY 2000: Because large numbers of families on welfare consist of mothers and children who receive little or no child support from fathers, state and federal officials are intensifying efforts to ensure that fathers pay the support amounts they owe. The table provides an indication of the relative significance of the resulting child support payments in each state.

Collections are reported by the Department of Health and Human Services in the *Child Support Enforcement Annual Report to Congress*. This report has not been issued yet for FY 1999 and FY 2000, instead the information is available on the Department's Administration for Children and Families Office of Child Support Enforcement website (www.acf.dhhs.gov). The per capita amounts are those collections divided by each state's population on April 1, 2000. While most differences among states are real, some reflect the different degrees to which individual states enforce child support requirements through centralized systems.

L-13 Child Support Collections Per Dollar of Administrative Costs, FY 2000: Nationwide, it costs about thirty cents to collect every dollar of child support. These data, from the same source as Table L-12, indicate that the effectiveness of collections efforts varies considerably among the states.

L-14 Children in Foster Care, FY 1999: During the one-year period ending on March 31, 1999, over 540,000 children were in "substitute care" (foster care). Most commonly, these are children who have been removed from their natural parent(s) because of suspected abuse or neglect. The count is from the U.S. Department of Health and Human Services' Administration for Children and Families. The statistics were supplied to *State Fact Finder* in a fax dated November 2, 1999.

High rankings are not necessarily good or bad. Having large numbers of children in foster care for long periods is generally viewed as undesirable because the alternatives (adoption, return to natural parents) provide more stability for the child than do temporary homes with strangers. However, having small numbers may indicate that child welfare authorities are leaving abused and neglected children in homes where they should not be left.

L-15 State and Local Welfare Spending, FY 1999: This table relates spending data to population and personal income in each state. The data come from the Census Bureau's electronic publication "State and Local Government Finance Estimates, by State," available on the Census website (www.census.gov). Population numbers, also from the census, are as of July 1, 1999, and personal income numbers are from the Department of Commerce. Based on census historical practices, *State Fact Finder* used calendar year 1998 numbers. See notes to Table F-1 for more extensive information on the source of the data. In addition to cash payments, the Bureau's definition of welfare spending includes Medicaid and other payments to vendors, administrative costs, and welfare-related social services.

L-16 State and Local Welfare Spending as a Percentage of General Spending, FY 1999: These data (see notes to Table L-15) show the importance of welfare spending relative to total spending of state and local governments for "general" activities, a category that excludes spending for certain trust funds such as unemployment compensation and municipal utilities.

L-17 Average Monthly Administrative Costs Per TANF Case, FY 2000: In FY 2000 the average monthly costs of administering welfare run about $94 per case, with substantial variation among the states. The information comes from unpublished tabulations by the Department of Health and Human Services (see notes to Table L-2).

Technology

Is there a word that cannot be revamped for the technological age by assigning it that ubiquitous prefix E-? There's e-commerce, e-business, e-government, e-zine, e-card, e-learning, e-museum, even e-soccer. The spate of dot-com failures did not seem to dampen our enthusiasm for the internet, though the bust encouraged us to reevaluate the role of the web and remind us that it is a work-in-progress. How the internet can be utilized for commercial purposes we are still figuring out, but it is clear that as a communication and information gathering device it has altered our world. Studies from the Census Bureau still show that the internet is used most often for these two purposes.

Access is one issue that continues to dominate discussion about technology. "Digital divide" is the oft-heard phrase used to describe the gulf between technology have and have-nots. More than half of the information in this chapter shares what is known, on the statistical front, about access, from at-home computer use (M-1 and M-2) to high-speed service (M-3) to technology in schools (M-7). Of course, having technology is one thing, having the tools to use it is another. This is an especially important issue in the schools, where educators and others are concerned with how technology is utilized and to what purposes.

The events of September 11th have heightened existing concerns about cyber-terrorism, as well as technology-dependent coordination of emergency response services. Governments, at all levels, are realizing the need for back-up plans should, for instance, telecommunications systems be compromised. September 11th also woke states up to the fact that public safety agencies need to be able to communicate with each other quickly and easily.

As more and more government and financial services are being offered on-line, expect to hear more about privacy concerns. Also of issue is the under utilization of fiber-optic lines that provide broadband service. Known as the "last mile" or the "last hundred feet," the issue is getting the high-speed lines connected to homes and businesses.

M-1 Percentage of Households with Computers, 2000

State	Percentage with computers	Rank
Alabama	44.2	44
Alaska	64.8	2
Arizona	53.5	20
Arkansas	37.3	49
California	56.6	11
Colorado	62.6	4
Connecticut	60.4	7
Delaware	58.6	8
Florida	50.1	29
Georgia	47.1	40
Hawaii	52.4	23
Idaho	54.5	14
Illinois	50.2	28
Indiana	48.8	31
Iowa	53.6	19
Kansas	55.8	12
Kentucky	46.2	41
Louisiana	41.2	48
Maine	54.7	13
Maryland	53.7	17
Massachusetts	53.0	21
Michigan	51.5	24
Minnesota	57.0	10
Mississippi	37.2	50
Missouri	52.6	22
Montana	51.5	24
Nebraska	48.5	34
Nevada	48.8	31
New Hampshire	54.3	15
New Jersey	48.7	33
New Mexico	63.7	3
New York	47.6	38
North Carolina	45.3	43
North Dakota	47.5	39
Ohio	49.5	30
Oklahoma	41.5	47
Oregon	61.1	5
Pennsylvania	48.4	35
Rhode Island	47.9	36
South Carolina	43.3	45
South Dakota	50.4	27
Tennessee	45.7	42
Texas	47.9	36
Utah	66.1	1
Vermont	53.7	17
Virginia	53.9	16
Washington	60.7	6
West Virginia	42.8	46
Wisconsin	50.9	26
Wyoming	58.2	9
50 States	n/a	
DC	48.8	
United States	51.0	

Rank in order by percentage	
1	Utah
2	Alaska
3	New Mexico
4	Colorado
5	Oregon
6	Washington
7	Connecticut
8	Delaware
9	Wyoming
10	Minnesota
11	California
12	Kansas
13	Maine
14	Idaho
15	New Hampshire
16	Virginia
17	Maryland
17	Vermont
19	Iowa
20	Arizona
21	Massachusetts
22	Missouri
23	Hawaii
24	Michigan
24	Montana
26	Wisconsin
27	South Dakota
28	Illinois
29	Florida
30	Ohio
31	Indiana
31	Nevada
33	New Jersey
34	Nebraska
35	Pennsylvania
36	Rhode Island
36	Texas
38	New York
39	North Dakota
40	Georgia
41	Kentucky
42	Tennessee
43	North Carolina
44	Alabama
45	South Carolina
46	West Virginia
47	Oklahoma
48	Louisiana
49	Arkansas
50	Mississippi

Note: Ties in ranking reflect ties in actual values.

M-2 Percentage of Households with Internet Access, 2000

State	Percentage with internet access	Rank
Alabama	35.5	43
Alaska	55.6	2
Arizona	42.5	21
Arkansas	26.5	49
California	46.7	10
Colorado	51.8	3
Connecticut	51.2	4
Delaware	50.7	6
Florida	43.2	17
Georgia	38.3	35
Hawaii	43.0	18
Idaho	42.3	23
Illinois	40.1	29
Indiana	39.4	32
Iowa	39.0	33
Kansas	43.9	15
Kentucky	36.6	40
Louisiana	30.2	48
Maine	42.6	20
Maryland	43.8	16
Massachusetts	45.5	12
Michigan	42.1	24
Minnesota	43.0	18
Mississippi	26.3	50
Missouri	42.5	21
Montana	40.6	27
Nebraska	37.0	39
Nevada	41.0	25
New Hampshire	56.0	1
New Jersey	39.8	31
New Mexico	47.8	9
New York	35.7	42
North Carolina	35.3	44
North Dakota	37.7	38
Ohio	40.7	26
Oklahoma	34.3	45
Oregon	50.8	5
Pennsylvania	40.1	29
Rhode Island	38.8	34
South Carolina	32.0	47
South Dakota	37.9	37
Tennessee	36.3	41
Texas	38.3	35
Utah	48.4	8
Vermont	46.7	10
Virginia	44.3	13
Washington	49.7	7
West Virginia	34.3	45
Wisconsin	40.6	27
Wyoming	44.1	14
50 States	n/a	
DC	39.6	
United States	41.5	

Rank in order by percentage

1 New Hampshire
2 Alaska
3 Colorado
4 Connecticut
5 Oregon
6 Delaware
7 Washington
8 Utah
9 New Mexico
10 California
10 Vermont
12 Massachusetts
13 Virginia
14 Wyoming
15 Kansas
16 Maryland
17 Florida
18 Hawaii
18 Minnesota
20 Maine
21 Arizona
21 Missouri
23 Idaho
24 Michigan
25 Nevada
26 Ohio
27 Montana
27 Wisconsin
29 Illinois
29 Pennsylvania
31 New Jersey
32 Indiana
33 Iowa
34 Rhode Island
35 Georgia
35 Texas
37 South Dakota
38 North Dakota
39 Nebraska
40 Kentucky
41 Tennessee
42 New York
43 Alabama
44 North Carolina
45 Oklahoma
45 West Virginia
47 South Carolina
48 Louisiana
49 Arkansas
50 Mississippi

Note: Ties in ranking reflect ties in actual values.

M-3 Percentage of Zip Codes with Broadband Telecommunications Service, 2000

State	Percentage of zipcodes with atleast one subscriber	Number of broadband providers	Rank by percentage
Alabama	51	6	31
Alaska	21	1-3	50
Arizona	74	8	11
Arkansas	27	5	45
California	72	20	12
Colorado	68	11	16
Connecticut	81	10	6
Delaware	100	5	1
Florida	87	15	4
Georgia	55	10	29
Hawaii	49	1-3	32
Idaho	37	13	38
Illinois	44	10	35
Indiana	63	6	22
Iowa	29	6	44
Kansas	44	6	35
Kentucky	35	9	41
Louisiana	57	7	28
Maine	23	5	49
Maryland	98	11	2
Massachusetts	81	14	6
Michigan	68	13	16
Minnesota	58	10	27
Mississippi	49	1-3	32
Missouri	37	7	38
Montana	27	1-3	45
Nebraska	30	6	43
Nevada	66	5	19
New Hampshire	63	6	22
New Jersey	97	11	3
New Mexico	46	1-3	34
New York	68	15	16
North Carolina	75	14	8
North Dakota	24	1-3	48
Ohio	75	11	8
Oklahoma	37	5	38
Oregon	61	12	24
Pennsylvania	75	20	8
Rhode Island	69	1-3	15
South Carolina	66	8	19
South Dakota	26	4	47
Tennessee	65	11	21
Texas	61	18	24
Utah	61	5	24
Vermont	34	4	42
Virginia	72	15	12
Washington	86	13	5
West Virginia	71	1-3	14
Wisconsin	55	7	29
Wyoming	40	1-3	37
50 States	n/a	n/a	
DC	100	7	
United States	59	105	

Rank in order by percentage

1	Delaware
2	Maryland
3	New Jersey
4	Florida
5	Washington
6	Connecticut
6	Massachusetts
8	North Carolina
8	Ohio
8	Pennsylvania
11	Arizona
12	California
12	Virginia
14	West Virginia
15	Rhode Island
16	Colorado
16	Michigan
16	New York
19	Nevada
19	South Carolina
21	Tennessee
22	Indiana
22	New Hampshire
24	Oregon
24	Texas
24	Utah
27	Minnesota
28	Louisiana
29	Georgia
29	Wisconsin
31	Alabama
32	Hawaii
32	Mississippi
34	New Mexico
35	Illinois
35	Kansas
37	Wyoming
38	Idaho
38	Missouri
38	Oklahoma
41	Kentucky
42	Vermont
43	Nebraska
44	Iowa
45	Arkansas
45	Montana
47	South Dakota
48	North Dakota
49	Maine
50	Alaska

Note: Ties in ranking reflect ties in actual values.

M-4 High-tech Jobs, 2000

State	Employment in the high-tech industry	High-tech employment per 1,000 private sector workers	Rank per 1,000 workers
Alabama	51,668	34	30
Alaska	5,428	26	38
Arizona	103,951	54	15
Arkansas	21,297	22	42
California	973,555	77	4
Colorado	180,866	97	1
Connecticut	77,482	53	16
Delaware	9,187	26	40
Florida	231,413	38	26
Georgia	167,821	51	18
Hawaii	8,353	19	46
Idaho	28,251	61	6
Illinois	220,952	43	22
Indiana	67,910	26	37
Iowa	45,034	37	28
Kansas	41,699	38	25
Kentucky	38,610	26	39
Louisiana	24,627	16	49
Maine	13,722	28	35
Maryland	114,864	58	11
Massachusetts	233,848	82	3
Michigan	105,626	27	36
Minnesota	138,007	61	7
Mississippi	16,813	18	47
Missouri	82,840	36	29
Montana	5,551	18	48
Nebraska	36,644	50	19
Nevada	19,803	22	43
New Hampshire	43,494	82	2
New Jersey	194,930	59	10
New Mexico	25,159	45	21
New York	339,131	48	20
North Carolina	132,318	40	23
North Dakota	7,681	30	33
Ohio	149,210	31	31
Oklahoma	35,583	31	32
Oregon	82,987	61	8
Pennsylvania	187,337	38	24
Rhode Island	15,139	37	27
South Carolina	36,781	24	41
South Dakota	15,915	53	17
Tennessee	48,188	21	44
Texas	440,718	57	13
Utah	47,869	55	14
Vermont	14,892	60	9
Virginia	210,889	75	5
Washington	130,305	58	12
West Virginia	10,685	19	45
Wisconsin	71,931	30	34
Wyoming	2,372	13	50
50 States	5,309,336	n/a	
DC	17,003	42	
United States*	5,317,884	48	

Due to rounding or data sources, the 50-state total plus D.C. may not equal the U.S. total. Please see introduction.

Rank in order per 1,000 workers	
1	Colorado
2	New Hampshire
3	Massachusetts
4	California
5	Virginia
6	Idaho
7	Minnesota
8	Oregon
9	Vermont
10	New Jersey
11	Maryland
12	Washington
13	Texas
14	Utah
15	Arizona
16	Connecticut
17	South Dakota
18	Georgia
19	Nebraska
20	New York
21	New Mexico
22	Illinois
23	North Carolina
24	Pennsylvania
25	Kansas
26	Florida
27	Rhode Island
28	Iowa
29	Missouri
30	Alabama
31	Ohio
32	Oklahoma
33	North Dakota
34	Wisconsin
35	Maine
36	Michigan
37	Indiana
38	Alaska
39	Kentucky
40	Delaware
41	South Carolina
42	Arkansas
43	Nevada
44	Tennessee
45	West Virginia
46	Hawaii
47	Mississippi
48	Montana
49	Louisiana
50	Wyoming

Note: Numbers that appear to be identical are rounded and vary slightly in actual value. The rankings reflect the actual values before rounding. See the introduction for more details.

M-5 Dot-com Domain Names, 2001

State	Number of domain names	Domain names per 1,000 population	Domain names per business firm	Rank per business firm
Alabama	108,225	24.3	1.3	40
Alaska	36,000	57.4	2.3	20
Arizona	308,325	60.1	3.4	4
Arkansas	53,850	20.1	1.0	47
California	3,179,025	93.9	5.0	1
Colorado	325,875	75.8	2.9	12
Connecticut	226,200	66.4	2.9	13
Delaware	47,775	61.0	2.5	19
Florida	1,046,025	65.4	3.0	9
Georgia	408,975	50.0	2.6	15
Hawaii	75,600	62.4	3.2	6
Idaho	49,725	38.4	1.6	32
Illinois	577,725	46.5	2.3	21
Indiana	164,400	27.0	1.4	35
Iowa	67,575	23.1	1.0	48
Kansas	93,750	34.9	1.5	34
Kentucky	88,125	21.8	1.2	43
Louisiana	110,400	24.7	1.3	38
Maine	55,875	43.8	1.7	31
Maryland	316,800	59.8	3.0	8
Massachusetts	500,925	78.9	3.6	3
Michigan	327,675	33.0	1.7	30
Minnesota	237,000	48.2	2.1	22
Mississippi	40,500	14.2	0.8	49
Missouri	186,300	33.3	1.6	33
Montana	31,650	35.1	1.2	44
Nebraska	53,250	31.1	1.3	42
Nevada	168,525	84.3	4.5	2
New Hampshire	83,025	67.2	2.6	16
New Jersey	526,875	62.6	2.6	14
New Mexico	65,250	35.9	1.8	26
New York	1,248,975	65.8	3.0	10
North Carolina	287,475	35.7	1.8	27
North Dakota	23,475	36.6	1.3	36
Ohio	376,275	33.1	1.8	28
Oklahoma	94,575	27.4	1.3	39
Oregon	212,175	62.0	2.5	18
Pennsylvania	453,525	36.9	1.9	23
Rhode Island	44,325	42.3	1.7	29
South Carolina	101,100	25.2	1.3	41
South Dakota	21,375	28.3	1.0	45
Tennessee	197,925	34.8	1.9	24
Texas	950,325	45.6	2.6	17
Utah	137,625	61.6	3.1	7
Vermont	35,325	58.0	1.9	25
Virginia	410,175	57.9	3.0	11
Washington	434,325	73.7	3.2	5
West Virginia	27,225	15.1	0.8	50
Wisconsin	155,325	29.0	1.3	37
Wyoming	16,500	33.4	1.0	46
50 States	14,789,250	52.7	2.6	
DC	136,275	238.2	8.3	
United States*	19,003,575	67.5	3.4	

Rank in order per business firm	
1	California
2	Nevada
3	Massachusetts
4	Arizona
5	Washington
6	Hawaii
7	Utah
8	Maryland
9	Florida
10	New York
11	Virginia
12	Colorado
13	Connecticut
14	New Jersey
15	Georgia
16	New Hampshire
17	Texas
18	Oregon
19	Delaware
20	Alaska
21	Illinois
22	Minnesota
23	Pennsylvania
24	Tennessee
25	Vermont
26	New Mexico
27	North Carolina
28	Ohio
29	Rhode Island
30	Michigan
31	Maine
32	Idaho
33	Missouri
34	Kansas
35	Indiana
36	North Dakota
37	Wisconsin
38	Louisiana
39	Oklahoma
40	Alabama
41	South Carolina
42	Nebraska
43	Kentucky
44	Montana
45	South Dakota
46	Wyoming
47	Arkansas
48	Iowa
49	Mississippi
50	West Virginia

Note: Numbers that appear to be identical are rounded and vary slightly in actual value. The rankings reflect the actual values before rounding. See the introduction for more details.

Due to rounding or data sources, the 50-state total plus D.C. may not equal the U.S. total. Please see introduction.

M-6 State Government Website Ratings, 2001

State	Website rating	Rank
Alabama	33.0	48
Alaska	37.2	39
Arizona	42.3	19
Arkansas	33.4	45
California	46.3	6
Colorado	40.5	29
Connecticut	41.4	24
Delaware	39.7	35
Florida	45.6	9
Georgia	39.1	37
Hawaii	38.1	38
Idaho	37.2	39
Illinois	39.5	36
Indiana	52.3	1
Iowa	41.8	22
Kansas	39.8	34
Kentucky	40.5	29
Louisiana	42.8	15
Maine	43.0	14
Maryland	40.6	28
Massachusetts	42.6	16
Michigan	51.3	2
Minnesota	40.4	31
Mississippi	35.5	42
Missouri	41.2	25
Montana	42.3	19
Nebraska	40.4	31
Nevada	40.2	33
New Hampshire	33.0	48
New Jersey	42.4	18
New Mexico	33.3	47
New York	45.8	7
North Carolina	44.1	11
North Dakota	44.0	12
Ohio	45.2	10
Oklahoma	33.4	45
Oregon	42.2	21
Pennsylvania	45.7	8
Rhode Island	34.8	44
South Carolina	40.7	27
South Dakota	41.8	22
Tennessee	49.0	4
Texas	50.9	3
Utah	42.6	16
Vermont	35.2	43
Virginia	43.2	13
Washington	47.6	5
West Virginia	36.5	41
Wisconsin	41.0	26
Wyoming	31.5	50
50 States	n/a	
DC	n/a	
United States	n/a	

Rank in order	
1	Indiana
2	Michigan
3	Texas
4	Tennessee
5	Washington
6	California
7	New York
8	Pennsylvania
9	Florida
10	Ohio
11	North Carolina
12	North Dakota
13	Virginia
14	Maine
15	Louisiana
16	Massachusetts
16	Utah
18	New Jersey
19	Arizona
19	Montana
21	Oregon
22	Iowa
22	South Dakota
24	Connecticut
25	Missouri
26	Wisconsin
27	South Carolina
28	Maryland
29	Colorado
29	Kentucky
31	Minnesota
31	Nebraska
33	Nevada
34	Kansas
35	Delaware
36	Illinois
37	Georgia
38	Hawaii
39	Alaska
39	Idaho
41	West Virginia
42	Mississippi
43	Vermont
44	Rhode Island
45	Arkansas
45	Oklahoma
47	New Mexico
48	Alabama
48	New Hampshire
50	Wyoming

Note: Ties in ranking reflect ties in actual values.

M-7 Students per Computer, 2000

State	Students per instructional computer	Students per internet connected instructional computer	Rank per instructional computer only
Alabama	5.0	11.6	18
Alaska	3.7	4.8	42
Arizona	4.8	6.1	23
Arkansas	5.1	8.1	16
California	7.2	12.4	1
Colorado	4.6	8.0	27
Connecticut	5.4	8.9	10
Delaware	4.4	5.1	33
Florida	4.2	9.0	36
Georgia	4.7	8.3	24
Hawaii	5.8	8.8	7
Idaho	3.8	6.5	40
Illinois	4.9	7.8	20
Indiana	3.7	6.8	42
Iowa	3.8	5.6	40
Kansas	3.3	6.0	47
Kentucky	4.2	7.1	36
Louisiana	6.8	11.4	2
Maine	4.6	6.2	27
Maryland	5.6	9.0	8
Massachusetts	5.2	9.0	13
Michigan	5.1	8.7	16
Minnesota	4.2	6.2	36
Mississippi	6.4	11.1	4
Missouri	4.5	6.6	32
Montana	3.1	6.9	49
Nebraska	3.7	5.1	42
Nevada	6.1	11.3	5
New Hampshire	6.1	10.4	5
New Jersey	4.6	8.9	27
New Mexico	4.9	9.3	20
New York	5.3	9.8	12
North Carolina	5.2	11.0	13
North Dakota	3.6	5.7	46
Ohio	4.4	4.9	33
Oklahoma	4.6	7.0	27
Oregon	5.2	8.1	13
Pennsylvania	4.6	8.8	27
Rhode Island	6.5	9.6	3
South Carolina	5.0	7.1	18
South Dakota	3.2	4.6	48
Tennessee	5.4	9.0	10
Texas	4.3	7.3	35
Utah	5.5	7.7	9
Vermont	4.9	6.4	20
Virginia	4.7	7.5	24
Washington	4.7	7.5	24
West Virginia	3.9	6.3	39
Wisconsin	3.7	6.7	42
Wyoming	3.0	4.9	50
50 States	n/a	n/a	
DC	5.8	12.6	
United States	4.9	7.9	

Rank in order per instructional computer	
1	California
2	Louisiana
3	Rhode Island
4	Mississippi
5	New Hampshire
5	Nevada
7	Hawaii
8	Maryland
9	Utah
10	Tennessee
10	Connecticut
12	New York
13	Oregon
13	North Carolina
13	Massachusetts
16	Michigan
16	Arkansas
18	South Carolina
18	Alabama
20	Vermont
20	New Mexico
20	Illinois
23	Arizona
24	Washington
24	Virginia
24	Georgia
27	Pennsylvania
27	Oklahoma
27	New Jersey
27	Maine
27	Colorado
32	Missouri
33	Ohio
33	Delaware
35	Texas
36	Minnesota
36	Kentucky
36	Florida
39	West Virginia
40	Iowa
40	Idaho
42	Wisconsin
42	Nebraska
42	Indiana
42	Alaska
46	North Dakota
47	Kansas
48	South Dakota
49	Montana
50	Wyoming

Note: Ties in ranking reflect ties in actual values.

Source Notes for Technology (Section M)

M-1 Percentage of Households with Computers, 2000: In 1995, the National Telecommunication and Information Administration (NTIA), an agency of the Department of Commerce, began publishing a series of reports on access to technology in the United States. The statistics on computer ownership are from the fourth and most recent report, *Falling through the Net: Toward Digital Inclusion*, released in October 2000 and available on the NTIA website (www.ntia.doc.gov). The data come from Census Bureau interviews with approximately 48,000 sample households. Besides geographical data the report contains information on computer ownership by race and ethnicity, income, and education. The report finds that in a little less than two years computer ownership has increased by 21 percent.

M-2 Percentage of Households with Internet Access, 2000: 41.5 percent of American households were connected to the internet in 2000, 10.7 percent of these were connected by a high-speed broadband service. This table is from the same NTIA report cited in the notes to Table B-36. According to the report, the most common use of the internet, whether connected at or away from home, is e-mail (79.9%). Over half of those "connected" use the internet on a regular basis to search for information (58.8%). Shopping and bill paying accounted for only 30 percent of online activity.

M-3 Percentage of Zip Codes with Broadband Telecommunications Service, 2000: High-speed, high-capacity, "always on" broadband telecommunications services allow large amounts of information to be transmitted quickly, providing at least the promise of increased productivity. The majority of these services are supplied by cable lines and digital subscriber lines (DSL), a small percentage come from satellite, wireless and other technologies. As many who live in rural areas know, broadband service is not yet universally available.

The Federal Communications Commission (FCC) began tracking access to broadband services in 1998. While it does not count individual subscribers, the FCC does keep statistics on the number of broadband providers in each zipcode. This information for the start of the year 2000 is provided in the table. The first column shows the percentage of zipcodes in each state that have one or more subscribers to one or more broadband services. According to the FCC report from which the data is culled ("Deployment of Advanced Telecommunications Capability: Second Report"), 91 percent of the U.S. population resides in those zipcodes. Because access can vary greatly within a zipcode—cable lines tend to be laid in residential rather than business and industrial areas, and one neighbor can be offered DSL while another is not—presumptions about access should be made with caution. The second column of the table shows the number of companies that supply broadband service within each state, providing some indication of competition in the broadband market.

M-4 High-tech Jobs, 2000: The recognized authority on employment statistics—the Bureau of Labor Statistics (BLS)—does not currently release "high-tech" industry data for states, but BLS does assign every category of job an employment code (Standard Industrial Classification, or SIC code). In order to create this table, the American Electronics Association (AeA) sifted through these SIC codes to create its own definition of the high-tech industry. In *Cyberstates 2001,* the source of the data in this table, AeA calls their definition "a solid, yet conservative, representation of the core components of today's high-tech industry." It includes high-tech manufacturing, communications services, and software and computer-related services. It does not include wholesale and retail trade of high-tech goods, nor does it include the biotechnology industry (due to the difficulty of separating "tech" from "bio" activities), temporary employees, consultants, or freelance workers. AeA's definition tends to overlook industries that utilize high-tech processes, such as drug, chemical, or architectural services, even if their product is not considered "high-tech." High-technology is not an easy industry to isolate. Other groups are bound to develop differing definitions.

M-5 Dot-com Domain Names, 2001: This table presents a count of commercial domain names (".coms") registered in each state. Anyone who pays a modest fee ($20-$50 a year) can register a domain name and use their website for virtually any purpose, such as sharing vacation photos, idolizing popstars, or espousing the latest conspiracy theory. Presumably, though, a large number of these domain names are used for commercial enterprises. Thus, domain names per business is included in this table as a subject of possible interest. The statistics are compiled by Matthew Zook at UC Berkeley using a sampling method. Large collections of domain names owned by a single entity were removed to reduce geographical bias. These and other domain name statistics are available at www.zooknic.com.

M-6 State Government Website Ratings, 2001: Citing the internet as an important means for governments to deliver information and services to citizens, Daniel M. West, Director of the Taubman Center for Public Policy at Brown University, has taken on the task of rating "e-government." West's report, "State and Federal E-Government in the United States, 2001," published on www.InsidePolitics.org, analyzes 1,680 government websites from a "citizen's perspective." Thirty-two measures were used to evaluate websites. These include the presence of on-line services, publications and databases, security and privacy measures, handicap-accessibility, and other services such as foreign language translation, digital signatures, credit card payments, and comment forms. Each state was given a score out of a possible 100. Indiana topped the scale with a score of 52.3.

M-7 Students per Computer, 2000: This table is one measure of student access to technology in public schools. The data come from *Education Week's* "Technology Counts 2001" (www.edweek.org), which includes additional information on how computers and the internet are used in the classroom. For more information on the capacity to use technology see also, the National Center for Education Statistics' report, "Teachers' Tools for the 21st Century: A Report on Teachers' Use of Technology."

State Rankings

Alabama

Alabama

Own-source General Revenue 49
Per Capita Non-tax Revenue 17
Per Capita Total Spending 34
General Spending as Percentage of
  Income 15
Per Capita General Spending 36
Change in General Expenditures 17
State Government General Revenue 35
State Government General Spending 32
State Government General Fund
  Spending 14
State and Local Debt 42
Debt as Percentage of Revenue 37
Per Capita Full Faith and Credit Debt 30
Bond Ratings 4
State Solvency Index 23
Pension Plan Assets 38
State Reserves 48
Capital Outlays and Interest 44
State Budget Process Quality 40
Relative State Spending "Needs" 41
Structural Deficits 31

Education - Section H

Math Proficiency, Eighth Grade 34
Science Proficiency, Eighth Grade 33
AFQT Ranks 46
SAT Scores n/a
ACT Scores 20
Over-25 Population with a High
  School Diploma 49
Students in Private Schools 26
High School Completion Rates 46
Pupil-Teacher Ratio 25
Public School Enrollment 28
Library Holdings Per Capita 38
Children with Disabilities 25
Education Spending Per Capita 36
Education Spending as a Percentage
  of Total 26
Spending Per Pupil 47
Average Teacher Salary 28
Sources of School Funds 44
State Aid Per Pupil 30
Higher Education Spending Per
  Capita 22
Higher Education Spending as
  Percentage of Total 16
Public Higher Education Enrollment 19
Per Pupil Support of Higher Education 16
Tuition and Fees 31
Average Professor Salary 40
Education Employees 33
R and D Spending 6
Library Operating Spending 44

Health - Section I

Immunization Rates 16
Infant Mortality Rates 3
State Health Rankings 45
Population Without Health
  Insurance 19
Abortions 28
Alcohol Consumption 44
Percentage of Adult Smokers 10
Percentage Obese 2
AIDS Cases 19
Physicians Per 100,000 Population 40
Hospital Beds Per 1,000 Population 11
Medicaid Recipients 24
Medicaid Recipients as Percentage of
  Poverty Population 42
Health and Hospital Spending 2
Health and Hospital Spending as
  Percentage of Total Spending 1
Per Capita Medicaid Spending 30
Medicaid Spending Per Aged
  Recipient 34
Medicaid Spending Per Child 48
Medicare Payment Per Hospital Day 13
Hospital Expense Per Inpatient Day 49
Population in HMOs 43

Crime - Section J

Crime Rate 15
Violent Crime Rate 20
Murder Rate 5
Property Crime Rate 15
Motor Vehicle Theft Rate 32
Violent Crime Rate Change 29
Prisoners 16
Change in Prisoners 36
Incarceration Rate 6
Juvenile Violent Crime Rate 40
Proportion of Sentence Served n/a
Law Enforcement Employees 24
Corrections Employees 45
State Corrections Spending 49
Increase in State Corrections
  Spending 3
Law Enforcement Spending 40
Law Enforcement Spending as
  Percentage of Total 39

Transportation - Section K

Travel on Interstates 39
Interstate Mileage in
  Unacceptable Condition 28
Deficient Bridges 15

Traffic Deaths 16
Seat Belt Use 22
Vehicle-miles Traveled Per Capita 3
Workers Using Public
  Transportation 48
Road and Street Miles 32
Highway Employees 19
Public Transit Employees 46
Highway Spending Per Capita 47
Highway Spending as Percentage
  of Total Spending 40

Welfare - Section L

Percentage of Births to Unwed
  Mothers 17
TANF Recipients as a Percentage
  of Population 34
Food Stamp Recipients as
  Percentage of Population 8
SSI Recipients as Percentage of
  Population 5
Change in TANF/AFDC
  Recipients 32
Condition of Children Index 46
Percentage of Families with Single
  Parent 10
Average Monthly TANF Payments 48
Welfare as Percentage of
  Poverty-level Income 41
State Supplements of SSI 34
State Income Tax Liability of Typical
  Family in Poverty 1
Child Support Collections 43
Child Support Collections Per
  $ of Administrative Costs 35
Children in Foster Care 35
Welfare Spending Per Capita 25
Welfare Spending as Percentage of
  Total Spending 16
Administrative Costs Per
  TANF Case 42

Technology - Section M

Percentage of Households with
  Computers 44
Percentage of Households with
  Internet Access 43
Zip codes with Broadband
  Service 31
High-tech Jobs 30
Dot-com Domain Names 40
State Government Website
  Ratings 48
Students per Computer 18

State Rankings 315

Alaska

Own-source General Revenue	1
Per Capita Non-tax Revenue	1
Per Capita Total Spending	1
General Spending as Percentage of Income	1
Per Capita General Spending	1
Change in General Expenditures	49
State Government General Revenue	1
State Government General Spending	1
State Government General Fund Spending	1
State and Local Debt	1
Debt as Percentage of Revenue	18
Per Capita Full Faith and Credit Debt	4
Bond Ratings	3
State Solvency Index	1
Pension Plan Assets	5
State Reserves	1
Capital Outlays and Interest	1
State Budget Process Quality	32
Relative State Spending "Needs"	38
Structural Deficits	49

Education - Section H

Math Proficiency, Eighth Grade	n/a
Science Proficiency, Eighth Grade	n/a
AFQT Ranks	17
SAT Scores	6
ACT Scores	n/a
Over-25 Population with a High School Diploma	5
Students in Private Schools	46
High School Completion Rates	3
Pupil-Teacher Ratio	12
Public School Enrollment	2
Library Holdings Per Capita	20
Children with Disabilities	24
Education Spending Per Capita	1
Education Spending as a Percentage of Total	50
Spending Per Pupil	4
Average Teacher Salary	11
Sources of School Funds	45
State Aid Per Pupil	4
Higher Education Spending Per Capita	16
Higher Education Spending as Percentage of Total	49
Public Higher Education Enrollment	31
Per Pupil Support of Higher Education	2
Tuition and Fees	30
Average Professor Salary	42
Education Employees	2
R and D Spending	17
Library Operating Spending	4

Health - Section I

Immunization Rates	28
Infant Mortality Rates	43
State Health Rankings	25
Population Without Health Insurance	7
Abortions	34
Alcohol Consumption	4
Percentage of Adult Smokers	12
Percentage Obese	21
AIDS Cases	41
Physicians Per 100,000 Population	42
Hospital Beds Per 1,000 Population	41
Medicaid Recipients	16
Medicaid Recipients as Percentage of Poverty Population	3
Health and Hospital Spending	23
Health and Hospital Spending as Percentage of Total Spending	47
Per Capita Medicaid Spending	14
Medicaid Spending Per Aged Recipient	21
Medicaid Spending Per Child	2
Medicare Payment Per Hospital Day	10
Hospital Expense Per Inpatient Day	1
Population in HMOs	50

Crime - Section J

Crime Rate	22
Violent Crime Rate	10
Murder Rate	26
Property Crime Rate	23
Motor Vehicle Theft Rate	24
Violent Crime Rate Change	38
Prisoners	40
Change in Prisoners	48
Incarceration Rate	32
Juvenile Violent Crime Rate	23
Proportion of Sentence Served	7
Law Enforcement Employees	35
Corrections Employees	10
State Corrections Spending	7
Increase in State Corrections Spending	46
Law Enforcement Spending	2
Law Enforcement Spending as Percentage of Total	45

Transportation - Section K

Travel on Interstates	5
Interstate Mileage in Unacceptable Condition	39
Deficient Bridges	23

Traffic Deaths	6
Seat Belt Use	39
Vehicle-miles Traveled Per Capita	48
Workers Using Public Transportation	17
Road and Street Miles	6
Highway Employees	1
Public Transit Employees	23
Highway Spending Per Capita	1
Highway Spending as Percentage of Total Spending	8

Welfare - Section L

Percentage of Births to Unwed Mothers	23
TANF Recipients as a Percentage of Population	5
Food Stamp Recipients as Percentage of Population	25
SSI Recipients as Percentage of Population	40
Change in TANF/AFDC Recipients	47
Condition of Children Index	26
Percentage of Families with Single Parent	18
Average Monthly TANF Payments	1
Welfare as Percentage of Poverty-level Income	1
State Supplements of SSI	3
State Income Tax Liability of Typical Family in Poverty	n/a
Child Support Collections	3
Child Support Collections Per $ of Administrative Costs	29
Children in Foster Care	25
Welfare Spending Per Capita	4
Welfare Spending as Percentage of Total Spending	47
Administrative Costs Per TANF Case	17

Technology - Section M

Percentage of Households with Computers	2
Percentage of Households with Internet Access	2
Zip codes with Broadband Service	50
High-tech Jobs	38
Dot-com Domain Names	20
State Government Website Ratings	39
Students per Computer	42

Arizona

Arkansas

California

Colorado

Connecticut

Delaware

Florida

Florida

Georgia

Hawaii

Idaho

Illinois

Own-source General Revenue	20
Per Capita Non-tax Revenue	48
Per Capita Total Spending	23
General Spending as Percentage of Income	46
Per Capita General Spending	24
Change in General Expenditures	20
State Government General Revenue	39
State Government General Spending	42
State Government General Fund Spending	45
State and Local Debt	17
Debt as Percentage of Revenue	15
Per Capita Full Faith and Credit Debt	9
Bond Ratings	3
State Solvency Index	38
Pension Plan Assets	31
State Reserves	29
Capital Outlays and Interest	18
State Budget Process Quality	41
Relative State Spending "Needs"	33
Structural Deficits	13

Education - Section H

Math Proficiency, Eighth Grade	16
Science Proficiency, Eighth Grade	19
AFQT Ranks	14
SAT Scores	n/a
ACT Scores	5
Over-25 Population with a High School Diploma	29
Students in Private Schools	10
High School Completion Rates	29
Pupil-Teacher Ratio	19
Public School Enrollment	26
Library Holdings Per Capita	15
Children with Disabilities	19
Education Spending Per Capita	27
Education Spending as a Percentage of Total	27
Spending Per Pupil	10
Average Teacher Salary	8
Sources of School Funds	2
State Aid Per Pupil	45
Higher Education Spending Per Capita	41
Higher Education Spending as Percentage of Total	40
Public Higher Education Enrollment	21
Per Pupil Support of Higher Education	32
Tuition and Fees	13
Average Professor Salary	11
Education Employees	37
R and D Spending	33
Library Operating Spending	8

Health - Section I

Immunization Rates	31
Infant Mortality Rates	7
State Health Rankings	30
Population Without Health Insurance	21
Abortions	15
Alcohol Consumption	21
Percentage of Adult Smokers	29
Percentage Obese	16
AIDS Cases	14
Physicians Per 100,000 Population	11
Hospital Beds Per 1,000 Population	23
Medicaid Recipients	27
Medicaid Recipients as Percentage of Poverty Population	20
Health and Hospital Spending	33
Health and Hospital Spending as Percentage of Total Spending	30
Per Capita Medicaid Spending	32
Medicaid Spending Per Aged Recipient	26
Medicaid Spending Per Child	19
Medicare Payment Per Hospital Day	8
Hospital Expense Per Inpatient Day	15
Population in HMOs	27

Crime - Section J

Crime Rate	20
Violent Crime Rate	8
Murder Rate	7
Property Crime Rate	27
Motor Vehicle Theft Rate	12
Violent Crime Rate Change	45
Prisoners	7
Change in Prisoners	30
Incarceration Rate	26
Juvenile Violent Crime Rate	1
Proportion of Sentence Served	35
Law Enforcement Employees	5
Corrections Employees	30
State Corrections Spending	31
Increase in State Corrections Spending	15
Law Enforcement Spending	17
Law Enforcement Spending as Percentage of Total	12

Transportation - Section K

Travel on Interstates	10
Interstate Mileage in Unacceptable Condition	18
Deficient Bridges	42

Traffic Deaths	33
Seat Belt Use	24
Vehicle-miles Traveled Per Capita	45
Workers Using Public Transportation	4
Road and Street Miles	31
Highway Employees	40
Public Transit Employees	2
Highway Spending Per Capita	40
Highway Spending as Percentage of Total Spending	39

Welfare - Section L

Percentage of Births to Unwed Mothers	15
TANF Recipients as a Percentage of Population	21
Food Stamp Recipients as Percentage of Population	22
SSI Recipients as Percentage of Population	24
Change in TANF/AFDC Recipients	18
Condition of Children Index	32
Percentage of Families with Single Parent	12
Average Monthly TANF Payments	25
Welfare as Percentage of Poverty-level Income	24
State Supplements of SSI	29
State Income Tax Liability of Typical Family in Poverty	12
Child Support Collections	49
Child Support Collections Per $ of Administrative Costs	49
Children in Foster Care	1
Welfare Spending Per Capita	28
Welfare Spending as Percentage of Total Spending	28
Administrative Costs Per TANF Case	15

Technology - Section M

Percentage of Households with Computers	28
Percentage of Households with Internet Access	29
Zip codes with Broadband Service	35
High-tech Jobs	22
Dot-com Domain Names	21
State Government Website Ratings	36
Students per Computer	20

Indiana

Iowa

Kansas

Kentucky

Own-source General Revenue	41
Per Capita Non-tax Revenue	38
Per Capita Total Spending	40
General Spending as Percentage of Income	19
Per Capita General Spending	38
Change in General Expenditures	8
State Government General Revenue	22
State Government General Spending	22
State Government General Fund Spending	20
State and Local Debt	13
Debt as Percentage of Revenue	5
Per Capita Full Faith and Credit Debt	48
Bond Ratings	3
State Solvency Index	31
Pension Plan Assets	36
State Reserves	37
Capital Outlays and Interest	13
State Budget Process Quality	19
Relative State Spending "Needs"	33
Structural Deficits	5

Education - Section H

Math Proficiency, Eighth Grade	25
Science Proficiency, Eighth Grade	17
AFQT Ranks	49
SAT Scores	n/a
ACT Scores	20
Over-25 Population with a High School Diploma	48
Students in Private Schools	17
High School Completion Rates	33
Pupil-Teacher Ratio	12
Public School Enrollment	42
Library Holdings Per Capita	38
Children with Disabilities	21
Education Spending Per Capita	47
Education Spending as a Percentage of Total	40
Spending Per Pupil	25
Average Teacher Salary	33
Sources of School Funds	40
State Aid Per Pupil	13
Higher Education Spending Per Capita	27
Higher Education Spending as Percentage of Total	23
Public Higher Education Enrollment	37
Per Pupil Support of Higher Education	6
Tuition and Fees	34
Average Professor Salary	30
Education Employees	8
R and D Spending	50
Library Operating Spending	40

Health - Section I

Immunization Rates	13
Infant Mortality Rates	17
State Health Rankings	39
Population Without Health Insurance	23
Abortions	45
Alcohol Consumption	47
Percentage of Adult Smokers	1
Percentage Obese	8
AIDS Cases	36
Physicians Per 100,000 Population	35
Hospital Beds Per 1,000 Population	12
Medicaid Recipients	13
Medicaid Recipients as Percentage of Poverty Population	19
Health and Hospital Spending	41
Health and Hospital Spending as Percentage of Total Spending	37
Per Capita Medicaid Spending	12
Medicaid Spending Per Aged Recipient	33
Medicaid Spending Per Child	11
Medicare Payment Per Hospital Day	38
Hospital Expense Per Inpatient Day	43
Population in HMOs	17

Crime - Section J

Crime Rate	45
Violent Crime Rate	36
Murder Rate	25
Property Crime Rate	42
Motor Vehicle Theft Rate	40
Violent Crime Rate Change	18
Prisoners	26
Change in Prisoners	29
Incarceration Rate	25
Juvenile Violent Crime Rate	4
Proportion of Sentence Served	25
Law Enforcement Employees	43
Corrections Employees	41
State Corrections Spending	35
Increase in State Corrections Spending	30
Law Enforcement Spending	42
Law Enforcement Spending as Percentage of Total	40

Transportation - Section K

Travel on Interstates	19
Interstate Mileage in Unacceptable Condition	24
Deficient Bridges	18

Traffic Deaths	17
Seat Belt Use	40
Vehicle-miles Traveled Per Capita	9
Workers Using Public Transportation	27
Road and Street Miles	8
Highway Employees	24
Public Transit Employees	28
Highway Spending Per Capita	22
Highway Spending as Percentage of Total Spending	16

Welfare - Section L

Percentage of Births to Unwed Mothers	29
TANF Recipients as a Percentage of Population	13
Food Stamp Recipients as Percentage of Population	3
SSI Recipients as Percentage of Population	2
Change in TANF/AFDC Recipients	29
Condition of Children Index	36
Percentage of Families with Single Parent	30
Average Monthly TANF Payments	38
Welfare as Percentage of Poverty-level Income	41
State Supplements of SSI	6
State Income Tax Liability of Typical Family in Poverty	2
Child Support Collections	27
Child Support Collections Per $ of Administrative Costs	27
Children in Foster Care	30
Welfare Spending Per Capita	11
Welfare Spending as Percentage of Total Spending	4
Administrative Costs Per TANF Case	45

Technology - Section M

Percentage of Households with Computers	41
Percentage of Households with Internet Access	40
Zip codes with Broadband Service	41
High-tech Jobs	39
Dot-com Domain Names	43
State Government Website Ratings	29
Students per Computer	36

Louisiana

Maine

Maryland

Massachusetts

Own-source General Revenue 8
Per Capita Non-tax Revenue 28
Per Capita Total Spending 7
General Spending as Percentage of Income 43
Per Capita General Spending 8
Change in General Expenditures 38
State Government General Revenue 8
State Government General Spending 7
State Government General Fund Spending 35
State and Local Debt 3
Debt as Percentage of Revenue 1
Per Capita Full Faith and Credit Debt 5
Bond Ratings 3
State Solvency Index 50
Pension Plan Assets 17
State Reserves 16
Capital Outlays and Interest 7
State Budget Process Quality 3
Relative State Spending "Needs" 14
Structural Deficits 11

Education - Section H

Math Proficiency, Eighth Grade 5
Science Proficiency, Eighth Grade 2
AFQT Ranks 50
SAT Scores 5
ACT Scores n/a
Over-25 Population with a High School Diploma 31
Students in Private Schools 14
High School Completion Rates 12
Pupil-Teacher Ratio 39
Public School Enrollment 43
Library Holdings Per Capita 4
Children with Disabilities 2
Education Spending Per Capita 31
Education Spending as a Percentage of Total 46
Spending Per Pupil 5
Average Teacher Salary 9
Sources of School Funds 12
State Aid Per Pupil 20
Higher Education Spending Per Capita 49
Higher Education Spending as Percentage of Total 48
Public Higher Education Enrollment 48
Per Pupil Support of Higher Education 11
Tuition and Fees 12
Average Professor Salary 8
Education Employees 28
R and D Spending 4
Library Operating Spending 11

Health - Section I

Immunization Rates 3
Infant Mortality Rates 47
State Health Rankings 5
Population Without Health Insurance 43
Abortions 6
Alcohol Consumption 11
Percentage of Adult Smokers 43
Percentage Obese 46
AIDS Cases 7
Physicians Per 100,000 Population 1
Hospital Beds Per 1,000 Population 34
Medicaid Recipients 12
Medicaid Recipients as Percentage of Poverty Population 17
Health and Hospital Spending 30
Health and Hospital Spending as Percentage of Total Spending 34
Per Capita Medicaid Spending 3
Medicaid Spending Per Aged Recipient 11
Medicaid Spending Per Child 14
Medicare Payment Per Hospital Day 30
Hospital Expense Per Inpatient Day 3
Population in HMOs 2

Crime - Section J

Crime Rate 42
Violent Crime Rate 21
Murder Rate 40
Property Crime Rate 44
Motor Vehicle Theft Rate 16
Violent Crime Rate Change 40
Prisoners 29
Change in Prisoners 47
Incarceration Rate 41
Juvenile Violent Crime Rate 7
Proportion of Sentence Served 15
Law Enforcement Employees 3
Corrections Employees 42
State Corrections Spending 1
Increase in State Corrections Spending 32
Law Enforcement Spending 18
Law Enforcement Spending as Percentage of Total 27

Transportation - Section K

Travel on Interstates 6
Interstate Mileage in Unacceptable Condition 28
Deficient Bridges 3

Traffic Deaths 50
Seat Belt Use 46
Vehicle-miles Traveled Per Capita 44
Workers Using Public Transportation 3
Road and Street Miles 47
Highway Employees 39
Public Transit Employees 6
Highway Spending Per Capita 16
Highway Spending as Percentage of Total Spending 28

Welfare - Section L

Percentage of Births to Unwed Mothers 44
TANF Recipients as a Percentage of Population 28
Food Stamp Recipients as Percentage of Population 46
SSI Recipients as Percentage of Population 12
Change in TANF/AFDC Recipients 15
Condition of Children Index 4
Percentage of Families with Single Parent 18
Average Monthly TANF Payments 14
Welfare as Percentage of Poverty-level Income 20
State Supplements of SSI 22
State Income Tax Liability of Typical Family in Poverty 35
Child Support Collections 32
Child Support Collections Per $ of Administrative Costs 38
Children in Foster Care 12
Welfare Spending Per Capita 7
Welfare Spending as Percentage of Total Spending 14
Administrative Costs Per TANF Case 30

Technology - Section M

Percentage of Households with Computers 21
Percentage of Households with Internet Access 12
Zip codes with Broadband Service 6
High-tech Jobs 3
Dot-com Domain Names 3
State Government Website Ratings 16
Students per Computer 13

Michigan

Minnesota

Mississippi

Own-source General Revenue	45
Per Capita Non-tax Revenue	26
Per Capita Total Spending	39
General Spending as Percentage of Income	5
Per Capita General Spending	34
Change in General Expenditures	2
State Government General Revenue	27
State Government General Spending	25
State Government General Fund Spending	9
State and Local Debt	47
Debt as Percentage of Revenue	42
Per Capita Full Faith and Credit Debt	21
Bond Ratings	4
State Solvency Index	28
Pension Plan Assets	44
State Reserves	25
Capital Outlays and Interest	39
State Budget Process Quality	32
Relative State Spending "Needs"	48
Structural Deficits	19

Education - Section H

Math Proficiency, Eighth Grade	39
Science Proficiency, Eighth Grade	36
AFQT Ranks	10
SAT Scores	n/a
ACT Scores	26
Over-25 Population with a High School Diploma	44
Students in Private Schools	25
High School Completion Rates	43
Pupil-Teacher Ratio	16
Public School Enrollment	12
Library Holdings Per Capita	41
Children with Disabilities	37
Education Spending Per Capita	40
Education Spending as a Percentage of Total	35
Spending Per Pupil	46
Average Teacher Salary	48
Sources of School Funds	34
State Aid Per Pupil	37
Higher Education Spending Per Capita	21
Higher Education Spending as Percentage of Total	17
Public Higher Education Enrollment	22
Per Pupil Support of Higher Education	5
Tuition and Fees	29
Average Professor Salary	46
Education Employees	7
R and D Spending	28
Library Operating Spending	50

Health - Section I

Immunization Rates	8
Infant Mortality Rates	2
State Health Rankings	49
Population Without Health Insurance	21
Abortions	46
Alcohol Consumption	33
Percentage of Adult Smokers	21
Percentage Obese	1
AIDS Cases	9
Physicians Per 100,000 Population	49
Hospital Beds Per 1,000 Population	3
Medicaid Recipients	5
Medicaid Recipients as Percentage of Poverty Population	33
Health and Hospital Spending	5
Health and Hospital Spending as Percentage of Total Spending	3
Per Capita Medicaid Spending	15
Medicaid Spending Per Aged Recipient	45
Medicaid Spending Per Child	36
Medicare Payment Per Hospital Day	48
Hospital Expense Per Inpatient Day	50
Population in HMOs	49

Crime - Section J

Crime Rate	27
Violent Crime Rate	27
Murder Rate	2
Property Crime Rate	26
Motor Vehicle Theft Rate	38
Violent Crime Rate Change	39
Prisoners	22
Change in Prisoners	4
Incarceration Rate	3
Juvenile Violent Crime Rate	37
Proportion of Sentence Served	30
Law Enforcement Employees	20
Corrections Employees	24
State Corrections Spending	48
Increase in State Corrections Spending	9
Law Enforcement Spending	38
Law Enforcement Spending as Percentage of Total	38

Transportation - Section K

Travel on Interstates	48
Interstate Mileage in Unacceptable Condition	13
Deficient Bridges	19

Traffic Deaths	1
Seat Belt Use	45
Vehicle-miles Traveled Per Capita	6
Workers Using Public Transportation	42
Road and Street Miles	25
Highway Employees	11
Public Transit Employees	45
Highway Spending Per Capita	19
Highway Spending as Percentage of Total Spending	14

Welfare - Section L

Percentage of Births to Unwed Mothers	1
TANF Recipients as a Percentage of Population	35
Food Stamp Recipients as Percentage of Population	5
SSI Recipients as Percentage of Population	1
Change in TANF/AFDC Recipients	6
Condition of Children Index	50
Percentage of Families with Single Parent	2
Average Monthly TANF Payments	50
Welfare as Percentage of Poverty-level Income	41
State Supplements of SSI	46
State Income Tax Liability of Typical Family in Poverty	17
Child Support Collections	31
Child Support Collections Per $ of Administrative Costs	10
Children in Foster Care	39
Welfare Spending Per Capita	26
Welfare Spending as Percentage of Total Spending	18
Administrative Costs Per TANF Case	49

Technology - Section M

Percentage of Households with Computers	50
Percentage of Households with Internet Access	50
Zip codes with Broadband Service	32
High-tech Jobs	47
Dot-com Domain Names	49
State Government Website Ratings	42
Students per Computer	4

Missouri

Montana

Nebraska

Nevada

New Hampshire

New Hampshire

Own-source General Revenue	38
Per Capita Non-tax Revenue	41
Per Capita Total Spending	46
General Spending as Percentage of Income	50
Per Capita General Spending	43
Change in General Expenditures	44
State Government General Revenue	50
State Government General Spending	49
State Government General Fund Spending	48
State and Local Debt	14
Debt as Percentage of Revenue	2
Per Capita Full Faith and Credit Debt	23
Bond Ratings	3
State Solvency Index	35
Pension Plan Assets	29
State Reserves	45
Capital Outlays and Interest	40
State Budget Process Quality	50
Relative State Spending "Needs"	1
Structural Deficits	41

Education - Section H

Math Proficiency, Eighth Grade	n/a
Science Proficiency, Eighth Grade	n/a
AFQT Ranks	41
SAT Scores	4
ACT Scores	n/a
Over-25 Population with a High School Diploma	14
Students in Private Schools	19
High School Completion Rates	36
Pupil-Teacher Ratio	34
Public School Enrollment	20
Library Holdings Per Capita	9
Children with Disabilities	14
Education Spending Per Capita	46
Education Spending as a Percentage of Total	31
Spending Per Pupil	21
Average Teacher Salary	26
Sources of School Funds	1
State Aid Per Pupil	21
Higher Education Spending Per Capita	46
Higher Education Spending as Percentage of Total	39
Public Higher Education Enrollment	49
Per Pupil Support of Higher Education	50
Tuition and Fees	2
Average Professor Salary	27
Education Employees	19
R and D Spending	12
Library Operating Spending	17

Health - Section I

Immunization Rates	5
Infant Mortality Rates	40
State Health Rankings	2
Population Without Health Insurance	49
Abortions	40
Alcohol Consumption	1
Percentage of Adult Smokers	9
Percentage Obese	42
AIDS Cases	45
Physicians Per 100,000 Population	24
Hospital Beds Per 1,000 Population	38
Medicaid Recipients	47
Medicaid Recipients as Percentage of Poverty Population	38
Health and Hospital Spending	48
Health and Hospital Spending as Percentage of Total Spending	48
Per Capita Medicaid Spending	16
Medicaid Spending Per Aged Recipient	3
Medicaid Spending Per Child	3
Medicare Payment Per Hospital Day	29
Hospital Expense Per Inpatient Day	5
Population in HMOs	4

Crime - Section J

Crime Rate	48
Violent Crime Rate	46
Murder Rate	43
Property Crime Rate	48
Motor Vehicle Theft Rate	44
Violent Crime Rate Change	n/a
Prisoners	46
Change in Prisoners	26
Incarceration Rate	47
Juvenile Violent Crime Rate	42
Proportion of Sentence Served	35
Law Enforcement Employees	8
Corrections Employees	47
State Corrections Spending	29
Increase in State Corrections Spending	22
Law Enforcement Spending	44
Law Enforcement Spending as Percentage of Total	37

Transportation - Section K

Travel on Interstates	31
Interstate Mileage in Unacceptable Condition	43
Deficient Bridges	13

Traffic Deaths	48
Seat Belt Use	n/a
Vehicle-miles Traveled Per Capita	32
Workers Using Public Transportation	43
Road and Street Miles	13
Highway Employees	9
Public Transit Employees	41
Highway Spending Per Capita	25
Highway Spending as Percentage of Total Spending	18

Welfare - Section L

Percentage of Births to Unwed Mothers	47
TANF Recipients as a Percentage of Population	38
Food Stamp Recipients as Percentage of Population	50
SSI Recipients as Percentage of Population	49
Change in TANF/AFDC Recipients	35
Condition of Children Index	1
Percentage of Families with Single Parent	37
Average Monthly TANF Payments	11
Welfare as Percentage of Poverty-level Income	13
State Supplements of SSI	31
State Income Tax Liability of Typical Family in Poverty	n/a
Child Support Collections	24
Child Support Collections Per $ of Administrative Costs	15
Children in Foster Care	40
Welfare Spending Per Capita	14
Welfare Spending as Percentage of Total Spending	7
Administrative Costs Per TANF Case	2

Technology - Section M

Percentage of Households with Computers	15
Percentage of Households with Internet Access	1
Zip codes with Broadband Service	22
High-tech Jobs	2
Dot-com Domain Names	16
State Government Website Ratings	48
Students per Computer	5

State Rankings   371

New Jersey

New Mexico

Own-source General Revenue 27
Per Capita Non-tax Revenue 6
Per Capita Total Spending 14
General Spending as Percentage of
  Income 3
Per Capita General Spending 14
Change in General Expenditures 14
State Government General Revenue 9
State Government General Spending 6
State Government General Fund
  Spending 2
State and Local Debt 30
Debt as Percentage of Revenue 34
Per Capita Full Faith and Credit Debt 36
Bond Ratings 2
State Solvency Index 3
Pension Plan Assets 27
State Reserves 15
Capital Outlays and Interest 23
State Budget Process Quality 22
Relative State Spending "Needs" 50
Structural Deficits 46

Education - Section H

Math Proficiency, Eighth Grade 37
Science Proficiency, Eighth Grade 34
AFQT Ranks 23
SAT Scores n/a
ACT Scores 24
Over-25 Population with a High
  School Diploma 39
Students in Private Schools 38
High School Completion Rates 41
Pupil-Teacher Ratio 19
Public School Enrollment 11
Library Holdings Per Capita 24
Children with Disabilities 5
Education Spending Per Capita 12
Education Spending as a Percentage
  of Total 29
Spending Per Pupil 34
Average Teacher Salary 46
Sources of School Funds 49
State Aid Per Pupil 6
Higher Education Spending Per
  Capita 5
Higher Education Spending as
  Percentage of Total 8
Public Higher Education Enrollment 1
Per Pupil Support of Higher Education 21
Tuition and Fees 44
Average Professor Salary 43
Education Employees 26
R and D Spending 2
Library Operating Spending 41

Health - Section I

Immunization Rates 49
Infant Mortality Rates 25
State Health Rankings 40
Population Without Health
  Insurance 1
Abortions 29
Alcohol Consumption 16
Percentage of Adult Smokers 20
Percentage Obese 30
AIDS Cases 27
Physicians Per 100,000 Population 33
Hospital Beds Per 1,000 Population 48
Medicaid Recipients 3
Medicaid Recipients as Percentage of
  Poverty Population 41
Health and Hospital Spending 12
Health and Hospital Spending as
  Percentage of Total Spending 18
Per Capita Medicaid Spending 20
Medicaid Spending Per Aged
  Recipient 40
Medicaid Spending Per Child 17
Medicare Payment Per Hospital Day 21
Hospital Expense Per Inpatient Day 16
Population in HMOs 21

Crime - Section J

Crime Rate 3
Violent Crime Rate 4
Murder Rate 5
Property Crime Rate 4
Motor Vehicle Theft Rate 19
Violent Crime Rate Change 9
Prisoners 38
Change in Prisoners 34
Incarceration Rate 38
Juvenile Violent Crime Rate 12
Proportion of Sentence Served 17
Law Enforcement Employees 22
Corrections Employees 6
State Corrections Spending 23
Increase in State Corrections
  Spending 38
Law Enforcement Spending 14
Law Enforcement Spending as
  Percentage of Total 22

Transportation - Section K

Travel on Interstates 9
Interstate Mileage in
  Unacceptable Condition 16
Deficient Bridges 45

Traffic Deaths 13
Seat Belt Use 2
Vehicle-miles Traveled Per Capita 5
Workers Using Public
  Transportation 30
Road and Street Miles 17
Highway Employees 22
Public Transit Employees 22
Highway Spending Per Capita 4
Highway Spending as Percentage
  of Total Spending 3

Welfare - Section L

Percentage of Births to Unwed
  Mothers 3
TANF Recipients as a Percentage
  of Population 3
Food Stamp Recipients as
  Percentage of Population 6
SSI Recipients as Percentage of
  Population 13
Change in TANF/AFDC
  Recipients 46
Condition of Children Index 48
Percentage of Families with Single
  Parent 4
Average Monthly TANF Payments 10
Welfare as Percentage of
  Poverty-level Income 15
State Supplements of SSI 17
State Income Tax Liability of Typical
  Family in Poverty 31
Child Support Collections 50
Child Support Collections Per
  $ of Administrative Costs 50
Children in Foster Care 49
Welfare Spending Per Capita 19
Welfare Spending as Percentage of
  Total Spending 27
Administrative Costs Per
  TANF Case 48

Technology - Section M

Percentage of Households with
  Computers 3
Percentage of Households with
  Internet Access 9
Zip codes with Broadband
  Service 34
High-tech Jobs 21
Dot-com Domain Names 26
State Government Website
  Ratings 47
Students per Computer 20

New York

Own-source General Revenue	2
Per Capita Non-tax Revenue	8
Per Capita Total Spending	2
General Spending as Percentage of Income	7
Per Capita General Spending	2
Change in General Expenditures	46
State Government General Revenue	7
State Government General Spending	5
State Government General Fund Spending	32
State and Local Debt	2
Debt as Percentage of Revenue	4
Per Capita Full Faith and Credit Debt	6
Bond Ratings	5
State Solvency Index	25
Pension Plan Assets	2
State Reserves	40
Capital Outlays and Interest	4
State Budget Process Quality	13
Relative State Spending "Needs"	41
Structural Deficits	8

Education - Section H

Math Proficiency, Eighth Grade	19
Science Proficiency, Eighth Grade	22
AFQT Ranks	32
SAT Scores	15
ACT Scores	n/a
Over-25 Population with a High School Diploma	38
Students in Private Schools	6
High School Completion Rates	32
Pupil-Teacher Ratio	38
Public School Enrollment	45
Library Holdings Per Capita	8
Children with Disabilities	8
Education Spending Per Capita	6
Education Spending as a Percentage of Total	48
Spending Per Pupil	2
Average Teacher Salary	3
Sources of School Funds	17
State Aid Per Pupil	8
Higher Education Spending Per Capita	50
Higher Education Spending as Percentage of Total	50
Public Higher Education Enrollment	45
Per Pupil Support of Higher Education	12
Tuition and Fees	14
Average Professor Salary	14
Education Employees	23
R and D Spending	25
Library Operating Spending	2

Health - Section I

Immunization Rates	33
Infant Mortality Rates	36
State Health Rankings	33
Population Without Health Insurance	12
Abortions	1
Alcohol Consumption	40
Percentage of Adult Smokers	33
Percentage Obese	40
AIDS Cases	1
Physicians Per 100,000 Population	3
Hospital Beds Per 1,000 Population	16
Medicaid Recipients	9
Medicaid Recipients as Percentage of Poverty Population	28
Health and Hospital Spending	7
Health and Hospital Spending as Percentage of Total Spending	23
Per Capita Medicaid Spending	1
Medicaid Spending Per Aged Recipient	2
Medicaid Spending Per Child	4
Medicare Payment Per Hospital Day	45
Hospital Expense Per Inpatient Day	36
Population in HMOs	9

Crime - Section J

Crime Rate	40
Violent Crime Rate	12
Murder Rate	23
Property Crime Rate	45
Motor Vehicle Theft Rate	33
Violent Crime Rate Change	46
Prisoners	4
Change in Prisoners	45
Incarceration Rate	23
Juvenile Violent Crime Rate	14
Proportion of Sentence Served	12
Law Enforcement Employees	1
Corrections Employees	3
State Corrections Spending	14
Increase in State Corrections Spending	47
Law Enforcement Spending	1
Law Enforcement Spending as Percentage of Total	10

Transportation - Section K

Travel on Interstates	46
Interstate Mileage in Unacceptable Condition	4
Deficient Bridges	7

Traffic Deaths	45
Seat Belt Use	11
Vehicle-miles Traveled Per Capita	50
Workers Using Public Transportation	1
Road and Street Miles	28
Highway Employees	31
Public Transit Employees	1
Highway Spending Per Capita	28
Highway Spending as Percentage of Total Spending	49

Welfare - Section L

Percentage of Births to Unwed Mothers	9
TANF Recipients as a Percentage of Population	4
Food Stamp Recipients as Percentage of Population	11
SSI Recipients as Percentage of Population	6
Change in TANF/AFDC Recipients	42
Condition of Children Index	33
Percentage of Families with Single Parent	4
Average Monthly TANF Payments	2
Welfare as Percentage of Poverty-level Income	9
State Supplements of SSI	24
State Income Tax Liability of Typical Family in Poverty	38
Child Support Collections	22
Child Support Collections Per $ of Administrative Costs	12
Children in Foster Care	4
Welfare Spending Per Capita	1
Welfare Spending as Percentage of Total Spending	2
Administrative Costs Per TANF Case	13

Technology - Section M

Percentage of Households with Computers	38
Percentage of Households with Internet Access	42
Zip codes with Broadband Service	16
High-tech Jobs	20
Dot-com Domain Names	10
State Government Website Ratings	7
Students per Computer	12

North Carolina

North Dakota

Ohio

Oklahoma

Own-source General Revenue	47
Per Capita Non-tax Revenue	39
Per Capita Total Spending	49
General Spending as Percentage of Income	31
Per Capita General Spending	50
Change in General Expenditures	30
State Government General Revenue	42
State Government General Spending	45
State Government General Fund Spending	18
State and Local Debt	41
Debt as Percentage of Revenue	33
Per Capita Full Faith and Credit Debt	47
Bond Ratings	4
State Solvency Index	37
Pension Plan Assets	34
State Reserves	8
Capital Outlays and Interest	48
State Budget Process Quality	27
Relative State Spending "Needs"	41
Structural Deficits	20

Education - Section H

Math Proficiency, Eighth Grade	25
Science Proficiency, Eighth Grade	22
AFQT Ranks	9
SAT Scores	n/a
ACT Scores	18
Over-25 Population with a High School Diploma	25
Students in Private Schools	45
High School Completion Rates	35
Pupil-Teacher Ratio	28
Public School Enrollment	6
Library Holdings Per Capita	36
Children with Disabilities	29
Education Spending Per Capita	37
Education Spending as a Percentage of Total	3
Spending Per Pupil	39
Average Teacher Salary	42
Sources of School Funds	36
State Aid Per Pupil	33
Higher Education Spending Per Capita	24
Higher Education Spending as Percentage of Total	10
Public Higher Education Enrollment	16
Per Pupil Support of Higher Education	35
Tuition and Fees	47
Average Professor Salary	35
Education Employees	13
R and D Spending	48
Library Operating Spending	42

Health - Section I

Immunization Rates	48
Infant Mortality Rates	7
State Health Rankings	41
Population Without Health Insurance	3
Abortions	44
Alcohol Consumption	48
Percentage of Adult Smokers	24
Percentage Obese	29
AIDS Cases	20
Physicians Per 100,000 Population	45
Hospital Beds Per 1,000 Population	19
Medicaid Recipients	20
Medicaid Recipients as Percentage of Poverty Population	30
Health and Hospital Spending	27
Health and Hospital Spending as Percentage of Total Spending	15
Per Capita Medicaid Spending	43
Medicaid Spending Per Aged Recipient	n/a
Medicaid Spending Per Child	n/a
Medicare Payment Per Hospital Day	35
Hospital Expense Per Inpatient Day	48
Population in HMOs	35

Crime - Section J

Crime Rate	14
Violent Crime Rate	17
Murder Rate	22
Property Crime Rate	14
Motor Vehicle Theft Rate	25
Violent Crime Rate Change	35
Prisoners	18
Change in Prisoners	16
Incarceration Rate	4
Juvenile Violent Crime Rate	n/a
Proportion of Sentence Served	39
Law Enforcement Employees	13
Corrections Employees	28
State Corrections Spending	43
Increase in State Corrections Spending	8
Law Enforcement Spending	37
Law Enforcement Spending as Percentage of Total	24

Transportation - Section K

Travel on Interstates	40
Interstate Mileage in Unacceptable Condition	8
Deficient Bridges	5

Traffic Deaths	27
Seat Belt Use	28
Vehicle-miles Traveled Per Capita	4
Workers Using Public Transportation	44
Road and Street Miles	34
Highway Employees	15
Public Transit Employees	43
Highway Spending Per Capita	35
Highway Spending as Percentage of Total Spending	23

Welfare - Section L

Percentage of Births to Unwed Mothers	19
TANF Recipients as a Percentage of Population	41
Food Stamp Recipients as Percentage of Population	14
SSI Recipients as Percentage of Population	21
Change in TANF/AFDC Recipients	3
Condition of Children Index	37
Percentage of Families with Single Parent	18
Average Monthly TANF Payments	18
Welfare as Percentage of Poverty-level Income	33
State Supplements of SSI	38
State Income Tax Liability of Typical Family in Poverty	8
Child Support Collections	48
Child Support Collections Per $ of Administrative Costs	47
Children in Foster Care	14
Welfare Spending Per Capita	47
Welfare Spending as Percentage of Total Spending	40
Administrative Costs Per TANF Case	9

Technology - Section M

Percentage of Households with Computers	47
Percentage of Households with Internet Access	45
Zip codes with Broadband Service	38
High-tech Jobs	32
Dot-com Domain Names	39
State Government Website Ratings	45
Students per Computer	27

Oregon

Education - Section H

Health - Section I

Crime - Section J

Transportation - Section K

Welfare - Section L

Technology - Section M

Pennsylvania

Own-source General Revenue	26
Per Capita Non-tax Revenue	35
Per Capita Total Spending	19
General Spending as Percentage of Income	30
Per Capita General Spending	20
Change in General Expenditures	25
State Government General Revenue	28
State Government General Spending	29
State Government General Fund Spending	39
State and Local Debt	12
Debt as Percentage of Revenue	9
Per Capita Full Faith and Credit Debt	11
Bond Ratings	3
State Solvency Index	33
Pension Plan Assets	3
State Reserves	23
Capital Outlays and Interest	26
State Budget Process Quality	31
Relative State Spending "Needs"	14
Structural Deficits	14

Education - Section H

Math Proficiency, Eighth Grade	n/a
Science Proficiency, Eighth Grade	n/a
AFQT Ranks	30
SAT Scores	19
ACT Scores	n/a
Over-25 Population with a High School Diploma	27
Students in Private Schools	2
High School Completion Rates	22
Pupil-Teacher Ratio	23
Public School Enrollment	49
Library Holdings Per Capita	36
Children with Disabilities	32
Education Spending Per Capita	18
Education Spending as a Percentage of Total	19
Spending Per Pupil	18
Average Teacher Salary	5
Sources of School Funds	9
State Aid Per Pupil	31
Higher Education Spending Per Capita	40
Higher Education Spending as Percentage of Total	41
Public Higher Education Enrollment	50
Per Pupil Support of Higher Education	14
Tuition and Fees	3
Average Professor Salary	14
Education Employees	47
R and D Spending	22
Library Operating Spending	32

Health - Section I

Immunization Rates	15
Infant Mortality Rates	21
State Health Rankings	26
Population Without Health Insurance	47
Abortions	20
Alcohol Consumption	42
Percentage of Adult Smokers	14
Percentage Obese	19
AIDS Cases	16
Physicians Per 100,000 Population	7
Hospital Beds Per 1,000 Population	17
Medicaid Recipients	25
Medicaid Recipients as Percentage of Poverty Population	12
Health and Hospital Spending	39
Health and Hospital Spending as Percentage of Total Spending	38
Per Capita Medicaid Spending	6
Medicaid Spending Per Aged Recipient	20
Medicaid Spending Per Child	12
Medicare Payment Per Hospital Day	7
Hospital Expense Per Inpatient Day	37
Population in HMOs	11

Crime - Section J

Crime Rate	43
Violent Crime Rate	23
Murder Rate	24
Property Crime Rate	43
Motor Vehicle Theft Rate	30
Violent Crime Rate Change	4
Prisoners	9
Change in Prisoners	28
Incarceration Rate	36
Juvenile Violent Crime Rate	8
Proportion of Sentence Served	13
Law Enforcement Employees	38
Corrections Employees	26
State Corrections Spending	11
Increase in State Corrections Spending	28
Law Enforcement Spending	19
Law Enforcement Spending as Percentage of Total	19

Transportation - Section K

Travel on Interstates	37
Interstate Mileage in Unacceptable Condition	18
Deficient Bridges	4

Traffic Deaths	29
Seat Belt Use	21
Vehicle-miles Traveled Per Capita	43
Workers Using Public Transportation	7
Road and Street Miles	9
Highway Employees	30
Public Transit Employees	5
Highway Spending Per Capita	39
Highway Spending as Percentage of Total Spending	41

Welfare - Section L

Percentage of Births to Unwed Mothers	24
TANF Recipients as a Percentage of Population	17
Food Stamp Recipients as Percentage of Population	21
SSI Recipients as Percentage of Population	18
Change in TANF/AFDC Recipients	22
Condition of Children Index	14
Percentage of Families with Single Parent	37
Average Monthly TANF Payments	8
Welfare as Percentage of Poverty-level Income	27
State Supplements of SSI	39
State Income Tax Liability of Typical Family in Poverty	17
Child Support Collections	6
Child Support Collections Per $ of Administrative Costs	4
Children in Foster Care	18
Welfare Spending Per Capita	8
Welfare Spending as Percentage of Total Spending	8
Administrative Costs Per TANF Case	26

Technology - Section M

Percentage of Households with Computers	35
Percentage of Households with Internet Access	29
Zip codes with Broadband Service	8
High-tech Jobs	24
Dot-com Domain Names	23
State Government Website Ratings	8
Students per Computer	27

Rhode Island

Own-source General Revenue	17
Per Capita Non-tax Revenue	46
Per Capita Total Spending	13
General Spending as Percentage of Income	28
Per Capita General Spending	16
Change in General Expenditures	47
State Government General Revenue	10
State Government General Spending	12
State Government General Fund Spending	15
State and Local Debt	6
Debt as Percentage of Revenue	10
Per Capita Full Faith and Credit Debt	17
Bond Ratings	4
State Solvency Index	45
Pension Plan Assets	4
State Reserves	22
Capital Outlays and Interest	42
State Budget Process Quality	10
Relative State Spending "Needs"	4
Structural Deficits	24

Education - Section H

Math Proficiency, Eighth Grade	24
Science Proficiency, Eighth Grade	19
AFQT Ranks	10
SAT Scores	15
ACT Scores	n/a
Over-25 Population with a High School Diploma	41
Students in Private Schools	7
High School Completion Rates	24
Pupil-Teacher Ratio	49
Public School Enrollment	48
Library Holdings Per Capita	12
Children with Disabilities	1
Education Spending Per Capita	22
Education Spending as a Percentage of Total	38
Spending Per Pupil	8
Average Teacher Salary	7
Sources of School Funds	5
State Aid Per Pupil	40
Higher Education Spending Per Capita	44
Higher Education Spending as Percentage of Total	44
Public Higher Education Enrollment	35
Per Pupil Support of Higher Education	43
Tuition and Fees	10
Average Professor Salary	29
Education Employees	14
R and D Spending	7
Library Operating Spending	12

Health - Section I

Immunization Rates	9
Infant Mortality Rates	43
State Health Rankings	14
Population Without Health Insurance	50
Abortions	4
Alcohol Consumption	18
Percentage of Adult Smokers	23
Percentage Obese	44
AIDS Cases	21
Physicians Per 100,000 Population	5
Hospital Beds Per 1,000 Population	39
Medicaid Recipients	21
Medicaid Recipients as Percentage of Poverty Population	13
Health and Hospital Spending	44
Health and Hospital Spending as Percentage of Total Spending	46
Per Capita Medicaid Spending	2
Medicaid Spending Per Aged Recipient	4
Medicaid Spending Per Child	20
Medicare Payment Per Hospital Day	34
Hospital Expense Per Inpatient Day	11
Population in HMOs	9

Crime - Section J

Crime Rate	33
Violent Crime Rate	35
Murder Rate	26
Property Crime Rate	32
Motor Vehicle Theft Rate	14
Violent Crime Rate Change	17
Prisoners	43
Change in Prisoners	46
Incarceration Rate	46
Juvenile Violent Crime Rate	29
Proportion of Sentence Served	8
Law Enforcement Employees	12
Corrections Employees	40
State Corrections Spending	5
Increase in State Corrections Spending	36
Law Enforcement Spending	24
Law Enforcement Spending as Percentage of Total	28

Transportation - Section K

Travel on Interstates	18
Interstate Mileage in Unacceptable Condition	26
Deficient Bridges	1

Traffic Deaths	49
Seat Belt Use	35
Vehicle-miles Traveled Per Capita	47
Workers Using Public Transportation	24
Road and Street Miles	16
Highway Employees	44
Public Transit Employees	13
Highway Spending Per Capita	44
Highway Spending as Percentage of Total Spending	46

Welfare - Section L

Percentage of Births to Unwed Mothers	17
TANF Recipients as a Percentage of Population	1
Food Stamp Recipients as Percentage of Population	15
SSI Recipients as Percentage of Population	11
Change in TANF/AFDC Recipients	50
Condition of Children Index	21
Percentage of Families with Single Parent	8
Average Monthly TANF Payments	12
Welfare as Percentage of Poverty-level Income	6
State Supplements of SSI	25
State Income Tax Liability of Typical Family in Poverty	17
Child Support Collections	38
Child Support Collections Per $ of Administrative Costs	21
Children in Foster Care	3
Welfare Spending Per Capita	5
Welfare Spending as Percentage of Total Spending	5
Administrative Costs Per TANF Case	40

Technology - Section M

Percentage of Households with Computers	36
Percentage of Households with Internet Access	34
Zip codes with Broadband Service	15
High-tech Jobs	27
Dot-com Domain Names	29
State Government Website Ratings	44
Students per Computer	3

South Carolina

South Dakota

Tennessee

Own-source General Revenue	50	**Health - Section I**		Traffic Deaths	11
Per Capita Non-tax Revenue	45			Seat Belt Use	41
Per Capita Total Spending	27	Immunization Rates	12	Vehicle-miles Traveled Per Capita	10
General Spending as Percentage of		Infant Mortality Rates	16	Workers Using Public	
Income	32	State Health Rankings	44	Transportation	36
Per Capita General Spending	45	Population Without Health		Road and Street Miles	23
Change in General Expenditures	11	Insurance	39	Highway Employees	33
State Government General Revenue	47	Abortions	24	Public Transit Employees	33
State Government General Spending	47	Alcohol Consumption	43	Highway Spending Per Capita	42
State Government General Fund		Percentage of Adult Smokers	8	Highway Spending as Percentage	
Spending	38	Percentage Obese	5	of Total Spending	31
State and Local Debt	45	AIDS Cases	9		
Debt as Percentage of Revenue	45	Physicians Per 100,000 Population	22	**Welfare - Section L**	
Per Capita Full Faith and Credit Debt	24	Hospital Beds Per 1,000 Population	14		
Bond Ratings	3	Medicaid Recipients	1	Percentage of Births to Unwed	
State Solvency Index	19	Medicaid Recipients as Percentage of		Mothers	15
Pension Plan Assets	15	Poverty Population	2	TANF Recipients as a Percentage	
State Reserves	43	Health and Hospital Spending	10	of Population	7
Capital Outlays and Interest	21	Health and Hospital Spending as		Food Stamp Recipients as	
State Budget Process Quality	43	Percentage of Total Spending	7	Percentage of Population	9
Relative State Spending "Needs"	38	Per Capita Medicaid Spending	8	SSI Recipients as Percentage of	
Structural Deficits	43	Medicaid Spending Per Aged		Population	9
		Recipient	38	Change in TANF/AFDC	
Education - Section H		Medicaid Spending Per Child	47	Recipients	40
		Medicare Payment Per Hospital Day	27	Condition of Children Index	43
Math Proficiency, Eighth Grade	32	Hospital Expense Per Inpatient Day	35	Percentage of Families with Single	
Science Proficiency, Eighth Grade	26	Population in HMOs	12	Parent	4
AFQT Ranks	43			Average Monthly TANF Payments	45
SAT Scores	n/a	**Crime - Section J**		Welfare as Percentage of	
ACT Scores	23			Poverty-level Income	28
Over-25 Population with a High		Crime Rate	10	State Supplements of SSI	46
School Diploma	45	Violent Crime Rate	5	State Income Tax Liability of Typical	
Students in Private Schools	24	Murder Rate	7	Family in Poverty	n/a
High School Completion Rates	22	Property Crime Rate	13	Child Support Collections	42
Pupil-Teacher Ratio	17	Motor Vehicle Theft Rate	9	Child Support Collections Per	
Public School Enrollment	39	Violent Crime Rate Change	10	$ of Administrative Costs	14
Library Holdings Per Capita	50	Prisoners	19	Children in Foster Care	17
Children with Disabilities	17	Change in Prisoners	9	Welfare Spending Per Capita	20
Education Spending Per Capita	49	Incarceration Rate	21	Welfare Spending as Percentage of	
Education Spending as a Percentage		Juvenile Violent Crime Rate	27	Total Spending	10
of Total	39	Proportion of Sentence Served	35	Administrative Costs Per	
Spending Per Pupil	42	Law Enforcement Employees	14	TANF Case	44
Average Teacher Salary	31	Corrections Employees	35		
Sources of School Funds	23	State Corrections Spending	40	**Technology - Section M**	
State Aid Per Pupil	42	Increase in State Corrections			
Higher Education Spending Per		Spending	34	Percentage of Households with	
Capita	37	Law Enforcement Spending	36	Computers	42
Higher Education Spending as		Law Enforcement Spending as		Percentage of Households with	
Percentage of Total	31	Percentage of Total	33	Internet Access	41
Public Higher Education Enrollment	41			Zip codes with Broadband	
Per Pupil Support of Higher Education	23	**Transportation - Section K**		Service	21
Tuition and Fees	35			High-tech Jobs	44
Average Professor Salary	28	Travel on Interstates	11	Dot-com Domain Names	24
Education Employees	40	Interstate Mileage in		State Government Website	
R and D Spending	30	Unacceptable Condition	34	Ratings	4
Library Operating Spending	46	Deficient Bridges	34	Students per Computer	10

Texas

Texas

Item	Rank
Own-source General Revenue	40
Per Capita Non-tax Revenue	31
Per Capita Total Spending	43
General Spending as Percentage of Income	42
Per Capita General Spending	47
Change in General Expenditures	16
State Government General Revenue	48
State Government General Spending	50
State Government General Fund Spending	47
State and Local Debt	25
Debt as Percentage of Revenue	19
Per Capita Full Faith and Credit Debt	13
Bond Ratings	2
State Solvency Index	14
Pension Plan Assets	26
State Reserves	n/a
Capital Outlays and Interest	27
State Budget Process Quality	28
Relative State Spending "Needs"	46
Structural Deficits	40

Education - Section H

Item	Rank
Math Proficiency, Eighth Grade	21
Science Proficiency, Eighth Grade	28
AFQT Ranks	6
SAT Scores	21
ACT Scores	n/a
Over-25 Population with a High School Diploma	46
Students in Private Schools	41
High School Completion Rates	48
Pupil-Teacher Ratio	33
Public School Enrollment	3
Library Holdings Per Capita	41
Children with Disabilities	31
Education Spending Per Capita	26
Education Spending as a Percentage of Total	5
Spending Per Pupil	26
Average Teacher Salary	25
Sources of School Funds	19
State Aid Per Pupil	34
Higher Education Spending Per Capita	30
Higher Education Spending as Percentage of Total	22
Public Higher Education Enrollment	26
Per Pupil Support of Higher Education	38
Tuition and Fees	36
Average Professor Salary	24
Education Employees	6
R and D Spending	16
Library Operating Spending	45

Health - Section I

Item	Rank
Immunization Rates	50
Infant Mortality Rates	37
State Health Rankings	36
Population Without Health Insurance	2
Abortions	22
Alcohol Consumption	19
Percentage of Adult Smokers	31
Percentage Obese	5
AIDS Cases	17
Physicians Per 100,000 Population	37
Hospital Beds Per 1,000 Population	32
Medicaid Recipients	31
Medicaid Recipients as Percentage of Poverty Population	45
Health and Hospital Spending	22
Health and Hospital Spending as Percentage of Total Spending	13
Per Capita Medicaid Spending	34
Medicaid Spending Per Aged Recipient	37
Medicaid Spending Per Child	35
Medicare Payment Per Hospital Day	9
Hospital Expense Per Inpatient Day	30
Population in HMOs	28

Crime - Section J

Item	Rank
Crime Rate	8
Violent Crime Rate	13
Murder Rate	17
Property Crime Rate	10
Motor Vehicle Theft Rate	13
Violent Crime Rate Change	15
Prisoners	2
Change in Prisoners	2
Incarceration Rate	2
Juvenile Violent Crime Rate	30
Proportion of Sentence Served	20
Law Enforcement Employees	30
Corrections Employees	1
State Corrections Spending	42
Increase in State Corrections Spending	21
Law Enforcement Spending	22
Law Enforcement Spending as Percentage of Total	6

Transportation - Section K

Item	Rank
Travel on Interstates	34
Interstate Mileage in Unacceptable Condition	32
Deficient Bridges	39
Traffic Deaths	19
Seat Belt Use	12
Vehicle-miles Traveled Per Capita	24
Workers Using Public Transportation	25
Road and Street Miles	12
Highway Employees	42
Public Transit Employees	18
Highway Spending Per Capita	46
Highway Spending as Percentage of Total Spending	37

Welfare - Section L

Item	Rank
Percentage of Births to Unwed Mothers	31
TANF Recipients as a Percentage of Population	24
Food Stamp Recipients as Percentage of Population	20
SSI Recipients as Percentage of Population	25
Change in TANF/AFDC Recipients	31
Condition of Children Index	38
Percentage of Families with Single Parent	18
Average Monthly TANF Payments	47
Welfare as Percentage of Poverty-level Income	41
State Supplements of SSI	46
State Income Tax Liability of Typical Family in Poverty	n/a
Child Support Collections	37
Child Support Collections Per $ of Administrative Costs	9
Children in Foster Care	46
Welfare Spending Per Capita	45
Welfare Spending as Percentage of Total Spending	36
Administrative Costs Per TANF Case	41

Technology - Section M

Item	Rank
Percentage of Households with Computers	36
Percentage of Households with Internet Access	35
Zip codes with Broadband Service	24
High-tech Jobs	13
Dot-com Domain Names	17
State Government Website Ratings	3
Students per Computer	35

Utah

Vermont

Virginia

Washington

Washington

Own-source General Revenue — 10
Per Capita Non-tax Revenue — 11
Per Capita Total Spending — 4
General Spending as Percentage of Income — 23
Per Capita General Spending — 9
Change in General Expenditures — 22
State Government General Revenue — 21
State Government General Spending — 14
State Government General Fund Spending — 28
State and Local Debt — 8
Debt as Percentage of Revenue — 16
Per Capita Full Faith and Credit Debt — 7
Bond Ratings — 2
State Solvency Index — 36
Pension Plan Assets — 10
State Reserves — 13
Capital Outlays and Interest — 5
State Budget Process Quality — 22
Relative State Spending "Needs" — 18
Structural Deficits — 36

Education - Section H

Math Proficiency, Eighth Grade — n/a
Science Proficiency, Eighth Grade — n/a
AFQT Ranks — 23
SAT Scores — 1
ACT Scores — n/a
Over-25 Population with a High School Diploma — 1
Students in Private Schools — 35
High School Completion Rates — 26
Pupil-Teacher Ratio — 3
Public School Enrollment — 17
Library Holdings Per Capita — 28
Children with Disabilities — 42
Education Spending Per Capita — 11
Education Spending as a Percentage of Total — 34
Spending Per Pupil — 23
Average Teacher Salary — 17
Sources of School Funds — 43
State Aid Per Pupil — 14
Higher Education Spending Per Capita — 17
Higher Education Spending as Percentage of Total — 26
Public Higher Education Enrollment — 17
Per Pupil Support of Higher Education — 31
Tuition and Fees — 21
Average Professor Salary — 16
Education Employees — 49
R and D Spending — 14
Library Operating Spending — 7

Health - Section I

Immunization Rates — 24
Infant Mortality Rates — 48
State Health Rankings — 12
Population Without Health Insurance — 18
Abortions — 7
Alcohol Consumption — 26
Percentage of Adult Smokers — 39
Percentage Obese — 32
AIDS Cases — 24
Physicians Per 100,000 Population — 25
Hospital Beds Per 1,000 Population — 50
Medicaid Recipients — 22
Medicaid Recipients as Percentage of Poverty Population — 9
Health and Hospital Spending — 9
Health and Hospital Spending as Percentage of Total Spending — 11
Per Capita Medicaid Spending — 23
Medicaid Spending Per Aged Recipient — 32
Medicaid Spending Per Child — 49
Medicare Payment Per Hospital Day — 20
Hospital Expense Per Inpatient Day — 2
Population in HMOs — 34

Crime - Section J

Crime Rate — 7
Violent Crime Rate — 26
Murder Rate — 31
Property Crime Rate — 6
Motor Vehicle Theft Rate — 3
Violent Crime Rate Change — 31
Prisoners — 27
Change in Prisoners — 19
Incarceration Rate — 42
Juvenile Violent Crime Rate — 15
Proportion of Sentence Served — 3
Law Enforcement Employees — 45
Corrections Employees — 27
State Corrections Spending — 10
Increase in State Corrections Spending — 33
Law Enforcement Spending — 20
Law Enforcement Spending as Percentage of Total — 30

Transportation - Section K

Travel on Interstates — 12
Interstate Mileage in Unacceptable Condition — 27
Deficient Bridges — 28

Traffic Deaths — 42
Seat Belt Use — 6
Vehicle-miles Traveled Per Capita — 40
Workers Using Public Transportation — 9
Road and Street Miles — 45
Highway Employees — 26
Public Transit Employees — 4
Highway Spending Per Capita — 24
Highway Spending as Percentage of Total Spending — 35

Welfare - Section L

Percentage of Births to Unwed Mothers — 40
TANF Recipients as a Percentage of Population — 9
Food Stamp Recipients as Percentage of Population — 31
SSI Recipients as Percentage of Population — 29
Change in TANF/AFDC Recipients — 37
Condition of Children Index — 9
Percentage of Families with Single Parent — 30
Average Monthly TANF Payments — 13
Welfare as Percentage of Poverty-level Income — 7
State Supplements of SSI — 41
State Income Tax Liability of Typical Family in Poverty — n/a
Child Support Collections — 7
Child Support Collections Per $ of Administrative Costs — 20
Children in Foster Care — 48
Welfare Spending Per Capita — 18
Welfare Spending as Percentage of Total Spending — 29
Administrative Costs Per TANF Case — 39

Technology - Section M

Percentage of Households with Computers — 6
Percentage of Households with Internet Access — 7
Zip codes with Broadband Service — 5
High-tech Jobs — 12
Dot-com Domain Names — 5
State Government Website Ratings — 5
Students per Computer — 24

State Rankings   407

West Virginia

Wisconsin

Education - Section H

Health - Section I

Crime - Section J

Transportation - Section K

Welfare - Section L

Technology - Section M

Wyoming

Population - Section A

Population 2000	50
Population Change 1999-2000	40
Population Change 1990-2000	32
Population 2005	1
Population 2015	50
Percentage 65 and Over	37
Percentage 17 and Under	17
Median Age	14
Percentage African American	44
Percentage Hispanic	20
Percentage in Poverty	19
Child Poverty Rate	25
Percentage Female	47
Birth Rates	41
Death Rates	25
Population Density	49
Illegal Immigrant Population	47

Economies - Section B

Personal Income 2000	50
Gross State Product	12
Per Capita Personal Income	27
Personal Income from Wages and Salaries	47
Average Annual Pay	45
Average Hourly Earnings	5
Value Added in Manufacturing	46
Cost of Living	25
Average Annual Pay in Manufacturing	42
Average Annual Pay in Retailing	46
Labor Force	6
Unemployment Rate	39
Employment Rate	12
Government Employment	2
Manufacturing Employment	48
Fortune 500 Companies	n/a
Forbes 500 Companies	n/a
Tourism Spending Per Capita	4
Exports Per Capita	41
Housing Permits	44
Percentage Change in Home Prices	41
Net Farm Income	42
Financial Institution Assets	27
Bankruptcy Filings	24
Patents Issued	39
WC Disability Payment	33
UC Average Weekly Benefit	34
Economic Momentum	12
Employment Change	3
Manufacturing Employment Change	5
Home Ownership	24

Gambling	46
Electricity Use Per Residential Customer	31
Cost Per Kwh	9
New Companies	9

Geography - Section C

Total Land Area	9
Federally Owned Land	8
State Park Acreage	25
State Park Visitors	10
Population Not Active	43
Hunters with Firearms	24
Registered Boats	49
State Spending for the Arts	32
Energy Consumption Per Capita	2
Toxic Chemical Release Per Capita	9
Hazardous Waste Sites	47
Polluted Rivers and Streams	50
Expired Surface Water Pollution Permits	50
Air Pollution Emissions	42

Government - Section D

Members of United States House	44
State Legislators	43
Legislators Per Million Population	4
Units of Government	5
Legislators Compensation	45
Female Legislators	41
Turnover in Legislatures	27
Term Limits	1
Legislative Session Length	36
Republicans in State Legislatures	48
Governor's Power Rating	21
Number of Statewide Elected Officials	9
State and Local Government Employees	1
State and Local Average Salaries	41
Local Employment	18
Local Spending Accountability	16
Registered Voters	47
Percentage of Population Voting	11
Statewide Initiatives	n/a
Campaign Costs Per Vote	37

Federal Impacts - Section E

Per Capita Federal Spending	11
Increase in Federal Spending	8
Per Capita Federal Grant Spending	2
Per Capita Federal Spending on Procurement	23

Per Capita Federal Spending on Payments to Individuals	39
Per Capita Federal Spending on Social Security and Medicare	38
Social Security Benefits	23
Federal Spending on Employee Wages and Salaries	9
Federal Grant Spending Per $ of State Tax Revenue	2
General Revenue from Federal Government	3
Federal Tax Burden Per Capita	19
Federal Spending Per Dollar of Taxes Paid	23
Highway Charges Returned to States	9
Terms of Trade	6
Federal Personal Income Taxes	14
Federal Share of Welfare and Medicaid	17

Taxes - Section F

Tax Revenue	16
Per Capita Tax Revenue	23
Tax Effort	48
Tax Capacity	3
Percentage Change in Taxes	48
Property Taxes as a Percentage of Income	7
Property Taxes Per Capita	11
Property Tax Revenue as a Percentage of 3-tax Revenues	5
Sales Taxes as Percentage of Income	17
Sales Taxes Per Capita	15
Sales Tax Revenue as a Percentage of 3-tax Revenues	14
Services with Sales Tax	17
Income Taxes as a Percentage of Income	n/a
Income Taxes Per Capita	n/a
Income Tax Revenue as a Percentage of 3-tax Revenues	n/a
Highest Personal Income Rate	n/a
Corporate Income Taxes	n/a
Motor Fuel Taxes	45
Tobacco Taxes	45
Tax Burden on Wealthy Family	50
Taxes in the Largest City in Each State	50
Progressivity of Taxes	4

Revenues & Finances - Section G

Per Capita Total Revenue	3
Per Capita General Revenue	3

Wyoming

Own-source General Revenue	5
Per Capita Non-tax Revenue	2
Per Capita Total Spending	3
General Spending as Percentage of Income	2
Per Capita General Spending	3
Change in General Expenditures	40
State Government General Revenue	4
State Government General Spending	4
State Government General Fund Spending	n/a
State and Local Debt	20
Debt as Percentage of Revenue	46
Per Capita Full Faith and Credit Debt	44
Bond Ratings	n/a
State Solvency Index	2
Pension Plan Assets	25
State Reserves	2
Capital Outlays and Interest	3
State Budget Process Quality	21
Relative State Spending "Needs"	33
Structural Deficits	45

Education - Section H

Math Proficiency, Eighth Grade	16
Science Proficiency, Eighth Grade	9
AFQT Ranks	2
SAT Scores	n/a
ACT Scores	8
Over-25 Population with a High School Diploma	7
Students in Private Schools	50
High School Completion Rates	30
Pupil-Teacher Ratio	45
Public School Enrollment	5
Library Holdings Per Capita	5
Children with Disabilities	15
Education Spending Per Capita	2
Education Spending as a Percentage of Total	37
Spending Per Pupil	14
Average Teacher Salary	41
Sources of School Funds	29
State Aid Per Pupil	19
Higher Education Spending Per Capita	9
Higher Education Spending as Percentage of Total	30
Public Higher Education Enrollment	3
Per Pupil Support of Higher Education	22
Tuition and Fees	43
Average Professor Salary	47
Education Employees	1
R and D Spending	39
Library Operating Spending	15

Health - Section I

Immunization Rates	22
Infant Mortality Rates	25
State Health Rankings	31
Population Without Health Insurance	14
Abortions	50
Alcohol Consumption	11
Percentage of Adult Smokers	18
Percentage Obese	37
AIDS Cases	46
Physicians Per 100,000 Population	48
Hospital Beds Per 1,000 Population	10
Medicaid Recipients	40
Medicaid Recipients as Percentage of Poverty Population	44
Health and Hospital Spending	1
Health and Hospital Spending as Percentage of Total Spending	6
Per Capita Medicaid Spending	46
Medicaid Spending Per Aged Recipient	10
Medicaid Spending Per Child	22
Medicare Payment Per Hospital Day	28
Hospital Expense Per Inpatient Day	7
Population in HMOs	47

Crime - Section J

Crime Rate	34
Violent Crime Rate	39
Murder Rate	39
Property Crime Rate	34
Motor Vehicle Theft Rate	48
Violent Crime Rate Change	3
Prisoners	48
Change in Prisoners	38
Incarceration Rate	29
Juvenile Violent Crime Rate	41
Proportion of Sentence Served	35
Law Enforcement Employees	7
Corrections Employees	23
State Corrections Spending	n/a
Increase in State Corrections Spending	n/a
Law Enforcement Spending	10
Law Enforcement Spending as Percentage of Total	32

Transportation - Section K

Travel on Interstates	2
Interstate Mileage in Unacceptable Condition	39
Deficient Bridges	40

Traffic Deaths	14
Seat Belt Use	29
Vehicle-miles Traveled Per Capita	1
Workers Using Public Transportation	31
Road and Street Miles	14
Highway Employees	2
Public Transit Employees	37
Highway Spending Per Capita	2
Highway Spending as Percentage of Total Spending	2

Welfare - Section L

Percentage of Births to Unwed Mothers	38
TANF Recipients as a Percentage of Population	49
Food Stamp Recipients as Percentage of Population	37
SSI Recipients as Percentage of Population	48
Change in TANF/AFDC Recipients	2
Condition of Children Index	30
Percentage of Families with Single Parent	37
Average Monthly TANF Payments	6
Welfare as Percentage of Poverty-level Income	37
State Supplements of SSI	43
State Income Tax Liability of Typical Family in Poverty	n/a
Child Support Collections	8
Child Support Collections Per $ of Administrative Costs	22
Children in Foster Care	29
Welfare Spending Per Capita	46
Welfare Spending as Percentage of Total Spending	50
Administrative Costs Per TANF Case	14

Technology - Section M

Percentage of Households with Computers	9
Percentage of Households with Internet Access	14
Zip codes with Broadband Service	37
High-tech Jobs	50
Dot-com Domain Names	46
State Government Website Ratings	50
Students per Computer	50

Index

A

AARP, 3
Abortions, 230
Acquired immunodeficiency syndrome (AIDS), 234. *See also* Health and health care
AFDC. *See* Aid to Families with Dependent Children
Age. *See* Population
Agriculture. *See* Farming and agriculture income
AIDS. *See* Acquired immunodeficiency syndrome
Aid to Families with Dependent Children (AFDC), 288,
Alabama, 5, 314-315
Alaska, 3, 5, 6, 11, 13, 316-317
Alcohol consumption, 233
American Demographics, 7
Annie B. Casey Foundation, 3
Arizona, 318-319
Arkansas, 320-321
Armed forces qualification test, 196
Arts. *See* Cultural attractions and recreation

B

Banks. *See* Financial institution assets
Benefits
    disability, 63
    federal payments to individuals, 124
    federal share of, 135
    Medicare, 125
    Social Security, 125-126
    state pensions, 184
    unemployment, 10, 64

Birth rates. *See* Social issues
Bridges. *See* Transportation
Broadband, 306
Budget Processes in the States, 10
Bureau of Labor Statistics, 2, 10
"Business climate," 9
Business issues. *See also* Decisionmaking; Economic issues; Taxes; Trade
    bankruptcy filings, 61
    business location, 6-7, 8
    costs, 7
    federal procurement, 123
    Forbes 500 companies, 54
    Fortune 500 companies, 53
    government regulation, 9
    manufacturing, 7, 8, 44, 46, 52, 67
    multistate firms, 8
    new companies, 72
    pro-business attitudes, 9
    productivity, 7
    retailing, 7, 47
    taxes, 10, 11
    transportation, 7, 9
    travel expenses, 7
    utility costs, 9, 71
    wages and salaries, 7-8, 41-43, 46-47

C

California, 3, 4, 5, 322-323
Capital punishment, 4. *See also* Crime; Law enforcement
Center for Budget and Policy Priorities, 11
Children. *See also* Decisionmaking; Education; Social issues; Welfare
    child support collections, 295-296
    Condition of Children Index, 289

    with disabilities, 205
    environment for, 3
    foster care, 297
    infant mortality rates, 227
    poverty rate, 29
Children's Defense Fund, 3
Colorado, 5, 324-325
Common Cause, 13
Computers
    internet access, 305
    ownership, 304
    in schools, 310
Connecticut, 13, 326-327
Construction industry, 1
Corporation for Enterprise Development, 9
Corrections. *See* Crime; Law enforcement
Cost of living index, 6, 45
County Business Patterns, 2, 10
Crime. *See also* Decisionmaking
    crime rates, 250-255
    employees, 261-262
    juvenile, 259
    prisons and prisoners, 256-257
    safety from, 5-6
    sentences, 260
    spending on, 263-266
Cultural attractions and recreation. *See also* Decisionmaking; Environment
    boats, 84
    government support of, 9
    hunting, 83
    opportunities for, 3-4
    retirement and, 3
    spending for the arts, 85
    state parks, 80-81